Mae'r eitem yma ar gael i chi hyd y dyddiad neu'r amser a nodir isod, oni bai fod darllenydd arall yn ei alw'n ôl ynghynt.

This item is on loan to you until the date or time shown below, unless it is recalled sooner by another borrower.

I'W DDEFNYDDIO YN Y LLYFRGELL YN UNIG

TO BE CONSULTED IN THE LIBRARY ONLY

AF734314

INTERNATIONAL COPYRIGHT AND NEIGHBOURING RIGHTS

VOLUME II

INTERNATIONAL COPYRIGHT AND NEIGHBOURING RIGHTS

The Berne Convention and Beyond

SECOND EDITION

Sam Ricketson and Jane C Ginsburg

VOLUME II

OXFORD
UNIVERSITY PRESS

LLYFRGELL
U.W.B LIBRAR

OXFORD
UNIVERSITY PRESS

Great Clarendon Street, Oxford OX2 6DP

Oxford University Press is a department of the University of Oxford.
It furthers the University's objective of excellence in research, scholarship,
and education by publishing worldwide in

Oxford New York

Auckland Cape Town Dar es Salaam Hong Kong Karachi
Kuala Lumpur Madrid Melbourne Mexico City Nairobi
New Delhi Shanghai Taipei Toronto

With offices in

Argentina Austria Brazil Chile Czech Republic France Greece
Guatemala Hungary Italy Japan Poland Portugal Singapore
South Korea Switzerland Thailand Turkey Ukraine Vietnam

Oxford is a registered trade mark of Oxford University Press
in the UK and in certain other countries

Published in the United States
by Oxford University Press Inc., New York

© Sam Ricketson and Jane C Ginsburg 2005

The moral rights of the authors have been asserted
Database right Oxford University Press (maker)

Crown copyright material is reproduced under Class Licence
Number C01P0000148 with the permission of OPSI
and the Queen's Printer for Scotland

First published 1987
Second edition 2006

All rights reserved. No part of this publication may be reproduced,
stored in a retrieval system, or transmitted, in any form or by any means,
without the prior permission in writing of Oxford University Press,
or as expressly permitted by law, or under terms agreed with the appropriate
reprographics rights organization. Enquiries concerning reproduction
outside the scope of the above should be sent to the Rights Department,
Oxford University Press, at the address above

You must not circulate this book in any other binding or cover
and you must impose this same condition on any acquirer

British Library Cataloguing in Publication Data
Data available

Library of Congress Cataloging in Publication Data
Data available

Typeset by RefineCatch Limited, Bungay, Suffolk
Printed in Great Britain
on acid-free paper by
Biddles Ltd, King's Lynn

ISBN 0–19–825946–8 978–0–19–825946–6

1 3 5 7 9 10 8 6 4 2

BU Law Library
K1412.2 .R52 2006
30110008068620

CONTENTS—SUMMARY

VOLUME I

CONTENTS

VOLUME II

IV OTHER CONVENTIONS ON COPYRIGHT AND NEIGHBOURING RIGHTS

All of the Appendices are available as documents to download from the companion website for the book. The following documents (listed in italics) are only available on the companion website of the book, which is freely available to readers at: **http://www.oup.com/uk/booksites/content/9780198259466/**

14

DEVELOPING COUNTRIES

A. Introduction

In this chapter, we shall consider the regime set out in the Appendix to the Paris Act of the Berne Convention which contains special provisions regarding developing countries. In essence, these allow those countries to adopt compulsory translation and reproduction licences, subject to certain conditions. As noted in Chapter 3 above, extensive provisions relating to these matters were introduced into the Convention at the time of the Stockholm Revision by way of a special protocol. This never came into force, and was replaced in the revision at Paris by the modified set of provisions now contained in the Appendix to the Paris Act. Compliance with the Appendix is also required as a condition of adherence to the World Trade Organization ('WTO') under the Agreement on Trade-Related Aspects of Intellectual Property Rights 1994 ('the TRIPs Agreement') as well as under the World Intellectual Property Organization ('WIPO') Copyright Treaty ('WCT'), regardless of whether the country in question is a Berne member. **14.01**

The relationship between the Berne Convention and developing countries raises difficult and complex issues.[1] The Convention is essentially concerned with the private interests of authors, and with raising the level of protection that is accorded to them. Such questions are not usually of great significance to developing countries. These are at varying stages of economic development, **14.02**

[1] For the general background on this question, see C Masouyé, 'Décolonisation, indépendence et droit d'auteur' (1962) 36 *RIDA* 85; N Ndiaye, 'Influence du droit d'auteur sur le développement de la culture dans les pays en voie de développement' (1975) 86 *RIDA* 59; I A Olian, 'International Copyright and the Needs of Developing Countries: The Awakening at Stockholm and Paris' (1974) 7 *Cornell Int L J* 81; A Dietz, *Urheberrecht und Entwicklungsländer* (1981); H P Kunz-Hallstein, 'Recent Trends in Copyright Legislation of Developing Countries' (1982) 13 *IIC* 689; N M Tocups, 'The Development of Special Provisions in International Copyright Law for the Benefit of Developing Countries' (1982) 29 *Journal of the Copyright Society of the USA* 402; J M Teran, 'International Copyright Developments: A Third World Perspective' (1982) 30 *Journal of the Copyright Society of the USA* 129; N M Kumar, 'Cultural Imperialism and Third World Publishing' [1983] *Copyright* 17.

with the consequence that the standard of living of their populations is generally much lower than that found in the developed countries. Economic development, even where this means no more than the attainment of a basic level of self-sufficiency, is therefore an overriding goal for these countries. Ways of achieving this object are through the promotion of literacy and through technical and vocational training, and these programmes, in turn, necessitate ready access to a wide range of educational and informational materials. The authors and publishers/providers of many of these works, however, will usually be resident in one of the developed countries, and the works themselves will generally be subject to copyright protection both in that country, as well as under Berne. This naturally causes problems for a developing nation, which is generally deficient in the foreign currency that is needed to buy stocks of these works, or to purchase authorization to reproduce, translate, or otherwise utilize them for their purposes. On a more practical level, the actual process of obtaining these supplies or permissions (which may always be refused) may involve considerable time delays or even prove impossible, although these difficulties may now be diminished with the advent of digital communications. From the point of view of authors and publishers, however, there is no particular reason why they should treat users in developing countries any differently from those in developed countries: these works are, after all, their property, and they are not in the business of providing free assistance to less developed countries. There is, of course, an obvious solution to these difficulties for any developing country: abstain from entering any international copyright relations and become a 'free rider', using the works of foreign copyright owners without any payment at all. The history of free riding is an ancient, if dubious, one, and the practice has been adopted by many countries, including a number that are now pillars of the international copyright establishment.[2] There may be some appeal to the proposition that what was good for yesterday's developing nations—such as the USA—should continue to hold for today's; that, like their predecessors, today's developing nations should enjoy free access to the works that will eventually enable them to join the ranks of more developed nations. Nevertheless, developing countries may find it more difficult to engage in that practice today, given the dependence of these countries on or interest in international trade in non-copyright subject matter. A would-be free-rider country today thus is more vulnerable to pressure from the developed nations, particularly where such a country seeks to become a member of the WTO, and thereby gain tariff-free access to foreign markets for its exports of goods or raw materials. Free riding will also prove counterproductive where such a country wishes to

[2] In their time, these included the USA, Belgium, and the Netherlands: see generally Chapter 1, and in particular, para 1.20ff above.

obtain protection for its own authors abroad. Even so, where a developing country decides to enter international copyright relations it will generally find that a perceptible gap remains between what is needed to satisfy its requirements and the standard of protection demanded by a multilateral instrument such as the Berne Convention. These tensions have been present since the inception of the Convention, but have become far more marked in the last forty years or so. The question which arises, therefore, is whether the Convention should contain any modification of its requirements in relation to those of its members that are developing countries. At the end of the 1960s, this was an issue that threatened to break up the entire international copyright system; at the present time, this threat has all but subsided, although the underlying conflict is still far from resolved.

B. The Position of Developing Countries Under the Earlier Acts of the Convention

From its inception, membership of the Convention has comprised countries which were at widely differing stages in their economic, social, and cultural development. Of the initial signatories of the Berne Act, two can be fairly regarded as falling within the category of what are today called developing countries. These were Tunisia and Haiti, and the membership of the UK brought another great developing country within the Union, namely India. In the years leading up to the Berlin Revision, another developing nation, Liberia,[3] joined the Berne Union, together with one rapidly industrializing nation, Japan.[4] There was also an intermediate group of Union countries whose literary and artistic development was at a lower level to that found in the principal industrialized states such as France, Germany, and the UK: these included the self-governing and predominantly English-speaking Dominions of the British Empire. In addition, at each of the early conferences there were present observers from a number of other developing countries, mainly from Central and South America.[5] In this period of widespread European colonization and domination, there were relatively few independent developing nations, and it was not until after World War II that these nations came to form a majority of the international community. Nevertheless, the Berne Convention was applied to many of these countries during the period they **14.03**

[3] 16 Oct 1908: [1908] *DA* 145. Note that Liberia denounced the Convention (the Berlin Act) on 22 Feb 1930: [1930] *DA* 1.

[4] 15 July 1899: [1899] *DA* 49.

[5] eg Argentina, Honduras, and Paraguay were represented at the 1885 Conference in Berne: see para 2.39 above.

were colonies or protectorates of European states that were members of the Union.[6]

14.04 While developing nations did not emerge as an identifiable bloc within the Berne Union—or, indeed, in other international forums—until after 1945, from its start the Convention had to take account of the relative differences in the levels of development of its members. In this regard, the Convention was a progressive instrument, which was seen as evolving steadily towards a high and comprehensive level of protection for authors.[7] Thus, it was not until the Berlin Act that translation rights were completely assimilated to the other rights of authors, the reason for this delay being a desire to accommodate the views of the Scandinavian nations.[8] Another area where the requirements of the Convention were relaxed was in relation to the use of articles and other works, particularly for purposes of teaching and public information.[9] Following the Berlin Revision, the system of reservations provided a further means of avoiding the full rigours of the requirements of the Convention by allowing states to retain lower levels of protection in certain key areas, notably the making of translations and exceptions to protection.[10] Even the Rome Act did not entirely end this system, as it allowed states to retain their existing reservations and for new member states to adopt a less rigorous regime with respect to translations.[11] Despite these ameliorations in the Convention system, it is still true to say that each revision of the Convention saw a steady augmentation in the level of protection required, and this made it an instrument that was increasingly less congenial to the interests of developing countries. This was particularly so in the years following the Brussels Revision.

(1) The Stockholm Protocol and its origins

14.05 The Brussels Conference came too soon after World War II for developing countries to play any significant role in this revision (although both India and

[6] See the list of colonies to which the Convention was applied in para 17.49 below. See also S P Ladas, *The International Protection of Literary and Artistic Property* (1938), 124–5. In terms of modern states now members of the Union, the Convention was applied to the following when they were dependent territories of other states which had acceded to the Union: as from 5 Dec 1887—Australia, Bahamas, Benin, Cameroon, Canada, Central African Republic, Chad, Congo, Fiji, Gabon, India, Ireland, Ivory Coast, Madagascar, Mali, Malta, Mauritania, New Zealand, Niger, Pakistan, Senegal, South Africa, Upper Volta; 1 Apr 1913—Suriname; as from 21 Mar 1924—Israel; 1 Aug 1924—Lebanon; 1 Aug 1931—Cyprus, Sri Lanka; 20 Dec 1948—Zaire; 22 May 1952—Togo (source: [1978] *Copyright* 22, n 1).

[7] See the statements to this effect by L Renault in his report to the Berlin Conference: *Actes* 1908, 272.

[8] See paras 2.29 and 2.44 above.

[9] See paras 2.30, 2.45, and 3.05 above.

[10] Berlin Act, arts 25 and 27.

[11] Rome Act, arts 25(1) and 27(2).

Pakistan participated for the first time as fully independent nations).[12] However, in the years immediately following, the process of decolonization brought into existence a large number of new independent states, notably in Africa and Asia. The majority of these had previously been subject to the provisions of the Berne Convention as dependent territories of metropolitan states that were members of the Berne Union. The question which therefore faced these new states was whether they would now continue as members in their own right, or would withdraw from the Union. In the case of some states, such as Indonesia,[13] the decision was made to withdraw, but a number of others, notably India, Pakistan, the Philippines, and many of the former French and Belgian African territories elected to remain bound by the Convention. The result was that, by the time of the Stockholm Conference, twenty-four members of the Union (with a total membership of fifty-seven)[14] could be regarded as developing countries within the terms of appropriate UN resolutions on the subject.[15] At the same time, it had become apparent that these countries were unhappy with the stringent requirements of the Convention, and felt that it did not take sufficient account of their particular needs. There was also a more general view that the future growth of the Union would be restricted unless some specific concessions were made in favour of developing countries, both inside and outside the Union.

(2) The effect of the Universal Copyright Convention

Against this background, it should also be borne in mind that since 1952 there had been in existence another multilateral copyright convention which embodied the same basic principle of national treatment as in the Berne Convention, but contained far fewer mandatory requirements as to the level of protection to be accorded to works claiming protection under it. This was the Universal Copyright Convention (the 'UCC') which had grown out of work done by UNESCO in the years immediately after World War II. Its purpose was **14.06**

[12] *Documents de la Conférence réunie à Bruxelles du 5 au 26 juin 1948* (1951), 57 and 58.

[13] Indonesia denounced the Convention on 19 Feb 1959 with effect from 19 Feb 1960: [1959] *DA* 79 and see further para 17.59 below.

[14] See *Records* 1967, vol I, 18 for the full list of member countries at the time of the opening of the Conference (11 June 1967).

[15] With their date of joining the Union specified in parentheses, these were Argentina (1967), Brazil (1952), Cameroon (1964), Ceylon (1886, 1959), Cyprus (1964), Congo (Brazzaville) (1962), Congo (Democratic Republic) (1963), Dahomey (1961), Gabon (1962), Upper Volta (1963), India (1886, 1958), Lebanon (1925), Madagascar (1966), Mali (1962), Morocco (1920), Mexico (1967), Niger (1962), Pakistan (1886, 1948), Philippines (1951), Senegal (1962), Thailand (1931), Tunisia (1886), Uruguay (1967), and Yugoslavia (1931). Note that Turkey and Israel, which were both members of the Convention, were not included in these lists. The source for this list is Resolution No 1897 (XVIII) of the 1265th plenary meeting of the United Nations General Assembly, which is set out in S D O'Hara, 'Developing Countries: A Definitional Exercise' (1967) 15 *Bull Cop Soc USA* 83, 101–2. See also A Françon, 'Le droit d'auteur et les pays en voie de développement' (1968) 95 *Journal de Droit International* 889, 897n.

to establish a broader-based convention that would bring together countries with widely differing levels of protection. It was particularly concerned to provide a means for the USA and the other American states to enter into international copyright relations with the more 'advanced' states that were members of the Berne Union. These matters are discussed in more detail in Chapter 18 below, but in the present context it should be noted that the UCC was potentially of great assistance to developing countries which wished to obtain protection for their works abroad but felt unable or unwilling to accord to foreign works the high level of protection required by the Berne Convention. By 1967, the new Convention had only two fewer members than the Berne Union, and, of these, thirty-three were members of both conventions.[16] As for the developing countries, twenty-six of these had, by this time, acceded to the UCC.[17] However, there was relatively little overlap between Berne and UCC membership in the case of these countries: only seven were members of both.[18] As a generalization, the former French African colonies and some of the former British Asian Dominions had preferred Berne, while the UCC had attracted the Central and South American countries and a number of former British dependent territories. Apart from its lower level of protection, the UCC also allowed the possibility of granting compulsory licences in respect of translations of works protected by the Convention. Under article V, these were available, subject to a number of conditions, where (i) no translation in the national language had been published within seven years of the original's first publication, or (ii) if such a translation had been published within seven years of the original's first publication but all editions of this translation were out of print after the expiration of this term of seven years. This provision was arguably less generous than the reservation which countries were permitted to make on acceding to the Berne Convention, the effect of which was that translation rights fell into the public domain after ten years if no authorized translation had been published in that period.[19] Furthermore, there was a significant discouragement to countries which were members of both conventions and which sought to withdraw from the Berne Convention in order to take advantage of the lower level of protection allowed

---

[16] These states were Argentina, Austria, Belgium, Brazil, Canada, Czechoslovakia, Denmark, Finland, France, the FRG, Greece, Holy See, Iceland, India, Ireland, Israel, Italy, Japan, Lebanon, Liechtenstein, Luxembourg, Mexico, Monaco, the Netherlands, New Zealand, Norway, Pakistan, Portugal, Spain, Sweden, Switzerland, the UK, and Yugoslavia: [1967] *Copyright* 141 (state of ratifications of UCC as at 1 July 1967).

[17] Argentina, Brazil, Cambodia, Chile, Costa Rica, Cuba, Ecuador, Ghana, Guatemala, Haiti, India, Kenya, Laos, Lebanon, Liberia, Malawi, Mexico, Nicaragua, Nigeria, Pakistan, Panama, Paraguay, Peru, Venezuela, Yugoslavia, and Zambia: [1967] *Copyright* 141.

[18] Argentina, Brazil, India, Lebanon, Mexico, Pakistan, and Yugoslavia.

[19] Brussels Act, art 25(3): these reservations, however, were understood to be made 'at least provisionally' (although no explanation of the meaning of this was given). Furthermore, they only applied to translations into the language or languages of the country in question.

under the UCC. Under the 'Berne safeguard clause', which was contained in the UCC, a country doing this was denied the protection of the UCC in those countries which were members of both conventions.[20] In 1967, this would have limited the number of countries which would have been bound to accord protection under the UCC in such a case to twenty-two—these being those countries which were bound by the UCC alone.[21]

(3) The first signs of interest in the problems of developing countries

As a matter of chronology, the question of providing special assistance to developing countries in relation to copyright was first raised in the context of the UCC rather than the Berne Union. This came at the initiative of the USA, and took the form of proposals to provide assistance to those countries which were not members of either convention in the drafting of copyright legislation and the training of personnel. These questions were discussed at successive meetings of the Intergovernmental Committee of the UCC,[22] and, at its General Conference of 1960, UNESCO adopted a resolution authorizing the Director General 'to participate, at the request of Member States, in their activities concerning the international and national protection of copyright'.[23] The same Conference also saw the emergence of India as a prominent advocate of special concessions in favour of developing countries. While not contending that works from the developed countries should be used without remuneration, India was concerned at the high prices and frequent unavailability of works from the developed countries. It therefore argued that some modification to their traditional view of copyright protection had to be made by those nations, so as to allow for the freer circulation of their works in developing countries.[24] A further resolution was then passed by the Conference, empowering the Director General: **14.07**

> . . . to undertake an early examination of these and allied problems in order to help in the formulation of suitable programmes for cheap production of scientific and technological books in the underdeveloped countries, on a national and a regional basis.[25]

---

[20] UCC, art XVII and the Appendix Declaration relating to art XVII. See further A Bogsch, *The Law of Copyright under the Universal Copyright Convention*, 3rd rev edn (1968), 111ff.

[21] See nn 17 and 18 above and paras 18.27ff below.

[22] Notably at its fourth session in Munich, 12–17 Oct 1959 (see [1959] *DA* 212) and its fifth session in London, 31 Oct–4 Nov 1960: see [1961] *DA* 46. See further C F Johnson, 'The Origins of the Stockholm Protocol' (1970) 18 *Bull Cop Soc USA* 91 ('Johnson (1970)') for a detailed account of these meetings.

[23] Resolution 4.32(b) of the eleventh General Conference of UNESCO, held in Paris, 14 Nov 1960: see *Records of the UNESCO General Conference, 11th session*, Resolutions, 51 and Johnson (1970), 94ff. Johnson notes that in 1960 UNESCO welcomed seventeen new African states to membership.

[24] Johnson (1970), 102–3.

[25] *Records* (n 23 above), Resolutions, 39.

Little immediate action followed the adoption of these resolutions, but a long-term consequence was the convening of a seminar on copyright for African countries in Brazzaville in 1963.[26]

(4) The Brazzaville meeting

14.08 The purpose of this meeting was to assist the new African states to formulate appropriate principles for the drafting of their own copyright laws. The Permanent Committee of the Berne Union ('BUPC') had also expressed interest in this undertaking, and the seminar was therefore jointly organized by both UNESCO and BIRPI.[27] Of the thirty African states invited, twenty-three attended,[28] and several non-African countries[29] and a number of non-governmental international organizations[30] were present as observers. Part of the seminar was purely educational and informational,[31] but the remainder was concerned with the problems of developing countries, in particular those on the African continent.[32] A series of recommendations and resolutions was adopted, which, in the words of one commentator, showed:

> . . . the appreciation of African representatives for the value of adopting domestic legislation. However, their opinion of the world copyright situation as of 1963 was that it was essentially European in orientation and therefore opposed to their interests. They expressed the view that the major conventions needed to be re-examined in light of the specific needs of the African continent. In this connection, they recommended that African experts be included at all international copyright meetings, especially the committees which were then preparing for the revision of the Berne Convention.[33]

Three specific recommendations in relation to this revision were then made: that the term of protection under article 7 should be reduced; that article 20 should be modified so as to enable the making of bilateral agreements in promoting exchanges in derogation of the text of that provision; and that special provisions should be included for the protection of African folklore, while

---

[26] Johnson (1970), 97, notes that the resolutions of the 1960 Conference were understood as meaning that such a conference should be called, but that there were delays in doing this: see further ibid, 98ff.

[27] The issue was raised at a joint session of the tenth session of the BUPC and the sixth session of the Intergovernmental Committee in Madrid, 25–30 Sept 1961: [1961] *Copyright* 318, 328. For a report of the meeting, see (1963) 16 *Copyright Bulletin* 171 and [1963] *DA* 250.

[28] Algeria, Burundi, Cameroon, Central African Republic, Chad, Congo (Brazzaville), Congo (Leopoldville), Dahomey, Ethiopia, Ghana, Guinea, Ivory Coast, Liberia, Malagasy Republic, Mali, Mauritius, Morocco, Niger, Sierra Leone, Tanganyika, Togo, Tunisia, and Uganda: [1963] *DA* 257.

[29] Czechoslovakia, Italy, and the USA: ibid.

[30] African Society of Culture, Union of African National Radio and Television Broadcasters (URTNA), European Broadcasting Union (EBU), ALAI, *CISAC*, and International Copyright Society (*INTERGU*): ibid.

[31] [1963] *DA* 251–3. [32] ibid, 253ff. [33] Johnson (1970), 107.

permitting the free use of protected works for educational and school purposes.[34] Finally, it was proposed that a model copyright law suitable for African conditions and needs should be developed, and that UNESCO and WIPO should assist in this task.[35]

While it is likely that the initial intentions of those states represented at Brazzaville was to seek accession to the UCC,[36] the discussions at that meeting saw this concern shift towards the Berne Union. In part, this was due to the impending revision of the Berne Convention, while none was then contemplated in relation to the UCC. Another reason may have been that the Berne Convention, in view of its longer history, was seen as the more prestigious instrument.[37] Up to the time of the Brazzaville meeting, however, the preparatory work for the Berne revision had taken no account of the problems of developing countries, and had been essentially concerned with the question of raising the level of protection offered by that Convention. Indeed, at this time, the major issue for the forthcoming revision was thought to be the achievement of a uniform regime governing cinematographic works.[38] Although the Brazzaville recommendations came too late for consideration by the Study Group in its first report of 1963, they were discussed by the Group of Experts which met later that year and their importance was further underlined by the Tunisian delegate[39] as well as in a lengthy submission presented by the European Broadcasting Union.[40] The latter organization, as the representative of a major group of copyright users, was very sympathetic to the interests of the developing nations, and suggested that special concessions should also be made in relation to broadcasting rights in those countries.[41] The Group of Experts expressed their hope that these matters would be examined by the Study Group or by a special committee appointed for that purpose.[42] Pressure for consideration of the position of developing countries was also maintained at the joint meeting of the BUPC and the IGC of the UCC which was held in New Delhi in December 1963.[43] The Indian delegation at this meeting proposed that there should be a study of the possibility of introducing compulsory licences into the Convention for the reproduction of protected works for educational purposes, as well as translation licences similar to those in the UCC.[44] The Committees duly invited **14.09**

[34] [1963] *DA* 258. [35] ibid, 259. [36] Johnson (1970), 109. [37] ibid.

[38] See C Masouyé, 'Prospects of Revision of the Berne Convention' (1964) 43 *RIDA* 28, 30.

[39] *Stockholm Conference, Committee of Experts (1963), Report of Debates,* Document DA/20/29rev, 18.

[40] Observations of the EBU on the Preliminary Proposals for Revision of the Berne Convention (submitted to the 1963 Committee of Experts), 39–43.

[41] ibid, 42. [42] *Report of Debates* (n 39 above), 18.

[43] Eleventh session of the BUPC and seventh session of the IGC, 2–7 Dec 1963, New Delhi: [1964] *DA* 50.

[44] ibid, 55.

the secretariats to make a study of these questions for consideration at their next joint meeting.[45] They also gave their general support to the work of the recent Brazzaville meeting, in particular the proposal for a draft model law for African countries.[46]

(5) The 1964 Study Group report

14.10 Against this background, it is not surprising that the 1964 report of the Study Group saw a considerable change in emphasis. This is clearly reflected in the Study Group's interpretation of article 24(1) of the Convention which dealt with the object of revision conferences, namely the introduction of 'improvements intended to perfect the system of the Union'. In its 1963 report, the Study Group had stated that it understood this to mean the 'enlargement of the protection granted to authors by the creation of new rights or by the increasing of rights which are already recognized'.[47] This statement was modified in the 1964 report as follows:

> However, it is also necessary to promote the general development of copyright by reforms intended to make the rules relating to it more simple to apply, as well as to adapt them to the social, technical and economic conditions of the contemporary community.[48]

The report then proposed the addition of a new article 25*bis*. This contained a number of modified regulations that might be adopted by developing countries. These took the form of reservations which these countries might make when acceding to the Convention, and were limited to a renewable term of ten years.[49] The expression 'developing country' was also defined as '[a]ny country which desires to accede to this Convention but which, with regard to the economic situation and its social needs, does not consider itself immediately in a position to make provision for the protection of all the rights forming the object of this Convention'.[50] The reservations that might be made by such a country were as follows:

1. *Translations*: article 5 of the Convention as revised at Paris in 1896 might be substituted for article 8 of the present Convention on the basis that these provisions were to apply 'only to translations into the language or languages of that country'.[51] This retained the substance of the reservation with

[45] Resolution 8.51 (VII): ibid 57. [46] ibid, 55.

[47] BIRPI, *General Report of the Swedish/BIRPI Study Group, 1 June 1963*, Document DA/20/2, 5.

[48] BIRPI, *General Report of the Swedish/BIRPI Study Group, 1 July 1964*, Document DA/22/2, 5 ('1964 SG').

[49] ibid, 83ff.

[50] ibid, 86. For text of proposals, see *Records* 1967, 137–8 (Document S/1).

[51] *Records* 1967, 137–8. See also 1964 SG (n 48 above), 87.

respect to translations that had been allowed under article 25(3) of the Brussels Act, but henceforth this was to apply only to developing countries.

2. *Duration*: article 7 of the Rome Act might be substituted for article 7 of the present Convention, with the result that the mandatory term of life plus fifty years would not be applicable.[52]
3. *Broadcasting*: article 11*bis* of the Rome Act might be substituted for article 11*bis* of the present Convention, with the result that developing countries would not have to protect all the more detailed rights specified in the Brussels Act. This proposal appeared to flow from the submission of the EBU, and was thought reasonable on the basis that the more limited provision of the Rome Act had been 'considered as adequate for industrialized countries between 1930 and 1940'.[53] On the other hand, the need for such a provision can be queried in view of the wide scope allowed for compulsory licences under article 11*bis*(2) of the Brussels Act.
4. *Educational use*: developing countries might reserve for themselves the determination of regulations 'for the protection of works covered by this Convention when such works are used for exclusively educational or scholastic purposes'.[54]
5. *Arrangements under article 20*: it was proposed here that developing countries might reserve for themselves the right to make agreements in derogation of article 20. This would allow them to make regional arrangements between themselves, even if the conditions of article 20 were not satisfied.[55]

No special proposals concerning folklore were made, but the Study Group pointed out that the present provisions of the Berne Convention placed no obstacles in the way of national legislation on the subject.[56]

In putting forward these proposals, it was clear that the Study Group was **14.11** endeavouring to keep and attract developing countries into the Berne Union, rather than the UCC, on the basis that the higher level of protection in the former would be of greater advantage to their authors.[57] At the same time, it is clear that the Study Group was also concerned with the likely future of the

[52] ibid. [53] ibid. [54] *Records* 1967, 138. See also 1964 SG (n 48 above), 87.
[55] ibid, 87–8. [56] ibid, 88.
[57] The following remark was made in this regard by the Study Group: 'The objection has of course been made that if the developing countries find themselves unable to organise protection as effective as accession to the Berne Convention would imply, they ought to become parties to the Universal Copyright Convention, instead of the Berne Convention. There is no doubt, however, that the adoption by the developing countries of copyright legislation within the framework of the Berne Convention would be of considerable advantage to the authors. Conditions in several of these countries will certainly eventually improve and one of the consequences of this development will be the increasing exploitation of literary and artistic works. In these circumstances, it will naturally be to the authors' advantage if protection has been organised from the start, on the pattern of the Berne Convention.': 1964 SG (n 48 above), 85.

Convention in the event that some concessions were not made by the developed nations.[58] The major authors' organizations represented in the Authors' Consultative Committee, however, were critical of its proposals. While appreciating the Group's preoccupation with facilitating membership of the Convention by developing countries, they thought that the proposed system of reservations (substantially abandoned in 1928) carried with it 'risks of degeneration' to the overall Convention.[59] They therefore proposed a number of restrictions to the proposed reservations, and urged strongly that the fifth reservation relating to arrangements in derogation of article 20 should be deleted altogether.[60] In the period following the Brazzaville meeting, in particular after the publication of the Study Group's 1964 Report, the opposition of authors' and publishers' organizations to the proposals intensified, and was reflected in a series of critical resolutions and efforts that sought to influence the policies of the governments of developed nations in their favour.[61]

(6) The 1965 Committee of Governmental Experts

14.12 Although the decisions of this Committee did not bind the governments represented, this was the first general meeting at which governmental representatives discussed the particular problems of developing countries in detail. The basis for these discussions was found in the proposals made by the Study Group in its 1964 Report and the responses to this, but a further proposal (the 'joint proposal') was presented by six developing nations that were Union members.[62] While this was based on the Study Group's proposals, it differed from it in a number of important respects, and, in the light of these proposals, the Committee adopted the following recommendations:

(a) The countries eligible to apply reservations

It was agreed that any developing country, whether already a member of the Union or not, should be eligible to apply the reservations under the proposed article 25*[bis]*. No agreement, however, could be reached on the criteria and

[58] In this regard, the Study Group noted that the Berne Convention did not govern the protection granted by countries to their nationals, and that developing countries were therefore free to grant their citizens inferior protection to that granted by the Convention: 1964 SG (n 48 above), 88.

[59] *Report of the ACC*, DA/22/7, 36 (contained in the documentation for the 1965 Committee of Governmental Experts).

[60] ibid. See further Johnson (1970), 124–5.

[61] See further ibid, 125–6.

[62] Joint proposal of Congo (Leopoldville), India, Lebanon, Morocco, Senegal and Tunisia: DA/22/28, contained in the documentation for the 1965 Committee of Governmental Experts. For the discussions, see the *Committee of Governmental Experts (1965), Report of the Debates*, Document DA/22/33, 15–21 and the summary in *Records* 1967, 139–42 (Document S/1).

procedure for determining which countries were to be regarded as 'developing' for this purpose.[63]

(b) The basis for a claim to eligibility

While no mechanism for determining the validity of a state's claim for eligibility to make reservations was adopted by the Committee, the characteristics on which a state might claim its entitlement to do so were expanded by the addition of a reference to cultural needs. The new wording proposed therefore was 'Any country . . . having regard to its economic, scientific, social and cultural needs . . .'.[64]

(c) The time for making of reservations

The joint proposal suggested that developing countries should be able to do this 'at any time', so as to avoid the need for these countries to make all these reservations at the moment of ratification or accession, without having time to decide whether it needed all of these, or only some.[65] This was rejected by the Committee, on the basis that authors required certainty as to their rights, and that this certainty would be undermined if a developing country was free to make further reservations after its accession to the Convention.[66]

(d) Duration of reservations

There was nothing in the joint proposal on this, but the Committee changed the Study Group's proposal for a renewable term of ten years, allowing the second period to extend until the entry into force of the next revised text of the Convention.[67]

(e) The nature of the reservations

The Committee accepted a suggestion in the joint proposal that reservations in respect of translation rights should apply to dramatic and dramatico-musical works.[68] With regard to both translations and the matter of duration, several delegations urged the Study Group to ensure that these reservations should not lead to regimes that were inferior to those in the UCC,[69] and these suggestions were endorsed by the Committee. As to the reservation concerning the use of works for educational or scholastic purposes, a suggestion in the joint proposal that this include 'cultural purposes' was rejected as being too wide and indefinite in scope.[70] A further suggestion that there should be an additional and more general reservation under which reproduction of works within the territory of a developing country should be permissible under the regime of a compulsory

[63] *Report of the 1965 CGE* (n 62 above), 16. [64] ibid. [65] ibid. [66] ibid.
[67] ibid, 17. [68] ibid. [69] Notably Italy and France: ibid.
[70] Rejected by eighteen to four, with four abstentions: ibid.

licence was also rejected, after evoking strong opposition from a number of delegations.[71]

(f) Special arrangements in derogation of article 20

There was considerable discussion of the extent to which such arrangements should be allowed. Under the joint proposal, any country which was eligible to make reservations under the proposed article 25*bis* was left free to enter such arrangements with any other country of the Union. Other delegations were opposed to this, saying that such arrangements would throw the Convention out of balance, and proposed that they should only operate between countries making reservations. Finally, a text proposed by the Lebanese delegation was adopted.[72]

(7) The programme for the Stockholm Revision

14.13 It will be apparent that, to this point, there had been a general readiness, albeit one tempered by a degree of wariness, on the part of the majority of Union members to accommodate the particular claims of the developing countries. While the Committee of Governmental Experts had not accepted all the recommendations contained in the joint proposal, the final recommendations

---

[71] France and Italy: ibid.

[72] ibid, 18–19. The text of the reservations proposed by the CGE were as follows:

(1) Any developing country which ratifies this Convention or accedes to it and which, having regard to its economic situation and its social or cultural needs, does not consider itself immediately in a position to make provision for the protection of all the rights forming the object of this Convention, may, by a notification deposited with the . . . at the time of ratification or accession, declare that it will, for a period of ten years from the ratification or accession,

(a) substitute for Article 8 of this Convention the provisions of Article 5 of the Convention as revised in Paris in 1896, in respect of translations into the language or languages of that country, and apply the same provisions to the translations referred to in paragraph (2) of Article II; (Alternative: text based on Article V of the Universal Copyright Convention)

(b) substitute for Article 7 of this Convention the provisions of Article 7 of the Convention as revised in Rome in 1928; (Alternative: text based on Article IV of the Universal Copyright Convention)

(c) substitute for Article 11*bis*, paragraphs (1) and (2), of this Convention the provisions of Article 11*bis* of the Convention as revised in Rome in 1928;

(d) reserve the right, for exclusively educational, scientific or scholastic purposes, to restrict the protection of literary and artistic works;

(e) reserve the right to make arrangements with any other country of the Union in derogation of Article 20 of this Convention, on condition that the arrangement concerns solely works the country of origin of which is a country party to that arrangement and relates only to the reservations mentioned above, each condition being operative only if a developed country is party to the said arrangement.

Any developing country fulfilling the conditions referred to above may avail itself of one, several or all of the reservations provided above.

Of the remaining paragraphs, para (2) provided for the renewal of reservations until the entry into force of the next revised text of the Convention; para (3) provided for the withdrawal of reservations; para (4) required that all notifications required to be made to give effect to these provisions should be communicated to all countries of the Union.

that they had made were quite favourable to the developing countries, and entailed considerable potential curtailments of authors' rights. These proposals, in turn, formed the basis for the Conference programme, which was drawn up by the Swedish/BIRPI Study Group, but contained some further significant modifications.[73] The first of these related to the form of the proposals. In the Committee of Governmental Experts, several delegates had argued that these should be in a separate protocol, rather than in the body of the Convention.[74] The reason for this was that these were conceived as being interim measures that would be abandoned by countries when they reached higher levels of development. As the provisions involved were quite extensive, there were also stylistic reasons for including them in a separate Protocol.[75] This approach was adopted in the programme, which also proposed there be a link provided with the Protocol in the Convention. This was done in a new article 20*bis* which stated that the Protocol formed an integral part of the Convention.[76] As to more substantive matters, the programme made the following changes.

First, with respect to the first and second reservations (translations and duration), the Study Group concluded that the substitution of the earlier texts of the Berne Convention would furnish authors with a lower level of protection than was available under the UCC. Accordingly, it was proposed that these reservations should be based on the UCC provisions alone.[77] In the case of translations, this now meant the proposed reservation took the form of a very detailed and lengthy regulation.[78] In the case of duration of protection, it meant that states might substitute a term of no less than twenty-five years for the period of life plus fifty years, and no less than ten years post publication for anonymous and pseudonymous works.[79]

Second, the reservation relating to special arrangements was deleted. This was on the basis that the arrangements proposed here could be classified in two categories: the first providing for limitations on copyright protection permissible under the Convention or the proposed Protocol, and the second being those intended to provide for wider restrictions. In the view of the Study Group, there was no need for any special provision for arrangements of the first kind as they were, in any event, permitted under article 20—they could not be regarded as 'contrary to the Convention' within the meaning of that article, as the Protocol would form an integral part of the Convention.[80] As for the second, these arrangements could theoretically lower copyright protection to any level whatsoever, or even abolish it completely in particular cases. The Study

[73] *Records* 1967, 142–4 and 165–6 (text of provisions) (Document S/1).
[74] eg France: *Report of the 1965 CGE* (n 62 above), 15.
[75] *Records* 1967, 142 (Document S/1). [76] ibid. [77] ibid, 143.
[78] See UCC, art V. [79] ibid, art IV. [80] *Records* 1967, 143 (Document S/1).

Group therefore took the view that it would be impossible to permit such arrangements, and deleted any mention of them in the programme.[81]

Finally, an additional reservation relating to the right freely to reproduce press articles was proposed. This was intended to take account of the proposal made elsewhere in the programme to delete article 9(2) which had previously provided for this. The Study Group took the view that it would be unfair if a non-member country adhering to the new text were unable to take advantage of this provision, while older members of the Union (including countries which were not developing nations) could continue to apply it so long as they remained bound by earlier Acts of the Convention. The new reservation which was proposed was therefore based in substance on article 9(2) of the present text of the Convention.[82]

No changes were made to the proposed reservations concerning broadcasting and educational uses;[83] likewise, the Committee's recommendations concerning the time at which reservations might be made, and their duration, were adopted unaltered.[84]

14.14 The programme for the Stockholm Conference was published in May 1966, but member states were slow in registering their observations on its provisions. By the end of March 1967, only eighteen governments had forwarded their responses to BIRPI, and of these only eleven dealt with the issues raised by the Protocol.[85] These governmental submissions have been described as 'less than profound', revealing that most of the developed nations had not formulated any coherent attitude to the claims of their developing neighbours.[86] Of these, the UK was the most determined critic of the Protocol, and suggested wide-ranging modifications to it. This antagonism was, no doubt, strongly influenced by the vigorous opposition to the Protocol that was emerging in that country among publishers' and authors' groups.[87] There was a more muted, but still critical,

[81] *Records* 1967, 143 (Document S/1).

[82] ibid, 143–4. [83] ibid, 143. [84] ibid, 144.

[85] These governmental observations on Document S/1 are to be found in Document S/13 (Austria, Belgium, Czechoslovakia, Denmark, France, the FRG, Ireland, Israel, Italy, Japan, Madagascar, Portugal, South Africa, and the UK) (*Records* 1967, 611) and Document S/17 (Bulgaria, Luxembourg, Switzerland, and Turkey) (*Records* 1967, 662). Only Czechoslovakia, Denmark, France, Israel, Italy, Japan, Portugal, the UK, Bulgaria, Luxembourg, and Turkey referred to the Protocol in their submissions, while South Africa reserved its position. For a general discussion of the governmental observations, see Johnson (1970), 142ff, and see also the summary of governmental observations prepared by BIRPI in Document S/18: *Records* 1967, 665.

[86] Johnson (1970), 142.

[87] See generally, R F Whale, *The Stockholm Act of the Berne Copyright Union: Protocol Regarding the Developing Countries* (1968) and H D Sacks, 'Crisis in International Copyright: The Protocol Regarding Developing Countries' [1969] *JBL* 26, 128. This situation had even received the attention of *The Times* (London), which on 28 Apr 1967 declared 'Copyright laws are one thing, aid to developing countries another. It is a mistake to entangle them.'

response from France,[88] but the comments from other developed nations were generally favourable, containing at least lip-service recognition of the problems of developing countries.[89] The non-governmental international organizations, however, were far less restrained in their response to the Protocol, as is revealed by this fiercely worded resolution of the Executive Committee of ALAI in November 1966:

> . . . the proposed Protocol appears to be useless and would even be capable, by discouraging the vocation of authors, of jeopardizing the cultural advancement of the countries in question.[90]

In the event the Protocol was adopted, the non-governmental international organizations urged that it should be made an independent Protocol, not linked to the Berne Convention, which might be acceded to by states at their option.[91] They also argued that emphasis should be placed on other forms of economic assistance to developing countries, or alternatively that the present proposals be pursued in the forum of the UCC rather than the Berne Union.[92] As for the developing countries themselves, many of these felt that the Protocol did not go far enough in meeting their needs. On the African continent, awareness of these matters had continued to be raised, in the period following the Brazzaville meeting, by the work that had been done on the drafting of a model copyright law. This was adapted to African conditions and contained a number of provisions allowing for lower levels of protection in such instances as the making of translations, educational use and the like.[93] Interest among the Asian nations had also been stimulated by the convening of an East Asia seminar on copyright which met in New Delhi in January 1967.[94] This was attended by delegates from fourteen Asian states, including a number of important countries that were not members of either international convention, such as Indonesia, Malaysia, Korea, and Iran.[95] At the motion of the delegation of Ceylon (now Sri Lanka), a

[88] Document S/13 (French observations) in *Records* 1967, 616.

[89] eg Denmark 'recommended' the Protocol 'in the desire to meet the special needs of developing countries' while Portugal 'commended' the proposals: *Records* 1967, 615 and 629. By contrast, the FRG stated, in an otherwise lengthy submission, that it had no comments on the Protocol: ibid, 620.

[90] Observations of ALAI submitted to BIRPI, quoted by Johnson (1970), 150. The observations of other international NGOs, such as *CISAC*, the International Writers Guild, IPA, IFPI, and INTERGU are reviewed by Johnson (1970), 150–8. Note, however, that the EBU continued to be favourable to the Protocol.

[91] ibid. [92] ibid.

[93] See the general report of the Committee of African Experts to Study a Draft Model Copyright Law (Geneva, 30 Nov–4 Dec 1964): [1965] *Copyright* 31 (including a draft model law at 36).

[94] New Delhi, 23–30 Jan 1967: [1967] *Copyright* 42.

[95] The following states attended: Afghanistan, Cambodia, Ceylon, India, Indonesia, Iran, Japan, Korea, Laos, Malaysia, Nepal, Philippines, Singapore, Thailand, and the USSR; Burma, Mongolia, Pakistan and Vietnam were invited but did not attend: ibid, 49.

resolution calling for modifications and extensions to the Protocol was adopted.[96] This resolution was to serve as the basis for a proposal which was to be made by ten developing Asian and African nations at the Stockholm Revision.[97]

(8) The prospects of UCC revision

14.15 One further factor that emerged in the period immediately prior to the Stockholm Conference was the possibility of a revision of the UCC. Although proposals for this had been made at the beginning of the decade, they had been rejected then as premature in view of the fact that the Convention had only recently come into force.[98] However, with the preparation of the Stockholm Protocol, concern began to be expressed in some quarters that the Berne Convention might be about to take over the role of the UCC in providing a bridge to international copyright relations for those countries with lower levels of protection. In addition, the developing countries themselves began to press for a more active role in the affairs of the IGC of the UCC, and attention was directed at the possibility of deleting article XVII (the Berne safeguard clause).[99] The issue finally came to a head at the fourteenth session of the General Conference of UNESCO in October 1966, where the Director General was asked to consult the relevant parties as to their views on the revision of articles XI (which dealt with the composition of the Intergovernmental Committee) and XVII.[100] This request was obviously of direct relevance to the forthcoming revision of the Berne Convention, and was the subject of lengthy discussion at an extraordinary meeting of the BUPC which was held in March 1967.[101] The Committee took the view that it would be premature for those members of the Union which were also members of the UCC to respond to the Director General's inquiry until the Stockholm Revision had been held.[102] While the question of a UCC revision was therefore deferred for the moment, it was to become of critical importance to the Berne Union after the unsatisfactory outcome of the Stockholm Revision.

---

[96] [1967] *Copyright*, 52–3. [97] Document S/160: *Records* 1967, 702.

[98] As early, in fact, as the fourth session of the IGC at its meeting in Munich in 1959: Johnson (1970) 166–7.

[99] As to which see paras 18.27ff below. See generally on these developments, Johnson (1970), 167ff; E M Braderman, 'International Copyright: A World View' (1970) 17 *Bull Cop Soc USA* 147, 151ff.

[100] Resolution 5.122, UNESCO General Conference, fourteenth session, Paris, 25 Oct–30 Nov 1966: quoted by Johnson (1970), 173.

[101] 14–16 Mar 1967, Geneva: [1967] *Copyright* 66. See also the report by the Director of BIRPI on this question at 70ff.

[102] ibid, 68 (for resolution adopted).

C. The Stockholm Revision Conference

(1) The parties' positions

The attitudes of the two sides had become more polarized by the time the Conference met. This was apparent in the opening statements made by delegates at the first session of Main Committee II which was the committee appointed to discuss the Protocol. In the view of some developing nations, particularly India, the Protocol was essential as a means of assisting in the promotion of national literacy and training: it was an area where there was an obligation on the part of the developed nations to help those that were less developed.[103] In this regard, the Indian delegation argued that the rights of authors should not be absolute, and that there should be no barrier to the adoption of compulsory licences in appropriate cases. Underlying this argument was the view that their lack of development was largely due to their colonial past, and that the obligation of the developed states to assist them was in the nature of a moral debt. At the same time, the Indian delegation sought to remove fears that the introduction of special concessions would weaken the Convention system, arguing that they were necessary at this stage in order to enable the developing countries to attain the high standards of protection required by the Convention. Thus, a person 'making a long jump took steps backward to enable him to make a greater leap forward'.[104] In the same way, 'any temporary lowering of the standards of the Convention would eventually be more than compensated for'.[105] As for the developed nations, there were differences in emphasis between them, although each affirmed its readiness to provide assistance of some kind to the developing countries.[106] As might be expected, the British delegation took the strongest stance, arguing that the Protocol appeared to be a way of giving economic assistance to developing nations at the expense of authors and that it was an inappropriate way of achieving this objective.[107] Even among the developing countries themselves there were considerable differences: in general, the African and Asian countries took a similar approach to that of India, with the general support of the socialist countries, but the three Latin American member states took quite an opposite approach, arguing that no intellectual or artistic progress would be possible if the protection of authors was weakened.[108] Finally, it is worth noting the role played by the Israeli delegation, a country at an intermediate stage of 14.16

[103] *Records* 1967, 947–52 (statements by delegates of India, Tunisia, Senegal, Ivory Coast, and Madagascar).

[104] ibid, 949 (Mr Krishnamurti of India).

[105] ibid.

[106] eg France, Italy, and Ireland: ibid, 949–52.

[107] ibid, 950 (Mr Wallace).

[108] Mexico, Argentina, and Uruguay; ibid, 949–50.

development, in seeking to achieve consensus between the different camps.[109] Although the minutes of Main Committee II only reveal intermittent glimpses of the strong passions that discussion of the Protocol proposals raised, it is clear that the atmosphere of the Committee's proceedings was highly charged and that there was considerable mutual mistrust between the protagonists.[110] This, no doubt, was simply a reflection of what had been happening in other international forums for a number of years, but there can be no doubt as to the deep divisions that existed between the parties in this debate. Failure has never been very far from the surface in many of the projects which have been undertaken by revision conferences of the Berne Union: in the present case, it was inevitable from the start.

14.17 Although a number of specific proposals were put forward by various delegations, the principal documents which formed the basis of the deliberations of Main Committee II were the programme proposals in Document S/1[111] and those made by ten developing countries in Document S/160.[112] Much of the work was done by two working groups. The first of these examined the critical question of the definition of developing country, and the second dealt with substantive matters.[113]

(2) The contents of the Stockholm Protocol

(a) The definition of a developing country

14.18 No clear proposal concerning this had been put forward in the preparatory work for the Conference, but it was obviously a question of critical importance. A wide range of proposals were made in this regard, but each had major weaknesses. Thus, a French proposal suggested a purely arbitrary amendment to the effect that any country that adhered to the Union after the signing and coming into force of the Brussels Act would be eligible to be a beneficiary of the Protocol.[114] An Italian proposal sought to place emphasis on technical criteria, such as the percentage of illiteracy and the rate of school attendance.[115] By

---

[109] *Records* 1967, 951. See also the lengthy submission which Israel had prepared, containing a large number of suggested changes to the Protocol: ibid, 683 (Document S/40).

[110] See the highly coloured description in J-L Tournier, 'Ryksdag 67, or the End of a Myth' (1968) 54–5 *RIDA* 709, 714. See further R Barker, 'The Stockholm Conference', *The Bookseller*, 8 July 1967 and B Ringer, 'The Role of the United States in International Copyright' [1968] *Copyright* 215, 223. The last-mentioned author refers to a 'febrile atmosphere of crisis and bitter debate'.

[111] *Records* 1967, 137ff.

[112] ibid, 702. These countries were Congo (Brazzaville), Congo (Kinshasa), Gabon, Ivory Coast, India, Madagascar, Morocco, Senegal, and Tunisia.

[113] Report on the Work of Main Committee II (*rapporteur*, V Strnad, Czechoslovakia): ibid, 1193.

[114] Document S/176: ibid, 704.

[115] Document S/213: ibid, 714.

contrast, two proposals by the UK and the Scandinavian countries suggested that the determination of whether a particular country was developing or not should be submitted to an appropriate international authority such as the Executive Committee of the Berne Union[116] or the UN General Assembly.[117] Other proposals included reference to the countries which were treated generally as developing countries by the UN or its agencies, such as the UN Conference on Trade and Development.[118] In the end, the Working Group proposed a text which referred to Resolution No 1897 of the UN General Assembly at its eighteenth session on 13 November 1963 which designated a long list of countries as developing countries.[119] To this was added, at the motion of the Ivory Coast, a further seven states that had become independent since this time.[120] This solution was hardly adequate, as the need to refer to UN resolutions would involve delays in the case of states which gained independence in the future. Finally, a proposal by the Scandinavian countries resulted in a more flexible formula which provided that a developing country would be considered to be any country regarded as such 'in conformity with the established practice of the General Assembly of the UN'.[121] It was further understood (though not stated) that the term 'established practice' implied that the country concerned received assistance from the UN Development Programme through the UN or its specialized agencies.[122] Even this formula is open to criticism, and is dealt with further below (see paras 14.51–14.55).[123]

---

[116] Document S/149 (UK): ibid, 700.

[117] Document S/253 (Denmark, Finland, Norway, and Sweden); ibid, 730.

[118] Preferred by Israel: ibid, 974–5 (minutes of Main Committee II).

[119] Document S/224: ibid, 716. These countries were Afghanistan, Algeria, Argentina, Bolivia, Brazil, Burma, Burundi, Cambodia, Cameroon, Central African Republic, Ceylon, Chad, Chile, Columbia, Congo (Brazzaville), Congo (Leopoldville), Costa Rica, Cyprus, Dahomey, Dominican Republic, Ecuador, El Salvador, Ethiopia, Gabon, Ghana, Guatemala, Guinea, Haiti, Honduras, India, Indonesia, Iran, Iraq, Jamaica, Jordan, Kuwait, Laos, Lebanon, Liberia, Libya, Madagascar, Malaysia, Mali, Mauritania, Mexico, Morocco, Nepal, New Zealand, Nicaragua, Niger, Nigeria, Pakistan, Panama, Paraguay, Peru, Philippines, Rwanda, Saudi Arabia, Senegal, Sierra Leone, Somalia, Sudan, Syria, Tanganyika, Thailand, Togo, Trinidad and Tobago, Tunisia, Uganda, United Arab Republic, Upper Volta, Uruguay, Venezuela, Yemen, and Yugoslavia: see O'Hara (n 15 above), 102. With the exception of New Zealand and the addition of Zambia, Kenya, and Korea, these were the developing nations that formed the original 'Group of 77' that signed the Joint Declaration of Developing Countries in Geneva in 1964, a group which has now been massively swollen in the intervening years: O'Hara (n 15 above), 103.

[120] Document S/234: ibid, 719. The countries were Botswana, Gambia, Ivory Coast, Kenya, Lesotho, Malawi, and Zambia.

[121] Document S/249: ibid, 726. See the Protocol, art 1 (preamble).

[122] Report of Main Committee II: ibid, 1194. Note that Israel made a self-denying statement that it would not seek to avail itself of the Protocol: ibid, 983. On the other hand, a Turkish request for it to be included on the list of developing countries was rejected: ibid, 974.

[123] See further O'Hara (n 15 above); D M Schrader, 'Analysis of the Protocol Regarding Developing Countries' (1970) 17 *Bull Cop Soc USA* 166ff ('Schrader (1970)').

(3) Reservations permitted

14.19 There were considerable changes made here to the proposals in the programme. The order in which the reservations appeared in the final text were also changed from that adopted in the programme. Article 1 of the Protocol now made provision for five distinct reservations: duration of protection (paragraph (a)), translation (paragraph (b)), reproduction (paragraph (c)), broadcasting (paragraph (d)), and general educational uses (paragraph (e)).

(a) Duration

14.20 No change from the programme was made here, but there was an Italian proposal to extend the term of protection from life plus twenty-five years to life plus thirty years, so as to make the Protocol a halfway house between the Berne Convention and the UCC on this point, rather than a mere replica of the latter.[124] This was decisively rejected, and the programme proposal was retained.[125] However, it should be noted that an anomaly arose here with respect to Union members who were bound, and remained bound, by the Rome Act only. These nations were not necessarily developing countries, but were free under that text to adopt whatever term of protection they thought fit.[126]

(b) Translations

14.21 The programme proposals on these were substantially amended, chiefly in the light of the proposals made by the ten developing countries in Document S/160. The latter sought to introduce to the programme proposal, which was based on the compulsory licence regime of article V of the UCC, some of the elements of article 5 of the Berne Act, as revised at Paris in 1896.[127] A number of other proposals were made,[128] but the final text proposed by the Working Group and adopted by the Committee strongly reflected the desires of the developing countries.[129] The new provision was long and detailed, but essentially contained two elements: the ending of translation rights in the event that these rights were not exercised within a given period of time, and the provision of compulsory licences. It provided as follows.

---

124 Document S/162: *Records* 1967, 703.

125 ibid, 959 (minutes of Main Committee II). The vote was twenty-six to four, with nine abstentions.

126 Rome Act, art 7(1) and (2).

127 *Records* 1967, 956–7 (minutes of Main Committee II).

128 Italy (Document S/162: ibid, 703); Denmark (Document S/146: ibid, 700); Greece (Document S/181: ibid, 708); Israel (Document S/199: ibid, 711); Japan (Document S/127: ibid, 698).

129 ibid, 1195 (report). See also Schrader (1970), 176ff.

(i) The ending of translation rights: These were to cease to exist after ten years from the date of publication of the original of his work, if, during this time, the copyright owner had not published, in one of the countries of the Union, a translation in the language for which protection was claimed.[130] This provision basically preserved the position under earlier texts of the Convention. It appeared unnecessary for the authorized translation to have been published in the country invoking the Protocol.[131]

(ii) Compulsory licences: The regime governing these was more complex, and provided as follows. If, after three years from the date of a work's first publication, or any longer period determined by the legislation of the developing country concerned, a translation of this work had not been published in that country in the 'national or official or regional language or languages of that country' by the owner of the translation right, or with his authorization, any national of such country might obtain a non-exclusive licence from the 'competent authority' to translate and publish the translation into any of the languages in which the work was unpublished.[132] The granting of these licences was subject to certain conditions:

1. The national seeking the licence was required to establish, in accordance with the procedure laid down in national legislation, that he had requested, and had been denied, authorization to make a translation, or that he had been unable to find the owner of the right 'after due diligence on his part'. In the event that the same conditions were fulfilled, a licence could also be granted where all previous editions of a translation in that language in that country were out of print.[133]
2. Where the owner could not be found, there was a procedure to be followed before the licence could be granted: appropriate notice was to be sent to the publisher whose name appeared on the work and, where the author's nationality was known, to the diplomatic or consular representative of the country of which he was a national.[134]
3. Provision was to be made by national legislation to 'assure to the owner of the right of translation a just compensation, to assure payment and transmittal of such compensation, subject to national currency regulations, and to assure a correct translation of the work'.[135] The reference to

[130] Protocol, art 1(b)(i).
[131] Schrader (1970), 181, expresses the opposite opinion, basing this on a comment in the report of the Main Committee II (*Records* 1967, 1196). But the comments in the report are directed at translation licences under art 1(b)(ii)–(ix), not at reservations to translation rights.
[132] Protocol, art 1(b)(ii)–(ix). [133] ibid, art 1(b)(ii). [134] ibid, art 1(b)(iii).
[135] ibid, art 1(b)(iv).

national currency regulations was to become a serious point of contention to publishers in the developed nations.

4. The author's right of attribution was to be acknowledged, with the printing of the original title and name of the author on each copy of the published translation.[136]
5. The licence was only valid for publication of the translation in the territory of the country of the Union where it had been applied for.[137] However, copies of the translation might be imported and sold in another country of the Union if one of the national or official or regional languages of that country was the same as that into which the work had been translated, and if the legislation of that country provided for similar licences and did not prohibit such importation or sale—in other words, if the country of importation was a developing country that had taken advantage of the reservation with respect to translations under the Protocol.[138] To give an example, if India were to provide for such translation licences under the Protocol, and an Indian national was granted a licence to translate an English work into Tamil, copies of these translations might be exported to Ceylon (Sri Lanka) if that country made provision for similar licences and did not prohibit that importation. The rationale for this provision appeared to be that no harm was done in such a case, as the work could have been made subject to an identical licence in the second country. However, there was extended debate over this in Main Committee II, as the developed nations were concerned to avoid the exportation of such translations for commercial profit or even back to the country of origin of the original work.
6. Licences were not to be transferable.[139]
7. Licences were not to be granted when the author had withdrawn all copies of his work from circulation.[140]
8. In the event that the author exercised his right of translation during the ten-year period from first publication of the original, the licence was to terminate on the date on which the author published his translation in the country where the licence had been granted.[141] The sale of translations already made under the licence was permitted.[142] In the event that all editions of the author's translation fell out of print, the right of any national of that country to obtain a non-exclusive licence to translate the work was revived, subject to observing the same conditions as were required for the original licence.[143]

[136] Protocol, art 1(b)(v). [137] ibid. [138] ibid. [139] ibid.
[140] ibid, art 1(b)(vi). [141] ibid, art 1(b)(vii). [142] ibid. [143] ibid, art 1(b)(ix).

9. The sting in the tail, however, was that where the author failed to publish such a translation within the said ten-year period, at the end of this time the obligation of the licensee to pay compensation came to an end.[144] This complemented the provisions of the Berne Act, as revised at Paris, under which translation rights came to an end after ten years of publication of the original work if a translation was not published in that period. However, it evoked considerable opposition from delegates of the developed nations.[145]
10. Licences could only be granted where the author had not published a translation in the country whose national was invoking the licence.[146] This differed from both the UCC and article 5 of the Paris Act of 1896, neither of which stated precisely where the publication should take place. The effect of this stipulation was that, if an author published a translation in the relevant language in a Union country, the licence could still be invoked in another Union country which had adopted the Protocol. On the other hand, the following clarification of the meaning of 'publication', as used in paragraph (b) of article I of the Protocol, is to be found in the report of Main Committee II. This was said not to be

> . . . printing in the strict sense; . . . an essential distinction for countries that do not possess even the technical means needed to publish translations or reproductions under the conditions laid down by the Protocol.[147]

In other words, it appeared feasible for an author to publish a translation of his work in the country in question by simply importing copies of the translation for sale in that country.

The operation of, and interrelationship between, these different components of the reservation provided under paragraph (b) was far from clear. For instance, the following questions arose: **14.22**

1. Did the author lose his whole right of translation after ten years from publication of the original if he had not published a translation in the language for which he claimed protection, or was his right cut back only in respect of translations into that language?
2. Did the author also lose his moral rights in such a case? This matter was not dealt with in the provision, but the correct view appeared to be that, in the absence of a clear contrary stipulation, the author was not to be divested of his moral rights under article 6*bis*.[148]
3. If the author published a translation in the relevant language within ten years of first publication of the original in any other country of the Union,

[144] ibid, art 1(b)(viii).
[145] *Records* 1967, 976–8 (the Netherlands, Italy).
[146] Protocol, art 1(b)(ii).
[147] *Records* 1967, 1196 (report of Main Committee II).
[148] Schrader (1970), 192–3.

he would not lose his protection for such translations in a country which invoked the Protocol. On the other hand, if he did not publish, in that country, a translation in the language within three years of publication of the original, that country was then free to grant compulsory licences for such translations. In such a case, the obligation to pay compensation under the licence came to an end ten years after publication of the original, even though the author had otherwise satisfied the requirements for the continuation of his right.

4. Problems of proof might arise in cases where the author alleged that he had withdrawn all copies of his work from circulation. This state of affairs might be indistinguishable from that where all copies of the work were out of print—a situation which justified the granting of a compulsory licence.

These matters, as well as many others, made the scope of the reservation in respect of translations unclear and uncertain.

(c) Reproduction licences

14.23 The programme proposal to allow for reservations in respect of reproductions permitted under article 9(2) of the Brussels Act was substantially changed. For a start, article 9(2) was retained, in substance, as article 10*bis* of the new Act. However, a far wider reservation relating to reproductions was added to the Protocol as article I(c), taking account of the concerns of developing countries to have ready access to copies of works in their original language as well as in translation (as permitted under article I(b)).[149] In essence, this provided that non-exclusive licences for the reproduction and publication of a literary or artistic work for 'educational or cultural purposes' might be granted by a 'competent authority' to any national of a developing country if, after the expiry of three years from the date of first publication of the work (or any longer period that might be determined by national legislation), it had not been published in that country 'in the original form in which it was created', by the owner of the right of reproduction or with his authorization.[150] These licences were distinct from the additional (and wider) reservations which were permitted in the case of educational uses (see article I(e)). According to the report of Main Committee I, the wording 'for educational or cultural purposes' was not to be interpreted in a restrictive manner: for this reason, it was stated that the words 'for exclusively . . . purposes' had been intentionally deleted.[151] On the other hand, it stressed that the expression 'educational or cultural purposes' excluded from its scope 'all works whose educational or cultural purpose is not apparent', for example, detective or adventure stories.[152] The procedure for obtaining such licences, and

[149] For a detailed commentary, see Schrader (1970) 196ff.
[150] Protocol, art 1(c)(i).
[151] *Records* 1967, 1196 (report).
[152] ibid.

the conditions under which this might be done, followed the same model as for translation licences under article I(b).[153]

(d) Broadcasting

Under article I(b), developing countries were permitted to substitute, for article 11*bis* of the Stockholm Act, the provisions of article 11*bis* (1) and (2) of the Rome Act. However, two changes to the Rome text were made here. The first was the substitution of the word 'broadcasting' for 'communication by radiodiffusion', thus making it clear that television transmissions were included.[154] Secondly, it was stipulated that the words 'communication to the public of the broadcast' applied only where this was made for 'profit-making purposes'.[155] Accordingly, while article 11*bis* (2) of the Rome Act allowed for the imposition of compulsory licences (subject to the payment of equitable remuneration) for profit-making communications, any non-profit-making communication could be freely made without the permission of the author or any requirement to pay equitable remuneration. **14.24**

(e) Educational uses

Although each of the foregoing reservations was the subject of controversy, the final one in article I(e) most clearly brought out the differences between developing and developed nations. The programme had proposed that developing countries should be able to reserve the right, 'for exclusively educational, scientific or scholastic purposes, to restrict the protection of literary or artistic works'.[156] There was no requirement to pay compensation under this formulation, but the purposes were strictly defined. The proposal of the ten developing countries in Document S/160 had gone further, proposing the imposition of compulsory licences generally, unless the use was for 'primarily educational, scientific or scholastic purposes'.[157] Neither proposal was restricted to the making of translations or reproductions: the reservation was to apply to all uses of protected works. The developing countries' rationale for their wider formulation was that they needed to be able to use works more generally than for strictly educational, scientific or scholastic purposes, as this would give the mass of their population, unable to attend schools and similar institutions, the opportunity of acquiring knowledge through adult literacy campaigns and other information programmes.[158] The response of the developed nations to this argument was that the proposed reservation went far beyond what could be reconciled with the aims of the Convention, and should be dealt with as part of a general programme of assistance to developing countries.[159] The final text adopted by **14.25**

[153] Protocol, art 1(c)(ii)–(vii).
[154] *Records* 1967, 1197 (report). [155] ibid. [156] Document S/1: ibid, 143.
[157] ibid, 702.
[158] ibid, 960 (speech by Mr Krishnamurti of India to Main Committee II).
[159] ibid, 960–1 (the UK and the Netherlands).

the Stockholm Conference did not go as far as Document S/160, but nonetheless embodied more concessions than had been proposed in the programme. In essence, it permitted developing countries to impose compulsory licences in respect of any protected use of literary or artistic works 'exclusively for teaching, study and research in all fields of education'.[160] There was a clear overlap here with the other reservations allowed under paragraphs (b), (c), and (d), but the licences under paragraph (e) extended to uses other than translations, reproductions, and broadcasts of protected works.[161] Furthermore, the requirement to pay compensation was differently formulated, in that it was to conform to the 'standards of payment made to national authors'.[162] While this put national and foreign authors on the same level, this was not necessarily the same as the 'just compensation' required to be paid under paragraphs (b) and (c), or the 'equitable remuneration' payable under paragraph (d). For example, if national authors were content, or were required, to receive nominal fees for the use of their works, the same fees could be paid to foreign authors whose works might in fact constitute the bulk of works used. The addition of the words 'in all fields of education' and the exclusivity of the purposes for which the reservation could be utilized indicated that industrial and commercial research lay outside its scope. On the other hand, the words 'in all fields of education' were still wide enough to apply to mass literacy and adult education campaigns extending far beyond the confines of the classroom. During the debates in Main Committee II, there had been attempts to confine the reservation to uses within established educational institutions, but these had been rejected.[163] Finally, as with paragraphs (b) and (c), paragraph (e) was subject to the same conditions as to payment and transmittal of compensation, but the export and sale of copies to other countries of the Union was only permitted if those countries had also invoked paragraph (e) or if this had the consent of the author or his successors in title.[164]

(4) **Length of reservations**

14.26 The programme had proposed that the duration of reservations should be for a period of ten years, which might be renewed, by notification to this effect before the end of this period, until 'the entry into force of the Act adopted by the next Revision Conference'.[165] There was considerable debate over this in Main Committee II, as the developing countries argued that it would deprive them of the benefit of reservations which they might still need, in the event that they did

[160] Protocol, art 1(e). [161] *Records* 1967, 1197 (report). [162] Protocol, art 1(e).

[163] *Records* 1967, 961 (French proposal to limit usage to the 'exclusive use of scholastic or educational institutions, vocational training centres and centres of a rural nature'). See also Document S/178: ibid, 704.

[164] See further Schrader (1970), 213–14. [165] Document S/1: *Records* 1967, 144.

not adhere to the next Act of Revision.[166] This was not necessarily as arbitrary as might first appear, as a new Act could only be formulated, in the first place, if all countries of the Union, including those which were developing, agreed to its provisions:[167] it would therefore be surprising if a new Act failed to make suitable provision for the continuance of reservations under the Protocol where these were necessary. The final wording adopted, however, was based on Document S/160 and allowed those countries which had made reservations to maintain any or all of them until they ratified or acceded to the Act adopted by the next conference of revision.[168] There was no requirement, as under the programme proposal, for the intention to maintain these reservations to be communicated to the Director General.[169] However, provision was made for withdrawal of reservations by notification deposited with the Director General when a country no longer needed to maintain them.[170]

(a) Dependent territories

In 1967, there were still a number of dependent and developing territories that had not attained the status of fully independent states. As the result of a UK proposal, a further article was added to the Protocol which allowed for its application to territories which otherwise satisfied the requirements of article 1 and to which the Convention had been applied by a declaration made by their protecting power under article 31(1).[171] Thus, the latter could declare, by notification to the Director General, that the territory in question would avail itself of one or more of the reservations permitted in the Protocol.[172] The delegations of Tunisia, Czechoslovakia, India, and Israel stated their opposition in principle to clauses of this kind,[173] and in the plenary of the Berne Union it was amended so as to indicate that the notification under the Protocol could only be made by a country which was itself bound by the provisions of the Protocol.[174] **14.27**

(5) Countries ceasing to be developing

This situation was covered by article 4 which applied the reverse test to that required for eligibility to invoke the provisions of the Protocol. If, in conformity with the established practice of the UN General Assembly, a country ceased to **14.28**

---

166 ibid, 967ff (India, Ivory Coast, Gabon).

167 ibid, 969 (remarks by Mr Bodenhausen, Director of BIRPI, to Main Committee II).

168 Protocol, art 3.

169 Note here the comments by Mr Krishnamurti of India that unforeseen natural and other crises might sometimes make it difficult for developing countries to manifest their wishes with respect to the continuation of their reservations within the required time if this was a condition for the maintenance of such reservations: *Records* 1967, 969.

170 Protocol, art 2. 171 ibid, art 6. 172 ibid.

173 *Records* 1967, 985 and 1198 (report). See also Schrader (1970), 229ff.

174 *Records* 1967, 809.

be regarded as developing, the Director General was to notify the country concerned and all other countries of the Union of this fact.[175] After six years from the date of this notification, the country in question would no longer have the right to maintain any reservations under the Protocol.[176]

(6) Provisions to hasten the application of the Protocol

14.29 There had always been a strong desire by developing countries to be able to take immediate advantage of the benefits of the new concessions allowed under the Protocol, without waiting for the new Act to come into force.[177] Article 5 of the Protocol therefore contained provisions which permitted both developing and developed countries to apply the Protocol voluntarily as between those which were so agreed from the date of signature[178] of the Convention and at any time before becoming bound by the Protocol. Under article 5(a), a developing country was able to declare that it intended to apply the provisions of the Protocol to works whose country of origin was a country of the Union which admitted the application of the reservations under the Protocol. Conversely, under article 5(b) a developed country was able to declare that it admitted the application of the Protocol to works of which it was the country of origin by a developing country which was either bound by the Protocol or had made a declaration under paragraph (a). This invitation to expedite the application of the Protocol was taken up by very few countries: by 1971, only Bulgaria and Sweden had deposited declarations under paragraph (b) and only Senegal and Pakistan under paragraph (a).[179]

(7) Status of the Protocol

14.30 This question was debated at length both before and during the Stockholm Conference.[180] The view of many of the developed countries was that the Protocol should be an independent instrument,[181] but for obvious reasons this was strongly resisted by the developing countries.[182] Under article 21(2), therefore,

[175] See further Schrader (1970), 221ff.

[176] As to the problems in applying this article, see ibid, 224ff.

[177] Document S/1: *Records* 1967, 144. See further Schrader (1970), 226ff.

[178] This meant the date of signature of the Convention (14 July 1967), not the date of signature by the country concerned to take advantage of the Protocol. This was the interpretation agreed upon in the thirteenth session of the BUPC which met in Geneva, 12–15 Dec 1967: [1968] *Copyright* 23, 24.

[179] Report by the Director General of WIPO (historical outline of the preparations for the revision of the Berne Convention), B/DC/3, in *Records* 1971, 34. 181 Johnson (1970), 178ff.

[180] ibid.

[181] This was the view of ALAI, expressed in a resolution at its 52nd Congress at Basle, 29 Mar–4 Apr 1967: [1967] *Copyright* 124.

[182] See the opening debates in Main Committee II: *Records* 1967, 947ff.

the Protocol was declared to be an integral part of the principal Act. However, the effect of this declaration was broken by article 28(1)(b)(i) which provided that any country acceding to, or ratifying, the new Act might do so only in part, by limiting its accession or ratification so as not to apply to articles 1 to 21 and the Protocol. It was further provided that these provisions might be subsequently adhered to, but the result was that a developed nation was left with the option of not acceding to, or ratifying, the Protocol. Such a course carried with it the penalty of being unable to adhere to the substantive provisions of articles 1 to 20, but this did not involve any great sacrifice as the level of protection already offered by the Brussels Act was, in some respects, higher than that offered by these provisions. Article 28(1)(b)(i) therefore provided a means for the developed nations to subvert the intended effects of the Protocol, and this is exactly what happened.

(8) Reservations with respect to translation rights

Under the Brussels Act, countries of the Union (the 'old countries') which acceded to that Act were allowed to retain the benefit of reservations previously made, while countries outside the Union (the 'new countries') were allowed to apply the provisions of article 5 of the Berne Act, as amended by article 1 of the Paris Additional Act, upon their accession.[183] In the programme for the Stockholm Revision, it was proposed that, while the old countries should continue to have the benefit of their previous reservations, there was no reason why new countries should be allowed to formulate reservations in respect of translation rights: after all, the latter had taken the decision to adhere to the Union on the basis of acceptance of its substantive provisions and there was no need to allow the continuance of this special concession.[184] This proposal evoked some opposition, and, at the request of Main Committee IV (the committee responsible for drafting the administrative and final clauses of the Convention),[185] a large majority of Main Committee I expressed the opinion that it would be better to give new countries the benefit of continuing to be able to formulate reservations as had hitherto been the case.[186] This was only an expression of opinion, and led to renewed discussion in Main Committee IV.[187] Finally, a new formulation was adopted in article 30(2)(b) whereby new countries were free to continue to make, upon their accession to the Union, reservations with respect to translations, but subject to the requirement of effective reciprocity. Thus, a rider to this paragraph provided that: **14.31**

[183] Brussels Act, art 25(3) ('new countries') and art 27(2) ('old countries').

[184] Article 25ter, Document S/9: *Records* 1967, 466–8.

[185] ibid, 1217–18 (report of Main Committee IV).

[186] ibid, 920 (Main Committee I), 943–5 (Main Committees I and IV).

[187] ibid, 1050–1.

> Any country of the Union has the right to apply, in relation to the right of translation of works whose country of origin is a country availing itself of such a reservation, a protection which is equivalent to the protection granted by the latter country.

This still left an imbalance as between old and new countries. If country X, being an old country, had previously made a reservation relating to translations, this could be maintained upon accession to the Stockholm Act by virtue of article 30(2)(a). In such a case, other countries of the Union were not free to impose corresponding restrictions with respect to translations into the language(s) of country X. On the other hand, if country Y, being a new country, limited translation rights in accordance with article 30(2)(b), similar limitations could be imposed by other Union countries with respect to works originating from country Y.

(9) Proposals for an authors' fund

14.32 Throughout the discussions at the Stockholm Revision Conference, a number of the delegates of the developed nations referred to the need for assistance to developing nations to take other forms than through the lowering of protection offered by the Berne Convention.[188] Few specific proposals were considered, but, at the instance of the Israeli delegation, the Conference gave its approval to a recommendation that the International Office of the Berne Union should investigate the concept of an authors' fund which would compensate authors for the use that might be made of their works in developing countries. The final resolution adopted by the Conference read as follows:

> The Intellectual Property Conference of Stockholm, Recognizing the special economic and cultural needs of developing countries, desirous of enabling developing countries to have the full use of works protected by copyright for educational requirements, having for this purpose adopted the Protocol Regarding Developing Countries, requests and authorizes the International Bureau to undertake in association with other governmental and non-governmental organizations a study of ways and means for creating financial machinery to ensure a fair and just return to authors.[189]

(10) The adoption of the Protocol

14.33 The adoption of the Protocol by the final plenary session of the Berne Union at the Stockholm Conference revealed little real satisfaction with what had been achieved. It also showed that the rancour between developing and developed nations that had suffused the sessions of Main Committee II had failed to subside. One of the most important of the developed nations, the UK,

[188] See, in particular, the opening comments of delegates in Main Committee II: ibid, 947ff.
[189] ibid, 987 (Main Committee II). For text of resolution, see Document S/228: ibid, 716.

abstained from voting on the Protocol,[190] and it has been suggested that it only refrained from voting against it because of fears of offending the developing nations, particularly those with large markets for English-language books such as India and Pakistan.[191] There were also abstentions from Mexico and Uruguay which had made clear their opposition to the Protocol throughout the Conference.[192] The delegation of France, by contrast, 'welcomed' the adoption of the Protocol as a suitable solution, within the framework of the Union, of the conflicting interests concerned.[193] Nevertheless, this country, over the next year or so, was to adopt a more critical view of the Protocol and was ultimately to refrain from ratifying it. As for the proponents of the Protocol, there was a view that not enough had been achieved, and that it was only a halfway step in the right direction.[194] In this regard, the Indian delegation made pointed reference to the failure of the UK to adopt a more positive attitude.[195] In the event, the provisions of the Protocol were to prove the largest concessions that developing countries were to attain in the context of the Berne Convention, and the lukewarm acquiescence of the developed nations was to be rapidly replaced by concerted opposition.

D. The Events Following the Adoption of the Stockholm Protocol

(1) The immediate reactions

It will be clear from the above that the Protocol commanded little real acceptance from any of the parties concerned in its formulation. The authors' and publishers' associations in the developed countries were implacably opposed to it, particularly in the UK,[196] and the international organizations representing their interests took a similar, if more restrained, attitude.[197] The prevailing view was that the Protocol embodied too many concessions in favour of the developing countries. Four particular areas of concern can be identified: the lack of any real guarantee that authors would be paid in cases of use for 'teaching, scholarship and research' and the problems that might arise with respect to the transmittal of compensation in the case of the other reservations; **14.34**

[190] ibid, 807 (Plenary Session of Berne Union).

[191] Sacks (n 87 above), 129, n 43, reproduces the following report from *The Times*, 20 July, that the 'Government had not vetoed the Protocol because of fears that countries such as India and Pakistan would withdraw from the Berne Convention on copyright, and that Britain would isolate herself from the underdeveloped countries who benefit from the Protocol'.

[192] *Records* 1967, 810.

[193] ibid, 814.

[194] ibid, 809–11 (Tunisia, Cameroon, and India).

[195] ibid, 811 (Mr Singh of India).

[196] Sacks (n 87 above), 130ff; Whale (n 87 above), 20ff.

[197] [1968] *Copyright* 146 and 188.

the provisions allowing export of copies to other developing countries; the inadequate definition of a developing country; and the lack of any direct incentive to developing countries to improve the level of protection beyond that offered by the Protocol.[198] It was also strongly argued that lowering the level of international copyright protection, at the expense of authors and publishers, was not the way to assist developing countries in their literacy and education programmes and that the real solution lay in the adoption of other forms of technical and economic assistance. Thus, in its Congress of 1968, the IPA called upon its member associations:

> . . . to urge their governments to provide such technical and economic aid as would eliminate any need to ratify or implement the Stockholm Protocol, and together with the publishing, to facilitate the local distribution of needed books in developing countries.[199]

CISAC was similarly opposed,[200] and ALAI confirmed its earlier opinion that:

> . . . the Protocol constitutes a sacrifice of the rights of authors in developed countries and jeopardizes the best interests of authors in developing countries.[201]

These views clearly had a strong influence on the governments of the developed nations, as was witnessed by their failure to ratify the Protocol. Another significant factor was a statement by the US Government in December 1967 that the Protocol, if adopted, would pose a near insurmountable barrier to that country's desired accession to the Convention.[202] The resulting situation of stalemate has rightly been called a 'crisis in international copyright'.[203] It seemed clear that the point had been reached where the needs and interests of developed and developing nations could no longer be accommodated within the one multilateral instrument. This might be seen as the result of a failure by the developed countries to recognize, in time, the problems of the developing countries and to formulate a coherent strategy for meeting these concerns through other forms of assistance. This failure now meant that, for the first time in its history, the Berne Convention had become 'politicized', and its status as one of the pre-eminent international conventions dealing with private rights in a generally non-partisan manner had been severely weakened. The surprising thing is that, within four years, this crisis was to be overcome through the display of an unusually high level of international co-operation and conciliation. In 1967, however, the

[198] These were the principal areas of concern highlighted by Mr A Kaminstein, the US Register of Copyrights, in a statement to the joint meeting of the BUPC and IGC in Geneva, 12–15 Dec 1967: (1967–8) 15 *Bull Cop Soc USA* 157, 159 (the 'Register's Statement').

[199] 18th Congress, Amsterdam, 9–15 June 1968: [1968] *Copyright* 188, 189.

[200] See the resolutions passed by the 26th Congress, Vienna, 23–9 June 1968: [1968] *Copyright* 189, 190.

[201] General Assembly of ALAI, 23 Apr 1968, Paris: [1968] *Copyright* 146.

[202] Register's Statement (n 198 above), 157.

[203] Sacks (n 87 above), 26.

future looked bleak, and it was unclear how the impasse might be breached. At this stage, several different scenarios appeared possible.

First, there was the possibility that the developing nations would leave the Berne Union (and perhaps the UCC, if they were also members of that Convention), and desert the international copyright system altogether, relying on the advantages to be derived from being a 'free rider'. There were 'respectable' precedents for remaining outside the international copyright system, as provided by the experience of the USA in the nineteenth century and the examples of China and the Soviet Union in the twentieth. Another possibility, only slightly less worrying, was that a system of special bilateral arrangements between individual developing and developed nations would develop, with all the confusion and uncertainty that this would entail.[204]

A second possible scenario was that the developing nations would leave the Berne Union and join the UCC, so as to take advantage of the lower level of protection of the latter. An obstacle here was the Berne safeguard clause (see further paras 18.27ff below), and a number of developing countries began to campaign more vigorously for its deletion in the period after the Stockholm Revision.[205] On the other hand, the USA and some other existing UCC members were concerned that this might make it harder to raise the level of protection offered by the UCC.[206]

A third possibility was the modification of the Stockholm Protocol so as to provide a compromise more acceptable to the developed nations, and thus to keep the Berne Union intact. In this scenario, it was clear that the developing nations would be required to make significant concessions on their earlier demands and would have to accept reductions in the gains they had made at Stockholm. They would therefore have to assess how much continued membership of the Berne Union was worth to them.

Finally, a more complex solution was to bring the Berne Convention and UCC closer together so as to take account of the respective interests of developed and developing nations. One possibility was a common protocol which members of both conventions might sign, with differing levels of protection applicable between different groups of states.[207] Another was for there to be a mechanism

[204] This possibility was referred to with 'genuine alarm' by Mr Kaminstein: Register's Statement (n 198 above), 159.

[205] See generally, E Ulmer, 'The Revision of the Copyright Conventions in the Light of the Washington Recommendation' (1970) 1 *IIC* 235, 236; R Hadl, 'Toward International Copyright Revision' (1970) 18 *Bull Cop Soc USA* 183, 184ff; Braderman (n 99 above).

[206] Register's Statement (n 198 above), 160.

[207] Such a proposal, indeed, was to be found in the detailed memorandum prepared by BIRPI for the meeting of the Joint Study Group in Washington in mid-1969: see para 14.40 below.

which allowed developing states to move from the Berne Union to the UCC, and then back again when they had ceased to be developing. There were further variants, and each was complicated by the desire of some UCC states (such as the USA) to raise the level of protection under the UCC. This fourth option, of joint revision, was the course that was ultimately taken.

(2) The steps in the revision of the Stockholm Protocol

14.35 The principal steps by which the different sides came to agree on a differently formulated set of provisions concerning developing countries were as follows.

(a) The meeting of the Permanent Committee of the Berne Union (thirteenth session, Geneva, 12–15 December 1967)[208]

14.36 This was the first formal opportunity for there to be an assessment of the results of the Stockholm Revision, in particular the Protocol Concerning Developing Countries. The meeting was also attended by a large number of states and non-governmental international organizations in an observer capacity, including a number of non-Berne states.[209] The reluctance of the developed nations to commit themselves to the Protocol became clear at this meeting,[210] although only the UK was prepared to state unreservedly that it would not ratify it.[211] The concern of the developing nations at the likely failure of the Protocol was also evident,[212] and was reflected in a resolution which was passed, at the motion of the Indian delegation.[213] This requested BIRPI to inquire of the developed states what were their intentions as regards the Protocol, and to inquire of the developing states the use they proposed to make of the Protocol.[214] However, a more positive measure adopted by the joint meeting of the BUPC and the IGC of the UCC held at the same time concerned the relationship between the Berne Convention and the UCC. This stemmed from a suggestion made by the US observer, and proposed the establishment of a joint group for the study of the relationship between the two conventions, with particular reference to the problems of developing countries.[215]

(b) The extraordinary sessions of the Permanent Committee of the Berne Union and the Intergovernmental Committee of the UCC (Paris, 3–7 February 1969)[216]

14.37 The following year (1968) saw no further meeting of an official nature, but a great deal of negotiation took place between the interested parties on an informal level.[217] During this time, the developing countries increased their

[208] [1968] *Copyright* 23. [209] Notably the USA: ibid, 31. [210] ibid, 24–5.
[211] ibid, 24. [212] ibid. [213] ibid. [214] ibid, 24 and 29 (Resolution No 1).
[215] ibid, 26–7 and 29 (Resolution No 2). [216] [1969] *Copyright* 48.
[217] Hadl (n 205 above), 186.

pressure for a revision of the UCC, in particular through the deletion of the Berne safeguard clause.[218] Support for this gradually grew, but some important developed nations, such as the USA, indicated that they would not be able to accept revision of the safeguard clause unless the general level of protection under the UCC was also raised.[219] At the same time, the concept of a joint study group was pursued. The next formal step in the saga therefore was an extraordinary session of both the BUPC and the IGC of the UCC in February 1969.[220] At the meeting of the IGC, it was unanimously decided to convene a conference for the purpose of revising the safeguard clause, and, at the invitation of the US Government, Washington was chosen as the venue. A sub-committee was established to examine the implications of this proposal, particularly with respect to its implications for the Berne Convention, and the following issues of relevance to our present discussion were referred to it:[221]

(1) whether the suspension of the safeguard clause should be limited to developing countries and, if so, how that term should be defined;
(2) whether the safeguard clause should be suspended indefinitely or for a specified period of time;
(3) whether a Berne Union member should be entitled to adjust the level of protection to that offered by a developing country under the suspension;
(4) whether any link between the Berne Union and the Universal Copyright Convention could or should be substituted for the safeguard clause;
(5) the majority necessary at a revision conference to revise the Universal Copyright Convention and particularly its Article XVII and the Appendix Declaration relating thereto.[222]

In addition to this, at the meeting of the two committees, a formal resolution was passed to constitute the joint study group referred to in the 1967 resolution, and to establish its terms of reference and composition.[223] Referring to the 'present serious and potential problems of multilateral copyright relations' and noting that the Stockholm Protocol had not yet been accepted by many member states of the Berne Union, the resolution established 'a group for the study of the entire situation of international relations in the field of copyright to be called the International Copyright Joint Study Group'.[224] It was further provided that the Group might examine 'any questions concerning international copyright relations and their practical implications', but as a matter of priority the Group was asked to consider the following matters at its first meeting: **14.38**

[218] Ringer (n 110 above), 226. Note that some seven UCC members had made a request for a revision to the Convention by the time of the Dec 1967 meeting of the IGC.

[219] Ulmer (n 205 above), 236 and Ringer (n 110 above), 226. See also the discussions in the joint meeting of the BUPC and IGC in Dec 1967: [1967] *Copyright* 26ff.

[220] [1969] *Copyright* 48 (BUPC), 70 (IGC). [221] ibid, 72. [222] ibid, 73.

[223] ibid, 51 and 52. [224] ibid, 52.

(a) the establishment of an international mechanism for permitting developing countries a greater degree of access to protected works while respecting the rights of authors;

(b) the needs of developing and developed countries in the international copyright field, particularly that of education, the effect of the regime of international copyright relations on the satisfaction of these needs, as well as any improvements that could be made in this respect, taking into account the interests of authors with a view to encouraging the creation of intellectual works;

(c) the problems arising from the existence of two copyright conventions of world-wide scope and possible methods for providing links between them.[225]

The first of these items did not really relate to the question of copyright, but was relevant to the practical measures that might be made to assist developing countries, for example, to hasten the obtaining of authorizations. The second two items, however, were of direct importance to the future development of both conventions. The date of the first meeting of the Joint Group was set for 29 September to 3 October 1969 in Washington, and representation on the Group was given to twenty-six states, members of both conventions.[226]

14.39 In the words of one distinguished participant, it is hard to realize from reading the reports and resolutions what 'an important corner was turned' at these meetings of February 1969.[227] Although a great amount of detailed work remained to be done, it was now clear that the solution of the problems of the developing countries under the Berne Convention was to be found in the framework of a revision of the UCC.[228] Furthermore, it appeared clear that the Stockholm Protocol was now generally regarded by all the concerned parties as a 'dying if not dead duck'.[229] Finally, on a more personal level, much of the hostility and suspicion that had been present at the Stockholm Revision Conference had subsided, with the result that the Paris meetings had been conducted 'in an atmosphere of cooperation and goodwill that was as gratifying as it was unusual'.[230] This represented a recognition by the developing nations that there was some value for them in remaining in the international copyright system, although it was clear that some surrender would have to be made of the benefits they had notionally gained in Stockholm.

---

225 *Copyright* 48, 52.

226 Argentina, Australia, Brazil, Canada, Ceylon, Czechoslovakia, France, the FRG, India, Italy, Ivory Coast, Japan, Kenya, Mexico, the Netherlands, Nigeria, Peru, Philippines, Romania, Senegal, Spain, Sweden, Tunisia, the UK, the USA, and Yugoslavia: ibid.

227 B Ringer, 'Recent Developments in International Copyright: The Paris Meetings of February 1969' (1968–9) 16 *Bull Cop Soc USA* 223.

228 ibid, 224. 229 ibid. 230 ibid.

(c) *The extraordinary session of the Permanent Committee of the Berne Union (Geneva, 20–1 June 1969)*[231]

This meeting immediately preceded the meeting of the sub-committee of the IGC which had been set up in February. Its purpose was to consider the advice which should be given by the Director of BIRPI to the sub-committee on the effects of the proposed revision with respect to the Berne Convention.[232] In a provisional report prepared by the Director, the latter had suggested that there should be a search under both conventions for 'common rules' which could be adopted in both conventions in relation to developing countries.[233] In this regard, a new protocol common to both conventions might be considered, or even a merging of the two, providing, at the same time, for the same concessions to developing countries. The discussions in the Committee, however, revealed that there was a strong body of opinion against any merger of the conventions and that they should each maintain their separate identity.[234] Nevertheless, it was accepted that any proposal to revise or suspend the safeguard clause of the UCC should not be carried out in isolation from the Berne Convention, and that some kind of link between the two conventions should be maintained.[235] With this in view, the Director of BIRPI (Professor Bodenhausen) proposed that, if the safeguard clause were to be revised, the two conventions should be revised simultaneously: the Berne Convention, in order to separate the Stockholm Protocol from it and to make certain of the provisions of the latter more precise, and the UCC, in order to introduce some minimum rights with exceptions identical to those which would be admitted under the revised and by then separate Stockholm Protocol.[236] These proposals were to prove prophetic of the course that the process of revision was eventually to take. For the present, however, the majority of the BUPC took the following view on the issues to be discussed by the forthcoming meeting of the sub-committee of the IGC (see above): **14.40**

1. Only developing countries should be able to benefit from any suspension of the safeguard clause, and the notion of a 'developing country' should be the same as in the Stockholm Protocol.
2. Any precise limitation as to times (of suspension) would be artificial, and should not be provided for.
3. That the application of any measure of material reciprocity depended upon the scope of the revision; if the revision was limited to the safeguard clause, the said reciprocity should be introduced; if the revision was broader, reciprocity should only apply between countries party to the Berne Convention alone and countries party to the UCC alone.

231 [1969] *Copyright* 146. 232 ibid. 233 ibid, 153.
234 ibid, 146ff (notably the delegation of France). 235 ibid. 236 ibid, 149.

4. That there should be some 'replacement link' adopted in place of the safeguard clause; and, in any case, the treatment accorded to developing countries under each of the two conventions must be the same.
5. That there should be a double vote on any proposal to revise the safeguard clause: one by members of the UCC and one by members of the Berne Union.[237]

(d) The meeting of the sub-committee of the Intergovernmental Committee (Paris, 23–7 June 1969)[238]

14.41 The conclusions of this sub-committee largely reflected the views that had been expressed by the BUPC at the extraordinary session that had been held immediately prior to it, but were more limited in their effect. In particular, it took the view that the suspension of the safeguard clause should not entail the cessation of the existing links between the two conventions, but that it was 'for further study by the Intergovernmental Copyright Committee and for decision by the revision conference whether or not to establish new links or not, and if so, to define their nature'.[239]

(e) The International Copyright Joint Study Group, first session (Washington, 29 September–3 October 1969)[240]

14.42 The two preceding meetings had clarified to some extent the kind of revision that was in contemplation for the UCC. The Joint Study Group meeting, however, provided the overall framework for the simultaneous revision of the two conventions in accordance with certain general principles. A preliminary matter discussed by the Group dealt with what may be called 'practical assistance' and was concerned with the establishment of an international mechanism to facilitate access to protected works by developing countries. There was general consensus on the need for such a measure, and, in the light of national experience and studies conducted by UNESCO, it was recommended that that body should 'establish, as soon as possible, an international copyright information centre'.[241] The guidelines for this body were laid down in the report of a working group, and were essentially concerned with the exchange of information concerning the availability of protected works and the terms on which they might be used.[242]

---

237 *Copyright*, 151 (summary made by Professor Bodenhausen).

238 [1969] *Copyright* 194. 239 ibid, 204.

240 [1969] *Copyright* 214. Although it was contemplated that further sessions would be held, this was, in fact, the only one.

241 ibid, 215. 242 ibid, 226–7. See further Ulmer (n 205 above), 239ff.

(f) The Washington Recommendation

This was the most important part of the Joint Group's achievement, and reflected the general agreement that was now emerging that both conventions should be revised simultaneously, with special attention being paid to the needs of developing countries. Although there were marked differences as to the nexus that should exist between the conventions, the following set of general principles to guide the proposed revisions were adopted. Entitled the 'Washington Recommendation', they provided as follows: **14.43**

> . . . as a matter of first priority, that the Universal Copyright Convention and the Berne Convention be simultaneously revised in revision conferences to be held at the same time and place so as to achieve the following:
>
> (I) In the Universal Copyright Convention:
> (1) Suspension of Article XVII and the Appendix Declaration for the benefit of developing countries;
> (2) Inclusion of author's basic rights of reproduction, of broadcasting, and of public performance;
> (3) Inclusion of rules permitting relaxation of those rights, as well as the right of translation, for the benefit of developing countries without material reciprocity.
>
> (II) In the Berne Convention:
> (1) Revision of Article 21 of the Stockholm Act to separate the Protocol Regarding Developing Countries from that Act;
> (2) Provision under which the revision of Article 21 can become effective only upon ratification of the revised Universal Copyright Convention by France, Spain, the United Kingdom and the United States of America;
> (3) Provision to allow developing countries members of the Berne Union to apply in their relations with other countries members of that Union the revised text of the Universal Copyright Convention;
> (4) Suspension of the obligation of paying contributions to the Berne Union by developing countries having chosen Class VI or VII for the purposes of contribution.[243]

This has been accurately described as a 'package deal',[244] and it will be seen that it was based on the following premises. First, no developing country was to be prevented from leaving the Berne Convention. Secondly, every developing country would be entitled to apply the same level of protection to foreign works, whether covered by the Berne or Universal Convention. Thirdly, the level of **14.44**

[243] ibid, 227. See further Ulmer (n 205 above), 242ff and R Fernay, 'La Recommendation de Washington' (1970) 63 *RIDA* 87.

[244] Ulmer (n 205 above), 244.

minimum protection provided by the UCC was to be raised, as a counterbalance to the suspension of the safeguard clause in the case of developing countries. Fourthly, there was a safeguard for developing countries to ensure that there should not be a stalemate similar to that which had arisen after the adoption of the Stockholm Protocol. Fifthly, there was to be no discrimination between developing states that were presently members of one of the conventions, and those acceding after the revisions. Finally, both revisions were to be simultaneous, it being understood that the revision of the UCC should precede that of the Berne Convention which would follow immediately afterward.[245]

(g) Preparations for the Paris Revision Conference

14.45 Considerable work remained to be done before a viable programme for the proposed revision conferences could be formulated. However, the Washington Recommendation set the terms and limits of these revisions. The proposed 'package deal' received the support of a large number of delegations at the joint meeting of the BUPC and the IGC of the UCC which was held in December 1969.[246] The UK, however, still had certain reservations,[247] while France, expressing its readiness to discuss with developing countries the circumstances under which they would remain in the Berne Union, declared its opposition to a solution which meant applying the UCC within the Berne Union.[248] Despite these reservations, both committees decided to appoint Ad Hoc Preparatory Committees to draw up detailed draft proposals for revision of the two conventions. These Ad Hoc Committees duly met in May 1970,[249] and they settled draft texts which were approved by extraordinary sessions of the BUPC[250] and the IGC[251] in September of that year. The two revision conferences were then scheduled for the middle of 1971, and commenced in Paris on 5 July.

(3) The programmes for the Paris Revision Conferences

14.46 After the turmoil and debates of the preceding eight years, the final work of revision was carried through in less than three weeks. As envisaged in the Washington Recommendation, the revision of both conventions proceeded

[245] To the same effect, see the summation by G Straschnov, the delegate for Kenya, at the joint session of the BUPC and IGC in Dec 1969: [1970] *Copyright* 21, 24.

[246] 15–19 Dec 1969, Paris: ibid. The meeting of the IGC alone was held from 12–15 Dec 1969, Paris: ibid, 51.

[247] ibid, 24. [248] ibid.

[249] Final Report, Ad Hoc Committee for the Revision of the Berne Convention (Geneva, 19–21 May 1970): [1970] *Copyright* 145, also reproduced in *Records* 1971, 37; 'Report, Ad Hoc Committee to Prepare a Draft Text of the Proposals for revision of the Universal Copyright Convention (Paris, 11–16 May 1970)' [1970] *Copyright* 161.

[250] Geneva, 14–18 Sept 1970: [1970] *Copyright* 209. Also reproduced in *Records* 1971, 47. See further Hadl (n 205 above).

[251] Paris, 2–11 Sept 1970: [1970] *Copyright* 223.

simultaneously.[252] The principal points in the draft texts contained in each programme were as follows.

(a) The Berne Convention

In the final draft prepared by the International Office on the basis of the draft adopted by the BUPC, two alternative formats for the revision were proposed. The first consisted of a completely new Act of the Convention with an Appendix. The Act contained the substantive clauses of the Stockholm Act (articles 1 to 20), which were left unchanged, and the administrative and final clauses of that Act (articles 22 to 38) which were revised to some extent.[253] The Appendix comprised a new set of provisions relating to developing countries which were incorporated into the new Act by article 21.[254] These were intended to replace the Stockholm Protocol and were a mirror image of the provisions concerning developing countries which it was proposed to introduce into the UCC at the complementary revision conference. In essence, the reservations allowed were more restrictive in character than those in the Stockholm Protocol, comprising compulsory licences in respect of translations and reproductions only.[255] The procedures and conditions for the obtaining of these licences were also more tightly regulated than in the Protocol.[256] The second draft text proposed by the International Office took the form of an additional Act which was intended to amend (not to replace) the Stockholm Act and Protocol, and consisted of the same provisions relating to developing countries as were proposed for the Appendix.[257] There were precedents for this kind of revision in the Paris Additional Act[258] and the Berne Additional Protocol,[259] but it had the obvious disadvantage that, after the revision, it would be necessary to consult two, rather than one, instrument. In the event, the Paris Conference chose the first approach, adopting a single instrument which was to be known as the 'Paris Act' rather than an 'Act additional to the Stockholm Act'.[260] The provisions of this new Act are discussed below (see para 14.49). **14.47**

(b) The UCC

In accordance with the Washington Recommendation, these proposals now extended to substantive matters. In particular, they involved recognition, for the **14.48**

[252] On the course of the two revisions, see E Ulmer, 'The Revisions of the Copyright Conventions' (1971) 2 *IIC* 345; R Fernay, 'Paris 1971, ou les aventures d'un 'package deal' (1971) 70 *RIDA* 3; G Roeber (ed), *Die Pariser Revisionen der Übereinkunfte zum internationalen Urheberrecht* (1975).

[253] Document B/DC/5, *Actes* 1971, 53.

[254] ibid, 64.

[255] Draft Appendix, arts II and III: ibid, 66.

[256] Draft Appendix, art IV: ibid, 70.

[257] ibid, 73.

[258] See paras 3.02ff above.

[259] See paras 3.21ff above.

[260] General report of Paris Conference, *Actes* 1971, 165, 167.

first time, of the 'basic rights constituting the author's economic right, including the rights of reproduction by any means, of public performance and of broadcasting of their works either in their original form or in any form recognizably derived from the original'.[261] As for developing countries, new provisions corresponding closely to those in the Berne programme were also proposed.[262] Finally, the safeguard clause was to be modified so as to allow for its suspension in the case of developing countries.[263] With some changes, these proposals were approved by the UCC revision conference and were adopted as part of the new UCC text.[264]

E. The Paris Act and Appendix

14.49 As our main concern here is obviously with the Berne rather than the Universal Copyright Convention, the rest of this chapter is concerned only with the provisions of the Paris Act and Appendix. However, it should be remembered that the provisions of the revised UCC relating to developing countries (articles V*bis* to V*quater*), in substance, parallel those of the Paris Appendix, and references to these provisions are therefore made in the accompanying footnotes. More importantly, the general report of the UCC Conference[265] is generally more informative on the interpretations to be attached to these provisions than the rather terser general report of the Berne Revision Conference which, on many points, simply refers the reader to the minutes of the Main Committee.[266] As there was a considerable overlap in the states represented at both conferences,[267] and the provisions adopted by each are much the same, it seems appropriate to refer to the UCC general report on matters of uncertainty where the general report and minutes of the Berne Revision Conference are silent.

261 To be art IV*bis*(1) in the revised UCC: 'Proposals for the Revision of the Universal Copyright Convention adopted by the Intergovernmental Copyright Committee, Extraordinary Session, Paris, 2–11 September 1970' [1970] *Copyright* 223, 231.

262 ibid, 231–2 (to be arts V*bis*, *ter*, and *quater*).

263 ibid, 233–4.

264 See the final text of the revised UCC in (1972) 19 *Bull Cop Soc USA*, 189.

265 Reproduced in (1972) 19 *Bull Cop Soc USA* 211 (A Kaminstein of the USA, *rapporteur général*) ('UCC general report'). Also in *Records of the Conference for the Revision of the Universal Copyright Convention, Paris, 5–24 July 1971*, 57–93.

266 ibid, 169. Another useful guide to the meaning of the provisions in both the Paris Appendix and the revised UCC is to be found in the 'Advisory Notes on the Implementation of the System of Translation and Reproduction Licences for Developing Countries under the Copyright Conventions' which were formulated by a Joint Working Group of both Conventions, 6–10 Dec 1982, Paris: [1983] *Copyright* 123. It is expressly stated that these do not form an official interpretation of these provisions: ibid, 126. Nevertheless, they contain useful points of assistance and are referred to hereafter as the 'WG Guidelines'.

267 See n 17 above.

One further preliminary point to note about the Appendix is that it only applies to translation and reproduction rights: unlike the Stockholm Protocol, broadcasting and public communication rights are not covered. Accordingly, online modes of delivery which might well be attractive to developing countries with large and widespread populations, do not come within its scope. As will be seen in the commentary below, the Appendix is essentially premised on traditional printing technologies and this may be another reason why, in practice, its provisions do not seem to have been taken up by the countries for which it was intended (see further para 14.106 below).

(1) Incorporation of the Appendix into the Paris Act

As under the Stockholm Act, article 21 refers directly to the Appendix which is declared, subject to the provisions of article 28(1)(b), to be an integral part of the new Act. Under the latter provision, a country may declare in its instrument of ratification or accession that this does not apply to articles 1 to 21 and the Appendix. Unlike the Stockholm Act, however, special provision was made under article 28(2)(a) to ensure that a similar situation to that following the Stockholm Revision should not arise. The effect of this was that articles 1 to 21 and the Appendix were not to enter into force until three months after at least five countries of the Union had ratified the Paris Act without making a declaration under article 28(1)(b). It was further required (as a cumulative condition) that France, Spain, the UK, and the USA should have become bound by the revised text of the UCC. This second requirement reflected one of the points of the Washington Recommendation,[268] although a reference to external events of this kind is unusual in an international instrument. **14.50**

(2) Definition of a developing country

Under article I(1) of the Appendix it is provided that the provisions of the Appendix may be invoked by: **14.51**

> Any country regarded as a developing country in conformity with the established practice of the General Assembly of the United Nations . . . and which, having regard to its economic situation and its social or cultural needs, does not consider itself immediately in a position to make provision for the protection of all the rights as provided for in this Act, . . .

The two criteria mentioned here are the same as those in article I of the Stockholm Protocol, where they had only been arrived at after considerable debate.[269] While the first was open to obvious criticism as being uncertain,

[268] See para 14.43 above. [269] See paras 14.18ff above.

there was no apparent alternative formulation to hand and the Paris Revision Conference retained it without much further discussion.[270] The report of Main Committee II at the Stockholm Conference stated that it was understood that the term 'established practice' implied that the country in question received assistance from the UN Development Programme through the UN or one of its specialized agencies.[271] This 'understanding' was not referred to in the general report of the Paris Revision Conference, but it does contain the following statement:

> It was understood that the expression 'country regarded as a developing country in conformity with the established practice of the General Assembly of the United Nations' did not allow for the drawing up of a list of such countries which would not be susceptible to changes in the future, not only because the stage of development of particular countries may change but also because the practice of the General Assembly may undergo changes in the sense that the criteria on which such practice is based may undergo changes. Whether any country is at any given time a developing country for the purposes of the Appendix would have to be decided on the basis of the practice of the General Assembly prevailing at the time relevant for deciding the question.[272]

The notion of 'established practice' therefore remains disturbingly vague. In the vast majority of cases, there will be little dispute, but there will be cases on the margin that will cause doubt. Reference to UN assistance programmes will certainly be one element to consider, but it has been argued that this should not be determinative of the issue as it may exclude countries that, on other criteria, would clearly be regarded as 'developing'.[273] Another relevant criterion was the three-yearly decisions of the UN Committee on Contributions concerning the contributions to be made by member countries and in which special consideration is given to those countries with an annual *per capita* income of less than $300.[274] Nevertheless, in the Main Committee, one delegate considered this to be too rigid a criterion,[275] and no mention of it was made in the report.

---

270 *Records* 1971, 146 (minutes of Main Committee).

271 *Records* 1967, 1194.

272 *Records* 1971, 169–70.

273 eg a country may be refused UNDP aid, yet still be a developing country by all other objective criteria: O'Hara (n 15 above), 97ff. See also Ulmer (n 252 above), 354; Schrader (1970), 166 and Z Sher, 'Reflections on Copyright in Developing Countries' (1968–9) 16 *Bull Cop Soc USA* 201, 203ff.

274 Following the Stockholm Conference, the Director of BIRPI had consultations with the UN Secretariat concerning the definition of a 'developing country in conformity with the established practice of the General Assembly of the United Nations', and it emerged from these that the most appropriate criterion would be one based on contributions of UN members. Using this as a guide, the Director submitted to the BUPC a list of countries that might be considered as developing within this criterion: Document DA/29/2 of 28 Dec 1968, reported to the BUPC at its extraordinary meeting in Feb 1969: [1969] *Copyright* 48, 49, and referred to in the minutes of the Main Committee in *Records* 1971, 146.

275 Mr Gabay of Israel: *Records* 1971, 146.

Likewise, in the UCC Revision Conference, when the *rapporteur*, Mr Kaminstein of the USA, suggested contributions as a possible criterion there was no unanimity among the delegates on this point[276] and it was deleted from his final report. All that can be said, therefore, is that the 'established practice' of the UN remains to be determined as and when every case arises, and that it will be necessary to look at all criteria that are taken account of by the General Assembly at that time. This raises the question of how, and by whom, these matters are to be decided in a contentious case. As the same issues arise where a country ceases to be regarded as a developing country, they are discussed together (see para 14.55 below).

The second criterion for a country wishing to take advantage of the Appendix is that, 'having regard to its economic situation and its social or cultural needs, [it] does not consider itself immediately in a position to make provision for the protection of all the rights as provided for in this Act, . . .'. This was considered as superfluous by some delegates in the Main Committee,[277] and, indeed, for this reason was not included in the corresponding provision of the revised UCC.[278] Nonetheless, there was still some preference for its retention in the Main Committee, on the basis, it seems, that it clearly left the decision whether to invoke the provisions of the Appendix to each country, once it was regarded as a 'developing country' in accordance with UN practice.[279] In the view of at least two delegates, it also indicated that cultural, as well as economic, factors were to be taken into account.[280] **14.52**

(a) Declaration to be made

To invoke the provisions of the Appendix, all that is necessary under article I(1) is for the developing country in question to deposit with the Director General a notification declaring that it will avail itself of either or both of the facilities provided in articles II and III (compulsory licences for translations and reproductions respectively). This declaration may be made at the time of ratification of, or accession to, the Paris Act, or at any time thereafter. In the second case, however, this is subject to the limitation contained in article V(1)(c) (see further para 14.101). A declaration under article I(1) may be made by a developing country that is already a member of the Union and is simply ratifying or acceding to the new Act, just as much as by a developing country that is acceding to the Union for the first time. **14.53**

[276] Ulmer (n 252 above), 354.
[277] *Records* 1971, 146 (Mr Balakrishnan of India).
[278] UCC general report (n 265 above), 228. See revised UCC, art V*bis*(1).
[279] *Records* 1971, 146 (remarks by Mr Bodenhausen, Director of BIRPI).
[280] ibid (delegates of Uruguay and Argentina).

(b) Duration of declarations

14.54 Declarations can be made for renewable periods of ten years.[281] In the first instance, where a declaration is made before the expiration of ten years from the entry into force of articles 1 to 21 and the Appendix, it will be valid until the end of that period, and then may be renewed in whole or in part for further periods of ten years.[282] In the same way, if a declaration is made after the expiry of the first ten-year period, it will be valid until the end of the ten-year period then running, and may then be renewed in the same way.[283] All renewals must be done by notification deposited with the Director General, and must be made no more than fifteen months, and no less than three months, before the expiration of the ten-year period then running.[284] The purpose of this requirement is to allow other states sufficient notice of whether the given ten-year period will expire on a particular date or not.

(3) Countries which cease to be developing

14.55 When a country which is entitled to make a declaration under article I(1), loses its character as a developing nation, it also loses the capacity to maintain its declaration. A period of grace is provided for this to happen: until the expiration of the ten-year period then running or until 'the expiration of three years after it has ceased to be regarded as a developing country, whichever period expires later'.[285] This happens whether or not the country in question formally withdraws its declaration, and the question which then arises is how the decision whether a country has ceased to be a developing country is to be made. Obviously, if the country itself recognizes that it is no longer a developing country, it will formally withdraw its declaration[286] and that will be an end to the matter. Where it does not do this, questions of some difficulty arise, and no guidance is provided as to how these are to be resolved. It will clearly be possible for the Director General or the Executive Committee to obtain advice from the Secretary General of the UN as to whether the country in question is regarded as a developing country in accordance with established UN practice or not, but what happens if the country disputes this? It is stipulated under article I(1) that the country's declaration will cease to have any effect, but there is no power in any of the organs of the Union to direct that country to cease to apply its compulsory licences to works from other Union countries, while the

[281] Appendix, art I(2)(a). Cf revised UCC, art 2*bis*(2).

[282] ibid. The question of which countries have made declarations and renewals thereof is dealt with in n 447 below.

[283] Appendix, art I(2)(b). [284] ibid, art I(2)(a).

[285] ibid, art I(3). Cf revised UCC, art V*bis*(3). See also Schrader (1970), 216ff; O'Hara (n 15 above), 98ff.

[286] The possibility of doing this is referred to in art I(3).

possibility of imposing material reciprocity or taking other sanctions is expressly forbidden by the Convention.[287] We enter here into the complex area of treaty implementation which is discussed below in Chapter 17.

(a) Stock in hand after declaration ends

Where a declaration ceases to have effect and there are still copies in stock which have been made under a licence granted by virtue of the Appendix, these copies may continue to be distributed until their stock is exhausted.[288] **14.56**

(b) Application of Appendix to territories

The provision concerning dependent territories which appeared in the Protocol[289] was retained in the Appendix. Any country which is bound by the Paris Act and which has deposited a declaration or notification under article 31(1) (applying the Convention to a territory for the external relations of which it is responsible) may also make a declaration invoking the provisions of the Appendix in respect of that territory, if the situation of that territory can be 'regarded as analogous' to that of a developing country.[290] The need for such a provision is probably negligible now, but at the time of the Paris Conference there were still several countries of the Berne Union with responsibility for a number of large territories that fell potentially within the scope of this provision.[291] **14.57**

(c) No requirement of material reciprocity

No member country is permitted to accord less protection to works of which the country of origin is a country which has availed itself of any of the faculties referred to in article I than it is obliged to grant under articles 1 to 20.[292] In other words, a member country is not entitled to apply material reciprocity in its relations with another member country that has applied the provisions of the Appendix. This provision is in accordance with the decisions that were reached at the various preparatory meetings for the Paris Revision.[293] However, it is noted in the general report of the Conference that it was understood that this sub-paragraph did 'not modify the right of any country to apply the so-called "comparison of terms" clause contained in Article 7(8)'.[294] This seems only reasonable, as the latter is a specific rule of material reciprocity that is **14.58**

---

[287] Paris Act, art 6: this applies only to retaliatory measures against non-member countries. See also paras 5.17ff above.

[288] Appendix, art 1(4). Cf revised UCC art V*bis*(4).

[289] Stockholm Protocol, art 6.

[290] Appendix, art I(5). Cf revised UCC, art V*bis*(5).

[291] In particular, the UK, France, Australia, Spain, Portugal, and South Africa.

[292] Appendix, art I(6)(a). This is not dealt with in the revised UCC, but is mentioned only in the UCC general report (n 265 above), 230–1.

[293] See para 14.43 above. [294] *Records* 1971, 170.

contained in the Convention: the application of material reciprocity is only prohibited in respect of restrictions that have been applied by a developing country under the Appendix. Article 7(8), however, is not the only rule of material reciprocity contained in articles 1 to 20, and it is to be presumed that the same approach applies to articles 2(7) (works of applied art) and 14ter (*droit de suite*).

14.59 A special problem arises with respect to the imposition of material reciprocity in the case of reservations made with respect to translation rights under article 30(2)(b). (This is discussed below at para 14.101.)

(4) Translation licences

14.60 These are dealt with under article II, and their scope is considerably restricted by comparison with the Protocol. Any country which has declared that it will avail itself of this faculty is entitled:

> . . . so far as works published in printed or analogous forms of reproduction are concerned, to substitute for the exclusive right of translation provided for in Article 8, a system of non-exclusive and non-transferable licences, granted by the competent authority under the following conditions and subject to Article IV.[295]

The procedures for applying for, and the conditions for the exercise of, licences under both articles II and III are contained in article IV, and are dealt with below (see paras 14.92ff). As for the conditions laid down in article II itself, the following points should be noted.

(a) Works covered by the licence

14.61 The translation licence applies only to published works; in addition, these must be 'works published in printed or analogous form'.[296] This indicates that copies of the work must be available in a form in which it can be read, and the licences therefore cannot provide for the translation of works which are, for example, embodied in a sound recording or in electronic form.[297] The acts that are permitted under the licences are limited in the same way, so as to apply to the publication of a translation in 'printed or analogous forms of reproduction'.[298]

---

295 Appendix, art II(1). Cf revised UCC, art $V^{ter}(1)$.

296 ibid. Note that in the revised UCC, the combined effect of arts V, V^{ter}, and VII is that only 'writings' can be covered by the licence, and, while these include literary works, they exclude musical, dramatic, and cinematographic works, and paintings, engravings, and sculptures: WG Guidelines, 128.

297 As to this, Ficsor comments pithily that this provision is 'without any relevance from the point of view of the "digital agenda" '; see M Ficsor, *The Law of Copyright and the Internet* (2001) ('Ficsor (2001)'), 278.

298 Appendix, art II(2)(a).

(b) Licences to be non-exclusive and non-transferable

These requirements seem straightforward. The licences must be granted to whoever satisfies the requirements of article II, and are purely personal to the licensee.[299] **14.62**

(c) Who may apply

'[A]ny national' of the country in question may apply for a licence.[300] It is stated in the general report that the term 'national' is not to be limited to natural persons, it being understood that it 'also covered legal entities, including the state itself, its national or local authorities, and enterprises owned by the state or such authorities'.[301] This interpretation appears to exclude other kinds of legal entity, such as private corporations or charitable organizations. On the other hand, the minutes of the Main Committee indicate that several of the delegates, including the chairman (Professor Ulmer) did not understand the term 'nationals' as being restricted in this sense, and there was no dissent from their view on the part of the other delegates.[302] It also appears from the general report of the UCC that the delegates at that Conference took a similar view to that expressed by Professor Ulmer.[303] **14.63**

(d) Circumstances in which an application for a licence may be made

The situations in which licences may be applied for are as follows. **14.64**

(i) After a period of three years, or any longer period determined by the national legislation of the country in question: After this period, commencing on the date of first publication of the work, if a translation of the work has not been published in a 'language in general use' in that country by the owner of the right of translation, or with his authorization.[304] Nothing is stipulated here as to where the publication of the authorized translation must take place for this condition to be avoided. It would seem therefore that, if the translation had been published within the three-year period in another country of the Union, a licence could not be granted. By contrast, under the reproduction licence in article III, the place in which the distribution is to take place is clearly specified.

(ii) If a translation in the language concerned has been published, but all editions of it are out of print:[305] The words 'out of print', which also appeared in the Stockholm Protocol, are a little vague, but presumably mean that no more copies of that translation can be purchased on the open market in any country

[299] ibid, art II(1). [300] ibid, art II(2)(a).
[301] *Records* 1971, 170. See further the WG Guidelines, 127. [302] ibid, 147.
[303] UCC general report (n 265 above), 227. [304] Appendix, art II(2)(a).
[305] ibid, art II(2)(b).

of the Union. In this regard, it would not be reasonable to take account of the availability of second-hand copies, as the supply of these would normally be small and uncertain.

(iii) Translations from the language of another developing country: In the case of translations into a language which is not in general use in one or more of the developed countries which are members of the Union, the three-year period described in paragraph (i) above may be replaced by a period of one year.[306] This shortened period will therefore only apply in the case of translations from the language of another developing country. The main area where this concession would be of use is probably translations from Arabic, a language which is in wide general use in a significant number of Union countries which are not developed countries. It will clearly be of far greater utility to developing countries following the accession of both China and the Russian Federation.

(iv) Other limited conditions: Under certain limited conditions, the three-year period described in paragraph (i) above may also be shortened to a period of not less than one year for translations in cases where the translation is from a language which is in general use in one of the developed countries.[307] These are as follows:

1. there must be the unanimous agreement of the developed countries in which that language is in general use—it would not be enough if only one of these countries agreed;
2. in any event, this shorter period will not apply where the language in question is English, French, or Spanish; and
3. any such agreement must be notified to the Director General by the governments which have concluded it.

The exclusion of translations from English, French, and Spanish significantly limits the scope for relaxation of time periods, and must be regarded as a considerable concession in favour of authors and publishers in those languages. Furthermore, the requirement that there must be the 'unanimous agreement' of all the developed countries in which the language translated is in general use imposes a considerable practical limitation. For instance, in the case of translations from German, the agreement of Germany, Austria, Switzerland, and Liechtenstein will be required, as each of these states is a member of the Union. On the other hand, if the developed countries in which English, French, or Spanish are in general use seek to enter an agreement with a developing country to shorten the required three-year period, this will not be permitted

[306] Appendix, art II(3)(a). Revised UCC, art V*ter*(1)(b).
[307] ibid, art II(3)(b). Cf revised UCC, art V*ter*(1)(b). See further, the WG Guidelines, 129.

by article 20 of the Paris Act, as such an agreement would be in derogation of this provision.

(e) 'Language in general use'

This expression is used in many places in the Appendix, and replaces the expression 'national or official or regional language' which appeared in article I of the Stockholm Protocol. The latter expression gave rise to difficulties in the case of some languages, such as English or French, which were widely used in some countries without being a national or official language, and certainly not a regional language. The same criticism could be made of the general translation licence of article V(2) of the UCC which referred to 'national language or where applicable, . . . one of the national languages of a Contracting State'. The wording proposed in the programme for the Paris Conference was simply 'language or . . . one of the languages of that country',[308] but the present wording was adopted on the proposal of the Tunisian delegate.[309] There were some reservations concerning the formulation 'language in general use' as it was feared that this might not cover a language which was used only in one part of the country.[310] To remove this fear, the following interpretation was inserted in the general report: **14.65**

> . . . it was understood that the notion of a 'language in general use' included languages in general use by less than the totality of the country's population. Thus, such a language could be a language in general use in a given geographic region of the country, the language of an ethnic group of the population, or a language generally used for particular purposes, such as government administration or education.[311]

It was further noted that wherever this expression appeared in other parts of the Paris Act it was to be understood in the same sense.[312] This interpretation seems wide enough to cover the vast majority of foreseeable situations, for example, translations into the language of a small aboriginal tribe, regional languages, and 'languages of government' such as English, French, Spanish, or Portuguese in many former colonial territories.

(f) Further time limits to be observed in the granting of licences

Before licences can be granted under article II, there are certain additional periods of time that must elapse once the above requirements have been satisfied.[313] These are 'grace periods' which enable the owner of the translation right to obviate the need for the grant of a licence by publishing his own translation. In the case of a licence obtainable after three years, the licence cannot be granted **14.66**

[308] *Records* 1971, 66. [309] ibid, 147.
[310] ibid (query by the chairman, Professor Ulmer). [311] ibid, 170. [312] ibid.
[313] Appendix, art II(4). Cf revised UCC, art V*ter*(2)(a).

until a 'further period of six months' has elapsed: (i) from the date on which the applicant has complied with the procedural requirements for the obtaining of the licence under article IV(1) (see paras 14.92ff below);[314] and (ii) where the identity or address of the owner of the translation right is unknown, from the date on which the applicant complies with the procedure in article IV(2) (see paras 14.92ff below).[315]

In the case of a licence obtainable after one year, a 'further period of nine months' from the above dates applies.[316] It is then provided that if, during these periods of six or nine months, a translation in the language in respect of which the licence application was made is published by the owner of the translation right or with his authorization, no licence under article II may be granted.[317] There is no indication as to the country in which the 'authorized' translation must be published. However, as the effect of the publication is to debar the grant of a licence in the developing country in question, it seems reasonable to assume that the owner of the translation right should publish his translation in that country, rather than his own or in another.

14.67 In the Main Committee of the Paris Conference, it was stated by the delegation of India that it interpreted this provision as meaning that the six- or nine-month period could begin running before the expiration of the initial one- or three-year period.[318] This interpretation is difficult to maintain, particularly in view of the use of the adjective 'further' in the phrases 'further period of six months' and 'further period of nine months'. It was also referred to in the general report in the following terms:

> . . . it was generally agreed that the six or nine months periods could not run concurrently with the three or one year periods since an application for a licence for translation could validly be presented only after the expiration of the three or one year period and because the sense of the word 'further' was to bring out clearly

[314] Appendix, art II(4)(a)(i). [315] ibid, art II(4)(a)(ii). [316] ibid, art II(4)(a).

[317] ibid, art II(4)(b). The WG Guidelines, 132, point to a difficulty of interpretation about these time periods in the case where a translation licence can be granted on the ground that all the editions of the translation published in the language concerned are out of print. Three possible interpretations are suggested: (i) that the going out of print gives rise to the right to apply for a licence, provided that the three- or one-year period has elapsed and the further six- or nine-month period is also observed, (ii) that the going out of print gives rise to the right to apply immediately for a licence on the ground that the six- or nine-month period is only relevant where the three- or one-year period is applicable, and (iii) the going out of print rules out every condition of admissibility (that is, the three- or one-year period) but this does not affect the rules of procedure governing applications for licences, and applicants must therefore comply with the six- or nine-month period if the waiting period would have normally been three or one years respectively. The Guidelines express no preference, but in view of the wording of art II(4)(a), which refers only to licences obtainable after three years or one year, the second interpretation seems to be correct.

[318] *Records* 1971, 148.

that the six or nine months period is necessarily subsequent to the three or one year period.[319]

(g) Limitation of purpose of licence

Translation licences may only be granted for 'the purpose of teaching, scholarship or research'.[320] This is a significant qualification of the licence allowed under the Stockholm Protocol,[321] and was another clear concession to the interests of authors and publishers in the developed countries, reflecting the understanding on this question that had been reached in the preparatory work for the Paris Revision.[322] It is of interest to note that a proposal by the Sri Lankan delegation which sought to expand the purposes for which these licences might be granted to the 'promotion of culture' was withdrawn after objections by the British and French delegations that this represented a fundamental change to the 'package deal' that had been agreed to as the basis for the dual revisions.[323] The translation licences under article V*ter* of the revised UCC are subject to the same qualification as to purpose, but the general report of that Conference offers more explanation on the scope to be given to it. It states here that: **14.68**

> . . . it was the understanding of the conference that the word 'scholarship' in this phrase refers not only to instructional activities at all levels in tutorial institutions, primary and secondary schools, colleges, and universities, but also to a wide range of organised educational activities intended for participation at any age level and devoted to the study of any subject.[324]

The UCC Conference also agreed that the word 'research' was not to be understood as extending to industrial or commercial research ('by industrial research institutes or by private corporations doing research for commercial purposes').[325] On the other hand, it is also relevant to note that this Conference rejected as too 'limitative' an Argentinian proposal to limit translations under article V*ter* to those works made 'for the benefit of official or officially recognized establishments of education or research'.[326]

(h) Termination of licences

The owner of the translation right may do this at his own election by publishing, or authorizing the publication of, a translation of the work in question.[327] This is subject to the following conditions. **14.69**

---

319 ibid, 170. See further WG Guidelines, 131.
320 Appendix, art II(5). Cf revised UCC, art V*ter*(3).
321 Stockholm Protocol, art I(b). 322 See para 14.43 above.
323 *Records* 1971, 148. The Sri Lankan proposal was in Document B/DC/17: ibid, 105.
324 UCC general report (n 265 above), 236.
325 ibid. See further WG Guidelines, 128.
326 UCC general report (n 265 above), 236.
327 Appendix, art II(6). Cf revised UCC, art V*ter*(6).

(i) **Reasonable price:** The translation must be sold at 'a price reasonably related to that normally charged in the country for comparable works'.[328] Although not stated, it seems reasonable to assume that this should be the price at which the translation of comparable works can actually be obtained in that country, not the price for which it may be obtained in another country of the Union, such as that of the work's country of origin. If the latter were the case, this could make a nonsense of this provision, as the owner of the translation right might publish the translation in his own country at a price comparable to that charged in the country which has granted the licence, but sell copies of this translation in the developing country at a greater price.

(ii) **In the same language:** The authorized translation must be in the same language as the licensed translation and have 'substantially the same content'.[329] In elaboration of this second requirement, the general report states that:

> . . . it was understood that this condition would be satisfied not only when the content of the translation of the owner was identical or almost so but also when the former contained certain improvements, as would be the case, for example, when the content of a school book is updated.[330]

(iii) **Reasonable notice:** The report also states that it was understood that the owner of the translation right should give 'reasonable notice' of the publication of the authorized translation, if the owner is aware of the existence of the licence.[331] The Appendix further provides that any copies already made before the termination of the licence may continue to be distributed until the stock is exhausted.[332]

(i) Works consisting mainly of illustrations

14.70 In the case of such works, a licence to publish a translation of the text may only be obtained if a corresponding licence under article III to reproduce and publish the illustrations is also obtained.[333]

(j) Withdrawal of copies by author

14.71 As under the Stockholm Protocol, protection of the author's moral right of repentance is provided by a stipulation that no translation licence is to be granted where the author has withdrawn from circulation all copies of his work.[334] This will, of course, only be effective in relation to works from countries where the author enjoys this particular moral right under the principle of

---

[328] Appendix, art II(6). [329] ibid. [330] *Records* 1971, 171. [331] ibid.
[332] Appendix, art II(6) (last sentence).
[333] ibid, art II(7). Cf revised UCC, art V*ter*(7). [334] ibid, art II(8).

national treatment.[335] As it is not recognized in all countries of the Union, it may prove a meaningless limitation as the author may not be able to withdraw all copies of his work if they have been circulated in countries of this kind.

(k) Translations for broadcasting purposes

At the Stockholm Conference, there was discussion of the extent to which various provisions of the Convention relating to restrictions on the use of works also comprised the right to impose restrictions with respect to translations of those works.[336] In the case of some provisions, it was generally agreed that this was so; for example, articles 9(2), 10, and 10*bis*.[337] In the case of broadcasts, however, there was uncertainty among the delegates as to whether the restrictions allowed under article 11*bis*(2) extended to the broadcasting of translations, and this question was therefore left open.[338] In the preparations for the Paris Revision, the reservations which had been made in the Stockholm Protocol in respect of broadcasting rights were deleted, on the basis that both paragraphs (2) and (3) of article 11*bis* allowed for reservations on these rights in any case.[339] However, there was no discussion of whether these provisions also extended to the broadcasting of translations. The latter was nevertheless a question of some significance to developing countries, as shortages of textbooks and teachers meant that broadcasting was often a very important part of their education programmes. This question was raised by Dr Straschnov, adviser to the Kenyan delegation, at the Paris UCC Revision Conference,[340] and the result was a precisely drafted and restricted provision which permits the granting of compulsory licences for the making of translations for the purposes of educational broadcasts. This appears in both article V*ter*(8) of the UCC and article II(9)(a) of the Appendix. **14.72**

This provision does not affect or modify in any way the provisions of article 11*bis* of the principal Act, in particular paragraph (2) which permits the imposition of compulsory licences for broadcasting and paragraph (3) which permits the making of ephemeral recordings.[341] Thus, if a translation has already been made, whether by the owner of the translation right or pursuant to a licence granted under article II, article II(9)(b) is quite irrelevant, as the translation may then be broadcast pursuant to a compulsory licence imposed by virtue of article 11*bis*(2). Article II(9)(a), by contrast, is concerned with the making of translations of works for the purposes of broadcasting, and applies where no authorized or **14.73**

335 On the basis that this particular moral right is not one of those required to be protected under art 6*bis* as one of the 'rights specially granted by this Convention' (art 5(1)).

336 See paras 13.83ff above.

337 Report of Main Committee I, Stockholm Conference: *Records* 1967, 1165.

338 ibid. 339 Ulmer (n 252 above), 363–4. 340 ibid.

341 *Records* 1971, 171 (general report).

licensed translation is available.[342] In such circumstances, it is open to any broadcasting organization which has its headquarters in a country which has imposed translation licences under article II to apply to the competent authority for a licence to translate a work which has been published in printed or analogous forms of reproduction.[343] The time limits and other conditions which apply to other translation licences under article II are obviously not relevant here, but a number of other stringent restrictions are applicable as follows.

(i) Must not be an infringing copy: The translation must be made from a copy made and acquired in accordance with the laws of the said country; this means that it must not be an infringing copy within the laws of the country granting the licence.[344]

(ii) Broadcasts must be intended exclusively for teaching etc: The translation must be for 'use in broadcasts intended exclusively for teaching or the dissemination of the results of specialised technical or scientific research to experts in a particular profession'.[345] It will be noted that the adverb 'exclusively' is used, rather than 'primarily', and that these strictly limited purposes would certainly not extend to translations made for programmes intended for the general 'promotion of culture'. As to the second of the uses specified ('the dissemination of the results . . .'), the same wording appears in article V*ter*(8) of the revised UCC, and the general report of the UCC Conference states that this formulation was found 'acceptable after several delegates had expressed dissatisfaction with a mere reference to "research" '.[346]

(iii) Broadcasts and recordings must be lawfully made: The translation must be used exclusively for the purposes referred to in paragraph (ii) above 'through broadcasts made lawfully and intended for recipients on the territory of the said country, including broadcasts made through the medium of sound or visual recordings lawfully and exclusively made for the purpose of such broadcasts'.[347] The reference to 'made lawfully' and 'lawfully . . . made' underline the comments made above with respect to article 11*bis*. The licences allowed under article II(9)(a) relate only to the making of the translation: the subsequent broadcasting must also be authorized by the owner of the broadcasting right or made pursuant to a compulsory licence allowed under article 11*bis*(2). The reference to 'broadcasts made lawfully' therefore covers broadcasts made in either situation. As for the reference to 'recordings lawfully . . . made', this must

342 Ulmer (n 252 above), 364.
343 Appendix, art I(9)(a) (preamble). Cf revised UCC, art V*ter*(8)(a).
344 ibid, art I(9)(a)(i). See also *Records* 1971, 171 (general report).
345 Appendix, art I(9)(a)(ii).
346 UCC general report (n 265 above), 239.
347 Appendix, art II(9)(a)(iii).

include recordings of the translation which have been lawfully made under article 11*bis*(3). It also seems not to matter if the broadcasts are received by listeners or viewers in other countries, as long as the broadcasts are intended for reception on the state's territory.[348] Subject to these conditions, there is no restriction as to the kind of broadcasting which may take place: this may be by radio or television, or consist of terrestrial or satellite relays.[349]

(iv) Without any commercial purpose: All uses made of the translation must be 'without any commercial purpose'.[350] In this regard, the UCC general report states that the UCC Conference was agreed that this phrase meant:

> . . . the organisation itself is not a private corporation operated for profit-making purposes and that no commercial advertising is included in the programme incorporating the translation. It was not, however, intended to preclude the organisation from broadcasting commercial advertising at other times, or to exclude the common situation where the owners of receiving sets are charged a fee.[351]

(l) Use of translations by other broadcasting organizations

Article II(9)(b) also permits the use of sound or visual recordings of licensed translations which have been made under article II(9)(a) by other broadcasting organizations that have their headquarters in the same country. This must be done with the consent of the organization which obtained the original licence, and the use must be for the purposes and subject to the conditions specified in article II(9)(a).[352] That is, such recordings cannot be sent outside the country, and must only be used for the purpose of educational broadcasts intended for reception in that country.[353] This provision therefore supplements article 11*bis*(3), as that paragraph confines the use of an ephemeral recording to the broadcasts of the organization that made it. **14.74**

(m) Limited aspect of translation licences for broadcasting

In the discussions on the equivalent provision of the revised UCC, particular emphasis was laid on the limited nature of these licences: they cover only the act of translation and nothing more.[354] Thus, they cannot extend to any act of adaptation, such as dramatization or novelization. In the same way, they do not apply to the broadcasting of the translation or the making of an ephemeral recording, as these rights arise under other provisions of the Convention.[355] These comments are equally applicable to article II(9) of the Paris Appendix. **14.75**

---

348 UCC general report (n 265 above), 240. 349 ibid.
350 Appendix, art II(9)(a)(iv).
351 UCC general report (n 265 above), 240.
352 Appendix, art II(9)(b). Cf revised UCC, art V*ter*(8)(iv).
353 UCC general report (n 265 above), 240.
354 ibid, 241. 355 ibid.

(n) *Translations of texts incorporated in an audio-visual fixation*

14.76 Article II(9)(c) deals with the making of translations for the purposes of broadcasting where the text is incorporated in an audio-visual fixation. This is a logical extension of the licence provided for under article II(9)(a), as educational texts are often embodied in training films, video cassettes, film strips, slides, and other kinds of visual aids as part of the soundtrack or written commentary.[356] The making of these translations is subject to the same conditions as apply to licences under article II(9)(a). For reasons that are not immediately obvious, it is required that the audio-visual fixation of the text which is translated should itself have been 'prepared and published for the sole purpose of being used in connection with systematic instructional activities'.[357] This phrase is also used in article III, and refers to both instruction in educational institutions as well as out-of-school instruction.[358] However, it represents an unnecessary discrimination against texts fixed in this form. Under article II(9)(a), any text 'published in printed or analogous forms of reproduction' may be translated where this is done for the purposes specified in that sub-paragraph. This leaves the decision of what texts are considered relevant for those purposes to the potential licensee. By contrast, under article II(9)(c), the audio-visual fixation must first have been made for those purposes, and this will exclude the translations of other kinds of texts which are fixed in this way, for example, documentary or feature films which it might be desired to use for the purposes of courses in history, literature, or some other discipline.

(o) *Application of remaining provisions of article II to licences granted under paragraph (9)*

14.77 Article II(9)(d) provides that, subject to sub-paragraphs (a), (b), and (c), the preceding paragraphs of article II apply to the grant and exercise of any licence granted under that paragraph. This provision is not clearly expressed, and requires some explanation. For example, the conditions and time limits under paragraphs (2) to (4) cannot be applicable to the making of translations under paragraph (9): if these conditions were satisfied, then there would be no need for the paragraph (9) licence, as it would simply be a question of fact whether a broadcasting organization was allowed to broadcast and record the translation under the provisions of article 11*bis*. In the same way, the more specialized purpose in paragraph (9)(a)(ii) must supersede that stated in paragraph (5). This leaves only paragraphs (6) to (8) as applicable to licences under paragraph (9).

---

356 UCC general report (n 265 above), 240–1.

357 Appendix, art II(9)(c). Cf revised UCC, art V*ter*(8)(b).

358 See para 14.86 below.

(5) Reproduction licences

These are provided for in article III, though in a more attenuated form than in the Stockholm Protocol. They are patterned on the translation licences under article II, but with some differences. Thus, it is provided that any country which has declared that it will avail itself of the faculty contained in this article may substitute for the exclusive reproduction right in article 9 'a system of non-exclusive and non-transferable licences, granted by the competent authority under the following conditions and subject to Article IV'.[359] **14.78**

(a) Works covered by the licence

These must be 'works published in printed or analogous forms of reproduction'.[360] Thus, works embodied in sound recordings are excluded, and the acts covered by the licence are limited in the same way: to the reproduction and publication of 'such editions'.[361] A special exception, however, is made in the case of the 'reproduction in audio-visual form of lawfully made audio-visual fixations' of protected works.[362] (This is discussed below at para 14.90.) **14.79**

(b) Licences to be non-exclusive and non-transferable

This is the same requirement as for translation licences under article II(1) (see para 14.62 above). **14.80**

(c) Who may apply

'Any national' of the country concerned may apply: this has the same meaning as in article II(1) (see para 14.63 above). **14.81**

(d) Circumstances in which a licence may be applied for

Article II contemplates the following situations here. **14.82**

(i) After five years if copies not distributed at a normal price: After five years from the date of first publication of 'a particular edition of the work' or any longer period determined by national legislation, if copies of this edition have not been 'distributed in that country to the general public, or in connection with systematic instructional activities, by the owner of the right of reproduction or with his authorization, at a price reasonably related to that normally charged in the country for comparable works . . .'.[363] It will be seen here that failure to distribute the edition at all during this period is not required: the

[359] Appendix, art III(1). See generally, revised UCC, art V^{quater}.

[360] Appendix, art III(7)(a).

[361] ibid, art III(2)(a). Cf revised UCC, art V^{quater}(1)(a). See further Ficsor (2001), 279: 'reproduction through digital transmissions might hardly be regarded as analogous to printing'.

[362] Appendix, art III(7)(b). [363] ibid, art III(2)(a).

criterion is availability at a price reasonably related to that normally charged in the country for comparable works (referred to in the ensuing discussion as the 'normal price'). This 'availability' may be satisfied from either locally made or imported copies, and it is possible that the distribution of copies through digital interactive networks might also be relevant here,[364] but problems may arise in determining what is the normal price of these copies. In many cases, there may be no locally made copies of comparable works in the country in question, because it either lacks indigenous printing facilities or it is not economic to produce them in that country. If this is so, then the only copies available for the purpose of comparison will be imported ones, and these may only be available at a much higher price which takes account of the cost of importation and production abroad. Is this, then, the normal price of those copies in that country? No guidance on this matter is to be found in the reports and records of either revision conference, and it therefore remains a matter to be determined by national legislation. This lack of certainty may therefore work against developing countries, as it is possible that the 'normal price' for comparable books in those countries is kept artificially high as the result of monopolistic activities on the part of overseas or local publishers or distributors. Nonetheless, as long as these prices are the 'norm' in that country, they will satisfy the criterion of a normal price.

(ii) Exceptions to the five-year period: The five-year period described in paragraph (i) does not apply in the following cases. First, for 'works of the natural and physical sciences, including mathematics and technology', the period is three years.[365] Second, for 'works of fiction, poetry, drama and music, and for art books', the period is seven years.[366] The French text is rather different here, referring to 'oeuvres qui appartiennent au domaine de l'imagination telles que romans, les oeuvres poétiques, dramatiques et musicales'. This difference was noted by the Conference, but it was agreed that it is:

> . . . merely one of form (unavoidable because 'works of fiction' had no exactly corresponding expression in French, and '*oeuvres qui appartiennent au domaine de l'imagination*' had no exactly corresponding expression in English) whereas in substance they meant the same, and, in particular, the absence of the word '*roman*' in English did not mean that they were not included, and that the use of the word '*roman*' in French did not mean that works of fiction shorter than novels were excluded.[367]

A further point that was approved by the Conference, but is not referred to in the general report, is that the term 'works of fiction' included all works generally

[364] Ficsor (2001), 279, although this writer goes on to say that he does not regard it necessary to analyse this issue in detail because the Appendix is 'hardly applied in practice'.
[365] Appendix, art III(3)(i). [366] ibid, art III(3)(ii). [367] *Records* 1971, 171.

referred to as '*belles lettres*' in French, and was also applicable to 'works based on documents but presented in an artistic manner'.[368]

The reasons for these differing periods are straightforward: the shorter period for technical and scientific works is merited in view of the most pressing needs of developing countries, while the longer period for works of fiction and the like are appropriate, given that these are more vulnerable in character and less necessary for the purposes of those countries.

(iii) Distributed edition not available for six months: If the edition has already been distributed within the various periods described in paragraphs (i) or (ii) above, a licence to reproduce and publish that edition may also be granted if, 'after the expiration of the applicable period, no authorized copies of that edition have been on sale for a period of six months in the country concerned to the general public or in connection with systematic instructional activities at a normal price'.[369] Thus, if an edition was distributed at this price within the prescribed period, a licence may subsequently be applied for at any time after this when a six-month period in which no copies of that edition are available at that price has elapsed. As described in paragraph (i) above, the determination of this price is a matter of uncertainty.

(e) 'Particular edition'

The significance of this phrase should not be overlooked: where a work is published in successive editions, separate time periods apply to each edition. Thus, even if the time period for an earlier edition has expired, a licence to reproduce the latest edition cannot be granted unless the time limits applicable to that edition have also expired.[370] **14.83**

(f) Periods of grace for right owners

As under article II, grace periods are provided for right owners to undertake their own distribution of copies of the edition at a 'normal price' before a compulsory licence pursuant to article III can be granted. In the case of licences granted after three years, this must be done within six months of the date on which the intending licensee has complied with the procedural requirements under article IV(1) or has taken the appropriate steps under article IV(2) in the case of an unknown or untraceable right owner.[371] No licence can be granted during this period, and, if an authorized distribution takes place, no licence can be subsequently granted until these copies have ceased to be available for a **14.84**

[368] ibid, 150 (point raised by Mr Wincke of Denmark).
[369] Appendix, art III(2)(b). Cf revised UCC, art V^{quater}(1)(b).
[370] UCC general report (n 265 above), 241.
[371] Appendix, art III(4)(a)(i) and (ii). Cf revised UCC, art V^{quater}(1)(d).

period of six months.[372] There is no grace period applicable in the case of five- or seven-year licences, except where the owner of the reproduction right cannot be found: in such a case, a period of three months from the date of compliance with the requirements of article IV(2) must elapse.[373] Unlike the grace periods applicable under article II, it appears that those under article III may commence before the expiry of the appropriate three-, five-, or seven-year period. This can be seen from the omission of the word 'further', which appears in article II(4), and it is also clearly stated in the UCC general report that this was the unanimous view of that Conference with respect to the equivalent provision in the revised UCC.[374] As with article II, it is also provided that a licence is not to be granted if the author has withdrawn from circulation all copies of the edition in respect of which the application has been made.[375]

(g) Restrictions on reproduction of translations

14.85 Licences for the reproduction of translations of works may be granted under article II, except in two cases. First, where the translation was not published by the owner of the right of translation or with his authorization.[376] This precludes a competent authority from granting a licence to reproduce a translation that itself has been made and published under an article II licence: a compulsory licence on a compulsory licence. The second case is where the translation is not in a language in general use in the country in which the licence is applied for.[377]

It should also be noted that, in principle, where reproduction of a translation is in question, two sets of rights are involved: those in the translation and those in the original work, and these rights may be in different hands. Although this is not referred to in article III(5) of the Appendix, at the UCC Conference it was accepted that 'where reproduction of a translation is involved, licences must be sought from the owner of copyright in both the original text and the translation . . .'.[378] This must also apply to article III(5) of the Paris Appendix, and will mean that an intending licensee under that article will need to make two requests for permission under the procedures laid down in article IV(1).

(h) Limitation of purpose of licence

14.86 The purpose for which licences may be granted under article III is also strictly limited. This must be for 'use in connection with systematic

372 Appendix, art III(4)(c) and (2)(a). Cf revised UCC art V*quater*(1)(e).
373 Appendix, art III(4)(b). Cf revised UCC, art V*quater*(1)(b).
374 UCC general report (n 265 above), 247.
375 Appendix, art III(4)(d). Cf revised UCC, art V*quater*(2)(d).
376 Appendix, art III(5)(i). Cf revised UCC, art V*quater*(1)(h)(i).
377 Appendix, art III(5)(ii). Cf revised UCC, art Vquater(1)(h)(ii).
378 UCC general report (n 265 above), 248.

instructional activities',[379] a phrase which appears in several other places in article III, as well as in article II(9)(c) (see para 14.76 above). The same term is used in article V*quater* of the revised UCC, while the expression '*enseignement scolaire et universitaire*' is used in the French texts of both conventions. No comment on the meaning of this expression is to be found in the general report or records of the Berne Convention, nor is there any explanation as to how this might differ from the phrase 'for the purpose of teaching, scholarship or research' in article II. However, the general report of the UCC Conference notes that it was 'intended to include not only activities connected with the formal and informal curriculum of an educational institution, but also systematic out-of-school education'.[380] Reproduction for purposes of research is therefore excluded. It should also be noted that the provision does not contemplate that licensed copies will be distributed in that country to the general public, although it is possible for the owner of the reproduction right to prevent a licence being granted where he (the owner) distributes, or authorizes, the distribution of, copies of the edition to the general public. In this regard, the UCC report comments that it was envisaged that copies made under a licence might be sold, but it was always for the competent authority to determine that the licence would fulfil the needs of 'specified instructional activities'. Consequently, a licence should be refused if these activities are 'in fact incidental to the actual purpose of the reproduction'.[381]

(i) Condition as to price of licensed copies

Copies reproduced and published under licence must be distributed at a normal or lower price.[382] This requirement corresponds to the condition as to price which must be satisfied before a licence can be applied for.[383] The uncertainty of this criterion has already been referred to (see para 14.82 above). **14.87**

(j) Termination of licence

This will happen if the owner of the reproduction right distributes, or authorizes the distribution of, copies of an edition of a work for which a licence has been granted in the country in question.[384] This may be by way of a distribution to the general public or a more limited distribution connected only with systematic instructional activities, but in both cases the price of the copies must be a normal price.[385] Furthermore, the edition must be in 'the same language and with substantially the same content' as the licensed edition.[386] These last two conditions are similar to those applicable in the case of translation licences, but **14.88**

379 Appendix, art III(2)(a). 380 UCC general report (n 265 above), 244.
381 ibid. 382 Appendix, art III(2)(a). 383 ibid.
384 ibid, art III(6). Cf revised UCC, art V*ter*(3)(a). 385 Appendix, art III(6).
386 ibid.

the words 'substantially the same content as the edition' may raise difficulties. In the case of article II(6), it was noted that the words 'substantially the same content as the translation' would include updated versions of the work.[387] In the case of a reproduction licence, however, such additions and revisions would surely constitute the making of a new edition. If this is so, the owner of the reproduction right would have published a new edition of his work, and the licence relating to the previous edition should not be affected. As in article II(6), article III(6) also provides that where a licence is terminated any copies already made before this time may continue to be distributed until their stock is exhausted. It is also to be assumed that, as under article II(6), the owner of the reproduction right should give 'reasonable notice' of the publication of the authorized reproduction if he is aware of the existence of the licence.[388]

(k) Reproductions in audio-visual form

14.89 The general rule is that article III licences only apply to works 'published in printed or analogous forms of reproduction'.[389] However, article III(7)(b) assimilates to these 'audio-visual fixations including any protected works incorporated therein', providing that licences may be granted for the 'reproduction in audio-visual form' of these fixations. This last limitation on the scope of the licence should be noted: it would not, for example, allow the reproduction of an audio-visual fixation in the form of a written text, even if all the other conditions for an article III licence were satisfied. The meaning of the term 'audio-visual fixation' is quite broad—a fixation containing both pictures and sounds, and would cover cinematographic films, video cassettes, and discs, but not sound recordings. It will also be seen that article III(7)(b) applies to audio-visual fixations where the fixation itself is a protected work or contains a protected work, that is, a cinematographic work or a distinct literary or artistic work that is embodied in a cinematographic film.[390] In many cases, this will mean that there will be two or more sets of rights involved in any audio-visual fixation, with the consequence that an intending licensee will need to send requests to each of these owners in accordance with the procedures laid down in article IV(1).[391] A final limitation on the grant of such licences is that the audio-visual fixations which are to be reproduced must themselves have been 'prepared and published for the sole purpose of being used in connection with systematic instructional activities'.[392]

[387] See para 14.69 above. [388] Appendix, art III(6).

[389] Appendix, art III(7)(a). Cf revised UCC, art V^{quater}(3)(a).

[390] Appendix, art III(7)(b): '. . . lawfully made audio-visual fixations including any protected works incorporated therein'.

[391] See paras 14.92ff below.

[392] Appendix, art III(7)(b). Cf revised UCC, art V^{quater}(3)(b). See further para 14.76 above.

(l) Translations of texts incorporated in audio-visual fixations

It is also provided that a reproduction licence in respect of an audio-visual **14.90**
fixation may extend to the 'translation of any incorporated text into a language in general use in the country in which the licence is applied for . . .'.[393] This overlaps with the translation licence permitted in respect of audio-visual fixations under article II(9)(c), and may therefore lead to confusion as to the time periods applicable to such licences. This matter was taken up in the UCC Conference with respect to the corresponding provisions of articles V^{ter}(8)(b) and V^{quater}(3)(b) of the revised UCC, and the following interpretation was provided in the general report of that Conference:

> (1) Under Article V^{ter} the licence can cover only the translation of text for broadcasting purposes. Typically, it would be employed for the translation of the sound track of a teaching film or video-tape that had been lawfully acquired on the market, and the use of the translation in a new ('dubbed') soundtrack or for visible sub-titles.
>
> (2) Under Article V^{quater}(3)(b), the licensee would reproduce the entire audio-visual fixation, and as part of the process he could translate the sound track and reproduce the translation aurally or visually along with his reproduction of the visual images. The periods applicable in that situation would vary depending upon the nature of the work in accordance with Article V^{quater}(1)(c).[394]

It was also understood that 'under no circumstances' could article V^{quater}(3)(b) serve as the basis for a compulsory licence allowing reproduction of commercial films or tapes produced for theatrical or other commercial purposes; nor could it extend to 'the reproduction of a cinematographic work based upon a dramatized work of fiction, since such works were not prepared and published for the sole purpose of use in systematic education'.[395] These comments are equally applicable to article III(7)(b) of the Paris Appendix.

The assimilation of audio-visual fixations to licences under article III may lead **14.91**
to some slight inconsistencies in the terminology used in the earlier paragraphs of that article. No particular problem arises with respect to the requirement that the fixation be 'published':[396] this should be interpreted in the same way as publication in the case of cinematographic works is interpreted under article 3(3) of the Paris Act.[397] The word 'edition', however, is not generally used with respect to audio-visual fixations: in the UCC general report, it is stated that this is considered to refer to a 'particular version of the work'.[398]

---

[393] Appendix, art III(7)(b). [394] UCC general report (n 265 above), 249–50.
[395] ibid, 250. [396] Appendix, art III(7)(a).
[397] See paras 6.36ff above.
[398] UCC general report (n 265 above), 250.

(6) Procedures for applications for licences

14.92 Article IV contains certain common requirements that apply to the grant of licences under both articles II and III.

(a) Preconditions for the grant of licences

14.93 Under article IV(1), licences may only be granted if the applicant, 'in accordance with the procedure of the country concerned', establishes one of two things. First, that he has requested, and been denied, authorization by the relevant right owner to make the translation or to reproduce and publish the edition, as the case may be.[399] At the same time as he makes this request, the applicant should inform any national or international information centre referred to in article IV(2). It is also stated in the general report that it was understood that the request for authorization addressed to the right owner must indicate that, if such authorization is denied, the denial may serve as a basis for applying for a licence under the Appendix.[400]

Second, that, 'after due diligence' on his (the applicant's) part, he was unable to find the owner of the right.[401] In the event that the owner cannot be found, the applicant is required to send by registered airmail copies of the application he has submitted to the competent authority to the publisher whose name appears on the work, as well as to any national or international information centre which may have been designated, in a notification to this effect deposited with the Director General, by the government of the country in which the publisher is believed to have his principal place of business.[402] In this regard, the equivalent revised UCC provision also refers to the international copyright information centre established by UNESCO.[403]

The purpose of these provisions is to ensure that the publisher, and through him, the author, is informed of the application. Although the way in which these requirements are to be established is left as a matter for national law, it would seem that no application can be validly made until they have been satisfied.[404] Furthermore, the general report states that, before an application can be made, the applicable period under article II(2)(a) or (3) or article III(3) should have expired.[405]

---

[399] Appendix, art IV(1). Cf revised UCC, arts V*ter*(1)(a) and V*quater*(1)(a). For an indication of the particulars to be included in an application, see the WG Guidelines, 132.

[400] ibid. The WG Guidelines also state that it is a matter for national legislation to determine a reasonable period in which no reply from the owners of the right is tantamount to a refusal.

[401] ibid.

[402] ibid, art IV(2). Cf revised UCC, arts V*ter*(1)(d) and V*quater*(1)(a).

[403] ibid. See further on the UNESCO Centre, Tocups (n 1 above), 416.

[404] *Records* 1971, 172 (general report). [405] ibid.

(b) Acknowledgement of author

It is required that the author's name and the title of the work should be indicated on all copies of the translation or reproduction published under an article II or III licence.[406] In the case of a translation, it is required, in any case, that the original title of the work should appear on these copies.[407] **14.94**

(c) Export of copies made under licence

The scope that was permitted with respect to the export of licensed copies under the Stockholm Protocol attracted some of the most bitter criticism made of the Protocol by the developed countries.[408] This situation was changed radically under the Appendix, where the matter of exports is dealt with in article IV(4). The basic position is that no licence granted under either article II or III extends to the export of any copies made under that licence: the latter is valid only for publication of the translation or reproduction in the territory of the country in which it is applied for.[409] The notion of 'export' also applies in the case of dependent territories in respect of which a country has made a declaration under article I(5): in the case of such territories, 'export' includes the sending of copies to the country which has made the declaration.[410] It follows from these territorial restrictions that a licensee will be excluded from having his translation or reproduction printed outside the territory of the country which has granted the licence. This limitation, in fact, was the cause of considerable discussion in both revision conferences, as a number of developing countries lacked the basic technical facilities for the printing and production of copies. For example, it was noted that, at this time, of the fourteen French-speaking African states, only two had such facilities.[411] Thus, an amendment (to be article IV(4)^{bis}) was proposed by five of the Francophone African countries under which two or more countries with the same language would be allowed, jointly, to request and obtain a licence for translation or reproduction of a work for the purpose of teaching, scholarship, or research.[412] The purpose of the amendment was to enable several states to pool their resources, but its consequence was that the circulation among these countries of licensed copies would not be regarded as 'exports' for the purposes of article IV(4). This proposal evoked a sharp response from the developed countries, notably the UK and USA,[413] as representing a major **14.95**

[406] Appendix, art IV(3). Cf revised UCC, art V^{quater}(1)(f).
[407] ibid. [408] See para 14.34 above.
[409] Appendix, art IV(4)(a). Cf revised UCC arts V^{quater}(1)(a) and V^{ter}(1)(f).
[410] Appendix, art IV(4)(b).
[411] *Records* 1971, 152 (statement by Mrs Liguer-Laubhoet of the Ivory Coast to the Main Committee).
[412] Document B/DC/25, *Records* 1971, 110 (proposed by Congo (Democratic Republic), Congo, Ivory Coast, Niger, and Senegal).
[413] ibid, 151 (Mr Wallace) and 152 (Miss Ringer).

departure from the guidelines of the agreed 'package deal'. The dangers of the open-ended circulation of licensed copies of works in widely spoken languages such as Swahili, Spanish, or Arabic was pointed to,[414] and a Joint Working Group (between the two conferences) was appointed to work out a compromise solution.[415] This Group eventually recommended that the general reports of both conferences should confirm that a licensee was not permitted to manufacture copies outside the territory of the country where the licence was in force, but that the reports should also indicate that this restriction was not to apply in certain, very limited, circumstances.[416] These are as follows:

> (a) the country granting the licence has, within its territory, no printing or reproduction facilities, or such facilities exist but are incapable for economic or practical reasons of reproducing the copies;
> (b) the country where the work of reproduction is done is a member of the Berne Union or a party to the Universal Copyright Convention;
> (c) all copies reproduced are sent, in one or more bulk shipments, to the licensee for distribution exclusively in the licensee's country and the contract between the licensee and the establishment doing the work of reproduction so requires and provides further that the establishment guarantees that the work of reproduction is lawful in the country where it is done;
> (d) the licensee does not entrust the work of reproduction to an establishment specially created for the purpose of having copies reproduced of works for which a licence has been granted under Article II or Article III; and
> (e) all copies reproduced bear a notice in accordance with Article IV(5).[417]

It was also understood that these conditions should apply only to works published in printed or analogous forms of reproduction and to the incorporation in audio-visual fixations of translated texts;[418] in other words, they did not apply to the reproduction of audio-visual fixations generally. It was further understood that these conditions did not require any country in which the copies were reproduced to permit 'what would otherwise be an infringement of copyright under its law'.[419] A final interpretation that was 'generally accepted' by both conferences related to the making of translations: nothing in article II, III, or IV was to be understood as prohibiting a compulsory licensee from employing a translator in another country, or other compulsory licensees, licensed to publish a translation in the same language in other countries, from using the same translation in other countries, 'assuming, of course, that the translation has not already been published'.[420] This interpretation was also stated to apply to 'persons entrusted with doing the preparatory editorial work'.[421] So detailed and

---

[414] *Records* 1971, 151–2 (Mr Kéréver, France). [415] ibid, 153.
[416] Document B/DC/35, *Records* 1971, 116.
[417] *Records* 1971, 172–3; UCC general report (n 265 above), 251.
[418] ibid. [419] ibid. [420] ibid. [421] ibid.

precise, in fact, are these 'interpretations' adopted by both revision conferences that they might as well have been embodied in the conventions themselves. They are very far from meeting the desire of developing countries for joint licences, although they do go some way to ameliorating the situations of those countries which lack any technical facilities of their own.

(d) Limited exception to the prohibition on exports

A further, very limited, exception to the ban on exports is provided in the case of translations into languages other than English, French, or Spanish.[422] Where copies of these translations are sent to another country by the governmental or other public entity which has granted the licence (in other words, the 'competent authority'), this will not constitute the 'export' of those copies if the following conditions are met: **14.96**

1. the recipients are nationals of the country where the licence was granted, or organizations of those nationals;[423]
2. the copies are only for use for the purposes of teaching, scholarship, or research;[424]
3. there is no 'commercial purpose' in the sending of the copies and their subsequent distribution;[425] this does not mean that no price may be charged by the competent authority: merely that the 'price, if any, should not include any profit or financial gain for the entity, but should merely enable it to recover its costs'.[426]
4. there is an agreement between the country to which the copies have been sent and the country whose competent authority granted the licence to allow the receipt or distribution of the copies, and this agreement has been notified to the Director General by the government of the said country.[427]

These conditions ensure that the export of copies will not go beyond what may be done with those copies in the country which has granted the licence, but it is difficult to conceive of cases where this will, in fact, occur. A possibility would be where a particular ethnic community wishes to keep up its own cultural traditions, and to obtain copies of works in its own language for use in special schools, for example, a Sikh community in England or Canada, or a Turkish community in Germany. In the first instance, it will be necessary for compulsory licences for the translation and publication of these works to have been granted in India or Turkey, as the case may be. Secondly, the Governments of India or Turkey will have to enter agreements with the Governments of England, Canada, or Germany, to allow the receipt and distribution of these

422 Appendix, art IV(4)(c). Cf revised UCC, art V*ter*(4)(c).
423 ibid, art IV(4)(c)(i).
424 ibid, art IV(4)(c)(ii).
425 ibid, art IV(4)(c)(iii).
426 *Records* 1971, 173.
427 Appendix, art IV(4)(c)(iv).

copies. Finally, it should be noted that the object of these licences may be thwarted by the fact that many of the potential recipients of the copies are no longer nationals of the country where the licence was granted. This would certainly be the case for many second- or third-generation immigrants who may have assumed the nationality of their host country:[428] in such a case, they would not be eligible to receive the copies which are exported. The rationale for allowing such communities access to these cheap translations may be doubted in any event, particularly if they are located in prosperous overseas communities. And, if the aim is to preserve the immigrants' home culture, why should this be done via translations of works from other countries, including perhaps the country in which they are now living, rather than works in the original language of their country of origin?

(e) Notice on copies

14.97 All licensed copies published under either article II or III must bear a notice in the appropriate language stating that the copies are only for distribution in the country or territory covered by the licence.[429]

(f) Payment of compensation

14.98 The conditions concerning this under the Stockholm Protocol were the subject of some of the most stringent criticism by the developed countries, particularly as the criteria for determining the level of royalties were vague and the transmittal of the compensation was left subject to national currency restrictions (meaning that it might be impossible to repatriate payments at all).[430] This position was changed in article IV of the Paris Appendix, which requires that 'due provision shall be made at the national level' to ensure that two stipulations are met. First, the licence must provide, in favour of the relevant right owner, for the payment of 'just compensation that is consistent with standards of royalties normally operating on licences freely negotiated between persons in the two countries concerned'.[431] No comment on the meaning of the expression 'just compensation' is to be found in the general reports of either conference, but the criterion which accompanies it is very expansive. Consistency with 'the standards of royalties normally operating on licences freely negotiated between the persons in the two countries concerned' can work directly against the interests of the licensee's country. Thus, if the royalty normally charged by publishers in a developed country to voluntary licensees in the developing country in question is the same as for other licensees, all that the developing country will obtain is

[428] In this regard, simply being born in a country may not be enough for the purposes of acquiring citizenship thereof: this will be a matter for the law of citizenship of the particular country concerned.

[429] ibid, art IV(5). Cf revised UCC, arts $V^{ter}(4)(b)$ and $V^{quater}(1)(f)$.

[430] See para 14.43 above.

[431] Appendix, art IV(6)(a)(i). Cf revised UCC, arts $V^{ter}(5)(a)$ and $V^{quater}(2)(i)$.

the dubious benefit of a compulsory licence with the obligation of paying a rate of royalty similar to that paid by licensees in developed countries. The response to this is that publishers in the developed countries do not usually charge the same royalties to all would-be licensees, and take into account the circumstances of the latter's country when determining their rates.[432] In such a case, the 'normal royalty' will probably be appropriate for the country in question. However, the fact remains that the formulation adopted in the Appendix notionally allows for the imposition of a higher rate.

Second, with respect to the transmittal of royalties, it is provided that, in the event this becomes difficult or impossible through the intervention of national currency regulations, it is required that the competent authority should 'make all efforts, by the use of international machinery, to ensure transmittal in internationally convertible currency or its equivalent'.[433]

(g) Accuracy of licensed translations or reproductions

14.99 To protect the author's moral right of integrity, national legislation is required to make 'due provision' to ensure the accuracy of licensed translations or reproductions.[434]

(h) The meaning of 'competent authority'

14.100 This phrase recurs throughout articles I to IV, but without any specific guidance as to its meaning. However, it is clear from the context of these provisions that the 'competent authority' is the body which is designated as the licence-granting body under the national legislation of any country which avails itself of the provisions of the Appendix. It is to be assumed that this will normally be a governmental or other public entity, but there are no restrictions expressed in this regard. Thus, it could equally well be a court or some kind of judicial or quasi-judicial body, or even possibly a private organization.[435]

(7) Substitution of reservations in respect of translations for licences under article II

14.101 Under article V, it is possible for countries entitled to avail themselves of the Appendix to substitute reservations in respect of translation rights for the

[432] See eg Whale (n 87 above), 20ff; 'CISAC's Comments on the Draft Text for the Revision of the Berne Convention' [1972] *Interauteurs* 23–4.

[433] Appendix, art IV(6)(a)(ii). Cf revised UCC, arts V^{ter}(5)(d) and V^{quater}(2)(b)(ii). See further WG Guidelines, 134.

[434] Appendix, art IV(6)(b).

[435] It may be of significance here to note that art IV(4)(c) refers to governmental or public entities (being competent authorities), thereby implying that for other provisions other kinds of bodies may be included. See further WG Guidelines, 128.

compulsory licences allowed under article II. The scope of this faculty differs slightly, depending upon whether a country has previously made such a reservation under an earlier text of the Convention, and first requires reference to article 30(2) of the Paris Act which deals generally with the question of reservations. The latter contains the following provisions.

(i) **Union countries:** In the case of a Union country ratifying or acceding to the Paris Act or Appendix, article 30(2)(a) permits it to retain the benefits of reservations previously formulated (including any with respect to translations) on condition that a declaration to this effect is made at the time of deposit of its instrument of ratification or accession. In the case of a reservation in respect of translation rights, this may have originally been made in the terms of article 5 of the Berne Act (with the effect that translation rights fall into the public domain after ten years from first publication of the original), or in terms of article 5, as modified by the Paris Additional Act (with the effect that these rights fall into the public domain after ten years unless an authorized translation is published during this period).

(ii) **Countries outside the Union:** In the case of a country outside the Union (that is, a country acceding to the Convention for the first time), under article 30(2)(b) it may make a declaration to the effect that it intends, temporarily at least, to substitute the provisions of article 5 of the Berne Act, as modified by the Paris Additional Act, for article 8 of the new Act. This faculty is more limited than that allowed under article 30(2)(a), as it is subject to the further limitation that such a reservation can only be made 'on the clear understanding that the said provisions are applicable to translations into a language in general use in the said country'. In addition, other Union states are entitled to impose material reciprocity in respect of works coming from a country which has made such a reservation.[436]

Developing countries may fall into either of the above categories; there may also be others which have not made any reservations at the time of their accession to the Union, and, which are, as a consequence, under these provisions estopped from making such declarations at any later time. Article V(1) of the Appendix therefore offers each of these classes of developing countries the possibility of substituting declarations under article 30(2) for compulsory translation licences under article II. This takes the form of an election, with the result that when a declaration under article 30(2) is made it becomes impossible to invoke the provisions of article II and vice versa.[437] In the case of countries which have previously made reservations, they simply retain the benefit of these by the

[436] Paris Act, art 30(2)(b) (last sentence).

[437] Appendix, art V(1)(c) and (2).

making of a declaration under article 30(2)(a). In the same way, a non-Union country which accedes to the Paris Act may make a declaration under article 30(2)(b), with the added advantage that other Union countries are prevented from applying material reciprocity so long as it remains developing.[438] This benefit is also extended to developing countries that are already Union members, but have not previously made any reservations: they, too, are permitted to make declarations under article 30(2)(b).[439] The making of these declarations are subject to four conditions. First, the developing country in question must decide at the time of its ratification or accession of the Paris Act whether it will make one of the declarations allowed under article 30(2): the declaration must be made at that time and not later.[440]

Second, when a country ceases to be developing, any declaration which it has made under article V(1) remains effective until the date on which the period applicable under article I(3) expires (this being the expiration of the ten-year period then running in respect of that country or the expiration of three years, whichever is the longer).[441] This seems to apply to both declarations under article 30(2)(a) and (b), with the result that a non-developing country that has made such a declaration will be able to maintain this indefinitely, but a developing country may not. However, as will be seen below, article V(3) provides a limited means for a country which has ceased to be developing to preserve any reservation it has made with respect to translation rights.

Third, once it has made a declaration under article 30(2), a country cannot later avail itself of the compulsory licensing provisions of article II of the Appendix, even if it withdraws the declaration.[442] By contrast, if it had not made the declaration, article I(1) leaves it free to adopt these provisions at any time, so long as it remains developing.

Finally, as a corollary, any country which has availed itself of article II cannot subsequently make a declaration under article 30(2).[443]

Nevertheless, under article V(3) a concession is allowed in the case of any country which has ceased to be developing, and which has consequently lost the advantage of any compulsory licences imposed under article II or any declaration under article 30(2). Not later than two years prior to the expiration of the period applicable under article I(3), it may make a declaration to the effect provided for in article 30(2)(b), even though it is no longer a developing country and is no longer a country outside the Union. This declaration takes effect on the date on which the period applicable under article I(3) expires. Once this

[438] ibid, art I(6)(b).
[439] ibid, art V(1)(a)(ii).
[440] ibid, art V(1)(a) (preamble).
[441] ibid, art V(3).
[442] ibid, art V(1)(c).
[443] ibid, art V(2).

happens, other countries of the Union are entitled to apply reciprocity of treatment in respect of works from that country.[444]

(a) Accelerated application of Appendix

14.102 Article VI of the Appendix replicates the provisions contained in article 5 of the Stockholm Protocol for the application of its provisions prior to its entry into force with the Act, and will not be dealt with here again (see para 14.29 above).

(8) Assessment of the Paris Appendix

14.103 The Paris Revision Conference brought to an end the crisis in international copyright that had arisen with the adoption of the Stockholm Protocol four years earlier. How is the Appendix to be assessed? Did it represent a fair settlement of the conflicting demands and interests of developing and developed countries? Or was it a victory for one side, and defeat for the other? These questions need to be examined from several perspectives.

(a) The immediate responses

14.104 Unlike the Stockholm Revision, the two Paris Conferences proceeded with a far greater display of goodwill on both sides. In great part, this had to do with the fact that most of the fundamental aspects of the proposed revision had been agreed to in advance as part of the 'package deal' embodied in the Washington Recommendation. From the point of view of the developed countries, this was something they could 'live with'; from that of the developing countries, it represented a reluctant admission that this was the most they were likely to be able to obtain. However, it is clear that the ultimate revision of the two conventions in Paris in 1971 was effected in a far friendlier and less grudging spirit than had been present in Stockholm in 1967, and there was much wider support for the final results on the part of all the principal parties concerned. In this, the linkage of the two revisions played an important role, because the UCC no longer remained a potential low-level refuge for the developing countries. On the other hand, these countries were no longer placed in the position under the Berne safeguard clause of being prevented from acceding to the UCC if this was what they wished. The advantages to developing countries under both conventions were now essentially the same, and there was no reason for them to move from one convention to the other. The immediate result was that all the major protagonists for concessions at the Stockholm Conference, chose to stay in the Berne Convention. Of the forty-nine countries which had ratified the Paris Act and Appendix, as of January 1986, twenty-eight were developing

[444] Paris Act, art 30(2)(b) and Appendix, art I(6)(b).

countries.[445] By 17 January 2005, all but eleven of the 159 member states had ratified both the Paris Act and Appendix, and well over half of these 148 'Paris' signatories could legitimately claim developing country status.[446]

(b) Legal consequences

In terms of the Convention's overall development as a major instrument regulating private rights in the area of international law, the form of the Appendix may be regretted. It is an extremely detailed set of provisions, which exceeds the original Berne Act in length. The need for such detail must be queried, particularly in a Convention which has traditionally been concerned with the prescription of general principles of protection. The detail of the compulsory licences allowed under the Appendix contrasts strangely with the generally framed provisions of articles 11*bis* and 13(1). **14.105**

(c) The practical consequences

It is hard to point to any obvious benefits that have flowed directly to developing countries from the adoption of the Appendix. Indeed, only a handful of developing countries have availed themselves of its provisions in the time since its adoption.[447] Furthermore, of those countries that have made the necessary declarations, very few actually seem to have implemented such licensing schemes in their domestic laws.[448] This fact, however, may mask the real **14.106**

[445] [1986] *Copyright* 6–8. These countries were Barbados, Benin, Brazil, Burkina Faso, Cameroon, Central African Republic, Chile, Congo, Costa Rica, Ivory Coast, Cyprus, Egypt, Gabon, Guinea, India, Mali, Mauritania, Mexico, Niger, Rwanda, Senegal, Suriname, Togo, Tunisia, Uruguay, Venezuela, Yugoslavia, and Zaire.

[446] See the list of accessions and ratifications at www.wipo.org. Note that, of the ten 'non-Paris' countries, the bulk are developing countries, namely: Bahamas, Chad, Fiji, Lebanon, Madagascar, Pakistan, South Africa, Sri Lanka, and Zimbabwe.

[447] As of Dec 2004, the following countries had made declarations (operative until Oct 2014) under Art I of the Appendix with respect to the facilities provided by arts II and III: Bangladesh (Berne Notification No 234), Cuba (Berne Notification No 238, renewing previous declaration to Oct 2004), Jordan (Berne Notification No 232, renewing previous declaration to Oct 2004), Mongolia (Berne Notification No 237, renewing previous declaration to Oct 2004), Oman (Berne Notification No 233), Philippines (Berne Notification No 235, renewing previous declaration to Oct 2004), Sudan (Berne Notification No 240), Syrian Arab Republic (Berne Notification No 245), United Arab Emirates (Berne Notification No 236), and Vietnam (Berne Notification No 241), while Thailand had made a declaration with respect to art II (to Oct 2014) (Berne Notification No 239, renewing previous declaration to Oct 2004): see generally www.wipo.int/edocs/notdocs/en/berne/. Note also that Cyprus and Slovenia have made reservations with respect to translations. Previous declarations under art I of the Appendix with respect to the facilities under arts II and III (to Oct 2004) had been made by Algeria (Berne Notification No 194), Bahrain (Berne Notification No 177), Democratic Peoples' Republic of Korea (Berne Notification No 224), and Singapore (Berne Notification No 198), but these have not been renewed).

[448] Thus, a brief survey of the laws of these countries that is available online at www.wipo.int ('Collection of Laws for Electronic Access') reveals that only Thailand, of those countries whose laws are available there, actually has provisions in Chapter 3 of the Copyright Act BE 2537 (1994)

consequences of the adoption of the Appendix. Its provisions represent a delicate compromise between widely differing conceptions of the role of copyright. The developing countries never argued for the abolition of copyright, but they did urge that its prescriptions should be lowered in certain circumstances so as to assist their economic development in the areas of education and training. The developed countries, or rather the authors' and publishers' organizations in those countries, argued in turn that their rights should not be used as a means of providing economic assistance to developing countries. To a great extent, the adoption of the Appendix represents the developing countries' acceptance of this argument: if economic assistance is to be given, it should not be at the expense of the relatively small group of persons who create and provide literary and artistic works.

On the other hand, the provisions of the Appendix also serve as a warning to this last group that they may add markedly to the burden and frustration of developing countries through their reluctance to provide copies of their works or to authorize others to translate or reproduce them at a reasonable price. The Appendix, then, can be seen as an incentive to authors and publishers in the developed countries to co-operate in the making of voluntary licensing arrangements: the compulsory licences remain in the background both as a reminder of the needs of developing countries and as a threat to be brought into operation if there is a reluctance to provide access.[449] The fact that, to date, so few developing countries have invoked the Appendix may be an indication that authors and publishers in the developed countries have been far more willing to license their works than was previously the case. Alternative explanations, that need to be properly tested in each instance, are (i) that the social and economic problems of some of these countries are so intense that concern about copyright matters is not going to be a high priority, as distinct from overcoming famine, drought, floods, earthquakes, or civil war; or (ii) that the advent of digital technologies and communications may now render the provisions of the Appendix unnecessary to meet the developmental needs of these countries, even though such uses may, in principle, come within the scope of its provisions and may therefore pose a different set of challenges for authors and rights owners from developed countries.

---

that gives effect to Thailand's declaration with respect to translation licences under art III of the Appendix. The other national laws available online seem to be silent on the point, although there are some that are not available at all. The question of implementation therefore would repay careful investigation to ascertain the extent to which these countries, if any at all, have availed themselves of the facilities that they have claimed.

[449] See further on this point, V de Sanctis, 'L'avenir du droit d'auteur international a la lumière des conférences de révision de juillet 1971' [1972] *Interauteurs* 39, 42ff; R E Barker, *Copyright: The New International Conventions* (1971), 7.

A further, and perhaps paradoxical, development is that many developing countries have, in the years since 1967 to 1971, adopted high levels of protection in their laws, particularly in Africa.[450] This phenomenon, indeed, led one distinguished African expert in 1986 to point to the difference that appeared to have emerged between developing and developed countries in this respect, with the latter being more concerned with the 'purity' of authors' rights, while in the former there were increasing demands for the lowering of protection in particular instances, as shown by the claims of consumers for rights of private use in the case of sound and video reproduction, and online uses more generally.[451] Indeed, the advent of the Internet has created an 'anti-copyright' atmosphere in some of the most developed economies that has little to do with the needs of developing countries.[452] The role of WIPO in the course of the last two decades or so must also be noted: with limited resources, this body has provided considerable assistance to developing countries in the formulation of their new laws, as well as undertaking extensive training programmes for local personnel.[453]

---

[450] See eg the Rwanda Law of 15 Nov 1983, the Benin Law of 15 Mar 1984, and the Burkina Faso Law of 29 Feb 1984. These laws are closely patterned on the Tunis Model Law on Copyright which was prepared under the auspices of WIPO.

[451] N Ndiaye, 'The Berne Convention and the Developing Countries' [1986] *Columbia-VLA Journal of Law and the Arts* 47.

[452] See eg Lawrence Lessig, *Free Culture: How Big Media Uses Technology and the Law to Lock Down Culture and Control Creativity* (2004); Lawrence Lessig, *The Future of Ideas: The Fate of the Commons in a Connected World* (2001); Siva Viadhyanathan, *Copyrights and Copywrongs: The Rise of Intellectual Property and How it Threatens Creativity* (2001).

[453] The achievements of WIPO in this area appear impressive, as a cursory survey of the periodical *Copyright* between the years 1972 and 1986 will show. There were regional seminars on copyright and neighbouring rights held in a variety of different countries, eg, for African countries at Nairobi (16–20 Oct 1972), for Arabic countries at Rabbat (23–6 May 1977), for Latin American and Caribbean countries at Buenos Aires (5–9 Nov 1979 and 6–10 Apr 1981), for Asian and Pacific states and territories at New Delhi (18–22 Dec 1978), for newly independent African countries at Bissau (19–22 May 1980) and again at Lomé, Togo (1–5 Dec 1980), for the Economic Community of the Great Lakes Countries at Gisenyi, Rwanda (2–4 Mar 1981), for English-speaking Caribbean states at Kingston, Jamaica (19–23 Oct 1981), for Arabic countries at Cairo (7–10 Oct 1985) and for Central American and Caribbean states at Mexico City (19–22 Feb 1985). More specialized training courses and workshops have also been held during this time, and since 1977 WIPO has had a Permanent Programme for Developing Countries related to Copyright and Neighbouring Rights, with a Permanent Committee that met first in March 1977, and has met annually since then. Other committees of experts have examined particular problems of developing countries, such as the application of the compulsory licences under the Appendix (see n 266 above) and the organization of authors' societies. Most important has been the work done on the formulation of a Model Copyright Law in Tunis, 23 Feb–2 Mar 1976: [1976] *Copyright* 139, 165. For a further survey of this work, see A Bogsch, 'The First Hundred Years of the Berne Convention for the Protection of Literary and Artistic Works' [1986] *Copyright* 291, 333ff. These activities have continued in the years since 1986, with the establishment of a specific development co-operation bureau within WIPO, and the holding of further regional training and technical assistance conferences and meetings. A significant recent development, initiated by the current Director General in 1998, was the formation of the WIPO Worldwide Academy, which offers courses and training to academics and administrators from developing countries: see further www.wipo.int/academy/en.

In purely quantitative terms, the great majority of accessions to the Convention since the adoption of the Paris Act and Appendix has been from developing countries and, while there may be other explanations for this, the most obvious is that the 1971 settlement did represent an acceptable and workable compromise for those countries. These matters are beyond the scope of the present work, but they provide some evidence, at least, that developing countries now see copyright protection as a useful means of encouraging and promoting their own authors and artists and cultural industries. Perhaps, then, the experience of the years 1963 to 1971 was a valuable one in the overall growth of the Berne Union, as it made both developed and developing countries more conscious of each others' needs and perspectives. The result has been that developing countries are more fully integrated into the Berne Union system than ever before, and this is to an extent that would have been inconceivable at the start of the 1970s. In this respect, it seems true to say that the Berne Convention has scored a significant victory.

F. Beyond the Berne Convention

(1) The TRIPs Agreement

14.107 An obligation to comply with 'Articles 1 through to 21 of the Berne Convention (1971) and the Appendix thereto' applies under article 9(1) of the TRIPs Agreement. While a similar obligation also applies under the WCT (see para 14.109 below), under TRIPs any failure by a developing country that is otherwise entitled to invoke the provisions of the Appendix to comply with some or any of its detailed requirements will be a matter that can be pursued by any other aggrieved WTO member through the dispute-settlement procedures of the WTO. So far, this has not happened.

14.108 It should also be noted that there are extended transitional periods that are given to developing and 'least developed' countries under articles 65 and 66 of the TRIPs Agreement for these countries to 'apply the provisions' of the Agreement. Under article 65(2), for developing countries this was a further period of four years from the expiry of one year from the date of entry into force of the WTO Agreement (1 January 1996). Thus, such countries had until 1 January 2000 to achieve compliance, subject to a further requirement during the transitional period that such countries should ensure that any changes to domestic laws, regulations, and practice do not 'result in a lesser degree of consistency with the provisions of this Agreement'.[454] It appears that the decision as to whether a

[454] See further Daniel Gervais, *The TRIPS Agreement: Drafting History and Analysis*, 2nd edn (2003) ('Gervais (2003)'), 348–9.

country is developing or developed under the WTO system is a matter for WTO members to determine for themselves, rather than to do so in accordance with any outside or 'official' determination.[455] 'Least-developed country members' have the benefit of a ten-year transition period and the TRIPs Council is empowered to accord extensions of this period 'upon duly motivated request by a least-developed country': article 66(1).[456] The paragraph provides some guidance as to what constitutes a 'least-developed country' by referring to their 'economic, financial and administrative constraints, and the need for flexibility to create a viable technological base', and it appears that the WTO 'traditionally' will accept the UN list of such countries, as modified from time to time by the UN General Assembly, as a strong presumption that a Member may be considered a 'least-developed country'.[457] Under article 66(2), developed country members are required to 'provide incentives to enterprises and institutions in their countries for the purpose of promoting and encouraging technology transfer to least-developed country Members in order to enable them to create a sound and viable technological base'.[458]

(2) The WCT

The fundamental obligation relating to developing countries under the WCT is the same as under the TRIPs Agreement: article 1(4) requires all contracting parties to comply with articles 1 to 21 and the Appendix of the Berne Convention. By way of clarification, article 1(3) provides that, in the following text, 'Berne Convention' refers to the 'Paris Act of July 24, 1971, of the Berne Convention for the Protection of Literary and Artistic Works'. There is no obligation here that contracting parties should actually accede to the Berne Convention, although in practice this will almost invariably be the case, given the current size of Berne membership. However, it should be noted that there was an ambiguity in the text of article 1(4) as originally presented to the **14.109**

[455] ibid, 349. See further the statements at www.wto.org. Note also that further transitional periods for developing countries are allowed in relation to product patent protection (art 65(4)) and for other members that are in 'the process of transformation from a centrally-planned into a market, free-enterprise economy and which . . . [are] undertaking structural reform of its intellectual property system and facing special problems in the preparation and implementation of intellectual property laws and regulations' (art 65(3)).

[456] An instance of such request, from the Maldives, is reported as having been made to the TRIPs Council in Sept 2004: see the 2004 Annual Report of the Council for TRIPs, paras 13–17, available at www.wto.org.

[457] Gervais (2003), 351.

[458] Further information on assistance to these countries, as well as on the progress made by them in conforming to TRIPs standards is to be found in the minutes of the TRIPs Council and the documents of the Committee on Trade and Development. See eg the 2004 Annual Report of the Council for TRIPs (n 456 above), paras 13–17.

Diplomatic Conference in December 1996.[459] This was phrased as follows: 'Contracting Parties *that are not countries of the Union established by the Berne Convention* shall comply with Articles 1 to 21 and the Appendix of the Berne Convention.' In the case of countries that were only parties to Acts of the Convention prior to Paris, it might have been possible to argue that they were still 'countries of the Union' within the meaning of this draft provision, although the wording of draft article 1(3) would have provided a basis for the opposite argument, namely that arguing that 'countries of the Union' meant only those that had acceded to the Paris Act. This ambiguity, however, was removed during the discussions in Main Committee I of the Conference[460] with the deletion of the words 'that are not countries of the Union established by the Berne Convention'[461] in the final text that was adopted by the Conference. It will be noted that the obligation under article 1(4) not only applies to 'countries', but to any intergovernmental organization, including the European Community, that is eligible to become a party to the WCT under article 17(2) and (3).

14.110 An interesting problem arises in relation to the meaning of the word 'comply' as it appears in article 1(4). In the case of a developing country which is not a member of the Paris Act of Berne, or even a Berne member at all, would it be entitled to make a declaration under article I of the Appendix? The entitlement under that article refers to a country which, apart from possessing the necessary qualification of being a 'developing country', has ratified or acceded to 'this Act, of which this Appendix forms an integral part'. Thus, if a country was not a signatory to the Paris Act, it would not be entitled to invoke the facilities provided under the Appendix, even if it otherwise met the 'developing country' qualification. On the other hand, article 1(4) of the WCT would require that it 'complies' with the requirements of the Appendix, insofar as recognizing that the validity of compulsory licences, etc, introduced in their domestic laws by other WCT members that were entitled to invoke the Appendix (because they are actually signatories to Paris). This scenario is probably of theoretical interest only, but it will be recalled that there are still a number of non-Paris members of Berne and that most of these would fall within the category of developing countries, namely Bahamas, Chad, Fiji, Lebanon, Madagascar, Pakistan, South Africa, Sri Lanka, and Zimbabwe. At the time of writing, none of these countries had adhered to the WCT, and it is

[459] *Records* 1996, vol I, 4.

[460] See here the intervention by Mr Reinbothe of the European Communities at ibid, vol II, 722, and then by Hungary at 723.

[461] Document CRNR/DC/82.Prov at ibid, vol I, 502; see also the explanation for this by Mr Visser (South Africa) at ibid, vol II, 753–4.

difficult to conceive that, if any of them did make such a decision, it would not also adhere to the Paris Act and Appendix at the same time. In any event, the possibility that adherence to the WCT would not carry with it the entitlement to invoke the provisions of the Paris Appendix would surely be a strong incentive to adhere to both instruments.

15

NEW INTERNATIONAL OBLIGATIONS: TECHNOLOGICAL PROTECTION MEASURES (WCT, ARTICLES 11 AND 12), RIGHTS MANAGEMENT INFORMATION, AND ENFORCEMENT

A. Introduction

15.01 Both the Agreement on Trade-Related Aspects of Intellectual Property Rights 1994 (the 'TRIPs Agreement') and the World Intellectual Property Organization ('WIPO') copyright treaties broaden the substantive minimum protections that member states undertake to provide to authors whose works originate in Berne Union and other World Trade Organization ('WTO') or WIPO Copyright Treaty ('WCT') or WIPO Performances and Phonograms Treaty ('WPPT') member states. The new (or, in some instances, 'clarified') minimum rights we have so far considered in Chapters 11 and 12 above come within the traditional copyright categories of rights of reproduction and distribution, and of communication to the public.[1] The WCT and WPPT, however, introduced two new obligations, that do not create or enlarge exclusive rights as such, but which enhance the exploitation and enforcement of exclusive rights in the digital environment. These provisions formed the core of WIPO's 'digital agenda'. The first obligation, set out at article 11 of the WCT and article 18 of the WPPT, provides legal protections for the technological protection measures that copyright owners may employ to prevent unlawful use of works of authorship.[2] The second, imposed by article 12 of the WCT and article 19 of the WPPT, requires member states to protect electronic rights management information against knowing and unauthorized removal or tampering that induces or enables infringement of economic or moral rights.[3] Variations on the first obligation had made an appearance in national and regional laws, starting in the early 1990s,[4] and WIPO experts had already in 1990 considered proposing some model provisions with regard to anti-copying equipment and other measures.[5] The WIPO Treaties further reinforced both old (clarified) and new international obligations by requiring, in article 14 of the WCT and article 32(1) of the WPTT, that member states ensure effective enforcement of treaty rights. This chapter will first address the policies and precursors to article 11 of the WCT and the development of the WCT text, before turning to that article's interpretation. The chapter will then take up the development and interpretation of the obligation under article 12 of the WCT to protect rights management information. The last part of this chapter deals briefly with the general domestic enforcement obligation imposed by article 14 of the WCT.

[1] In addition to mandating compliance with existing Berne minima, the TRIPs Agreement requires WTO members to accord rental rights in computer software, phonograms, and, under certain circumstances, cinematographic works (art 11). See discussion at paras 11.81–11.84 above. The WCT sets out a general right of distribution (art 6), discussed at paras 11.88–11.94 above, and expands the right of communication to the public to cover the gaps left by arts 11, 11*bis*, 14, and 14*bis* of the Berne Convention, as well as clarifies that right's application to on-demand 'making available' of works (art 8), discussed at paras 12.57ff above.

[2] See further Chapter 19 below.

[3] See further Chapter 19 below.

[4] See Council Directive 91/250/EEC of 14 May 1991 on the legal protection of computer programs, *Official Journal* L 122, 17/05/1991 P 0042–0046 (the 'Software Directive'), art 7(1)(c); US Audio Home Recording Act of 1992, 17 USC § 1002(c).

[5] See Committee of Experts on Model Provisions in the Field of Copyright, third session, Geneva, 2–13 July 1990 at [1990] *Copyright* 241 (preparatory document at 278, report at 299–300).

B. Technological Protection Measures

15.02 Article 11 of the WCT obligation stems from the recognition that works made available in digital formats may be especially vulnerable to unauthorized copying and redistribution; unless the digital file can be secured against these acts, its susceptibility to unauthorized recirculation may discourage authors from making it digitally available to the general public. But supplying a technological lock may offer only short-lived solace: the measure may be effective only for so long as it takes to develop and distribute a device to break it. International copyright policymakers thus confronted the question whether international norms should reinforce authors' and copyright owners' efforts to prevent unauthorized copying, or whether technology and the market should be left to devise defences and counter-ripostes, leading to a technological 'arms race',[6] if need be. Such an arms race arguably diverts creative resources that might be better directed toward developing original works of authorship. In any event, the WCT's drafters were not writing on an entirely clean slate, for WIPO had itself considered proposing dispositions prohibiting the distribution of 'unauthorized decoders' of encrypted television transmissions.[7] Moreover, the European Commission had in 1991 already required member states to prohibit 'any act of putting into circulation, or the possession for commercial purposes of, any means the sole intended purpose of which is to facilitate the unauthorized removal or circumvention of any technical device which may have been applied to protect a computer program'.[8] Similarly, in 1992, the US Audio Home Recording Act required all 'digital audio recording devices' to be equipped with the 'serial copying management system', which disabled multigenerational copying of digital musical recordings. The Act also prohibited the distribution of any device or provision of any service 'the primary purpose or effect of which is to . . . circumvent' the system.[9] More generally, many national laws contained a variety of provisions in their tort or unfair competition laws, as well as in their telecommunication and penal laws, prohibiting a range of circumvention-related conduct such as the sale of satellite descramblers, and computer hacking.[10]

---

[6] I Trotter Hardy, 'Property (and Copyright) in Cyberspace' (1996) *U Chi Legal F* 217, 251.

[7] See preparatory document (n 5 above), paras 319–38. The Committee of Experts also considered requiring the provision of equipment that would limit the ability of home-recording machines to make successive generations of digital copies; ibid, paras 303–17. The proposal would have included an early form of copyright management information; ibid, para 312.

[8] Software Directive (n 4 above), art 7(1)(c).

[9] 17 USC § 1002(c).

[10] For a detailed discussion, see Séverine Dusollier, 'General Report—Situating Legal Protections for Copyright-Related Technological Measures in the Broader Legal Landscape: Anti Circumvention Protection outside Copyright', in Jane Ginsburg and June Besek (eds), *Adjuncts and Alternatives to Copyright, Proceedings of the 2001 ALAI Congress* (2002), 123. See also the questionnaire related to the general report, ibid at 110.

15.03 The contours of the EU and US prohibitions differ from each other and from the approach ultimately adopted in the WCT, but the same perceptions and policy determinations inform all three. In the digital environment, the ease of copying renders legal protection *simpliciter* inadequate. In the past, copying technology was too rudimentary, cumbersome, or expensive to enable users to copy and redisseminate on the scale that digital media make possible.[11] Copyright law's prohibition thus generally sufficed, because right holders could enforce the law against the commercial intermediaries who engaged in large-scale copying and dissemination, while whatever copying end-users engaged in was unlikely to rival the copyright owner's control of markets for the work. When digital media changed the technological balance, they also altered legal relationships, for now economically significant infringing acts were no longer the sole province of entities higher up the distribution chain. To redress the shift, it might be necessary to reinforce the legal prohibition with a layer of technological protection, disabling end-users from availing themselves of some of the copying technology's potential for reproducing and redistributing copyrighted works. But if end-users may easily procure the means to circumvent those impediments, then we are back where we started, without a middleman against whom copyright may effectively be enforced. Hence the conclusion followed that legal protection supplemented by technological protection will fail unless the technological protection is in turn backed up by further legal protection against the provision of circumvention devices or services.[12] When the copyists are so diffuse, the intermediary whom the enforcement efforts target now becomes the distributor of the means to circumvent technological protections.

(1) The development of WCT, article 11

15.04 As WIPO's efforts at drafting a model copyright law evolved into proposing a 'Protocol to the Berne Convention', and ultimately into the draft WCT, WIPO did not initially pursue its initiative to draft provisions against unauthorized decoders of encrypted television transmissions, despite general expressions of

[11] See Hardy (n 6 above), 224–5 (discussing 'state of the art' limitations on unauthorized copying and exploitation).

[12] For an evocation and analysis of this three-layer approach, see eg Alain Strowel, *La protection des mesures techniques: une couche en trop? Auteurs & Médias* (2001), 90–5. Séverine Dusollier, *Droit d'auteur et protection des oeuvres dans l'univers numérique: Droits et exceptions à la lumière des dispositifs de verrouillage des oeuvres* (2005). As Professor Sirinelli has observed, 'Technology comes to the aid of rights threatened by technology. But can it do everything? In order to be really effective, the devices themselves have to be protected. The WIPO Treaties . . . provide such measures. In a never-ending game of mirrors, rights come to the aid of technology so as to allow the latter to come to the aid of rights . . . !!!'. Pierre Sirinelli, 'Exceptions and Limitations to Copyright and Neighboring Rights', report presented to the Workshop on Implementation Issues of the WCT and the WPPT, Geneva, 6–7 Dec 1999, WIPO Document WCT-WPPT/IMP/1 (3 Dec 1999), 28.

concern that illicit decoders were promoting piracy.[13] The first version of the draft 'protocol' included no provision prohibiting the circumvention of technological protection measures, decoders, or otherwise.[14] The succeeding versions, however, returned to the problem, gradually elevating it from general provisions on enforcement of copyright, to a series of specific proposals defining the object and scope of the prohibition.[15] Both of those issues, however, proved controversial, and the final text of what became article 11 of the WCT differs significantly in a number of respects from the draft text proposed to the Diplomatic Conference.

15.05 The Basic Proposal set out the following as article 13 'Obligations concerning Technological Measures':

> (1) Contracting Parties shall make unlawful the importation, manufacture or distribution of protection-defeating devices, or the offer of performance of any service having the same effect, by any person knowing or having reasonable grounds to know that the device or service will be used for, or in the course of, the exercise of rights provided under this Treaty that is not authorized by the rightholder or the law.
>
> (2) Contracting Parties shall provide for appropriate and effective remedies against the unlawful acts referred to in paragraph (1).
>
> (3) As used in this Article, 'protection-defeating device' means any device, product or component incorporated into a device or product, the primary purpose or primary effect of which is to circumvent any process, treatment, mechanism or system that prevents or inhibits any of the acts covered by the rights under this Treaty.

(a) The object of the Basic Proposal's prohibition

15.06 The Basic Proposal defined 'protection defeating device' to comprehend three elements. First, that the protection which the proscribed device defeats be 'any process, treatment, mechanism or system'; second, that the 'primary purpose or effect' of the device be to circumvent; and third, that the device defeat a protection measure that 'prevents or inhibits any of the acts covered by the rights under this Treaty'. The nature of the protection measure appears to have

---

[13] See 1990 Report of the Committee of Experts on Model Provisions in the Field of Copyright (n 5 above), paras 168–71.

[14] See Committee of Experts on a Possible Protocol to the Berne Convention for the Protection of Literary and Artistic Works (first session, Geneva, 4–8 Nov 1991; second session, Geneva, 10–17 Feb, 1992): [1992] *Copyright* 30, 66.

[15] For a detailed description of the several stages leading up to the text of the Basic Proposal for the Substantive Provisions of the Treaty on Certain Questions Concerning the Protection of Literary and Artistic Works to be Considered by the Diplomatic Conference, in *Records* 1996 at 217, WIPO Document CRNR/DC/4, see Jörg Reinbothe and Silke von Lewinski, *The WIPO Treaties 1996* (2002) ('Reinbothe and von Lewinski (2002)'), 135–7; Mihály Ficsor, *The Law of Copyright and the Internet: The 1996 WIPO Treaties, Their Interpretation and Implementation* (2003) ('Ficsor (2003)'), 359–406.

been defined very broadly in order to cover the maximum variety of protective measures.

With respect to the second element—the nexus between the device and the prohibited circumvention—the drafters rejected the 'sole intended purpose' standard incorporated in the EU Software Directive,[16] and the 'specifically or predominantly designed or adapted to circumvent' standard expressed in an earlier version of the proposed Protocol.[17] Both of those standards incorporated a requirement of proving intent. While in most cases one might expect that a circumvention device will have been produced with the intent of overriding copy or other protection, the purpose of the prohibition is not to punish bad states of mind, but to protect the works of authorship. As a result, a more objective standard, inquiring into either intent (primary purpose) or result (primary effect) seems better adapted to the task at hand. Similarly, the 'sole intended purpose' test may be too narrow, for the device designer may adduce an additional, non-circumventing, purpose. In light of the goal of the prohibition, however, the additional purpose should be irrelevant if the device is in fact predominantly used to circumvent.

The third element may be the most elusive. While the Basic Proposal included a provision obliging contracting parties who were not already Union countries to comply with articles 1 to 21 of the Berne Convention,[18] Berne Convention rights are arguably not 'rights under this Treaty'. Thus, measures that protect rights found in the Berne Convention but not in the Basic Proposal might not have been covered by this provision. On the other hand, the nature and scope of the rights set out in the Basic Proposal was more comprehensive than in the final version. For example, it included a reproduction right (see the earlier discussion at para 11.72). Nonetheless, the formulation may have left some gaps and ambiguities as to its coverage.

(b) The scope of the Basic Proposal's prohibition

In prohibiting the 'importation, manufacture or distribution of protection-defeating devices, or the offer or performance of any service having the same effect', the text primarily targeted the dissemination of these devices. The term 'manufacture' may suggest that the prohibition addressed the large-scale or commercial creation of circumvention devices, but did not extend to more discrete development of the devices, such as might occur among researchers **15.07**

[16] See Software Directive (n 4 above), art 7(1)(c).

[17] See WIPO Memorandum for the Third Session of the Committee of Experts on a Possible Protocol to the Berne Convention: [1993] *Copyright* 95, para 75. See also Notes on Article 13 of the Basic Proposal: *Records* 1996 at 216, para 13.06.

[18] See Basic Proposal, art 1(4)

studying decryption. The extension of the prohibition to the provision of services covered what might otherwise have been a significant gap, but did not include a similar limitation to the commercial or general public context. A limitation on the scope of the prohibition occurred in the knowledge standard imposed on the person making or disseminating the circumvention device or offering circumvention services. This was not an intent standard (though intent might be inferred from knowledge), and by assimilating those 'with reasonable grounds to know' what the device will be used for, the standard covered wilful blindness. The Notes to the Basic Proposal explain that the 'knowledge requirement therefore focuses on the purpose for which the device or service will be used', and that the standard 'has the same meaning as the expression "knowingly or with reasonable grounds to know" in the provisions on enforcement in the TRIPs Agreement'.[19]

Finally, the purpose of which the provider of the devices or services was to have knowledge was the use of the device 'for, or in the course of, the exercise of rights provided under this Treaty that is not authorized by the rightholder or the law'. This language contained significant ambiguities. First, the range of the rights concerned remained uncertain (as discussed in para 15.06 above in connection with the definition of 'protection-defeating device'). Secondly, and most importantly, the phrase 'not authorized by . . . the law' seems to indicate that the prohibition did not extend to the provision of circumvention devices or services used to engage in an act permitted by law, for example, copying for a purpose covered by a copyright exception. As a practical matter, however, at least with respect to mass-production devices, or mass-provision services, the provider of goods or services which could be used for permitted purposes may well have reasonable grounds to know that its customers will not be using the device primarily for purposes such as news reporting or illustrations for teaching.

(c) Remedies

15.08 The Basic Proposal left it to contracting parties to define and implement 'appropriate and effective remedies' against unlawful provision of circumvention devices or services.

(d) From the Basic Proposal to the final text

15.09 As the above analysis of the text of the Basic Proposal indicates, there were sufficient uncertainties regarding the object and scope of the prohibition to provoke considerable controversy. Delegates expressed concern that the prohibition was overbroad and would lead to abuses by copyright holders, particularly

[19] Basic Proposal, Notes on Article 13 (n 17 above), para 13.02

if the prohibition could be applied to prevent non-infringing uses of protected works.[20] The delegation of South Africa, supported by the delegations of other African nations, offered a proposal that received general acceptance. The provision 'should have three characteristics: first, they should be effective technological measures; second, they should be used by right holders in connection with the exercise of their rights under the Treaties; and, third, they should restrict acts which were not authorized by the right holders or not permitted by law'.[21] The amendment which followed closely tracked this proposal:

> Contracting Parties shall provide adequate legal protection and effective legal remedies against the circumvention of effective technological measures that are used by right holders in connection with the exercise of their rights under this Treaty and that restrict acts, in respect of their works, which are not authorized by the rights holders concerned or permitted by law.[22]

This text differs from that ultimately adopted in only two respects. First, in the final version 'authors' are substituted for 'right holders', a change more consonant with the Berne Convention. Secondly, the final version adds 'or the Berne Convention' to 'rights under', thus avoiding the ambiguity as to the provision's coverage (discussed above at para 15.06).

(2) Analysis of WCT, article 11

Article 11 provides: **15.10**

> Contracting Parties shall provide adequate legal protection and effective legal remedies against the circumvention of effective technological measures that are used by authors in connection with the exercise of their rights under this treaty or the Berne Convention and that restrict acts, in respect of their works, which are not authorized by the authors concerned or permitted by law.

We will consider the subject matter as well as the scope of protection that the WCT requires member states to provide. Compared to the Basic Proposal, the final text is much less detailed, but in some respects is more precise. It also leaves considerable room to member states to delineate the types of circumvention prohibited, as well as the remedies.

(a) Subject matter protected: 'effective technological measures'

The WCT does not define what makes a technological protection measure **15.11**
'effective'. The term, which recurs in national and regional laws implementing

[20] See *Records* 1996, 709–16, and especially the remarks of the delegates of Ghana (para 517), Korea (para 518), 523 (Canada), 526–7 (Singapore), 536 (Australia).

[21] ibid, 710–11, para 519 (Mr Visser).

[22] ibid, 445, WIPO Document CRNR/DC/56 (12 Dec 1996).

article 11,[23] is not self-explanatory.[24] The one thing it cannot mean is 'impervious'. That is, were the measure not 'effective' unless it resisted attempts to circumvent it, there would be no need for legal protection; the technology would take care of itself. If 'effective' simply means that it hinders or prevents the relevant copyright-implicating act[25]—copying, distributing, communicating to the public—then it is not clear what the term adds.[26] By contrast, the approach taken in the European Union defines the term to describe the universe of protected measures: in the EU, an 'effective' technological measure is one 'where the use of a protected work or other subject matter is controlled by the right holders through application of an access control or protection process, such as encryption, scrambling, or other transformation of the work or other subject matter or a copy-control mechanism, which achieves the protection objective'.[27] This definition resolves the question, discussed later (see paras 15.13–15.16 below), of coverage of types of technological measures. It implies, however, that a technological measure that controls neither access nor copying, would not be 'effective' (no matter how well it functioned), and therefore would not be protected against circumvention.[28]

(b) 'Used by authors . . .'

15.12 In this context, the term 'authors' comprehends authors' successors in title (see

[23] See eg 17 USC § 1201(a)(1)(A), 1201(b)(1)(A); Directive 2001/29/EC of the European Parliament and of the Council of 22 May 2001 on the harmonisation of certain aspects of copyright and related rights in the information society, *Official Journal* L 167, 22/06/2001 (the 'Information Society Directive'), art 6

[24] For a variety of interpretations, see Jacques de Werra, 'The Legal System of Technological Protection Measures under the WIPO Treaties, the Digital Millennium Copyright Act, he European Union Directives, and other National Laws (Japan, Australia)', in Ginsburg and Besek (n 10 above), 198, 207.

[25] See eg 17 USC § 1201(b)(2)(B) ('a technological measure "effectively protects a right of a copyright owner under this title" if the measure, in the ordinary course of its operation, prevents, restricts, or otherwise limits the exercise of a right of a copyright owner under this title').

[26] Reinbothe and von Lewinski (2002), 145, suggest that malfunctioning technological measures need not be protected against circumvention, nor should those which 'interfere with the normal functioning of the equipment or services', giving the example of a copy control mechanism that interferes with the playability of a television or VCR.

Perhaps a technological measure is not 'effective', even if it functions properly, if access may be gained by means other than circumventing the device, that is, if the access device controls one 'door' to a work, but another 'door' exists and is not technologically locked, then locking only one 'door' is not 'effective'. See *Lexmark Int'l* v *Static Control Components, Inc*, 387 F 3d 522 (6th Cir, 2004) (employing door metaphor).

[27] Information Society Directive (n 23 above), art 6(3).

[28] It is not clear that such a measure in fact does or will exist. Devices that control distribution come to mind, but in the digital environment, distribution (or making available) probably implies copying. For the same reasons, technological measures protecting the moral right of integrity will probably be covered by the EU's definition of 'effective'. By contrast, a technological measure that protects the attribution right might not. Moreover such a device would not necessarily be within the scope of protection for copyright management information under WCT, art 12; see the further discussion at para 15.31 below.

Berne Convention, article 2(6)). While authors themselves may increasingly apply technological protection measures that enable them to market their works directly to the public without resort to intermediaries who require them to transfer all or part of their copyrights,[29] the WCT text should not be read to limit the protection of technological measures only to those actually applied by authors. Such a reading would disqualify protection of devices used by intermediaries on behalf of authors, thus defeating the WCT's author-protective goals. Moreover, the difficulty of knowing whether a particular protection measure has been used by the author or by her successor in title would make such an interpretation unworkable.

Assuming that 'used by authors' includes authors' successors in title, does it also extend to persons authorized by the author to exploit the work, but who may not be successors in title, such as grantees of non exclusive rights? It may be over-stretching the 'successors' category to comprehend those who are not title holders, but technological protection measures used by non-exclusive licensees would nonetheless be covered for reasons both practical and textual. If the goal of protecting technological measures is to favour e-commerce in works of authorship, then it should not matter whether the user is an exclusive or non-exclusive grantee. Moreover, as with successors in title, the would-be circumventor may not know the status of the licensee who employs the measure. Finally, the text of Berne article 2(6) provides that 'protection shall operate *for the benefit* of the author and his successors in title' (emphasis added). A non-exclusive licensee who employs technological measures benefits the author (or successor) by protecting the work, and thereby endeavoring to secure the royalty stream in which the author (or successor) may share.

(c) '. . . in connection with the exercise of their rights under this Treaty or the Berne Convention'

This phrase concerns the types of technological protection measures covered. A measure that prevents or hinders any of the acts covered within Berne or WCT economic or moral rights with respect to protected works would come within article 11's scope. Thus, measures protecting against copying (Berne Convention, article 9), adapting (Berne Convention, article 12), distributing of physical copies, including by means of rental (WCT, article 6), publicly communicating (Berne Convention, articles 11, 11*bis*, 11*ter*, 14, 14*bis*; WCT, article 8), and against **15.13**

[29] In the digital environment, many of the tasks publishers performed that were unrelated to the production and distribution of hard copies, such as promoting the works and accounting for sales, may be undertaken by agents or other new businesses whose compensation need not derive from owning the author's copyrights. See eg Jane Ginsburg, 'Copyright and Control over New Technologies of Dissemination' (2001) 101 *Colum L Rev* 1613, 1645–7; Raymond Shih Ray Ku, 'The Creative Destruction of Copyright: Napster and the New Economics of Digital Technology' (2002) 69 *U Chi L Rev* 263, 274–5.

violations of the integrity and attribution rights (Berne Convention, art 6bis) would all be covered.

But a particularly significant subset of technological protection measures addresses an arguably different act; these regulate access to a work of authorship.[30] In the digital environment, works may be made available not only in traditional formats permitting unlimited access, but also in access-controlled formats that limit the user's apprehension of the work to a certain number of viewings or hearings, or to a certain time period. A technological measure shuts off access after the designated time period or number of consultations. The copy of the work may remain in the user's hard drive or on a CD-Rom or similar external medium, but the user may be required to pay an additional fee or supply additional information before access will be restored. These sorts of formats may be particularly appealing to users who do not need or desire unlimited viewings or hearings of the work, assuming that a reduction in price accompanies the reduction in access. Whatever the business justifications for access controls, the question for the interpretation of article 11 of the WCT is whether it prohibits the circumvention of these measures as well.

(d) Coverage of access controls

15.14 The response turns on whether access controls are 'used by authors in connection with the exercise of their rights under the Treaty or the Berne Convention'. We will consider, first, whether accessing a work comes within the Berne-WCT minimum rights. Next, we will address whether access controls are 'used . . . in connection with' the exercise of those rights. In connection with the first question, it is important to distinguish accessing a *work* from accessing a *copy* of a work, as access controls generally apply to the former. Suppose a user purchases a CD-Rom containing a copyrighted work, such as a video game. She has acquired a copy, the physical medium in which the work is embodied. But the medium is not the work. The work is the video game; to access this, she needs to load the game into her computer or video-game player; when the game's sounds are heard and the images appear on the screen, she will have accessed the work. If a technological measure included on the CD-Rom does not permit her to play her copy of

[30] For a description and analysis of technological protection measures, see eg June Besek, 'Anti-Circumvention Laws and Copyright: A Report From the Kernochan Center for Law, Media and the Arts' (2004) 27 *Colum JL & the Arts* 389, 446–66; Jeffrey Cunard, 'Technological Protection of Copyrighted Works and Copyright Management Systems: A Brief Survey of the Landscape', in Ginsburg and Besek (n 10 above), 24; de Werra (n 24 above), 200–5; Gillian Davies, 'Technical Devices as a Solution to Private Copying', in Irini Stamatudi and Paul Torremans (eds), *Copyright in the New Digital Environment* (2000), 163, 173–8; Dean Marks and Bruce Turnbull, 'Technical Protection Measures: The Intersection of Technology, Law and Commercial Licenses', WIPO Workshop on Implementation Issues of the WCT and the WPPT, Geneva, 6–7 Dec, 1999, WIPO Document WCT-WPPT/IMP/3.

the game unless, for example, she enters a password, or plays the game only on certain designated computers, that is a measure controlling access to the work.

In light of this distinction, can it be said that the Berne Convention or the WCT establish a right to control access to a work? The WCT introduces a right of distribution of copies to the public, but this right addresses material (rather than electronic) copies; it would not extend beyond conferring a right to control access to a physical *copy*, rather than to a *work*.[31] The WCT also synthesizes the Berne Convention's various provisions on public performance into a general right of 'communication to the public', including by digital delivery.[32] This right would appear to cover 'access' to a work through online media; it is considerably less clear that it would also cover subsequent apprehension of a work once the user downloads a copy to the user's storage medium, or once the user acquires a free-standing copy, such as a CD-Rom.[33] The subsequent acts may 'perform' or 'communicate' the works, but not in or to the public. Neither the Berne Convention nor the WCT requires member states to extend exclusive rights to private performances or communications. **15.15**

Accessing a work expressed in digital form might nonetheless implicate the reproduction right under the Berne Convention: each apprehension of the work implies the creation of a temporary copy in the user's RAM. As the earlier discussion of the scope of the article 9(1) reproduction right indicated (see paras 11.27, 11.69–11.71 above), that provision's reference to 'any manner or form' may well cover temporary digital copies of this kind. But the scope of the reproduction right proved sufficiently controversial at the diplomatic conference that produced the WCT, so that many signatories to the WCT may not subscribe to a characterization of the scope of the reproduction right that would embrace a right to control access to a work (see paras 11.72–11.75 above).

Given the continuing uncertainty in some quarters regarding the scope of the reproduction right, does it follow that WCT member states are not obliged to protect access controls against circumvention? Not necessarily, because one must next ask whether access controls are technological measures 'used in connection with the exercise' of exclusive rights. Here the case for WCT coverage appears stronger. For example, access controls may be said to be used in connection with the exercise of the reproduction and communication rights, because **15.16**

[31] See WCT, art 6 and accompanying agreed statement. See generally paras 11.88ff above.

[32] See WCT, art 8 ('authors of literary or artistic works shall enjoy the exclusive right of authorizing any communication to the public of their works, by wire or wireless means, including the making available to the public of their works in such a way that members of the public may *access* those works from a place and at a time individually chosen by them.' (emphasis added)). See generally paras 12.57ff above.

[33] Article 6 of the 2001 EU Information Society Directive (n 23 above), however, implements WCT, art 11 by protecting access controls.

an access-controlled copy, even if reproduced or communicated without authorization, will yield its copyist or recipient no benefits; that person will not be able to apprehend the work.[34] Thus, access controls underpin the reproduction, communication, and distribution rights.

(e) Acts prohibited

15.17 (i) **'the circumvention'**: The text appears most directly to cover the acts of removing, breaking, or bypassing a technological measure. But relatively few individual users are likely to be able to engage in these acts unaided by a device that will overcome the protection. The question therefore arises whether the formulation 'the circumvention' covers only that act, or also reaches the more economically significant activity of 'preparatory acts', including supplying a device that will enable the circumvention. As discussed earlier (see paras 15.05–15.06 above), the Basic Proposal specifically targeted circumvention devices; should one infer from the final version's more abstract expression a rejection of the liability of manufacturers and distributors of devices?[35]

Such an inference seems unwarranted, because it would significantly diminish the effectiveness of the prohibition. First, limiting the prohibition to the act of circumvention would mean that copyright owners would need to discover and prove the commission of acts that may often occur in private, at the user's home. This seems both difficult for copyright owners and undesirable to users.[36] Second, outlawing the device as well as the activity is likely to have a greater impact on the provision of circumvention devices; without the device, less circumvention is likely to occur, and it is more effective to pursue a small number of device

---

[34] See *Kabushiki Kaisha Sony Computer Entertainment* v *Stevens* [2003] FCAFC 157 (30 July 2003). In an action under s 116A of the Australian Copyright Act, which gives copyright owners a right of action against sellers of devices whose purpose is to circumvent technological protection measures, the court construed 'technological protection measure' to include controls that block access to unauthorized copies because the controls 'prevent or inhibit the infringement of copyright in a work'. A technological measure that 'renders the infringing copies . . . useless', meets the statutory requirement of preventing infringement 'by rendering the sale of the copy "impracticable or impossible by anticipatory action"'.

This decision also exemplifies the uncertainty regarding the relationship of RAM copying to the reproduction right; two of three judges held that temporary storage in RAM did not produce a copy 'in material form', and therefore no reproduction within the meaning of the Act had occurred.

[35] See eg Thomas C Vijne, 'Copyright Imperilled?' (1999) 21 *EIPR* 192, 201; Alain Strowel and Séverine Dusollier, 'Legal Protection of Technological Systems', Workshop on Implementation Issues of the WCT and the WPPT, Geneva, 6–7 Dec 1999, WIPO Document WCT-WPPT/IMP/2 at 7, available at: www.wipo.int/documents. Contra, Kamiel Koelman, A Hard Nut to Crack: The Protection of Technological Measures (2000) 22 *EIPR* 272, 273 (whether WCT, art 11 requires member states to prohibit the act of circumvention is 'debatable').

[36] See eg Marks and Turnbull (n 30 above), 6 (pointing out privacy and practical concerns underlying the monitoring of private activity that a prohibition limited to the act of circumvention would entail).

suppliers than the large numbers of their customers.[37] Moreover, the formulation 'the circumvention' should be read in the context of the sentence in which it appears. An interpretation that disfavours effective protection against circumvention by limiting the prohibited conduct to the sole act of circumvention, rather than encompassing the provision of devices as well, would be inconsistent with article 11's direction that member states 'shall provide adequate legal protection and effective legal remedies against the circumvention . . .'.[38]

(ii) Circumvention of technological measures 'that restrict acts, in respect of their works, which are not authorized by the authors concerned or permitted by law': Not all acts of circumvention are violations of article 11; member states incur no obligation to prohibit circumventions that allow the user to exploit a work in the public domain, or to engage in an act authorized by the right holder, or, more importantly, that allow the user to engage in a non-infringing act, such as accessing a work in the public domain, or copying for purposes endorsed by articles 10 and 10*bis*. Article 11 delegates to member states' laws the determination of permissible acts, but these must remain consonant with the scope of exceptions and limitations allowed under article 10 of the WCT and articles 9(2), 10, 10*bis*, 11*bis*, and 13 of the Berne Convention (see further the discussion of these matters at paras 13.129ff above). **15.18**

The difficulty in implementing article 11 of the WCT arises with respect to the prohibition of circumvention devices and services. These may be used to engage in acts that infringe, but they may also be used for permitted purposes. If the prohibition sweeps too broadly, it may bar the manufacture and dissemination of devices or services that have legitimate uses other than to circumvent controls on access to or copying of copyrighted works. Too extensive a prohibition may frustrate whatever legitimate activities the devices may permit. Equally importantly, too broad a prohibition may hamper the development of useful new technologies. On the other hand, if national law provided that a device may be distributed so long as it is capable of being put to use for non-infringing purposes, the prohibition would likely become meaningless. This in turn would put the national law in tension with article 11, for that law's protection of the technological measure would be neither 'adequate' nor 'effective'. **15.19**

For example, an access-circumvention device may be used to decrypt motion pictures in the public domain, but the same device can be employed to decrypt works still under copyright. A device that circumvents copy controls may be used to copy limited portions for purposes of illustration for teaching, but it may also be used to make unlimited complete copies to distribute to one's

[37] Accord, Reinbothe and von Lewinski (2002), 144.
[38] Accord, ibid, 145; Ficsor (2003), 549.

friends (or to the world over the Internet) for purposes of personal enjoyment. In most instances, and especially for mass-market devices, the maker or provider of the device will not know, at the time the device is made available, the nature of the use to which it will be put (although he or she might well anticipate that the market for the device is not likely to be limited to researchers, teachers, and librarians).[39] Even if the device is designed in good faith to allow the public to decrypt DVDs of *The Sheik* or *Birth of a Nation* or other silent-era motion pictures in the public domain, it is equally capable, and probably more likely, to be used to unlock the digitized oeuvre of Federico Fellini or Woody Allen.

15.20 The Basic Proposal sought to address the problem of intended purpose or likely utilization by defining the prohibited device as one whose 'primary purpose or effect' was to circumvent. This drew considerable opposition, however, notably from delegations who urged a 'sole purpose or effect' standard.[40] The final version of article 11 avoids that controversy by declining to define targeted devices (indeed, not mentioning devices at all), and leaving it to member states to determine how to protect against 'the circumvention. . .'. As the analysis above (see paras 15.17, 15.19), suggests, however, the 'adequate and effective' proviso would seem to require member states to bar the general circulation of circumvention devices. For the same reason, it also appears to disallow a 'sole intended purpose' standard. While that standard might have proved too coarse a sieve, the opposite risk remains, that, in the absence of Treaty guidance on the preservation of non-infringing uses, national implementing laws will design so fine a mesh that too few non-infringing applications will succeed in passing through. The challenge for national laws, then, is to determine how to regulate the creation and dissemination of circumvention devices without effectively cutting off the fair uses that at least some devices, in the right hands, would permit. This conundrum was explored further in Chapter 13 (see paras 13.129ff above), although ultimately it will be seen that there is little here in the WCT text or in Berne itself that will provide guidance to national legislators and policymakers.

(f) 'Effective legal remedies'

15.21 Article 11 of the WCT does not instruct member states regarding the nature of the sanction for violating the anti-circumvention norm. Thus, the WCT does

---

[39] The context of the production or provision of the device may be determinative in certain circumstances. For example, if a university's information technology department supplies a circumvention device to university teaching or library staff for purposes of research or preservation, the uses of the device will likely be limited to those 'permitted by law', and the provision of the device should therefore be permissible as well. Problems would arise, however, were the same device distributed to the general public, because the activities of the recipients of the device would no longer be likely to be confined to non-infringing acts.

[40] See *Records* 1996, 711–14; proposed amendment to substitute 'sole intended purpose' for 'primary purpose or effect' (submitted by Singapore), WIPO Document CRNR/DC/12 at *Records* 1996, 712, para 526.

not specify whether member states must grant injunctive relief against the distribution of circumvention devices or offering of circumvention services. In many cases, that relief may be necessary to ensure 'adequate and effective' protection, but there may be situations in which a lesser course, such as permitting the distribution of the device, subject to remunerating right owners, might be envisioned. As a general matter, the provisions of articles 41 to 61 of the TRIPs Agreement on the enforcement of intellectual property rights indicate the range of remedies that constitute effective relief. It is worth noting that the WCT does not require that protections for technological measures be enacted as part of national copyright laws; that certainly is one route, but so too are *sui generis* laws, or inclusion of protections within the scope of more general laws, such as those addressing unfair competition.[41]

One matter, discussed in connection with the Basic Proposal, was whether member states should be obliged to impose design mandates on consumer equipment, so that mass-market playback devices would interact successfully with technological protection measures applied to the content of the works played back. Mandates of this sort had been posited and debated as early as the WIPO Draft Model Law of 1990.[42] But those debates occurred in the context of discussions over mandated protection measures, such as the Serial Copy Management System ultimately required for digital audio tape players by the 1992 US Audio Home Recording Act.[43] Once the drafters determined to leave the design of protection measures to the member states, design mandates were no longer at issue at the international level. Member states remain free to impose such requirements as a means of domestic implementation of the anti-circumvention norm, but they have no duty to do so. The trend, in fact, is the other way: both the USA and the European Union have explicitly dispensed the designers of playback or other devices from having to comply with the specifications of the protection measure, so long as they do not circumvent it.[44] Non co-operation is fully permissible; aggressive hostilities are not.

---

[41] eg Japan has divided coverage of technological measures between the copyright law and the unfair competition law. See Copyright Law (Law No 48, promulgated on 6 May 1970, as amended through 12 June 1988), art 120*bis* (i); Unfair Competition Prevention Law (No 47 of 19 May 1993, as last amended on 23 Apr 1999), art 2(x)–(xi), discussed in Besek (n 30 above), 431–6. Australia has done this solely within the provisions of the Copyright Act 1968 (ss 116A and D) but makes them the subject of separate rights of action that may be brought by the copyright owner.

[42] See Memorandum prepared for the Committee of Experts on Model Provisions in the Field of Copyright (n 5 above), paras 312–18; Report, ibid, 299–300, paras 159–67.

[43] See ibid, 279, paras 309–10 (Memorandum); 300, para 164 (Report); 17 USC § 1002.

[44] See 17 USC § 1201(c) ('no mandate' clause); Information Society Directive (n 23 above), recital 48.

(3) Assessment of article 11

15.22 We have considered the policy underlying article 11 of the WCT (see paras 15.02–15.03 above); it is appropriate now to inquire whether the WCT successfully implements that policy. If the goal was to promote the digital distribution of works of authorship by giving authors some sense of security that copy- or access-protected formats will not be vulnerable to piracy, it remains to be seen how effective national implementations of article 11[45] prove to be in preventing or forestalling circumvention activities or devices. If the companion goal was to ensure that privileged unauthorized uses could continue to be made notwithstanding authors' resort to technological protections, it remains to be seen whether the various member state attempts to reconcile meaningful protection with preservation of copyright exceptions and limitations achieve a successful balance. In any event, the subsequent development of high-speed, high-volume peer-to-peer file 'sharing', may call into question the efficacy of any technological protections or the legal regimes intended to reinforce those protections. Potentially, so long as one decrypted or protection-stripped copy is made available over a file-'sharing' network, millions of end-users may rapidly acquire and redistribute the work, unhampered by the protection measures attached to copies made available through lawful means of distribution. In this scenario, the application of technological protections becomes, if not completely irrelevant, then confined to those users who quaintly continue to pay for their enjoyment of works of authorship.[46]

15.23 But one may envisage equally bleak scenarios at the other extreme. In this dystopia, yet another legal regime will come to overlay the strata of technological and legal protections already secured through the WCT. Rather than circulating freely (with or without remuneration), works will be made available only in protected formats and under onerous contractual conditions that preclude exercise of the non-infringing uses otherwise authorized by local laws and by the Berne Convention and WCT. Copyright owners thus would 'contract out' of fair use and other copyright limitations, and technological measures—backed up by law—would make the contract stick. Copyrighted works, 'thus trebly

[45] See eg 17 USC § 1201(d)–(j); Information Society Directive (n 23 above), art 6(4).

[46] Several scholars in the US have suggested that the solution is to substitute a levy scheme for technologically protected exclusive rights; this would ensure both that authors are remunerated, and that the public has untrammelled access to works. Most of these suggestions, however, do not analyse the compatibility of such proposals with the Berne Convention and the TRIPs Agreement. See eg William Fisher, *Promises to Keep: Technology, Law, and the Future of Entertainment* (2004), 199–258; Neil Netanel, 'Impose a Noncommercial Use Levy to Allow Free Peer-to-Peer File Sharing' (2003) 17 *Harv JL & Tech* 1. But see Jessica Litman, 'Sharing and Stealing' (2004) 27 *Hastings Comm & Ent LJ* 1, 17, 45–6 and n 166 (endeavouring to work through Berne-compatibility of a levy proposal).

insured',[47] would become the objects of the 'digital lockup' that some critics feared the WCT and its national implementing laws would promote.[48] This dire scene presupposes that works will no longer be available in non-protected formats, which may not soon be likely, but for works that are 'digital originals', it is at least conceivable. It is generally a matter for local law to determine whether parties may contractually override copyright limitations,[49] as, apart from Berne article 2(8) (news of the day) and 10(1) (quotation rights) neither Berne nor the WCT contain mandatory limitations. But the European Union Information Society Directive may portend a grim future in this regard. Article 6(4), which sets out the general terms of protection for technological measures, requires member states to accommodate a variety of copyright exceptions, but then provides that this obligation 'shall not apply to works or other subject-matter made available to the public on agreed contractual terms in such a way that members of the public may access them from a place and at a time individually chosen by them'.[50] This would mean that if the work is made available to the public online on an on-demand basis, the copyright owner may impose conditions incompatible with the exceptions otherwise explicitly preserved by the Directive, and the member states, when implementing the Directive, must similarly honour these contractual overrides. So long as copies are available through other means of distribution, the Directive may betoken no more than eventual inconvenience in exercising privileged uses. The Directive does not, notably, enshrine 'shrink wrap' licences attached to digital hard copies such as CD-Roms. Member states remain free to enforce, or to reject, such 'agreements'. Hence not all digital formats are insulated from copyright limitations. If, however, online on-demand delivery ultimately displaces other forms of digital

[47] The phrase is Judge Learned Hand's, but the context is completely different, see *Nichols* v *Universal Pictures Corp*, 45 F 2d 119, 120 (2d Cir 1930) (referring to marriage, thrice-performed, of Jewish-Irish lovers in *Abie's Irish Rose*).

[48] See eg Jessica Litman, *Digital Copyright* (2001), 81–6; Julie E Cohen, 'WIPO Copyright Treaty Implementation in the United States: Will Fair Use Survive' [1999] *European Intellectual Property Review* 236; Julie E Cohen, 'Copyright and the Jurisprudence of Self-Help' (1998) 13 *Berkeley Tech LJ* 1089; Niva Elkin-Koren, 'Copyrights in Cyberspace: Rights Without Laws?' (1998) 73 *Chi-Kent L Rev* 1155.

[49] See eg Jaap H Spoor, 'General Aspects of Exceptions and Limitations to Copyright: General Report', in Libby Baulch et al (eds), *ALAI Study Days: The Boundaries of Copyright: Its Proper Limitations and Exceptions* (1998), 27 (summarizing national reports setting forth various positions on whether copyright exceptions are mandatory; Lucie M C R Guibault, 'Contract and Copyright Exemptions', in P Bernt Hugenholz and K Koelman (eds), *Copyright and Electronic Commerce* (2000), 125, 126. For a detailed analysis of the general problem, see Lucie Guibault, *Copyright Limitations and Contracts: An Analysis of the Contractual Overridability of Limitations on Copyright* (Information Law Series, vol 9) (2002).

[50] Information Society Directive (n 23 above), art 6(4), para 4. For commentary on art 6(4), see eg Alvise Maria Casellati, 'The Evolution of Article 6.4 of the European Information Society Copyright Directive' (2001) 24 *Colum J Law & the Arts* 369.

distribution, then the 'click wrap' licence that expands copyright beyond statutory limitations could result in overprotection.

15.24 A technological protection-measured future need not, however, forebode either anarchy or apocalypse. A more optimistic forecast would focus on the opportunities extended to individual authors to disseminate their works, and to condition further copying or exploitation on remunerating the creators. Digital media, by making the means of production and dissemination available to any computer-equipped author, give authors a realistic opportunity to bring their works to the public without having to put themselves in thrall to traditional intermediaries. The technological measures that reinforce legal control may enable and encourage authorial entrepreneurship, because authors may be able to rely on these measures to secure the distribution of and payment for their works, and new business models may therefore emerge. Shifting control from publishers (writ large) to authors not only enhances the moral appeal of the exercise of copyright, it also may offer the public an increased quantity and variety of works of authorship, as authors whom the traditional intermediary-controlled distribution system may have excluded now or soon may directly propose to the public (and be compensated for) their creations.

15.25 For the moment, it is up to national law to find the balances that will promote the realization of the happy last of these three scenarios, rather than its two dismal alternatives. But it remains to be seen whether any domestic legislation or judicial interpretation will be able to achieve this outcome, not only because it will be difficult locally, but also, and especially, because a more articulated balance may need to be set at a supra-national level.[51] Whether the content is works of authorship or circumvention software, digital formats easily permeate borders, and disparate national solutions to the scope of protection of technological protection measures may resist predictable implementation in practice. But obtaining international agreement on the scope of protection of technological protection measures may imply a predicate agreement on the content of exceptions. As Chapter 13 above amply demonstrates, until now, the Berne Convention, the TRIPs Agreement and the WCT have simply furnished a general framework, describing the outer limits, but leaving to national law the design of the regime that fits within the frame. It remains to be seen whether a technique so solicitous of national peculiarities can successfully match with the new legal protection for what appear to be the less nuanced workings of access and

[51] For a variety of domestic and international proposals, see the discussion in Besek (n 30 above), 485–96.

copy controls.[52] If the marriage fails, new international substantive guidelines may be needed.

C. Rights Management Information

The second new obligation the WCT imposes on its member states is to protect 'rights management information' against removal or alteration. The 'digital agenda' sought to further the digital dissemination of works not only by protecting digital formats against circumvention of accompanying technological measures, but also to secure the information identifying the work and the terms and conditions of its exploitation. For those who seek to make lawful use of copyrighted works in the digital environment, easy acquisition of accurate and reliable information about the availability and price of rights enhances the likelihood that new formats or new versions will be disseminated to the public. The protection of rights management information against falsification thus advances important goals whose achievement will further both the interests of authors and of the broader public in the digital communication of works of authorship. In that light, we will consider the evolution and the interpretation of article 12 of the WCT. **15.26**

(1) Basic Proposal

Unlike technological measures, rights management information did not have WIPO draft precursors. As Dr Ficsor recounts, during the early 1990s, some national studies and WIPO workshops began to examine the question of technological measures, and copyright management information was occasionally raised as an adjunct.[53] Rights management information did not figure in the deliberations of the Committee of Experts on a Possible Protocol to the Berne Convention until the fourth session in December 1994, and then only in rather vague terms. Treaty language was first proposed in February 1996, at the sixth session of the Berne Protocol Committee. The US, Canada, and a group of Latin American and Caribbean countries all proposed Treaty language. The Basic Proposal for a new article 14 essentially merged the US language articulating the prohibited acts with some of the Canadian language defining rights management information (perhaps notably, the Basic Proposal's definition omitted the **15.27**

[52] For an attempt to make the match, see EU Information Society Directive (n 23 above), arts 5 and 6. Commentators' prognoses of successful accommodation, however, have not been sanguine. See eg Bernt Hugenholtz, 'Why the Copyright Directive is Unimportant, and Possibly Invalid' [2000] EIPR 501.

[53] See Ficsor (2003), 373–84.

name of the author; by contrast, this element of information was highlighted in both the Canadian and the Latin American proposals of February 1996):

> Obligations concerning Rights Management Information
>
> (1) Contracting Parties shall make it unlawful for any person knowingly to perform any of the following acts:
> (i) to remove or alter any electronic rights management information without authority
> (iii) to distribute, import for distribution or communicate to the public, without authority, copies of works from which electronic rights management information has been removed without authority.
>
> (2) As used in this Article, 'rights management information' means information which identifies the work, the owner of any right in the work, and any numbers or codes that represent such information, when any of these items of information are attached to a copy of a work or appear in connection with the communication of the work to the public.[54]

15.28 The Notes to the Basic Proposal raised three points. First, that the protected subject matter was electronic rights management information. Second, that liability turned on the knowing removal or alteration of the information. Third, that member states enjoy broad leeway to define the scope of the obligation. In that connection, the right holder's application of rights management information was purely voluntary; member states need not require authors or their successors to append any rights management information to digital copies.

A few observations are in order. Regarding the subject matter, the limitation to *electronic* rights management information makes clear that the relevant universe is works of authorship in digital form; removing a copyright notice from printed copies, for example, thus would not implicate this obligation. Regarding the state-of-mind prerequisite, this proved particularly contentious, and resulted in the most substantively significant amendment to the Basic Proposal. Finally, the margin given to member states in designing the implementation of the prohibition on removing rights management information not only left to them the determination of the remedies for a violation, but also the decision whether to designate the technical means of appending that information. That is, implicitly, the Basic Proposal rejected imposing any uniform technology mandates, although it permitted member states to impose them as a matter of domestic law.[55] This mirrors the approach taken with respect to technological protection measures (see the earlier discussion at para 15.21 above).

[54] *Records* 1996, 219.

[55] An amendment proposed by the USA would have made a no-mandate provision explicit, and would have barred member states from imposing local mandates, see *Records* 1996, 427.

(2) Amendments made at the Diplomatic Conference[56]

The principal changes to the text of the Basic Proposal concerned the standard of knowledge requisite to committing a violation. Both the USA and the European Union proposed amendments linking the element of knowledge to the commission of a copyright violation. That is, for a violation to occur, it would not suffice that the person concerned knowingly removed or altered the rights management information; it would also be necessary to show that he or she knew that the change would enable or facilitate infringement.[57] A US amendment added to the definition 'information about the terms and conditions of use of the work'.[58] The amendment prompted no discussion, but reflected the goals earlier expressed in the US White Paper, which had reviewed the adaptability of current copyright law to the digital communication of works, and which made several proposals for amending the law to clarify its application to those communications and to facilitate new digitally-based business models, specifically defining copyright management information to include 'terms and conditions for uses of the work'.[59] One amendment that did provoke some disagreement was the US proposal to add to the prohibition on removing rights management information which induces, enables, or facilitates infringement 'or the avoidance of payment to a right holder'.[60] The language could have been understood as referring to statutory remuneration rights, or to contractual obligations; delegates deemed the latter extension inappropriate.[61] The proposal, rephrased, and augmented to include a caution against the institution of mandatory formalities, was adopted as an agreed statement. **15.29**

(3) The text of article 12 and its agreed statement

We will examine the obligations and implications of the final WCT text. Article 12 provides: **15.30**

> Obligations concerning Rights Management Information
>
> (1) Contracting Parties shall provide adequate and effective legal remedies against any person knowingly performing any of the following acts knowing, or with respect to civil remedies, having reasonable grounds to know, that it will induce, enable, facilitate or conceal an infringement of any right covered by this Treaty or the Berne Convention:

[56] For a fully detailed discussion, see Ficsor (2003), 396–406. See also Reinbothe and von Lewinski (2002), 149–51.

[57] See *Records* 1996, 427 (US), 491–2 (EU).

[58] ibid, 427.

[59] See *Intellectual Property and the National Information Infrastructure: The Report of the Working Group on Intellectual Property Rights* (Sept 1995), Appendix 1 at 7 (www.uspto.gov/web/).

[60] *Records* 1996, 427.

[61] See Reinbothe and von Lewinski (2002), 150.

(i) to remove or alter any electronic rights management information without authority

(ii) to distribute, import for distribution, broadcast or communicate to the public, without authority, works or copies of works knowing that electronic rights management information has been removed or altered without authority.

(2) As used in this Article 'rights management information' means information which identifies the work, the author of the work, the owner of any right in the work, or information about the terms and conditions of use of the work, and any numbers or codes that represent such information, when any of these items of information is attached to a copy of a work or appears in connection with the communication of a work to the public.

Agreed statement concerning article 12

It is understood that the reference to 'infringement of any right covered by this Treaty or the Berne Convention' includes both exclusive rights and rights of remuneration.

It is further understood that Contracting Parties will not rely on this Article to devise or implement rights management systems that would have the effect of imposing formalities which are not permitted under the Berne Convention or this Treaty, prohibiting the free movement of goods or impeding the enjoyment of rights under this Treaty.

(a) Subject matter covered: definition of electronic rights management information

15.31 The electronic information to be protected is of two kinds: information identifying the work and its author and right holders, and information pertinent to the grant of permission to exploit a work. Unlike the Basic Proposal, the text as enacted includes author-identifying information among the listed elements to be protected. But there is no obligation to include any or all of the listed information. The protective obligation extends to whatever rights management information the right holder chooses to include. As a result, if the right holder includes its name, but not that of the author, article 12 gives the author no basis to demand her name's inclusion (although local moral rights laws may). Article 12 is not a shadow right of attribution.

15.32 The information is protected if it comes together with the work. This suggests that information contained in a separate registry, maintained, for example, by a government agency or a collecting society, is not covered by article 12. In the digital context, the phrase 'attached to a copy of the work' may seem peculiar. The information may be 'attached' to the packaging of a work in digital format, such as the documentation accompanying a CD-Rom, but it may also be embedded in the digital file, for example, by means of watermarking. While 'attached' may evoke a more physical connection, it would be absurd to interpret the text as failing to reach the stripping-out or falsification of information within a digital file, because that is precisely the information whose reliability the proponents of the 'digital agenda' sought to ensure. The second element of the same phrase 'or appears in connection with the communication of a work to the public', seems more readily to cover the gamut of information, whether embedded in the communicated file, or conveyed, for example, on a website from which the public would access the communication.

Would the second element of the definition also cover information in digital form about works of authorship, but not 'attached to copies', such as information from an online catalogue? If the catalogue allowed users to click on titles to receive a 'communication' of the work, it would seem that the catalogue information does appear 'in connection with' that communication. This should be true even if the communication does not necessarily emanate from the site of the catalogue, as might be the case if the catalogue aggregated information from a variety of sites, and linked the user to the site which actually communicates the work. This interpretation is also consistent with the overall goal of ensuring the reliability of the digital information that consumers encounter. But this general objective may be broader than the language of article 12. Because the information must appear in connection with the 'communication' of the work, it seems that article 12's protections would not reach the information in an online catalogue through which consumers would order the delivery of hard copies. These are distributed, not 'communicated'. The consumer interest in accuracy does not change with the mode of dissemination or the format of the copy, but the scope of the international obligation apparently does. On the other hand, member states are free to extend the protection to deliveries and copies of any kind.[62] **15.33**

(b) Conduct prohibited

Article 12 requires proof of the alleged bad actor's knowledge at three levels. The right holder must show: **15.34**

1. That the defendant *knowingly*, and without authority, *removed* or altered protected information from a copy of the work, or that the defendant *knowingly* and without permission *distributed* altered copies or *communicated the work to the public* without the protected information.

---

[62] See eg 17 USC § 1202(c) (definition of 'copyright management information' 'means any of the following information conveyed in connection with copies or phonorecords of a work or performances or displays of a work, including in digital form . . .'); Information Society Directive (n 23 above), art 7(2), para 2 (right management information is protected 'when any of these items of information is associated with a copy of, or appears in connection with the communication to the public of, a work'). Some delegations had supported expanding the ambit of article 12 'to include more than electronic right information'. See *Records* 1996, 711, para 520 (South Africa); 521 (Nigeria); 522 (Senegal).

2. In the case of distribution or communication, that the defendant *knew that the information was altered or removed without authority*.
3. That the defendant *knew or had reasonable grounds to know* that the removal or alteration will *induce, enable, facilitate, or conceal an infringement of any moral or economic right* under the Berne Convention or the WCT.

With respect to the first and second levels, 'without authority' would mean both 'without permission' and 'absent a legal right or privilege'.[63] Regarding permission to delete or alter rights management information, potential complications arise when the work is co-authored: must the information-alterer obtain the permission of all co-authors? This would seem to be a question of national law, and the answer may be different, depending on whether the country at issue allows one co-author independently to license rights in the work, or requires a common accord of all co-authors. (As for which national law applies, given the inherently multinational context of electronic communications, see the further discussion in paras 20.40ff below.) Regarding the right or privilege to delete or change rights management information, this factor may anticipate the key element of the third level of knowledge: that the alteration will induce infringement. If there is no infringement to induce, for example, because the work is in the public domain, there is no violation.

(c) Knowledge requirements

15.35 The first element of knowledge seems rather straightforward and reasonable. A user who accidentally erases rights management information should not be held to task, even if she subsequently recirculates her altered copy. Similarly, the person communicating an altered version should not be liable if she did not know of the change. But one may also inquire whether the first and second knowledge standards are not effectively subsumed in the third. That is, the accidental information-remover or recirculator may be unlikely to know that the unwitting removal of the information or the recycling of information-stripped copies will induce a third party's infringement. Establishing the third element may in practice occasionally prove elusive. This is because the link between the actions of deleting or distorting rights management information and infringement may not always be apparent. It depends on the nature of the alteration of the information. For example, a person who substitutes her name for that of the author may be committing a moral rights violation, and presumably knows it. A person who, without authorization, substitutes her name for that of the right holder may well be facilitating infringement if she purports to grant licences to engage in copyright-implicating acts. If she is purporting to

[63] See Reinbothe and von Lewinski (2002), 155.

grant rights that she does not have, then she is or should be aware that she is enabling others to infringe.[64] Similarly, some unauthorized alterations of the terms and conditions of the licence, such as its duration, geographic extent, or the number of copies or communications permitted, would seem to lead to infringements, and the person effecting the alteration should know that. But this may not be true for all alterations to terms and conditions. For example, a person who knowingly alters pricing information from copies of the work may knowingly be compromising the accuracy of the information, and may knowingly be frustrating the efficacy of electronic commerce, but is she inducing or facilitating infringement?

(d) Scope of 'induce . . . infringement'

The conclusion that alteration of pricing information might not violate article 11 does, however, seem at odds with the general purpose of that article, to promote and ensure the reliability of electronic commerce in copyrighted works. The agreed statement to article 11 may help dispel this quandary. The statement explains that article 11 should be interpreted to cover 'both exclusive rights and rights of remuneration'. This may be understood in two ways. First, it may refer to statutory remuneration rights, such as those permitted by Berne Convention, articles 11*bis* for retransmissions, and 13 for 'mechanical' reproduction rights. Thus, for example, if the substitution of the right holder's name with respect to a broadcast work would lead to payment of the retransmission remuneration fee to a person other than the holder of the communication rights in the work, this would violate article 11. It is not clear, however, how likely this situation is to transpire, at least in systems where the statutory licence is obtained from a government agency, or government-approved collecting society, which, presumably, will have the correct information regarding right holders. Moreover, the ordinary meaning of 'rights covered by the Berne Convention' would in any event extend to rights to remuneration that would arise under compulsory licences imposed pursuant to articles 11*bis* and 13 as well as to exclusive rights.[65] Thus, it is not clear that this reading of the agreed statement adds anything. **15.36**

This brings us to the second understanding of the agreed statement, as extending to contractual as well as statutory remuneration rights. It will be recalled that the **15.37**

[64] Indeed, in some countries, the unauthorized granting of licences would itself be an infringing act of 'authorization'. See eg UK Copyright, Designs and Patents Act 1988, s 16(2) ('Copyright in a work is infringed by a person who without the licence of the copyright owner does, *or authorises another to do*, any of the acts restricted by the copyright' (emphasis added); Australian Copyright Act, art 36(1) ('copyright . . . is infringed by a person who, not being the owner of the copyright, and without the licence of the owner of the copyright, does in Australia, *or authorizes the doing* in Australia of, any act comprised in the copyright' (emphasis added)).

[65] See eg David Vaver, 'The National Treatment Requirements of the Berne and Universal Copyright Conventions (Part Two)' (1986) 17 *IIC* 715, 717.

US delegation had urged making contractual rights to payment part of the text of article 11, but that the delegates compromised by displacing the proposed amendment to an agreed statement (see the earlier discussion at para 15.29 above). Some contractual remuneration rights will be directly linked to infringement; for example, if, in exchange for a given sum, the licence limits the right granted to communicate a work to the public to a certain duration, an unauthorized change in the copyright management information to lengthen the term of the licence would not only affect the remuneration (the co-contractant now would get more time for the same price), but would also infringe the copyright (the co-contractant would continue to communicate the work after the license has lapsed). In the case of an alteration to the pricing information (other than an alteration that purports to make the price zero), the connection to infringement is questionable, but the effect on the remuneration is apparent. If, by virtue of the agreed statement, these alterations also 'infringe', then knowing unauthorized changes to rights management information that affect pricing would also be covered by article 11. While this interpretation is consistent with the underlying goals of article 14, and would, moreover, give independent meaning to the agreed statement, the term 'rights of remuneration' does not ineluctably evoke contractual obligations.[66] There remains, therefore, some ambiguity regarding the meaning of 'induce . . . infringement'.[67]

(e) Remedies

15.38 Article 11 generally directs member states to 'provide adequate and effective legal remedies', without specifying what those are to be. One may infer that they include civil actions, because the text refers to 'civil remedies' with respect to the requisite knowledge standard. That same reference may permit an inference that criminal penalties are also contemplated, though this remains a matter for the determination of the member states. Within the range of civil remedies, injunctive relief, for example, to require correction of falsified rights management information, might be essential to any scheme of 'adequate and effective legal remedies', but it is not clear that member states' courts would be prepared to order and supervise the execution of the correction.[68]

---

[66] See also WPPT, art 15(1) (employing the term 'right to a single equitable remuneration') in a statutory licensing context; this may cut against interpreting the WCT, art 12 agreed statement to extend beyond compulsory licensing regimes to contractual rights).

[67] But see Reinbothe and von Lewinski (2002), 156 (reading the agreed statement to cover contractual rights of remuneration).

[68] eg under s 116D(1) of the Copyright Act 1968, an Australian court may award injunctive relief against alterations, etc of electronic rights management information, but such restraining orders would not ordinarily extend to requiring a defendant to take positive steps to correct such alterations. By contrast, in the case of infringements of the moral rights against false attribution of authorship and derogatory treatment that are protected under Part IX of the same

(f) Relationship to formalities

15.39 The elements of rights management information listed in article 11(2) bear some resemblance to the kinds of information sought for copyright notices and registries.[69] Indeed, rights management information and copyright registration systems share the policy goal of enabling the user to identify right holders in order to facilitate rights clearance. (Registration systems also endeavour to facilitate ascertaining the copyright status of works.) But rights management information should not be confused with the formalities prohibited by article 5(2) of the Berne Convention. The former is voluntary while the latter are mandatory and condition the availability or exercise of copyright upon compliance. The agreed statement to article 11 reminds member states not to 'rely' on article 11 as a direction, or a pretext, to institute Berne-prohibited formalities. Thus, member states are to offer copyright owners the protection of whatever copyright management information they choose to include, but the states may not oblige copyright owners to include any or all of it as a condition of enjoyment of *copyright*. On the other hand, it may be possible for member states to condition the protection of *rights management information* on compliance with the national law definition of what that information is to include. Article 11 lists items of information but does not require all of it to be protected, instead leaving the choice to the copyright owner to 'attach' whatever combination of information she chooses. But member states may, consistent with article 11, require, for example, that if a copyright owner chooses to include copyright management information, then that information must include the name(s) of the author(s).

In any event, article 11 could not furnish an obligation, or pretext, to institute formalities in violation of article 5(2) of the Berne Convention, because article 20 of Berne, to which the WCT is subject (see article 1(1) of the WCT), prohibits cutting back on Berne protections, and because, for non-Berne states joining the WCT, article 1(4) requires compliance with articles 1 to 21 of the Berne Convention, thus including article 5(2).

(g) Other elements of the agreed statement

15.40 The agreed statement also reminds member states that they are not to 'devise or to implement rights management systems that would have the effect of . . .

Act there is a specific power for courts to order a reversal of a false attribution or derogatory treatment of a work: see s 195AZA(1)(e) (the equivalent of what common law courts exercising equitable jurisdiction would regard as a mandatory injunction).

[69] See eg 17 USC § 401 (notice of copyright to include year of publication and name of copyright owner); 409 (application for copyright registration to include the name and address of the claimant, the name and domicile of the author, the title, and any other information requested by the Copyright Office regarding the ownership and duration of copyright in the work).

prohibiting the free movement of goods or impeding the enjoyment of rights under this Treaty'. This language, proposed by the USA, was accepted without discussion.[70] It is unclear, however, what it means. First—and this observation applies to the formalities issue as well—in most instances, it is not likely to be the member *states* who devise or implement rights management systems, but rather the right owners. The role of the states would not be to create the systems, but to outline their content, and to protect the results. Second, with respect to the effects that the systems are not to have, it is not clear how a rights management system (as opposed to a technological measure) would impede the free movement of goods. Were, however, an impediment to result, article 11 would not supply a justification for the adverse effect on free movement. Either the copyright law itself justifies the effect, or the competing free movement norm (where applicable) would prevail. Third, it is also not apparent how a rights management system would 'impede the enjoyment of rights under this Treaty'. (Note that the agreed statement does not include the enjoyment of rights under the Berne Convention, although these may be implicitly incorporated by virtue of WCT art 1(4).) It is conceivable that a rights management system might have some impact on the enjoyment of an exception or limitation allowed by article 10 of the WCT, but these are not 'rights' under the Treaty.

D. Enforcement

15.41 Detailed provisions dealing with enforcement of rights at the national level were a major component of the TRIPs Agreement, filling a gap that had long existed under Berne: see generally Part III of that instrument and para 4.37 above. Coming on the heels of TRIPs, the WCT Basic Proposal included alternative proposals to incorporate the relevant TRIPs provisions by reference or to have similar provisions contained in an Annex.[71] There was some concern at the Diplomatic Conference over the matter of duplication,[72] and the final provision adopted, as article 14(2) of the WCT, is expressed succinctly as a general obligation that Contracting Parties are:

> to ensure that enforcement procedures are available under their law so as to permit effective action against any act of infringement of rights covered by this Treaty,

[70] *Records* 1996, 780.

[71] Document CRNR/DC/4 at *Records* 1996, vol I, 223ff. Note that proposals for such provisions were originally contained in the WIPO Memorandum for the Third Session of the Committee of Experts on a Possible Protocol for the Berne Convention: see [1993] *Copyright* 72, 91, and 105, and Reinbothe and von Lewinski (2002), 168ff.

[72] *Records* 1996, vol II, 716–721 (Minutes, Main Committee), in particular Kushan, USA, at para 544. Note, however, that a number of delegates strongly supported the inclusion of enforcement provisions: see the summary by the Chairman (Liedes) at para 575.

> including expeditious remedies to prevent infringements and remedies which constitute a deterrent to further infringements.

While it may be concluded that this requires the domestic availability of civil remedies and procedures of the kind detailed in Part III of TRIPs, it will be less certain whether these extend to criminal procedures unless the latter can be justified by reference to the term 'deterrent'. The expression 'the rights covered by this Treaty' is broad enough to include all the incorporated Berne rights—including moral rights—that are to be protected under article 1(4), not just those specifically granted under the articles 6–8.[73] On the other hand, because articles 11 and 12 already require member states to provide adequate and effective legal remedies, article 14(2) adds nothing to these provisions.[74]

[73] Accord: Reinbothe and von Lewinski (2002), 174.
[74] Accord: Reinbothe and von Lewinski (2002), 175.

16

ADMINISTRATIVE AND FINANCIAL PROVISIONS

A. Introduction

For the first eighty years of its existence, the administrative and financial arrangements of the Berne Union remained substantially the same. Although the Union could be regarded as an international organization, possessing a limited kind of international legal personality,[1] it did not possess a permanent governing body, apart from the conferences of revision which met at irregular intervals. There was a permanent secretariat, the International Office, which, after 1893, was combined with the International Office of the Paris Union (later known as 'BIRPI'—the abbreviation of the French expression '*Bureaux internationaux réunis pour la protection de la propriété intellectuelle*').[2] This acted as a clearing house for information on copyright and related matters, and carried out the necessary preparatory and administrative arrangements for the revision conferences. After the Brussels Revision, this situation was altered, with the informal constitution of an advisory committee (the Permanent Committee) of member states elected on a rotating basis.[3] Furthermore, in 1962, co-ordination between the activities of the Berne and Paris Unions was enhanced by the constitution of an Interunion Coordinating Committee.[4] More fundamental changes were made at the Stockholm Conference, however, with the establishment of both an Assembly and an Executive Committee which were to meet on a regular basis.[5] This had first been proposed in October 1962 by a joint meeting of the Berne Permanent Committee and the Permanent Office of the Paris Union,[6] and grew out of the work of a series of expert committees which had proposed the programme for the Stockholm Revision.[7] Parallel changes 16.01

[1] See paras 4.29ff above.

[2] C Masouyé, *Guide to the Berne Convention for the Protection of Literary and Artistic Works* (1978) ('Masouyé (1978)'), 113.

[3] *Documents de la Conférence réunie à Bruxelles du 5 au 26 juin 1948* (1951) ('*Documents 1948* (1951)'), 425–6.

[4] Resolution of the extraordinary session of the BUPC, 15 Oct 1962: [1962] *DA* 282.

[5] Stockholm Act, arts 22 and 23.

[6] 15–19 Oct 1962, Geneva: [1962] *DA* 278.

[7] The joint meeting recommended the appointment of a working party to prepare these proposals, and then the appointment of a committee of governmental experts. The Working Party met in May 1964, and the Committee of Governmental Experts in Mar–Apr 1965 (the '1965 Committee') and in May 1966 (the '1966 Committee'). The work of these groups was reported to the yearly sessions of the Interunion Coordination Committees in 1963, 1964, and 1965, and the final proposals (with some changes) were contained in Document S/9 in the programme for the Stockholm Revision. For fuller details on the history of these preparations, see *Records* 1967,

were also made to the administrative provisions of the Paris Convention and the other industrial property conventions administered by BIRPI. At the same time, the World Intellectual Property Organization ('WIPO') was constituted, becoming responsible for the administrative functions of both the Berne Union and the other industrial property unions. Finally, the financial and budgetary arrangements of each of the unions were revised. These provisions were retained unchanged in the Paris Revision of the Berne Convention, and, in the case of the administrative clauses, have provided the model for similar provisions in the WIPO Copyright Treaty ('WCT') and the WIPO Performances and Phonograms Treaty ('WPPT'). The present chapter deals primarily with the position under the Berne Union, but concludes with a brief treatment of the position under the WCT and WPPT. The arrangements under the Agreement on Trade-Related Aspects of Intellectual Property Rights 1994 (the 'TRIPs Agreement') are noted in passing, while those under the the Rome Convention for the Protection of Performers, Producers of Phonograms and Broadcasting Organizations 1961 (the 'Rome Convention') are dealt with in a later chapter (see para 19.18 below).

B. The Administration of the Berne Union

(1) Conferences of revision

(a) Background

16.02 Prior to the Stockholm Revision, the only forum in which the affairs of the Union could be discussed between member states was the conference of

423–5. At the Conference itself, these proposals, and the parallel ones affecting the other Unions were discussed in Main Committee IV (chairman: F Savignon of France; *rapporteur:* V de Sanctis of Italy). For further background reading on the administrative changes made at the Stockholm Revision, see: G Beguin, 'L'Organisation des Bureaux internationaux réunis pour la protection de la propriété industrielle, littéraire et artistique' [1962] *DA* 9; J Sécretan, 'Évolution structurelle des Unions internationales pour la protection de la propriété intellectuelle' [1962] *DA* 131; L Malapate and J Vilbois, 'Réforme de la structure administrative des Unions de Berne et de Paris et des Bureaux réunis' (1965) 46 *RIDA* 5; G H C Bodenhausen, 'Evolution of the United International Bureaux' [1963] *DA* (General Studies) 91; 'New International Organization for Intellectual Property? Efforts to Modify the Structure of the Paris and Berne Unions' [1966] *Industrial Property* 37; M G Luzzati, 'Réforme des clauses administratives des unions et l'institution de l'organisation mondiale de la propriété intellectuelle' (1967) 101 *Annales de la propriété industrielle, artistique et littéraire* 344; H Desbois, 'L'organisation mondiale de la propriété intellectuelle' (1967–8) 54–5 *RIDA* 573; C Joubert, 'Les clauses administratives et les clauses finales' (1967–8) 54–5 *RIDA* 427; A Troller, 'Aufgabe und Organisation des Berner Verbandes zum Schutze der Rechte der Urheber an ihren Werken der Literatur und Kunst' (1962) 39 *UFITA* 173. See also W Nordemann, K Vinck, and P W Hertin, *Internationales Urheberrecht und Leistungsschutzrecht der deutschsprachigen Länder unter Berücksichtigung auch der Staaten der Europäischen Gemeinschaft, Kommentar* (1977), 134ff and J Ekedi-Samnik, *L'Organisation mondiale de la propriété intellectuelle (OMPI)* (1975).

revision.[8] This was a full-scale diplomatic conference of sovereign states, and the nature of the proceedings was legislative, in that its principal function was to amend or add to the provisions of the Convention. This was in keeping with the progressive nature of the Convention, whereby it was to be revised 'upwards' at regular intervals.[9] As a consequence, there were considerable periods of time between conferences, because of the time needed to prepare these amendments and, more importantly, because of the delays that often occurred in the ratification of the preceding revision by member states.[10] In the case of the Rome and Brussels Revisions, war also caused the postponement of these meetings for over a decade or more.[11] These long delays therefore meant that, in the intervening periods, there was no opportunity for member states to meet on a less formal basis to consider the general operation of the Convention, and to assess the areas in which change was required. On two occasions only were special revision conferences called at relatively short notice to deal with particular problems: that of 1914, which adopted the provisions concerning retaliation against non-member states, and that of 1971, which adopted the provisions dealing with developing countries.[12]

(b) The obligation to revise the Convention

Under article 27(1), it is provided that the Convention 'shall be submitted to revision with a view to the introduction of amendments designed to improve the system of the Union'. This wording, which was introduced at the time of the Stockholm Revision, differs slightly from that used in the earlier texts where less mandatory terms were used ('. . . may be submitted to revision').[13] Neither text, however, makes it clear on whom the obligation to initiate a revision lies: while the Stockholm and Paris Acts contain certain directions as to how the revision is to be carried out (see paras 16.04 and 16.10 below), there is silence as to who is to begin the process. This obligation must therefore rest on all the members of **16.03**

---

[8] Brussels Act, art 24.

[9] See here the comments of Louis Renault in his report to the Berlin Conference: *Actes* 1908, 272 and 276.

[10] This was particularly so in the case of those member countries where treaties were not self-executing, and where, in consequence, legislative changes in their domestic laws were required in order to be able to accede to the revised text.

[11] The Rome Conference was originally to be held within six to ten years after the Berlin Conference: *Actes* 1908, 219. The Brussels Conference was similarly scheduled for 1935 or 1936: *Actes* 1928, 314–15.

[12] A further conference to prepare a special protocol to enable the readier accession of the USA following that country's adoption of new legislation in 1976 was considered in the period 1978–80, but was finally not proceeded with: A Bogsch, 'The First Hundred Years of the Berne Convention for the Protection of Literary and Artistic Works' [1986] *Copyright* 291, 299 ('Bogsch (1986)').

[13] Brussels Act, art 24(1).

the Union.[14] Furthermore, while the earlier texts spoke of the purpose of the revision as being 'to perfect the system of the Union',[15] the present wording embodies a more modest objective ('the introduction of amendments designed to improve the system of the Union'). The earlier texts also required the conference of revision to consider those questions 'which are of interest to the Union in other respects'.[16] With the establishment of the Assembly under the Stockholm Act, this second function is now undertaken by that body,[17] and is no longer given to the revision conference.

(c) Time and place of conference

16.04 No particular interval for the holding of conferences is specified, but article 27(2) provides generally that they are to be held 'successively in one of the countries of the Union among delegates of the said countries'. Apart from the Final Protocol of the Berne Act, where Paris was designated as the venue for the first revision conference and a time for this was stipulated,[18] these matters have been decided by resolution at each conference.[19] For the reasons mentioned above (see para 16.02), these conferences have usually been delayed. Prior to the Stockholm Act, the programme for each conference was prepared by the administration of the host country with the assistance of the International Office. There was no obligation for these parties to engage in wider consultation among Union members or other interested groups, such as authors' and users' groups, to ascertain what revisions to the Convention were required. In practice, this occurred,[20] and efforts were made to ensure the programme proposals were circulated in advance, with ample time for the making of counter-proposals and other amendments.[21] In addition, advisory committees were often appointed to assist in the process of preparation.[22] The most involved process of consultation

---

[14] There was a suggestion by several delegates in Main Committee IV that this responsibility henceforth was that of BIRPI and its successor, WIPO: *Records* 1967, 1044 (Brazil). But, in view of art 22(2)(a)(ii), which gives the Assembly power to give directions to the International Bureau concerning the preparations for a conference of revision, it seems reasonable to assume that the proposal to initiate such a conference in the first place will come from members of the Union represented in the Assembly.

[15] Brussels Act, art 24(1).

[16] ibid, art 24(2).

[17] Stockholm, Paris Acts, art 22(2)(a)(i). See further para 16.10 below.

[18] Berne Act, Final Protocol, para 6.

[19] See n 11 above.

[20] See generally S P Ladas, *The International Protection of Literary and Artistic Property* (1938) ('Ladas (1938)'), 134–7.

[21] Beginning with the Paris Conference, the International Office circulated detailed preparatory studies of the principal problems to be addressed in the coming revision: *Études sur la Convention de Berne* (1896) (published beforehand in *DA* during 1895). Member states, however, were usually slow in responding with their observations and counter-proposals: Ladas (1938), 136–7. See further paras 3.08, 3.22, and 3.33 above.

[22] This was first done by the French Government in 1892 to prepare for the Paris Revision: [1892] *DA* 67. In the event, this committee did not meet until 1896: Ladas (1938), 134.

took place at the time of the Stockholm Revision itself, with the calling of two separate committees of experts and the constitution of a special authors' consultative committee.[23] Nevertheless, these arrangements were essentially ad hoc, and depended upon the wishes of the host country and International Office. This situation was changed in the Stockholm Act, and the responsibility for preparing the revision programme now rests on all member countries, acting through the Assembly which is required to give the appropriate directions for this to the International Office.[24] These 'directions' will necessarily contain instructions as to whether and how consultation on the contents of the programme is to be sought. As for the place of the next revision, there was a view expressed at the Stockholm Conference that this should be at the place where the International Office was located (Geneva).[25] However, this matter was left in abeyance, to be re-examined at the time of the next revision conference of the Paris Union which had been scheduled to be held at Vienna.[26] This conference had not been held at the time of writing.

(d) The rule of unanimity

No revision of the Paris Act (including the Appendix) may be made without a **16.05**
'unanimity of the votes cast'.[27] This does not apply in the case of revisions to the administrative articles (articles 22–5), which are governed by a different procedure specified in article 26 (see paras 16.49ff below). Unanimity has always been a basic principle of the Berne Convention, and, although not expressly provided for in the Paris Convention, has always been applied in practice in revisions of that instrument.[28] The principle may be defended on several levels. First, it ensures that no increased obligation may be laid upon member states without their consent. Secondly, it may have the contrary effect of preventing any lowering of protection. The result may often be stalemate and it may work unfairly against the wishes of an overwhelming majority of member states if one state insists on exercising its veto. It may also lead to the adoption of bland compromise provisions that are either ambiguous or leave it to each state to formulate its own rules.[29] Nevertheless, the requirement of unanimity has served

---

[23] See paras 3.49–3.52 above. See further J Vilbois, 'La procédure de révision de la Convention de Berne' (1962) 36 *RIDA* 33.

[24] Stockholm, Paris Acts, art 22(2)(a)(ii).

[25] *Records* 1967, 1044 (proposal by Argentina, Brazil, Madagascar, Senegal, and Uruguay in Main Committee IV: Document S/94, ibid, 695). This proposal, in fact, related to the Paris Convention.

[26] *Records* 1967, 1211 (report of Main Committee IV).

[27] Paris Act, art 27(3).

[28] See further H Ballreich and H P Kunz-Hallstein, 'Revision of the Paris Convention: The Principle of Unanimity' (1978) 9 *IIC* 21.

[29] See eg the controversies over works of applied art and moral rights discussed at paras 8.59ff and 10.07ff above.

to ensure that laws of Union members do not get too far out of equilibrium with each other, and that those changes which are adopted reflect changes in broad international practice. This can be seen in the provisions governing duration which were steadily strengthened over the course of three revision conferences, as well as in the formulation of the provisions dealing with substantive rights and exceptions to those rights.[30] On the other hand, the failure of successive attempted compromises on such matters as the protection of works of applied art show the operation of the unanimity rule in a poor light.[31] It can also be said that the rule becomes less appropriate and easy to apply as the size of Union membership increases. Thus, provision for majority voting has been made in many international bodies since 1945.[32] Nevertheless, attempts to substitute a different rule allowing for revision by special majority votes were unsuccessful at both the Brussels and Stockholm Revisions, and the rule of unanimity was retained.[33] It should be noted, however, that the wording of the present provision differs from that used prior to the Stockholm, Paris Acts. The former refers to a 'unanimity of votes cast', while the earlier Acts provided that no alteration in the Convention should be 'binding on the Union except by the unanimous consent of the countries composing it'.[34] The previous wording therefore was much broader, requiring the consent of all members of the Convention to any change, irrespective of whether they were represented at the Conference. It also seemed to require that all states should have voted in favour of the change, in the sense that it is difficult to talk of there being 'unanimous consent' to a particular proposition where one or more states simply abstain, without voting for or against it. In practice, however, these requirements were ignored, and a number of revisions, including that of Brussels, proceeded in the absence of several member states, without there being any challenge to the validity of the changes made.[35] Nevertheless, if there is uncertainty as to the meaning of the earlier wording, this is removed by the present formulation which expressly takes account of (i) the possibility that states may not be present at the particular revision conference, and (ii) that some may abstain from voting on a particular proposition without depriving it of the necessary unanimity. By contrast, in the

---

30 See generally Chapters 7–9 above.

31 See paras 6.47ff above.

32 See further H G Schermers, *International Institutional Law* (1980), 391–438.

33 *Documents 1948* (1951), 388–92 (rejection of programme proposal for a five-sixths majority); *Records* 1967, 1045 (rejection of proposal by the FRG, the Netherlands, and Switzerland for a nine-tenths majority in relation to the Paris Convention understood as applying equally to the Berne Convention: see Document S/106, ibid, 696). See also G Ronga, 'Règle de l'unaminité pour la révision des Conventions des Paris et Berne' (1961) 33 *RIDA* 13.

34 Brussels Act, art 24(3).

35 Thus, Germany was not represented, except in an observer capacity by the British Control Commission, at Brussels: *Documents 1948* (1951), 60. At Rome, neither Liberia nor Haiti were represented (although both denounced the Convention shortly after this).

case of the 1996 Diplomatic Conference on the Internet Treaties, as this was a *de nova* meeting and not a revision of the Berne Convention, it was possible for that Conference to adopt a general rule of a 'two-thirds of the Member Delegations present and voting' to be applied in voting on the adoption of the treaties, in the absence of consensus.[36]

(e) Indirect methods of changing the Convention

Although it is undoubtedly true that the requirement of unanimity has frequently stifled a number of innovations to the Convention, this has not prevented the making of changes in less direct ways. Although these methods have often had undesirable effects, they still remain open to a revision conference under the present Act. The first is through the adoption of an Additional Act or protocol which contains the desired changes and to which the states in favour may adhere separately. This was done at the Paris Conference of 1896, in Berne in 1914, and at Stockholm in 1967. The result is that states become bound by different texts, which leads to considerable confusion, and thereby defeats the main purpose of the Convention as a multilateral instrument which contains a set of common provisions to be applied by all its signatories. The second indirect method of achieving change is through the adoption of a system of reservations, under which the desired new provision is adopted into the revised Convention text. Having done this, however, states are then free to make reservations to that provision. This method was freely adopted in the period 1896 to 1928, as a means of retaining and expanding the membership of the Union while still raising its level of protection.[37] Nevertheless, the result was one of confusion, with member states being governed, in their relations, by slightly different versions of the Convention. At the same time, the method had some success as a strategy for upgrading the requirements of the Convention, in that the general principle of the proposed change was enshrined in the Convention itself and, in this way, could have an educative effect on those states which presently refused to accept it.[38] Finally, it should be borne in mind that a Union member always remains free to continue to be bound by an earlier Act of the Convention, even when it has agreed to the adoption of a new Act at a revision conference. In such a case, the relations of this state with other Union members are governed by the latest text which binds them both.[39] This is not an uncommon situation for states where treaties are not directly incorporated into municipal law, and the **16.06**

[36] Rule 34(2), Rules of Procedure of the Diplomatic Conference, as adopted on 3 Dec 1996 and amended on 5 Dec 1996 by the Diplomatic Conference: Document CRNR/DC/9 Rev in *Records* 1996, vol I, 390.

[37] See paras 3.19ff above.

[38] This certainly could be said of art 7, dealing with the question of duration.

[39] Paris, Act, art 32(1). See further paras 17.69ff below.

necessary legislative changes to achieve this result may take some time. As a consequence, a considerable period of time may often elapse before these states become bound by a new Act.[40] At the time of writing, some thirty-four years after the adoption of the most recent Act of Paris, of 159 members only eleven countries have not yet adhered to that text.

(f) Procedure at conferences

16.07 There is no general regulation concerning this contained in the Convention, and the practice has been for each Conference to adopt its own regulation at the outset of its proceedings.[41] At the Stockholm Conference, this was done in the form of a common set of rules of procedure that were used in all the meetings of the different unions that took place on that occasion.[42] At the Paris Revision, draft rules were prepared in advance by the Permanent Committee of the Union.[43] The details of these rules fall outside the scope of the present work, and, in any case, may vary from conference to conference. However, the matters invariably dealt with are: the election of officers, the appointment of committees and sub-committees, the secretariat, the conduct of proceedings, including quorums, the putting of motions and voting, the working languages to be used, the taking of minutes, and observers. In particular, the following points may be noted.

(i) **Meeting in plenary session**: Because of the number of delegates, all recent conferences have chosen to meet in plenary session and in 'committees of the whole' (called 'Main Committees' in the Stockholm and Paris Conferences). A preliminary task required of each plenary session has been the appointment of a Credentials Committee to consider the credentials of each delegation presenting itself to the Conference.[44] The most important bodies, however, are the Main Committees: these conduct the working sessions in which the draft texts of the new provisions are discussed and formulated, and are then submitted for approval by the plenary session.[45] In the meetings of the Main Committees, unanimity of votes cast has not been insisted upon, but this must obviously be

[40] This is particularly true of the common law countries: the UK did not accede to the Brussels Act until 1957, following the passing of the Copyright Act 1956: [1957] *DA* 225. Australia was even more dilatory in passing the necessary legislation: this did not happen until 1968, and it therefore acceded to the Brussels Act in 1969: [1969] *DA* 94 and see further G Sawyer, 'Australia: Embarrassing Interlude' (1964) 11 *Bull Cop Soc USA* 313. New Zealand is still bound by the Rome Act: [1986] *Copyright* 7.

[41] *Actes* 1884, 22; *Actes* 1885, 15; *Actes* 1896, 98–9; *Actes* 1908, 154; *Actes* 1928, 155–6; *Documents 1948* (1951), 67–8.

[42] Document S/MISC/1/Rev: *Records* 1967, 770.

[43] Document B/DC/8: *Records* 1971, 100.

[44] 1971 Rules, rr 3 and 7. [45] ibid, r 8.

so in the plenary session where the final decision whether or not to adopt a particular text is made.[46] In addition, each Main Committee has the power to appoint Working Groups (called sub-committees in earlier conferences) to consider particular problems.[47] Finally, each Main Committee is required to elect, from its members, a Drafting Committee to settle the final draft text to be considered by the plenary session.[48]

(ii) Election of President of the Conference: It has always been the practice to elect as President of the Conference a member of the delegation of the host government.[49] This has not always been done in the case of the chairmen of the Main Committees. For example, at the Stockholm Conference, there can be little doubt that the effectiveness of Main Committee I was enhanced by the appointment of the distinguished German scholar, Professor Eugen Ulmer, as Chairman.[50]

(iii) Appointment of a *rapporteur*: The appointment of a *rapporteur* has always been a matter of the utmost importance, as the report has been the principal document to which recourse could be had for the purposes of interpretation. For this reason, the preparation of a report is clearly a most difficult task, and there are differences in the detail and emphases which successive *rapporteurs* have included in their reports at Berne revision conferences. In the case of some reports, such as that of Caselli at the Rome Conference[51] and Goundiam[52] at the Paris Revision, there are gaps in relation to a number of important points. In others, such as those of Plaisant at Brussels[53] and Bergström at Stockholm,[54] the explanations are sometimes difficult to follow or deliberately bland or vague (in view of the obvious differences of opinion among delegates). The two reports of Renault at the Paris and Berlin Revisions[55] remain the clearest and most useful of their kind, but this may simply be a reflection of

[46] In the case of the 1996 Diplomatic Conference, it may be noted that the two-thirds majority rule adopted there applied only to meetings in plenary and certain other meetings, but that otherwise all decisions of all bodies required only a simple majority of member delegations present and voting: Rules of Procedure (n 36 above), r 34(2).

[47] ibid, r 6. [48] ibid, r 10.

[49] Thus, Numa Droz (Switzerland) was the President of the Berne Conferences of 1884–6; de Freycinet (France) presided at Paris in 1896; von Studt (Germany) at Berlin in 1908; Scialoja (Italy) at Rome in 1928; Kuypers (Belgium) at Brussels in 1948. At Stockholm, Kling (Sweden) was President of the Plenary of the whole Conference, but Grant of the UK was President of the Berne Plenary; Charpentier of France, however, was President of the Paris Conference of 1971.

[50] *Records* 1967, 1131 (report of Main Committee I). [51] *Actes* 1928, 192–220.

[52] *Records* 1971, 165–73. The brevity of this report stands in sharp contrast to the detail of that of Kaminstein at the UCC Revision Conference of 1971: UCC general report.

[53] *Documents 1948* (1951), 93–109. [54] *Records* 1967, 1131–91.

[55] *Actes* 1896, 159–81; *Actes* 1908, 225–77.

less complicated times when there were fewer delegates and consensus was easier.[56]

(iv) Observers: From the first conference of revision, non-member states have been freely admitted as observers, with rights of addressing the delegates but without voting rights.[57] The position regarding other observers was more restrictive, and has gradually been liberalized over successive conferences. The sessions of the early conferences were closed to non-state observers, but at the Rome and Brussels Conferences observer status, with the right to address the conference, was accorded to representatives of relevant international organizations, such as the International Institute for Intellectual Cooperation and League of Nations at Rome[58] and UNESCO at Brussels.[59] Non-governmental international organizations, however, did not obtain this privilege until the Stockholm Conference, when a large number of relevant bodies, including ALAI, IPA, and *CISAC*, were specifically invited to attend.[60] This exclusion from previous conferences had been the cause of some complaint, but it should be noted that, from the earliest revision conference, the International Office always ensured that member and non-member states attending each conference were circulated with the resolutions and motions of these organizations. In addition, representatives of these organizations were frequently included on the delegations of some states, and therefore had an opportunity of directly participating in the proceedings.[61] One notable contributor to three conferences of revision has been a member of two separate delegations, and a member of yet another at the Universal Copyright Convention ('UCC') Revision Conference in Paris.[62] It goes without saying that the Director of BIRPI has always had the right of attendance and speaking at conferences, and has the same right in his or her capacity as the Director General of WIPO.[63]

---

[56] It may be noted that at the 1996 Diplomatic Conference there were no reports, although the closing remarks of the chairs of the different committees often are of considerable interpretative value. There can be no doubt that these chairs, in particular the chair of Main Committee I had significant influence in the preparation of draft texts and compromise positions.

[57] *Actes* 1896, 98–9. [58] *Actes* 1928, 139.

[59] *Documents 1948* (1951), 61.

[60] *Records* 1967, 577 (list of intergovernmental organizations invited by the Swedish Government), 582 (list of intergovernmental and international non-governmental organizations invited by BIRPI), and 594–5 (observers present).

[61] See eg the list of members of delegations for the Brussels Conference, notably those of Belgium, France, and Italy: *Documents 1948* (1951), 54–60.

[62] Dr Georges Straschnov, member of the Monégasque delegations at Brussels and Stockholm, adviser to the delegation of Cyprus at the Paris Conference, and adviser to that of Kenya at the UCC Revision Conference.

[63] Berne Act, Closing Protocol, para 5; Brussels Act, art 24(2); Paris Act, art 24(7)(c).

(2) The Assembly

This was established at the Stockholm Revision, together with the Executive Committee.[64] The purpose was to provide the Union with a supreme governing body that would meet regularly between revision conferences. It was also intended that this body should have ultimate responsibility for the activities of the International Office which, until this time, had been placed under the supervision of the Swiss Government.[65] With the establishment of WIPO at the same diplomatic conference, it was desired to amend the administrative and financial provisions of the various intellectual and industrial property conventions administered by BIRPI, so that each union would become fully autonomous under the umbrella of the new organization which would take over the administrative functions formerly fulfilled for each union by BIRPI.[66] **16.08**

Under article 21, the Assembly of the Berne Union is constituted of those countries of the Union bound by articles 22 to 26. In this regard, it should be noted that it is possible for countries to ratify or accede to articles 22 to 38 of the Act only, without becoming bound by the substantive provisions of articles 1 to 21 and the Appendix.[67] In the years immediately following the Paris Revision Conference, this was done by a number of countries, which otherwise remained bound by the substantive provisions of one of the earlier Acts of the Convention.[68] Each country which is entitled to be a member of the Assembly is **16.09**

[64] Stockholm, Paris Acts, art 22(1). For a thorough description of the history and present operation of the administrative and financial provisions of the Convention, see Bogsch (1986).

[65] Brussels Act, art 21(2). See further the programme for the Stockholm Conference, Document S/9: *Records* 1967, 438ff.

[66] ibid. See further on the general question of the governing bodies of international organizations: Schermers (n 32 above), ch 5.

[67] Paris Act, art 28(1)(b). See further, paras 17.05ff below.

[68] Note here that arts 22–6 of the Stockholm Act are exactly the same, and a number of countries remain bound by the Stockholm, rather than the Paris Act, in this respect. As of 1 Jan 1986 (the year before publication of the first edition of this commentary), these countries were Argentina (still bound by substantive provisions of the Brussels Act), Bahamas (Brussels), Belgium (bound by arts 22–38 of the Stockholm Act and substantive provisions of the Brussels Act), Canada (substantive provisions of Rome Act and arts 22–38 of the Stockholm Act), Chad, Fiji, and Finland (Brussels and Stockholm), Iceland, and Malta (Rome and Paris), Ireland, Israel, Liechtenstein, and Morocco (Brussels and Stockholm), Madagascar (Brussels alone), Pakistan (Rome and Stockholm), Philippines (Brussels and Paris), Romania (Rome and Stockholm), South Africa (Brussels and Paris), Sri Lanka (Rome and Paris), Switzerland (Brussels and Stockholm), Thailand (Berlin and Paris), UK (Brussels and Stockholm), and Zimbabwe (Rome and Paris): [1986] *Copyright* 6–8. As of Jan 2005 (the year before the second edition of this commentary), with a total membership of 159, only the following countries remained bound by the substantive provisions of an earlier Act; Chad and Fiji (Brussels and arts 22–38 of Stockholm), Lebanon (Rome), Madagascar (Brussels alone), Malta, Sri Lanka, and Zimbabwe (Rome and arts 22–38 of Paris), New Zealand (Rome alone), Pakistan (Rome and arts 22–38 of Stockholm), Bahamas and South Africa (Brussels and arts 22–38 of Paris): Berne Convention for the Protection of Literary and Artistic Works, status on 2 Dec 2004: www.wipo.int/treaties/en.

represented by one delegate, but there is provision for this delegate to be assisted by alternate delegates, advisers, and experts.[69] The expenses of each delegation are borne by its own country.[70] As membership of the Berne Union is open only to 'countries' (see further para 5.76 above), so too is membership of the Assembly limited to 'countries of the Union', meaning that it is not possible to have intergovernmental organizations as members, such as the European Union or other regional organizations. This problem does not arise in the case of the WCT (see further para 17.97 below).

(a) Functions

16.10 The Assembly is required to do the following things

(i) 'Deal with all matters concerning the maintenance and development of the Union and the implementation of the Convention':[71] This is the general task of the Assembly, looking to the future of the Union as well as to the present operation of the Convention. In particular, it provides a forum in which member states may identify and raise problems, and decide upon what action should be taken in relation to them. It was suggested (see para 5.35 above) that this implies a power in the Assembly to provide authoritative interpretations of the provisions of the Convention, although to date such a power, if it exists, has not been exercised.[72] In this regard, it is also relevant to have regard to a more limited view that was expressed in the preparatory documents for the Stockholm Revision Conference that the phrase 'implementation of the Convention' in the draft text for article 22(2)(a)(i) should not be misunderstood: it was not intended to refer to the application of the Convention under the domestic laws of Union members—a matter falling outside the Assembly's jurisdiction—but to 'implementation by the Secretariat and other organs as far as those provisions of the Convention are concerned which call for the performance of tasks by such organs'.[73]

(ii) 'Give directions concerning the preparation for conferences of revision to the International Bureau of Intellectual Property (hereinafter designated as 'the International Bureau') referred to in the Convention Establishing the World Intellectual Property Organization (hereinafter designated as 'the Organization'), due account being taken of any comments made by those countries of the Union which are not bound by Articles 22 to 26':[74] This now means that all member countries, through their representation on the

[69] Paris Act, art 22(1)(b). [70] ibid, art 22(1)(c). [71] ibid, art 22(2)(a)(i).

[72] That this could be done by the Assembly was the view of the former Director General, Dr Bogsch: see Bogsch (1986), 36 and is also supported by Dr Ficsor in his commentary: M Ficsor, *The Law of Copyright and the Internet* (2001) ('Ficsor (2001)'), 652–3.

[73] Document S/9: *Records* 1967, 440. [74] Paris Act, art 22(2)(a)(ii).

Assembly, are involved in the process of preparing for a revision of the Convention. The Assembly determines how this is to be done, including such matters as the degree of consultation with interested groups, and the International Bureau then carries out these directions. This is a considerable advance from the pre-Stockholm position, as it takes the burden of preparation away from the government of the country which is hosting the revision conference.[75] So far, this provision has only been applied once, in the direction which was given by the Assembly at its first session in September 1970 for the holding of the diplomatic conference which prepared the Paris Act.[76] The reference which is made to the comments of member countries not bound by articles 22 to 26 takes account of the fact that these countries are not members of the Assembly, and otherwise would lack any formal means for putting forward their views on the proposed revision. As at January 2005, there were only three member states that fell into this category: Lebanon (bound by the Rome Act), Madagascar (Brussels), and New Zealand (Rome).[77] Three other countries are technically not bound by articles 22 to 26 of the Paris Act, but by articles 22 to 26 of the Stockholm Act which are identical: Chad, Fiji, and Pakistan.[78]

(iii) 'Review and approve the reports and activities of the Director General of the Organization concerning the Union, and give him all necessary instructions concerning the matters within the competence of the Union':[79] the Director General of WIPO is the chief executive officer of the Union, and takes over the role previously played by the Director of BIRPI.[80] Prior to the Stockholm Act, the countries of the Union, other than the Swiss Government as the supervising power, had no control over the activities of the Director.[81] This item therefore makes it clear that the Director General is subject to the authority of the Assembly in all matters relating to the Berne Union.

(iv) 'Elect the members of the Executive Committee':[82] this body is of limited membership, and is elected from the ranks of the Assembly. It meets between sessions of the Assembly, and has various responsibilities, including the overseeing of the activities of the Union. The details of its constitution and functions are set out in article 23 (see paras 16.15ff below), although at the present time it serves no useful function and there have been proposals made for its abolition (see further para 16.28 below).

[75] Cf Brussels Act, art 24(2). [76] [1970] *Copyright* 242.
[77] Berne Convention for the Protection of Literary and Artistic Works, status on 19 Jan 2005: www.wipo.int/treaties/en.
[78] ibid. [79] Paris Act, art 22(2)(a)(iii). [80] ibid, art 24(1)(c).
[81] Brussels Act, art 21(2). [82] Paris Act, art 22(2)(a)(iv).

(v) **'Review and approve the reports and activities of its Executive Committee and give instructions to such Committee':**[83] this confirms that the Executive Committee, as an emanation of the Assembly, is subject to its control and supervision.[84] In practice, reports on the activities of the Executive Committee are covered in the reports of the Director General referred to in the preceding item.[85] As a matter of practice, it will be seen below that the Executive Committee no longer plays any useful function (see para 16.28 below).

(vi) **'Determine the program and adopt the biennial budget of the Union, and approve its final accounts':**[86] this power is commonplace in most other international organizations, but was absent from both the Berne and Paris Conventions prior to the Stockholm Revision. Control over these matters was vested in the Swiss Government as supervising power, which approved the budget of BIRPI and audited its accounts.[87] From 1962 on, a measure of informal collective control was exercised through the Interunion Coordination Committee, which comprised some twenty member countries of both the Berne and Paris Unions, and which rendered 'advice' on the programmes and budgets of the Unions.[88] There was no legal basis to this Committee in either of the conventions, although its 'advice' was generally followed by the Swiss Government.[89] This item therefore vests the formal power of control over these matters in all member countries through the Assembly, 'not only as a matter of expressing advice but as a matter of sovereign concern . . .'.[90] As originally adopted by the Stockholm Conference, the budget of the Union was triennial. This was changed to biennial by the Assembly in 1979,[91] using the procedure contained in article 26 (see further para 16.49 below), and was applied immediately, without waiting for its entry into force in accordance with the requirements of article 26(3).[92] The matter of the budget of the Union is dealt with below (see paras 16.37ff). As for the 'programme of the Union', the significance of this expression should not be overlooked: it indicates clearly that the Union is to have a plan or timetable for action, and that this is to be worked out in advance, not adopted in ad hoc fashion as the need arises. In the words of Dr Bogsch, a former Director General, the main parts of the programme deal with:

> . . . the promotion of accessions to the Berne Convention, with cooperation, for the development of developing countries, with the collection and dissemination of information (publication of the monthly periodical *Copyright*, collection and publication of legislative texts), and with matters of topical interest. The budget

[83] ibid, art 22(2)(a)(v). [84] Document S/9: *Records* 1967, 440.
[85] Bogsch (1986), 303. [86] Paris Act, art 22(2)(a)(vi). [87] Brussels Act, art 23(5).
[88] See n 4 above. See further Bodenhausen (n 7 above), 93.
[89] Document S/9: *Records* 1967, 482.
[90] ibid, 440. [91] Bogsch (1986), 314. [92] ibid.

> allocates specific amounts for each of the corresponding activities that take different forms: meetings, . . . courses, seminars, individual training, study missions, surveys, publications, etc.[93]

(vii) 'Adopt the financial regulations of the Union':[94] this was done at the first session of the Assembly in October 1970.[95] These regulations were originally those of BIRPI, and are now common to WIPO and all the unions administered by WIPO.[96] They are revised from time to time, and such changes, insofar as they affect the Berne Union, require adoption by the Assembly.[97]

(viii) 'Establish such committees of experts and working groups as may be necessary for the work of the Union':[98] an example of this would be the appointment of a committee to assist in the preparation of the programme for a revision.[99] However, the power extends much further, to the appointment of committees and working groups on any subject that may be of relevance to the Union, for example, the problems of satellite communications, computer programs, and folklore.[100] In this regard, it should be noted that there is a large number of committees and working groups that are appointed under the general auspices of WIPO,[101] and the areas covered by these overlap or even fall entirely within the areas of concern of the Berne Union.[102] In the case of the committees of experts, more properly speaking, a 1998 WIPO memorandum viewed this as being the preparatory stage leading to an ultimate treaty or international agreement, describing the WIPO practice in this regard as follows:

> If and when the work of a Committee of Experts has reached a sufficiently mature stage, a diplomatic conference has been convened to conclude the treaty on the subject matter that has been considered by the Committee of Experts. The

[93] ibid. [94] Paris Act, art 22(2)(a)(vii).

[95] [1970] *Copyright* 243. [96] WIPO Document X85.

[97] Bogsch (1986), 314. [98] Paris Act, art 22(2)(a)(viii).

[99] Document S/9: *Records* 1967, 442.

[100] See eg the annual review of the activities of the Berne Union for 1975: 'The Berne Union and International Copyright and Neighbouring Rights in 1975' [1976] *Copyright* 14, 15ff. In more recent years, the most notable example has been the Committee of Experts on a Protocol to the Berne Convention, which preceded the 1996 Diplomatic Conference. Two other committees which sprang from the same source were the Committee of Experts on a Possible Instrument on the Protection of the Rights of Performers and on a Protocol concerning Audiovisual Performances: see 'The Governance Structure of WIPO', *Memorandum of WIPO*, A/32/INF/2 (20 Feb 1998) (the 'Governance Memorandum').

[101] There is no express power for the organs of WIPO to appoint such committees, but this nonetheless seems a power that is necessarily implied from their functions: see generally WIPO Convention, arts 6 (General Assembly), 7 (Conference), 8 (Coordination Committee), and 9 (International Bureau).

[102] See here the yearly index of *Copyright* up until 1996 for the reports of meetings of these committees and groups, and, for reports of current meetings, consult the WIPO website at www.wipo.int. See further Bogsch (1986), 327ff.

> Committee of Experts has thus been an ad hoc body in the sense that its mission and life are intended to be of limited duration.[103]

In the same memorandum, there was a proposal to replace the system of ad hoc Committees of Experts by Standing Committees in the main substantive areas of intellectual property. In the case of copyright, this is the Standing Committee on Copyright and Related Rights ('SCCR') which was described as being the 'vehicle for the progressive development of international intellectual property law (that is, the establishment of norms)', and would henceforth 'determine, within its sphere of competence and in accordance with the program and budget, its own agenda of items on which work should proceed. . . . When work on a particular area reaches a sufficiently mature stage, the Standing Committee would recommend to the WIPO General Assembly and the Assembly of any concerned Union the further action it considered appropriate in respect of that area, such as, for example, the convening of a diplomatic conference for the purposes of making a treaty or the adoption of a resolution or guidelines by the WIPO General Assembly or other Assembly.'[104] The SCCR has met regularly since its establishment, and has been the principal forum for discussion of issues relating to copyright and related rights, including the formulation of draft treaty proposals in the areas of audiovisual performances and broadcasting organizations (see further paras 19.82ff and 19.87ff below). So far as its relation to the Berne Convention is concerned, in formal terms, this seems simply another committee within the general scope of article 22(2)(a)(viii).

(ix) 'Determine which countries not members of the Union and which intergovernmental and international non-governmental organizations shall be admitted to its meetings as observers':[105] Guidelines on these matters were adopted by the first session of the Assembly in October 1970.[106] These guidelines have been changed from time to time, and comprise the following basic categories:

1. states which are members of the Union but not of the Assembly: these have an automatic right of admission under article 22(3)(g);
2. states which are not members of the Union, but are members of WIPO;
3. invited intergovernmental organizations;
4. invited international non-governmental organizations.

In a general information memorandum circulated by the International Bureau of WIPO for the extraordinary session of the Berne Assembly held in September

[103] Governance Memorandum (n 100 above), 6. [104] ibid, 8.
[105] Paris Act, art 22(2)(a)(ix). [106] [1970] *Copyright* 243.

1986 (for the centenary of the Convention),[107] five states were listed under the first of these categories,[108] thirty-eight came under the second,[109] while twelve international organizations were catalogued under the third[110] and fifty-two non-governmental organizations under the fourth.[111] By January 2005 (for those readers who like statistics!), there were six states in the first category, and twenty-two in the second, but these can be expected gradually to reduce as these states adhere to the Convention. So far as non-state observers are concerned, the various WIPO assemblies, including the Berne Assembly, have adopted a set of

[107] *Governing Bodies of WIPO and the Unions administered by WIPO, Seventeenth Series of Meetings, Geneva, September 8 to 12, 1986, General Information, Memorandum of the International Bureau*, Document AB/XVII/INF/1, 20 May 1986 (referred to hereafter as the '*IB Memorandum*').

[108] Lebanon, Madagascar, New Zealand, Poland, Turkey: *IB Memorandum* (n 107 above), 3.

[109] Algeria, Burundi, Byelorussian SSR, Peoples' Republic of China, Colombia, Cuba, Democratic Peoples' Republic of Korea, El Salvador, Gambia, Ghana, Guatemala, Haiti, Honduras, Indonesia, Iraq, Jamaica, Jordan, Kenya, Malawi, Mauritius, Mongolia, Peru, Qatar, Republic of Korea, Saudi Arabia, Somalia, USSR, Sudan, Turkey, Uganda, Ukrainian SSR, United Arab Emirates, Tanzania, USA, Vietnam, Yemen, Zambia: *IB Memorandum* (n 107 above), 4 and see also [1986] *Copyright* 3–5.

[110] The most important of these organizations were the UN, ILO, UNESCO, WHO, GATT, the African Intellectual Property Organisation (AIPO), and the Arab States Broadcasting Union (ASBU): *IB Memorandum* (n 107 above), 5.

[111] These were: Asia-Pacific Broadcasting Union, Council of the Professional Photographers of Europe, European Broadcasting Union, European Tape Industry Council, Ibero-American Television Organisation, Independent Film Producers International Association, Inter-American Association of Broadcasters, Inter-American Copyright Institute, International Alliance for Diffusion by Wire, International Association of Authors of Comics and Cartoons, International Association of Conference Interpreters, International Bureau of Societies Administering the Rights of Mechanical Recording and Reproduction, International Conference of Authors and Composers (*CISAC*), International Copyright Society (*INTERGU*), International Council for Reprography, International Council on Archives, International Federation of Actors, International Federation of Associations of Film Distributors, International Federation of Film Producers Associations, International Federation of Journalists, International Federation of Library Associations and Institutions, International Federation of Musicians, International Federation of Newspaper Publishers, International Federation of Phonograms and Videogram Producers (IFPI), International Federation of Translators, International Group of Scientific, Technical and Medical Publishers, International Hotel Association, International Institute of Communications, International Literary and Artistic Association (ALAI), International PEN, International Publishers' Association (IPA), International Radio and Television Organisation, International Secretariat for Arts, Mass Media and Entertainment Trade Unions, International Union of Architects, International Union of Cinemas, International Organisation of Hotel and Restaurant Associations, International Writers Guild, Latin American Federation of Performers, Union of National Radio and Television Organisations of Africa, World Blind Union, European Association of Advertising Agencies, European Computer Manufacturers Association, International Association for the Advancement of Teaching and Research in Intellectual Property, International Chamber of Commerce, International Confederation of Free Trade Unions, International Confederation of Professional and Intellectual Workers, International Federation for Documentation, International Law Association, International League for Competition Law, International Organization for Standardization, Law Association for Asia and the Western Pacific, Max-Planck Institute for Foreign and International Patent, Copyright and Competition Law: *IB Memorandum* (n 107 above), 5–6.

principles over recent years to govern the question of admission of observers.[112] These deal, in turn, with (i) intergovernmental organizations, (ii) international non-governmental organizations, and (iii) national non-governmental organizations. As to the first of these (intergovernmental organizations), these are grouped in three categories: Category A (United Nations System of Organizations), Category B (Industrial Property or Copyright), and Category C (Other Intergovernmental Organizations, Worldwide or Regional) and, 'depending upon the Assembly concerned and the category to which the intergovernmental organization belongs, an invitation is extended by the Director General to that organization to attend, as an observer, the meetings of that Assembly in accordance with the criteria set forth in the principles applicable to that Body'.[113] Principles have also been adopted with respect to the admission of international non-governmental organizations,[114] and it is noteworthy to see an increasing number of user and public advocacy groups.[115] The third group of national non-governmental organizations is the most recent to be given observer status, although this is not a matter strictly covered by article 22(2)(a)(ix), which refers only to 'intergovermental and international non-governmental organisations'.[116]

[112] These are set out in Annexe I of WIPO Document AB/XII/5.

[113] See Memorandum of the Director General on 'Admission of Observers', WIPO Document A/40/40/5 (20 Aug 2004), prepared for the fortieth series of meetings of the assemblies of member states of WIPO, 27 Sept–5 Oct 2004; and for the list of organizations invited to attend these last series of meetings, see WIPO Document A/40/INF/1. Clearly, an important member of Category C is the EU; an interesting addition at the fortieth series of meetings was the Commonwealth Secretariat.

[114] Memorandum (n 113 above), para 8 (containing references to earlier WIPO documents).

[115] Thus, note the following bodies that sought admission to the fortieth series of meetings: Civil Society Coalition, Foundation for Free Information Infrastructure and Free Software Foundation Europe: Memorandum (n 113 above), para 11.

[116] Such a power, however, could be inferred from the other provisions of art 22(2)(a), in particular sub-paragraphs (i) and (xi). In any event, the principles adopted for admission of such national non-governmental organizations are carefully framed so as to take account of the sensitivities of member states. These were adopted by the thirty-seventh series of meetings of the assemblies in Sept 2002 (Document A/37/14) and are as follows:

(a) The organization shall be essentially concerned with intellectual property matters falling within the competence of WIPO and shall, in the view of the Director General, be able to offer constructive, substantive contributions to the deliberations of the Assemblies of WIPO;
(b) The aims and purposes of the organization shall be in conformity with the spirit, purposes and principles of WIPO and of the United Nations;
(c) The organization shall have an established headquarters. It shall have democratically adopted statutes, adopted in conformity with the legislation of the Member State from which the NGO originates. One copy of the statutes shall be submitted to WIPO;
(d) The organization shall have authority to speak for its members through its authorized representatives and in accordance with the rules governing observer status; and
(e) The admission of national NGOs to observer status shall be the subject of prior consultations between Member States and the Secretariat.

At the fortieth series of meetings in Oct 2004, two national organizations with an interest in Berne that sought admission under this category were the Electronic Frontier Foundation and the Picture Archive Council of America: WIPO Document A/40/5, para 15.

Admission to observer status also entails invitations to associated meetings, such as those of committees and working groups where their subject matter seems to be of direct interest to that organization.

(x) **'Adopt amendments to Articles 22 to 26'**:[117] although the unanimous decision of a conference of revision is required for the amendment of other provisions of the Convention, it was thought at the Stockholm Revision that the administrative and financial provisions of articles 22 to 26 were not so important and that there would be advantages in allowing for a speedier and less formal method of amending them.[118] This may be done by the Assembly, in accordance with the procedure laid down in article 26 (see para 16.49 below) and has been done now on several occasions.

(xi) 'Take any other appropriate action designed to further the objectives of the Union':[119] this was described in the programme as 'a general authorization for the Assembly to undertake programmes which are designed to further the objectives of the Union, that is, better, cheaper, simpler, more efficient, protection of copyright'.[120] It was further said that the difference between this item and item (i) was that the former was concerned with action taken within the framework of the Union, for example, the examination of the desirability of revising the Convention. By contrast, examination of the desirability of creating special agreements on some particular aspect of the protection of copyright would fall under the present head.[121] This, indeed, is what the Assembly did in May 1996, leading to the convening of the 1996 Diplomatic Conference in Geneva.[122]

(xii) 'Exercise such other functions as are appropriate under this Convention':[123] this refers to functions which may be conferred on the Assembly other than under the present article. An example is found in article 23(5)(c), which requires the Assembly to establish rules governing the election and re-election of members of the Executive Committee. Others are the determination of the amount and terms of payment of each member country's initial contribution to the working capital fund of the Union,[124] and the level of any increase to this amount.[125]

---

[117] Paris Act, art 22(2)(a)(x). [118] Document S/9: *Records* 1967, 442, 458.

[119] Paris Act, art 22(2)(a)(xi). [120] Document S/9: *Records* 1967, 442.

[121] ibid. See further Bogsch (1986), 304, 326ff.

[122] 24–6 May 1996 meeting of the Berne Assembly, General Assembly of WIPO and the Preparatory Committee: see Document CRNR/DC/4, para 11: *Records* 1996, 162.

[123] Paris Act, art 22(2)(a)(xii). [124] ibid, art 25(6)(a).

[125] ibid, art 25(6)(c). A further power possessed by the Assembly is the designation of further languages for the establishment of official texts of the Convention: art 37(1)(b).

(xiii) 'Subject to its acceptance, exercise such rights as are given to it in the Convention establishing the Organization':[126] under the latter instrument, the assent of the Assembly is required for the following matters: (i) the appointment and conditions of appointment of the Director General,[127] (ii) the assumption by WIPO of responsibility for the administration of any additional international agreements,[128] and (iii) the transfer of the WIPO headquarters.[129] These matters are self-explanatory: each raises issues that are of vital importance to the Union in relation to the personnel and allocation of resources by WIPO.

(b) Advice of the Coordination Committee

16.11 Under the WIPO Convention, a 'Coordination Committee' was set up, and, subject to certain limitations as to numbers, it consists of those states which are members of the Executive Committees of the Berne and Paris Unions.[130] It fulfils, in part, a similar function to that played by the Executive Committees of both Unions in relation to their respective Assemblies.[131] However, it also takes over the advisory role that was carried out by the previous Interunion Coordination Committee.[132] Thus, it is required to:

> . . . give advice to the organs of the various Unions, . . . on all administrative, financial and other matters of common interest to two or more of the Unions, or to one or more of the Unions and the Organization, and in particular on the budget of expenses common to the Unions.[133]

A corresponding provision is contained in the Berne Convention, under which, with respect to 'matters which are of interest also to other Unions administered by the Organization', the Assembly shall only make its decisions after 'having heard the advice of the Coordination Committee . . .'.[134] There is nothing binding about the advice of the Committee, but, in the words of the programme for the Stockholm Conference, the provision is 'merely a reminder that the advice be considered before action is taken'.[135]

(c) Voting and procedures of the Assembly

16.12 Unlike the provisions concerning conferences of revision, article 22 contains quite detailed prescriptions as to these matters. The same model is also adopted for the assemblies established under the other industrial property conventions

[126] Paris Act, art 22(2)(1)(xiii). [127] WIPO Convention, art 6(2)(i) and (3)(g).

[128] ibid, art 6(2)(v) and (3)(g). Two examples of such agreements that have come under the administration of WIPO are the Geneva Phonograms Convention 1971 and the Vienna Agreement for the Protection of Typefaces and their International Deposit 1973: [1973] *Copyright* 237 (second ordinary session, General Assembly of WIPO).

[129] WIPO Convention, arts 10 and 6(3)(g). [130] ibid, art 8(1)(a).

[131] ibid, art 8(3)(ii)–(iv). [132] See n 4 above. [133] WIPO Convention, art 8(3)(i).

[134] Paris Act, art 22(2)(b). [135] Document S/9: *Records* 1967, 442.

revised at Stockholm,[136] as well as for the General Assembly and Conference of WIPO.[137]

(i) **Voting:** Each country member of the Assembly has one vote.[138] Equality of voting among members is therefore established, although the financial contributions of countries to the budget of the Union may vary widely.[139] However, there is provision for the suspension of the voting rights of a member state which is in arrears in paying its contribution.[140]

(ii) **Quorum:** This is one-half of the countries who are members of the Assembly.[141] The original proposal in the programme was for this to be one-third,[142] but this was amended in Main Committee IV after certain countries argued that the smaller quorum gave rise to the possibility of the affairs of the Assembly being taken over by a minority of countries.[143] Nevertheless, there is special provision for the subsequent validation of decisions where a quorum of less than half is missing: if the numbers actually present are equal to or more than one-third of the membership of the Assembly, it may make decisions if these are then communicated by the International Bureau to those countries which were absent.[144] The latter may then submit a written vote or abstention within three months of the date of this communication. If, at the end of this time, the number of countries that have expressed their vote or abstained attains the number for the required quorum at that session, the decisions shall take effect.[145] This is subject to the necessary majority for that decision having also been attained.[146] This validation procedure cannot be used in the case of decisions made by the Assembly concerning its own procedures.[147]

(iii) **Majority for decisions of Assembly:** These require two-thirds of the votes cast, and abstentions are not considered as votes.[148] It is also provided that a delegate may only represent and vote in the name of one country;[149] accordingly, it is not possible for the government of one member country to give its proxy vote to the delegation of another country (a procedure that may have been

136 Stockholm Act of the Paris Convention for the Protection of Industrial Property, art 13(4)–(8).

137 WIPO Convention, arts 6(3)(a)–(f) and (4) (Assembly) and 7(3) and (4) (Conference). Somewhat different and more flexible models, however, have been adopted for the assemblies of the WCT and WPPT: see further para 16.52.

138 Paris Act, art 22(3)(a).

139 ibid, art 25(4). See further paras 16.40ff below.

140 Paris Act, art 25(4)(e).

141 ibid, art 22(4)(b).

142 Document S/9: *Records* 1967, 442. The programme notes here that 'Based on past experience, one-third seems to be the maximum practical'.

143 ibid, 1013 and 1021–4 (Bulgaria, Poland, Czechoslovakia, France).

144 Paris Act, art 22(3)(c).

145 ibid.

146 ibid.

147 ibid.

148 ibid, art 22(3)(d) and (e).

149 ibid, art 22(3)(f).

useful in the case of countries from the same region or with similar economic and social backgrounds).[150] The original proposals in the programme for the Stockholm Conference envisaged that a simple majority should suffice, except for decisions on the admission of observers and on increases in the financial obligations of member countries (which would require two-thirds majorities).[151] This was thought desirable, particularly by BIRPI, as it would avoid the danger of the affairs of the Union, particularly in relation to the budget, falling into stalemate in the event that a larger majority was required and could not be attained.[152] However, it attracted considerable opposition in Main Committee IV on the ground that it might lead to instability and the making of unrepresentative decisions.[153] A working group on voting was appointed,[154] and the two-thirds majority was accepted, subject to a provision allowing for the continuation of the budget levels from the preceding year in the event that a proposed budget for the succeeding financial period was not adopted in time.[155]

(iv) **Observers:** It is expressly provided that Union countries that are not members of the Assembly are to be admitted as observers.[156] At the present time, these countries are Lebanon, Madagascar, and New Zealand.[157] The power of the Assembly to determine conditions for the admission of other observers has already been discussed (see para 16.10 above).

(v) **Meetings**: These are held once in every second calendar year and are convoked by the Director General.[158] This was formerly every third calendar year, but the two-year interval was adopted by the Assembly in an amendment to this provision in 1979, and accords with the general practice of most other UN organizations.[159] Apart from exceptional circumstances, sessions of the Assembly are held at the same time as those of the General Assembly of WIPO.[160] There have been thirty such sessions, including sixteen ordinary sessions, since 1970,[161] and these have also been held in conjunction with the

[150] This was the reason behind a proposed amendment to art 13 of the Paris Convention by the Malagasy Republic for states which were grouped together under the terms of an international agreement in an Intellectual Property Office to be represented by a single delegation or by that common organ: Document S/37, *Records* 1967, 683. This was eventually defeated: ibid, 1041–3, 1056–7.

[151] Document S/9: ibid, 442–3.

[152] *Records* 1967, 1015 (Professor Bodenhausen to Main Committee IV).

[153] ibid, 1014 (delegates of Hungary and Czechoslovakia). See also ibid, 1021–3.

[154] ibid, 1023.

[155] ibid, 1204. See now Paris Act, art 25(4)(f) and para 16.44 below.

[156] Paris Act, art 22(3)(g).

[157] [1986] *Copyright* 6–8.

[158] Paris Act, art 22(4)(b).

[159] Paris Act, art 22(4)(a). See further para 16.49 below.

[160] [1970] *Copyright* 243.

[161] The most recent taking place in Geneva from 27 Sept–5 Oct 2004: for the documents of these meetings, see www.wipo/int.

assemblies of the Paris and other Special Unions, as well as the WIPO Coordination Committee.[162] An extraordinary session to mark the centenary of the Berne Convention was held in September 1986.[163]

(vi) Extra meetings: These may be convoked by the Director General, or upon the request of one-quarter of the members of the Assembly.[164]

(vii) Rules of procedure: The Assembly controls its own procedure, and appropriate rules were adopted at its first session in 1970.[165] These apply equally to all the governing bodies of WIPO and the unions administered by that body, and have been revised from time to time.[166]

(d) Transitional provisions

It was inevitable that some period of time would elapse before all members of the Union had acceded to the Stockholm and Paris Acts, thereby becoming members of the Assembly. Both Acts therefore contained certain provisions to facilitate this process. The first was article 28(1)(b) which permitted present members of the Union to limit their ratification or accession to articles 22 to 38, in which case they remained bound by the substantive provisions of the last Act to which they were party. As the new administrative and financial provisions were largely uncontroversial, this gave states the opportunity to adopt these provisions rapidly without having to make an immediate decision concerning the substantive provisions of articles 1 to 21 and the Appendix. This was of particular value to those member countries where treaties were not automatically incorporated into municipal law, and where adherence to the new provisions would require considerable changes to their domestic laws. The second provision gave hesitating states the opportunity of participating in the Assembly for a **16.13**

[162] The reports of these sessions are to be found in *Copyright/Le Droit d'Auteur* up to 1995, then in *Industrial Property and Copyright*, and from 1997, are to be found on the WIPO website at www.wipo.int, the most recent general report being WIPO Document A/40/7 (5 Oct 2004). Since 1973, these have been contained in one joint report of all the assemblies of conventions administered by WIPO, namely the WIPO General Assembly, the Paris Union Assembly, the Madrid Union Assembly, the Hague Union Assembly, the Nice Union Assembly, the Lisbon Union Assembly, the Locarno Union Assembly, the IPC Union Assembly, the PCT Union Assembly, the Budapest Union Assembly, the Vienna Union Assembly, and, since 2002, the WCT and WPPT Assemblies: see general report, thirty-ninth series of meetings, 22 Sept–1 Oct 2003: WIPO Document A/39/15 (1 Oct 2003). These meetings have also been held jointly with meetings of the WIPO Coordination Committee and the Executive Committees of Paris and Berne.

[163] Geneva, 8–12 Sept 1986: [1986] *Copyright* 367, 376.

[164] Paris Act, art 22(4)(b). [165] [1970] *Copyright* 243.

[166] OMPI/WIPO *Régles Générales de Procèdure/General Rules of Procedure*, Document 399 (FE) Rev 3 (1984 edition). These were supplemented by further rules adopted on 28 Sept 1970 and reproduced in the compilation of 'Special Rules of Procedure of the Governing Bodies' prepared by WIPO for the seventeenth series of meetings of Governing Bodies of WIPO on 8–12 Sept 1986: Document AB/XVII/INF/2, dated 20 May 1986, 15–16.

limited period of time as 'deemed members', even though they had not become bound by articles 22 to 26. Until 26 April 1975, these states were permitted to exercise, if they so desired, 'the rights provided for under the said Articles as if they were bound by them'.[167] All that was required was that this desire be notified to the Director General, and it was effective from the date of the receipt of this communication.[168] Having done this, they were then entitled, among other things, to participate in the sessions of the Assembly.[169] This deemed membership, however, expired on 28 April 1975, giving these states, in practice, the right to participate in the first two sessions of the Assembly (those of 1970 and 1973).

(e) Conference of Representatives

16.14 The arrangements described in the preceding paragraph did not completely fill the gap that was caused by the delay of some states to adhere to the administrative provisions of the Paris Act, particularly after the passing of the 1975 deadline. For various reasons, some states refrained from doing this, and potentially they were denied a forum for expressing their views on the activities and budget of the Union. There was, of course, the possibility of them using their guaranteed observer status in the Assembly for this purpose, but it was thought that some more formal gathering was necessary. Accordingly, reference was had to precedents found under other conventions, and, at the time of the meeting of the first session of the Berne Assembly in October 1970, those member countries which were not members of the Assembly constituted themselves a 'Conference of Representatives'.[170] The model for this was found under the WIPO Convention, where there is provision for the establishment of a 'Conference of Representatives' in addition to the General Assembly.[171] This consists of all states that are party to the Convention, whether or not they are members of any of the Unions (only Union members are members of the General Assembly).[172] The model for this body, in turn, was to be found in the Lisbon Act of the Paris Convention,[173] although the purpose of the Conference set up under that Act was really to provide a forum for discussion between revision conferences,[174] a function that was taken over by the Assembly of the

[167] Paris Act, art 38(1). This was five years from the date the WIPO Convention came into force under the provision of art 15(1) of that Convention. The period allowed under the Stockholm Act, art 38(2) was simply five years from this time, as it was not possible then to nominate an exact date.

[168] Paris Act, art 38(1). These communications were duly published in *Le Droit d'Auteur* and *Copyright:* see eg the notifications with respect to India and Uruguay made on 10 Dec 1973: [1973] *Copyright* 240.

[169] Paris Act, art 38(1).

[170] [1970] *Copyright* 243.

[171] WIPO Convention, art 7.

[172] ibid, art 7(1)(a).

[173] Lisbon Act, art 14(5).

[174] ibid, art 14(5)(a).

Paris Union established under the Stockholm Act of the Paris Convention.[175] Although the Conference was not retained in this Act, it still continued in existence in relation to those member states of the Paris Union that remained bound by the Lisbon Act.[176] The Conference of Representatives of the Berne Union which was constituted in 1970 was therefore envisaged as a temporary forum that would continue in existence until such time as all its members had become members of the Assembly. As its constitution had no legal basis in any of the provisions of the pre-Stockholm Acts of the Convention, it was placed directly under the supervision of the Swiss Government. These matters were reflected in the terms of the following resolution:

> 1. The countries members of the International Union for the Protection of Literary and Artistic Works (Berne Union) which are not members of the Assembly of the said Union;
> 2. *Meeting* in Geneva from September 21 to 28, 1970;
> 3. *Resolve* to establish a Conference of Representatives of the Berne Union;
> 4. *Decide* that the members of this Conference shall be those member countries of the Berne Union which are not members of the Assembly of the Berne Union, and that any member country of the Berne Union which, in the future, shall become a member of the Assembly of the Berne Union shall automatically cease to be a member of the Conference of Representatives;
> 5. *Decide* that the Conference of Representatives shall meet every three years in ordinary session in order to draw up, for each three-year period to come, a report on the foreseeable expenditure of the International Bureau as far as the Berne Union is concerned, and to consider questions relating to the protection and the development of the said Union;
> 6. *Resolve* that the Conference of Representatives may modify, by unanimous decision, the maximum annual amount of the expenditure of the International Bureau as far as the countries members of the Conference of Representatives are concerned, provided that it meets as a Conference of Plenipotentiaries upon convocation by the Government of the Swiss Confederation;
> 7. *Resolve* that the Conference of Representatives shall establish its own rules of procedure.[177]

This Conference has met at the same time as the triennial, and now biennial, sessions of the Assembly, but with a steadily diminishing membership: fourteen

[175] Stockholm Act, art 13(2).

[176] The Conference of the Paris Union has thus continued to meet at the same time as the Assemblies of the Paris and Berne Unions, and the General Assembly of WIPO: thus, the third ordinary session was held at the same time as the first ordinary sessions of the WIPO General Assembly and the Berne Assembly: [1970] *Industrial Property* 365.

[177] [1970] *Copyright* 243.

states were represented at the first session in September 1970,[178] and, of the five members remaining by 1986, only four attended the seventh session in September 1985.[179] By 2000, only three members remained (Lebanon and New Zealand, bound by Rome, and Madagascar, bound by Brussels). In practice, there had never been a separate meeting of the Conference to consider an item of substantive business, and in 2000, a Working Group on Constitutional Reform appointed by the 1999 meeting of the WIPO General Assembly recommended its dissolution (along with the dissolution of residual counterpart Conferences of Representatives in the Paris, Hague, and Nice Unions).[180] Subsequently, at its twentieth (sixth extraordinary) session, held as part of the thirty-fifth series of meetings of WIPO member assemblies, the Berne Conference of Representatives decided to dissolve itself.[181]

(3) The Executive Committee

(a) The Permanent Committee

16.15 This was established by a resolution passed at the Brussels Conference.[182] It had originally been proposed by the Italian delegation that a provision to this effect be inserted in the Convention itself, or in an accompanying protocol.[183] However, there was opposition to this from a number of delegations who were anxious to maintain the integrity of the International Offices, and were also concerned about the possible expense that might be involved.[184] The resolution which was adopted was therefore cautiously phrased, and limited the proposed committee's role to an advisory one:

> So as to assist the office of the Union in the task which is conferred on it by article 24, paragraph 2, of the Convention signed at Brussels, on this day, a committee is hereby constituted, to be composed of twelve members from twelve countries of the Union chosen in such a way as to give an equitable representation

[178] [1970] *Copyright* 243. Bogsch gives the membership of the Conference at this time as twenty-five. As the total membership of the Union was then sixty, this meant that the Assembly had thirty-five members (thirteen by virtue of acceptance of the administrative clauses of the Stockholm and Paris Acts and twenty-two 'deemed members'): Bogsch (1986), 304.

[179] [1985] *Copyright* 419–21 (the fifth member, Lebanon, was absent).

[180] WIPO Document A/35/5 (26 May 2000), 'Proposed Discontinuation of the Conferences of Representatives of the Paris, Berne, Hague and Nice Unions and of the Lisbon Union Council: Memorandum of the Secretariat'.

[181] WIPO Document A/35/15, general report of the thirty-fifth series of meetings, 25 Sept-3 Oct 2000, para 136. Similar decisions were made by the Hague and Nice Conferences (with five and two members respectively). Interestingly, the Paris Conference and the Lisbon Union Council decided 'not to meet in future and each requested the Director General not to convene it'. Each of the states that were members of these conferences henceforth will be able to attend Assembly meetings as observers, pursuant to art 22(2)(a)(ix).

[182] *Documents 1948* (1951), 425–6. See further, Bodenhausen (n 7 above), 91 and note in [1948] *DA* 123–4.

[183] *Documents 1948* (1951), 425.

[184] ibid, 425 (the British and Spanish delegations).

> to the different parts of the world. A third of the Committee will be renewed, every three years, in the way to be established. The retiring members will not be immediately eligible for re-election. The duties of a member of the committee are honorary.[185]

The following countries were the foundation members of the committee: Brazil, Canada, Czechoslovakia, France, Hungary, India, Italy, Norway, the Netherlands, Portugal, Switzerland, and the UK.[186] The Committee met, usually at yearly intervals, beginning in September 1949,[187] and provided a useful focus for continuing discussion of the operation of the Convention. In particular, it gave much needed support to the activities of the International Office which, hitherto, had operated in a kind of vacuum between conferences of revision. Despite its informal basis, the Committee was better able to reflect the views of member countries, and to provide important advice on the questions which should be considered by the Office. It commissioned various studies and convened committees of experts to examine particular problems;[188] in addition, in 1951, it established a small sub-committee that met between 1951 and 1955 and studied a range of matters.[189] In 1952, a similar body was set up under the new UCC, but with more defined powers.[190] This was the Intergovernmental Copyright Committee, and from 1959 the two committees began to hold their meetings at the same time and place so that they could hold joint sessions.[191] In the years leading up to the Stockholm Revision, and particularly in the years 1967 to 1970, the Permanent Committee's role was of crucial importance.[192] This body was then given formal status as the Executive Committee of the Assembly under article 23 of the Stockholm Act.

(b) The Executive Committee

This consists of 'countries elected by the Assembly from among countries members of the Assembly',[193] with provision for *ex officio* membership by the **16.16**

---

[185] ibid. [186] ibid.

[187] 28–30 Sept 1949, Neuchâtel: [1949] *DA* 130. Thereafter, the Permanent Committee usually met in a different city in a member country: 1950 in Lisbon: [1950] *DA* 127 and 141; 1951 in Paris: [1951] *DA* 122; 1952 in Neuchâtel: [1952] *DA* 100; 1954 in Lugano: [1954] *DA* 141; 1956 in Paris: [1956] *DA* 69; 1958 in Geneva: [1958] *DA* 188; 1959 in Munich: [1959] *DA* 206; 1960 in London: [1960] *DA* 324; 1961 in Madrid: [1961] *DA* 318; 1964 in New Delhi: [1964] *DA* 50; 1965 in Paris: [1966] *Copyright* 9; 1967 in Geneva: [1968] *Copyright* 23; 1969 in Paris: [1970] *Copyright* 21.

[188] eg the 'consultations' and committees of experts that investigated the question of cinematographic works prior to the Stockholm Revision had their origin in a resolution of the fourth session of the Committee at Neuchâtel, 1–3 July 1952: [1952] *DA* 100, 103.

[189] This met six times, and for reports of its activities see [1951] *DA* 35; [1951] *DA* 122; [1952] *DA* 100; [1953] *DA* 81; [1955] *DA* 52.

[190] UCC, art XI. [191] 12–17 Oct 1959, Munich: [1959] *DA* 206, 212.

[192] See generally Chapter 14 above on the progress of the revision of the Stockholm Protocol concerning developing countries.

[193] Paris Act, art 23(2)(a).

country on whose territory the headquarters of WIPO is situated.[194] This last is Switzerland, which has been the host country, first for the International Office, and now for WIPO, since the foundation of the Convention. The reason for this *ex officio* membership is that, as host country, the Swiss Government undertakes certain financial obligations in relation to the Union,[195] and therefore has an interest in being fully informed of all the activities of the Union.[196] This membership comes to an end in the event that these obligations are denounced by Switzerland, and this matter is discussed further below (see para 16.47). The general provision regarding membership of the Committee is the same as for the Assembly: each state which is a member is represented by one delegate, who may be assisted by alternate delegates, advisers, and experts.[197] The expenses of each delegation are similarly borne by the country concerned.[198]

(c) Size of the Committee

16.17 The basic rule is that this is one-fourth of the number of countries that are members of the Assembly.[199] In establishing the number of seats to be filled, remainders after the division by four are to be disregarded.[200] Thus, to take the example given in the programme, if there are eighty-two members of the Assembly, eighty-two divided by four gives 20.5, and, after discarding the 0.5, this leaves twenty seats for election to the Executive Committee.[201] This would then be increased to twenty-one, with the addition of the *ex officio* membership of Switzerland.[202] As of 1 January 1986, there were seventy-one members of the Assembly, which meant that, with Switzerland, there were eighteen members of the Executive Committee. By January 2005, with 156 members of the Assembly, this meant that the potential membership of the Committee, with Switzerland, was forty. On any view, this is a cumbersome number, a kind of mini-assembly, and, as will be seen below, subsequent developments in the wider organization of WIPO and its governing structures have led to the Executive Committee ceasing to have any meaningful role. Nonetheless, it remains a formal part of the governing organs of the Berne Union, and the provisions of the Convention concerned with this are considered first, before we consider more recent changes that have occurred.

(d) Mode of selection of members

16.18 In electing the members of the Committee, the Assembly is required to have 'due regard to an equitable geographical distribution and to the need for countries

[194] Paris Act, art 23(2)(a).

[195] ibid, art 25(7)(a) (the making of advances in the event that there are insufficiencies in the working capital fund of the Union).

[196] Document S/9: *Records* 1967, 456.

[197] Paris Act, art 23(2)(b).

[198] ibid, art 22(2)(c).

[199] ibid, art 23(3).

[200] ibid.

[201] Document S/9: *Records* 1967, 446.

[202] ibid.

party to the Special Agreements which might be established in relation with the Union to be among the countries constituting the Executive Committee'.[203] The first of these criteria is a fairly customary requirement for all intergovernmental organizations.[204] This remains in the realm of moral stricture, as no sanction is provided in the event that it is ignored. In the main, the requirement has been observed: as the list of membership for its first sixteen years that was set out in the first edition of this commentary reveals.[205] The second criterion, however, has no present application, as, unlike the Paris Union, there are no Special Unions established under the Berne Convention.

(e) Term and re-election of members

Each member of the Committee serves from the close of the session of the Assembly that elects it to the close of the next ordinary session of the Assembly.[206] This will therefore usually mean that each member will serve a two-year term.[207] There is no bar on the re-election of members, except that no more than two-thirds can be re-elected at any one time.[208] In other words, at each election, one-third of the membership must be renewed. In practice, with the exception of Switzerland, as an *ex officio* member, some countries, such as France, Italy, Germany, India, and the UK, which have been members for most of the time, have voluntarily withdrawn from membership for certain periods. **16.19**

Apart from the one-third rule with respect to new members, it is left to the Assembly to establish the rules for election and possible re-election of members of the Executive Committee.[209] A set of draft rules for inclusion in the Convention itself was presented to the 1966 Committee, but the Committee thought that these were too detailed and did not recommend their inclusion.[210] However, at its first session, the Assembly adopted rules based on the 1966 proposals, and these have been used since this time.[211] **16.20**

---

203 [1986] *Copyright* 6–8. Thus, in the seventh ordinary session of the Assembly in the preceding year, seventeen members were elected to the Committee, with Switzerland making the eighteenth member: [1985] *Copyright* 419.

204 Document S/9: *Records* 1967, 446.

205 Sam Ricketson, *The Berne Convention 1886–1986* (1987), 720.

206 Paris Act, art 23(5)(a).

207 Noting that since 1979, Assemblies have been held at two-, rather than three-year, intervals: see further para 16.10 above.

208 Paris Act, art 23(3)(b). 209 ibid, art 23(5)(c).

210 Document S/9: *Records* 1971, 446–7.

211 See WIPO Document AB/XVII/INF/2 of 20 May 1986 (n 166 above), at 15: under r 3 of the supplementary rule of procedure adopted by the Assembly on 28 Sept 1970, it is provided that: '(3) Except where the procedure provided for in Article 34(1) of the General Rules of Procedure is observed, selection shall take place in the following manner: the member States shall be called in the alphabetical order of their names in French, after the letter of the alphabet at which the roll-call is to start shall have been drawn by lot; on the calling of the name of each State, the Assembly shall decide whether or not it is re-elected; if necessary, the State last called shall be

(f) Functions

16.21 The Executive Committee is required to do the following:

(i) prepare the draft agenda of the Assembly;
(ii) submit proposals to the Assembly respecting the draft programme and biennial budget of the Union prepared by the Director General;
(iii) [this provision was deleted by the Assembly in 1979 when the change to biennial budgets and sessions was made. Prior to this time, it read as follows: 'approve, within the limits of the program and the triennial budget, the specific yearly budgets and programs prepared by the Director General';]
(iv) submit, with appropriate comments, to the Assembly the periodical reports of the Director General and the yearly audit reports on the accounts;
(v) in accordance with the decisions of the Assembly and having regard to circumstances arising between two ordinary sessions of the Assembly, take all necessary measures to ensure the execution of the programme of the Union by the Director General;
(vi) perform such other functions as are allocated to it under this Convention.[212]

These functions are largely self-explanatory, underlining that the intended role of the Executive Committee was to be an intermediary body which organizes the material that goes ultimately before the Assembly, while acting as its delegate between its sessions. Item (i) is a standard kind of provision, which makes the Executive Committee the agenda committee for the Assembly. In practice, however, it appears that the final form of the agenda is ultimately determined by the Director General, in the light of events which occur between the meetings of the Committee and the sessions of the Assembly.[213] Items (ii), (iii), and (v) spell out in some detail the role of the Executive Committee in supervising the activities of the Director General in his capacity as chief executive officer of the Union. In doing this, the Committee is acting on behalf of the Assembly, which remains the supreme governing body of the Union. Once again, in practice, it seems that, from 1979, with the Assembly meeting every second year, this made these functions of the Committee largely unnecessary. Thus, in 1986, the then Director General, Dr Bogsch, indicated in his centenary study of the Convention, that the role of the Committee in relation to the budget and programme had become purely formal, with the Assembly usually proceeding directly to

excluded from re-election if such exclusion is necessary to ensure that the proportion of two-thirds shall not be exceeded; the Assembly shall then elect the number of new members required to attain the total number to be elected.'

[212] Paris Act, art 23(6)(a). [213] Bogsch (1986), 306.

consideration of these items without any substantive proposals coming from the Committee.[214] In addition, the reports of the Director General were only separately considered by the Committee every second year when the Assembly did not meet.[215] As for item (v), it seems that so far no measures of the kind described in this item have yet been taken by the Committee.[216] Finally, with respect to item (vi), the two main functions allocated to the Committee under the Convention are potentially important, namely the role which it is given in the preparations for a conference of revision,[217] and the right which it has to initiate amendments to the administrative clauses of the Convention under article 26.[218] As will be seen below, however, these too have proved to be of little practical importance in the administration and development of the Convention.

(g) Advice of the Coordination Committee

Where matters arise that are of interest to other unions administered by WIPO, the Committee is required not to make any decision until 'after having heard the advice of the Coordination Committee'.[219] This is the same requirement that applies to decisions of the Assembly.[220] The advice of the Committee is in no way binding, and after having heard it the Committee may disregard it altogether. As a practical matter, this is highly unlikely, as all the members of the Executive Committee are members of the Coordination Committee.[221] **16.22**

(h) Meetings

The Committee meets every year in ordinary session upon convocation by the Director General.[222] It is further provided that it should meet (and it usually does) at the same time and place as the Coordination Committee of WIPO.[223] Extraordinary sessions may also be convoked at any time by the Director General,[224] either at his own initiative or at the request of its chairman or of one-quarter of its members.[225] Such extraordinary sessions have been held from time to time.[226] **16.23**

(i) Voting

Each member of the Committee has one vote,[227] and a quorum is one-half of the membership.[228] Decisions are made by a simple majority, on the basis that **16.24**

214 ibid. 215 ibid. 216 ibid. 217 Paris Act, art 24(7)(a).
218 ibid, arts 24(7)(a) and 26(1). 219 ibid, art 23(6)(b).
220 ibid, art 22(2)(b). 221 WIPO Convention, art 8(1)(a).
222 Paris Act, art 23(7)(a). 223 ibid. 224 ibid, 23(7)(b). 225 ibid.
226 There were nine such sessions to 1986, namely in 1971, 1973, 1975, 1977, 1979 (two), 1981, 1983, and 1985: Bogsch (1986), 306. Since this time, there have been another three, with the thirty-fifth ordinary session of the Executive Committee being held on 27 Sept–5 Oct 2004: WIPO Document A/40/7 (general report, 5 Oct 2004).
227 Paris Act, art 23(8)(a). 228 ibid, art 23(8)(b).

these are not, by definition, as important as those made by the Assembly.[229] There is no possibility of a member exercising a proxy vote on behalf of an absent member: it is expressly provided that a delegate may represent and vote in the name of one country only.[230]

(j) Observers

16.25 Union members that are not members of the Executive Committee have the right to be admitted to its meetings as observers.[231] The admission of other observers, such as international and non-governmental organizations, is left to the discretion of the Committee, which has the power to adopt its own rules of procedure.[232] In this regard, the same guidelines as those adopted by the WIPO Assembly and the governing bodies of the other Unions administered by WIPO are applied.[233]

(k) Procedures

16.26 The Committee is master of its own procedures, and appropriate rules were adopted at its first ordinary session.[234] These deal, among other things, with the officers of the Committee and voting procedures, as well as providing for the publication of the report, or a summary of the report, of the work of each session.[235] They also make special provision for the role of associate members, providing that, as might be expected, only the votes of ordinary members are to be taken into account.[236]

(l) Transitional

16.27 The provisions described above (see para 16.13) in relation to 'deemed membership' of the Assembly also applied to the Executive Committee.[237] Since 28 April 1975, they have obviously ceased to be of any relevance.

(m) Proposal to abolish the Executive Committee

16.28 As noted above, WIPO, as the UN agency responsible for intellectual property agreements generally, has sought to streamline the administrative and logistical

---

229 Paris Act, art 23(8)(c). See further Document S/9: *Records* 1967, 448.

230 Paris Act, art 23(8)(e). 231 ibid, art 23(9). 232 ibid, art 23(10).

233 See generally the *IB Memorandum* (n 107 above) and, in relation to current meetings, see 'Admission of Observers: Memorandum of the Director General' (n 113 above), prepared for the fortieth series of WIPO Assemblies, including the Berne Executive Committee.

234 Paris Act, art 23(10). Supplementary rules to the General Rules of Procedure applicable to the Governing Bodies of WIPO and its Unions were adopted on 28 Sept 1970 and amended on 24 Oct 1979: Document AB/XVII/INF/2 of 20 May 1986, 21–2.

235 ibid, rr 3, 5 and 6. Formerly, these were published in *Copyright/Le Droit d'auteur*, but are now made available online at www.wipo.int.

236 ibid, rr 4 and 5. 237 ibid, art 38(1).

problems in organizing so many different governing body meetings by holding these together at the same time each year. By and large, the administrative (and financial) provisions of the WIPO conventions now follow the same template, and it is obvious that the holding of common meetings will save the purses of member countries if they need only send one delegation that can attend the various sessions, which can be held seriatum at the one time. This system of joint meetings was already well established by the first edition of this commentary, but has now become much more extensive with the creation of newer unions and agreements. Accordingly, in 1999, the WIPO General Assembly recommended that the Director General establish a working group to consider and study proposals concerning constitutional reform and to report on its progress to the 2000 assemblies meetings.[238] This working group met a number of times from 2000 to 2002, with an interim report to the 2001 meeting.[239] Among other things, it recommended the discontinuance of the Conferences of Representatives (see para 16.14 above), the abolition of the WIPO Conference, formalization of the unitary contribution system and changes in contribution classes (as to which, see para 16.41 below), and that the ordinary sessions of the various assemblies (including Berne) take place annually rather than biennially. The last of these recommendations has obvious ramifications for the Executive Committee of Berne, which is mandated under the Convention to meet annually as well, so a logical further recommendation would have been to abolish that Committee (as well as the Executive Committee of Paris). While there was general agreement in the Working Group that these committees served 'no useful function', one obstacle to this was that the Executive Committees provided the primary means by which membership of the WIPO Coordination Committee was constituted: see article 8(1) of the WIPO Convention. As there was no consensus as to how composition of the Coordination Committee might otherwise be determined, the Working Group agreed to maintain the status quo in relation to the three bodies,[240] with the consequence that the Executive Committee of Berne remains in formal existence and continues to meet annually at the same time as the other governing bodies. A further proposal for a unitary assembly was also discussed by the Working Group and while a majority of members believed that this would result in a 'simplified and a more efficient and effective governance and constitutional structure of the Organization [WIPO]', a number of delegations doubted the efficacy of such a proposal and so no recommendation in this respect was formulated by the Working Group.[241]

---

[238] WIPO Document A/34/10, para 159.
[239] The final report of the Working Group is WIPO Document A/37/5 (24 July 2002).
[240] ibid, para 13. [241] ibid, para 14.

(4) The International Bureau

(a) Background

16.29 There has been an 'Office of the International Union for the Protection of Literary and Artistic Works' in existence almost since the Convention came into force. This was provided for in the earliest draft proposals prepared by ALAI,[242] and was duly established by article 16 of the Berne Act which placed it under the 'high authority of the Superior Administration of the Swiss Government'.[243] It was further provided that its functions should be determined by common accord between the countries of the Union,[244] and more detail as to this was given in paragraph 5 of the Final Protocol of that Act. Among other things, this provided:

> The organisation of the International Office established by virtue of Article 16 of the Convention shall be fixed by a regulation which shall be drawn up by the Government of the Swiss Confederation.
>
> The official language of the International Office shall be French.
>
> The International Office will collect every kind of information relative to the protection of the rights of authors over their literary and artistic works. It will arrange and publish such information. It will undertake the study of questions of general interest concerning the Union, and, by the aid of documents placed at its disposal by the different Administrations, will edit a periodical publication in the French language on the questions which concern the purposes of the Union. The Governments of the countries of the Union reserve to themselves the power to authorise, by common accord, the publication by the Office of an edition in one or more languages if experience should show this to be requisite.
>
> The International Office will always hold itself at the disposal of members of the Union with a view to furnishing them with any special information they may require relative to the protection of literary and artistic works.

The remaining parts of paragraph 5 were concerned with the finances of the International Office, but there was a further requirement for the Director to make an annual report on his administration to all members of the Union.[245]

16.30 When the Convention entered into force on 5 December 1887, the Swiss Federal Council decided that it would combine the International Office set up under this with the Office constituted under the recently formed Paris Convention.[246]

---

242 *Actes* 1884, 8: art 10 of the ALAI draft convention.

243 Berne Act, art 16, para 2. On the general background of the relationship of the Swiss Government's relations with the International Office and WIPO, see J Voyame, 'Les rapports de la Convention avec le Bureau de l'Union internationale pour la protection des oeuvres littéraires et artistiques ainsi qu'avec l'Organisation mondiale de la proprieté intellectuelle', in M Rehbinder and W Larese (eds), *Die Berner Übereinkunft und die Schweiz* (1986).

244 Berne Act, art 16, para 2.

245 Closing Protocol, para 5(5).

246 [1888] *DA* 1. See further *L'Union internationale pour la protection des oeuvres littéraires et artistiques: son fondation et son développement—Mémoire 1886–1936* (1936) ('*Mémoire* (1936)'), 103–4.

Reasons of economy lay mainly behind this decision, as well as the fact that the subjects covered by both conventions were closely related.[247] Nevertheless, the Federal Council delayed for some time in finalizing this organization of the two offices, as it wished to see how it would work in practice.[248] The International Office of the Berne Union began its operations on 1 January 1888, and was administered, together with the Paris Office, by a 'secretary general' of the two offices. This was Henri Morel, a former member of the Swiss National Council and former president of the Federal Assembly.[249] He was assisted by a 'secretary-translator' and a registrar-secretary.[250] The distinguished Swiss official, Numa Droz, was made responsible for the oversight of these offices.[251] This interim arrangement was succeeded by a more permanent one that was set out in a regulation of the Swiss Federal Council on 11 November 1892.[252] The two offices were combined, and the post of Director was created.[253] Morel was appointed to this, and Léon Poinsard, a Frenchman, was named as secretary-general.[254] A number of other staff appointments were made at the same time, including two secretaries to be responsible for the industrial property and copyright sections respectively.[255] Overall powers of supervision were vested in the Swiss Federal Council, but supervision over less important matters was delegated to the Swiss Department of Foreign Affairs.[256] This was done by reference to the ordinances of the Federal Council concerning the International Offices of the Postal and Telegraph Unions, and included provisions for such matters as salaries and conditions of employment, travel, rental of premises, the preparation of budgets and accounts, staff disputes, and life insurance policies.[257] There was no reference to the combined or united offices in any of the successive Acts of the Convention, but indirect recognition of their existence is to be found in article 24(1)(a) of the Stockholm, Paris Acts which states that the International Bureau of WIPO is the continuation of the 'Bureau of the Union united with the Bureau of the Union established by the International Convention for the Protection of Industrial Property' (see further below). In the late 1950s, the title '*Bureaux internationaux réunis pour la protection de la propriété intellectuelle*' and the abbreviation 'BIRPI' began to be used to refer to the

[247] ibid. See also the paper on the 'Organisation et Fonctionnement du Bureau International de l'Union pour la Protection des Oeuvres Littéraires et Artistiques' in *Actes* 1896, 205ff.

[248] ibid. [249] ibid.

[250] The secretary-translator was Ernst Röthlisberger, who later became the Director and was also a distinguished commentator on the Convention: *Mémoire* (1936) 103.

[251] [1888] *DA* 1. [252] This is set out in *Actes* 1896, 206–7.

[253] Regulation, art 1. [254] *Mémoire* (1936), 103. See further [1892] *DA* 131.

[255] Regulation, art 2. [256] ibid, arts 1 and 3.

[257] Article 3 of the Regulation incorporated arts 3, 4, and 5 of the Ordinance of the Federal Council of 7 Dec 1885 relating to the international offices of posts and telegraphs: *Actes* 1896, 206–7.

combined offices, but, once again, no official reference to these usages is to be found in any of the Acts of the Berne or Paris Conventions.[258]

16.31 The provisions of the Convention concerning the International Office remained substantially unchanged in successive revisions of the Convention, although from the Berlin Act on they appeared in a more simplified form in articles 21 and 22. Successive revision conferences addressed themselves to certain matters concerning personnel,[259] but essentially the organization of the joint secretariat remained the same. Although it operated under strict financial constraints throughout this period, the professionalism and dedication of the staff of BIRPI was impressive, particularly with respect to the work that went into the production of learned commentaries and comparative surveys,[260] the publication of the monthly journal, *Le Droit d'Auteur*, and the preparation of the programmes for revision conferences. These activities were, of course, duplicated with respect to the Paris Union and the Special Unions that were set up in relation to that Union. By the late 1950s, however, it was clear that new administrative and financial arrangements were required, and one of the main goals of the Stockholm Revision therefore was the constitution of a new international organization which would undertake this responsibility for all the unions. This was done with the establishment of WIPO, which replaced BIRPI, taking over the administrative tasks of the Berne and other unions. In essence, these tasks remain little changed from the Berne Act, but they were restated in a more coherent fashion and the financial provisions relating to them were radically revised.

(b) The International Bureau under the Stockholm and Paris Acts

16.32 Under these Acts, the Convention now contains a provision corresponding to that in the WIPO Convention.[261] This stipulates that the 'administrative tasks with respect to the Union' are to be performed by the International Bureau, which is the secretariat of WIPO.[262] It is further provided that this body is a

---

[258] Masouyé (1978), 113. Dr Bogsch states that these were probably the invention of Jacques Sécretan, Director of the combined offices from 1953 to 1963, and the 'official' title for the combined offices (or 'United Bureaux') was 'United International Bureaux for the Protection of Industrial, Literary and Artistic Property': Bogsch (1986), 308. At the same place, Dr Bogsch also notes that the International Office was often referred to simply as 'Secretariat' of the Berne Union and, prior to its move to Geneva, as the 'Berne Bureau'.

[259] eg the Berlin Conference considered and approved of certain benefit funds for employees of the joint offices: *Actes* 1908, 301ff. In 1948, the Brussels Conference passed a resolution requesting that the Swiss Government take account of the terms and conditions of employees in other international organizations: *Documents 1948* (1951), 587.

[260] In the early years of the Union, the *Études* produced for the Paris Conference of 1896 were of a very high standard, as was the *Recueil* of 1904: *Études sur la Convention de Berne* (1896) and *Recueil des conventions et traités concernant la propriété littéraire et artistique, publiés en français et dans les langues des pays contractants avec une introduction et des notices* (1904).

[261] WIPO Convention, art 4(ii) (functions of WIPO).

[262] Paris Act, art 24(1)(a).

'continuation of the Bureau of the Union united with the Bureau of the Union established by the International Convention for the Protection of Industrial Property'.[263] The significance of the word 'continuation' seems to be that it was not contemplated that the International Bureau would carry any additional tasks to that of BIRPI, and a comparison of the functions listed in article 22 of the Brussels Act confirms this.[264] However, what is the significance of this change with respect to member countries that remain bound by Acts earlier than those of Stockholm and Paris? Does this mean that there is no longer any international secretariat which serves the administrative requirements of these countries? If the latter have acceded to the WIPO Convention, no problem arises, as the effect of articles 4(ii) and 9(1) of that Convention is that the International Bureau is to undertake the administrative tasks of the Union. In consequence, the administrative tasks under the Berne Convention with respect to those countries are now performed by that body. In the case of member countries that do not become members of WIPO, however, a potential void arises. Provision is therefore made under the Stockholm and Paris Acts for the continued existence of the International Office set up under the earlier Acts. Article 38(2) stipulates that as long as all countries of the Union have not become members of WIPO, the International Bureau is also to function as the Office of the Union and the Director General as the Director of the said Office. Corresponding provision to this effect is also made in the WIPO Convention.[265] Until this happens, the International Bureau has a dual legal capacity, although the physical facilities and personnel involved in the discharge of the functions of the International Bureau and Office are the same. From a legal point of view, it also means that the supervisory role of the Swiss Government over the Office continues, while the affairs of the International Bureau are supervised by the member states that are members of the Assembly. This division of responsibilities is of little practical consequence, as in the 1966 Committee the Swiss Government declared that, during this interim period, it would do its utmost to ensure that its decisions coincided with those of the Assembly.[266] It was also noted in the programme that the Interunion Coordination Committee would have considerable *de facto* influence on the supervision of the Office, as its 'advices' covered almost all facets of that body's activities (budget, programme, appointment of Director, and so on), and were generally followed by the Swiss Government.[267] This transitional period of dual supervision was still in operation as of 1 January 1986, the date of the first edition of this commentary, as two

[263] ibid. [264] Document S/9: *Records* 1967, 450.

[265] WIPO Convention, art 21(1). [266] Document S/9: *Records* 1967, 482.

[267] ibid. Dr Bogsch, moreover, states that, in practice, since 1970 the Swiss Government has ceased to exercise any supervisory function and that the Director General of WIPO no longer uses his former title of Director of the International Office of the Berne Union: Bogsch (1986), 308.

member states bound by earlier Acts (Madagascar and Lebanon) had not then joined WIPO.[268] It ceased at the end of 1989 when Madagascar acceded to the WIPO Convention, Lebanon having done so at the end of 1986.[269] Once this occurred, the rights, obligations, and property of the Office devolved on the International Bureau.[270]

(c) The Director General

16.33 The Director General of WIPO is the chief executive of the Union, and has the role of representing the Union.[271] A number of specific duties are assigned to him or her under various provisions, most importantly with respect to the preparation of budgets,[272] the execution of the programme of the Union,[273] and the submission of periodic reports.[274] This is also the person to whom ratifications, accessions, and other notices and declarations are addressed for deposit and notification to members of the Union.[275] In practice, the Director General will, of course, act through subordinate officials, but is, ultimately, the official responsible for the discharge of these functions to the Executive Committee and Assembly.[276] In the case of any Union members who are not yet members of WIPO, the Director General still fills the position of Director of BIRPI and is subject, in this capacity, to the supervision of the Swiss Government,[277] although, as noted above, this situation no longer appears to arise. The Director General is appointed by the WIPO General Assembly, upon the nomination of the Coordination Committee[278] on which the members of the Executive Committee of the Berne Union are represented.[279] In addition, the appointment must have the approval of the Berne Assembly.[280] The period of appointment is for a fixed term of not less than six years,[281] and the conditions are fixed by the WIPO General Assembly.[282] The Director General, and any staff member designated by him or her, is authorized to participate, without any right to vote, in all meetings of the Assembly, Executive Committee, and any other committee of

268 [1986] *Copyright* 6–8.

269 Convention Establishing the World Intellectual Property Organization (1967), amended in 1979, status on 15 July 2003: www.wipo.int.

270 Paris Act, art 38(3).

271 ibid, art 24(1)(c).

272 ibid, art 23(6)(a)(ii).

273 ibid, art 23(6)(a)(v).

274 ibid, art 23(6)(a)(iv). Prior to the Stockholm Act, the Director of BIRPI was required to make an annual report on his administration: Brussels Act, art 22(3). The reference to 'periodic' in the Paris Act does not necessarily mean 'annual', but in practice an annual report on the state of the Union appears in *Copyright* and *Le Droit d'Auteur*.

275 See generally, Paris Act, arts 28, 29, 30, 31, 33, 35, and 37.

276 ibid, art 23(6)(a).

277 Brussels Act, art 21(2) and Paris Act, art 38(2). See further Bogsch (1986), 317ff.

278 WIPO Convention, art 6(2)(i).

279 ibid, art 8(1)(a).

280 ibid, art 6(3)(g). The approval of the Assembly of the Paris Union is also required.

281 ibid, art 9(3).

282 ibid.

experts or working group.[283] In addition, the Director General or his delegate act as the *ex officio* secretary of these bodies.[284]

Since 1970, there have been three Directors General of WIPO: Georg Bodenhausen of the Netherlands (1970–3), Arpad Bogsch of the USA (1973–98), and Kamal Idris of the Sudan (1998–). Prior to this, there had been seven Directors of the International Office since 1893, including Bodenhausen who was the last. They were, in chronological order: **16.34**

Henri Morel (1838–1912): 1 January 1893–31 March 1912,[285]
Roberte Comtesse (1847–1922): 1 April 1912–31 December 1921,[286]
Ernst Röthlisberger (1858–1926): 1 January 1922–29 January 1926,[287]
Fritz Ostertag (1868–1948): 1 April 1926–30 April 1938,[288]
Bénigne Mentha (1888–1974): 1 May 1938–1 May 1953,[289]
Jacques Sécretan (1897–1964): 1 May 1959–15 January 1963,[290]
Georg Bodenhausen (1905–): 16 January 1963–30 November 1973.[291]

All these, except for Bodenhausen, were Swiss citizens, and all were highly qualified and erudite men. Three of them—Morel, Comtesse and Ostertag—had had distinguished public careers in Switzerland prior to their appointment.[292] Two others—Röthlisberger and Mentha—had served in the International Office for most of their working lives, rising through the ranks to the Directorship. Of the later Directors, both Secrétan and Bodenhausen had had notable legal and academic careers before their appointment, and Bodenhausen had served as a delegate for the Netherlands at a number of international conferences on intellectual property during the 1940s and 1950s. The second Director General, Dr Bogsch, had also held various important positions in UNESCO and the US Copyright Office before his appointment as Deputy Director of BIRPI in 1963. In addition, he had been a member of the Hungarian delegation at the Brussels Conference of 1948. Up to and including Dr Bogsch, each successive Director and Director General has made significant contributions to the literature dealing with international copyright protection, through the pages

283 Paris Act, art 24(6). 284 ibid.

285 Morel, in fact, had served as 'secretary-general' of the Office since its inception in 1888. For further details on his career, see his obituary in [1912] *DA* 87.

286 For further details, see his obituary in [1922] *DA* 153.

287 Obituary in [1926] *DA* 13. 288 Obituary in [1948] *DA* 60.

289 Obituary in [1974] *Copyright* 202. 290 Obituary in [1964] *DA* 237.

291 For further details on Professor Bodenhausen's achievements as the first Director General of WIPO, see the tribute made to him on his retirement in [1973] *Copyright* 235.

292 Morel had been a member of the lower house of the Swiss Federal Parliament and had also served as president of that body; Comtesse had been a minister (federal councillor) of the Swiss Federal Council and had been President of the Swiss Confederation; Ostertag had been President of the Swiss Federal Tribunal.

of *Le Droit d'Auteur* and in separate publications.[293] Of particular note in this regard are the exhaustive commentaries of Röthlisberger and the provocative studies of Ostertag, while Dr Bogsch was the author of the leading commentary on the sister convention to Berne, the Universal Copyright Convention.[294] Although he never held the highest office, mention should also be made here of the writings of the late Claude Masouyé who was a long serving and senior official of both BIRPI and WIPO. Another distinguished official was Dr Mihaly Ficsor, author of a comprehensive treatise on the 1996 Internet Treaties.[295]

(d) Functions of the International Bureau

16.35 The principal tasks of the International Bureau remain very much the same as those outlined in the original Act of 1886. They are as follows.

(i) To 'provide the secretariat of the various organs of the Union':[296] These include the Assembly, Executive Committee, and any other committee of experts, working group, and ad hoc advisory group that may be set up.

(ii) To 'assemble and publish information concerning the protection of copyright':[297] There is a corresponding obligation imposed here on each member state promptly to communicate to the International Bureau all new laws and official texts concerning the protection of copyright.[298] Until 1995, the function of publishing this information was carried out to a large extent through the pages of *Le Droit d'Auteur/Copyright*, which contains a priceless collection of all the laws of member countries (as well as many others) over the past century, as well as current amendments or revisions to those laws.[299] However, the International Bureau also publishes separately surveys and summaries of national laws, the texts of conventions, and the drafts of model laws.[300] An effort is made to do this in the principal languages used in the Union.[301] With the advent of digital technology, the WIPO website (www.wipo.int) now contains electronic versions of all treaty documents, notifications by parties, and an increasingly comprehensive collection of national laws.

---

[293] See further the Bibliography.

[294] A Bogsch, *The Law of Copyright under the Universal Copyright Convention*, Sijthoff, Leyden, and Bowker, New York (3rd rev ed, 1972)

[295] Ficsor (2001).

[296] Paris Act, art 24(1)(b).

[297] ibid, art 24(2).

[298] ibid.

[299] The principal language for this was French prior to 1965, but after this date it was published in both French and English. From 1995, it was amalgamated with *Industrial Property* and published under the title *Industrial Property and Copyright*, but from 1999 it was replaced by the more 'newsy' *WIPO Magazine*, with all the documentary material being made available electronically on the WIPO website: www.wipo.int.

[300] For a full list of WIPO publications, see the annual catalogues published by the Organization.

[301] ibid.

(iii) To 'publish a monthly periodical':[302] This was *Le Droit d'Auteur/ Copyright*, which was published monthly from January 1888 to 1996. The value of this journal as a source of primary and secondary material relating to the operation and implementation of the Convention cannot be exaggerated. Although the format and arrangement of material obviously changed over its 108 years of existence, the content remained relatively constant, including the following items:

1. the texts of all ratifications, accessions, and denunciations of the Convention;
2. the minutes or reports of, or notes on, all meetings of bodies connected with the Berne Union;
3. notes on all meetings and resolutions of relevant international and national bodies (both governmental and non-governmental) concerned with copyright and neighbouring rights;
4. reports on the meetings of the governing bodies of other relevant unions, as well as of meetings of the ICC of the UCC;
5. the texts of new national laws and other multilateral and bilateral conventions relating to copyright, whether or not between member countries of the Union;
6. reports on the jurisprudence of different countries (not only Union members): these ceased to be reported systematically by the late 1960s, but the gaps were filled by occasional 'Letters' from various countries which presented these developments in a more useful synoptic form;
7. reports and articles prepared either by members of the International Bureau or by independent experts. In the earlier years of the Union, commentaries prepared by the members of the International Office were quite common and served as useful guides to the interpretation of particular provisions of the Convention.[303] Commentaries of this kind became rarer, if not non-existent, in the later years of the journal and this was possibly a reflection of the growing size and professionalism of WIPO and its increased awareness of the need to act as the impartial servant of the Union. This is not to say, however,

302 Paris Act, art 24(3).

303 For a list of the most important of these commentaries, see the Bibliography below. It may also be observed that the International Office in some of its published comments was less than diplomatic in its references to those countries which remained outside the Union: see eg its remarks on the position of Russia in [1894] *DA* 23 and [1898] *DA* 76. In the words of one commentator, *Le Droit d'Auteur* often 'sketched a sort of picture that presented Union members like good people belonging to the only true Church while those staying outside the Union were somewhat regarded as the contrary': F Majoros, 'Some Considerations on the Future of International Copyright Arising upon the Paris Acts of 1971' (1978) 49 *Diritto di Autore* 291, 297.

that the views of WIPO staff members do not strongly influence the working papers and reports prepared for various meetings of the Union. This can hardly be a ground for criticism, as the governments of member countries have their own expert advisers and should benefit from a positive, rather than a bland, presentation of policy options by the International Bureau.

8. book reviews and extensive bibliographical information relating to copyright and matters of related concern.

From its inception, *Le Droit d'Auteur* was published in French, but in the 1950s English translations of particular articles began to appear, and in 1964 the BUPC took the decision to publish the journal in English as well as French.[304] As the name of the journal is not referred to in the Convention, there is no barrier to it being published in other languages as well, although to date this has not occurred.[305] With the extension of the Berne Union membership to the Spanish-and Arabic-speaking countries, these languages would be the obvious ones for additional translations of the journal. In 1995, *Le Droit d'Auteur/ Copyright* was combined with *La propriete industrielle Industrial Property* (the journal of the Paris Union) as a joint monthly publication, but this no longer carried the studies and commentaries that had distinguished both journals throughout their previous individual existences. With the advent of digital technology, however, the function of these publications as a 'journal of record' has now been taken over by the WIPO website, and the only monthly journal covering the activities of the Berne Union that is now published is the *WIPO Magazine*, a more glossy and newsy publication than its more scholarly predecessors. As its name would suggest, the *WIPO Magazine* covers the activities of WIPO generally, so the more serious inquirer after knowledge needs to interrogate the electronic sources available on the WIPO website. As noted above, these are now extensive and well presented, and it is far easier to identify and track down information relating to the Berne Convention than it was, even less than a decade previously. It should also be noted that WIPO has maintained an impressive list of hard-copy publications, many of which are relevant to copyright and neighbouring rights.

(iv) To furnish, on request, 'information to any country of the Union on matters concerning the protection of copyright':[306] in this regard, the International Bureau has performed a considerable role in supplying information and assistance to developing countries in the formulation of new laws.[307]

304 Eleventh session, 2–7 Dec 1963: [1964] *DA* 50, 56.

305 Document S/9: *Records* 1967, 450.

306 Paris Act, art 24(4).

307 See eg the 'World Intellectual Property Organization in 1984' (report of the activities of WIPO in copyright and neighbouring rights): [1984] *Copyright* 85 and yearly updates of a similar character since this time

(v) To conduct studies and provide services 'designed to facilitate the protection of copyright':[308] this overlaps to some extent with the previous task, and a number of notable studies have been carried out by the International Bureau.[309] As regards the provision of services, the training of personnel, particularly in developing countries, and the translation of texts should be noted.[310]

(vi) 'To make the preparations for the conferences of revision':[311] Here the International Bureau acts under the direction of the Assembly, and 'in cooperation with the Executive Committee'.[312] The words 'in cooperation with' are interesting, suggesting that the International Bureau is responsible ultimately in these matters only to the Assembly, and not to the Executive Committee as well. It is also provided that, in preparing for these conferences, the International Bureau may consult with intergovernmental and international non-governmental organizations:[313] obvious examples of these would be UNESCO, the ILO, and the sundry authors' and publishers' organizations whose doings were reported regularly in the pages of *Le Droit d'Auteur.* The Director General, or any person designated by him, has the right to take part, without voting, in these conferences.[314] As noted above, the preparatory work for recent WIPO treaties, including the 1996 WCT and WPPT, has been carried on through ad hoc committees of experts, although the role of the International Bureau in formulating programmes of proposals and draft texts has been central.

(vii) To 'carry out any other tasks assigned to it':[315] An example here would be the establishment of official translations of the Convention.[316]

Prior to the Stockholm Act, it was specifically provided that the 'official language' of the International Office was French.[317] This is no longer specified under the Stockholm, Paris Acts, as it is now left to the General Assembly of WIPO to determine the working languages of the secretariat (the International Bureau) 'taking into consideration the practice of the United Nations'.[318] At present, the main languages used by the International Bureau are English and French, while Spanish, Arabic, Russian and Chinese are also widely used.[319]

---

308 Paris Act, art 24(5).

309 In this regard, the excellent *Guide to the Berne Convention* (1978) by the late Claude Masouyé should not be overlooked. Another study which was of great value, although now overtaken by the plethora of electronic materials now available on the WIPO website, was the *Copyright Law Survey* (1979) (2nd supplement, 1982).

310 See the *Catalogue of WIPO Publications* carried on the WIPO website under the heading 'Electronic Bookshop' (go to 'News and Information Resources').

311 Paris Act, art 24(7)(a). 312 ibid. 313 ibid, art 24(7)(b).

314 ibid, art 24(7)(c). 315 ibid, art 24(8).

316 ibid, art 37(1)(b): this task, in fact, is given to the Director General.

317 Brussels Act, art 21(3). 318 WIPO Convention, art 6(2)(vii).

319 See further Bogsch (1986), 310–11.

(e) Relations with other international organizations and states

16.36 Apart from the power to consult in relation to preparations for revision conferences, no power is conferred on either the Director General or the International Bureau under the Convention to enter into agreements with states and other international organizations. Although no express power to do this was conferred under the earlier Acts, agreements with a number of international organizations were, in fact, made by the Directors of BIRPI prior to 1967.[320] These mainly related to such matters as the exchange of documentation and reciprocal representation at each other's meetings. The making of agreements of this kind is one of the characteristics of international legal personality, and is now expressly conferred on WIPO under its own Convention.[321] Thus, agreements affecting the Berne Union may be made by the International Bureau as the WIPO secretariat, although there is no provision in the Berne Convention requiring consultation with the governing organs of the Berne Union before this occurs. A number of agreements with other international organizations have been made by WIPO, notably with UNESCO,[322] the UN,[323] and the WTO.[324] Under the second of these, WIPO was recognized as a specialized agency of the UN,[325] and this carries with it a number of advantages relating to the provision of information,[326] reciprocal representation,[327] co-ordination of staffing arrangements and conditions,[328] and the use of the UN 'laisser passer' by WIPO personnel.[329] As for relations with other states, WIPO enjoys, on the territory of each member state, in conformity with the laws of that state, such legal capacity as may be necessary for the fulfilment of its objectives and for the exercise of its functions.[330] For practical purposes, the most important state in this regard is Switzerland where the headquarters of WIPO is situated. To this end, a headquarters agreement was concluded between WIPO and the Swiss Government in 1970, and this regulates the legal position of WIPO under Swiss law.[331]

---

[320] At least eleven of these had been entered into by Directors prior to the Stockholm Act. These generally took the form of an exchange of letters, in which the terms of a working accord were set out. The ones of most relevance to the Berne Union were with the UN, ILO, UNESCO, Council of Europe, and the Pan-American Union. See BIRPI, *Recueil des Accords de Travail entre les BIRPI et les autres organisations internationales* (1967) (WIPO Library).

[321] WIPO Convention, art 13. WIPO also has limited capacity to enter into bilateral or multilateral agreements with member states in matters relating to the discharge of its functions, as well as a headquarters agreement with the Swiss Confederation as the host country: ibid, art 12.

[322] Working Agreement, 22 Sept–12 Oct 1970: [1970] *Copyright* 145. Succeeded by the Agreement of 1974: [1974] *Copyright* 3.

[323] Agreement, 12 Mar 1974: [1974] *Copyright* 63.

[324] Agreement of Cooperation between WIPO and WTO, dated 22 Dec 1995, reproduced in D Gervais, *The TRIPS Agreement: Drafting History and Analysis*, 2nd edn (2004) ('Gervais (2003)'), Annex 8, 467.

[325] Agreement of 1974, art 1. [326] ibid, art 6. [327] ibid, art 3.

[328] ibid, arts 14 and 15. [329] ibid, art 17. [330] WIPO Convention, art 12(1).

[331] The conclusion of such an agreement is required by art 12(2).

C. Finances of the Berne Union

(1) Background

The financial arrangements of the Union were the weakest part of its administrative structure prior to the Stockholm Act, and had remained essentially unchanged from the time of the Berne Act. A ceiling of yearly contributions was fixed, and these were paid by member countries in proportions that were worked out in accordance with a classification system in which states placed themselves in one of six classes.[332] In practice, the Swiss Government, as the supervising power, authorized the expenditures of the Office as they arose, advancing the necessary funds to pay these expenses; it then rendered annual accounts to member countries which paid their dues in accordance with the shares worked out under the classification system.[333] However, the global ceiling of yearly contributions could only be changed by the decision of a conference of revision,[334] and this led to considerable problems in periods of rising costs and inflation. Thus, the limit of 60,000 Swiss francs fixed by the Berne Conference of 1886,[335] and retained by the Berlin Conference in 1908,[336] had become quite inadequate by 1921, and for the years 1921 and 1922 the level of contributions was increased voluntarily to 100,000 Swiss francs at the request of the Swiss Government.[337] At the Rome Conference, the Swiss Government therefore moved to increase the ceiling to 120,000 Swiss francs.[338] This was duly done, but an amendment made at the same time (also at the request of the Swiss Government) made it more difficult for this limit to be increased at future conferences.[339] This amendment required such an increase to be approved by the unanimous decision of a conference of revision, rather than by a simple majority decision as under the earlier Acts.[340] In the years following the Rome Conference, the International Office continued to suffer from a shortage of funds, particularly in consequence of delayed payments of contributions by members.[341] This was obviously a disturbed period, but the problem of defaulting 16.37

[332] Berne Act, Closing Protocol, para 5(7). [333] Bogsch (1986), 311.

[334] Berne Act, Closing Protocol, para 5(6).

[335] ibid, para 5(7). In fact, the level of contributions for the first year of the Office's operation (1888) was only 23,506 Swiss francs, but by 1908 this had increased to 43,847 Swiss francs: see the table of yearly expenses and contributions (1888–1986) in Bogsch (1986), 313.

[336] Berlin Act, art 23(1).

[337] *Actes* 1928, 274. See also the table in Bogsch (1986), 313.

[338] *Actes* 1928, 274. In this regard, it was noted that the share of the total expenses of the two offices by the Berne Office was only 23%.

[339] ibid. [340] Rome Act, art 23(1). Cf Berlin Act, art 23(1).

[341] The table given by Dr Bogsch reveals that in nearly every year there was a gap between the level of expenses incurred by the International Office and the contributions received: Bogsch (1986), 313.

members was raised by the UK Government at the Brussels Conference and ways of penalizing them were discussed (such as publication of names in *Le Droit d'Auteur*).[342] No change in this regard was finally made at the Conference, but the ceiling was altered to 120,000 gold francs.[343] It was also provided that this sum might be subsequently increased by 'the unanimous decision of the countries of the Union'.[344] In the ultimate analysis, these financial arrangements were still unsatisfactory, and left the International Office in a constant state of uncertainty about its financial position. They also involved the Swiss Government, as supervising power, in considerable potential liability as it was required to make (and, in fact, did make) advances to the Office to cover any shortfalls.[345] Thus, in the period 1956 to 1965 the ceiling of contributions was voluntarily raised three times at the request of the Swiss Government.[346] In consequence, the reform of these financial provisions was one of the chief objectives of the Stockholm Revision (bearing in mind that similar situations also arose with respect to the other unions).[347] The changes proposed in the programme were adopted by the Conference, with little alteration. These were accompanied by corresponding changes in the Paris Convention[348] and were linked closely to the financial provisions of the new WIPO Convention.[349]

(2) The present financial provisions

(a) The budget of the Union

16.38 Under article 25(1), the Union has a budget which includes both the income and expenses of the Union. This is distinct and separate from the budgets of the other unions as well as that of WIPO. The expenses of the Union are grouped under three heads.

(i) The 'expenses proper to the Union':[350] In the programme for the Stockholm Conference, the following examples of such expenses were given: the expenses of a meeting relating solely to matters dealing with the Berne Union

[342] *Documents 1948* (1951), 385.

[343] ibid, 387. This was approximately worth 171,400 Swiss francs: Document S/12: *Records* 1967, 565.

[344] Brussels Act, art 23(1). [345] ibid, art 23(5).

[346] The ceilings in force between 1951 and 1967 were as follows (in Swiss francs): 1951–6: 171,000; 1957–61: 231,000; 1962–4: 400,000; 1965: 700,000 (Document S/12, 'Proposals concerning the Ceiling of Contributions in the Paris and Berne Unions', *Records* 1967, 565).

[347] Document S/9: *Records* 1967, 452ff. Until these provisions came into force, the following increases (in Swiss francs) for the years 1968–70 were approved by resolution of the Stockholm Conference: 1968: 800,000; 1969: 900,000; 1970: 1,000,000 (*Records* 1967, 1501).

[348] Paris Act, art 25; Paris Convention, Stockholm Act, art 16.

[349] WIPO Convention, art 11. [350] Paris Act, art 25(1)(b).

and the salaries of employees of the International Bureau solely concerned with Berne Union matters.[351]

(ii) The contributions of the Union to the budget of 'expenses common to the Unions':[352] This expression is defined as 'expenses not attributable exclusively to the Union but also to one or more other Unions administered by the Organization'.[353] The share of the Union in these common expenses is to be 'in proportion to the interest the Union has in them', and parallel provisions are found in the budgetary arrangements of the other unions. Examples of common expenses would be the salary of the Director General of WIPO and other officials who serve all the unions and WIPO as such, the costs relating to the common accounting, mailing, personnel, telephone, typing, and translation services, and the maintenance of the headquarters building in Geneva.[354] In the light of these common expenses, it is specifically provided that the Union budget is to be established with 'due regard to the requirements of coordination with the budgets of the other Unions administered by the Organization'.[355]

(iii) Where applicable, the sum made available to the budget of the WIPO Conference:[356] this is important, as members of the Union do not contribute directly to the budget of WIPO, but only indirectly through the allocation of a sum in the Union budget to the budget of WIPO.[357] This is in accordance with the concept of WIPO as the umbrella organization of all the unions which it serves.

(b) Income of the Union

Unlike the budgetary provisions of the pre-Stockholm texts where reference was made only to the contributions of Union members,[358] the present text now identifies five items of income. **16.39**

(i) 'Contributions of the countries of the Union':[359] The determination of the size of these is discussed below (see para 16.40).

(ii) 'Fees and charges due for services performed by the International Bureau in relation to the Union':[360] Examples of such services might be the furnishing of translations of the texts of laws and other documents.

(iii) 'Sale of, or royalties on, the publications of the International Bureau concerning the Union':[361] There are a number of these, such as commentaries

---

[351] Document S/9: *Records* 1967, 452. [352] Paris Act, art 25(1)(b).
[353] ibid, art 25(1)(c). [354] Document S/9: *Records* 1967, 452.
[355] Paris Act, art 25(1)(b). [356] ibid, art 25(1)(b).
[357] Document S/9: *Records* 1967, 452. See further the WIPO Convention, art 11(2)(b)(i) and Document S/10: *Records* 1967, 520.
[358] Brussels Act, art 23(1). [359] Paris Act, art 25(3)(i). [360] ibid, art 25(3)(ii).
[361] ibid, art 25(3)(iii).

on the Berne Convention, guides and draft model laws, and comparative surveys of national legislation.

(iv) 'Gifts, bequests, and subventions'[362]

(v) 'Rents, interests, and other miscellaneous income'[363]

(c) Level and share of contributions

16.40 There is no longer any ceiling specified in the Convention. The total level of contributions is now fixed in the biennial budgets prepared by the Director General and approved by the Assembly.[364] This system provides far more flexibility than the pre-Stockholm arrangements, and provides an essential underpinning to the control of the Union by its member states. The contribution of each country, however, is still worked out on the basis of the classification system adopted in the Berne Act of 1886, and in 1967 a seventh class was added to the original six. Thus, under article 25(4) of the Stockholm and Paris Acts, each country was required to belong to a class, and its annual contribution was to be assessed on the basis of a number of units fixed as follows:[365]

Class I	25
Class II	20
Class III	15
Class IV	10
Class V	5
Class VI	3
Class VII	1

On ratifying or acceding to the Convention, each country was required to indicate the class to which it was to belong, unless it had already done this.[366] Its annual contribution then equalled 'an amount in the same proportion to the total sum to be contributed to the annual budget of the Union by all countries as the number of its units is to the total of the units of all contributing countries'.[367] In other words, a country in Class VII would be required to contribute 1/25 of the contribution of a country placed in Class I, while a country in Class III would pay 15/25 of the contribution of the Class I country. Thus, if the total number of units for all countries was, for example, 3,000, the share of a

[362] Paris Act, art 25(3)(iv). [363] ibid, art 25(3)(v).

[364] ibid, arts 22(2)(a)(vi) and 23(6)(ii). Prior to 1979, art 23(6)(iii) (now deleted) required also the preparation of specific yearly budgets by the Director General and approval of these by the Executive Committee.

[365] ibid, art 23(4)(a). [366] ibid, art 23(4)(b).

[367] ibid, art 23(4)(c). On the methods of assessment of contributions used in other international organizations, see generally Schermers (n 32 above), 472ff.

country in Class I would be 25/3,000 of the total sum of contributions which had been fixed in the budget, while that of a country in Class VII would only be 1/3,000. This system was intended to take account of the differing financial capacities of countries, and to enable each to determine for itself the class to which it would belong.[368] At the same time, each country was to have an equal voice in the affairs of the Union.[369] Since the Rome Act,[370] countries have been free to change their class, but if they choose a lower class this must be announced to the Assembly at one of its ordinary sessions and this change takes effect at the beginning of the calendar year following the session.[371] The reason for this is to give other member countries reasonable notice of the intended change, as this will mean that each will have to pay a correspondingly higher proportion of the contribution.[372]

As of 1 January 1986 (the first edition of this commentary), there were three countries in Class I,[373] two in Class II,[374] seven in Class III,[375] nine in Class IV,[376] four in Class V,[377] twenty-two in Class VI,[378] and twenty-nine in Class VII.[379] As a matter of historical interest, six of the original signatories of the Convention have remained in the same class they nominated upon their ratification of the Berne Act: France and the UK (Class I), Spain (Class II), Belgium and Switzerland (Class III), and Tunisia (Class IV). Germany, an original member, was also placed in Class I, and the FRG remained in this class although prior to reunification the former GDR was now placed in Class V. Italy, another original signatory which was in Class I, had moved to Class III.[380] In that year (1986), Dr Bogsch, the former Director General of WIPO, noted that the contribution of each Class I member was 5.88 per cent of the total contributions, while that of a Class VII member was 0.24 per cent.[381] He also noted that the question of contributions had been under review by WIPO and its various bodies, pointing

[368] Masouyé (1978), 117.

[369] Paris Act, art 23(3)(a) (Assembly). See further Bogsch (1986), 313–14, on the systems used in the UN and other Specialized Agencies. See further Schermers (n 32 above), 472ff.

[370] Rome Act, art 23(4).

[371] ibid, art 25(4)(b).

[372] Document S/9: *Records* 1967, 454.

[373] France, the FRG, the UK: see table in Bogsch (1986), 312.

[374] Japan, Spain: ibid.

[375] Australia, Belgium, Canada, Italy, the Netherlands, Sweden, Switzerland: ibid.

[376] Brazil, Czechoslovakia, Denmark, Finland, India, Ireland, Mexico, Norway, South Africa: ibid.

[377] GDR, New Zealand, Portugal, Venezuela: ibid.

[378] Argentina, Austria, Bulgaria, Cameroon, Chile, Cote d'Ivoire, Greece, Hungary, Israel, Lebanon, Libya, Madagascar, Morocco, Pakistan, Philippines, Poland, Romania, Senegal, Tunisia, Turkey, Yugoslavia, Zaire: ibid.

[379] Bahamas, Barbados, Benin, Burkina Faso, Central African Republic, Chad, Congo, Costa Rica, Cyprus, Egypt, Fiji, Gabon, Guinea, Holy See, Iceland, Liechtenstein, Luxembourg, Mali, Malta, Mauritania, Monaco, Niger, Rwanda, Sri Lanka, Surinam, Thailand, Togo, Uruguay, Zimbabwe: ibid.

[380] Bogsch (1986), 311 (list of original classifications).

[381] ibid, 312.

to systems of contributions adopted by other UN bodies where these were mainly assessed on the basis of relative wealth of members.[382]

16.41 As of 1 January 1994, the change in the contributions system foreshadowed by Dr Bogsch in 1986 was finally adopted by the WIPO Governing Bodies, including the Berne Union Assembly (fourteenth session) for a trial period of four years, covering the bienniums 1994 to 1995 and 1996 to 1997. This method of 'unitary contributions' replaced the separate contributions of different amounts paid by WIPO members in respect of the 'contribution-financed Unions' to which they belonged.[383] This was intended to simplify the administration of contributions and to provide 'an incentive for state members of fewer than all of the contribution-financed Unions to join additional Unions, since adherence to the additional Unions will not increase the amount of their contributions'.[384] Each state would henceforth pay only one contribution, regardless of however many contribution-financed unions to which it belonged, and the number of classes for contributions was increased to fourteen, with the effect that many developing countries could now be in a lower contribution class then before, it being suggested that there could be a reduction in yearly contributions of as much as 75 per cent.[385] This system of unitary contributions has been maintained to present, with the following classes and units of contribution (indicated in brackets) : I (25), II (20), III (15), IV (10), IV*bis* (7.5), V(5), VI (3), VI*bis* (2), VII (1), VIII (1/2), IX (1/4), S (1/8), S*bis* (1/16), and S*ter* (1/32). As of 15 October 2004, the 181 member states of WIPO were allocated to classes according to this list, and this number obviously includes all the present 159 Berne Union members. So far as the latter are concerned, there have been some movements up (or into) and down (or into) classes as compared with the sevenfold classification in operation in 1986. While the more discerning reader might be moved to think that the classifications do not reflect entirely the relative wealth and capacity to pay of members, the following allocations as between Berne Union members applied at 15 October 2004:[386]

Class I: France, Germany, Japan (up from Class II), United Kingdom, and

[382] Bogsch (1986), 312.

[383] Apart from Berne, there were five other unions established respectively under the Paris Convention for the Protection of Industrial Property, the International Patent Classification Treaty, the Nice Agreement Concerning the International Classification of Goods and Services for the Purposes of the Registration of Marks, Locarno Agreement Establishing an International Classification for Industrial Designs, and the Vienna Agreement Establishing an International Classification of the Figurative Elements of Marks.

[384] Governing Bodies of WIPO, twenty-fourth series of meetings, Geneva, 20–9 Sept 1993: [1993] *Copyright* 273–4.

[385] ibid.

[386] Derived from *Contribution Classes of States Members of WIPO and/or the Paris and/or Berne Unions*, as at 15 Oct 2004: www.wipo.int.

the United States of America (Spain, a former member, has moved to class IV);

Class II: none;

Class III: Australia, Belgium, Italy, the Netherlands, Sweden, Switzerland (unchanged, except for the move of Canada into class IV);

Class IV: Canada, Denmark, Finland, Ireland, Norway, Russian Federation, and Spain;

Class IV*bis* (new): Austria, China, Mexico, and South Africa;

Class V: no members;

Class VI: Greece, Hungary, Poland, and Slovakia;

Class VI*bis*: Brazil, Bulgaria, India, Romania, Turkey;

Class VII: Indonesia, Iran, Luxembourg, Republic of Korea, Saudi Arabia, and Slovenia;

Class VIII (new): Croatia, Holy See, Iceland, Liechtenstein, Malaysia, Serbia and Montenegro, the former Yuogoslav Republic of Macedonia;

Class IX (new): Albania, Andorra, Azerbaijan, Belarus, Chile, Columbia, Estonia, Georgia, Kazakhstan, Kuwait, Kyrgyzstan, Latvia, Lithuania, Paraguay, Republic of Moldova, Singapore, Tajikistan, Thailand, Ukraine, United Arab Emirates, Uzbekistan, Venezuela;

Class S (new): Algeria, Costa Rica, Cuba, Cyprus, Dominican Republic, Ecuador, Egypt, Guatemala, Libya, Morocco, Nigeria, Oman, Pakistan, Philippines, Qatar, Syria, Tunisia and Uruguay;

Class S*bis* (new): Bahamas, Bahrain, Barbados, Belize, Bolivia, Bosnia and Herzegovina, Botswana, Cameroon, Congo, Cote d'Ivoire, Democratic Peoples' Republic of Korea, Dominica, El Salvador, Fiji, Gabon, Ghana, Grenada, Guyana, Honduras, Jamaica, Jordan, Kenya, Lebanon, Malta, Mauritius, Micronesia (Federated States), Mongolia, Namibia, Nicaragua, Panama, Paraguay, Saint Kitts and Nevis, Saint Lucia, Saint Vincent and the Grenadines, Sri Lanka, Suriname, Swaziland, Tonga, Trinidad and Tobago, Vietnam, Zimbabwe;

Class S*ter* (new): Bangladesh, Benin, Bhutan, Burkina Faso, Cape Verde, Central African Republic, Chad, Democratic Republic of the Congo, Djibouti, Equatorial Guinea, Gambia, Guinea, Guinea-Bissau, Lesotho, Liberia, Madagascar, Malawi, Mali, Mauritania, Niger, Rwanda, São Tome and Príncipe, Senegal, Sierra Leone, Sudan, Togo, Tonga, United Republic of Tanzania, and Zambia.

Amendments to article 25(4)(a) in order to bring its text into accordance with the above new system of unitary contributions were adopted by the Berne Assembly in October 2003, using the amendment procedure provided under article 26 (as to which, see para 16.49 below), but had not come into formal operation at the time of writing.[387]

(d) Time for payment of contributions

16.42 This is 1 January of each year,[388] and this is understood to mean the start of each financial year.[389] This represents an important change from the pre-Stockholm position under which countries paid their contributions approximately six months after the close of the financial year.[390] In consequence, this meant that the Union did not receive its contributions until some time after the expenses of that year had been incurred. There was provision for the Swiss Government, as the supervising power, to make advances to cover these shortfalls,[391] but the system placed unnecessary burdens on both the International Office and the Swiss Government. The intention behind the present arrangements is that the contributions are in hand before the expenditure in question is made.

(e) Arrears in payment of contributions

16.43 Prior to the Stockholm Act, there was no sanction which could be applied against states which were in arrears with their contributions. Once again, these shortfalls could be (and were) covered by advances from the Swiss Government.[392] Under the present Act, however, once the amount of arrears equals two years' contributions, the country in question loses its vote in all organs of the Union.[393] It is left open to each organ to suspend this sanction 'if, and as long as, it is satisfied that the delay in payment is due to exceptional and unavoidable circumstances'.[394]

(f) Failure to adopt the budget

16.44 One of the fears of BIRPI, expressed in the debates of Main Committee IV in the Stockholm Conference on the majority needed for decisions of the Assembly, concerned the fate of the budget in the event that the necessary two-thirds majority for its approval was not attained.[395] The solution finally adopted to meet this eventuality provides that, in such a case, the budget for this period will be fixed automatically at the same level as the budget for the preceding year.[396]

---

[387] Assembly of Berne Union, thirty-ninth series of meetings of WIPO Assemblies, Geneva, 22 Sept–1 Oct 2003, General Report, para 167: Document A/39/15. The text of the amendments is in Document A/39/3.

[388] Paris Act, art 25(4)(d).

[389] Document S/9: *Records* 1967, 454. See also Bogsch (1986), 312 and the Financial Regulations of WIPO, arts 1 and 2.

[390] ibid. [391] Brussels Act, art 23(5). See further the table in Bogsch (1986), 313.

[392] ibid. [393] Paris Act, art 25(4)(e). [394] ibid.

[395] *Records* 1967, 1015 (Professor Bodenhausen to Management Committee IV).

[396] Paris Act, art 25(4)(f). A slight change of wording to this has been made in the amendments referred to in para 16.41 above, providing that an errant member shall 'not exercise its vote' rather than 'shall have no vote . . .'.

Thus, there will be no gap in the income of the Union and the level of contributions will be maintained at the same level as in the preceding year.

(g) Fees and charges for services rendered by the Union

These are fixed by the Director General of the Union, who is obliged to report **16.45** them to the Assembly and the Executive Committee.[397] There is no provision for either of these bodies to disapprove of these fees and charges, but the requirement of reporting is clearly intended to ensure that they are kept to reasonable levels.

(h) Working capital fund

Provision was made for this for the first time in the Stockholm Act, and is **16.46** intended to enable the International Bureau to continue operating during the short period between the time when the normal contributions become due and are in fact received.[398] It is constituted by a single payment made by each country of the Union,[399] the amount of which is defined by reference to a proportion of the contribution of each member country for the year in which the fund is established.[400] This proportion and the terms of its payment are fixed by the Assembly on the proposal of the Director General and after it has heard the advice of the Coordination Committee.[401] Likewise, if the fund becomes insufficient, the Assembly is required to fix the amount of any increase.[402] In such a case, the participation of each country in the increase is a proportion of the contribution of that country for the year in which the increase is decided.[403]

(i) Advances by the Swiss Government

The role of the Swiss Government as the financial 'safety net' of the Union still **16.47** remains under the Stockholm and Paris Acts. Thus, the headquarters agreement between WIPO and the Swiss Government provides that whenever the working capital fund is insufficient, the latter will grant advances.[404] The amount of these advances and the conditions on which they are granted are dealt with in separate agreements between the Swiss Government and WIPO.[405] It is in consequence of the assumption of this obligation that the Swiss Government receives its *ex officio* membership of the Executive Committee.[406] However, during the discussions in the 1966 Committee, the Swiss Government requested that this obligation should be renounceable, arguing that it was only necessary for it to be irrevocable

[397] ibid, art 25(5). [398] Bodenhausen (n 7 above), 186.
[399] Paris Act, art 25(6)(a). [400] ibid, art 25(6)(b). [401] ibid, art 25(6)(c).
[402] ibid, art 25(6)(a). [403] ibid, art 25(6)(b).
[404] ibid, art 25(7)(a). This provision requires such a stipulation to be included in the headquarters agreement.
[405] ibid. [406] ibid.

so long as Switzerland remained in its old capacity as supervising power.[407] Provision is therefore made for denunciation of this obligation, and this takes effect three years after the end of the year in which it has been notified.[408]

(j) Auditing of accounts

16.48 This is to be done by one or more of the countries of the Union or by external auditors.[409] At the first ordinary session of the Assembly, the Swiss Government was designated as the auditing power,[410] and has continued to fulfil this role since then.[411] 'Terms of Reference Governing Audit' are contained in the WIPO Financial Regulations that, in turn, are consistent with the audit requirements applied to the UN Specialized Agencies, and are reviewed regularly by the WIPO Governing Assemblies, including the Berne Union Assembly.[412]

D. Special Method of Amendment for Berne Administrative Provisions

16.49 Article 26 provides for a speedier and easier method of amendment of the administrative provisions of the Convention (articles 22 to 26). The reason for this is that it was thought, at the time of the Stockholm Revision, that these provisions were not so important as they did not affect private interests in the same way as the other substantive provisions of the Convention. Amendments to the former, however, might be required urgently to make the administration of the Convention and its organs more efficient.[413] In such cases, it was thought that an easier method of amendment was necessary, and the following procedure was adopted.

(i) **Initiation of amendments:** Proposals for amendments of articles 22 to 26 may be initiated by any country member of the Assembly, by the Executive Committee, or by the Director General.[414] They must be communicated by the

---

[407] Document S/9: *Records* 1967, 456. [408] Paris Act, art 25(7)(b).

[409] ibid, art 25(8). See further the Financial Regulations and the Annexe to these dealing with the terms of reference of the audit.

[410] [1970] *Copyright* 243. In the programme for the Stockholm Conference, it was understood that this would only be until the second ordinary session of the Berne Assembly: Document S/9: *Records* 1967, 456. However, the appointment of the Swiss Government was renewed regularly after this date.

[411] The Swiss Government was most recently reappointed as auditor for all the WIPO Unions until 2007 at the thirty-ninth series of WIPO Assembly Meetings: Document A/39/15, paras 192–5 (22 Sept–1 Oct 2003).

[412] See eg the amended terms of reference concerning external auditors adopted by the thirty-third series of WIPO Assembly meetings in Sept 1998: Document A/33/6 (17 July 1998).

[413] Document S/9: *Records* 1967, 458. [414] Paris Act, art 26(1).

Director General to the member countries of the Assembly at least six months prior to their consideration by that body.[415]

(ii) Adoption of amendments: This may be done by the Assembly by three-quarters of the votes cast;[416] in the case of amendments to article 22 (which concerns the Assembly) and article 26(2) (which concerns the majorities required for the making of amendments to the administrative provisions) a four-fifths majority of the votes cast is required.[417]

(iii) Entry into effect of amendments: Amendments made in the above way do not enter into force until one month after three-quarters of the countries have notified the Director General in writing of their acceptance of the amendment.[418] Once this has happened, the amendment binds all countries which were members of the Assembly at this time as well as all countries which may subsequently become members.[419] However, in the case of any amendment which increases the financial obligations of Union countries, this only binds those countries which notify their acceptance of the amendment.[420]

This procedure was used for the first time in 1979, when the Assembly decided to adopt biennial, instead of triennial, budgets and to hold its ordinary sessions every two years. This involved amendments to articles 22(2)(a)(vi) and (4)(a) and 23(6)(a)(ii) and (iii) which entered into force on 19 November 1984. In actual fact, these amendments were applied from the moment of their adoption, by virtue of unanimous decision of the Assembly.[421] Further amendments to articles 22(4) and 25(1)–(4) were also adopted in 2003 with respect to the periodicity of ordinary sessions of the WIPO assemblies (including Berne) and the formalization of the unitary system of contributions that had been applied since 1994.[422] These amendments, which were adopted by the Berne Assembly at its meeting in September 2003,[423] had not come into force at the time of writing and it may be expected that this will not occur for some time, given the slowness with which member states notify their approval in accordance with the requirements of article 26.

E. Beyond the Berne Convention

(1) The TRIPs Agreement

A brief description of the institutional structures associated with the TRIPs Agreement has already been given (see para 4.39 above). For more detailed 16.50

[415] ibid. [416] ibid, art 26(2). [417] ibid. [418] ibid, art 26(3). [419] ibid.
[420] ibid. [421] Bogsch (1986), 314. [422] WIPO Document A/39/3 (24 Feb 2003).
[423] WIPO Document A/39/15, General Report of 39th series of meetings of WIPO Assemblies, Geneva, 22 Sept–1 Oct 2003, par 167.

examination of these matters, readers are directed to the relevant specialist commentaries.[424]

(2) The WCT

(a) In general

16.51 The WCT has little of the elaborate administrative machinery and none of the financial provisions of the kind found in the Berne Convention, as there is no separate legal entity or 'union' established by the Treaty which is simply an agreement between 'Contracting Parties'. Nonetheless, there is an assembly established under article 15, while the role of the International Bureau of WIPO is dealt with in article 16. These provisions are replicated in articles 24 and 25 respectively of the WPPT.

(b) The WCT Assembly

16.52 (i) **Establishment:** Initially, there was no proposal for the establishment of an assembly for the WCT in the Draft Final Clauses for the new treaty that were submitted to the meeting of the Preparatory Committee that was held on 20 and 21 May 1996.[425] The reason for this, it appears, was concern about the possible membership of the new treaty by the European Union (EU) and its member states. Membership of the EU was desired, but there was the anomaly that the EU could not be a member of the Berne Union and Assembly (see para 16.09 above) and there were also queries about the way in which the EU might exercise its voting rights, in particular whether it would have a vote in its own right in addition to its member states. The Preparatory Committee, however, favoured the establishment of an assembly for the new treaty as a useful forum for periodic review of the treaty and its implementation, while the EU made it clear that it did not expect to have a vote on its own in the assembly but would only wish to exercise the rights of member states in areas where it (the EU) had competence.[426] Accordingly, on the basis of the discussions in the Preparatory Committee, a draft article to establish an assembly for the new treaty was prepared and submitted to the Diplomatic Conference and ultimately adopted, with minimal changes.[427] This is now found in article 15(1)(a) which provides that the contracting parties 'shall have an Assembly', in which each contracting

[424] In particular, see Gervais (2003), Part VII.

[425] Draft Final Clauses of the Treaty to be Considered by the Diplomatic Conference, WIPO Document CRNR/PM/2, 3 Apr 1996, 4, 6, described in Reinbothe and Silke von Lewinski, *The WIPO Treaties 1996* (2002) ('Reinbothe and von Lewinski (2002)'), 177.

[426] Report of the Preparatory Committee, WIPO Document CRNR/PM/8, 24 May 1996, 4, described in Reinbothe and von Lewinski (2002), 178.

[427] Document CRNR/DC/3, 30 Aug 1996, Basic Proposal for the Administrative and Final Clauses of the Treaty to be Considered by the Diplomatic Conference in *Records* 1996, vol I, 133.

party is to be represented by one delegate who may be 'assisted by alternative delegates, advisors and experts'.[428] The expenses of each delegation are to be borne by the contracting party in question, but there is provision for the Assembly to request financial assistance from WIPO to facilitate the participation of delegations from contracting parties that are developing countries or transitional economies, ie former socialist bloc countries that are moving to free-market economies.[429]

(ii) **Functions:** Under article 15(2), the Assembly has three principal functions: 16.53

To 'deal with matters concerning the maintenance and development of this Treaty and the application and operation of this Treaty': article 15(2)(a). This is a similar, but differently worded, obligation to that in article 22(2)(a)(i) of the Berne Convention which requires the Berne Assembly to 'deal with all matters concerning the maintenance and development of the Union and the implementation of this Convention'. The reference in article 15(2)(a) to 'matters concerning the maintenance and development of this Treaty' clearly underlines the primary function of the Assembly as a forum for discussion and consideration of matters relating to the WCT, including identification of problems and gaps, while the words 'deal with' clearly imply that the Assembly can take action with respect to these matters, eg through the formulation of proposals for future action. As for the reference to dealing with matters concerning 'the application and operation of this Treaty', it was noted above (see para 16.10) that the similar wording in article 22(2)(a)(i) of the Berne Convention might imply a power for the Berne Assembly to provide opinions or rulings on the interpretation of provisions of the Berne Convention, although it was also noted there that it was arguable that such an interpretation was not contemplated at the time that provision was inserted in the Stockholm Act. More recently, Dr Ficsor has argued that these words, in relation to the WCT, do include the possibility of the WCT Assembly 'expressing an opinion on what—according to it—is the correct interpretation of this or that given provision'.[430] Whether or not this is a correct characterization of the scope of article 15(2)(a) of the WCT, it is difficult to disagree with Dr Ficsor's further point that the effect of any opinion or view expressed by the Assembly on a matter of Treaty interpretation, at least where this was by consensus, could be regarded as a 'subsequent agreement between the parties regarding the

[428] Article 15(1)(b).

[429] Article 15(1)(c). Reinbothe and von Lewinski note that this assistance is not to be granted automatically or *ex gratia* as a matter purely of WIPO's discretion, but only on the basis of a decision taken by the Assembly on a request to WIPO to this end: Reinbothe and von Lewinski (2002), 184, n 13.

[430] Ficsor (2001), 653.

interpretation of the treaty or the application of its provisions' within the meaning of article 31(3)(a) of the Vienna Convention on the Law of Treaties and would need to be taken into account in the primary task of treaty interpretation under article 31(1) of that instrument.[431]

To perform the function allocated to it under article 17(2) of the WCT with respect to the admission of certain intergovernmental organizations to become party to the Treaty: article 15(2)(b). The criteria for admission that are set under article 17(2) are considered below (see paras 17.95ff).

To decide the convocation of a revision conference for the Treaty and to give the necessary instructions to the Director General of WIPO for the preparations of the conference: article 15(2)(c). This clearly extends the scope of the Assembly's 'maintenance and development' function under article 15(2)(a), and the reference to the Assembly giving the 'necessary instructions' to the WIPO Director General indicates that it is the Assembly that should be the guiding hand in any revision process that is undertaken. As with article 22(2)(a)(ii) of the Berne Convention, this implies that the membership of the Treaty as a whole, acting through the Assembly, should be involved, rather than a host country acting in conjunction with the International Office, as in the pre-Stockholm period.

16.54 **(iii) Voting:** The arrangements here are more complicated, given the possibility that intergovernmental organizations may become contracting parties. The primary position is that each contracting party that is a state has one vote and is to vote only in its name: article 15(3)(a). However, where an intergovernmental organization is a contracting party it may participate in voting in place of its member states, with an equal number of votes to the number of its member states which are party to the WCT: article 15(3)(b). The words 'in place' here are significant, as they indicate clearly that the votes of the intergovernmental organization are 'derived'[432] from those of its members, rather than independent or additional votes exercised by the organization itself. This is underlined by the next requirement of article 15(3)(b) that if any one of its member states 'exercises its right to vote and vice versa', the intergovernmental organization is not to participate in the vote. The intent of the provision seems clear: the intergovernmental organization cannot vote in a situation where any of its member states exercises its right to vote as a sovereign state. Given that the intergovernmental organization, when it does vote, has as many votes as it has member states,

[431] Reinbothe and von Lewinski (2002), 185, para 18, take a similar cautious view of the effect of such interpretations by the Assembly, stating that the latter cannot be considered 'as having the mandate to provide for authentic and binding interpretations of the WCT provisions'.

[432] ibid, 187.

it will then be possible for a dissenting member state of the intergovernmental organization to disenfranchise the other member states, unless they, too, are prepared to vote in their own right (which they can always do under article 15(3)(a)). There is no allowance here for the possibility of the intergovernmental organization exercising the rights of the balance of its member states.[433] The effect of the words 'and vice versa' at the end of article 15(3)(b), however, is not entirely clear. Two commentators, Reinbothe and von Lewinski, state that their effect is that 'with the same logic, a Member State of such an organisation cannot exercise its own voting right, if the intergovernmental organisation that it is a member of casts the vote for it'.[434] Obviously, there cannot be a duplication of voting, with the member state and intergovernmental organization both voting at the same time and having their votes counted. But the effect of the provision appears to be that, in the forum of the Assembly, the member state's vote should be able to trump and, indeed, render ineffective the collective votes of the intergovernmental organization, regardless of whatever internal dissensions or contraventions might have occurred within the intergovernmental organization on the matter in question. The words 'and vice versa' therefore seem better understood as directed to the issue of timing and to imply some requirement of notice by the member state as to its intention to vote. Thus, it should not be open to the member state to decide spontaneously to vote on an issue at the same time as the intergovernmental organization which otherwise would have been entitled to vote on behalf of the member state (along with all other member states). In such a case, only the intergovernmental organization should be able to vote. On the other hand, if the member state had given prior notice of its intention to exercise its vote on the matter in question, the intergovernmental organization would then be disentitled to vote at all, with the resultant disenfranchisement of all of the other non-voting member states referred to above. The repercussions of such an action by a member state would then be a matter for the internal governance of the intergovernmental organization.

A further matter to note in relation to article 15(3)(b) is that the original draft that was put to the Diplomatic Conference contained a requirement that the number of votes exercised by an intergovernmental organization should be both 'equal to the number of its Member States which are party to this Treaty and whose delegates are present at the time the vote is taken'.[435] The 'physical presence' requirement was apparently a matter of some controversy at the

[433] See further the discussions in Main Committee II at the 1996 Diplomatic Conference: *Records* 1996, vol II, 813.

[434] Reinbothe and von Lewinski (2002), 188, para 24.

[435] Document CRNR/DC/3, 30 Aug 1996, Basic Proposal for the Administrative and Final Clauses of the Treaty to be Considered by the Diplomatic Conference in *Records* 1996, vol I, 139, draft art 198(3)(b).

Diplomatic Conference, where it appears the concern was to avoid the possibility of intergovernmental organization voting becoming a kind of *de facto* proxy voting which is otherwise impermissible in WIPO meetings.[436] On the other hand, in the case of the EU, the most immediately relevant intergovernmental organization in this context, it is clear that the latter has its own areas of competence and legislation binding on its member states with respect to matters covered by the WCT, and 'proxy' would be a misdescription of its capacity here. Accordingly, a requirement of physical presence in respect of its member states, when voting on matters in respect of which it has its own competence, would be inconsistent with the internal relations between EU members as well as with the specific recognition given to the EU and other intergovernmental organizations for the purposes of the WCT itself under article 17 (see further para 17.96 below).[437] For these reasons, the requirement of a physical presence was removed from article 15(3)(b) as finally approved by the Diplomatic Conference.[438]

16.55 (iv) **Other matters:** The frequency of Assembly meetings is every two years in ordinary session upon convocation by the Director General of WIPO: article 15(4). At the date of writing, the first ordinary session of the Assembly was held in 2003, as part of the thirty-ninth series of meetings of WIPO assemblies,[439] with the next ordinary session scheduled for 2005. Unlike the Berne Assembly, which has specific rules in article 22(3) specifying such matters as the convocation of extraordinary sessions, quorum requirements and the majorities required for particular decisions, these are left as matters for the WCT Assembly to determine through its own rules of procedure: article 15(5). It has been remarked that the Assembly's discretion here cannot be 'unlimited', in the sense that the Berne provisions on these matters should 'at least serve as a guideline' to the rules adopted by the WCT Assembly, on the basis that the Berne rules themselves were only adopted after intensive discussions.[440] However, it also seems clear that the WCT Assembly's rule-making power goes beyond the matters of extraordinary sessions, quorums, and majorities, as these are only referred to inclusively in article 15(5). Other matters that could be covered by the rules would be the conduct of proceedings, the admission of observers, and notice requirements. The limiting factor, however, would be that these were only matters of a procedural nature, and it would not be open to the Assembly here to adopt rules that had the effect of modifying or abridging other specific stipulations of article 15, such as those in relation to voting rights under article 15(3).[441]

436 See further Reinbothe and von Lewinski (2002), 180–1. 437 ibid.

438 *Records* 1996, 814, para 81 (Main Committee II).

439 WIPO Document A/39/15 (1 Oct 2003).

440 Reinbothe and von Lewinski (2002), 189, para 26.

441 In this regard, Reinbothe and von Lewinski (ibid, 189) note that it would be impermissible here for the Assembly to reintroduce a 'presence' requirement for voting under art 15(3)(b), on

(c) *International Bureau*

Under article 16, it is provided that the International Bureau of WIPO shall perform the administrative tasks concerning the Treaty. This provision appeared for the first time only in the Basic Proposal concerning final and administrative clauses that was presented to the Diplomatic Conference,[442] as prior to this there had not been any proposals for the establishment of an assembly: see para 16.52 above. The only explanatory note accompanying the Basic Proposal draft was that this 'follows a tradition established in several WIPO-administered treaties' and there was no substantive discussion of it during the Diplomatic Conference. **16.56**

For present purposes, there is little more to be said about article 16, other than to say that the issue of what are the 'administrative tasks concerning the treaty' will follow from a consideration of what is required under article 15 in relation to the Assembly (clearly, WIPO is to provide the necessary administrative and logistical support for the convocation and conduct of these meetings and those of sub-committees and other working groups, the preparation of documentation and translations, etc, and any other reports or action that may be required by the Assembly). Furthermore, it should be noted that the Director General of WIPO, the official ultimately responsible for WIPO, is also given certain formal functions under the WCT,[443] functions that will presumably be carried out in practice by other officials of that organization. These include that of 'depositary of this Treaty' under article 25 for the purpose of receiving signatures under article 19, ratifications or accessions under article 20, and denunciations under article 23.[444] In addition, under article 24(2) the Director General is required, 'on the request of an interested party' to 'establish' official texts of the Treaty in languages other than the 'authentic versions' referred to under article 24(1). (The requirements of article 24 are discussed in more detail at para 17.104 below.)

(d) *Financial provisions (or the lack thereof)*

The short point to be made here is that contracting parties to the WCT have no financial obligations of the kind found under article 25 of the Berne Convention. As noted above, participation in the Assembly is at each contracting party's **16.57**

---

the basis that such a requirement was originally included in the Basic Proposal but was not adopted by the Diplomatic Conference: see further para 16.53 above.

[442] Document CRNR/DC/3, 30 Aug 1996, Basic Proposal for the Administrative and Final Clauses of the Treaty to be Considered by the Diplomatic Conference in *Records* 1996, vol I, 139, draft art 199.

[443] Reinbothe and von Lewinski (2002), 191, para 7, refer to these aptly as 'status-related tasks'.

[444] Note further the requirements of arts 76–7 of the Vienna Convention on Treaties, with respect to the functions of depositaries, including the general duty of act impartially (art 76(2)).

own expense: see article 15(1)(c). On the other hand, the administrative expenses of holding and supporting Assembly meetings will be borne by WIPO in the first place as the body responsible for performing the administrative tasks concerning the Treaty. While WIPO membership is not a prerequisite for joining the WCT, in practice it can be expected that this will almost always be the case, with the consequence that contracting parties will contribute to the expenses involved with the WCT through their WIPO membership contributions.

(3) The WPPT

16.58 Although consideration of this instrument is left to another chapter of this commentary (see generally Chapter 19 below), it can be noted briefly here that articles 24 and 25 of the WPPT which deal respectively with the WPPT Assembly and the International Bureau under that treaty are in identical terms to articles 15 and 16 of the WCT. Accordingly, the above commentary on the latter provisions is equally applicable.

17

MEMBERSHIP, TERRITORY, AND APPLICATION OF THE BERNE CONVENTION AND LATER AGREEMENTS (THE FINAL CLAUSES)

A. Introduction

17.01 In this chapter, we are concerned with the 'final clauses' of the Berne Convention and the later agreements. These cover a miscellany of matters, but are primarily concerned with questions of membership (eligibility and obligations) and the territorial application of each convention. As it is the oldest of the conventions, most of our discussion will focus on the Berne Convention, but interesting issues also arise with respect to the World Intellectual Property Organization ('WIPO') Copyright Treaty ('WCT'), the WIPO Performances and Phonograms Treaty ('WPPT'), and the Agreement on Trade-Related Aspects of Intellectual Property Rights 1994 ('TRIPs Agreement').

B. The Berne Convention

(1) Membership and territory of the Union

17.02 When the first edition of this commentary was written (on the centenary of the Convention), the membership of the Convention had changed extensively since

1886, but with the strange consequence that, while the number of Union members had increased over sevenfold in this time, the territory of the Union has not been significantly enlarged. Nearly twenty years on, membership has doubled again, while the reach of the Convention is nearly universal, with the accession of three of the largest nations (USA, China, and the Russian Federation). As will be seen below, the matter of membership raises some complex issues of international law, particularly in relation to the question of state succession. The relevant articles of the Paris Act which regulate these questions are: article 28, which is concerned with ratification of the Act by existing members of the Union; article 29, which is concerned with accessions by non-Union states; article 30, which deals with the reservations that may be made by countries ratifying or acceding to the Act; article 31, which is concerned with the application of the Act to dependent territories; and article 35, which is concerned with denunciations of the Convention. The territorial extent of the Union is closely related to these provisions, and is dealt with here as well.

(2) Ratification and accession

(a) In general

The provisions of the Convention concerning ratification and accession have become more detailed with each successive revision. In a formal sense, it is necessary to distinguish between the acts of ratification and accession, although the legal consequences of both are the same, in the sense that each results in a state becoming bound by the treaty in question.[1] The first of these is the act by which a state confirms that it will be bound by an instrument which it has signed. A time is usually fixed for this, as well as a place for the deposit of the ratification and the person who will act as the depository (usually a government or international organization). By contrast, the second is the act by which a state indicates its intention to be bound by an instrument which it has not signed, that is, an Act to which it was not originally a party. Its capacity to make such an act of accession will, of course, depend upon whether this is provided for in the agreement itself, but this is a common feature of many multilateral conventions, including the Berne Convention under which accession has always been open to any state which has been prepared to give effect to the provisions of the Convention (see further para 17.17 below). In a practical sense, the distinction between ratification and accession may be of some importance. A state which has been party to the making of an international agreement has had the opportunity to influence the shape and content of the provisions of that agreement. On the **17.03**

[1] See art 11 of the Vienna Convention on the Law of Treaties 1969 (the 'Vienna Convention'), which treats each of the acts of signature, exchange of instruments, ratification, approval, and accession as being effective to constitute consent by a state to be bound to a treaty.

other hand, a state which has not been a party to an agreement can usually only approach it on a 'take it or leave it' basis. Furthermore, while a signatory state may be given the capacity, by the instrument in question, to make its ratification subject to conditions or reservations, this capacity may be limited or denied completely in the case of a state which accedes subsequently (see further para 17.22 below). As a consequence, there may be considerable differences between the status of signatory and non-signatory states.

(b) The early Acts

17.04 These matters were dealt with in different ways under successive Acts of the Berne Convention. As an invariable rule, ratification within a particular period of time or by a particular number of states has been made the criterion for the initial entry into force of each Act. Thus, the Berne and Paris Additional Acts provided for their ratification within a year of signature and for their entry into force three months after this,[2] while under the Berlin, Rome, and Brussels Acts specific dates for these events were stipulated.[3] Furthermore, under each, there was provision for accession by non-Union states, although this accession was ineffective unless the Act was already in force among the ratifying states.[4] Under the Berlin and Rome Acts, however, a gap existed in relation to countries which were already members of the Union but failed to ratify these Acts within the specified time. There was no provision for these countries to make a subsequent ratification or to accede in the same way as non-Union states, although it was provided that these states remained bound by the Acts previously in force (see further paras 17.69ff below).[5] In practice, this omission did not prevent these states from adhering to the new Act after the time for ratification. These subsequent acts of adhesion were simply treated as accessions by the International Office, and there were no objections to this from other Union members.[6] Under the Brussels Act, however, this gap was covered by a specific provision to the effect that, after the time for ratification had passed (1 July 1951), Union countries which had not ratified the Act by that date might thereafter accede to it in the same way as non-Union states.[7] However, accession by a Union country in these circumstances did not differ from ratification in that such a country was permitted to retain the benefit of any reservations it had made under earlier

---

[2] Berne Act, art 20; Paris Additional Act, art 4.

[3] Berlin Act, art 28(1) (no later than 1 July 1910); Rome Act, art 28(1) (no later than 1 July 1931); Brussels Act, art 28(1) (no later than 1 July 1951).

[4] Berne Act, art 18; Berlin, Rome, and Brussels Acts, art 25(1). Note, however, that accession to the Paris Additional Act was only open to Union countries which were not parties to that Act: art 3.

[5] See eg Berlin, Rome, and Brussels Acts, art 27(1).

[6] See eg the accession by France to the Rome Act on 22 Dec 1933: [1933] *DA* 133.

[7] Brussels Act, art 28(3).

Acts[8] (by contrast, the capacity for reservations by non-Union states was extremely limited: see further paras 17.25–17.26 below). Similar treatment was also accorded, under the Rome and Brussels Acts, to Union members which had failed to sign those Acts altogether: these states were permitted subsequently to accede to these Acts while retaining the benefit of any prior reservations.[9] This facility preserved the position of a number of important Union members, notably that of Germany which was not represented at the Brussels Revision Conference.

(c) Adherence to the Stockholm and Paris Acts by Union countries

The provisions of the Stockholm and Paris Acts concerning ratification and accession are more complex than those in the earlier Acts. The same distinction is drawn between ratification and accession by Union and non-Union countries respectively, but the provisions relating to the first category also provide for the possibility of adhesion to different parts of the Convention at different points in time. In this regard, the provisions of article 28 of the Paris Act are largely modelled upon those of the Stockholm Act, and have already been referred to in Chapter 14 above. In substance, they provide as follows. **17.05**

(i) Any Union country which has signed the Paris Act may ratify it, or, if it has not signed it, may accede to it:[10] These instruments of ratification or accession are to be deposited with the Director General.[11] This system differs from that adopted under the Brussels Act (see para 17.04 above), in that a Union country which has signed the Paris Act may later ratify it at any time, whereas under the earlier Act such a country had to make an act of accession once the due date for ratification had passed. In a strict sense, this is a more correct use of terminology than in the Brussels Act, as there is no reason why the signature of an instrument, once made, cannot be ratified at any later time, whenever this may be. Such signature is clear evidence of that country's future intention to accept the Act, but, in many countries, particularly those where treaties are not received directly into municipal law, it may take these countries considerable time to bring their domestic law into conformity with what is required by the new Act. This was certainly true of the UK where this process took eight years before that country acceded to the Brussels Act,[12] and the FRG

[8] ibid. [9] Rome and Brussels Acts, art 27(3). [10] Paris Act, art 28(1)(a).

[11] ibid. This provision reflected the constitution of the new international organization known as WIPO, which henceforth was able to act as the depository for all ratifications, accessions, and other notifications that were required to be made under the Convention. Prior to this, ratifications had been deposited at the place where the particular revision conference had been held (eg Berlin, Rome, or Brussels), but the Swiss Government, as supervising power of the International Office, had received all other communications and had the general obligation of informing Union members of these: see eg Brussels Act, art 28(1).

[12] 15 Dec 1957: [1957] *DA* 225.

where nearly seventeen years elapsed.[13] On the other hand, the term 'accession' is more correctly applied to a Union country which has not signed the Act (usually because it has not been present at the conference in question), as such a country is in a similar position to that of a non-Union country which wishes to adhere to the Convention. In this respect, the Paris Act continues the practice adopted in the Rome and Brussels Acts, treating this as an accession while allowing such states to retain the benefit of any prior reservations.[14]

(ii) Limited ratification or accession: Now of mainly historical interest in view of the numbers that have ratified or acceded to the whole of the Paris Act and Appendix, ratification or accession by Union countries may be limited so as not to apply to articles 1 to 21 and the Appendix.[15] This must be done by a declaration in the instrument of ratification or accession, and continues the system originally adopted in the Stockholm Act in relation to the Protocol Regarding Developing Countries.[16] It should be noted that this provision gives a Union country the choice only of accepting or refusing articles 1 to 21 and the Appendix *en bloc*: it cannot refuse to accept some of these provisions while accepting others. Such an interpretation, however, was feasible on the draft of article 28(1) that was included in the programme for the Paris Conference,[17] and directions were given to the drafting committee by the Main Committee of the Conference to avoid such a result.[18] In the event that a country has previously made a declaration under article VI(1) of the Appendix (admitting the application of the Appendix before that country actually becomes bound by those provisions), it may only limit its subsequent instrument of ratification or accession so as not to apply to articles 1 to 21.[19] In other words, such a country, having already admitted the application of the Appendix, cannot withdraw this admission. This provision applies to three Union countries which made declarations under article VI(1) of the Appendix: the FRG,[20] Norway,[21] and the UK.[22]

(iii) Extension of ratification or accession: Any Union country which has excluded articles 1 to 21 and the Appendix from the effect of its ratification or accession may, at any subsequent time, extend the effect of its ratification or accession to those provisions. This can be done simply by the making of a declaration which is to be deposited with the Director General.[23]

[13] 10 Dec 1966: [1966] *Copyright* 242. [14] Paris Act, art 30(2)(a).
[15] ibid. [16] Stockholm Act, art 28(1)(b).
[17] The offending paragraph was art 28(1)(c): *Records* 1971, 56 (Document B/DC/5).
[18] ibid, 142. [19] Paris Act, art 28(1)(b).
[20] 18 Oct 1973: [1973] *Copyright* 214 (note, however, that the FRG became bound by arts 1–20 and the Appendix when these came into force on 10 Oct 1974).
[21] 8 Mar 1974: [1974] *Copyright* 65. [22] 27 Sept 1971: [1971] *Copyright* 189.
[23] Paris Act, art 28(1)(c).

(d) Entry into force

The provisions governing this are also complicated. Under earlier Acts, the general position was that the Act would come into force, among those countries which had ratified it, at a fixed time (usually one or three months) after the date fixed for ratification.[24] Under the Rome and Brussels Acts, it was also provided that this could occur earlier, if, before this date, the Convention had been ratified by six Union members: in this event, the Act entered into force one month after the deposit of the sixth ratification.[25] Under the Paris Act, the applicable provisions reflect the terms of the 'package deal' agreed between developed and developing countries at the Paris Conference of 1971, and are as follows. **17.06**

(i) **Three months after the fulfilment of two conditions:** Articles 1 to 21 and the Appendix were to enter into force three months after the fulfilment of both the following conditions: (i) ratification by at least five Union countries without making a declaration under article 28(1)(b), that is, a declaration that their ratification was not to apply to articles 1 to 21 and the Appendix; and (ii) the following four countries became bound by the revised Universal Copyright Convention ('UCC'): France, Spain, the UK, and the USA.[26]

This entry into force applied to each Union country which, at least three months before this event, had deposited an instrument of ratification or accession without making a declaration under article 28(1)(b).[27] These twin conditions were satisfied on 10 July 1974 on which date some seven Union members had ratified the Paris Act unconditionally and the four countries in question had become bound by the revised text of the UCC.[28] Accordingly, articles 1 to 21 and the Appendix entered into force with respect to these seven Union members on 10 October 1974.[29]

(ii) **Subsequent ratification or accession without limitation:** In the case of a Union country which subsequently ratifies or accedes to the Act without limiting that ratification or accession under article 28(1)(b), articles 1 to 21 and the Appendix enter into force three months from the date on which the Director General notifies the governments of all Union countries of the deposit with him of the relevant instrument of ratification or accession.[30] Does this mean the date

---

[24] Berne Act, art 20 (three months after exchange of ratifications); Paris Additional Act, art 4(3) (same); Berlin Act, art 29 (same); Berne Additional Protocol, art 5 (one month after ratification).

[25] Rome and Brussels Acts, art 28(2).

[26] Paris Act, art 28(2)(a).

[27] ibid, art 28(2)(b).

[28] These countries were Cameroon, France, the FRG, Hungary, Ivory Coast, Spain, and Sweden: [1974] *Copyright* 156.

[29] ibid.

[30] Paris Act, art 28(2)(c).

on which the Director General sends off his notifications, or the date on which these have been received by all Union members? No indication as to which of these alternatives is correct is to be found in the records of the Paris Conference. However, given the difficulties of ascertaining the date of receipt under the second, common sense indicates that the relevant date must be that on which the notifications are dispatched.[31] It is also open to a country to nominate in its instrument of ratification or accession a 'subsequent date' for the application to it of articles 1 to 21 and the Appendix.[32] The adjective 'subsequent' here clearly means 'subsequent to the date on which the Director General notifies the deposit of the instrument of ratification or accession'.

(iii) The application of article VI of the Appendix: It is provided that neither of the preceding provisions affect the application of article VI of the Appendix.[33] Thus, the fact that articles 1 to 21 and the Appendix have now come into force does not affect the application of the Appendix by a country which has made a declaration under article VI but has not deposited an instrument of ratification or accession with respect to these provisions.

(iv) Articles 22 to 38: As for these articles no conditions were set for them to enter into force. Accordingly, this happens with respect to any Union country which ratifies or accedes to the Paris Act either three months after the Director General has notified other Union countries of the deposit of its instrument of ratification or accession or on any subsequent date which that country has indicated in its instrument.[34] The entry into force of these provisions is unaffected by any limitation that the country in question may have made concerning articles 1 to 21 and the Appendix. For the first fifteen years of or after the Paris Act was negotiated, relatively few countries, in fact, took advantage of the faculty provided under the Paris Act to adhere only to articles 22 to 38. As of 1 January 1986, there were only ten Union members out of the then membership of seventy-six which had chosen to do this,[35] while there were thirteen states which were bound by articles 22 to 38 of the Stockholm Act which are broadly the same.[36] This meant that the great majority of Union members were then bound by the same provisions concerning the administration and finances of the Union. As at January 2005, with 159 member states, there were only six

[31] This has been the invariable practice of WIPO in relation to ratifications and accessions under the Paris Act: see generally *Copyright* for the period 1973–80.

[32] Paris Act, art 28(2)(c). [33] ibid, art 28(2)(d). [34] ibid, art 28(3).

[35] Argentina, Bahamas, Iceland, Malta, Norway, Philippines, South Africa, Sri Lanka, Thailand, and Zimbabwe: [1986] *Copyright* 6–8.

[36] Belgium, Canada, Chad, Fiji, Finland, Ireland, Israel, Liechtenstein, Morocco, Pakistan, Romania, Switzerland, and the UK: [1986] *Copyright* 6–8.

states that remained bound by articles 22 to 38 of Paris[37] and three by articles 22 to 38 of Stockholm.[38]

(e) Adherence to the Paris Act by non-Union countries

This is covered by article 29 which provides simply for accession by countries outside the Union by the deposit of an instrument of accession with the Director General.[39] There is no possibility of accession to part only of the Act: such a country is required to accept the whole Act, including the Appendix. The Act enters into force either three months after the Director General has notified other Union countries of the accession, or on any subsequent date that is indicated in the instrument of accession.[40] The effect of accession is to make the country in question 'a party to the Convention and a member of the Union'.[41] This is a significant point, as it is possible for a country to be one 'to which this Convention applies' and thus a part of the Union, without being either a party to the Convention or a member of the Union. (This has already been referred to in para 5.76 above, and is considered further at para 17.45 below in relation to former colonial and dependent territories of Union members.) **17.07**

(f) The status of earlier Acts

Given the small numbers of states that now remain outside the Berne Union, or which, being members, remain bound by earlier Acts of the Convention, this next section is of decreasing practical importance. Nevertheless, the provisions to be discussed are critical in 'closing off' earlier Acts of the Convention and ensuring that the Paris Act becomes the prevailing text throughout the Union, and therefore continue to require careful consideration in the present treatise. Under article 34(1) of the Paris Act, it is provided that no country can accede to earlier Acts of the Convention once articles 1 to 21 and the Appendix have entered into force, that is, after 10 October 1974. Article 34(2) further provides that, following this date, it is no longer possible for a country to make a declaration under article 5 of the Protocol of the Stockholm Act, that is, a declaration which applies, or accepts the application of, the Protocol to that country in advance of its entry into force (an event that never, in fact, occurred, and, under this provision, can no longer do so). The intended effect of these provisions is to close off all earlier Acts of the Convention, and this 'closure' is intended to apply equally to Union and non-Union countries. However, it is important to note that this prohibition does not affect the continued application of these Acts to **17.08**

[37] These were all members of the 1986 list, namely Argentina, Bahamas, Malta, South Africa, Sri Lanka, and Zimbabwe: www.wipo.int.

[38] These, again, were all members of the 1986 list, namely Chad, Fiji, and Pakistan: www.wipo.int.

[39] Paris Act, art 29(1).

[40] ibid, art 29(2)(a).

[41] ibid, art 29(1).

those countries which previously ratified or acceded to them and which have not yet ratified or acceded to the Paris Act. The application of these Acts is expressly preserved by article 32, which also provides that these Acts may continue to govern the Conventional relations between these states and those states which have ratified or acceded to the Paris Act (see further paras 17.69ff below). The relationship between articles 32 and 34 gives rise to some difficulties and these are explored further below. However, the intended effects of article 34 can be stated as follows. As of 10 October 1974, a country which is bound by the Rome or Berlin Act can no longer increase its Conventional obligations in stages by acceding first to the Brussels Act and then subsequently to the Paris Act. It must make an election to accede to the Paris Act or to remain bound by the Rome Act. The same restriction applies to non-Union countries: these have no choice as to the 'level' at which they can join the Convention and must either accede to the Paris Act or continue to remain outside the Union. The following justifications for these limitations can be advanced.

First, as far as Union countries are concerned, the requirement of unanimity for revisions of the Convention means that, once a new revision has been made, this represents the latest thinking of all Union members on the subject of international copyright protection. It would therefore be anomalous to allow these states to have the continued faculty of acceding to earlier Acts which, by definition, have been superseded by the new Act. It would be equally anomalous to allow non-Union countries to accede to earlier Acts which no longer reflect the latest views of member countries on the desirable level of international copyright protection.[42]

The second justification is that if accession to earlier Acts is permitted, this will clearly delay the general acceptance of the new Act and will serve to confuse further the already complex relationships that exist between member countries that are bound by different Acts of the Convention.[43]

However, while these justifications may be defended as a matter of policy, it is not completely certain that article 34 achieves these stated effects. This requires a further examination of the background to article 34, as well as a consideration of the effect of article 32.

17.09 (i) **Background to article 34**: The Convention has contained a provision concerning the closure of earlier Acts since the Rome Act, although the problem theoretically arose in the case of the Berlin Act which was the first revision of the Convention to result in an entirely new Act. While article 27 of the latter Act

[42] See further Document S/9 for the Stockholm Conference: *Records* 1967, 476.
[43] ibid.

stated that, as between contracting states, it was to replace the Berne and Paris Additional Acts, the operation of these earlier Acts was preserved with respect to those states which did not ratify the Berlin Act and there was no express prohibition on accession to these Acts by non-Union states. Such a prohibition, however, was hardly necessary, in view of the generous reservations which non-Union states were permitted to make upon accession to the Berlin Act. Thus, article 25 permitted these states to indicate which of the provisions of the Berne or Paris Additional Acts they thought 'necessary to substitute, provisionally at least, for the corresponding provisions of the present Convention'. Accordingly, there was no advantage for a non-Union country to seek to join the Union by accession to the Berne and Paris Additional Acts, and, following the Berlin Act, no state sought to do so. As the same scope for reservations was accorded to existing Union members,[44] by the time of the Rome Revision Conference there were no longer any members of the Union that were bound by the Berne and Paris Additional Acts only.

The issue of closure arose directly at the Rome Conference, where the need for it **17.10** became more obvious. One of the aims of this revision was to reduce the scope for reservations under the Convention, and this was achieved, at least partially, in articles 25(3) and 27(2) of the Rome Act. The first of these provisions restricted non-Union countries to reservations concerning translation rights, while the second permitted Union countries to retain those reservations which they had already made under earlier Acts (see further para 17.25 below). In the case of non-Union countries, it will be clear that there was now an advantage to be obtained if it continued to be possible for them to accede to the Berlin Act alone after the entry into force of the Rome Act. This would not only absolve them from having to comply with the increased requirements of the Rome Act with respect to such matters as the protection of moral rights and broadcasting rights. It would also permit them to take advantage of the generous reservations system of the Berlin Act and apply the even less rigorous requirements of the Berne and Paris Additional Acts, for example, in relation to retroactivity and exceptions to protection. In view of this, the commission at the Rome Conference decided to close off accessions to the Berlin Act by non-Union countries once the Rome Act had entered into force.[45] The latter event was to occur no later than 1 August 1931, this being one month after the date set for ratification, but it was also provided this might happen earlier, namely one month after the sixth ratification, if six ratifications of the Act had been deposited before 1 July 1931.[46] However, the commission decided to set the closure date for accession to the Berlin Act at 1 August 1931, even in the event that the Rome Act had

[44] Berlin Act, art 27(2). [45] Rome Act, arts 280–1. [46] ibid, 281.

entered into force at an earlier date.[47] The reason for this decision is a curious footnote to the history of the Berne Convention, as it arose out of a request from the US observer who had declared the intention of his country's government to accede to the Convention. However, at this stage, the USA felt that it could only adhere to the Berlin Act, and it explained that the necessary Congressional approval for this would be difficult to obtain before 1931.[48] Accordingly, the deadline of 1 August 1931 was set purely to accommodate the USA, which ultimately was unable to take advantage of this extension of time. Several other states, however, did do so, including Yugoslavia which acceded to the Berlin Act on 17 June 1930,[49] Thailand on 17 July 1931,[50] and Liechtenstein on 30 July 1931.[51] There was also a purported accession by Turkey on 20 June 1931, which is discussed further below (see para 17.18).

17.11 The closure provision of the Rome Act (article 28(3)) was repeated in the Brussels Act (also article 28(3)), where it was provided that, up to 1 July 1951, non-Union countries might accede to either the Rome or Brussels Act, but from that date they could accede only to the Brussels Act. This left the technical possibility that a Union country which was bound only by the Berlin Act might still accede to the Rome Act after this date. There were, in fact, two situations to be considered here. The first concerned a country which had signed the Rome Act, but had not ratified it within the prescribed time under article 28(1) of that Act. No express provision was made in that Act for subsequent accessions by such countries, although in practice these were accepted by the Swiss Government (the depository government) and were not objected to by other Union members.[52] After 1 July 1951, however, it would have been open to the Swiss Government to refuse a purported accession from such a country to the Rome Act, and for other Union members to refuse to acknowledge its validity. The basis for these refusals would have been (i) that there was no provision for subsequent ratification or accession by Union countries in the Rome Act itself, and (ii) that the practice before 1 July 1951 was a necessary one that had been adopted in order to achieve the largest possible number of adherences to the Rome Act, but that this necessity had completely disappeared with the entry into force of the Brussels Act. In the second situation, however, a different result obtained. This was the case of a country bound by the Berlin Act which had not signed the Rome Act: under article 27(3) of the latter instrument, such a country was permitted to 'adhere to' the Convention 'at any time'. As a result, there seemed to be no reason why such a country should not be able to accede to the Rome Act after 1 July 1951. With the exception of a number of 'declarations of

[47] ibid. [48] ibid.

[49] [1930] *DA* 85. This country also adhered to the Rome Act at the same time.

[50] [1931] *DA* 85. [51] ibid. [52] See n 6 above.

continued adherence' to the Rome Act which have been made after this date by newly independent states (see further para 17.58 below), no purported accessions to the Rome Act were made by states falling into this second category. However, there was one state that, in theory, was in a position to do so. This was Thailand which did not sign the Rome Act, although it was present at the Rome Conference in an observer capacity, and acceded to the Berlin Act before the deadline of 1 August 1931.

(ii) The Stockholm Revision Conference: By the time of this Conference, another problem concerning article 28(3) of the Brussels Act had become apparent: if non-Union states could no longer adhere to the Rome Act, this meant they did not have any text in common with those member states of the Union which were bound only by that Act or the Berlin Act.[53] This problem was addressed in the programme for the Stockholm Conference where the view was taken that the effect of article 28(3) of the Brussels Act went further than had been intended, in allowing non-Union countries to accede only to the Brussels Act after 1 July 1951. It was further stated that the desirable aim was rather that these states should not be allowed to accede 'only to Acts earlier than the Act resulting from the most recent revision'. On the other hand, they should be allowed to accede to earlier Acts where they did so at the same time they acceded to the most recent Act. The reason for this was quite simple: **17.12**

> . . . because otherwise there might be no substantive copyright link between a country acceding to the Stockholm Act and a country which is still bound only by one or more Acts earlier than the Stockholm Act. The lack of substantive copyright link would mean, of course, that there is no guarantee, flowing from membership in the Berne Union, that works of which one of these countries was the country of origin would receive copyright protection in the other country.[54]

In consequence, the programme proposed the adoption of the following provision:

> After the entry into force of this Act in its entirety, a country may accede to earlier Acts of this Convention only in conjunction with ratification of, or accession to, this Act.[55]

This proposal raised important questions going right to the basis of relations between Union members that are parties to different Acts of the Union, but was withdrawn by BIRPI and the Swedish Government without any clear reason for this change being given. In its place, the following provision was proposed and adopted by the Conference as article 34 of the Stockholm Act:

[53] eg the Philippines, which adhered to the Brussels Act on 1 Aug 1951: [1950] *DA* 97, had no text in common with New Zealand which remained bound by the Rome Act.

[54] Document S/9: *Records* 1967, 476. [55] ibid, 477.

> After the entry into force of this Act in its entirety, a country may not accede to earlier Acts of this Convention.[56]

In the view of BIRPI and the Swedish Government, this simply preserved the essence of article 28(3) of the Brussels Act, giving states the option of acceding to either the Brussels or Stockholm Act, or both, before the entry into force of the latter, just as article 28(3) had permitted a period of grace for states to accede to either the Rome or Brussels Act.[57] Nevertheless, there were significant differences between the two provisions. First, article 34 of the Stockholm Act was potentially open-ended, as no precise date was set for the entry into force of that Act (unlike article 28(3) of the Brussels Act which set a definite deadline). Secondly, article 34 spoke generally of 'a country' and could therefore include Union members as well as non-Union countries, while article 28(3) was clearly confined to the second category. However, the most puzzling aspect of this change is the failure of BIRPI and the Swedish Government to give any reason for withdrawing their original proposal. The answer to this does not emerge clearly from the Conference records, but must be linked to the extensive discussions which took place in relation to the provision that became article 32 and which dealt with relations between member states who were parties to different texts of the Convention. This matter is considered in detail below,[58] but it suffices to note, for our present purposes, that there was a lack of consensus among delegates as to the exact legal basis for these relations, in particular when Union members were not party to a common text. In this regard, the original programme proposal for article 34 would have embodied a clear solution to these matters, but at the risk of causing considerable disruption to the Convention. Thus, if such a provision were necessary, this would have implied that there was a gap under earlier Acts, with the result that difficult questions as to the availability of protection in one country vis-à-vis another would have arisen. The withdrawal of the original proposal for article 34 obviously avoided this threatened disentanglement of inter-Union relations, but the question of the basis for these relations still remains unsettled and is discussed below in relation to article 32. As for article 34 of the Stockholm Act, this was retained in the same form in article 34 of the Paris Act, with the addition of paragraph (2) concerning declarations under article 5 of the Stockholm Protocol.

17.13 **(iii) Effect of article 34:** Does article 34, in fact, achieve its aim of preventing countries from adhering to earlier Acts of the Convention in lieu of adherence to the Paris Act? This question is now of much more limited practical significance

[56] ibid, 487.

[57] ibid. Note here the precedent of Yugoslavia which, in 1931, before the closure of the Berlin Act, had acceded to both the Berlin and Rome Acts: [1930] *DA* 85.

[58] See paras 17.69ff.

than at the time of the first edition of this commentary when a great many countries still remained outside the Union, but the same issue would again move centre stage in the future if there was a revision of the Paris Act and the adoption of a new text. The issue for consideration arises as follows.

Each successive Act of the Convention has been stated to remain in force without limitation, although there is provision in each for its denunciation by any country which is bound by it (see further para 17.34 below). The making of a new Act, however, does not bring the earlier Act to an end, and ratification of, or accession to, the new Act does not operate as a denunciation of the preceding Act. As noted above, this is confirmed by article 32 which specifically preserves the operation of earlier Acts in relation to those states which remain bound by them, and these Acts continue to govern the relations between these states and the states which have adhered to the new Act. In consequence, the Brussels and Rome Acts are still in force today with respect to certain states[59] and regulate the relations of those states with other Union members. In the absence, therefore, of any provision in an Act forbidding accession to it after the entry into force of a later Act, it must theoretically remain open to accession by any other state at any time. In this regard, the closure provisions in the Brussels Act can be of no effect, as it purports to prohibit accession to an earlier and separate instrument. To prevent this occurring, the provision in question would need to be contained in the Brussels Act itself, and the effect of article 28(3) of that Act, therefore, can only be to bar accession to the earlier Act (Rome) when it is sought to do this at the same time as acceding to the later Act. Likewise, the prohibition in article 34 of the Paris Act can only be effective where a state wishes to adhere to that Act, in which case article 34 clearly makes it a condition of accession that the states in question should not adhere to any earlier Act. However, in the event that one of the few states remaining outside the Berne Union altogether desired to adhere only to an earlier Act, it is difficult to see how that state could be affected by a provision in an instrument to which it is not a party. If this reasoning is correct, it means that the Rome and Brussels Acts remain open to accession, although this would not be the case with the Stockholm Act as the substantive provisions of that Act never entered into force. Furthermore, these possibilities should be open to existing Union members and non-Union states alike. It should therefore be possible for a Union country, such as New Zealand or Lebanon, to adhere to the Brussels Act if it does not wish to undertake the full level of obligations required for accession to the Paris Act. Likewise, a developing country, such as Ethiopia, Myanmar, or Eritrea, which is not presently a Union member could choose to adhere to an earlier Act, such as that of Rome or Brussels, and

[59] Until 2 Sept 1995, this was also true of the Berlin Act to which Thailand was a signatory.

thereby relieve itself of having to comply with the detailed licensing provisions of the Paris Appendix. This might have particular advantages in the case of reproduction rights, as there was no requirement to protect these prior to the Stockholm Act.

17.14 If the foregoing analysis is correct, its consequences are far-reaching and unpredictable, to say the least. Nevertheless, as a matter of practice, since the entry into force of the Paris Act, no country has sought to adhere to any other Act of the Convention. Furthermore, in the event that there was an attempt to do so, there are a number of grounds for arguing that such an accession would be ineffective. For a start, it would be in contradiction to the wishes of successive revision conferences which, since that of Rome, have made it clear that accession to earlier Acts of the Convention should be barred once the later Act has come into force. The policy reasons for this have already been outlined (see para 17.08 above), and they were underlined in the Rome and Brussels Acts by the provision of specific 'grace periods' allowing for accession to the preceding Act in the period immediately following the signature of the new Act. In consequence, if accession to any Act of the Convention also means becoming a member of the wider Union, this could be regarded as a breach of the fundamental (though unwritten) rules of that Union. In this regard, it would be open to countries bound by the Paris Act to refuse to have any relations with a non-Union country which sought to join the Union in this way. However, as this last argument involves reference to other provisions of the Convention that have not yet been examined in depth (in particular, article 32), this discussion is best deferred until this has been done (see paras 17.69ff below).

(g) Ratification of, or accession to, the Stockholm Act

17.15 Of all the earlier Acts of the Convention, the Stockholm Act never entered into effect in its entirety. The reasons for this related to the adoption of the Protocol Concerning Developing Countries, and have already been dealt with at some length in Chapter 14. However, like article 28 of the Paris Act, article 28 of the Stockholm Act provided for the administrative and final clauses of the latter Act to come into force separately, and this event occurred on 26 February 1970.[60] As these provisions are essentially the same as articles 22 to 38 of the Paris Act, a number of countries which are not yet ready to accede to the substantive provisions of the Paris Act have not taken advantage of the opportunity to accede separately to articles 22 to 38 of the Paris Act. As of 1 January 1986, there were some thirteen countries in this position;[61] as of December 2004, this number

[60] [1969] *Copyright* 236. Alternatively, this was 29 Jan 1970 if the accession of the GDR was accepted: see paras 17.67ff below.
[61] See n 37 above.

had reduced to three.[62] The latter are not placed at any disadvantage by their failure to adhere to the administrative and final clauses of the Paris Act. On the contrary, there was a potential detriment to countries which, not having adhered to articles 22 to 38 of the Stockholm Act, subsequently adhered to the Paris Act. This arose from the fact that, under article 14(2) of the WIPO Convention, it was provided that a country which was a party to the Berne Convention but not to the Paris Convention for the Protection of Industrial Property could only become a party to the WIPO Convention if it had ratified or acceded to the Stockholm Act either in entirety or at least the administrative and final clauses of that Act. With the rapid revision of the Berne Convention at Paris in 1971, the absurd position arose that countries which adhered only to that Act might not be able to become a party to the WIPO Convention. To overcome this possibility, the Paris Conference adopted a special provision (article 29*bis*) containing a legal fiction under which ratification of, or accession to, the Paris Act by a country not bound by articles 22 to 38 of the Stockholm Act was, for the sole purpose of article 14(2) of the WIPO Convention, to be treated as a ratification of, or accession to, the Stockholm Act.[63] Article 34 is made subject to this, and for this limited purpose states adhering to the Paris Act can adhere also to an earlier Act.

(h) Accession to the Brussels Act in certain circumstances

Under both the Stockholm and Paris Acts, accession to the Brussels Act remained possible until the entry into force of each of these later Acts in its entirety. Thus, Australia acceded to the Brussels Act in 1969,[64] the Netherlands in 1973,[65] and Japan in 1974[66] (just before the entry into force of the Paris Act). However, the faculty that was allowed to countries under both the Stockholm and Paris Acts to ratify or accede to different parts of each Act at different times gave rise to certain problems as it was provided that these parts might come into force on different dates. In the case of the Stockholm Act, ratification or accession and entry into force could occur in three stages (not necessarily in this order): articles 1 to 21 and the Protocol, articles 22 to 26 (the administrative clauses) and articles 27 to 38 (the final clauses).[67] In the case of the Paris Act, two stages were possible: articles 1 to 21 and the Appendix and articles 22 to 38.[68] What happened, therefore, when one set of provisions entered into force before the other (or others) had done so? No problem arose with respect to an existing Union member: this country was bound by the provisions of the Act now in force, while for the rest it continued to be bound by the provisions of the **17.16**

62 Chad, Fiji, and Pakistan: www.wipo.int.

63 See further *Records* 1971, 58 (Document B/DC/5).

64 [1969] *Copyright* 94.

65 [1973] *Copyright* 22.

66 [1974] *Copyright* 157.

67 Stockholm Act, art 28(1).

68 Paris Act, art 28(1).

earlier Act to which it had adhered.[69] With a new Union member, however, the possibility arose that some period of time might elapse before it was bound by the whole of the new Act, and until this happened this country might be left in limbo, for example, where the final and administrative clauses had entered into force but not the substantive clauses. This, in fact, happened in the case of the Stockholm Act, due to the reluctance of many Union members to ratify the Protocol. To fill this gap, article 29(2)(a) of that Act therefore provided that such countries should be bound by articles 1 to 20 of the Brussels Act (until such time as articles 1 to 21 and the Protocol of the Stockholm Act entered into force) and by articles 21 to 24 of the Brussels Act (until articles 22 to 26 of the Stockholm Act entered into force). In this interim period, therefore, there was a notional accession to the earlier Act. This provision affected a number of countries which acceded to the Stockholm Act in full: while these countries became bound by articles 22 to 38 of that Act as from early 1970, in view of the fact that articles 1 to 21 and the Protocol never came into force, they were bound by articles 1 to 20 of the Brussels Act until such time as they acceded to the Paris Act. Originally, this provision affected two countries: Chad[70] and Mauritania,[71] although it was arguable that it also applied to the former GDR.[72] Pakistan,[73] Romania,[74] and Senegal[75] also ratified the Stockholm Act in whole, but as they were parties to previous Acts they were not affected. At present, only Chad continues to be bound, by virtue of this provision, by articles 1 to 20 of the Brussels Act and articles 22 to 38 of the Stockholm Act.[76] A similar provision was required for the Paris Act, in view of the fact that articles 22 to 38 of that Act entered into force almost immediately after ratification or accession by each country, while the entry into force of the substantive provisions was to take place at a later date.[77] Thus, article 29(2) of the Paris Act also provided for the application of articles 1 to 20 of the Brussels Act until such time as articles 1 to 21 and the Appendix of the Paris Act came into force. In the event, this provision was only required for a short period, as the whole Paris Act was in force by 10 October 1974.

---

[69] Paris Act, art 32(1). [70] [1971] *Copyright* 168. [71] [1972] *Copyright* 240.

[72] [1968] *Copyright* 155. The membership of the GDR to the Berne Union was disputed at this time, although it had previously declared that it continued to apply the Rome Act in its territory ([1955] *DA* 149). In the event that it was not bound by the Convention at the time it acceded to the Stockholm Act, then it would have been bound by arts 1–20 of the Brussels Act in the same way as Chad and Mauritania. However, this accession was itself disputed (see [1969] *Copyright* 236), so the position of the GDR at this time remains unclear. See further para 17.67 below.

[73] [1969] *Copyright* 234. [74] ibid, 235. [75] ibid, 236.

[76] [1986] *Copyright* 6–8. Fiji also remains bound by the Brussels Act, but this is by virtue a declaration of continued adherence to the Brussels Act that was made by that state on 1 Dec 1971 upon achieving independence: [1972] *Copyright* 128.

[77] Document B/DC/5: *Records* 1971, 57–8.

(3) The validity of ratifications and accessions

(a) Failure to give effect to the Convention

In keeping with its objective of achieving the widest possible international protection of literary and artistic works, the Berne Convention has traditionally been open to accession by all countries. In this respect, it differs from many other multilateral conventions where strict conditions for membership are laid down, for example, a particular geographical location, membership of some other international organization or convention, compliance with certain economic or social criteria, or, more generally, positive acceptance by the present parties or a certain proportion thereof.[78] The Berne Convention, by contrast, contains no specific limitations of these kinds. Nevertheless, as a general principle of international law, the consent of the existing parties to the adherence of a new party is crucial to the validity of that adherence.[79] This is no less the case with the Berne Convention, although here it can be said that this consent has been given in advance by article 29 which provides for the accession of these countries to the Paris Act.[80] This advance consent, however, is not given unconditionally, as article 36(2) provides: **17.17**

> It is understood that, at the time a country becomes bound by this Convention, it will be in a position under its domestic law to give effect to the provisions of this Convention.

A further obligation is to be found in article 36(1), but this applies to existing members and its effect is discussed further below (see para 17.80). As for article 36(2), the Convention has contained a similar provision since its inception,[81] but this has only been the subject of a separate article since the Stockholm, Paris Acts.

What is the effect of a purported ratification of, or accession to, the Paris Act by a country which does not give effect to the provisions of the Convention under its domestic law? Before answering this, it is important to consider the circumstances under which this question may arise. As a general matter, it may often be difficult to be certain whether a particular country fails to do this as it will require a detailed knowledge of that country's domestic law and constitutional requirements as to treaty implementation.[82] Thus, the fact that the statutory law **17.18**

[78] See generally H G Schermers, *International Institutional Law* (1980).

[79] Lord McNair, *The Law of Treaties* (1961), 151.

[80] S P Ladas, *The International Protection of Literary and Artistic Property* (1938) ('Ladas (1938)'), 119.

[81] Thus, the Berne Act, art 18, provided that 'Countries which have not become parties to the present Convention, and which make provision by the domestic law for the protection of the rights forming the object of the present Convention, shall be admitted to accede thereto on request to that effect.'

[82] See further para 5.09 above.

of the country fails to give effect to a particular provision of the Convention will be of no account if that provision is self-executing and can be directly applied by the courts of that country. Even in the case of the common law countries, it may be hard to point to a specific failure if the provision can be given effect to under some other head of protection, as in the case of moral rights. In consequence, where a country adheres unconditionally to the Paris Act, this adhesion will usually have to be accepted as a declaration by that country that it complies with the obligation contained in article 36(2). However, this would not be so if the adhesion is made subject to conditions that are clearly inconsistent with the provisions of the Convention. This occurred in the case of Turkey which purported to accede to the Berlin Act in 1931, and made a reservation which had the effect that it would not comply with article 8 in relation to translation rights.[83] There can be little doubt that the reason behind the Turkish reservation was the desire of the Turkish Government to have ready access to foreign literature for developmental purposes. However, there can equally be no doubt that the proposed reservation was inconsistent with the reservations which were allowed under the Berlin Act and which the Turkish Government could have readily made. This, indeed, was the course followed by Thailand, another developing country, which had acceded to the Berlin Act at the same time as Turkey.[84] In the case of the Turkish reservation, however, both the Swiss Federal Council and the International Office took the view that the Turkish reservation was impermissible and that its accession was therefore ineffective.[85] Nevertheless, they notified other Union members of the purported accession, and received, in reply, a number of objections from states which declared that, if the reservation was maintained, they would not consider themselves bound to Turkey under the Convention.[86] Turkey did not withdraw its reservation, and was never listed in *Le Droit d'Auteur* as a Union member. Subsequently she attended the Brussels

[83] [1931] *DA* 74. This accession was made 'subject to the conditions and reservations stipulated in art 14 of the Commercial Convention signed at Lausanne on July 24, 1923'. This Convention provided for Turkey to accede to the Berne Convention and Additional Berne Protocol subject to 'such reservation as Turkey might formulate concerning the provisions of the aforementioned Convention and Protocol, with reference to the right of translation into the Turkish language, if the other signatory Powers of the Convention and Protocol have not themselves opposed the said reservation in the course of the year following the entry into force' of the Convention of Lausanne. The parties to this Convention were Turkey, France, the UK, Greece, Italy, Japan, Romania, and Yugoslavia.

[84] This accession was made subject to no less than six reservations, all permitted under the Berlin Act: [1931] *DA* 85 and see further para 17.29 below.

[85] See the editorial notes in [1931] *DA* 74 and [1952] *DA* 133–4.

[86] These were made by Austria, Belgium, Czechoslovakia, Danzig, the Netherlands, Poland, Portugal, and Spain: [1932] *DA* 109, [1933] *DA* 3, 37, and 61. None of the Union countries that had been parties to the Lausanne Convention objected, although, in fact, Turkey had failed to accede to the Berne Convention within the one-year period required by the Lausanne Convention: see further Ladas (1938), 120 and the note in [1928] *DA* 128.

Conference in an observer capacity and acceded to the Brussels Act in 1952 with a correctly formulated reservation in relation to translation rights.[87]

The Turkish example does not indicate clearly what is the effect of an accession which is made subject to an inconsistent reservation or condition. Is it to make the accession void *ab initio*, on the basis that there is a clear failure to comply with the requirements of article 36(2)? Or does it only make the accession voidable at the option of the other Union members, who must therefore ensure that they register their objections? Furthermore, if only some countries object, does the accession remain effective as between the country which makes it and those which do not object? The principles of customary international law governing the making of reservations have evolved considerably over the past fifty years, particularly in relation to treaties which contain no provisions dealing with the question. As now embodied in the Vienna Convention, the rules concerning the effect of reservations are quite complex and may have differing consequences as between those countries which accept them and those which do not.[88] However, in the case of a convention which contains clear prescriptions as to the number and kind of reservations which can be made, such as the Berne Convention, it seems clear that a reservation which is inconsistent with these prescriptions has no effect and the accession to which it is attached is a nullity: the country which is making it must either withdraw the reservation or refrain from entering the treaty.[89] In this regard, it would seem irrelevant that some states have failed to object: they have already agreed in advance on the reservations that new members may make on joining the Convention and it cannot be argued that they have varied this agreement by a simple failure to object to a purported accession of this kind. The same result will obviously also apply in the case of a Union member which attempts to ratify or accede to the Paris Act subject to a reservation which is not permitted by that text: its ratification or accession will be ineffective and it will continue to be bound by the earlier Act to which it is a party. To date, no instance of the latter kind has occurred. **17.19**

Another possible ground on which Union members may refuse to accept an accession to the Convention arises where the country purporting to do so is not a 'country' within the sense that this term is used in the Convention. It is noteworthy here that the Convention refers throughout to 'country' rather than 'state', although the latter term is used in most current multilateral conventions, **17.20**

[87] [1952] *DA* 133.

[88] Vienna Convention, arts 19–23. See further I Sinclair, *The Vienna Convention on the Law of Treaties*, 2nd edn (1984), ch III. See further J K Gamble, 'Reservations to Multilateral Treaties: A Macroscopic View of State Practice' [1980] *AJIL* 372.

[89] This appeared to be the view of the International Law Commission in 1962: see Sinclair (n 88 above), 60.

including that constituting WIPO.[90] While the meaning of 'state' is now fairly well settled in international law,[91] 'country' is a more flexible term and is capable of possessing a wider meaning. Thus, 'state' is used generally to describe an international entity with certain characteristics, such as a defined territory, a permanent population, some form of organized government, the capacity to enter into relations with other states, and, above all, independence.[92] By contrast, with the exception of a defined territory, the other characteristics need not be present in the case of a 'country'. Nevertheless, it has been suggested that, at least so far as the current text of the Convention is concerned, 'country' should now be interpreted as meaning the same as 'state', with the consequence that only states should be able to accede to and be party to the Convention.[93] While this argument is borne out to a very large extent by a perusal of the present membership of the Union, it has not always been so and it seems clear, even now, that the use of the word 'country' in the Convention allows for a wider class of members than would be so if it were required that members can only be states. In this regard, the past practice of the Union is instructive. Thus, in its first fifty years of existence, there were accessions by a number of countries that were not states in the strict sense. These included the following:

1. Of the original signatories of the Berne Act, Tunisia was under the supervision of France which had declared a protectorate over that country in 1883.[94]
2. In 1889, the Principality of Monaco acceded to the Berne Act,[95] although in a number of respects its administration was integrated with and controlled by that of its neighbour, France.
3. In 1917, that part of Morocco which had been subject to a French protectorate since 1912 acceded to the Berlin Act.[96]
4. In 1924, Syria and Lebanon acceded to the Berlin Act.[97] Both countries had been formerly Turkish provinces and, at the time of their accession, were under the supervision of France pursuant to a League of Nations mandate.
5. In 1922, the Free City of Danzig, whose status as an independent state was, to say the least, unusual in view of its relations with both the League of Nations and Poland, acceded to the Berlin Act.[98]

---

[90] WIPO Convention, art 5.

[91] See generally J Crawford, *The Creation of States in International Law* (1979), chs 1–3.

[92] ibid, 31ff.

[93] C Masouyé, *Guide to the Berne Convention for the Protection of Literary and Artistic Works* (1978) ('Masouyé (1978)'), 8.

[94] [1887] *DA* 8. At the Berne Conferences of 1885 and 1886, Tunisia was represented by the distinguished French international lawyer, Louis Renault.

[95] [1889] *DA* 94. [96] [1917] *DA* 73. [97] [1924] *DA* 85.

[98] [1922] *DA* 77. See further Crawford (n 91 above), 160ff.

6. In 1928, five self-governing Dominions of the British Empire acceded to the Berlin Act in their own right: Australia,[99] Canada,[100] India,[101] New Zealand,[102] and South Africa.[103]
7. In 1931, Liechtenstein acceded to the Berlin Act,[104] although it had previously been denied admission to the League of Nations on the ground that it was too small to carry out its obligations under the Covenant of that body.[105]
8. In 1935, the Holy See, as the government of the Vatican City State, acceded to the Rome Act,[106] although its possession of statehood was disputed in a number of other international contexts.[107]

None of these accessions was opposed by the existing membership of the Union, although it was arguable that they were not strictly 'states' because of their lack of complete independence and that they therefore fell outside the expression 'Contracting States' which was used in both the Berne and Berlin Acts of the Convention.[108] Accordingly, in the Rome Act this expression was replaced by the expression 'countries to which the present Convention applies' which was apt to cover each of the examples given above. It was also apt to describe other colonial and dependent territories to which the Convention might be applied by the power responsible for them (see further para 17.45 below). Nevertheless, within a relatively short time after this change to the Convention, most of the 'countries' referred to above had attained the undisputed status of fully independent states: this was already the *de facto* situation in the cases of Australia, Canada, New Zealand, and South Africa,[109] while India acquired full independence in 1947,[110] Lebanon and Syria in 1944,[111] and Morocco and Tunisia in 1964.[112] Furthermore, there can be little doubt that the new members of the Union that acceded to it in the years after 1945 were states in the usual sense of the word, even if many of them were former colonial or dependent possessions of other Union members and had previously been 'countries to which this Convention applies'. However, in view of the continued membership of Liechtenstein, Monaco, and the Holy See, it must be said that, even now, the word 'country' is more appropriate to describe these entities than the word **17.21**

[99] [1928] *DA* 57. [100] ibid. [101] ibid, 58. [102] ibid, 78.
[103] ibid, 133. [104] [1931] *DA* 85.
[105] See generally Crawford (n 91 above), 139 on the general problem of 'micro-states', and see further M H Mendelsohn, 'Diminutive States in the United Nations' (1972) 21 *ICLQ* 609.
[106] [1935] *DA* 97. [107] See further Crawford (n 91 above), 195.
[108] Berne and Berlin Acts, art 1. [109] Crawford (n 91 above), 238ff.
[110] *The Europa Year Book 1985* (1985), vol II, 1775 ('*EYB*').
[111] *EYB* (n 110 above), 2032 and 2946 (in fact, it does not seem that full independence from France, in the case of Syria, was achieved until 17 Apr 1946). See further Crawford (n 91 above), 66–8.
[112] *EYB* (n 110 above), 2204 (Morocco) and 2715 (Tunisia).

'state', and, to this extent, it cannot be treated as having an identical meaning. The retention of the word 'country' in the present Act therefore provides a useful flexibility that avoids the need to inquire too closely into the question of whether an intending Union member possesses the requisite characteristics of statehood. Nonetheless, it is possible to conceive of certain cases where this flexibility may give rise to problems. While mostly in the realm of the hypothetical, the likelihood of such instances arising cannot be lightly dismissed, and is therefore deserving of brief consideration here.

(i) Accessions by 'puppet states': These are entities which can in no way be regarded as states, in that their independence is bogus and their affairs are effectively controlled by an external power. This was the case with a number of entities which were created by the Axis Powers in World War II, such as Manchukuo, Croatia, and Slovakia.[113] The last of these did, in fact, adhere to the Berne Convention in May 1944, and the accession was welcomed by the International Office.[114] This was on the basis that, with the dismemberment of Czechoslovakia in 1939 and the creation of the newly 'independent' state of Slovakia from former Czech territory, the latter had then ceased to be part of the Union.[115] While most commentators would dispute the International Office's view that Slovakia was really an independent state,[116] it can still be defended on the ground that it was nonetheless a 'country' and difficult to distinguish from the various protectorates which had previously been allowed to accede to the Berne and Berlin Acts. In the event, Slovakia's membership of the Union lasted less than a year as it was extinguished in April 1945, and thereafter its territory was absorbed in the reconstituted state of Czechoslovakia which remained a member of the Union (see further para 17.37 below).

(ii) The former South African homelands policy: A possibility that was considered in the first edition of this commentary, but which now has disappeared concerned the policy of the Republic of South Africa, in the apartheid period, to make purported grants of independence to 'states' which had been carved out of its existing territory.[117] It has been argued that these grants were illusory and made in pursuance of a policy which was illegal under international law.[118] Accordingly, recognition was not generally accorded to these entities by other states. On the other hand, in the period prior to the election of Nelson Mandela as President of a fully democratic South Africa, it could have been argued that

[113] See Crawford (n 91 above), 62–5, 119.

[114] [1944] *DA* 61 and accompanying editorial note.

[115] ibid. See further K Marek, *Identity and Continuity of States in Public International Law* (1954), 290–1.

[116] See Crawford (n 91 above), 63 and references cited therein.

[117] Crawford (n 91 above), 222–7.

[118] Discussed by Crawford, ibid.

these factors did not necessarily provide an obstacle to these entities being regarded as 'countries' for the purposes of accession to the Union. Clearly, there would have been widespread objections to attempts by any of these homeland states to accede to the Convention (see further para 17.91 below). Nonetheless, the juridical basis for such objections is not easy to formulate. While dependent to a large degree on South Africa, such homelands still possessed a considerable amount of autonomy and to this extent did not differ greatly from countries such as Monaco or Liechtenstein. A more fruitful ground of objection may have been that they lacked the necessary territorial character of a 'country', in that many of them consisted of a string of small parcels of land surrounded by South African territory. These questions clearly would not arise if membership of the Union was confined to states, and never, in fact, arose as an issue for the Union in view of the political changes that occurred in South Africa from 1994 on.

(iii) Federal states: A final situation concerns the constituent states, provinces, or *Länder* of federal states. Federations, confederations, and unions of different kinds are to be found in a number of countries, both Union and non-Union members alike. The degree of autonomy possessed by these entities varies greatly, but in some cases the entry into a federal relationship has not deprived them entirely of capacity to enter international relations. For example, this appeared to be the case with the former states of Germany after they were incorporated in the new German Empire in 1871,[119] and, in the case of the former Soviet Union, it was true in respect of two republics of the USSR—Byelorussia and the Ukraine—which were members of the UN and were signatories to a number of other international conventions.[120] In the case of most other federal states, however, the possibility of their constituent parts purporting to enter into international relations on their own behalf does not arise as they are excluded from doing so under their internal constitutional arrangements.[121] So far as the Berne Union is concerned, the question now seems moot, given the break-up of several important federal states that occurred at the end of the 1980s and early 1990s. Although the possibility of accession by the Byelorussian and Ukrainian Republics to the Berne Union remained a live possibility in the period before the break-up of the Soviet Union,[122] both are now fully independent nations and have acceded to the Berne Convention in their own right.[123]

[119] See D P O'Connell, *State Succession in Municipal and International Law, II: International Relations* (1967), 56ff.

[120] Including the WIPO Convention: [1969] *Industrial Property* 78 (Byelorussian Republic) and [1969] *Industrial Property* 62 (Ukrainian Republic).

[121] See generally O'Connell (n 119 above), ch 4.

[122] Both had been admitted to the UN and had also acceded to the WIPO Convention, which confines membership to states: WIPO Convention, art 5(1). For the background to the UN membership of these two 'nations', see Crawford (n 91 above), 132.

[123] Belarus on 12 Dec 1997 and Ukraine on 25 Oct 1995.

The same is true of a number of other republics of the former Soviet Union,[124] and Yugoslavia.[125]

(4) Reservations to ratifications or accessions

(a) In general

17.22 The making of reservations has already been referred to at various points in the text, notably in Chapter 14 above, and it has been seen that this has been an important issue throughout the history of the Convention. As to the meaning of the term, the following definition is to be found in the Vienna Convention:

> 'reservation' means a unilateral statement, however phrased or named, made by a State, when signing, ratifying, accepting, approving or acceding to a treaty whereby it purports to exclude or to modify the legal effect of certain provisions of the treaty in their application to that State; . . .'[126]

This is consistent with the meaning that is given to the term under customary international law, but some further explanation is required. In essence, a reservation is a declaration external to the text of a treaty, and, while unilateral at the time of its formulation, it will 'produce no legal effect until accepted, in one form or another, by other contracting states'.[127] In this respect, it is important to distinguish a reservation from other kinds of declarations which states may make in the course of negotiating, signing, ratifying, or acceding to a treaty. The legal effect of a declaration containing the interpretation which a state proposes to apply to a particular provision has already been referred to (see para 5.41 above); in general, where the meaning of a provision is uncertain or imprecise, such a declaration will not serve to exclude or modify its legal effect and will not therefore constitute a reservation. Other declarations may be of a more general and often rhetorical character, and have no effect at all on the application or interpretation of the provision in question (see further para 17.33 below). Since the Berlin Act, the making of reservations to the Berne Convention has been wholly regulated by the terms of the Convention itself, and the scope for this has

[124] The following former constituent republics are now Berne members: Armenia (19 Oct 2000); Azerbaijan (4 June 1999); Estonia (26 Oct 1994); Georgia (16 May 1995); Kazakhstan (12 Apr 1999); Kyrgyzstan (8 July 1999); Latvia (11 Aug 1995); Lithuania (14 Dec 1994); Mongolia (12 Mar 1998); Republic of Moldova (2 Nov 1995); Russian Federation (13 Feb 1995); Tajikistan (9 Mar 2000): www.wipo.int. The only former republic now remaining outside the Berne Union (as at June 2005) is Turkmenistan.

[125] The following former republics of Yugoslavia are now members of the Berne Convention: Bosnia and Herzegovina (1 Mar 1992); Croatia (8 Oct 1991); Serbia and Montenegro (27 Apr 1992); Slovenia (25 June 1991); the Former Yugoslav Republic of Macedonia (8 Sept 1991).

[126] Vienna Convention, art 2. See further Sinclair (n 88 above), ch 3; McNair (n 79 above), ch 9; P-H Imbert, *Les Réserves aux Traités Multilatéraux* (1978), Introduction and 31–3 (on the Berne Convention).

[127] Sinclair (n 88 above), 51. Imbert (n 126 above), 10.

been successively narrowed and widened. The stages by which this has occurred can be summarized as follows.

(b) The Berne and Paris Additional Acts

Neither of these contained any provision relating to the making of reservations. Accordingly, the validity and effect of any reservations would have fallen to be considered under the general principles of customary international law which were then applicable. Essentially, this would have required an inquiry into whether the reservation in question was accepted by other Union members and would have entitled them to apply a similar restriction in protection vis-à-vis the country making the reservation.[128] In fact, these questions did not arise as no country ratifying or acceding to either Act made any reservations. **17.23**

(c) The Berlin Act

This was the first text to deal expressly with the question of reservations. Articles 25 and 27 set broad guidelines within which reservations to the new Act might be made by non-Union countries and Union members respectively. Their effect was to permit both categories of countries to apply, or to continue to apply, specific provisions of the previous two Acts in place of the corresponding provisions of the new Act. However, the precise scope of the reservations permitted in respect of the two categories of countries differed slightly. **17.24**

(i) Non-Union countries: In the case of non-Union countries acceding to the Berlin Act, they were permitted to indicate which of the provisions of the Berne Act or Paris Additional Act they judged 'necessary to substitute, provisionally at least, for the corresponding provisions of the present Convention'.[129] This gave those countries a choice as to whether to apply the provisions of the Berne Act in their original form, or in their amended form as modified by the Paris Additional Act.

(ii) Union countries: in the case of Union countries ratifying the Berlin Act, their scope for reservations was more limited, as they were only permitted to declare, on ratification, that they desired 'to remain bound, as regards any specific point, by the provisions of the Conventions which they have previously signed'.[130] In other words, if these countries were bound by both the Berne and Paris Additional Acts, they could not choose to remain bound only by the unmodified provisions of the Berne Act.

In both instances, however, the effect of these provisions was to codify completely the conditions under which countries might make reservations to the

[128] Sinclair (n 88 above), 54ff.

[129] Berlin Act, art 25(3).

[130] ibid, art 37(2).

new Act. This had two principal consequences. The first was that there was no need for other Union countries to 'accept' these reservations, so long as they had been made within the limits of the above provisions: this acceptance was deemed to have been given in advance by the adoption of those provisions. In other words, it would not be a valid ground of objection for a Union country to oppose the accession of another country to the Convention where the latter made its accession subject to a reservation that fell within these provisions.[131] The second consequence was that existing Union countries were excluded from applying reciprocal reservations in respect of the reservant countries. The policy that lay behind the adoption of this regime has already been discussed (see para 3.19 above): the desire to increase the membership of the Union, without placing too many obstacles in the way of accession by those countries which required changes to their domestic laws in order to implement the provisions of the new Act. While this objective was certainly attained, an unfortunate consequence of the new provisions was that a large number of countries made reservations upon ratifying or acceding to the Berlin Act.[132] This introduced a considerable complexity into the *inter se* relations of Union members.

(d) The Rome Act

17.25 One of the aims of the Rome Revision was to reduce or eliminate the reservations system embodied in the Berlin Act, but this was only partially achieved with the imposition of the following limitations on the capacity of countries to make reservations.

(i) Existing Union members: Existing Union members were permitted to retain the benefit of reservations previously formulated provided they made a declaration to this effect at the time of deposit of their ratification.[133] This preserved the status quo, and meant that a Union member which had not previously made a reservation under the Berlin Act could no longer make any reservation at all. In the absence of an express declaration that such a country was retaining its prior reservation, it was also clear the latter no longer had any effect.[134]

(ii) Non-Union countries: Non-Union countries were permitted, on accession, to indicate that they wished to substitute

> . . . provisionally, at least, for Article 8 which relates to translations, the provisions of Article 5 of the Convention of 1886 revised at Paris in 1896, on the

[131] See further Imbert (n 126 above), 32.

[132] See the list of reservations given in *Actes* 1928, 12. This listed eighteen reservant countries, with a total of twenty-seven reservations between them.

[133] Rome Act, art 27(2). [134] ibid.

understanding that those provisions shall apply only to translations into the language or languages of that country.[135]

It will be noted that the scope of this reservation was more limited than the reservations with respect to translation rights that might be made by either Union or non-Union countries under the Berlin Act and retained upon ratification of the Rome Act. For example, a non-Union country acceding to the Berlin Act was free to formulate its reservation only in the terms of article 5 of the Berne Act (see above), and this had the effect that translation rights might be brought to an end ten years after publication. A country which had made a reservation in these terms, which it retained under the Rome Act, was Greece.[136] On the other hand, while the scope of reservations with respect to translations was more limited in the case of a Union country which had been bound by both the Berne and Paris Additional Acts and which then ratified the Berlin Act, this was still wider than the scope provided to non-Union countries under the Rome Act. Thus, the former country could provide for the termination of translation rights in respect of languages other than its own, if no authorized translations in those languages had been published within ten years from publication of the original. Japan was a country which had made a reservation in these terms under the Berlin Act and it retained this under the Rome Act.[137]

Following the adoption of the Rome Act, however, a number of Union members abandoned reservations which they had made previously under the Berlin Act. These included Italy,[138] the UK,[139] Norway,[140] Sweden,[141] and Denmark.[142] By the time of the Brussels Conference, there were only six countries bound by the Rome Act which had reservations to it.[143]

(e) The Brussels Act

The provisions of the Rome Act were continued unchanged in this Act.[144] **17.26**

(f) The Stockholm, Paris Acts

The same basic regime concerning the making of reservations was retained in these Acts, but this was extended considerably with the adoption of the new **17.27**

[135] ibid, art 27(3). [136] [1932] *DA* 13. [137] [1931] *DA* 73.

[138] With respect to translations and the representation of translations, as from 1 Aug 1931: [1932] *DA* 40.

[139] With respect to retroactivity, as from 1 Aug 1931: [1931] *DA* 96, 105.

[140] With respect to architectural works, newspaper articles and retroactivity, as from 1 Aug 1931: [1931] *DA* 96.

[141] With respect to newspaper articles, as from 1 Aug 1931: [1931] *DA* 96.

[142] With respect to newspaper articles, as from 16 Sept 1933: [1933] *DA* 97.

[143] France (works of applied art); Greece (translations and performing rights); Ireland (translations); Japan (translations); Tunisia (works of applied art); Yugoslavia (translations): *Documents de la Conférence réunie à Bruxelles du 5 au 26 juin 1948* (1951) ('*Documents 1948* (1951)'), 20–1.

[144] Brussels Act, arts 25(3) and 27(2).

restrictions allowed, first by the Protocol, and then by the Appendix, as well as certain other limitations which are described below. Under the Paris Act, the general principle is that ratification or accession automatically entails 'acceptance of all the provisions and admission to all the advantages of this Convention' (article 30(1)). However, exceptions to this are allowed under the following provisions.

(i) **Article** 7(7): This provision permits countries bound by the Rome Act to maintain shorter terms of protection when ratifying or acceding to the Act; there is no express requirement that the intention to maintain such a term should be declared in the instrument of ratification or accession, but this can be implied as a general matter of the good faith that should apply between states in their treaty relationships.[145] The retention of a shorter term under this provision clearly has the same effect as making a reservation to article 7, and can be made the subject of reciprocal provisions by other Union members under article 7(8).

(ii) **Article 30(2)**: This provides as follows. Union countries may still, upon ratification or accession, retain the benefit of reservations previously formulated if they make a declaration to this effect at the time of deposit of their instrument of ratification or accession.[146] In the case of a Union member which is also a developing country, if it has previously made a reservation with respect to translation rights it may make a declaration retaining this reservation in substitution for availing itself of the compulsory licensing provisions of article II of the Appendix.[147] In other words, it may continue to maintain a reservation based on article 5 of the Berne Act or article 5 as modified by the Paris Additional Act (as the case may be). However, a country in this position is required to make an election. In the event that it makes a declaration retaining the benefit of a reservation with respect to translations, it cannot later (even if the declaration is withdrawn) avail itself of the benefit of a compulsory licence under article II.[148] Likewise, if it avails itself first of article II, it cannot subsequently make a reservation.[149] The latter prohibition would, for example, affect India which availed itself of the provisions of both articles II and III of the Appendix upon its ratification of the substantive provisions of the Paris Act in 1984.[150]

Non-Union countries acceding to the Convention still retain the right to make the reservation with respect to translations which was first permitted under the Rome Act, but with a slight modification in its terms. Thus, they may substitute, 'temporarily at least', the provisions of article 5 of the Berne Act 'as

[145] Vienna Convention, art 26. [146] Paris Act, art 30(2)(a).
[147] Appendix, art V(1)(a). [148] ibid, art V(1)(c). [149] ibid, art V(2).
[150] [1984] *Copyright* 111.

completed at Paris in 1896, on the clear understanding that the said provisions are applicable only to translations into a language in general use in the said country'.[151] It is difficult to know what precise meaning to attach to the words 'temporarily at least', or whether any mandatory force can be given to them. On the other hand, they provide a general reminder to countries making a reservation of this kind that it should not be imposed permanently and is only intended to operate as a transitional measure.[152] The expression 'language in general use', however, is more exact, and corresponds with the terminology used in the Appendix (see para 14.65 above). Nonetheless, it should be noted that the reservation provided for here applies equally to developed as to developing countries. Under article V(1)(a)(ii) of the Appendix, it may also be made by a developing country which is already a Union member but has not previously made a reservation which it can retain pursuant to article 30(2)(b). However, in the case of developed countries it is further provided that other Union countries have the right to impose a similar restriction with respect to translations of works the country of origin of which is the country which has made the reservation allowed under this provision.[153] As a result, reciprocity—the usual rule for reservations in customary international law—is applicable here, although article I(6)(b) of the Appendix grants developing countries an immunity from this reciprocity so long as they retain that status. Reciprocity, moreover, cannot be applied in the case of Union members (whether developed or developing) which have previously made a reservation with respect to translations under earlier Acts, namely the Rome or Brussels Act, which they retain the benefit of, pursuant to article 30(2)(a) of the Paris Act.

(iii) **Article 28(1)(b)**: This provision permits Union countries to limit their acceptance of the Paris Act to the administrative and final clauses (see para 17.06 above).

(iv) **Article 33(2)**: This provision is concerned with the settlement of disputes between Union countries (see para 17.85 below).

(v) **Exceptions**: The exceptions to protection which may be imposed by developing countries pursuant to the Appendix (see generally Chapter 14 above).

(5) The current state of reservations under the Convention

The following paragraphs list the reservations that are presently applied by Union members. **17.28**

---

[151] Paris Act, art 30(2)(b).

[152] See here the comments of Louis Renault in his report to the Berlin Conference: *Actes* 1908, 273.

[153] Paris Act, art 30(2)(b).

(a) Countries still bound by the Berlin Act

17.29 Since 1995, there have been no countries in this category. Up to 2 September of that year, however, Thailand was a signatory to Berlin only, and retained all the reservations that it made on its accession in 1931. The effect of this was to continue to apply a substantial number of the provisions of the Berne and Paris Additional Acts, concerning the following matters: retroactivity, newspaper articles, works of applied art, translations, formalities, and performing rights.[154]

(b) Countries still bound by the Rome Act

17.30 Until relatively recently, there were only two reservations made by countries bound by this Act. The first of these has now disappeared with the accession of the country in question (Iceland) to the Paris Act in August 1999, while the second (by Sri Lanka) is of uncertain status.

(i) **Iceland**: In place of article 8 of the Berlin Act, this country reserved the right to apply article 5 of the Berne Act as modified by article 1(III) of the Paris Additional Act 'in respect of the exclusive right of translation into the Icelandic language'.[155] As stated above, this country is now a party to the Paris Act, and the reservation no longer applies.

(ii) **Sri Lanka (formerly Ceylon)**: In making its declaration of continuity with respect to the Rome Act in 1959 (see further para 17.58 below), this country declared that it reserved for itself 'the right to enact local legislation for the translation of educational, scientific and technical books into the national language'.[156] The status of this reservation, however, is uncertain, on several counts: first, as to the meaning of the purported reservation and, secondly, the capacity of Sri Lanka to make such a reservation in the first place.

It made no reference to article 5 of the Berne Act as modified by the Paris Additional Act which provided the basis for the reservation with respect to translations by a non-Union country under article 25(3) of the Rome Act. This was not, in itself, fatal, if the effect of the reservation was to fall within the terms of these provisions. However, its wording made this difficult to determine, and it was arguable that it allowed for the enactment of legislation which would disregard translation rights entirely so far as translations into the national language of these classes of works were concerned. If this were so, it would be an impermissible reservation of the kind that Turkey purported to make in 1931, with the effect that Sri Lanka's declaration of continuity would be ineffective. On the other hand, given the generality of the Sri Lankan reservation, it would be reasonable to argue for the adoption of an interpretation which allows it to be

154 [1931] *DA* 85. 155 [1935] *DA* 61. 156 [1959] *DA* 205.

effective. This would mean construing it as being subject to the conditions of article 5 of the Berne Act as modified by the Paris Additional Act.

Even if it is permissible to interpret the Sri Lankan reservation in the second way suggested above, it must also be doubted whether that country was entitled to make such a declaration anyway. The Rome Act had been applied to Sri Lanka by the UK in 1931 when it was still the British colony of Ceylon.[157] Strictly speaking, Sri Lanka was then part of the Union at the time it notified the Swiss Government that it continued to be bound by the Rome Act. This notification, although described by the then Government of Ceylon as an 'accession' was treated as a 'declaration of continuity' by the International Office. The making of these declarations is discussed further below (see para 17.58), but for the moment it suffices to note that their effect is to declare that the Act of the Convention which was applied to the country in question at the time that it was a colonial or dependent territory continues to apply. Furthermore, it has continued to apply to that country since its independence, and the declaration simply serves to confirm that fact. If the latter is so, the consequence is that Sri Lanka, at the time it made its declaration, was already part of the Union and was not acceding to the Rome Act. This is only logical, because if it were not a Union country, it should not have been able to accede to the Rome Act in 1959, because of the closure provision in article 28(3) of the Brussels Act (for a contrary argument, see para 17.11 above). In such a case, it could only have acceded to the Brussels Act, although, of course, a suitable reservation with respect to translations would still have been permitted under that Act.[158] However, if the true conclusion is that Sri Lanka was already a country of the Union in 1959, this leaves the effect of its reservation completely uncertain. Had the UK previously made a reservation, on its behalf with respect to translations, which the UK had then retained on its ratification of the Rome Act, in 1959 Sri Lanka could simply have stated that it was retaining the benefit of that reservation. No such reservation, however, was made by the UK, and the conclusion must be that Sri Lanka was not in a position to continue or to make such reservation afresh in its 1959 declaration. In this respect, its position appears to be similar to that of Turkey in 1931, but with the following differences: Sri Lanka had long been a country of the Union, whereas Turkey was not; no objection was made to the Sri Lankan reservation; and it has continued to exercise the rights of a member country and to be listed as such by the International Office in *Le Droit d'Auteur*. On the other hand, in the same lists the International Office has refrained from referring to the reservation and this continues to be the case. As a matter of practice, therefore, it can be said that the Sri Lankan reservation has quietly fallen into limbo, while no question has been

[157] [1932] *DA* 38.

[158] Brussels Act, art 25(3).

raised about its entitlement to be a Union member. In view of the fact that Sri Lanka now has the option of adhering to the Paris Act and taking advantage of the provisions of the Appendix with respect to restrictions on translation rights, it may be doubted whether any dispute is likely to arise over any action which it may take that falls within the limits of those provisions (even if it remains bound only by the Rome Act).

(c) Countries still bound by the Brussels Act

17.31 Until its accession to the Paris Act in January 1996, the only country which continued to apply a reservation under this Act was Turkey. This country acceded to Brussels in 1952, subject to a correctly formulated reservation which replaced article 8 of the Brussels Act by article 5 of the Berne Act as modified by article 1(III) of the Paris Additional Act 'with respect to the translations into the Turkish language'.[159] However, the UK accession to the Brussels Act was also made subject to the

> . . . specific declaration that the Government of this country accepts the provisions of Article 11 of the Act on the understanding that it remains free to enact such legislation as it considers necessary in the public interest to prevent or deal with any abuse of the monopoly rights conferred upon owners of copyright by the law of the United Kingdom.[160]

If this had the same effect as a reservation, it would fall outside what is permitted by article 27 of the Brussels Act and would render the UK's ratification as ineffective as the Turkish accession in 1931. However, it was suggested above (see para 13.91) that the UK declaration is not to be interpreted as a reservation, because it does not purport to modify or exclude the legal effects of article 11 but is simply a statement that the UK stands ready to apply its public laws to the exercise of private rights under that article. As such, it can also be argued that the declaration was unnecessary, but has the advantage of allowing other Union countries to know in advance of the UK Government's attitude. Since January 1990, the UK has been a member of the Paris Act, but has not indicated a change in policy in relation to anti-monopoly measures.

(d) The Paris Act

17.32 The range of possible reservations is now wider, and, according to WIPO, the following remain in force:

(i) The retention of a term of protection less than life plus fifty years (article 7(7) of the Paris Act): No reservations are maintained under this provision.

[159] [1951] *DA* 133.

[160] [1957] *DA* 225. Note that similar declarations were also made on their ratification and accession by South Africa: [1950] *DA* 61; and Australia: [1969] *Copyright* 94.

However, a similar reservation was also permitted under article 7(7) of the Stockholm Act, and, in ratifying the whole of that Act in 1969, Romania declared that it would retain its current term in accordance with article 7(7).[161] However, articles 1 to 21 and the Protocol of that Act never entered into force, and the Romanian declaration was of no effect. As long as that country had not acceded to the Paris Act, it still remained bound by the substantive provisions of the Rome Act and under this was entitled to keep its shorter term of protection. It acceded to the Paris Act on 9 September 1998, and must now apply the term of life plus fifty years.

(ii) Administrative and final clauses only: The following five countries have limited their ratification of, or accession to, the Paris Act to the administrative and final clauses only: Bahamas, Malta, South Africa, Sri Lanka, and Zimbabwe.[162]

(iii) Jurisdiction of the International Court of Justice: The following twenty-two countries have made reservations in the form allowed by article 33(2) with respect to the jurisdiction of the International Court of Justice: Algeria, Bahamas, Egypt, Guatemala, India, Indonesia, Israel, Lesotho, Libya, Lithuania, Malta, Mauritius, Mongolia, Oman, Saint Lucia, South Africa, Tanzania, Thailand, Tunisia, Turkey, Venezuela, and Vietnam.[163] (The effect of this reservation is discussed further at para 17.88 below.)

(iv) Faculties provided by articles II and III: Following the entry into force of the Appendix (10 October 1974), five countries gave notification that they intended to avail themselves of the faculties provided by articles II and III: Mexico,[164] Suriname,[165] Niger,[166] Guinea,[167] and India.[168] These declarations expired on 10 October 1984, and were maintained until 10 October 1994 by India[169] and Mexico[170] only. As of December 2004, the following countries had made declarations (operative until October 2014) under article I of the Appendix with respect to the faculties provided by articles II and III: Bangladesh,[171] Cuba,[172] Jordan,[173] Mongolia,[174] Oman,[175] Philippines,[176]

[161] [1969] *Copyright* 235.
[162] See the list of Union membership in [1986] *Copyright* 6–8.
[163] See the list of Berne members as at 2 Dec 2004 at www.wipo.int.
[164] [1976] *Copyright* 187. [165] ibid, 275. [166] [1978] *Copyright* 119.
[167] [1980] *Copyright* 306. [168] [1984] *Copyright* 111. [169] ibid.
[170] [1984] *Copyright* 217.
[171] Berne Notification No 234. (This notification and those listed in the notes that follow are available at www.wipo.int/edocs/notdocs/en/berne/.)
[172] Berne Notification No 238, renewing previous declaration to Oct 2004.
[173] Berne Notification No 232, renewing previous declaration to Oct 2004.
[174] Berne Notification No 237, renewing previous declaration to Oct 2004.
[175] Berne Notification No 233.
[176] Berne Notification No 235, renewing previous declaration to Oct 2004.

Sudan,[177] Syrian Arab Republic,[178] United Arab Emirates,[179] and Vietnam,[180] while Thailand had made a declaration with respect to article II.[181] Previous declarations under article I of the Appendix with respect to the faculties under articles II and III (to October 2004) had been made by Algeria,[182] Bahrain,[183] Democratic Peoples' Republic of Korea,[184] and Singapore,[185] but these were not renewed when they expired.

(v) **Translation rights**: The following four countries have made or retained reservations with respect to translation rights in accordance with the provisions of article 30(2): Bosnia and Herzegovina, Cyprus, Serbia and Montenegro, and Slovenia.[186] Japan also had made such a reservation, but this was only retained until 31 December 1980.[187]

17.33 Several other declarations have been made by countries ratifying or acceding to the Paris Act. As these are not expressly authorized by the provisions above, their legal effect deserves brief consideration. First, at the Stockholm and Paris Conferences, a number of countries made known their opposition to the retention of article 31 which allowed Union members to apply the Convention to dependent territories. This was seen to be a relic of colonialism and contrary to the policy of the United Nations which was embodied in a Declaration of the General Assembly of the United Nations made in 1960.[188] Accordingly, it was made the subject of declarations by certain countries in depositing their instruments of ratification or accession to the Paris Act.[189] The terms of these declarations vary to some extent, but their purpose appears to be simply that of condemning the philosophy underlying article 31. Thus, the declaration by Hungary stated that it regards the provision as 'contrary to the Declaration on the Granting of Independence to Colonial Countries and Peoples, contained in United Nations General Assembly resolution 1514(XV) of December 14, 1960'.[190] There was no statement, however, by Hungary as to the legal consequences which it attached to this contradiction, and whether it intended to exclude or modify the effect of article 31 with respect to countries which apply the provision to their dependent territories. Consequently, it is difficult to

[177] Berne Notification No 240. [178] Berne Notification No 245.

[179] Berne Notification No 236. [180] Berne Notification No 241.

[181] To Oct 2014: Berne Notification No 239, renewing previous declaration to Oct 2004.

[182] Berne Notification No 194. [183] Berne Notification No 177.

[184] Berne Notification No 224. [185] Berne Notification No 198.

[186] www.wipo.int. [187] [1975] *Copyright* 43.

[188] Declaration on the Granting of Independence to Colonial Countries and Peoples, contained in Resolution 1514(XV) of 14 Dec 1969 of the General Assembly of the United Nations.

[189] Hungary, 15 Dec 1972: [1972] *Copyright* 199; Bulgaria, 4 Dec 1974: [1974] *Copyright* 233; GDR, 18 Feb 1978: [1977] *Copyright* 331; Czechoslovakia, 11 Apr 1980: [1980] *Copyright* 84.

[190] See n 188 above.

regard such a statement as a reservation, and the question of whether it endangers the validity of Hungary's ratification of the Paris Act does not arise. Furthermore, the making of a declaration in these terms seems justified by a new paragraph which was added to article 31 at the time of the Paris Revision.[191] This provides that:

> (4) This Article shall in no way be understood as implying the recognition or tacit acceptance by a country of the Union of the factual situation concerning a territory to which this Convention is made applicable by another country of the Union by virtue of a declaration under paragraph (1).

There are precedents for such a provision in other industrial property conventions, such as the Patent Cooperation Treaty.[192] However, this does not permit other Union countries to disregard any declaration that is made under article 31(1): they are still obliged to protect works which have as their country of origin a country which is the subject of such a declaration. Its effect, therefore, is simply to state that acceptance of such a declaration cannot operate in any way as recognition of the dependent or colonial status of the territory in question. This view is clearly expressed in the following declaration in relation to article 31 which was made by the former GDR at the time of its accession to the Paris Act:

> The German Democratic Republic, in its attitude towards Article 31 of the Convention, in so far as it concerns the application of the Convention to colonial and other dependent territories, is guided by the stipulations of the United Nations Declaration on the Granting of Independence to Colonial Territories and Countries (res. 1514(XV) of 14 December 1960), which proclaims the necessity of bringing to a speedy and unconditional end colonialism in all its forms and manifestations.[193]

Second, in extending the effects of its ratification to articles 1 to 21 and the Appendix of the Paris Act in 1984, India declared that its ratification was not to apply to the provisions of article 14bis(2)(b) which deals with the presumption of legitimation for authors who have made contributions to the making of a cinematographic film.[194] On its face, this appears to be an unauthorized reservation to the Act, but on closer examination this is not the case. The presumption of legitimation in article 14bis(2)(b) is applicable to some Union countries only: those whose laws include authors who have brought contributions to the making of a cinematographic work among the owners of copyright in that work. In consequence, there is nothing in the provision which is applicable to those Union countries, such as India, which do not provide for this under their

191 *Records* 1971, 59–60 (Document B/DC/5).
192 Patent Cooperation Treaty 1970, art 62(4).
193 See n 188 above.
194 [1984] *Copyright* 111.

laws.[195] Accordingly, it is difficult to see that India's declaration operates in any way to exclude or modify the effect of article $14^{bis}(2)(b)$: it is simply a statement informing other Union countries of the status of Indian law on the matter of ownership of copyright in cinematographic works.

(6) Denunciation of the Convention

17.34 Under article 35(1), no time limit is set on the duration of the Convention. This has been the case since the Berne Act, but there has also been accompanying provision for countries to leave the Union by denouncing the Convention.[196] This position continues under the Paris Act, and member countries can do this by a simple notification to the Director General.[197] Such a denunciation not only applies to the Act which currently binds the country in question, but to all previous Acts as well,[198] thereby excluding the possibility of a Union member seeking to downgrade its Union obligations by denouncing the latest Act binding it, while remaining bound by an earlier Act. Denunciation has effect only with respect to the denouncing country, and does not have any impact on the relations between the remaining Union members.[199] Thus, article 35(2) provides that the Convention remains 'in full force and effect as regards the other countries of the Union'. This last provision underlines the fundamental notion of the Union as a continuing and autonomous association of countries which is unaffected by changes in its membership. Denunciation takes effect one year after the day on which the notification is received by the Director General.[200] However, the right of denunciation may not be exercised until the country in question has been a member of the Union for at least five years.[201] The result of this last provision is that a new member must remain in the Union for at least six years following its accession. In the lifetime of the Convention, there have been only six formal denunciations given in accordance with article 35 and its predecessors: Montenegro (1900),[202] Liberia (1930),[203] Haiti (1943),[204] Indonesia (1960),[205] Syria (1962),[206] and Upper Volta (1970).[207] Each of these countries has now rejoined,[208] in the case of Montenegro as part of the former Yugoslavia

---

195 Indian Copyright Act 1957, s 2(d).

196 Berne Act, art 20; Berlin, Rome, and Brussels Acts, art 29.

197 Paris Act, art 35(2). 198 ibid. 199 ibid. 200 ibid, art 35(3).

201 ibid, art 35(4). This time limit was first instituted in art 29(3) of the Brussels Act, but was differently formulated so as to be five years from the date of ratification or accession of that Act, not five years from the date of joining the Union.

202 [1899] *DA* 61 (it was stated that this action was taken 'for reasons of economy').

203 [1929] *DA* 37. 204 [1942] *DA* 73. 205 [1959] *DA* 79.

206 [1961] *DA* 70. 207 [1969] *Copyright* 235.

208 These accessions have all occurred since the first edition of this commentary: Montenegro as part of the former Yugoslavia in 1931 ([1031] *DA* 85) and then together with Serbia in 1992; Liberia in 1989; Haiti in 1996; Indonesia in 1997; Syria in 2004; and Upper Volta as Burkino Faso in 1976 ([1975] *Copyright* 203).

in 1975 and now together with Serbia (since 1992). A seventh state, Mauritius, has also left the Union, although its 'denunciation' in this case took the form of a declaration of the non-application of the Convention, following the application of the Brussels Act to its territory by the UK prior to its independence.[209] A number of other countries have also left the Union, either involuntarily (through extinction) or by implication (following the grant of independence to former colonial or dependent territories). These last two situations are discussed below (see paras 17.37 and 17.65). As a general matter of customary international law, it should be noted that the Convention (or an Act of the Convention), once it has entered into force, does not come to an end if the number of countries which are party to it falls below the number required for it to come into force.[210]

(7) Succession of states in Union membership and application of the Convention

Over its lifetime, the membership of the Union has not only increased to cover almost all the nations of the globe, but many of the members have themselves undergone profound changes. Of the original signatories in 1886, only two—Switzerland and the UK—have not undergone any major constitutional or political upheaval. As a general rule, however, changes of government, even where these result from revolution or *coup d'état*, do not affect the continuity of a state and its ability to enter into and be bound by international treaty commitments.[211] Thus, the fact that France has experienced three successive constitutional regimes since 1886 or that Spain has suffered civil war and has had successively monarchical, republican, and then monarchical forms of government in this time does not affect the continuance of France and Spain as states in international law. In the same way, increases or decreases in the size of a state do not generally affect its continued identity as a state or the international obligations which bind that state. On the other hand, states can cease to exist in a number of ways, such as through conquest and annexation by another state or through the breakup of their component parts, as in the case of the dissolution of a former empire or confederation. As a corollary, new states can come into existence in a variety of ways, such as dismemberment of a state that no longer exists, separation from another state or through joining with another state or states to form a new sovereign entity. They may also come into existence as the result of a grant of independence from a former colonial or protecting power. In addition, it is possible for states to cease to exist for a period and then to be re-established. In each of these instances, the question arises as to whether, and to **17.35**

[209] [1970] *Copyright* 208. Mauritius rejoined the Union in 1989.
[210] Vienna Convention, art 55.
[211] See generally Crawford (n 91 above), 405ff.

what extent, the new state succeeds to the rights and obligations of treaties binding its predecessor. In the case of the Berne Convention, of course, 'statehood' is not a prerequisite for membership of the Union, or for the application of the Convention to a particular territory (as in the case of dependent territories). Nevertheless, even if the term 'country' means something less than 'state', the general principles of state succession to treaty obligations are highly relevant, and require further consideration.

(a) Increases and decreases in territory

17.36 The general principle is that these changes do not affect the international obligations of a state.[212] In the course of the twentieth century, many members of the Union have experienced significant territorial changes. Prominent examples within the European sphere are: the separation of most of Ireland from the UK in 1921; the loss of Alsace and Lorraine by Germany to France and the corresponding increase in French territory after World War I; the extension of German territory through the annexation of Austria and Bohemia and Moravia in 1938 and 1939; the loss of Polish territory to the former Soviet Union after World War II and the gains by Poland and the former Czechoslovakia of territory that had formerly belonged to Germany; and the separation of Algeria from metropolitan France in 1962. In some of these cases, the transfer of sovereignty from one state did not affect the continued application of the Convention in the territory in question. Thus, in the case of Alsace and Lorraine, as both Germany and France were members of the Union, the passing of sovereignty to France meant only that from this time the Convention applied to these areas as part of France (and subject to the conditions governing French adherence to the Convention), rather than as part of Germany. On the other hand, the Convention no longer continued to apply to Algeria and the former Polish territories, as neither the new independent state of Algeria nor the Soviet Union were members of the Union.

(b) The extinction and re-establishment of states

17.37 Several Union members have ceased to exist entirely, and as a result their membership of the Union and the application of the Convention in their former territory has come to an end. Thus, Estonia and Latvia, which joined the Union in 1927[213] and 1937[214] respectively, were annexed by the Soviet Union in 1940. While the legality of this action and the consequent extinction of the international legal personality of these states was strongly disputed by many

[212] See generally McNair (n 79 above), 633ff and references cited therein. Note also the general principle in relation to succession in respect of part of territory now contained in art 15 of the Vienna Convention on Succession of States in Respect of Treaties, 1978.

[213] [1927] *DA* 89.

[214] [1937] *DA* 4.

countries,[215] there can be little doubt as to the factual situation which prevailed in both cases: territory which was formerly governed by independent states now passed under the control of a state that was not a member of the Berne Union and the Convention therefore ceased to apply in those countries. Another wartime victim of annexation was the Free City of Danzig, which was annexed by Germany in 1939 and eventually became part of Poland after 1945.[216] In this case, however, the Berne Convention continued to apply to the territory of the former Free City by virtue of the fact that both Germany and Poland were Union members. On the other hand, there are instances where member countries of the Union have ceased temporarily to exist, but have been re-established after a period of time. This, indeed, happened in the cases of Estonia and Latvia, which re-emerged as independent states after the breakup of the former Soviet Union in 1990 to 1991, and soon after rejoined Berne.[217] It also occurred in the case of Austria, which was annexed by Germany in 1938 and the former Czechoslovakia, parts of which were annexed by Germany in 1938 and 1939 and the remainder made into the puppet state of Slovakia. Unlike the Baltic states and Danzig, these two states were reconstituted after World War II and it is generally considered that there was no break in their continued existence.[218] So far as the Berne Union is concerned, however, a different view was adopted at the time of these occurrences by the International Office. Thus, Austria was treated as part of Germany from the time of its annexation (13 March 1938),[219] and the same attitude was taken to Danzig (after 1 September 1939).[220] A different approach, however, was adopted towards Czechoslovakia. Parts of this (the Sudetenland) had been annexed by Germany in 1938 and the Convention therefore applied to them as part of Germany.[221] On the other hand, Czechoslovakia, with its reduced territory, was still in existence and was still regarded as a member of the Union.[222] In 1939, however, following further German intervention, the country was divided into two parts: the Protectorate of Bohemia and Moravia

---

[215] See generally Crawford (n 91 above), 419–20. See also [1941] *DA* 3, where it was reported that the International Office for Industrial Property had received a notification from the USSR, dated 6 Aug 1940, saying that from this date the previously independent Republic of Estonia was no longer bound by conventions to which it had previously adhered. It was also reported that no note from Latvia had been received, but it was to be assumed that the same position applied to that state, following its incorporation into the USSR. See further Marek (n 115 above), ch VIII.

[216] Crawford (n 91 above), 163–6.

[217] In 1994 and 1995 respectively: www.wipo.int.

[218] Crawford (n 91 above), 418–19.

[219] Thus, in the list of Union members from 1939 to 1945, *Le Droit d'Auteur* treated Austria as part of Germany. In the list for 1939, Austria was simply omitted: [1939] *DA* 1–2; but from 1940, it was clearly indicated that it had been incorporated in Germany: [1940] *DA* 1–2.

[220] In the lists of Union membership from 1940–5, Danzig was treated in the same way as Austria: see eg [1940] *DA* 1–2.

[221] For the details of the partition of Czechoslovakia, see M Gilbert, *Recent Historical Atlas 1860 to 1960*, revd edn (1977), maps 53 and 54.

[222] See list of members as at 1 Jan 1939: [1939] *DA* 1–2.

and the nominally independent state of Slovakia. The International Office took the view that the first of these territories continued to be bound by the rights and obligations previously binding on Czechoslovakia.[223] However, it regarded Slovakia as an independent state which had come about as a result of the dismemberment of Czechoslovakia and was therefore no longer bound by the treaty obligations of that state.[224] Accordingly, Slovakia had now left the Union and the Convention no longer applied in its territory. With respect to the first of these views, it is not entirely clear whether the International Office considered that the Protectorate of Bohemia and Moravia was bound by the Convention (i) as a new state which had succeeded to the treaty obligations of its now extinguished state of Czechoslovakia or (ii) whether this was simply the state of Czechoslovakia that still continued, albeit under a different name, in the capacity of a protected state and with a vastly reduced territory. As the basis for the first of these alternatives is not clear, the second appears more likely, particularly as membership of the Union under the Rome Act was open to countries, rather than states,[225] and there were other member countries, such as Morocco and Tunisia, which were also protectorates. Under this view, therefore, Czechoslovakia had not ceased to be a member of the Union and the Convention was still applicable in its territory. Following World War II, however, both Austria and Czechoslovakia regained their status of independent states, and duly notified the International Office of their continued membership of the Union. Both declarations went on to state that they regarded their membership to have been maintained

> . . . without any interruption and with all the consequences deriving from their uninterrupted participation in the Union, the continuity of Austrian [Czechoslovak] laws in this regard remaining unaffected by the German occupation of Austrian territory [by the enemy occupation of Czechoslovak territories whether effected directly or indirectly in the form of the proclamation of the independent state of Slovakia].[226]

As a consequence, both Austria and Czechoslovakia were now regarded as having been members of the Union without interruption since their respective dates of accession to the Berlin Act in 1920 and 1921 respectively.[227] Furthermore, their declarations had the consequence that works which had Austria and

---

223 [1939] *DA*, 1, n 4.

224 See editorial note in [1944] *DA* 61, following the purported accession of Slovakia to the Convention. See further Marek (n 115 above), 290ff.

225 Rome Act, art 25(1).

226 [1948] *DA* 61 (declaration by Austria); [1947] *DA* 137 (declaration by Czechoslovakia).

227 From 1946, Czechoslovakia was restored to the list of members (before its declaration of 1947); Austria was not reinstated until 1949, although it was present and participated at the Brussels Conference: [1949] *DA* 1 and *Documents 1948* (1951), 54. See further Marek (n 115 above), 323–30.

Czechoslovakia as their countries of origin in the period 1938 to 1945 should continue to receive protection in other countries of the Union. The position of Czechoslovakia then changed in 1993 with the 'velvet divorce' between its Czech and Slovak components (see further para 17.43 below).

A distinct, though analogous, situation to those described in the preceding paragraph concerns the occupation of states by enemy forces during time of war, but without any formal act of annexation. The most obvious examples of this occurred in World War II where the territories of a number of Union members were occupied wholly or in part and at various times by German and Italian forces, notably France, Belgium, the Netherlands, Norway, Denmark, Poland, Yugoslavia, Greece, Finland, Bulgaria, Hungary, and Romania. In each case, the states themselves continued to exist, despite their occupation by enemy forces, while the occupations were, in any event, strongly disputed both internally and externally. Furthermore, at the end of the War these enemy forces had been expelled, and there were once again independent governments exercising control in each of these countries. The general principle appears to be that, although a state of war may interfere with a state's performance of its international obligations under a multilateral treaty such as the Berne Convention, it does not bring these obligations to an end[228] (see further para 17.92 below). The same conclusion should therefore follow where a state is temporarily occupied by belligerent forces during wartime. This was certainly the view of the International Office which continued to list all the occupied countries referred to above as members of the Berne Union, throughout the War.[229] **17.38**

(c) The creation of new states

Particular problems arise where new states come into existence. Although there are exceptions, new states are usually created from territory which was previously part of another state or was territory dependent on another state. Consequently, if the provisions of international conventions, such as that of Berne, applied in that territory before its accession to statehood, it is necessary to ask if those provisions continue to apply to that territory after this **17.39**

[228] See generally McNair (n 79 above), ch 43; Crawford (n 91 above), 407.

[229] See the lists of membership published in *Le Droit d'Auteur* between 1941 and 1945. Note, however, that in June 1941, the German Government made a specific communication to the International Office confirming the continued application of the Rome Act in the Government General of Poland which had replaced the 'former Republic of Poland' in Sept 1939: [1941] *DA* 85. This last statement would certainly not have been accepted by the Polish Government in exile: see further Crawford (n 91 above), 311–12 and 409–12 (the international disputes after 1945 about Poland concerned the composition of the Polish Government, rather than the continuity of the state of Poland). For further background on Poland between 1939 and 1945, see Marek (n 115 above), ch IX.

time.[230] The applicable principles of international law are far from clear here, although, as a general proposition, it is usually asserted that new states begin their existence with a clean sheet unencumbered by the treaty obligations that bound their predecessors.[231] However, this proposition is subject to so many qualifications that it is only of limited assistance in the present context. First, it seems that a 'tendency towards succession' is to be found in the case of at least some categories of multilateral conventions, although the criteria for determining which of these shall be transmissible are uncertain and it is therefore difficult to discern any generally applicable rule of customary international law.[232] As a general matter, however, it can be said that the sociological justification for a presumption of continuity in the case of multilateral conventions is obvious.[233] Thus, D P O'Connell observed, with reference to the newly independent states of Africa in the early 1960s:

> . . . the complex structure of treaty law, upon which the dynamism of the economic, moral and technological universe depends, cannot be permitted to disintegrate upon the arrival to maturity of a whole continent the size of Africa.[234]

Secondly, account must be taken of any provision in the convention itself concerning the succession of parties to that convention, as well as any provision in an instrument of devolution that seeks to specify the agreements of its predecessor by which a new state is bound. As instruments of this second kind were quite common in the case of grants of independence to former dependent territories, they will obviously be highly relevant for our present purposes. With respect to the Berne Convention itself, however, there is no provision which seeks to deal with this question, although such provisions are sometimes to be found in other multilateral treaties.[235] Thirdly, state practice will be the most

---

[230] One of most recent waves of new state creation, in the wake of the dissolution of the former Soviet Union, does not affect the following discussion, as the USSR was never a member of Berne. However, it is noteworthy that the great majority of the former Soviet republics have now acceded to the Paris Act of Berne: see para 17.21 above.

[231] This 'clean slate' principle was accepted by the International Law Commission in its preparatory work for the Vienna Convention on the Succession of States in respect of Treaties and is now contained in art 16 of that Convention: see generally I Sinclair, 'Some Reflections on the Vienna Convention on Succession of States in respect of Treaties', in *Essays in Honour of Erik Castren* (1979), 149, 158ff. See also K Yasseen, 'La Convention de Vienne sur la Succession d'États en Matière de Traites' [1978] 24 *Annuaire français de droit international* 59, 108ff.

[232] See generally O'Connell (n 119 above), 212. The provisions of arts 17–23 of the Vienna Convention on Succession of States in respect of Treaties also bear this out. However, these provisions do not apply to state successions occurring before its entry into force (art 7), so these provisions provide a guide only to the generally applicable rules of customary international law: see generally Sinclair (n 231 above).

[233] C W Jenks, 'State Succession in Respect of Law Making Treaties' (1952) 29 *BYIL* 105, 106.

[234] O'Connell (n 119 above), 213–17.

[235] See eg the second International Tin Agreement 1961, art XXII(b), referred to by O'Connell (n 119 above), 219.

important indicator of the way in which, if at all, new states may succeed to the obligations of a predecessor under a convention. This will not only include the attitude of the state itself to the continuance of these obligations, but also the acceptance of this by other states which are parties to that convention. In this regard, the role of a body, such as the International Office, may be of critical importance in defining this practice. Fourthly, in the case of the Berne Convention, where membership of the Union and application of the legal regime established under the Convention can be quite distinct, it becomes necessary to distinguish between the question of succession to membership and the continued application of the Convention to the territories of successor states or countries.

It will be clear from the preceding paragraph that our first concern here must be to survey the past practice of Berne Union members with regard to the question of succession. Only when this has been done will it be possible to deduce any rules that may be generally applicable and the juridical basis (if any) for these rules. It is therefore useful to distinguish between a number of situations in which new states may come into existence and to use these as a framework for our discussion. These situations are as follows. **17.40**

1. The creation of two or more new states, following the dismemberment of a previously existing state.
2. Creation of two or more new states through the dissolution of a union or federation.
3. Creation of a new state through separation or secession from another state (which still continues to exist).
4. Creation of a new state from the union or federation of several previously existing states.
5. Creation of a new state following the grant of independence to a former colonial or dependent territory (at the date of the first edition of this work (1987), this was the most important category and, for ease of discussion, can include territories placed under mandate or trust by the League of Nations or the United Nations).
6. The division of a state into two new states.

(d) Creation following dismemberment

The principal instance of this among the membership of the Berne Union was the creation of the separate states of Austria, Hungary, Czechoslovakia, Poland (in part), and Yugoslavia (in part) from the territories of the former Austro-Hungarian Empire at the end of World War II. In general, it seems that both Austria and Hungary considered themselves bound by imperial treaties insofar as they affected their respective territories, on the basis that these had been entered into by the Dual Monarchy, but this was not the attitude taken by **17.41**

Czechoslovakia or Poland.[236] However, from the point of view of the Berne Union, these matters were of no relevance as the Austro-Hungarian Empire had not acceded to the Convention and no question of state succession therefore arose. It was, in fact, made a condition of the Treaty of Peace of Saint Germain between Austria and the Allies that Austria would adhere to the Berne and Paris Conventions within a given period of time.[237] Austria did this in 1920,[238] along with Poland,[239] followed by Czechoslovakia in 1921,[240] Hungary in 1922,[241] and Yugoslavia in 1930.[242] The other instance of dismemberment which has arisen in the history of the Berne Convention is that of the former Czechoslovakia between the years 1938 and 1945. For the purposes of our analysis and for reasons which have already been referred to (see para 17.37 above), this belongs more correctly to the third category of separation or secession, which is discussed below (see para 17.43).

(e) Creation following dissolution of a union or federation

17.42 There has been a number of significant instances of dissolution in the history of the Berne Union, but these did not cause any particular problems with respect to succession.

(i) **Norway and Sweden**: These countries were joined together by a personal union of their respective crowns, but it appears that generally they were governed quite autonomously.[243] The personal union was dissolved in 1905, and both countries then became separate kingdoms. Although the status of prior treaties entered into by Norway and Sweden was questioned by the UK Government on the basis that the personal union had made them a distinct international legal personality, it appears that, in practice, both the Governments of Norway and Sweden acted quite independently of each other in the execution of their treaty engagements.[244] Furthermore, both had acceded separately to the Berne Act,[245] and had been regarded as separate members of the Union. Accordingly, the dissolution of the personal union between their respective crowns had no effect on their status as separate members of the Berne Union.

(ii) **Syria and Lebanon**: The relations of these countries to the Berne Union raise a number of important issues. Both were former Turkish territories which

---

[236] O'Connell (n 119 above), 179.

[237] Treaty of Peace between the Allied Powers and their Associates and Austria, 10 Sept 1919, art 239: [1920] *DA* 97, 98.

[238] [1920] *DA* 2. [239] ibid, 25. [240] [1921] *DA* 25. [241] [1922] *DA* 25.

[242] [1930] *DA* 85. Yugoslavia adhered to the Berlin Act as from 17 June 1930, and then, as from 1 Aug 1931, to the Rome Act.

[243] O'Connell (n 119 above), 168–9. [244] ibid.

[245] Norway on 13 Apr 1896: [1896] *DA* 65; Sweden on 1 Aug 1904: [1904] *DA* 89. Both countries were separately represented at the Berne Conferences of 1884–6: *Actes* 1884, 16, and *Actes* 1885, 8.

had been placed under French mandate by the League of Nations following World War I. Both were administered jointly by France, but to a very great extent kept their separate identities.[246] When France acceded to the Berne Convention on their behalf in 1924, there was some uncertainty about this action on the part of the International Office. There was an ambiguity about the French accession, as it purported to do this in accordance with article 26 of the Berlin Act (the dependent territories clause), but also nominated a class for the payment of contributions by the two countries.[247] However, it was uncertain whether France, as the mandatory power, could apply the Convention to these countries under article 26(1) which then only referred to 'Colonies or foreign possessions'. On the other hand, it was equally uncertain whether they could accede to the Convention in their own right, as article 25 of the Berlin Act applied only to 'states'. These problems were solved by appropriate amendments to the Rome Act (see para 17.21 above), and the accession of Syria and Lebanon to the Convention was not disputed. However, they were treated as one member, paying contribution fees on this basis,[248] and France again acceded on their behalf to the Rome Act in 1933.[249] In 1944, both countries became separate and independent states, and in 1947 Lebanon acceded to the Convention in its own name.[250] In the view of the International Office, this was not a new entry into the Union as this had occurred in 1924. The purported accession therefore was simply a communication to the Union that henceforth Lebanon and Syria were separate states.[251] The International Office also regarded this separation as being different from the creation of a new state through dismemberment or secession, treating both Lebanon and Syria as equal parts of a composite entity to which the Convention applied.[252] In other words, the Convention applied in both countries and continued to do so after their separation. It follows from this view that there was no need for the Lebanese act of 'accession'. This was confirmed in the case of Syria which refrained from making a similar declaration, but was still regarded as a separate member of the Union until its denunciation of the Convention in 1962.[253] On the other hand, the 'accession' of Lebanon certainly made it easier for the International Office to treat Lebanon and Syria henceforth as separate members, with the consequences that this entailed, rather than reaching this conclusion on its own authority. This underlines, in turn, the fact

[246] Crawford (n 91 above), 66.

[247] [1924] *DA* 85. The same question arose shortly afterwards when the UK acceded to the Berlin Act on behalf of its mandated territory of Palestine, but did so without stating whether this was pursuant to art 25 or 26: [1924] *DA* 97.

[248] As per the terms of the original accession of 1 Aug 1924 where France requested that this 'group of states' be placed in the sixth class for contributions: [1924] *DA* 85.

[249] [1933] *DA* 133. [250] [1947] *DA* 109. [251] ibid. [252] ibid.

[253] [1961] *DA* 70. See further C Masouyé, 'Décolonisation, indépendence et droit d'auteur' (1962) 36 *RIDA* 85, 92ff. Note that Syria rejoined the Union in 2004.

that the question of membership is distinct from that of the continued application of the Convention in particular territories. This point is taken up further below.

(iii) The dissolution of the former federal state of Yugoslavia: This state had joined as the Kingdom of Yugoslavia in 1930, and had acceded to both the Brussels and Paris Acts as a federal republic in 1951[254] and 1975[255] respectively. Upon the dissolution of the federal state, each of the former constituent republics acceded separately to the Paris Act within a few months of each other: Bosnia and Herzegovina,[256] Croatia,[257] Slovenia,[258] Serbia and Montegro,[259] and the former Yugoslav Republic of Macedonia.[260]

(f) Separation or secession from an existing state

17.43 There are a number of notable examples where new states have come into existence as the result of separation or secession from a state which is already a member of the Berne Union. These examples generally are in accordance with the proposition that new states are not bound by the treaty obligations of their predecessors.

(i) The separation of Ireland from the United Kingdom: The Convention applied to Ireland from the time of the UK's ratification of the original Berne Act, as Ireland was then an integral part of the UK. After the Anglo-Irish Treaty of 1921, the Irish Free State came into existence as a Dominion within 'the Community of Nations known as the British Empire', but in 1948 became completely independent as the Republic of Eire.[261] Although the other 'older British Dominions' such as Australia, Canada, and New Zealand generally took the view that they succeeded to British treaties formerly binding on their territory, it does not seem that the Irish Free State automatically adopted this approach.[262] However, according to a statement of the Irish Prime Minister in 1933, it accepted the position created by commercial and administrative conventions of the UK, until such time as the individual treaties or conventions were terminated or amended.[263] The Berne Convention would clearly fall into this category, and it seems reasonable therefore to conclude that the Irish Free State remained bound by the Berlin Act after 1921 although it was not formally a member country of the Union. However, in 1927, the Irish Free State acceded to the Berlin Act in its own name, subject to a reservation as to translation rights,[264] and this led the International Office to conclude that the

254 1 Aug 1951: [1951] *DA* 98, 110.
255 2 Sept 1975: [1975] *Copyright* 123.
256 1 Mar 1992.
257 8 Oct 1991.
258 25 June 1991.
259 27 Apr 1992.
260 8 Sept 1991.
261 See O'Connell (n 119 above), 123–4.
262 ibid, 122–3.
263 Statement by Mr De Valera quoted by O'Connell (n 119 above), 123.
264 [1927] *DA* 125.

Irish Free State had left the Union upon becoming a 'new state' in 1921, and that this was therefore the accession of a new member to the Union.[265] In the light of the general attitude adopted by the Irish Government with respect to commercial treaties, this view of the International Office must be doubted, as must its assumption that the Irish Free State had become fully independent by 1921.

(ii) The creation of the puppet state of Slovakia from Czechoslovakia: The circumstances of the creation of this state have already been discussed (see para 17.37 above). The view of the International Office was that Slovakia was an independent state and no longer a part of the Union was confirmed by Slovakia's accession to the Convention in 1944. As noted above (see para 17.37), Slovakia in truth became an independent state in 1993, following its separation from the now Czech Republic: both countries now list their date of accession to Berne as from 1 January 1993.

(iii) The creation of Pakistan from India: This event occurred simultaneously with the achievement of independence by India in August 1947. Prior to this, the territory of the new state had been part of British India which had been a member of the Berne Convention from 1928 and had had the Convention applied to it since the time of the UK's ratification of the Berne Act in 1887. The creation of Pakistan, however, led to considerable uncertainty as to whether that state could succeed to the rights and obligations of treaties that had bound British India (and that continued to apply to India after its accession to full independence).[266] To resolve this uncertainty with respect to the Berne Convention, Pakistan acceded to the Rome Act in 1948.[267] This accession implies that, in the brief period between its creation (15 August 1947) and the coming into force of its accession (5 July 1948), Pakistan was not bound by the Berne Convention. In this respect, its situation is analogous to that of Israel (see para 17.60 below). Another way of analysing its position would be to say that the Rome Act continued to operate in its territory during this period, and that the effect of its accession was simply to make it a member country of the Union. This argument is applicable in the case of a newly independent state to which the Convention was applied by its former colonial or protecting power (see further para 17.58 below). However, in the case of Pakistan, there was no identifiable country of Pakistan in existence prior to 1947 and so this argument does not seem sustainable.[268] Accordingly, the better view must be that, during this period, the Berne Convention did not apply to Pakistan.

[265] ibid. [266] O'Connell (n 119 above), 128–9. [267] [1948] *DA* 61.

[268] See further O'Connell (n 119 above), 184–7, on the debates over Pakistan's admission to the UN.

(iv) The creation of Algeria from France: Algeria had been 'attached' to metropolitan France since the nineteenth century, but, after a war of independence beginning in the mid-1950s, formal independence was granted by France in 1962.[269] Up to this time, there appears to be little doubt that the Berne Convention applied in Algeria as part of France. After its independence, however, the new state was generally unprepared to affirm any previous treaty commitments affecting its territory that had been entered into by France,[270] and there is no indication of any different approach being applied with respect to the Berne Convention. Accordingly, by analogy with the position in other new states created by secession, the only conclusion must be that the Berne Convention was no longer in force in Algeria. Subsequently, Algeria acceded to the Paris Act on 19 April 1998.[271]

(v) The creation of Bangladesh from Pakistan: Prior to 1971, the present state of Bangladesh was part of the state of Pakistan (as East Pakistan). However, in that year it seceded after a bloody war and was recognized as an independent state.[272] There can be no doubt that, up to this time, the Berne Convention applied to the present territory of Bangladesh as part of Pakistan. After 1971, it seems equally clear, by analogy with the creation of Pakistan itself, that Bangladesh was no longer bound by the Berne Convention. It did not accede to the Convention until 4 May 1999.[273]

(vi) The separation of Iceland from Denmark: Iceland was formerly part of Denmark, but entered into a real union with that state in 1918, becoming completely independent in 1944.[274] However, when Denmark acceded to the Convention in 1903, this did not extend to Iceland,[275] and this position was maintained in the Danish accession to the Berlin Act in 1912.[276] Accordingly, Iceland was not bound by the Convention until 1947 when it acceded to the Rome Act as an independent state.[277]

(g) Formation of a union or federation

17.44 The question of succession to treaty obligations can raise difficult issues when a state enters into a union or federation with other states, with the consequence that a new state comes into existence. This has been the case with a number of Union members, but the acts of union or federation have generally occurred prior to their entry into the Union. Prominent examples of states in this category are Germany, the former Yugoslavia (now disaggregated), and Canada. Several former British Dominions were also formed by unions or federations of

[269] Crawford (n 91 above), 259–60. [270] O'Connell (n 119 above), 113.
[271] www.wipo.int. [272] Crawford (n 91 above), 115–18. [273] www.wipo.int.
[274] O'Connell (n 119 above), 111. [275] [1903] *DA* 73. [276] [1912] *DA* 89.
[277] [1947] *DA* 85.

previous colonies, as in the case of Australia and South Africa. In their 'colonial' period, the Convention was applied to each of them (with their consent) by the UK,[278] but at the time of their separate accessions to the Convention, these acts of union or federation had already occurred. Several other unions or federations have occurred in the case of countries already bound by the Convention, but these are of little significance. Thus, in 1958 Syria entered into a union with Egypt to form the United Arab Republic.[279] However, no question of whether the Convention now extended to Egypt arose as it was expressly provided in the provisional constitution of the new state that treaties binding both states continued in force in relation to their respective territories.[280] The union was dissolved in 1961, and in the same year Syria denounced the Convention.[281] Another ephemeral example of a federation of Union countries occurred in the case of Senegal and French Soudan, both countries to which the Convention had been applied by France, their former metropolitan power.[282] This entity was formed in 1959 under the title of the Federation of Mali, but was dissolved in the following year.[283] There was no accession to the Berne Union by the new state, and subsequently Senegal and Soudan (now Mali) adhered to the Convention in their own right (see further paras 17.58 and 17.60 below).

(h) Grants of independence to former dependent territories

One of the most significant phenomenon in international affairs after 1945 has **17.45**
been the accession to independence of a large number of new states that were formerly the colonies or foreign possessions of other states. While the process of decolonization had largely concluded by the end of the 1960s,[284] the question of the succession of these states to the treaty obligations of their former governors can lead to considerable difficulties.[285] Of the original signatories of the Berne Act in 1886, four were European colonial powers with extensive overseas territories, chiefly in Africa and Asia. These were France, Germany, Spain, and the UK, while two other original signatories—Belgium and Italy—were shortly afterwards to acquire considerable foreign possessions. By 1914, the accessions of the

---

278 See para 17.49 below.

279 O'Connell (n 119 above), 169–70. See also Masouyé (n 253 above), 92ff.

280 Article 69 of the Provincial Constitution of the United Arab Republic referred to in O'Connell (n 119 above), 169.

281 With effect from 12 Jan 1962: [1961] *DA* 70.

282 O'Connell (n 119 above), 170ff.

283 ibid.

284 Significant new states to gain independence at later dates, either from their former metropolitan power or from UN trust status, were Papua-New Guinea (1975), Zimbabwe (1980), and Namibia (1990).

285 See generally O'Connell (n 119 above), chs 8 and 9. See further the detailed studies of O'Connell entitled 'Independence and Succession to Treaties' (1962) 38 *BYIL* 84 and 'State Succession and the Effect upon Treaties of Entry into a Composite Relationship' (1963) 39 *BYIL* 54.

Netherlands and Portugal had added two more large colonial empires to the Union, while several other new members, such as Japan and Denmark, had various external territories under their sovereignty. While the adjective 'colonial' is often used as a general description of the way in which these territories were governed, there were, in fact, many variations in their legal character and the degree of control that was exercised. Some were 'colonies' in the true sense, with governors appointed by the metropolitan power and exercising full control over the territory in question, but a number of these had developed into self-governing and largely autonomous entities by the late nineteenth century, particularly in the British Empire where they began to be described as 'Dominions'.[286] Others were referred to as 'protectorates', but this term came to have a very flexible meaning, ranging from the traditional situation where one state assumed responsibility for the 'protection' of another state which still retained a considerable degree of autonomy (as in the case of the British protectorate over Egypt and the French protectorates over Tunisia and Morocco) to cases where 'protectorate' really meant nothing more than disguised colonial control (as in the case of many of the sub-Saharan African territories).[287] Other territories, again, were simply placed under the overall sovereignty or suzerainty of another power, while still retaining a nominal independence, as in the case of the princely states of India.[288] On the other hand, some were actually 'attached' to or incorporated in the territory of the metropolitan power, the most notable example here being Algeria and France.[289] Finally, following World War I, the former territories of the German and Turkish Empires were placed under the control of certain of the Allied Powers which, among other things, were given an implicit mandate to bring these territories to self-government and independence.[290]

17.46 It was against this background that the UK delegation proposed at the 1885 Conference that provision should be made in the draft text of the Berne Act for the Convention to be extended to colonies and other possessions.[291] Article 19 therefore allowed states acceding to the Convention to accede thereto at any time for their 'Colonies and foreign possessions'. It was further provided that this could be done

> . . . either by a general Declaration comprising in the accession all their Colonies or possessions, or by specially naming those comprised therein, or by simply indicating those which are excluded.

---

[286] Crawford (n 91 above), ch 7.

[287] eg the British protectorates over Uganda, Swaziland, and Somaliland: see further Crawford (n 91 above), 198–201.

[288] ibid, 209–11.

[289] For background on the relationship of Algeria to France, see the various studies published in the *Annuaire Français de Droit International* between 1959–63.

[290] Crawford (n 91 above), ch 13.

[291] *Actes* 1885, 53.

No provision of this kind was contained in the Paris Additional Act concerning its application to colonies and other possessions. However, as this was a modification of the Berne Act and not a new Act, it seems reasonable to suppose that any ratification or accession to the Additional Act automatically extended to any colonies or possessions which had been the subject of a declaration under article 19 of the Berne Act. The latter provision was retained in essentially the same form as article 26 of the new Berlin Act, but was modified in a number of respects in the Rome Act. First, a more extensive description was included of the kinds of dependent territories that might be the subject of a declaration, so as to conform more closely 'with the political circumstances of such countries in relation to the metropolitan state'.[292] While the previous expression 'Colonies and foreign possessions' was quite general, some doubts had been raised as to whether this embraced territories under League of Nations mandates.[293] Furthermore, the Japanese delegation requested that reference be made to territories that were under the general sovereignty or suzerainty of another state, an expression which appeared more accurately to describe the relationship of Japan to countries such as Korea and Formosa.[294] The composite expression adopted in the Rome Act therefore referred to 'colonies, protectorates, territories under mandate or any other territories subject to its sovereignty or to its authority, or any territories under suzerainty'. The second change was to provide that the effect of a declaration by a Union country under this section would be to 'apply' the Convention to all or any of the territories named in the declaration, rather than to be an accession to the Convention for those territories. This change seems consistent with other changes in terminology that were made in the Convention at this time. Thus, to speak of 'accession' in the case of a colony or foreign possession, as under the Berne and Berlin Acts, was not accurate, as only contracting states could do this. In reality, what happened under these Acts was that the state extended the application of the Convention to these territories, which, in the language of the Rome Act, now became 'countries of the Union' without being regarded as members thereof and without the financial obligations entailed in this. The third change made in article 26 of the Rome Act was to declare explicitly that a notification made under the section only applied to the territories named therein, and, failing such notification, this notification was not to apply to those territories. Finally, it was provided that further notification might be made at any time stating that the previous notification was to cease to apply to all or any of the named territories and that this application would cease twelve months following the receipt of the second notification by the Swiss Government.[295]

[292] *Actes* 1928, 215 (report of E Piola Caselli). [293] [1924] *DA* 85.
[294] *Actes* 1928, 277. [295] Rome Act, art 26(2).

17.47 This provision was retained in much the same form in article 26 of the Brussels Act, except that the description of territories was changed again to be consistent with the terminology that was now current in the practice of the newly constituted United Nations. Thus, article 26(1) now referred to the application of the Convention to a Union country's 'overseas territories, colonies, protectorates, territories under its trusteeship, or to any other territory for the international relations of which it is responsible'. This wording was further modified in article 31(1) of the Stockholm, Paris Acts, which now provides for the application of the Convention to 'all or part of those territories, . . . for the external relations of which it [the Union country] is responsible'. The same provision for the withdrawal of notifications is retained under article 31(2), but more precise provision is now made for the coming into effect of these notifications under article 31(3). Finally, in the Paris Act, a new paragraph (4) was added, to accommodate the strong objections that had been made by a number of Union members to the 'colonialist' philosophy which they alleged was still embodied in the provision. (The background to these objections, and the effect of the new paragraph are referred to at para 17.73 below.)

17.48 At the present time, there are very few territories of any significance covered by notifications under article 31, although it should be noted that a number of Union countries still possess a string of small dependent territories or 'dependencies' which, because of their size and close links with the metropolitan country, will probably never succeed to viable independence and will therefore continue to fall within article 31.[296] However, from the beginning of the Convention, there was a large number of notifications made under the predecessors of article 31, and the Convention was applied to a wide range of dependent territories. It is therefore important to determine two matters: first, the territories which were covered by these notifications, and second, the status of these territories with respect to the Convention following their independence. The first is largely a factual question, which may have significance in relation to the present protection under the Convention of works that have been produced in these countries during the time the Convention was applied to them. The second is a more specifically legal question, but also has obvious practical implications with respect to the present protection of works under the Convention. (As to the first of these questions, the notifications made under the different Acts of the Convention are detailed in paras 17.49–17.54 below. The second of these questions is considered at paras 17.55ff below.)

[296] See the list of such territories under the entries for Australia, France, Denmark, the UK, US, New Zealand, Spain, and Portugal in *EYB* (n 110 above), vols I and II.

(i) The Berne Act

Only three of the original members took advantage of article 19 at the time of signature or ratification: **17.49**

(i) Spain: Spain, in its ratification, included 'all territories dependent on the Spanish Crown'.[297] Apart from Spain's African territories, these included the Philippines, Cuba, and Puerto Rico which passed out of Spanish dominion in 1899 and 1898 respectively, following the Spanish-American War.[298] The Convention therefore ceased to apply to these countries after this time, although the Republic of Philippines acceded to the Brussels Act in its own right in 1951.[299]

(ii) France: At the time of signature, France declared that its accession included 'all the colonies of France'.[300] This expression was of uncertain extent, and appeared to exclude French overseas territories that were protectorates, such as Madagascar and Cambodia. As will be seen below, the French territories covered by this declaration were not listed specifically until 1930.

(iii) United Kingdom: The UK, at the time of signature, declared that its accession comprehended 'the United Kingdom of Great Britain and Ireland and all the colonies and possessions of Her Britannic Majesty'.[301] This formulation was wider than that of France and seemed adequate to cover all British territories, even if these were not specified individually. On the other hand, before it made its accession in these terms, the UK Government had sought the consent of each of its self-governing colonies and possessions to its inclusion in the accession. These were: India, the Dominion of Canada, the Cape, Natal, New South Wales, Victoria, Queensland, Tasmania, South Australia, Western Australia, and New Zealand.[302] In addition, the UK Government expressly reserved its right to separate denunciation of the Convention with respect to one or several of these colonies or possessions.[303] This procedure accorded with the developing practice of the UK in relation to its self-governing Dominions.[304]

(iv) Germany: In 1909, Germany acceded to the Convention in respect of all its protectorates ('*pays de protectorat*' or '*Schutzgebiet*').[305] It had earlier been the

[297] [1888] *DA* 8. [298] [1899] *DA* 77. See also Gilbert (n 221 above), maps 17 and 104.
[299] [1950] *DA* 97. [300] [1888] *DA* 7–8. See also *Actes* 1886, 21.
[301] ibid, 8. See also *Actes* 1886, 21.
[302] ibid. For the consents given by these colonies, see *Further Correspondence Respecting the Formation of an International Copyright Union*, C-4856 (1886), 8–17. See further [1889] *DA* 48 and [1890] *DA* 21.
[303] [1888] *DA* 8.
[304] See Crawford (n 91 above), 238ff and McNair (n 79 above), 111–17, and the references cited therein.
[305] [1908] *DA* 157.

view of the International Office that these countries had been covered by the earlier accession of the 'German Empire', but the making of this separate accession indicated that this was incorrect.[306]

A possible objection to the above declarations might be made on the basis that they were not made at the time of the accession to the Convention by these four states, as each was an original signatory and therefore ratified the Convention, rather than acceding to it. Nonetheless, it is clear that the intention of the Berne Conference of 1885 was that any member state with foreign possessions should be able to avail itself of the benefit of article 19 and that the word 'accession' was therefore used in that provision with a wider meaning than was usual.[307] This view is confirmed by the fact that it was left open to these states to accede to the Convention at a later date with respect to any of their colonies and possessions. Accordingly, 'accession' for the purposes of article 19 was a distinct act in the case of colonies and possessions which could be carried out at any time. For this reason, no significance is to be attached to the fact that France and the UK made their declaration of accession at the time of their signature of the Berne Act, while at that time Spain reserved its position and made its declaration at the time of exchange of ratifications. Another issue raised by article 19 was whether a declaration made under it applied to colonies and possessions that might be obtained in the future by a member country. In view of the fact that each of the declarations made above was couched in general terms, the answer to this was in the affirmative, and this was confirmed by the UK in 1903 when it notified the International Office that its declaration of 1886 now included its new colonies of Transvaal and Orange River.[308]

(j) The Paris Additional Act

17.50 As suggested above, it would seem that no renewed declaration was required to accede to the provisions of this Act and the Interpretative Declaration as they were simply modifications of the earlier Act. The only member country which made a declaration to this effect was the UK, which did so when depositing its ratification.[309]

(k) The Berlin Act

17.51 The following declarations were made.

(i) **Spain:** Spain again acceded to the Act in respect of 'all territories dependent on the Spanish Crown'.[310]

306 See the earlier views of the International Office in [1899] *DA* 77 and [1900] *DA* 13.
307 *Actes* 1885, 53. 308 [1903] *DA* 49. 309 [1907] *DA* 109.
310 [1910] *DA* 90.

(ii) Denmark: Denmark, acceding to the Convention for the first time, did so in relation to the Faeroe Islands, but excluded Iceland, Greenland, and the Danish Antilles from its accession.[311]

(iii) Portugal: The accession of Portugal, also for the first time, extended to all its colonies.[312]

(iv) United Kingdom: The accession of the UK was made applicable to all British colonies and possessions,[313] but the following self-governing Dominions were excluded from this declaration, although a separate declaration was made with respect to each at a later date: India (1912),[314] Canada (1924),[315] Australia, including Papua and Norfolk Island (1912),[316] New Zealand (1914),[317] Newfoundland (1913),[318] South Africa (1920),[319] and the Channel Isles (1914).[320] The UK accession was also made expressly applicable to Cyprus and the following British protectorates: Bechuanaland, East Africa, Gambia, Gilbert and Ellice Islands, Northern Nigeria, Southern Nigeria, Territories of the Gold Coast, Nyasaland, Northern Rhodesia, Southern Rhodesia, Sierra Leone, Somaliland, Solomon Islands, Swaziland, Uganda and Weihaiwei (in China).[321] Subsequently, the UK acceded to the Berlin Act in respect of the mandated territory of Palestine. This included the territory of Transjordan which was administered separately as part of the Palestine mandate.[322] Some uncertainty was expressed by the International Office concerning the basis for this act in view of the wording of article 26 of the Berlin Act[323] and the latter was amended accordingly in the Rome Revision (compare the French approach with respect to Syria and Lebanon: see para 17.42 above). Immediately prior to the Rome Conference, the self-governing Dominions of Australia,[324] Canada,[325] New Zealand,[326] and India[327] acceded to the Berlin Act in their own right, being preceded in 1927 by the Irish Free State.[328] In the case of India, it should be noted that Aden and Burma were then included in its territory;[329] whether the Indian accession also extended to the princely and native states under British suzerainty is less certain.[330] Finally, following the Rome Conference, South Africa also acceded to the Berlin Act in its own right.[331]

---

311 [1912] *DA* 89. 312 [1911] *DA* 45. 313 [1912] *DA* 90.
314 [1914] *DA* 33 (from 30 Oct 1912). 315 [1924] *DA* 13 (from 1 Jan 1924).
316 [1913] *DA* 165. 317 [1914] *DA* 46. 318 [1913] *DA* 149.
319 [1920] *DA* 49. 320 [1914] *DA* 33. 321 [1912] *DA* 90.
322 [1924] *DA* 97.
323 ibid. See further 'La situation des pays sous mandat dans les unions pour la protection de la propriété industrielle et des droits des auteurs' [1926] *DA* 62.
324 [1928] *DA* 57. 325 ibid. 326 [1928] *DA* 78. 327 [1928] *DA* 58.
328 [1927] *DA* 125.
329 See letter from the UK Government to the International Office referred to in [1939] *DA* 5.
330 See further Crawford (n 91 above), 210–11. 331 [1928] *DA* 133.

(v) The Netherlands: Acceding to the Convention for the first time, the Netherlands did so with respect to the European part of the Netherlands,[332] and then later for its territories of the Dutch East Indies, Curaçao, and Suriname.[333]

(vi) France: In acceding to the Berlin Act in 1910, France made no reference to its colonies and other possessions.[334] For some time, the International Office took the view that this was an oversight and the French accession was to be interpreted as having this effect in view of its original declaration when signing the Berne Act.[335] Subsequently, this view was shown to be mistaken as France acceded to the Berlin Act in 1930 in respect of its colonies and protectorates.[336] In consequence, it appears that, up to this time, French colonies (though arguably not protectorates; see para 17.49 above) were only covered by the French accession to the Berne Act, as modified by the Paris Additional Act.[337] In the case of Algeria, however, it seems clear that this would have been covered by the earlier French accession in respect of its metropolitan territory.[338] France also acceded to the Berlin Act in 1924 on behalf of its mandated territory of Syria and Lebanon.[339] However, this was not an application of article 26, but of article 25 and Syria and Lebanon thereby became member countries of the Union (see further para 17.42 above).

(vii) South Africa: In October 1931, South Africa extended its accession in respect of the Berlin Act and Berne Protocol so as to apply to its mandated territory of South West Africa.[340]

(l) The Rome Act

17.52 The following declarations were made under this Act.

(i) Japan: Japan, on ratification, declared the application of the Act to Korea (Chosen), Formosa (Taiwan), Sakaline (South) (Karafulo), and Kwantung (Kwanto).[341]

(ii) The Netherlands: The Netherlands, on ratification, retained its declarations with respect to the Dutch East Indies, Suriname, and Curaçao.[342]

(iii) United Kingdom: The UK, on ratification, declared the Convention applicable to Southern Rhodesia, the Channel Islands, and to British colonies and protectorates as well as to British mandated territories as follows: Bahamas, Barbados, Bermuda, British Guinea (Guyana), British Honduras, Ceylon,

---

332 [1912] *DA* 146.
333 [1913] *DA* 17 (Dutch East Indies); [1913] *DA* 29 (Curaçao); [1913] *DA* 61 (Suriname).
334 [1910] *DA* 86. 335 [1929] *DA* 60. See further [1930] *DA* 73.
336 [1930] *DA* 73. 337 ibid. 338 ibid. 339 [1924] *DA* 85.
340 [1932] *DA* 14 (from 28 Oct 1931). 341 [1932] *DA* 40 (from 1 Aug 1931).
342 [1931] *DA* 106 (from 1 Aug 1931).

Cyprus, Falkland Islands and dependencies, Fiji Islands, Gambia (colony and protectorate), Gibraltar, Gold Coast (comprising the Gold Coast colony, Ashanti Territory, Northern Territories and the British Mandated Territory of Togo), Hong Kong, Jamaica (including Turks and Caicos Islands and Cayenne Islands), Kenya (colony and protectorate), Leeward Islands (Antigua, Dominica, Montserrat, St Christopher and Neves, Virgin Islands), Malta, Mauritius, Nigeria (colony, protectorate and Mandated Territory of British Cameroon), Northern Rhodesia, Nyasaland (protectorate), Mandated Territory of Palestine (including Transjordan), St Helena and Ascension, Seychelles, Sierra Leone (colony and protectorate), Somalia (protectorate), Territories of the High Commission of South Africa (Basutoland, protectorate of Bechuanaland and Swaziland), Straits Settlements, Mandated Territory of Tanganyika, Trinidad and Tobago, Uganda (protectorate), West Pacific Islands (protectorate of British Solomons and colony of Gilbert and Ellice Islands), and the Windward Islands (Grenada, St Lucia and St Vincent).[343] Subsequent to this notification, the UK declared the Rome Act applicable to Newfoundland and the Federated Malay States,[344] Aden and Burma (following the separation of these territories from British India in 1937),[345] and British North Borneo and Sarawak.[346]

(iv) Spain: Spain, after acceding to the Act in 1933, in the following year declared it applicable to the Spanish zone of the protectorate of Morocco and to all Spanish colonies.[347]

(v) France: France, in acceding to the Act, declared it applicable to 'French colonies, as well as to protected countries and territories under the control of the French Minister of Colonies'.[348]

(vi) Denmark: Denmark, on accession, again made a declaration with respect to the Faeroe Islands.[349]

(vii) Australia: Australia, after its accession, declared it applicable to its territories of Papua and Norfolk Island and the Mandated Territories of New Guinea and Nauru.[350]

(viii) New Zealand: New Zealand, on accession, declared it applicable to its Mandated Territory of Western Somoa,[351] and much later to its dependent territories of Cook and Tokelau Islands.[352]

---

343 [1932] *DA* 38.

344 [1933] *DA* 134 (from 11 Dec 1933) (Newfoundland) and [1933] *DA* 3 (from 10 Jan 1933) (Federated Malay States).

345 [1939] *DA* 5 (from 1 Apr 1937).

346 [1938] *DA* 125 (from 1 Jan 1939).

347 [1934] *DA* 133 (from 8 Dec 1934).

348 [1933] *DA* 133 (from 22 Dec 1933).

349 [1933] *DA* 97 (from 16 Sept 1933).

350 [1936] *DA* 73 (from 29 July 1936).

351 [1948] *DA* 105 (from 4 Dec 1947) (note the earlier notification in [1947] *DA* 121 where the International Office erroneously assumed that the UK was the trustee power for this territory).

352 [1965] *Copyright* 55 (from 18 Mar 1965).

(ix) Belgium: Belgium, fourteen years after its own accession, applied the Act for the first time to the Belgian Congo and the UN Trust Territories of Ruanda-Urundi.[353]

(m) The Brussels Act

17.53 As this was adopted at the start of the post-World War II decolonization process, the number of declarations made under article 26 of this Act were more limited as metropolitan powers were reluctant to impose fresh treaty obligations on territories that were now rapidly moving towards independence. This reticence, however, did not affect the continuance of declarations made under earlier Acts (see further para 17.55 below).

(i) Belgium: Belgium, after its ratification of the Brussels Act, applied it to the Belgian Congo and the Trust Territory of Ruanda-Urundi.[354]

(ii) France: France, after ratification declared the Act applicable to its possessions, enumerating (for the first time) the following overseas territories: French West Africa (Senegal, French Soudan, French Guinea, Ivory Coast, Niger, Upper Volta, Dahomey, Mauritania), French Equatorial Africa (Gabon, Middle Congo, Oubangui-Chari, Chad), Madagascar and dependencies, Comoros, New Caledonia and dependencies, the French establishments in India, the French establishments in Oceania, the French coast of Somalia, the islands of St-Pierre and Miquelon, the French Trust Territories of Cameroon and Togo, and the Franco-British Condominium of New Hebrides.[355] The French declaration also referred to Tunisia and Morocco, but, as these were already member countries of the Union, the International Office regarded the French declaration as a ratification under article 25 on behalf of these countries.[356] Algeria was also not mentioned in the declaration, but as part of metropolitan France it was covered directly by the French ratification.

(iii) Portugal: Portugal, on accession, applied the Act to all 'overseas Portuguese provinces'.[357]

(iv) United Kingdom: The UK made no declarations on its accession in 1957, but thereafter made the following limited number of declarations: Channel Islands,[358] Fiji and Sarawak,[359] Bahamas,[360] Virgin Islands,[361] Falkland

353 [1948] *DA* 141 (from 20 Dec 1948).
354 [1952] *DA* 13 (from 14 Feb 1952).
355 [1952] *DA* 39 (from 22 May 1952).
356 ibid. 357 [1956] *DA* 109 (from 3 Aug 1956).
358 [1962] *DA* 46 (from 28 Nov 1961).
359 ibid.
360 [1963] *DA* 156 (from 19 Aug 1963). 361 ibid.

Islands,[362] Kenya,[363] St Helena,[364] Seychelles,[365] Mauritius,[366] Bechuanaland,[367] Grenada,[368] Cayman Islands,[369] British Guinea,[370] British Honduras,[371] St Vincent,[372] and Hong Kong.[373]

(n) Paris Act

The only declaration that has been made under article 31 was that by the Netherlands with respect to Suriname and the Netherlands Antilles.[374] This was limited to articles 22 to 38 of that Act. **17.54**

(o) Application of Convention following independence

The application of the different Acts of the Convention to the dependent territories of Union members resemble the layers of a cake, each made of slightly different ingredients. The following points should be noted. First, for any Act of the Convention to apply to these territories, it was essential that a declaration mentioning them either specifically or in general terms should be made. The effect of the omission of France to make such a declaration at the time of her accession to the Berlin Act has already been noted. Again, in the case of the German Empire, a ratification made in the name of that entity did not include its dependencies until these were specifically mentioned. This point is also important under later Acts; for example, Belgium did not declare the Convention applicable to its territories until 1948, and Portugal did not make any declaration with respect to its territories under the Rome Act. Thus, the effect of article 31 and its predecessors was to underline the distinction between membership of the Union and its territorial extent. In the absence of specific notifications, ratification or accession to the Convention only bound the metropolitan territory of the country ratifying or acceding, and did not automatically extend to its subject territories. Secondly, except where a declaration was made in general terms, those territories not specifically mentioned were not to be regarded as covered by the declaration. In this regard, the later British, Belgian, and the Netherlands declarations were the most specific. On the other hand, with general declarations it may require detailed research to establish exactly which territories were, for example, French or Spanish colonies, at the time of the making of the declaration. Problems of terminology may also arise, such as the distinction between 'colonies' and 'protectorates' or 'protected countries', **17.55**

[362] [1963] *DA* 238 (from 18 Oct 1963). [363] ibid (from 4 Nov 1963).
[364] ibid (from 18 Oct 1963). [365] ibid.
[366] [1964] *DA* 296 (from 27 Dec 1964). [367] [1966] *Copyright* 67 (from 4 Apr 1966).
[368] ibid, 90 (from 1 May 1966). [369] ibid, 91 (from 4 June 1966).
[370] ibid, 92 (from 5 June 1966). [371] [1967] *Copyright* 208 (from 1 Nov 1967).
[372] [1966] *Copyright* 242 (from 16 Oct 1966).
[373] [1973] *Copyright* 35 (from 5 May 1973).
[374] [1974] *Copyright* 251 (from 10 Jan 1975).

although these problems disappeared after the adoption of the redrafted article 26 of the Rome Act. A final point concerns the continued application of declarations to territories, if these were not included in a subsequent declaration made by their metropolitan power under a later Act. The example of France indicates that these earlier declarations continued to apply, even where the metropolitan power and other dependent territories had become bound by the new Act. As a matter of theory this must be correct, as prior Acts of the Convention still continue in force, and therefore can still be applied to those territories.[375] As a result, member countries had the option to exclude their dependent territories from the application of a later Act where a lower level of protection might seem more appropriate because of the developing character of these territories.

17.56 Following World War II, the vast majority of the territories referred to in the previous paragraphs attained their independence, although the ways in which this occurred varied considerably from country to country. As a general matter, however, it is possible to identify two broad categories of independent states: those which achieved it through an orderly transfer of power, and those which did so through force of arms. In the first category, the question of treaty succession was often dealt with by specific agreements between the new state and its former metropolitan power. In such cases, therefore, the inclusion of a convention or class of conventions (such as 'commercial treaties') in one of these lists provided some *prima facie* evidence of its continued application in that country.[376] On the other hand, a number of countries in this category took a more cautious attitude to the treaties of their predecessors, being prepared to regard them in force only as an interim measure subject to their examination for the purposes of subsequent confirmation or repudiation.[377] In the case of states falling into the second category, the position was clearer: by analogy with cases of secession (see para 17.43 above), it was easier to argue that these new states began their existence unbound by the treaties of their predecessors. In general, these classifications are reflected in the practice of the Berne Union, although a significant middle area still remains where the question of succession to the Berne Convention may be quite uncertain. In those areas where the situation is clearer, however, the International Office has played an important role in defining the practice.

17.57 **(i) The practice with respect to the older British Dominions:** This has already been referred to above (see para 17.49), but is worth reiterating, as these

---

[375] *Actes* 1908, 273.

[376] See generally O'Connell (n 119 above), chs 8 and 20. At the same time, it should be noted that succession to treaties under devolution agreements did not automatically bind other states that were parties to these treaties: see now Vienna Convention on Succession of States, art 9.

[377] As eg with the 'Nyerere doctrine' discussed by O'Connell (n 119 above), 116ff.

were the first dependent territories to join the Union as independent states. Their attainment of independence was an evolutionary process extending over more than fifty years, from the initial grant of limited self-government to the final acknowledgement of their capacity to engage in international relations on their own behalf.[378] Nevertheless, even by 1886 the UK Government would only enter into treaty commitments binding these territories with their consent.[379] This was done in 1886 and 1896,[380] and again with the Berlin Act where the UK Government, in accordance with the wishes of each Dominion, made separate notifications of the application of that Act to that Dominion.[381] These notifications were still made under article 26, but in 1928 Australia, Canada, New Zealand, and South Africa each acceded to the Convention in their own right under article 25.[382] It was made clear that this entailed no interruption in the application of the Act to their territories, but in the view of the International Office the effect of their accession was to make them contracting states of the Union.[383] In other words, while they had previously been part of the territory of the Union as British possessions, they were now full members with the rights and obligations attached to this status and, from 1929 on, were included in the list of Union members published annually by the International Office.[384] This succession to the rights and obligations previously exercised by the UK in relation to their territories is consistent with the almost universal succession to the treaties of the UK that is regarded as having occurred with respect to each of these Dominions.[385] In the case of the Berne Convention, however, it may be doubted that the word 'accession' was really appropriate to describe the act by which they acquired this status. Certainly, they did not accede to the Convention in the sense in article 25 of the Berlin Act, as they were not countries outside the Union. In reality, the effect of their actions was to confirm the application of the Convention to their territories and to undertake the

378 Crawford (n 91 above), 330ff; McNair (n 79 above), 640–54.

379 See generally O'Connell (n 285 above), 89ff.

380 See n 302 above. With respect to the 1896 Conference, there is no official correspondence in the published British records which refers to direct consultation with the self-governing colonies, but the attitude of the British delegation throughout the Conference was that it was very reluctant to entertain any proposal that might not be accepted by those colonies: *Actes* 1896, 36. See further *Correspondence Respecting the Copyright Conference at Paris*, C-8441 (1897).

381 See nn 314–20 above.

382 See nn 314–20 above.

383 See eg the accompanying comment made by the International Office in relation to the accessions of Australia, Canada, and India and their nomination of classes for the purposes of contributions: 'This double declaration implies a change in the situation of Australia [Canada, India] in the bosom of the Union. From 14 Apr 1928, . . . Australia has, in effect, become a contracting country, while previously it was only part of the Union as a non-autonomous British colony': [1928] *DA* 57. The last part of this statement, referring to the lack of autonomy of these countries, reflects a clear misunderstanding of the internal constitutional arrangements of these countries.

384 [1929] *DA* 1–2.

385 O'Connell (n 119 above), 122ff.

obligations of Union membership. In subsequent practice, this act has come to be known as a 'declaration of continued adherence', and this appears a more accurate description (see para 17.58 below).

17.58 **(ii) States declaring their continued adherence to the Convention:** From 1960 on, a number of newly independent states which had been covered by notifications under article 26 of the Rome or Brussels Act made declarations indicating the continued application of these Acts in their territory. It seems that the form of these declarations was adopted at the suggestion of the International Office,[386] and a similar practice had been followed in the case of other multilateral conventions.[387] For the most part, each declaration referred to the previous notification and confirmed that this had continued in force from the date of independence of the country making the declaration. They also specified the class in which the new state wished to be placed for the purpose of annual contributions. In substance, these declarations were indistinguishable from the accessions which had been made by the older British Dominions in 1928, except that in the case of the latter countries their achievement of independence had been a more evolutionary process and it was difficult to give an exact date for the occurrence of this event. In addition, as Table 17.1 shows, the declarations of continued adherence made in the post-1960 period were often made some time after the formal date of independence of the country making the declaration. In several other instances, the International Office took the course of describing an act of accession as a declaration of continuity. These were Ceylon (Sri Lanka) and the Ivory Coast. In the case of the first, the purported accession (dated 24 June 1959) was to the Rome Act, and, in view of the closure provision in article 28(3) of the Brussels Act, the logical conclusion was that this was in fact a declaration of the continuity of the Rome Act to Ceylon following the application of that Act to Ceylon by the UK in 1931.[388] The corollary to this was that the Rome Act had continued to apply to Ceylon in the period between its independence (in 1948) and the date of its purported accession, a state of affairs that was in no way disputed by Ceylon. In the case of the Ivory Coast, which had become independent on 7 August 1960, its accession was expressed to take effect from 1 January 1962.[389] While the implication to be drawn from an act of accession is that the country in question is not bound by the Act of the Convention and, furthermore, that it is a country outside the Union, the interpretation of the International Office overcame the problem that, for a period of eighteen months, the Ivory Coast would otherwise have ceased to be

---

[386] See the description of the letters sent by the Director of BIRPI to these countries on 31 Mar and 5 Dec 1960 in [1960] *Copyright* 336. See further G Ronga, 'Les colonies et l'Union de Berne' [1956] *DA* 21.

[387] See eg the declaration made by Dahomey (Benin) in [1961] *DA* 69.

[388] [1959] *DA* 205. [389] [1961] *DA* 257.

Table 17.1

Country	*Date of independence*	*Date of declaration*	*Act continued*
Dahomey (Benin)	1 August 1960	3 January 1961[1]	Brussels
Congo (B)	15 August 1960	8 May 1962[2]	Brussels
Mali (Fr Soudan)	20 June 1960	20 June 1960[3]	Brussels
Niger	3 August 1960	2 May 1962[4]	Brussels
Congo (L) (Zaire)	15 August 1960	8 October 1963[5]	Brussels
Cyprus	16 August 1960	25 February 1964/18 June 1968[6]	Brussels/Rome
Cameroon	1 January 1960	21 September 1964[7]	Brussels
Madagascar (Malagasy Rep)	26 June 1960	11 February 1966[8]	Brussels
Malta	21 September 1964	29 May 1968[9]	Rome
Fiji	10 October 1970	1 December 1971[10]	Brussels
Bahamas	10 July 1973	5 July 1976[11]	Brussels
Zimbabwe	18 April 1980	18 September 1981[12]	Rome
Namibia	21 March 1990	21 September 1993[13]	Berlin[14]

[1] [1961] *DA* 69.
[2] [1962] *DA* 146.
[3] ibid, 146.
[4] ibid, 170.
[5] [1963] *DA* 291.
[6] The first declaration of 1964 purported to continue the Brussels Act, which the UK Government had not extended to Cyprus: [1964] *DA* 127. This was, in fact, treated by the International Office as a declaration of continuity with respect to the Rome Act and as an accession to the Brussels Act: [1965] *DA* 3. However, in its later note of 1968, Cyprus indicated that it had been mistaken as to the effect of the previous declaration by the UK Government with respect to its territory, and wished to remain bound by the Rome Act only: [1968] *Copyright* 194.
[7] [1964] *DA* 273.
[8] [1960] *Copyright* 90.
[9] [1968] *Copyright* 178.
[10] [1972] *Copyright* 128.
[11] [1976] *Copyright* 363.
[12] [1981] *Copyright* 286.
[13] [1993] *Copyright* 243.
[14] Together with Berne Protocol of 1914 and the reservations made pursuant to art 27 of the Berlin Act, allowing for substitution of article 18 thereof, with respect to works not fallen into the public domain of their country of origin, by art 14 of the Berne Act 1886 as amended by para 4 of the Final Protocol of the Additional Act of Paris 1896: see [1993] *Copyright* 243. At the same time as making its declaration of continued application of the Berlin Act as from the date of independence Namibia acceded to the Paris Act, with effect from 24 Dec 1993.

bound by the Convention. In other instances of accession by newly independent states, however, the International Office has refrained from making any comments, leading to the conclusion that the Convention ceased to apply in the countries in question in the period between independence and accession (see further para 17.60 below).

(iii) Denunciations by newly independent countries: Denunciation of the Convention is, by definition, only necessary if the Convention is in force in the country making the denunciation. This therefore provides incontrovertible confirmation of the continued operation of the Convention in a newly **17.59**

Table 17.2

Country	*Date of independence*	*Date of denunciation*	*Act denounced*
Indonesia	27 December 1949	19 February 1960[1]	Rome
Syria	1 January 1944	12 January 1962[2]	Rome
Mauritius	12 May 1968	18 August 1971[3]	Brussels

[1] [1959] *DA* 79. See further on the background to the application of the Convention to Indonesia by the Netherlands, G Ronga, 'Les colonies et l'Union de Berne' [1956] *DA* 21, and G Ronga, 'The Position in the Berne Union of Countries which have Recently Become Independent' [1960] *DA* 320. See also [1956] *DA* 93.
[2] [1961] *DA* 70.
[3] [1970] *DA* 208.

independent state up to the time of the denunciation.[390] As Table 17.2 shows, this has happened in a number of cases, usually a considerable time after the date of independence.

This list does not include Upper Volta which became independent on 5 August 1960, acceded to the Brussels Act with effect from 19 August 1963[391] and then denounced it from 20 September 1970.[392] As noted above (see para 17.34), each of these countries has now re-entered the Berne fold.

17.60 (iv) **Accession by newly independent countries:** Accession to an Act of the Convention is only necessary where the country in question is not bound by that Act. In consequence, where a country accedes to an Act by which it was bound immediately prior to independence by virtue of an article 26 notification, the clear implication is that the Act has ceased to apply to that country upon its independence. This implication is easier to draw in the case of a country which has come into existence through secession or separation from an existing country (as in the case of Pakistan) or where the country has attained independence after a period of hostilities with its former colonial or protecting power. A classic instance of the second category is Israel, which was created out of the former British mandated territory of Palestine and came into existence without any orderly transfer of power.[393] The Berlin Act had been applied to this territory (along with Transjordan) by an article 26 notification made by the UK in 1926 and a similar declaration had been given in 1932[394] in respect of the Rome Act.[395] Following its attainment of independence on 15 May 1948, the new state sought to accede to the Rome Act in December 1949.[396] It stated further that its accession was to have retroactive effect as from the date of independence.[397] There would clearly have been no need for such retroactive

[390] See generally Masouyé (n 253 above), 90ff. [391] [1963] *DA* 156.
[392] [1970] *DA* 235. [393] See O'Connell (n 119 above), 155ff.
[394] [1924] *DA* 97. [395] [1932] *DA* 38. [396] [1950] *DA* 25. [397] ibid.

operation, if the declaration of the UK had still been effective. In this respect, then, it is clear that the Rome Act had ceased to apply in Israel in the period after its independence. However, there was no provision for the making of a retroactive accession in the Rome Act (nor, indeed, in any other Act of the Convention), and, for this reason, there were objections to the Israeli accession by several Union countries. In consequence, the International Office treated the Israeli accession as taking effect only three months after the date of its receipt, in accordance with article 25(3) of the Rome Act.[398] The result is that the Rome Act did not apply to Israel in the period from 15 May 1948 to 24 March 1950.

In addition to Israel, the following states listed in Table 17.3 acceded to Acts of the Convention by which they had been bound prior to their independence by an article 26 notification, although in none of these cases did the state achieve independence in circumstances similar to Israel.

Table 17.3

Country	*Date of independence*	*Date of accession*	*Act acceded to*
Senegal	20 June 1960	30 June 1962[1]	Brussels
Upper Volta	5 August 1960	19 August 1963[2]	Brussels
Gabon	17 August 1960	19 December 1961[3]	Brussels
Mauritania	28 August 1960	10 October 1972[4]	Brussels/Paris
Chad	11 August 1960	25 November 1971[5]	Brussels/Paris
Suriname	25 November 1975	25 February 1977[6]	Paris

[1] [1962] *DA* 170.
[2] [1963] *DA* 156.
[3] [1962] *DA* 70.
[4] [1971] *Copyright* 168.
[5] [1972] *Copyright* 240.
[6] [1976] *Copyright* 275

In each of these instances, the conclusion must be that the Convention ceased to apply in the period between the dates of independence and the coming into effect of the instrument of accession. To these countries must be added another group of newly independent states covered by article 26 notifications that have acceded to later Acts not covered by the notification (see Table 17.4). Each of these accessions has been treated by the International Office as an accession by a country outside the Union with the consequence that a similar break in the application of the Convention with respect to these countries has also occurred (see further, however, para 17.61 below).

[398] [1950] *DA* 62 (from 24 Mar 1950). See further Masouyé (1978), 96.

Table 17.4

Country	*Date of independence*	*Date of accession*	*Act adhered to*	*Act applied under article 26*
Togo	27 April 1960	30 April 1975	Paris[1]	Brussels
CAR	13 August 1960	3 September 1977	Paris[2]	Brussels
Guinea	28 September 1960	20 November 1980	Paris[3]	Rome
Barbados	30 November 1966	30 July 1984	Paris[4]	Brussels
Rwanda	1 June 1962	1 March 1984	Paris[5]	Brussels
Trinidad & Tobago	31 August 1961	16 August 1988	Paris	Paris
Lesotho	30 September 1966	28 September 1989	Paris	Rome
Guinea-Bissau	26 September 1973	22 July 1991	Paris	Brussels
Ghana	6 March 1957	11 October 1991	Paris	Rome
Malawi	6 July 1964	12 October 1991	Paris	Rome
Zambia	26 October 1964	2 January 1992	Paris	Rome
Gambia	18 February 1965	7 March 1993	Paris	Rome
Kenya	12 December 1963	11 June 1993	Paris	Rome
Nigeria	1 October 1960	14 September 1993	Paris	Rome
Jamaica	6 August 1962	1 January 1994	Paris	Rome
Guyana	26 May 1966	25 October 1994	Paris	Brussels
Equatorial Guinea	12 October 1968	26 June 1997	Paris	Brussels
Cape Verde Islands	5 July 1966	7 July 1997	Paris	Brussels
Botswana	30 September 1966	15 April 1998	Paris	Brussels
Grenada	7 February 1974	22 September 1998	Paris	Brussels
Swaziland	6 September 1968	14 December 1998	Paris	Rome
Singapore	9 August 1965	21 December 1998	Paris	Rome
Jordan	6 August 1962	28 July 1999	Paris	Rome
Belize	11 November 1981	17 June 2000	Paris	Brussels
Djbouti	26 June 1977	13 May 2002	Paris	Brussels
Korea, Dem Rep	12 December 1945	28 April 2003	Paris	Rome

[1] [1975] *Copyright* 44.
[2] [1977] *Copyright* 150.
[3] [1980] *Copyright* 306.
[4] [1983] *Copyright* 164.
[5] [1984] *Copyright* 16.

(p) The role of the International Office

17.61 This has clearly been considerable. In December 1960, the Office identified thirty-one newly independent states, fifteen of which had been the subject of notifications under the Rome Act and sixteen under the Brussels Act.[399] Rather

[399] Those countries notified under the Rome Act were: Burma, Cambodia, Cyprus, North Korea, South Korea, Formosa, Ghana, Jordan, Laos, Malaya, Nigeria, Federation of Rhodesia and Nyasaland, Somalia, North Vietnam, South Vietnam. Those countries notified under the Brussels Act were: Cameroon, Central African Republic, Congo (Léopoldville), Congo (Brazzaville), Ivory Coast, Dahomey, Gabon, Guinea, Upper Volta, Madagascar, Mali, Mauritania, Niger, Senegal, Chad, Togo. See generally [1960] *DA* 336. This list was amended, with respect to a number of dates of application of the Convention in [1961] *Copyright* 28.

than waiting passively for these countries to indicate, at their convenience, their position in relation to the Convention, the International Office took the initiative and communicated with these states to confirm whether or not they still applied the rules of the Convention in their country.[400] In this regard, the declaration of continued adherence, which had already been invoked in the case of the two post-World War II German states (see para 17.67 below) as well as that of Ceylon, was a useful device, although no express basis for the making of such a declaration is to be found in the Convention itself. Within five years, eight of the thirty-one states in the Office's list, had made clear their position by making these declarations,[401] three had deposited instruments of accession,[402] while three others (South Vietnam, South Korea, and Cambodia) had replied that they did not consider themselves bound by the Convention following their independence[403] and a further communication from China stated that it regarded the Japanese notification with respect to Formosa as having ceased to have any effect, following the date of reinstatement of that territory into the Republic of China.[404] The Federation of Malaya had also replied that it was presently studying the question of adopting draft legislation on copyright, and had not yet given consideration to 'the question of reciprocal copyright protection on an international basis'.[405] It therefore stated that it was not in a position to advise on 'the Government's intention regarding accession to the Union', a clear indication that it did not regard the Convention as continuing to apply in its territory.[406] By contrast, a communication from Nigeria implied that the Convention was still applicable in its territory, as this stated that Nigeria was presently considering the question of membership of international organizations, and that as soon as a decision was reached 'about our continued membership in your organisation' this would be communicated to BIRPI.[407] This last letter, however, has the imprint of a *pro forma* communication, and was equivocal in the sense that it was concerned with the question of membership rather than application of the Convention (as per the original letter of inquiry from the International Office).

Of the original list of thirty-one states compiled by the International Office in December 1960, a further six joined the Union in the period after 1965, either by the device of making a declaration of continuity or by depositing an instrument of accession.[408] However, the list itself was steadily augmented in the following decade, particularly with the attainment of formal independence by many former British territories. In the following decade, this process slowed **17.62**

[400] [1960] *DA* 336. [401] See Table 17.1. [402] See Table 17.3.

[403] [1960] *DA* 337 (letter of 17 June 1960 from South Vietnam, letter of 15 July 1960 from South Korea, and letter of 28 Sept 1960 from Cambodia).

[404] [1961] *DA* 27 (from 25 Oct 1945). [405] [1961] *DA* 134 (letter of 12 Jan 1961).

[406] ibid. [407] ibid. [408] See Tables 17.1, 17.2, and 17.3.

down, although there was a sudden spate of new state creation with the independence of the former Portuguese territories in 1974 and 1975. As of 2005 (and, indeed, at the date of the first edition of this commentary), there are very few territories which have yet to achieve independence, and which are likely to do so in the immediate future.[409] Table 17.5 therefore attempts to list all those states, formerly under the protection or control of older Berne members, which have become independent since 1945, and which have not made any formal indication of their attitude with respect to the continued application of the Berne Convention in their territory. This table is a modified version of the table that appeared in the first edition, and, for ease of reference, includes those states that have now acceded to the Berne Convention (Paris). These states, which also appear in Table 17.4 above, are represented in Table 17.5 with a line through them.

(q) The effect of state practice

17.63 In the light of the above, this may be summarized as follows.

(i) **Declaration of continued adherence:** Where a country makes a declaration of continued adherence, this confirms that the pre-independence application of the Act in question continues in force. It also has the effect that this country henceforth acquires the status of a member country of the Union. Although the making of these declarations is not expressly authorized by the Convention, there has been no objection to the practice by any existing Union member, and it has also been adopted in the case of a number of other multilateral conventions, including the Paris Union. It also has the consequence that the declarant country may remain bound by an Act of the Convention which has now become 'closed', as well as retain the benefits of any reservations that may have been contained in the original notification.

(ii) **Denunciation:** Where a country denounces the Convention following its independence or declares that the article 26 notification no longer applies, this also confirms the continued application of the Convention in the period between independence and the date of the denunciation or declaration.

(iii) **Accession:** Where a country accedes to the Convention after its independence, the implication is that the Convention was not applicable in that country after its independence. The same is obviously true when a country makes it clear, as in the case of the Republic of Korea (South Korea) and Vietnam, that it does not regard a pre-independence declaration as having any force from the date of independence.

[409] Several contentious examples include the Falkland Islands (UK) and the French Pacific Territories.

Table 17.5[1]

Country	*Date of independence*	*First Act applied under article 26*	*Last Act in force pre-independence*
Angola	11 November 1975	Berlin	Brussels
~~Belize~~	~~11 November 1981~~	~~Berne/Paris~~	~~Brussels~~
~~Botswana~~	~~30 September 1966~~	~~Berne/Paris~~	~~Brussels~~
Brunei	30 September 1984	Berne/Paris	Brussels?
Burma	4 January 1948	Berne/Paris	Brussels
Burundi	1 June 1962	Berne/Paris	Brussels
~~Cape Verde Islands~~	~~5 July 1975~~	~~Berlin~~	~~Brussels~~
Comoros	5 July 1975	Berne/Paris	Brussels
~~Djibouti~~	~~26 June 1977~~	~~Berne/Paris~~	~~Brussels~~
East Timor	1999	Berlin/Paris	Brussels/Paris[2]
~~Equatorial Guinea~~	~~12 October 1968~~	~~Berne/Paris~~	~~Rome~~
~~Gambia~~	~~18 February 1965~~	~~Berne/Paris~~	~~Rome~~
~~Ghana~~	~~6 March 1957~~	~~Berne/Paris~~	~~Rome~~
~~Grenada~~	~~7 February 1974~~	~~Berne/Paris~~	~~Brussels~~
~~Guinea-Bissau~~	~~26 September 1973~~	~~Berne/Paris~~	~~Brussels~~
~~Guyana~~	~~26 May 1966~~	~~Berne/Paris~~	~~Brussels~~
~~Jamaica~~	~~6 August 1962~~	~~Berne/Paris~~	~~Rome~~
~~Jordan~~	~~6 August 1962~~	~~Berne/Paris~~	~~Rome~~
~~Kenya~~	~~12 December 1963~~	~~Berlin~~	~~Rome~~
~~Korea, Dem Rep~~	~~12 December 1945~~	~~Rome~~	
Laos	19 July 1949	Berlin	Rome
~~Lesotho~~	~~30 September 1966~~	~~Berne/Paris~~	~~Rome~~
~~Malawi~~	~~6 July 1964~~	~~Berlin~~	~~Rome~~
Maldives	6 July 1964	Berne/Paris	Rome
Mozambique	25 June 1975	Berlin	Brussels
Nauru	31 December 1968	Berlin	Brussels
~~Nigeria~~	~~1 October 1960~~	~~Berlin~~	~~Rome~~
Papua-New Guinea	16 September 1975	Berne/Paris	Rome
São Tomé & Príncipe	12 July 1975	Berlin	Brussels
Seychelles	29 June 1976	Berne/Paris	Brussels
~~Singapore~~	~~9 August 1976~~	~~Berne/Paris~~	~~Rome~~
Somalia	1 July 1960	Berne/Paris	Rome
Southern Yemen	30 November 1967	Berne/Paris	Rome
~~Swaziland~~	~~6 September 1968~~	~~Berlin~~	~~Rome~~
Tanzania	9 September 1961	Berne/Paris	Rome
~~Trinidad~~	~~31 August 1961~~	~~Berne/Paris~~	~~Rome~~
Uganda	9 October 1962	Berlin	Rome
Western Samoa	1 January 1962	Berne/Paris	Rome
~~Zambia~~	~~26 October 1964~~	~~Berlin~~	~~Rome~~

[1] Derived from [1960] *DA* 336 and J Crawford, *The Creation of States in International Law* (1979), Appendices 1–3.
[2] See further the discussion in n 424 below as to which Act may have been the last applying in this country, depending upon whether the former colonial/occupying power was Portugal or Indonesia.

(r) The applicable legal principles

What legal principles, if any, underlie the practice described above? Furthermore, what assistance do they provide in the case of countries which have made no indication of their position with respect to the Convention? As to the first of **17.64** these questions, it should be noted that the International Office has played an important role in defining the present practice, in particular through the device of the declaration of continued adherence. While the practical advantages of these declarations are clear, there is also a firm legal basis that can be ascribed to them. The Acts of the Convention possess the character of 'regulatory treaty or treaty law'.[410] They do not have a political character, being concerned rather with private rights and the protection of these rights within certain defined territories. In the words of Masouyé:

> The result is an international law of which the conditions of application are clearly defined, it being left to the States to fit them within the framework of their national laws. When the present State separates from the colony or overseas territory and grants it independence, continuity must be normally assured. The new State must continue to benefit from the advantages provided by the Convention in question and to remain bound by the obligations derived from it, except for contrary provisions inserted in the acts of transfer of sovereignty. This continuity is all the more necessary as the rights acquired by third parties must be safeguarded.[411]

This view is also confirmed by the distinction which the Convention has traditionally drawn between member countries (or 'Contracting States' under the earlier texts) and the territorial application of the Union (under article 31 and its predecessors in respect of territories which have been regarded as part of the Union and therefore 'countries of the Union'). For these reasons, it is possible to postulate a presumption of continuity which should apply in the case of a newly independent country that has not indicated its attitude to the Convention. Accordingly, the making of a declaration of continued adherence simply confirms an existing state of affairs and does not represent any kind of novation or alteration of a country's obligations under the Convention. On this view, such a declaration is strictly unnecessary, but it has the effect of removing the uncertainty that inevitably exists in the period between independence and the making of the declaration. Furthermore, there are certain situations in which the presumption of continuity will clearly be regarded as displaced (see para 17.65 below). In this regard, it is of interest to compare the position under the Paris Convention where the International Bureau of that Union appeared to take a contrary view, namely that the Convention and its related Agreements did not automatically continue to apply after independence, and that it was necessary for a new state to take some formal step to become an independent member of the Union in accordance with article 16 of the Hague Act of that

---

410 See generally Masouyé (n 253 above), 122ff; Ronga (n 386 above), 23ff; O'Connell (n 119 above), 213ff.

411 Masouyé (n 253 above), 122.

Convention.[412] In the view of O'Connell, the policy of the Bureau was 'puzzling' from a jurisprudential point of view:

> A declaration of continuity is regarded by it as continuing the *de facto* legal situation between the date of independence and the date of the declaration. Failure to make a declaration is regarded as an indication of the lapse of the convention's application upon independence. But since years elapse before declarations are made no one knows whether in fact the convention continues to apply.[413]

The fallacy of this view is clear: in the absence of some clear time limit, it becomes impossible to determine when a country has failed to make a declaration and is therefore no longer bound by the Convention. In the case of the Berne Convention, however, the International Office has refrained from drawing any conclusions from the fact that no declaration of continuity or notice of denunciation has been made. In consequence, it should be possible for any of the states listed in Table 17.5 that have not subsequently acceded to make declarations of continued adherence to the Convention at any time they wish. While this leaves considerable uncertainty, it has the virtue of consistency and the advantage that, on the making of a declaration, no break in the application of the Convention will have occurred in the period before the making of the declaration. Uncertainty in this interim period is therefore replaced by the benefit of unbroken continuity once the declaration is made.

This presumption of continuity is no more than a presumption: in any particular case, the attitude of the country itself, once this becomes evident, must be decisive in confirming or rebutting it. In addition, as consent lies at the basis of any international agreement, there must be acceptance of this attitude by other Union members. The following situations have to be considered here. **17.65**

(i) **Later accession to the Convention**: This is the clearest indication that a country can give that it has ceased to be bound by the Convention in the period following independence. With a couple of exceptions (see para 17.58 above), the International Office has not sought to oppose this inference, and has treated these countries as being bound by the Convention only from the date of accession. An opposite inference, however, can be drawn in the case of an accession to a later Act: it could still be argued here that the presumption of continuity should operate in respect of any earlier Act which had been applied to that country by an article 26 notification. This has logical force, and therefore remains an area of uncertainty. There is no inference to be drawn here either way from the official publications of BIRPI or WIPO.

[412] See the review of practice with respect to the Paris Convention in O'Connell (n 119 above), 206–8.
[413] ibid, 207–8.

(ii) The general attitude of the new state with respect to prior treaty obligations: In the absence of any indication by a new state as to its attitude to the continued application of the Convention, it might be possible to find support for the confirmation or displacement of the presumption of continuity in the general practice of that state with respect to the treaty obligations of its predecessor. This will require detailed investigation in each case, and even then it may be difficult to reach a considered view. However, guidance may be gained from a number of possible sources. First, the provisions of any instrument of devolution between the new state and its former metropolitan power dealing with the question of succession to treaties: the terms of many of these instruments, however, are quite general, and often leave the new state with considerable latitude for independent decision.[414] Second, the practice of the new state with respect to other conventions, particularly those of a multilateral character: if the general practice has been to confirm these treaties, this might indicate that the state in question is still bound by the Berne Convention.[415] Finally, the circumstances of the state's attainment of independence: where this has occurred after a period of conflict or armed hostilities with the former governing power, it is far easier to conclude that the new state has begun its international existence free of the treaty obligations of its predecessor. This view was obviously correct in the case of Israel and is clearly evidenced in the communications made by Vietnam and the Republic of Korea to the International Office (see para 17.61 above). It may well be applicable to a number of countries in Table 17.5, such as Yemen and the former Portuguese possessions.

(iii) Conduct: If a newly independent state continues to protect the works of Union authors, this will be evidence of the continued application of the Convention in that country. On the other hand, the adoption of municipal legislation that is inconsistent with the obligations of the Convention could be regarded as clear evidence to the contrary.[416] This has happened in the case of several countries, notably Ghana.[417] Whether this is to be regarded as a *de facto* denunciation of the Convention or simply as confirmation that the Convention ceased to apply to that country upon its independence is another question. However, it may have implications in relation to the UCC, if the country later adheres to that Convention. This relates to the effect of the 'Berne Safeguard Clause' and is discussed further below (see paras 18.27ff).[418]

---

[414] O'Connell (n 119 above), 114ff and 358ff. [415] ibid, 223ff.

[416] See further Masouyé (n 253 above), 128ff.

[417] In the view of Straschnov, the view was taken in the drafting of the new Ghanaian Copyright Act 1961 that Ghana would no longer be bound by the Berne Convention. Instead, it acceded in 1962 to the UCC. See generally G Straschnov, 'La loi ghanéenne sur le droit d'auteur' [1962] *DA* 156, and Masouyé (n 253 above), 134ff. Subsequently, Ghana acceded to the Paris Act of the Berne Convention: 11 Oct 1991.

[418] See further Masouyé (n 253 above), 125ff.

(iv) Failure to pay contributions: While it is true that membership of the Berne Union involves the obligation to pay annual contributions, failure to pay these does not affect the continuance of this membership, although under the Stockholm, Paris Acts it may lead to the suspension of the voting rights of that member in various organs of the Union.[419] Furthermore, the fact that a country may be a part of the Union and a 'country of the Union', but without actually being a member of the Union, means that there is a recognized category of countries which do not pay contributions. Accordingly, no inference as to the continued application of the Convention can be drawn one way or the other from the failure of a newly independent country to pay contributions. In this regard, it appears that Indonesia did not pay contributions in the period after its independence from the Netherlands,[420] although there seems little doubt that it continued to be bound by the Convention and was, in fact, regarded as a member by the International Office until its denunciation in 1960. The letters sent out by the Director of BIRPI to newly independent countries in 1960 also confirm the irrelevance of contributions in this regard, as those letters made it clear that the obligation to pay contributions would only arise once a declaration of continued adherence had been made.[421] On the other hand, at the time they made such declarations, those countries have invariably indicated their willingness to make such payments by nominating the class in which they wish to be placed. This is obviously of great practical importance, as a new state will rarely wish to be bound by the class adopted by its previous metropolitan power.[422]

(v) The lapse of time: Although it has been suggested that no inference of non-application should be drawn from the simple fact that a state fails to make a declaration of continued adherence or to give some indication of its attitude to the Convention, could it be argued that this inference becomes irresistible after the lapse of a lengthy period of time? If, during this period, other states have acted on the assumption that the country in question was outside the Union, the basis for such an argument could be estoppel.[423] Lapse of time in itself, however, is probably not enough. Thus, eleven years had passed since its independence in the case of the declaration by Ceylon, and in the case of Zimbabwe it is possible to argue that fifteen years had elapsed (at least, since the date of its illegal independence). In both cases, however, there was no objection by any Union member to the continued application of the Convention in these countries.

[419] Paris Act, art 25(4)(e). [420] Masouyé (n 253 above), 120. [421] [1960] *DA* 336.

[422] Particularly as the large former colonial powers such as France and the UK have always been placed in the first class for contributions: [1986] *Copyright* 311–12.

[423] See generally McNair (n 79 above), 485–9; D Bowett (1957) 33 *BYIL* 176; Sinclair (n 88 above), 168–9.

(s) Conclusions

17.66 The continued application of the Convention to newly independent states raises many difficult questions of a practical and theoretical kind, making this a shadow area where firm conclusions are impossible. The actions of the International Office have done much to clarify the situation, particularly through the device of the declaration of continued adherence as well as through the general development co-operation projects of WIPO which have been directed towards gaining adherents to the Convention among recently independent states. The present practice of WIPO is to refrain from adopting any posture on the position of countries which have not made declarations of continued adherence or deposited instruments of accession. Thus, no reference to these states is made in any of the lists of member countries published by WIPO. This seems sound, from a practical point of view, and would clearly provide the basis for the estoppel argument referred to above (see para 17.65), in the event that one of these countries sought now to make a declaration of continued adherence. Nonetheless, the possibility that this may occur remains, particularly where the making of a declaration might allow the country to undertake a lower level of obligation than is embodied in the Paris Act, for example, in relation to the matter of duration under the Rome Act.[424]

(t) Divided states

17.67 One particular problem in the period from 1945 to 1973 was raised by the existence of two 'Germanys' following the division of the former German Reich.[425] After the collapse of German resistance in 1945, there was no longer an effective or recognized German Government. The country was divided into four Zones of Occupation, with a special regime for Berlin, which was placed under quadpartite control. There was no act of annexation or assumption of sovereignty over the former German Reich by any of the occupying powers, but effective authority was exercised by the Commander-in-Chief in

[424] An interesting instance might arise with respect to East Timor, the most recent independent state in Table 17.5. Until 1975, this was a Portuguese territory, and in that year was incorporated into Indonesia. Following a referendum on 30 Aug 1999, there was a majority vote for independence, and, following considerable civil unrest, the territory was placed under United Nations control and finally achieved independence in 1999. During the period of its incorporation in Indonesia, it can be presumed that the Berne Convention did not apply as Indonesia had denounced the Convention. However, Indonesia acceded to the Paris Act of Berne on 5 Sept 1997, and presumably the Convention was then applied to East Timor, albeit without the consent of that country. Does East Timor therefore succeed to the obligations of its former occupying power, Indonesia, or could it still claim to be bound only by the lesser obligations of Portugal, which had declared the Brussels Act to apply to its territory? Or could it accede afresh?

[425] See generally F A Mann, 'Germany's Present Legal Status Revisited' (1967) 16 *ICLQ* 761; J A Frowein, 'Legal Problems of the German Ostpolitik' (1974) 23 *ICLQ* 105; Crawford (n 91 above), ch 10.

each Occupation Zone. Rapidly, however, as relations between the Allies deteriorated, these Zones became divided into the Western and Soviet Zones of Germany, and by 1949 two new 'states' had come into existence on their territories: the Federal Republic of Germany (FRG) in the West (24 May 1949) and the German Democratic Republic (GDR) in the East (7 October 1949).[426] Such were the political conditions of the time that, while the FRG received widespread recognition as a state (including recognition from the USSR), the GDR did not receive any recognition other than from members of the then Soviet bloc and its existence as a state in international law was therefore extremely doubtful. This remained the case until the early 1970s, when the Ostpolitik of Chancellor Brandt led to a normalization of relations between the two Germanys and the countries of Eastern Europe.[427] Following this, the GDR came to receive recognition from the Western states, culminating with the unopposed admission of both countries to the UN on 18 September 1973. Although the question of which German state was the successor to the treaty obligations of the former German Reich was a highly contentious one,[428] it does not seem that any argument of this kind arose directly in the context of the Berne Union. However, in 1950 the FRG addressed a letter to the Swiss Government, through the Allied Control Commission, declaring that it recognized the unrestricted applicability of the Berne Convention in its territory.[429] A declaration to the same effect was also made at a later date with respect to the Land of Berlin.[430] These declarations evoked objections from Czechoslovakia and Poland, which refused to accept them.[431] However, these were insignificant by comparison with the string of objections lodged by Union members when, in 1955, the GDR made a simple declaration that it considered the Rome Act to be in force in its territory.[432] In general, these objections refused to 'note' the GDR declaration, on the basis of the objecting states' non-recognition of the GDR.[433] From the date of its declaration, however, the FRG played an important role in the affairs of the Union, both in the newly constituted Permanent Committee and in the preparations for the Stockholm Conference. In 1966, the FRG also acceded to the Brussels Act, applying it again to Berlin;[434] the latter

426 Crawford (n 91 above), 275–6.

427 See generally Frowein (n 425 above).

428 Crawford (n 91 above), 280. It does not seem that the GDR has ever claimed identity with pre-1945 Germany.

429 [1950] *DA* 73 (letter of 7 Feb from Konrad Adenauer to the Allied High Commission).

430 [1954] *DA* 27.

431 [1950] *DA* 121 (Czechoslovakia) and [1951] *DA* 25 (Poland).

432 [1955] *DA* 149 (declaration dated 11 May 1955).

433 [1956] *DA* 105 (from New Zealand, the FRG, the Netherlands, Turkey, Thailand, Switzerland, France, Canada, Spain, Ireland, and Pakistan); [1957] *DA* 174 (Philippines, Italy, Norway, the UK, South Africa, Portugal, Denmark, Iceland, Luxembourg, Australia, Austria, and Brazil). Note that the declarations made by Austria and Switzerland were more reserved in their tone.

434 [1966] *Copyright* 242.

part of this accession was objected to by five Eastern European member countries,[435] but its validity was strongly maintained by the FRG, France, and the UK (the last two being two of the Allied Powers responsible for the overall administration of Berlin).[436] The GDR was not invited to the Stockholm Conference, but it deposited an instrument of accession to articles 22 to 38 of the Stockholm Act in 1968.[437] A number of objections were again made to this, and, in consequence, the Director of BIRPI made the following statement, when notifying members of the accession:

> This notification does not mean that the Director of *BIRPI* has adopted any position on the question of whether the GDR is or is not a party to the said Convention. The Governments of the member countries of the Berne Union are in disagreement on this question.[438]

For this reason, BIRPI listed two dates for the coming into force of articles 22 to 38 of the Stockholm Act: 26 February 1970 or 29 January 1970, if the validity of the instrument of accession deposited by the GDR was accepted.[439] Nonetheless, in the period immediately following, the GDR came to receive general recognition, and there were no objections when it acceded to the Paris Act in 1978.[440] While there can be little doubt about the validity of this accession, it seems likely that, from 1970 on, the application of the Convention (under the Rome and Stockholm texts) to the GDR was accepted by an increasing number of Union members.

17.68 Was the GDR a member country of the Berne Union in the period from 1949 to 1970? If the criterion for membership were 'statehood', the answer to this would probably be negative, as the GDR lacked general international recognition. On the other hand, it is hard to deny that the GDR was a 'country' in the sense in which this term is used in the Convention, and was therefore capable of being a member. While there are no specific restrictions on Berne Union membership (see para 17.17 above), it still seems clear that the consent of the existing membership to the admission or recognition of a new member is necessary; and,

---

[435] [1967] *Copyright* 208 (notification of 19 Aug 1967 from Bulgaria, Czechoslovakia, Hungary, Poland, and Romania).

[436] [1968] *Copyright* 62. [437] [1968] *Copyright* 155 (20 May 1968). [438] ibid.

[439] [1969] *Copyright* 236.

[440] [1977] *Copyright* 331 (from 18 Feb 1978), noting that the FRG had already acceded as from 10 Oct 1974 for arts 1–21 and 18 Oct 1973 for the Appendix and as from 22 Jan 1974 for arts 22–38. It seems clear that the GDR took the view that it was bound by the Rome Act from the time of its creation. See generally H Püschel, 'The International Law of the Berne Convention and the National Copyright Law of Member States with Particular Reference to the Legislation of the German Democratic Republic' [1986] *Copyright* 144 and the opinion of A Troller and H Rollin in [1967] *Staat und Recht* 138 arguing that the GDR was a member of the Union and therefore entitled to attend the Stockholm Conference: 'Gutachten über die Mitgliedschaft der Deutschen Demokratischen Republik in der internationalen Konventionen für den gewerblichen Rechtsschutz und der Schutz der Urheberschaft'.

in the case of the GDR, twenty-five members were unprepared to accept its declaration in relation to the continued application of the Rome Act in its territory. As this destroyed the basis of acceptance into the Union, it seems logical to say that the GDR was not a member during the period in which this acceptance was lacking. Accordingly, no member country, whether an objector or not, was obliged to apply the Convention to the GDR. On the other hand, in view of the GDR's declaration that it remained bound by the Rome Act, this provided a basis on which non-objecting member countries could regulate their relations towards the GDR in a bilateral fashion, if they so desired. In this respect, it must be added that the case of the GDR was a special one, and might have been more readily resolved if the issue had not been so bedevilled by the political passions generated by the Cold War. In any event, after 1990, this debate has become a thing of the past, with the reunification of the two Germanys, and the International Office now has one entry for 'Germany' with a date of 10 October 1974 for the coming into force of articles 1 to 21 and 22 January 1974 for articles 22 to 38 (these being the relevant dates for the accession by the FRG).[441]

(8) Relations between Union members

(a) The application of the different Acts of the Convention

(i) Background to the problem: As not all member countries of the Union are bound by the same Act of the Convention, this raises questions as to the links, if any, that exist between these countries, as well as the nature and extent of these links. At the time of writing of the first edition of this commentary (1986), this was an important practical issue as there were still significant numbers of members bound by pre-Paris Acts of the Convention. While this is no longer the case, there are small groups of members bound by the Rome and Paris Acts respectively, so the following discussion still remains of relevance. There are two particular situations where problems may arise here. First, where country A and country B are both bound by an earlier Act, and country B accedes to a later Act while country A does not. And, second, where country A is bound by an earlier Act, and country B, being a non-Union country, accedes to the latest Act. **17.69**

In the first of these cases, the countries have been bound, at one time, by a common text. In the second case, however, there is no text in common between them, and there appears to be no legal relationship which binds them. Under the Berlin, Rome, and Brussels Acts, only the first of these problems was directly addressed. Thus, article 27(1) of the Berlin Act provided:

[441] As at Dec 2004: www.wipo.int.

> The present Convention shall replace, in regard to the relations between the Contracting States, the Convention of Berne of the 9th September, 1886, including the Additional Article and the Final Protocol of the same date, as well as the Additional Act and the Interpretative Declaration of the 4th May, 1896. These Instruments shall remain in force in regard to relations with States which do not ratify the present Convention.

In the Rome Act, the wording of this provision was changed to accommodate the fact that the Berlin Act was now to be replaced, in addition to the earlier Acts of Berne and Paris. The new wording was retained in the Brussels Act, and was as follows:

> (1) The present Convention shall replace, in regard to the relations between the countries of the Union, the Convention of Berne of the 9th September, 1886, and the subsequent revisions thereof. The instruments previously in force shall continue to be applicable in regard to relations with countries which do not ratify the present Convention.

17.70 The meaning of the first sentence of this provision seems clear enough: countries ratifying or acceding to the new Act were to be governed, in their *inter se* relations, entirely by its provisions. As the second sentence indicates, however, this did not, and could not, have the effect of terminating the earlier Acts in force as not all Union countries would ratify the new Act or, at the very least, there might be a considerable length of time before they did so. In consequence, these earlier Acts were to remain in force 'in regard to relations with countries which do not ratify the present Convention'. As the new Act could not affect the *inter se* relations of countries that remained bound only by the earlier Acts, the effect of this sentence was simply to require countries that acceded to the new Act to continue to apply the earlier Acts in their relations with the first group of countries. As long as the countries which acceded to the new Act had also been bound by the earlier Acts, this presented no problem and provided them with a common text to regulate their relations with those countries which had not acceded to the new Act. However, the membership of the Union was hardly likely to remain static, and there soon came into existence a group of countries which had entered the Union after the entry into force of the latest Act (whether this was the Rome or Berlin Act), and were bound only by that text. So far as those countries were concerned, there was no text in common between them and those countries which remained bound by the earlier Acts only. What were the relations under the Convention, if any, between these groups of countries? Two interpretations were possible.

First, the strictly legal view that, as these countries were not bound by a common text and never had been, there were no legal links between them in a conventional sense. Accordingly, a country bound only by the Brussels Act was under no obligation to extend the protection of that Act to authors from a country that was bound only by the Berlin or Brussels Act. If it did do so, it was free to make this subject to a requirement of reciprocity or to do so simply on the basis of national treatment. This attitude was adopted by a number of countries, including France.

The second possible interpretation was that, despite the lack of a common interest, these countries were still members of the one Union, and this provided the basis for a legal link between them. The problem still remained of determining the terms on which this relationship should be regulated, and the view adopted by a number of Union members was that their mutual relations should be governed by the latest text to which each was party. This could lead to obvious imbalances, as, between each Act, there were differences in the level of protection required. At the same time, however, there was a solid corpus of provisions that were common to each Act, and in this sense they were really successive versions of the one Convention rather than totally separate instruments. Furthermore, this approach (sometimes called the 'Union interpretation')[442] was simple to apply in practice.

These matters did not give rise to extended discussion among Union members until the Stockholm Conference, although both interpretations described above were applied by member countries. In this regard, the annual report on the 'State of the International Union' that was published by BIRPI in *Le Droit d'Auteur* dealt only with the relations between states that were bound by a common text, and did not make any statements concerning the relations between states that were not so bound. Thus, the 'State of the International Union on January 1, 1967' declared that the fifty-five member countries of the Union applied three Acts (Berlin, Rome, and Brussels) in their mutual relations.[443] These were as follows: **17.71**

Berlin Act: Thailand, which had acceded to neither the Rome nor Brussels Act, was obliged to apply this Act to other Union countries which had acceded to the latter Act and to the dependencies of those countries which continued to apply the Berlin Act (SW Africa).[444]

Rome Act: This was stated to apply between fourteen countries which had acceded to the Rome Act,[445] as well as to the relations between these fourteen countries and twenty-six other countries which 'after having acceded to this Act have ratified the Brussels Act or have acceded to it'.[446] To this figure of

[442] So called by the Swedish delegate, T Hesser, in the debates in Main Committees II and IV at the Stockholm Conference: *Records* 1967, 993.
[443] [1967] *Copyright* 2–3. See further C Joubert, 'La applicabilité des actes successifs de la Convention de Berne' (1968) 58 *RIDA* 4.
[444] [1967] *Copyright*, 2. [445] ibid. [446] ibid.

twenty-six were added eight former colonies which had made declarations of continued adherence to the Rome Act.[447]

Brussels Act: Forty countries applied the Brussels Act in their mutual relations.[448]

It was therefore clear that there was an obvious gap in the Convention system, and that something needed to be done to place the relations between Union countries bound by different texts of the Convention on a more rational basis.

17.72 **(ii) The debates at Stockholm:** An attempt to do this was made in the programme for the Stockholm Conference, which proposed a new article consisting of three paragraphs to replace article 27(1) of the Brussels Act.[449] The first paragraph replicated article 27(1), with the addition of the words 'to the extent that it applies' to take account of the fact that it would be possible to adhere to the Stockholm Act either in whole or in part, with the effect that, where the latter occurred, the countries in question would continue to be bound by the Act which previously applied to them. The second paragraph then set out a series of rules concerning the relations between the Union countries that adhered to the Stockholm Act and those that remained bound by earlier Acts. The effect of these rules was essentially that the relations of these countries would be bound by the latest Act which both had in common. Thus, in the case of the UK (bound by Brussels, but previously by Rome) and New Zealand (bound by Rome), if the UK were to adhere to the Stockholm Act both countries would continue to apply the Rome Act in their mutual dealings as the UK would still remain bound by the latter Act. This meant that countries would find themselves obliged to apply different Acts to different countries, even though they had adhered to the Stockholm Act, and therefore represented a departure from the practice which had been applied by many countries under the Rome and Brussels Acts of applying to all Union countries the latest Act by which they were bound.[450] The third paragraph of the programme proposal was concerned with the problem of countries outside the Union which acceded to the Stockholm Act and their relations to Union countries which remained bound by earlier Acts. In accordance with another proposed change to article 28(3) of the Brussels Act which provided that countries outside the Union should also be allowed to accede, simultaneously, to earlier Acts of the Convention, this paragraph provided that where this did not occur, these countries should

[447] [1967] *Copyright*, 2–3. [448] ibid, 3. [449] *Records* 1967, 470 (Document S/9).
[450] eg the UK: Copyright (International Conventions) Order 1957, SI 1957/1523.

> . . . subject to reciprocal protection, apply the present Act in their relations with countries of the Union which are not party to this Act or which, although party to this Act made a declaration as permitted by Article 25(1)(b) [that is, countries which had acceded to part only of the Stockholm Act].[451]

The solution proposed in the programme was involved, but was based essentially on the view that, unless there was some text in common between the parties, there could be no legal basis for relations between them under the Convention in the absence of some requirement of reciprocity. In consequence, the programme proposals were criticized by several of these countries, notably the UK, which (i) objected to the requirement to apply different texts to other countries not bound by the Stockholm Act, rather than simply the latest text binding each country, and (ii) took the view that the requirement of reciprocity was unnecessary as the necessary legal link between these countries was provided by their common membership of the Union.[452] However, the proposals received the support of countries such as France which took the 'strictly legal' view that relations between countries which were not parties to a common text could only be governed on the basis of reciprocity and that the Stockholm Act could not purport to bind countries which did not ratify or accede to it.[453] These countries were, in turn, opposed to a further proposal that was made in a corrigendum to the programme. This simplified the original programme proposals by proposing the deletion of paragraphs (2) and (3) and the addition of a second sentence to paragraph (1), which now reads:

> The present Act shall, as regards the relations between the countries to which it applies, and the extent that it applies, replace the Convention of Berne of September 9, 1886, and the subsequent Acts of revision. The Acts previously in force shall continue to be applicable, in their entirety or to the extent that the present Act does not replace them by virtue of the preceding sentence, in relations with countries which do not ratify or accede to this Act.[454]

It was argued that this preserved the substance of article 27(1) of the Brussels Act, and that there was no need to depart from this text which had 'proved its worth ever since it came into existence'.[455] It was further argued that this had

> . . . the advantage of not weakening the 'generally accepted interpretation' according to which:
>
> (i) works originating in one country of the Union shall be protected under the Convention in any other country of the Union; and
> (ii) each country of the Union grants protection to works originating in any country of the Union according to the provisions of the most recent Act to which the former country has acceded.[456]

---

[451] *Records* 1967, 473 (Document S/9).
[452] ibid, 993 (UK delegate in Main Committees II and IV).
[453] ibid, 992. [454] ibid, 486. [455] ibid. [456] ibid.

This, in fact, represented a complete reversal of the assumptions which had underlain the original proposals, and, for this reason, came under strong opposition from the French delegation.[457] In particular, the latter was opposed to the possibility that states which had not ratified the Stockholm Act might still have it applied to them by those states which had ratified it.[458] This concern was aggravated by the fact that, in some respects, the Stockholm Act represented a diminution in the protection of authors' rights in comparison with earlier Acts. However, the drafters of the amended programme proposal did not think that they were departing from the basic rule of article 27(1) of the Brussels Act which, hitherto, had accommodated the different interpretations represented by the French and UK delegations. Thus, the minutes of Main Committees II and IV noted the following explanation that was given by the Swedish delegate (Hesser):

> The discussion seemed to suggest that the corrigendum proposed revolutionary changes; actually it was seeking to maintain the Berne Convention text with drafting changes. There was room in the Berne text for the different interpretations said to exist, although in practice the interpretation or rather application explained by the United Kingdom, was mainly applied, namely the Union system, whereby a country entering the Union should claim protection for works in all other countries, on the basis of the latest text of the Berne Convention the other country had adhered to, while each Union country could do likewise in the new member country.[459]

These differing interpretations were fully discussed in a joint meeting of Committees II and IV, as the question of application of earlier Acts also arose in the context of the Paris Convention.[460] No consensus was reached, and finally a working group was appointed to consider the matter further.[461] This group concluded that it was impossible to reach agreement on any text other than that of the Brussels Act, and that it should be left to each country to apply its own interpretation of this with respect to the relations of countries outside the Union which acceded to the Stockholm Act and those countries in the Union which remained bound by earlier Acts.[462] This led to further discussion in Main Committee IV, and it was finally decided, on the basis of a Swiss amendment,[463] that reciprocity should be permitted on the part of countries not bound by the Stockholm Act in the event that that Act was applied to them by countries

---

457 *Records* 1967, 992. 458 ibid. 459 ibid.

460 Paris Convention, Lisbon Act, art 18 (the original programme proposal in Document S/9 for the Stockholm Revision was essentially based on this provision).

461 *Records* 1967, 993.

462 Document S/265: ibid, 733; for the verbal report of the chairman of the Working Group (Voyame of Switzerland) to Main Committee IV, see ibid, 1076.

463 Document S/268: ibid, 734. See further ibid, 1079 (discussion in Main Committee IV).

outside the Union which acceded to that Act alone.[464] It was therefore proposed that countries which were parties to the Stockholm Act should accept that countries which were parties to earlier Acts of the Convention were free to 'adapt the level of protection' of the last Act to which they were party to the level guaranteed by the Stockholm Act.[465] The rationale for this was that it would remove the likelihood of any prejudice to non-Stockholm countries that might flow from the fact that the new Act generally embodied a lower level of protection than that in the Brussels Act. The provision that was finally adapted as article 32 of the Stockholm Act read as follows:

> (1) The present Act shall, as regards the relations between the countries of the Union, and to the extent that it applies, replace the Berne Convention of September 9, 1886, and the subsequent Acts of revision. The Acts previously in force shall continue to be applicable, in their entirety or to the extent that the present Act does not replace them by virtue of the preceding sentence, in relations with countries of the Union which do not ratify or accede to this Act.
> (2) Countries outside the Union which become party to this Act shall, subject to the provisions of paragraph (3), apply it with respect to any country of the Union not party to this Act or which, although party to this Act, has made a declaration pursuant to Article 28(1)(b). Such countries recognize that the said country of the Union, in its relations with them:
> (i) may apply the provisions of the most recent Act to which it is party, and
> (ii) has the right to adapt its protection to the level provided for by this Act.

A third paragraph then dealt with the application of the provisions of the Stockholm Protocol (see further para 17.75 below).

It will be seen that this provision still allowed for the application of the two conflicting interpretations that had been discussed in Main Committees II and IV, but did so in more explicit terms than had article 27(1) of the Brussels Act. It allowed countries to apply the latest text that bound them (a considerable advance), but also acknowledged that countries bound by earlier Acts might adopt the principle of reciprocity with respect to countries bound only by the Stockholm Act. In this regard, several countries which had strong views on the interpretation of the provision made declarations in Main Committee IV stating how they proposed to apply the provision. Thus, the French delegation stated that it had only accepted the text of article 32 **17.73**

> . . . in order to facilitate the work of the Stockholm Conference. It wishes to state, however, that, in accordance with the rules of international law, the Government of the French Republic is required only to comply with those agreements to which

[464] ibid. [465] ibid.

> France has definitely become a party or which France has decided to apply temporarily in its relations with certain states, by virtue of domestic legislation, provided that, in the absence of any stipulation to the contrary which may have been agreed by France, the other Union member State concerned grants to works of French origin or works created, within the meaning of the Union Convention, by a French national, a protection which is not less than that granted by French law to works of the same nature.[466]

On the other side, the UK delegation declared that it considered:

> . . . that under Article 32(1) of the Berne Convention, countries party to the Stockholm Act are entitled to apply the latest Act in their relations with other members of the Union, whether or not they are party to the Stockholm Act. Similarly, the Delegation of the United Kingdom considers that countries of the Union are entitled to apply the latest Act to which they are parties in their relations with other countries of the Union.[467]

And a similar declaration was made by the Australian delegation.[468] A further exegesis on the effect of the new provision was to be found in the report of Valerio de Sanctis, the *rapporteur* of Main Committee IV:

> The solution envisaged by the Committee takes its inspiration from the following general principle: as this matter is not one of different treaties but of successive Acts of a Union of countries (see Article 1 of the Berne and Paris Conventions: 'The countries . . . constitute a Union . . .'), all of the Union countries must always have some links with one another, even if they are not bound by a common Act. Moreover, the successive Acts of a Union Convention always contain more or less parallel provisions, so that, from a practical point of view, the question arises only with respect to provisions that differ from one another, especially when the more recent Act to which a Union country has not acceded contains provisions regarding minimum rights that are far removed from the level of protection guaranteed by the previous Act. Only in such a case did it seem reasonable and legally correct for the countries outside the Union but parties to the Stockholm Act, in conformity with the above-mentioned Swiss proposal, to apply that Act in their relations with all of the Union countries, even those that have not acceded to the Stockholm Act, while the latter countries, in their relations with the former, apply the provisions of the later Act to which they are party, with the possibility, however, of adapting its level of protection to the level guaranteed by the Stockholm Act. Texts based on these principles were adapted by the Committee.
>
> — Consequently, as regards the relations between countries that accede only to the Stockholm Act and countries of the Union that do not accede to it, or that do so only later, . . . the Berne Convention . . . provide[s] that the former shall apply the Stockholm Act, and that the latter shall apply the most recent Act to which they have acceded.
>
> — Furthermore, I repeat, the Stockholm Act of the Berne Convention also provides that the countries of the second group mentioned above have the

---

[466] *Records* 1967, 1084 (closing declaration by Labry of France).

[467] ibid (Bowen of the UK). [468] ibid (Petersson of Australia).

> possibility of adjusting the level of protection they grant, on the basis of the most recent Act, to the level of protection provided by the Stockholm Act. The Committee felt that this provision was justified because, in certain respects, the level of protection guaranteed by the Stockholm Act is not as high as that guaranteed by earlier Acts.[469]

(iii) The practical application of article 32: This article was left unchanged in the Paris Act, with the exception of certain changes that were made to take account of the replacement of the Protocol by the Appendix.[470] As stated above, it does little to resolve the question of interpretation that was so hotly debated at Stockholm. Thus, the French view that a country cannot be bound by a text to which it is not a party remains intact, while the concept of an overall obligation existing between all Union countries on the basis of their common membership of the Union has neither been confirmed or rejected. In other words, countries remain free to adopt whichever interpretation they prefer, with the proviso that a country bound by the Paris Act undertakes, nonetheless, to accept the application to it of an 'adapted Paris Act' by a country which is not bound by that Act. The application of the provision can be illustrated by the following examples, which set out the relations between country A (bound by the Paris Act), country B (bound by Paris and Brussels), country C (by Brussels), country D (by Brussels and Rome), and country E (by Rome and Berlin). With the accession of Thailand to the Paris Act in September 1995 and Namibia in March 1990, it is no longer necessary to consider the case of country F (bound only by Berlin). **17.74**

1. *Countries A and B*: these are clearly bound by the Paris Act for the entirety of their relations as a direct result of the application of article 32(1).
2. *Countries A and C*: A will apply the Paris Act and C may apply Brussels (the latest text by which it is bound), with the option of 'adapting' the protection it offers from authors of A to that provided under the Paris Act. The same position will arise with respect to A's relations with D and E. Under the strict view preferred by the French Government, however, there is no obligation on any of these countries to accord protection to each other's authors, as there is no common text which binds them. In this respect, the provisions of article 32(2) cannot have a binding effect on these countries.
3. *Countries B and D:* both will apply the Brussels Act, as this text binds them both. Nonetheless, if B adopts the Union interpretation, it will simply apply the Paris Act to D, accepting in return that D may adapt its protection accordingly. The same position applies with respect to D's relations with E, the common text here being the Rome Act.

[469] ibid, 1215. [470] *Records* 1971, 60–1 (Document B/DC/5).

Finally, for purposes of ready reference, the following paragraphs set out the latest text governing member countries of the Union as at January 2005. It does not, however, purport to stipulate which Act each country should apply to each other Union country (see the examples above):

Rome Act: Lebanon, Malta, New Zealand, Pakistan, Sri Lanka, Zimbabwe.

Brussels Act: Bahamas, Chad, Fiji, Madagascar, South Africa.

Stockholm Act (*articles 22 to 38*): Chad, Fiji, Pakistan.

Paris Act (all): Albania, Algeria, Andorra, Antigua and Barbuda, Argentina, Armenia, Australia, Austria, Azerbaijan, Barbados, Bahrain, Bangladesh, Belarus, Belgium, Belize, Benin, Bhutan, Bolivia, Bosnia and Herzegovina, Botswana, Brazil, Bulgaria, Burkina Faso, Cameroon, Canada, Cape Verde, Central African Republic, Chile, China, Columbia, Congo, Costa Rica, Cote d'Ivoire, Croatia, Cuba, Cyprus, Czech Republic, Democratic Peoples' Republic of Korea, Democratic Republic of the Congo, Denmark, Djibouti, Dominica, Dominican Republic, Ecuador, Egypt, El Salvador, Equatorial Guinea, Estonia, Finland, France, Gabon, Gambia, Georgia, Germany, Ghana, Greece, Grenada, Guatemala, Guinea, Guyana, Haiti, Holy See, Honduras, Hungary, Iceland, India, Indonesia, Ireland, Israel, Italy, Jamaica, Japan, Jordan, Kazakhstan, Kenya, Kyrgyzstan, Latvia, Lesotho, Liberia, Libya, Liechtenstein, Lithuania, Luxembourg, Malawi, Malaysia, Mali, Malta, Mauritania, Mauritius, Mexico, Micronesia (Federated States of), Monaco, Mongolia, Morocco, Namibia, Netherlands, Nicaragua, Niger, Nigeria, Norway, Oman, Panama, Paraguay, Peru, Philippines, Poland, Portugal, Qatar, Republic of Korea, Republic of Moldova, Romania, Russian Federation, Rwanda, Saint Kitts and Nevis, Saint Lucia, Saint Vincent and the Grenadines, Saudi Arabia, Senegal, Serbia and Montenegro, Singapore, Slovakia, Slovenia, Spain, Sudan, Suriname, Swaziland, Sweden, Switzerland, Syrian Arab Republic, Tajikistan, Thailand, The Former Yugoslav Republic of Macedonia, Togo, Tonga, Trinidad and Tobago, Tunisia, Turkey, Ukraine, United Arab Emirates, United Kingdom, United Republic of Tanzania, United States of America, Uruguay, Venezuela, Vietnam, Zambia, Zimbabwe.

Paris Act (*articles 22 to 38)*: Bahamas, Malta, South Africa, Sri Lanka, Zimbabwe.

(b) 'Adaptation' of protection to the level of the Paris Act

17.75 Under article 32(2)(ii), countries bound by the Paris Act alone are obliged to accept the application to them of reciprocal protection on the part of a Union country not bound by that Act in the event that the latter does not simply apply the provisions of the most recent Act by which it is bound. Thus, article 32(2)(ii) permits such a country to 'adapt' the level of its protection to that accorded by the Paris Act. Such adaptations, if made, will usually be to the benefit of the Paris Act country, given that there are certain rights and subject matter recognized and protected under Paris that were not protected under the earlier Acts (for example, the right of reproduction). On the other hand, it might be argued that the protection offered by the Paris Act is modified by the availability of the compulsory licences that are allowable under the Appendix in the case of developing countries (see further paras 14.49ff).

As at December 2004, the options offered by article 32(2)(ii) are potentially relevant to the eleven non-Paris countries listed above: Lebanon, Pakistan, Sri Lanka, Zimbabwe (Rome) and Bahamas, Chad, Fiji, Madagascar, South Africa (Brussels). Under either alternative, some imbalance in protection may occur, but it is worth remembering that these are not different conventions, but simply successive revisions of the same convention and have a majority of provisions in common.

(c) Application in part or whole

The words 'to the extent that' in article 32(1) take account of the fact that the Paris Act could be ratified or acceded to in whole or in part (with a limitation with respect to articles 1 to 20 and the Appendix). This only applies to countries which are already Union members, as countries outside the Union can only accede to the whole of the Paris Act. Thus, where a country bound by the Brussels or Rome Act ratifies or accedes to articles 22 to 38 of the Paris Act, in its relations with other Union countries it will continue to apply the substantive provisions of the Brussels or Rome Act, as the case may be. In the examples given above (see para 17.74), if country B has acceded only to articles 22 to 38 of the Paris Act, its relations with country A will be governed by articles 22 to 38, which they have in common. For the rest, A will apply articles 1 to 21 and the Appendix of the Paris Acts to B, while the latter can continue to apply articles 1 to 20 of the Brussels Act to A or (at its option) an adapted Paris Act. **17.76**

(d) Application of the Appendix Concerning Developing Countries

Article 32 contains two provisions concerning the effect of the Appendix on countries not bound by the Paris Act. The first is found in paragraph 32(3), which provides that a developing country which has availed itself of the faculties provided in the Appendix may apply these provisions in its relations with countries not bound by the Paris Act as long as the latter has accepted their application. Declarations to this effect were made by several important developed countries prior to their accession to the Paris Act, most notably the UK.[471] The **17.77**

[471] [1971] *DA* 189 (as from 21 Sept 1971). Similar declarations were made by Germany on 18 Oct 1973 ([1974] *Copyright* 156) and Norway on 8 Mar 1974.

second is in paragraph 32(2)(ii) (see para 17.76 above), under which countries bound by the Paris Act recognize the right of countries not so bound to elect to adapt the level that they accord to that of the Paris Act. This is made subject to article I(6) of the Appendix, and the combined effect of these provisions seems to be as follows. First, if country A is a developing country bound only by the Paris Act and has, in addition, availed itself of the provisions of the Appendix in relation to country B which is not bound by the Paris Act, the latter should not seek to apply full reciprocity in its relations with A if it seeks to adapt to the level of protection offered by the Paris Act. This can, in no sense, be a mandatory requirement, as B remains free under paragraph (2) to refrain from offering any protection at all to A's works. However, as B will have accepted the application of the provisions of the Appendix to it in the first place under paragraph (3), to seek to extend the reciprocal protection which it may accord under paragraph (2)(ii) so as to take account of the effect of the Appendix would be churlish, to say the least.

Second, if country A has made a reservation with respect to translations under article V of the Appendix, country B should also refrain from applying reciprocity in this regard until such time as country A has ceased to be regarded as a developing country. Once again, as country B is not actually bound by the Paris Act, this can only be a moral obligation.

(e) Application of reservations on an inter se *basis*

17.78 Under customary international law, it is necessary for a reservation which is made by any party to a treaty to be accepted by the other party or parties.[472] In addition, it is generally permissible for the latter to apply reciprocal restrictions in relation to the reservant state.[473] By contrast, under the Berne Convention, where the making of reservations has been wholly regulated by the terms of that instrument since the Berlin Act, there has only been provision for this since the Stockholm Act.[474] In consequence, any country which acceded to the Berlin, Rome, or Brussels Act was obliged to accept, without the possibility of applying reciprocal restrictions, reservations which were made in accordance with those Acts by other countries. Any imbalance which this caused, however, was thought to be of a temporary or transitional character, as it was envisaged that all countries would move eventually to the same plateau of protection and would renounce their reservations.[475] This position has now been altered under the Paris Act, and a degree of reciprocity is now allowed on the part of non-reservant states. This applies in the case of new reservations with respect to

[472] See generally Sinclair (n 88 above), 54ff; McNair (n 79 above), 158; Vienna Convention, art 20.
[473] ibid. [474] See para 17.27 above. [475] *Actes* 1908, 273 (report of Louis Renault).

translations (see para 17.77 above) and with respect to the jurisdiction of the International Court of Justice (see para 17.87 below). In the case of prior reservations which are retained on ratification or accession by existing Union members, no reciprocity may be applied. Thus, even where countries are now bound by the Paris Act, there may still be differences in the level of protection which each is obliged to accord the other under that Act.

(f) Continuance of prior reservations where abandoned upon becoming bound by a new Act

Where a Union country abandons its prior reservations upon ratification of a new Act, this does not affect the continuance of those reservations with respect to its relations with countries remaining bound by the Act under which the reservations were formulated.[476] For the latter to cease to have effect in this regard, it is necessary for the country in question to declare expressly that they no longer apply.[477] This may be a point of some importance for newly independent states that were previously bound by the Convention pursuant to a notification made under article 26 of the Rome or Brussels Act. If the benefit of a reservation made by their former metropolitan power was thereby extended to these countries (which was often the case), the reservation would still remain in force if the former state abandoned this when it adhered to a later Act but made no express renunciation of the reservation with respect to its dependent territories.[478] Accordingly, it would be possible for these territories, when they became independent, to continue the reservation when they made a declaration of continued adherence.[479] **17.79**

---

[476] See the note of the International Office in [1936] *DA* 3 and see also Ladas (1938), 145.

[477] Thus, in 1931, Norway ratified the Rome Act without maintaining its prior reservations: [1931] *DA* 36. This did not have the effect of renouncing these reservations with respect to its relations with countries still bound by the Berlin Act, but six months later Norway expressly renounced these reservations as well: [1932] *DA* 3 (and accompanying note by the International Office). Note, however, the view of Ladas that a country could not make a reservation with respect to a colony alone, if it did not at the same time apply this to its metropolitan territory: Ladas (1938), 144. This view, however, did not seem to be shared by the International Office which suggested that a country making an art 26 notification could continue to apply a prior reservation to its colony and even make a separate reservation with respect to translation rights (by analogy with a new country acceding to the Union): [1933] *DA* 3 and 134.

[478] eg France applied its reservation concerning works of applied art to its territories when it extended the Berlin Act to them in 1930: [1930] *DA* 73. This was subsequently expressly retained when France acceded to the Rome Act in 1933, applying this Act at the same time to its colonies: [1933] *DA* 133. In another instance, South Africa made a reservation concerning retroactivity when it acceded to the Berlin Act in respect of SW Africa in 1931: [1932] *DA* 17. This reservation was maintained, however, when South Africa subsequently acceded to the Rome Act without extending this to SW Africa and, at the same time, abandoning its own reservation with respect to retroactivity: [1935] *DA* 49 (note by the International Office).

[479] This was not, in fact, a practical possibility, as all the major colonial powers had abandoned their own reservations by the time of the Brussels Act, and therefore could not maintain

(9) The obligations of Union membership: implementation of the Convention

(a) Generally

17.80 Subject to the exceptions relating to reservations and the application of the Appendix which have been discussed above, article 30(1) provides that ratification or accession to the Paris Act entails 'acceptance of all the provisions and admission to all the advantages of this Convention'. At this stage of our study, it is hardly necessary to reiterate the advantages of Union membership, in particular the benefit of protection of a country's authors in other Union countries and the opportunity for participation in the organs of the Union. However, the matter of a country's obligations under the Convention merits further consideration, particularly the question of implementation. 'Acceptance' of the provisions of the Convention is one thing; how these provisions are to be given effect to, and how this is to be assured, raise issues of quite a different character. The Paris Act contains two provisions which are of relevance in this regard. The first, article 36(2), deals with the undertaking that each country makes, when it becomes bound by the Convention, that it will be in a position under its domestic law to give effect to its provisions. This has already been discussed above (see para 17.18), and it was suggested there that this provides the basis for member countries to refuse admission to the Union in certain cases (such as Turkey, in 1931). The second, article 36(1), has only been in the Convention since the Stockholm Revision, and provides:

> (1) Any country party to this Convention undertakes to adopt, in accordance with its constitution, the measures necessary to ensure the application of this Convention.

Although at first sight, this appears to overlap with article 36(2), it is in fact directed at countries which are already Union countries and underlines the fact that 'conformity with the requirements of the Convention is a continuing obligation and must exist also when a country of the Union ratifies or accedes to a new Act'.[480] Our present concern in this section, therefore, is with the question of how it is to be ensured that Union countries comply with this undertaking.

---

them in respect of any notifications made under art 26 extending the Convention to their dependent territories. See, in relation to France, the note of the International Office in [1952] *DA* 49 on the application of the Brussels Act to those territories. The same was true of the UK applications of the Rome Act to its dependent territories: [1932] *DA* 38. In this respect, then, the reservation made by Ceylon with respect to translation rights when making its declaration of continuity in 1959 would seem unjustified: [1959] *DA* 205, but see also the last sentence of note 477 above.

[480] *Records* 1967, 478 (Document S/9).

17.81 In this regard, it is useful to refer to our previous discussion of the implementation of treaty obligations (see paras 5.08ff). It was noted there that the ways in which countries carry this out vary considerably, and depends upon their internal constitutional requirements. In some countries, treaties are incorporated into municipal law and, where this is possible, may be directly applied by national courts. In other countries, however, it is necessary for treaty obligations to be implemented through domestic legislation, and, in the absence of such measures, the protection of the treaty cannot be invoked in that country. As a consequence, the question of whether a country is complying with its obligations under the Berne Convention involves a detailed examination of the way in which treaty obligations are given effect to in that country. In a country where direct application is possible, the absence of any enabling domestic legislation will be of no account as the courts in that country will still be obliged to apply the provisions of the Convention.[481] On the other hand, a legislative lacuna of this kind may lead to an irresistible inference of non-compliance in a country where treaty obligations require implementation by municipal law. At the same time, it needs to be borne in mind that many provisions of the Berne Convention leave considerable room for national legislation to apply its own solutions, and the fact that countries differ here will not amount to non-compliance unless the course followed by one country clearly falls outside what is allowed by the Convention. Furthermore, it should be remembered that in some instances, such as the protection of moral rights, the Convention envisages that protection may be accorded under other heads than copyright, and this may make it very difficult to determine whether a particular country is complying with its obligations under the Convention. Accordingly, a claim of non-compliance requires careful scrutiny in each case, and involves consideration of the following questions:

1. Is the country one where treaty provisions can be self-executing?
2. If so, is this such a provision (bearing in mind that many treaty provisions

[481] Prominent Berne Union countries where this is so include three of the original signatories: Switzerland, Spain, and Belgium. In each of these countries, at various times, the direct application of the Convention to Union authors has resulted in the latter being better treated than native authors. See further A Troller, 'The Hundredth Anniversary of the Berne Convention: the Development of Law in the Copyright Field through the Interaction of the Convention and Swiss Legislation' [1986] *Copyright* 208; A Bercovitz, 'The Relationship between the Berne Convention and Intellectual Property Law in Spain' [1986] *Copyright* 345; J Corbet, 'The Berne Convention and the Belgian Copyright Law' [1986] *Copyright* 260. The question of whether the Convention, or parts of it, would be directly applicable under US law was a matter which was carefully considered in the context of likely US accession to the Convention in the mid-1980s: see generally the Preliminary Report of the Ad Hoc Working Group on US Adherence to the Berne Convention (Dec 1985), ch XII.

still require further measures in national legislation for their implementation)?
3. If national legislation is required, what is the precise meaning of the particular Convention obligation and what scope for its application is left to national legislation?
4. In the light of the answer to 3, to what extent does the national legislation of the country vary from, or fail to give effect to, this obligation?

The answers to these questions may not be easy, and this is particularly so in the case of the third. It will therefore be clear that, in many instances, allegations of non-compliance are often hard to establish, particularly where divergent interpretations of particular treaty provisions are possible. But, assuming that a failure on the part of a Union country to comply with a provision of the Convention can be shown, what is the consequence of this?

17.82 A cynical response, at least in the days before the TRIPs Agreement, was that very little, if anything, flowed from a showing of non-compliance. Certain cases have become notorious in the history of the Convention, notably that of the common law countries' failure to protect moral rights to the extent required by article 6*bis*. Nonetheless, apart from evoking the occasional outrage of commentators,[482] this breach of a Convention obligation did not lead Union countries to examine the avenues that might be open to them to rectify this situation.[483] In large part, this is due to political and economic considerations (see below), and this is both reflected and compounded by the fact that the Convention contains no provisions dealing expressly with the question of breach and has no formal sanctions that may be applied against defaulting countries. It is therefore necessary to seek solutions to these questions against the background of state practice and the general principles of customary international law. The limitations thereby revealed will then highlight the significant role that the TRIPs Agreement and the dispute-resolution machinery of the WTO can play (see further paras 4.38 above 17.93 below).

---

[482] In relation to Australia, see eg S Ricketson, 'Is Australia in Breach of its International Obligations with Respect to the Protection of Moral Rights?' (1990) 17 *Melbourne University Law Review* 462; D Vaver, 'Moral Rights and the Copyright Law Review Committee's Report: W[h]ither such Rights Now?' (1988) 14 *Monash University Law Review* 384.

[483] See generally T Collovà and J-L Tournier, 'Des sanctions et la notion de réciprocité dans la Convention de Berne' [1964] *DA* 11. See further with respect to the Paris Convention, G R Gansser, 'Violations of the Paris Convention for the Protection of Industrial Property' (1980) 11 *IIC* 1.

(b) The context in which problems of non-compliance arise

Although the Convention is an agreement among countries, who are the only parties, it is essentially concerned with the protection of private rights. While it is true that governments are concerned with the overall gains that are to be made through the international protection of authors and their works, this is only one among a range of matters that states must have regard to in their internal and international policies. As a consequence, the persons who will be most intimately interested in the question of compliance with the Convention are authors and their representatives, and the context in which this concern will become crystallized is where the legislature or courts of a Union country fail to give effect to a provision of the Convention in a particular case. It is also possible that, in some instances, the complainants will be users or user groups who assert that they have not been accorded, in a particular Union country, the latitude which the Convention requires they be given, for example, in relation to rights of quotation. However, as none of these persons or groups are parties to the Convention, they have no *locus standi* or international forum in which to press their complaints. In practice, they will seek to do this in one or more of the following ways: **17.83**

1. By making representations to the government of the country concerned, either individually or through the medium of some national or international non-governmental organization that represents their interests, such as *CISAC* or ALAI.
2. By prevailing upon the government of a 'sympathetic' Union country to press their complaint on an official or unofficial diplomatic level with the government of the offending country.
3. By using the observer status they may possess in any of the organs of the Union (in the case of a non-governmental international organization) to bring their complaints to the notice of Union members generally.
4. By requesting WIPO to act as an intermediary in passing their complaint on to the country concerned.
5. In the context of an impending revision of the Convention (not relevant at the present moment), bringing pressure to bear on national governments to promote amendments designed to overcome their problem, or, alternatively using any influence which they may have by virtue of membership of advisory committees and the like to promote such amendments. In this regard, it has been seen that the role of such bodies as ALAI has been considerable in each revision of the Convention, to say nothing of the part played by ALAI in initiating the Convention.

Each of the above methods may be of use in removing a cause of complaint. Nonetheless, as a remedy depends ultimately upon action at state level, we need to consider further the means of resolution that exist within the framework of the Convention. These are: the conference of revision and the Assembly, and the possibility of invoking the jurisdiction of the International Court of Justice. We must then look at the remedies available under customary international law, leaving discussion of the solutions now available under the TRIPs Agreement until the end of this chapter.

(c) Revision conferences and the Assembly

17.84 Both these bodies, which have been discussed in detail in Chapter 16 above, provide a more formal forum for questions of compliance to be examined, particularly where the issue is really concerned with a dispute over the interpretation of a particular provision. We have seen that, on occasion, these matters have been resolved by the adoption of an appropriate amendment to the Convention or by agreement on the meaning that is to be given to a particular provision.[484] On the other hand, the results of a revision conference may often be a compromise solution which accommodates conflicting interpretations.[485] As for the Assembly, the potential role for this body to provide interpretations of provisions of the Convention has already been discussed (see para 16.10 above). To date, this power has not been invoked, and, in any event, the Assembly has no power to enforce any decision it may reach upon a recalcitrant member.

(d) Settlement of disputes by the International Court of Justice

17.85 The possibility of member countries bringing disputes before the International Court of Justice has existed since the Brussels Act and is now dealt with in article 33 of the Paris Act. However, proposals for the adoption of this procedure were first made by the Norwegian and Swedish delegations at the time of the Rome Conference.[486] This received strong support from a number of smaller Union members as well as from the International Institute of Intellectual Cooperation,[487] but was opposed by some of the larger states which were concerned at the conflicts that might arise between the decisions of the Court and the national legislation of countries which were not involved in the dispute.[488] Finally, the proposal was deferred for consideration at the Brussels Revision Conference, where a more detailed proposal was again made by the Norwegian and Swedish delegations.[489] Among other things, this proposed that

---

[484] See eg the Interpretative Declaration of Paris, 1896, and the successive definitions of 'published works' that have been inserted in the Convention.

[485] See eg Rome Act, art 6*bis* and Stockholm, Paris Acts, art 14*ter*.

[486] *Actes* 1928, 113, 124.

[487] Notably Finland, Czechoslovakia, Switzerland, the Netherlands, and Denmark: ibid, 279.

[488] eg Italy: ibid.

[489] *Documents 1948* (1951), 401–2. For further background to the campaign for international jurisdiction that was conducted after the 1928 Conference, see Collovà and Tournier (n 483 above), 10–11.

the International Court of Justice should exercise a compulsory jurisdiction over the disputes of Union members and that there should be a right for other member countries to intervene in the proceedings.[490] A simpler and modified proposition, which still embodied the principle of compulsory arbitration, was finally accepted and this became article 27*bis* of the Brussels Act:

> A dispute between two or more countries of the Union concerning the interpretation or application of this Convention, not settled by negotiation, shall be brought before the International Court of Justice for determination by it, unless the countries concerned agree on some other method of settlement. The country requesting that the dispute should be brought before the Court shall inform the International Office; the Office shall bring the matter before it to the attention of the other countries of the Union.[491]

In the period following the Brussels Conference, no use was made of this **17.86** provision, although by the time of the Stockholm Conference thirty-nine out of fifty-five Union members had accepted the jurisdiction of the International Court under this provision through their ratification of or accession to the Brussels Act.[492] Nevertheless, it appeared that one of the reasons for the reluctance of the remaining members to become bound by the Brussels Act was their objection to the principle of compulsory jurisdiction (although this was not necessarily an objection to the principle of international arbitration itself).[493] Accordingly, the programme for the Stockholm Revision contained a series of alternative proposals for article 27*bis*: retention in its present form, deletion, the making of its application optional, and its placement in a protocol to the new Act which could be separately signed and adhered to.[494] After considerable debate in Main Committee IV, it became clear that there was a considerable body of opinion that remained opposed to compulsory jurisdiction.[495] On the basis of a Dutch and Swiss proposal, therefore, a compromise provision was adopted as article 33 of the Stockholm Act.[496] This made acceptance of the jurisdiction of the International Court optional, through the device of a reservation which might be applied reciprocally by other states. This provision was left unchanged in the Paris Act and provides as follows:

> (1) Any dispute between two or more countries of the Union concerning the interpretation or application of this Convention, not settled by negotiation, may, by any one of the countries concerned, be brought before the International Court of Justice by application in conformity with the Statute of the Court, unless the countries concerned agree on some other

[490] *Documents 1948* (1951), 402. [491] ibid, 404.

[492] *Records* 1967, 472 (Document S/9). See also the *Report of the Sub-Committee Charged with the Study of Sanctions and Reciprocity in the Convention of Berne*, submitted to the fifth meeting of the Authors' Consultative Committee, 28 Feb and 1 Mar 1963.

[493] *Records* 1967, 472. [494] ibid, 473. [495] ibid, 1060–2.

[496] Document S/222: ibid, 715.

method of settlement. The country bringing the dispute before the Court shall inform the International Bureau; the International Bureau shall bring the matter to the attention of the other countries of the Union.

(2) Each country may, at the time it signs this Act or deposits its instrument of ratification or accession, declare that it does not consider itself bound by the provisions of paragraph (1). With regard to any dispute between such country and any other country of the Union, the provisions of paragraph (1) shall not apply.

(3) Any country having made a declaration in accordance with the provisions of paragraph (2) may, at any time, withdraw its declaration by notification addressed to the Director-General.

17.87 (i) **The scope of the present provision:** The description of disputes in article 33 is in quite general terms: those 'concerning the interpretation or application of this Convention'. This therefore covers (i) cases where two or more countries are in genuine dispute over the way in which a particular provision is to be interpreted, and (ii) cases of non-compliance, where, if the state of facts as claimed by country A is true, country B is failing to comply with its obligations under the Convention (the 'application' of the Convention). An implied condition for the application of the jurisdiction of the International Court is that the countries in question have first sought to resolve their dispute through negotiation. It is also provided that the parties may agree on an alternative to this jurisdiction, that is, 'on some other method of settlement'. In Main Committee IV, it was suggested by the Italian delegation that these words be replaced by 'to settle the question by means of arbitration'.[497] However, the more general wording was preferred, and they seem adequate to cover any means of settlement that might be suggested by the parties, including arbitration by the Permanent International Court of Arbitration constituted under the Hague Convention of 1907 or an international arbitrator appointed by mutual agreement between the parties. The principle of *res judicata* applies to any decision of the International Court of Justice which is made under this provision, that is, it can only be binding on the parties to the dispute. As a means of ensuring uniformity of interpretation throughout the Union, this may be regretted. Nevertheless, the provisions for bringing the matter to the attention of other Union members ensures that they are apprised of the Court's decision and can seek to apply any interpretation which it embodies in their own laws.

17.88 As a means of ensuring compliance with the Convention, article 33 is of limited use and has not, to date, been invoked. Only Union countries may bring disputes before the Court, and the provisions allowing for the making of

[497] *Records* 1967, 1074.

reservations with respect to the application of this jurisdiction means that there is a number of member countries which do not accept this jurisdiction.[498] Nonetheless, as a proportion of total membership (twenty-one out of 159, 13.2 per cent), this is a smaller proportion than at the time of the first edition of this commentary (1987) when it was fourteen out of seventy-six (18.4 per cent). While there are some significantly sized reservants in the present list, such as Algeria, Egypt, India, Indonesia, Thailand, and Turkey, it is also noteworthy that other large members such as the USA, Russian Federation, China, the states of the EC, and most of the African, Asian, and Latin American members have not made such reservations. Accordingly, the option of an ICJ application should not be automatically discarded. While it will be relatively rarely that countries will be inclined to pursue disputes at the behest of private individuals or organizations whose interests have been damaged by the failure of another member country to comply with the Convention, it is possible to see article 33 being of potential value in relation to the interpretation of the provisions of the Paris Act. This is particularly so in the case of the Appendix. In principle, at least, the operation of these provisions is of intimate concern to the governments of developing countries, and an application to the International Court might be a useful means of resolving these questions, for example, through the provision of advisory opinions.[499] In this respect, it should be noted that an application under article 33(1) may be made by only one of the parties concerned in a dispute, and that the other party will be bound to accept the jurisdiction of the Court if it has not made a reservation with respect to article 33(1).[500]

(e) The applicable rules of customary international law

Outside the avenues provided within the Convention itself (and leaving aside the TRIPs Agreement/WTO machinery), recourse can only be to the general principles of customary international law concerning the breach of treaty obligations. The relevant rules are to be found as expressed in article 60 of the Vienna Convention which permits the termination or suspension of a multilateral treaty in the event of 'a material breach' of that treaty. In more detail, paragraphs 2 and 3 of article 60 provide as follows: **17.89**

> 2 A material breach of a multilateral treaty by one of the parties entitles:
> (a) the other parties by unanimous agreement to suspend the operation of the treaty in whole or in part or to terminate it either:

[498] Namely Algeria, Bahamas, Egypt, Guatemala, India, Indonesia, Israel, Lesotho, Libya, Lithuania, Malta, Mauritius, Mongolia, Oman, Saint Lucia, South Africa, Tanzania, Thailand, Tunisia, Turkey, Venezuela, and Vietnam: see para 17.32 above.

[499] Statute of the International Court of Justice, art 65.

[500] ibid. On the ICJ generally, see further S Rosenne, *The Law and Practice of the International Court* (1965) and T O Elias, *The International Court of Justice and Some Contemporary Problems* (1983).

(i) in the relations between themselves and the defaulting State, or
(ii) as between all the parties;

(b) a party specially affected by the breach to invoke it as a ground for suspending the operation of the treaty in whole or in part in the relations between itself and the defaulting State;

(c) any party other than the defaulting State to invoke the breach as a ground for suspending the operation of the treaty in whole or in part with respect to itself if the treaty is of such a character that a material breach of its provisions by one party radically changes the position of every party with respect to the further performance of its obligations under the treaty.

3 A material breach of a treaty, for the purposes of this article, consists in:
(a) . . .
(b) the violation of a provision essential to the accomplishment of the object or purpose of the treaty.[501]

17.90 To date, no situation has arisen in which any member of the Union has sought to suspend or terminate its obligations under the Convention with respect to another member country on the ground of 'material breach'. The widespread non-recognition of the application of the Convention to the GDR is not such a case, as there was no allegation there that the GDR was failing to give effect to its obligations under the Convention. This is not to deny that instances of non-compliance have occurred throughout the history of the Convention, but simply that Union members have preferred not to take such drastic action and have kept their Convention obligations with the defaulting country alive. The reasons for these decisions (if, indeed, they have been consciously made) are legion, and may reflect an underlying acknowledgement that none of these breaches have been so 'material' as to justify the final sanction of suspension or termination of Convention relations with that country. Indeed, it would seem that a strong motivation has been a desire to keep the Union intact (particularly in the case of the common law countries) and to keep its doors open to new entrants. Thus, acquiescence in many alleged instances of non-compliance may now make it difficult to insist on a strict application of the Convention.[502] There are sound reasons for flexibility in this regard, and this is a central thread that runs through the history of the Union. It is possible to view the story of US accession to Berne in the late 1980s as providing a striking example of this 'flexibility', particularly in relation to such matters as formalities, moral rights, and retroactivity. On the other hand, the consideration of Berne compliance issues by US legislators and policy-makers was both detailed and conscientious and, above all things, fully exposed for the world to see (see further paras 4.50ff). It is also noteworthy that

[501] See further Sinclair (n 88 above), 188ff.
[502] Vienna Convention, art 45. See also Sinclair (n 88 above), 168–9, 180–1.

the USA subsequently took legislative action to amend an area of non-compliance with respect to retroactivity and Berne compliance issues have been central to that country's policymaking in the international copyright sphere.

(f) Refusal to invite certain states to meetings of Union organs

Although not related to questions of non-compliance, reference should be made here to the decisions that have been made by Union members on several occasions not to invite certain member states to meetings of Union organs. After World War II, the question was raised of Spain's entitlement to participate in the Brussels Conference in view of the widespread disapproval of the Franco Government, but eventually the Spanish Government was invited and participated fully in the Conference.[503] It will also be recalled that the GDR was not invited to either the Stockholm or Paris Conference, although this could be distinguished from the Spanish case on the ground that the GDR was not generally recognized as a state and its membership of the Union was therefore hotly disputed (see further para 17.67 above). Again, until the abolition of its apartheid policies, the South African Government was not invited to attend meetings of Union organs.[504] In the last case, there did not seem to be any question that South Africa had failed to comply with its obligations under the Convention or to meet its annual contributions. The basis for the decision was simply disapproval of the South African Government and its policies, and was in line with similar decisions that have been taken in a wide range of international forums and organizations.[505] It does not appear that South Africa insisted on its right to attend meetings and there is no reason for concluding that this country has ceased to be bound by the Convention or that other Union countries no longer have obligations under the Convention with respect to South Africa. Certainly, there has been issue in this regard since 1994. **17.91**

(10) The effect of war

One final problem which deserves brief consideration is the effect of war on relations between Union members. As a general principle, there is no reason to suppose that war automatically terminates the relations of countries towards each other under a convention, particularly where this is a multilateral **17.92**

[503] See British Foreign Office Records: FO 371/68958(1948), UE 4893/406/53 on the background to this question.

[504] In 1977, the WIPO Coordination Committee put on the agenda of the governing bodies of WIPO, and the unions administered by it, a resolution to exclude South Africa from participation in all meetings in accordance with UN resolutions on the matter: [1977] *Copyright* 296. This failed to obtain the necessary two-thirds majority of the WIPO Conference at its meeting of 1979. Nevertheless, the decision of the WIPO Coordination Committee not to invite South Africa to meetings was not repealed and continued to be applied: [1979] *Copyright* 8.

[505] See further Schermers (n 78 above), 718ff.

convention.[506] This is certainly true of the Berne Convention, which has continued in existence despite the occurrence of two major world wars and a series of minor wars involving its members. These have not led to any termination of Convention relations, particularly with respect to the relations of belligerents and neutrals, and even among the belligerents themselves it seems that the most that has happened has been a temporary suspension of relations.[507] Thus, authors should not cease to be protected against infringement of their rights in another Union country, even when that country is at war with the country of the author. In this respect, the action of the UK Government in vesting the literary and artistic property of enemy authors in an official custodian during World War I was not regarded by the International Office as a breach of the Convention, as this maintained the protection of the works and these copyrights were revested in the authors at the end of the War.[508] It should also be noted that wartime interferences with the exercise of rights protected under the Convention are permitted under the police power in article 17, for example, where the circulation or dissemination of protected works is prohibited through censorship or national security regulations.[509]

C. Beyond the Berne Convention

(1) The TRIPs Agreement

17.93 The 'steel in the spine' provided by the dispute-resolution procedures of the TRIPs Agreement have already been commented upon in other parts of this commentary (see, in particular, para 4.38 above). For more detail on these matters, readers should refer to the specialist commentaries.[510]

---

[506] McNair (n 79 above), 696. See generally ibid, ch 43.

[507] See generally 'Union internationale: les rapports unionistes pendant la guerre' [1915] *DA* 5–7, 116–17; 'De la situation des droits d'auteur et d'édition durant et après la guerre' [1917] *DA* 15, 29; 'L'Union internationale après la guerre' [1918] *DA* 15; 'La bilan de la guerre mondiale en matière de propriété intellectuelle' [1920] *DA* 37, 50 and 66; [1939] *DA* 109.

[508] Trading with the Enemy (Copyright) Act 1916 and the Order in Council of 9 Feb 1920 (made under the Termination of the Present War (Definition) Act 1918) revesting these rights: discussed further in *Copinger on the Law of Copyright*, 6th edn (1927), 296–7. See further [1920] *DA* 38 and [1939] *DA* 109, 110. Note also that the various treaties of peace at the end of the two world wars also dealt with the question of revesting of enemy copyrights confiscated during the course of hostilities.

[509] See generally the review of these controls in different belligerent countries during World War I in [1920] *DA* 50ff.

[510] In particular, D Gervais, *The TRIPS Agreement: Drafting History and Analysis*, 2nd edn (2004), 332–49.

(2) The WCT and WPPT

(a) In general

The final clauses of these two treaties—articles 17 to 25 of the WCT and articles 26 to 33 of the WPPT—are identical and will be treated together below. They deal with the following matters: eligibility to become a party to the treaty in question; rights and obligations under the treaty; signature and entry into force; effective date of becoming a party; reservations and denunciation; languages; and depository. The last two of these matters have already been dealt with above (see paras 5.14 and 16.56); the others are dealt with below. **17.94**

(b) Eligibility (WCT, article 17 and WPPT, article 26)

The eligibility criteria here are different from the Berne Convention, being limited to member states of WIPO, intergovernmental organizations that meet certain criteria, and the European Community. **17.95**

(i) **Member states of WIPO**: This is now a very large potential pool, numbering some 182 states as at December 2004.[511] Even in July 1996, at the time of the preparation of the Basic Proposal for the Administrative and Final Clauses,[512] there were 151 member states and this had grown to 161 by the time of the Diplomatic Conference. Of these, all the then 119 members of Berne were WIPO member states, while all but one of fifty-one Rome Convention states were WIPO member states.[513] The limitation to WIPO member states was described, not surprisingly, in the WIPO Memorandum prepared for the Preparatory Committee in May 1996, as a 'logical requirement' in view of the role of that organization in organizing and making the preparations for the Diplomatic Conference.[514] It also seemed logical in view of the almost complete overlap in membership between the Berne, Rome, and WIPO Conventions, as well as the general administrative roles of WIPO in relation to both the Berne and Rome Conventions. The proposal was adopted by consensus by the Preparatory Committee in May 1996,[515] and then appeared in article 100(1) of the Basic Proposal submitted to the Diplomatic Conference. Nonetheless, there was some opposition to the proposal in Main Committee, stemming mainly from the Latin American and Caribbean countries who wanted membership of the WCT tied to Berne membership, with a view to maintaining the close **17.96**

---

[511] www.wipo.int/treaties/en.

[512] Document CRNR/DC/3 in *Records* 1996, vol I, 133.

[513] The missing one was the Dominican Republic which joined WIPO on 27 June 2000.

[514] Draft Final Clauses of the Treaty to be Considered by the Diplomatic Conference, WIPO Document CRNR/PM/2, 3 Apr 1996.

[515] Report of Preparatory Committee, WIPO Document CRNR/PM/8, 24 May 1996.

linkage between the two instruments.[516] Logically, it followed that membership of the WPPT should be limited to Rome Convention states as well. These views, however, called forth strong interventions from the then Director General of WIPO, Dr Bogsch, who argued that such limitations would then exclude significant numbers of states that were already WIPO member states, but not parties to Berne (or Rome). In the case of Berne, this would exclude some forty states, as the numbers then stood.[517] Significant opposition continued to be expressed in the Committee, notably by Columbia, whose delegate pointed to the need to have an 'effective linkage' with Berne and that one way of increasing membership of Berne would be to make it obligatory for a new member to accede to Berne in the event that it wished to join the new treaty. An obvious answer to this was that compliance with articles 1 to 21 of Berne was, in any event, a requirement of article 1(4) of the proposed treaty,[518] and other delegates pointed to the risk that the WCT, and even more so the WPPT, might become 'exclusive clubs' if the membership limitations were adopted.[519] Eventually, after time for informal 'consultations' of the kind that never find their way into official conference records, article 100(1), now article 102(1), was adopted without objection.[520] From the perspective of 2005, this debate seems to have been about very little, given that the memberships of the WCT and Berne are now much greater and almost completely overlap. Even in the case of Rome, membership of this has increased significantly since 1996 and all Rome members are WIPO members.[521]

17.97 **(ii) Intergovernmental organizations and the European Community:** The competence and ever-growing interest of the European Community in copyright matters had been evident for some time prior to the 1996 Diplomatic Conference, and, for this reason was included as an eligible member in the Draft Final Clauses in the WIPO Memorandum prepared for the Preparatory Committee in May 1996.[522] No particular conditions for EC membership were proposed, although it was noted that this might be desirable, and no proposal with respect to intergovernmental organizations other than the EC was included, on the basis that no other organization had shown an interest in membership or had the same legislative competence in copyright matters as the EC.[523] While the Preparatory Committee was agreed on the EC, it also thought

[516] Rogers (Chile) in Main Committee II, second meeting, 18 Dec 1996, in *Records* 1996, vol II, 803, para 28.

[517] ibid, 801–2, para 28.

[518] ibid, 805, para 36 (Dr Bogsch).

[519] ibid, 806, para 39 (Yambao, Philippines).

[520] ibid, 814, para 81.

[521] Seventy-nine as at June 2005 (see www.wipo.int/treaties).

[522] Draft Final Clauses of the Treaty to be Considered by the Diplomatic Conference, WIPO Document CRNR/PM/2, 3 Apr 1996.

[523] J Reinbothe and S von Lewinski, *The WIPO Treaties 1996* (2002) ('Reinbothe and von Lewinski (2002)'), 194, 1.

that other intergovernmental organizations should be included, although there were differences of opinion as to the conditions of eligibility for such organizations (including the EC).[524] The Basic Proposal submitted to the Diplomatic Conference[525] proposed in draft article 100(2) that the EC should be eligible without condition, but subject to draft article 100(4) in square brackets which reflected a concern about competence that had been expressed in the Preparatory Committee by the group of African states. Under draft article 100(4), the EC, on depositing its instrument of ratification or accession would have been required to inform the Director General of WIPO of its competence and legislation with respect to the matters covered by the Treaty, as well as to do the same with respect to any subsequent changes that might occur. In the case of other intergovernmental organizations, there was now a proposal for their admission subject to a decision by the Assembly (proposed article 100(3), with a square brackets proposal that the organization have the relevant competence and legislation binding on its members, as well as the authority of its members to become a party; again, it seems, that this proposed draft accommodated the views of the African countries in the Preparatory Committee).[526] While there were further informal 'consultations' about the wording of this draft, the redrafted final text[527] was adopted with no further formal debate by Main Committee II,[528] and this now appears as article 17(2) and (3) of the WCT and article 26(2) and (3) of the WPPT. These paragraphs deal with: (i) intergovernmental organizations generally, with the exception of the EC; and (ii) the EC specifically.

(iii) **Intergovernmental organizations**: The general requirements here under articles 17(2) (WCT) and 26(2) (WPPT) respectively are that the decision on admission to become a party is to be made by the Assembly of the contracting parties for each treaty (see also articles 15(2)(b) (WCT) and 24(2)(b) (WPPT)). The Assembly has full discretion on this question, and no specific guidelines or criteria are specified. However, a precondition for the Assembly to decide is that the organization membership 'declares' that is 'competent in respect of, and has its own legislation binding on all its own Members, on matters covered by this Treaty'. Moreover, the declaration will need to state that the organization has been 'duly authorised, in accordance with its internal procedures, to become party to this Treaty'. It is to be supposed that these would be matters that the Assembly could inquire into further if it so desired, but under the wording of the paragraph it would be enough that the declaration had been made. In fact, **17.98**

[524] Report of Preparatory Committee, WIPO Document CRNR/PM/8, 24 May 1996, paras 12–17.

[525] Document CRNR/DC/3 in *Records* 1996, vol I, 143.

[526] ibid.

[527] Document CRNR/DC/83, *Records* 1996, vol I, 514, draft art 102(2) and (3).

[528] *Records* 1996, vol II, 814, para 81.

the organization that in 1996 most readily met these criteria was the EC, but this organization is actually treated separately in the next paragraph.

17.99 (iv) **The EC:** Under articles 17(3) (WCT) and 26(3) (WPPT), it is provided that the EC, 'having made the declaration referred to in the preceding paragraph in the Diplomatic Conference that has adopted this Treaty, may become party to this Treaty'. The reference to the 'declaration' made by the EC is to the declaration made by the EC delegation (J Stoodley) to the final meeting of the plenary of the Diplomatic Conference that

> . . . on behalf of the European Community, he wished, in connection with the Articles in both Treaties dealing with the Contracting Party status of the European Community, to make the statement for the records of the Conference that the European Community was competent in respect of, and had its own legislation binding on all of its Member States, on the matters covered by the treaties. Moreover, the European Community had the capacity to become party to the treaties.[529]

As noted by Reinbothe and von Lewinski, there had never been any doubt throughout the Diplomatic Conference, and the preceding preparations, that the EC would be capable of becoming a contracting party: negotiations rather had focused on whether there should be conditions set for other intergovernmental organizations.[530] Under articles 17(3) and 26(3), no decision of the Assembly is required for the purposes of admission of the EC, but this was made subject to the making of the above declaration at the Diplomatic Conference. While there can be no doubt as to the growing competence of the EC in the area of copyright, it may be questioned whether the declaration of the EC delegation at the Diplomatic Conference was fully justified. Thus, its 'competence' in the area is not a full plenary power such as is found in some national federal constitutions, such as those of the USA[531] or Australia,[532] where there is power to legislate generally with respect to copyright. Legislative competence in the EC has grown bit by bit as it has formulated new Directives and regulations on different copyright topics,[533] and it could not have been said in 1996 that existing EC Directives binding on its members covered all the matters covered by the treaties, an obvious gap being in relation to those matters covered by the

[529] *Records* 1996, vol II, 630, para 518.

[530] Reinbothe and von Lewinski (2002), 197–8, para 8.

[531] US Constitution, art 1, sec 8, cl 8: 'to promote the progress of science and the useful arts by for limited times to authors and inventors the exclusive right to their respective writings and discoveries'.

[532] Commonwealth Constitution, s 51(xviii): power for the Commonwealth (federal) parliament to legislate with respect to '. . . copyright'.

[533] In the words of Reinbothe and von Lewinski (2002), at 199, para 9, 'The internal competence of the EC in relation to its Member States is also gradually evolving in the area of copyright and neighbouring rights. The basis for this competence also tends to get more solid with every piece of Community legislation in this field.'

Information Society Directive several years later. At the same time, EC membership in the new treaties was clearly a 'good thing' that caused no particular concern to delegates at the Diplomatic Conference (apart from issues to do with voting rights, as to which see para 16.54 above). Moreover, the EC has contracting party status in the WTO and was one of the first parties as from 1 January 1995, so its formal exclusion from older intellectual property conventions, such as Berne, begins to look anomalous. Automatic eligibility for the WCT and WPPT, without Assembly approval, was therefore not a stumbling block. At the time of writing, however, the EC had not yet acceded to either treaty.

(c) Rights and obligations

Articles 18 (WCT) and 27 (WPPT) provide that: **17.100**

> Subject to any specific provision to the contrary in this Treaty, each Contracting Party shall enjoy all of the rights and assume all of the obligations under this Treaty.[534]

In the case of sovereign states, these articles are simply a restatement of the general requirements under public international law: as article 27 of the Vienna Convention states '[E]very treaty in force is binding upon the parties to it and must be performed by them in good faith' (*Pacta sunt servanda*). On the other hand, there is a problem that potentially arises in the case of intergovernmental organizations that wish to become contracting parties to a treaty: other contracting parties may be unsure as to the extent of their competence to undertake treaty obligations, particularly where this may raise complicated questions as to the internal constitutional structures of the organization in question and where some or all of its member states are also contracting parties. No provision along the lines of articles 18 and 27 was contained in the preparatory documents for the Diplomatic Conference, but the concerns that had been expressed by some delegations about the competence of intergovernmental organizations to become contracting parties have already been discussed above (see paras 17.98 and 17.99). Against whom would issues of treaty compliance be pursued where an intergovernmental organization such as the EC became a contracting party? Would this be the intergovernmental organization itself, or would it be the member states themselves, or would there be some kind of joint liability? Article 100(4) of the Basic Proposal (see para 17.96 above) had been an attempt to deal with this question in the context of eligibility, but questions still arose as to issues of joint liability and the differences that might arise from the undoubted

[534] General compliance obligations on Contracting Parties to the WCT and WPPT to 'adopt, in accordance with their legal systems, the measures necessary to ensure the application of this Treaty' are contained in articles 14(1) and 23(1) of the WCT and WPPT respectively. See further paras 5.11ff above, and Reinbothe and von Lewinski (2002), 172 and 449.

status of sovereign states and the more limited authority that might be enjoyed by intergovernmental organizations under their constituent instruments.[535] A compromise that was ultimately arrived at informally was the proposal for a provision on rights and obligations that would be separate from the eligibility requirements, but that would require all contracting parties, including intergovernmental organizations, to comply, as a matter of general international law, with their obligations under the treaties. The text of articles 18 and 27 was therefore based on an amendment proposed by the EC and its member states 'to substitute for a declaration of competence'[536] that was adopted with a slight change of wording by Main Committee II.[537] A further EC proposal allowing contracting parties to request of any other contracting party 'information concerning its implementation of any provision of this Treaty' and a requirement of the party receiving the request to provide this information 'within a reasonable time' was not proceeded with.[538]

17.101 Although the background sketched in the preceding paragraph does not clearly arise from the formal records of the Diplomatic Conference, articles 18 and 27 can therefore be seen as 'locking in' the requirement that all contracting parties must be able to assume all obligations under the Treaty, and that, in the case of non-state members, such as intergovernmental organizations, other contracting parties can look directly to them, rather than having to concern themselves with questions of internal constitutional authority and competence: regardless of whether the organization in question has the required authority, it will have the full international obligation of treaty compliance under articles 18 and 27. At the same time, each member state of the organization that is a contracting party is under the same obligation, so in principle all gaps in relation to compliance are closed.[539] In the case of the EC and its member states, it made a further declaration as follows to Plenary of the Diplomatic Conference:

> The European Community and its Member States hereby indicate their intention, when acceding, to deposit their instruments of ratification or accession simultaneously.[540]

---

535 Reinbothe and von Lewinski (2002), 203–4, para 3.

536 CRNR/DC/81, 18 Dec 1996, *Records* 1996, vol I, 499, as proposed new art 100*bis*.

537 CRNR/DC/83, *Records* 1996, vol I, 514, art 103, substituting the word 'assume all of the obligations under this Treaty' for 'bear all of the responsibilities under this Treaty' as in the EC draft art 100*bis*.

538 CRNR/DC/81, 18 Dec 1996, *Records* 1996, vol I, 499, as proposed new art 100*ter*.

539 Reinbothe and von Lewinski (2002), 205, n 6. As these authors note, obviously each state member will only be under such an obligation with respect to its national territory, while the intergovernmental organization will have responsibility for all of the territory of its member states.

540 *Records* 1996, vol II, 634, para 533 (Hennessy, Ireland, speaking on behalf of the EC and member states). Although, at the time of writing, accession by the EC and member states, had not occurred, this was approved by the EC Council on 16 Mar 2000: OJ L 89/6, 11 Apr 2000 (recital 7 reiterates the declaration made at the Diplomatic Conference as to simultaneous accession.

It should also be noted that these articles are subject to any specific contrary provision in the treaties. The most significant contrary provisions to note here are those relating to voting rights, namely articles 15(3)(b) and 24(3)(b), which allow intergovernmental organizations a number of votes equal to the number of member states that are contracting parties to the treaty (see para 16.50 above). Specific provisions concerning the effective date for becoming a party to the treaties in the case of intergovernmental organizations are contained in articles 21 and 26 (see further para 17.103 below).

(d) Signature and entry into force

In both cases, the WCT and WPPT remained open for signature until 31 December 1997 by any member state and by the European Community: articles 19 (WCT) and 28 (WPPT). Both came into force three months after the deposit of thirty instruments of ratification or accession: articles 20 (WCT) and 29 (WPPT). This happened on 6 March 2002 for the WCT and on 20 May 2002 for the WPPT. **17.102**

(e) Effective date of becoming a party

This is dealt with in identical provisions in articles 21 (WCT) and 30 (WPPT). The situations provided for are as follows: **17.103**

1. For the thirty states that have deposited accessions or ratifications in accordance with articles 20 and 29 respectively, the Treaty binds these states from the time it has entered into force, ie as from 6 March 2002 and 20 May 2002.
2. For states that subsequently become parties, they are bound from the expiration of three months from the deposit of the relevant instrument with the Director General.
3. For the EC, this happens three months after the deposit of its instrument of ratification or accession.
4. A similar three-month period applies in the case of other intergovernmental organizations that are admitted to become party to the treaties.

(f) Reservations and denunciation

Learning from the experience of Berne, there is no facility for the making of reservations under the WCT: article 22. A similar rule applies in the case of the WPPT (article 21), subject to the reservations that are allowable with respect to the right of remuneration for broadcasting and public communication of phonograms and performances fixed in phonograms under article 15(3) (as to this, see further para 19.68 below). **17.104**

Denunciations of either treaty are to be made by notification addressed to the

Director General of WIPO and take effect one year from the date of receipt: articles 23 (WCT) and 31 (WPPT).

(g) Languages

17.105 There are six 'equally authentic' versions of the WCT and WPPT, in English, Arabic, Chinese, French, Russian, and Spanish, with no single text being given priority with respect to conflicts in interpretation: articles 24(1) (WCT) and 32(1) (WPPT). In such an event, the appropriate rule to apply would therefore be that contained in article 33(4) of the Vienna Convention. This provides that 'the meaning which best reconciles the texts, having regard to the object and purpose of the treaty, shall be adopted' (see further the discussion at para 5.14 above).

Provision is also made for the establishment of official texts in other languages by the Director General at the request of an interested party, after consultation with all the interested parties: articles 24(2) (WCT) and 32(1) (WPPT).

Part IV

OTHER CONVENTIONS ON COPYRIGHT AND NEIGHBOURING RIGHTS

18

THE BERNE CONVENTION AND OTHER RELATED INTERNATIONAL CONVENTIONS ON COPYRIGHT

A. Introduction

18.01 Following World War II, five major conventions on copyright and neighbouring rights have sprung from the side of the Berne Convention. These are the Universal Copyright Convention (the 'UCC'), the Rome Convention for the Protection of Performers, Producers of Phonograms and Broadcasting Organizations 1961 (the 'Rome Convention'), the Convention for the Protection of Producers of Phonograms against Unauthorized Duplication of their Phonograms 1971 (the 'Phonograms Convention'), the World Intellectual Property Organization ('WIPO') Copyright Treaty (the 'WCT'), and the WIPO Performances and Phonograms Treaty (the 'WPPT'). They have been accompanied by a cluster of less important treaties dealing with such subjects as the international deposit of industrial designs, the protection of typefaces, the distribution of programme-carrying signals by means of satellite, and the avoidance of double taxation of copyright royalties. Finally, of course, there is the Agreement on Trade-Related Aspects of Intellectual Property Rights 1994 (the 'TRIPs Agreement'). None of these later conventions stands in contradiction to the Berne Convention: on the contrary, each can be seen as an important supplement to the international system of protection established by that Convention. In this regard, they fall into two broad categories and their objects can be described as follows: (i) attempts to increase the number of states in the international copyright system, even if this entails a lower level of protection than that offered by the Berne Convention: this was the principal aim of the UCC and is now largely a matter of history; and (ii) attempts to provide protection for subject matter and/or rights falling outside the traditional ambit of the Berne Convention, the notable instances here being the Rome and Phonograms Conventions, the WCT and WPPT, and those dealing with such matters as taxation, typefaces, and the like.

It is not intended to examine the provisions of these treaties in detail. In the case of the texts of the WCT and the TRIPs Agreement, this has already been done in the preceding chapters, and, in the case of the UCC and Rome Conventions, there are a number of significant commentaries that are available.[1] Our aim here is more limited: to consider the origins of these treaties and the way in which they extend the fundamental international copyright system established under Berne. For ease of exposition, the present chapter deals with other copyright

[1] See eg S Stewart, *International Copyright and Neighbouring Rights*, 2nd edn (1989) ('Stewart (1989)'); C Masouyé, *Guide to the Rome Convention and to the Phonograms Convention* (1981); A Bogsch, *The Law of Copyright under the Universal Convention*, 3rd rev edn (1972). See also J A L Sterling, *Intellectual Property Rights in Sound Recordings, Film & Video* (1992).

agreements, notably the UCC and its Pan-American predecessors. As will be seen, this is now a topic that is largely of historical interest, but the role that the UCC has played as a 'stepping stone' to Berne has been of considerable importance. The treaties concerned with neighbouring rights, in particular the Rome Convention and the WPPT, are considered separately in the following chapter.

B. The Universal Copyright Convention

(1) Origins

These are to be found in the parallel system of multilateral copyright conventions which grew up between the various American republics in the years from 1889 to 1928. The primary aim of the UCC was to provide a common instrument which would govern the copyright relations of these countries with the countries of the Berne Union. This was not achieved without a great deal of preliminary work which had to await the end of World War II before it came to fruition. **18.02**

(a) The Montevideo Convention

Shortly after the coming into force of the Berne Convention, a second multilateral copyright convention was adopted at a conference of seven South American states at Montevideo in 1889.[2] Several of these states, in fact, had been involved, at various stages, in the preparatory work for the Berne Convention but had not signed that Convention on the ground that they did not feel that its provisions were appropriate for countries at their present stages of literary and artistic development.[3] In consequence, the Berne Convention was almost a wholly European instrument, with Haiti being the only member state (and then only briefly) from the Americas. Nonetheless, the adoption of Berne clearly influenced the South American republics to make a treaty of their own and the resultant Montevideo Convention was largely modelled on the provisions of the Berne Convention. In a number of important respects, however, it was different and in several instances was more progressive. Thus, photographic and choreographic works were specifically protected[4] and there was complete assimilation of translation rights.[5] There was no reference to compliance with formalities, with the consequence that persons claiming under the Convention, unlike the Berne Convention, did not have to prove compliance with the formalities of the country of origin of the work.[6] On the other hand, there was no protection for **18.03**

---

[2] These states were Argentina, Bolivia, Brazil, Chile, Paraguay, Peru, and Uruguay: S P Ladas, *The International Protection of Literary and Artistic Property* (1938) ('Ladas (1938)'), 635. For the text of the Convention, see [1889] *DA* 52ff.

[3] See paras 2.21 and 2.39 above.

[4] Montevideo Convention, art 5.

[5] ibid, art 3.

[6] Ladas (1938), 655.

unpublished works and the nature and extent of protection accorded to works first published in a contracting country was determined by the law of that country, rather than the law of the country where protection was claimed (as under the Berne Convention).[7] Furthermore, the Montevideo Convention did not appear to have a retrospective application[8] and, unlike the Berne Convention, did not create a Union with a central office. Finally, membership was confined to signatory states which ratified the Convention and to non-signatory states whose relations, under the Convention, were restricted to those signatory states who accepted their accession.[9] This last was an important restriction. Of the five signatory states which ratified the Convention (Paraguay, Peru, Uruguay, Argentina, and Bolivia), two (Uruguay and Peru) adopted the policy of refusing to accept accessions by non-Latin American states.[10] It is clear, however, that European states were keen to enter into copyright relations with Latin American countries, as is evidenced by the accession of seven European states (each a member of the Berne Union) to the Montevideo Convention between 1896 and 1931.[11] This only achieved relations with a maximum of three Latin American states, and, for the majority of these European states, with only one or two of the signatory states.[12] Furthermore, despite a resolution of the first International American Conference meeting in Washington in October 1889 to the effect that all American governments should accede to the Montevideo Convention, no other American state chose to do so.[13] In consequence, the new Convention fell far short of realizing its potential of an all-American multilateral convention that could also provide a bridge to the countries of the Old World.

(b) Subsequent conventions on the American continent

18.04 In the forty years following the adoption of the Montevideo Convention, a succession of other multilateral copyright conventions came into existence between the states of South and Central America as well as the USA. The provisions of these instruments differed considerably, as did the parties to them, and none succeeded in gaining the adherence of all the American states. Nonetheless, by the time of the Rome Revision Conference of the Berne Convention,

[7] Ladas (1938), 655–6. [8] ibid, 654.

[9] Montevideo Convention, arts 13, 16 and Additional Protocol, art 6.

[10] Ladas (1938), 636.

[11] France (accession accepted by Argentina 1896 and Paraguay 1900); Italy and Spain (accession accepted by Argentina and Paraguay 1900); Belgium (accession accepted by Argentina 1903); Austria (accession accepted by Argentina 1923, Paraguay 1928, and Bolivia 1930); Germany (accession accepted by Argentina, Paraguay, and Bolivia 1927); and Hungary (accession accepted by Argentina, Paraguay, and Bolivia 1931) (sources: *Recueil des Conventions et Traités* (International Office), *Le Droit d'Auteur*, and Ladas (1938), 636).

[12] See n 11 above.

[13] *Minutes of the International American Conference* (1890), 81, 92, 220, 227, 235. See also Ladas (1938), 639.

there were a considerable number of multilateral conventions in force between the various American republics and the great majority were party to at least one instrument. Several of these were restricted to the South American and Central American republics respectively; a series of other agreements, known as the Pan-American Conventions, sought to bring all the American republics into copyright relations with each other.

(c) The Caracas Convention

This was signed on 17 July 1911 by the five South American republics founded by Simon Bolivar on the occasion of the first centenary of their independence.[14] It was modelled on the Montevideo Convention, with the following exceptions. Protection was accorded only to citizens of contracting countries and not to all persons publishing their works in these countries (as under the Montevideo Convention).[15] This restriction of protection, on the grounds of nationality, was to become a recurrent theme in other multilateral copyright conventions on the American continent. With respect to formalities, authors were required to give notice of the reservation of their rights and to comply with the formalities of each country where protection was claimed.[16] The Caracas Convention was ratified by only three of the five signatory states.[17] **18.05**

(d) The Central American conventions

Even before the Montevideo Convention, article 20 of the Treaty of Peace of 16 February 1887 between the five Central American republics had assured national treatment to authors in each country.[18] A special convention on literary, artistic, and industrial property was adopted in 1901, but failed to come into effect.[19] Following the hostilities of 1906 and 1907, earlier agreements concerning protection of copyright among the Central American republics were abrogated in the Treaty of Peace and Amity signed at Washington on 20 December 1907, but national treatment for authors of each country was maintained on a more restricted basis, namely that such authors must be resident in the country where they sought protection.[20] More substantive copyright relations, however, subsisted between the Central American republics under the successive Pan-American Conventions of 1902, 1906, 1910, and 1928 (see below). **18.06**

---

[14] Ecuador, Bolivia, Peru, Colombia, and Venezuela: 'L'Union bolivienne et le protection de la propriété intellectuelle' [1912] *DA* 58. See also Ladas (1938), 637.

[15] [1912] *DA* 58. [16] ibid.

[17] Venezuela, Peru, and Ecuador: Ladas (1938), 657. [18] ibid, 637.

[19] See notes in [1898] *DA* 87, [1902] *DA* 94, [1902] *DA* 138 and [1903] *DA* 106.

[20] Treaty of Peace and Amity, 20 Dec 1907, art VIII. See further 'La protection international de la propriété intellectuelle dans l'Amérique Centrale' [1911] *DA* 45.

(e) The Pan-American Convention of 1902

18.07 This was an attempt by the second Pan-American Conference, meeting in Mexico City in 1901 to 1902, to succeed where the Montevideo Convention had failed in attracting the adherence of all American states. The Conference adopted a new Convention on 27 January 1902 and this was signed by seventeen American republics, including the USA, the five Central American republics, Mexico, Haiti, and the Dominican Republic.[21] This instrument was more closely modelled on the Berne Convention than its predecessor of Montevideo. Thus, a union for the recognition and creation of authors' rights was established (though without a central office)[22] and the principle of national treatment was adopted.[23] However, as under the Berne Act, the law of the country of origin continued to govern the matter of duration[24] and, in substance, this law also applied with respect to the question of formalities.[25] This new Convention was no more successful than the Montevideo Convention in attracting adherences: by 1908 it had been ratified only by the USA, the Dominican Republic, and the five Central American republics and, as between the last five states, was abrogated by the Treaty of Peace of 1907 which ended the fighting in Central America (see above).[26]

(f) The Pan-American Convention of 1906

18.08 The third Pan-American Conference which met at Rio de Janeiro in 1906 decided to consolidate the subjects of patents, trade marks, and copyright in a single instrument. To this end, a new Convention on Patents of Invention, Drawings, Industrial Models, Trade Marks and Literary and Artistic Property was signed by the representatives of nineteen American republics participating in the Conference.[27] As far as copyright was concerned, article 1 of the Convention incorporated the Convention of 1902 and articles II to XI dealt with the creation of two offices for the Union (one in Havana and the other in Rio de Janeiro) which were to have the task, among other things, of centralizing the registration of literary and artistic works. This was to have the effect of gaining protection throughout all countries of the Union, although the procedure was to be optional and interested persons were left free to obtain registration of their

---

[21] The other states were Argentina, Bolivia, Chile, Colombia, Ecuador, Paraguay, Peru, and Uruguay: Ladas (1938), 640. See generally 'Les Conventions pan-américaines concernant la protection de la propriété intellectuelle: Mexico 1902, Rio de Janeiro 1906, Buenos Aires 1910' [1911] *DA* 58 (with texts of conventions).

[22] Pan-American Convention 1902, art 1. [23] ibid, art 3. [24] ibid, art 5.

[25] ibid, art 4. [26] See [1911] *DA* 45, 47; Ladas (1938), 641.

[27] These were the USA, Mexico, Cuba, Dominican Republic, Salvador, Honduras, Nicaragua, Costa Rica, Guatemala, Panama, Colombia, Brazil, Uruguay, Argentina, Paraguay, Bolivia, Chile, Peru, and Ecuador. Haiti and Venezuela did not attend the Conference: Ladas (1938), 643–4.

works directly in any or all of the countries belonging to the Union.[28] The other principal advance enshrined in the new Convention was the specification of a minimum term of protection of twenty-five years *post mortem auctoris*.[29] Like its predecessors, however, the Convention of 1906 was only partially successful. Only nine countries ratified it[30] and this was insufficient to permit the establishment of the proposed offices of the Union.[31] The effect of this was that the provisions of the Convention of 1902 were alone applicable to the relations between these states.[32]

(g) The Pan-American Convention of 1910

This was adopted by the fourth Pan-American Conference which met at Buenos Aires in 1910 and was signed by twenty American republics, including the USA.[33] It abandoned the idea of establishing a union for the protection of authors' rights as well as the notion of a central office. Unlike the Convention of 1902, it was also restricted to countries on the American continent.[34] This nationalistic approach was further reflected in the provisions concerning the persons protected by the Convention: these required that authors and their legal representatives should be nationals of one of the contracting countries and that foreigners claiming protection should be domiciled in a contracting country.[35] In addition, it was necessary that the work in question be first published in a contracting country.[36] Compliance with the formalities of the country of origin of a work was required,[37] as under the Berne Act, and the remaining provisions were closely modelled on that Act. This was the most successful of the Pan-American Conventions, as it was ratified by fourteen of the twenty states which had signed it: of these, the USA and Brazil were the most important.[38] **18.09**

(h) The Pan-American Convention of 1928

Although it had obtained the largest number of ratifications of any of the previous Pan-American Conventions, the Buenos Aires Convention of 1910 still fell short of its goal of a truly Pan-American Convention. In consequence, another attempt at such an instrument was made by the Sixth International Conference of American States which met in Havana in 1928. This took the **18.10**

---

[28] Pan-American Convention 1906, art II. [29] ibid, art VII.

[30] Costa Rica (1908), Guatemala (1907), Salvador (1907), Honduras (1907), Nicaragua (1909), Chile (1909), Ecuador (1909), Panama (1911), and Brazil (1911): Ladas (1938), 643.

[31] See Pan-American Convention 1906, art X. [32] ibid, art VII.

[33] With the exception of Bolivia: see Ladas (1938), 644 and note in [1911] *DA* 58ff.

[34] Ladas (1938), 660. [35] Pan-American Convention 1910, art 6.

[36] ibid, art 7. [37] ibid, art 4.

[38] The others being Colombia (1936), Costa Rica (1916), Dominican Republic (1912), Ecuador (1914), Guatemala (1912), Haiti (1918), Honduras (1913), Nicaragua (1913), Panama (1913), Paraguay (1917), Peru (1920), and Uruguay (1919): Ladas (1938), 645.

form of a review of the 1910 Convention and adopted, unchanged, most of the provisions of that Convention, but with a number of significant amendments and additions. The range of works to be protected was extended and included cinematographic works and 'arts applied to any human activity' (rather than 'works of art applied to industry' as under the Berlin/Rome Acts).[39] Furthermore, the basic principle of the Montevideo Convention, that is, application of the law of the country of origin of a work, was substituted for that of national treatment.[40] The requirements in relation to formalities were also increased, rather than reduced,[41] and the term of protection was set at fifty years *post mortem auctoris* (although this was not mandatory).[42] Finally, the rights to be protected by each contracting country were defined with more precision and moral rights were recognized for the first time so far as the right of integrity was concerned. Following its adoption, the new Convention was ratified by four states in the period up to 1934. Each of these was a Central American republic that had previously been a signatory to the Convention of 1910.[43]

(i) The position by 1928 with respect to the American states

18.11 The copyright relations between the different American states by the time of the Rome Conference of 1928 were complex and confusing. Several important states remained outside the Pan-American Conventions, such as Argentina and Bolivia (bound only by the Montevideo Convention), while the copyright relations of some states bound by the early Pan-American Conventions remained extremely restricted as they had not ratified the later texts. As stated above, the Convention of 1910 had the largest reach as it had come into force among fourteen states, but again these did not include some of the more important countries such as Argentina and Chile. It is not easy to identify the reasons for these delays in achieving an all-American copyright system, particularly between the Spanish-speaking republics. However, Ladas points to the lack of preparatory studies before each Convention as one possible reason, comparing the approach of the Pan-American Conferences unfavourably with that of the Berne Union in this respect.[44] He also notes that there was no American counterpart to ALAI which could bring pressure to bear on governments to adopt uniform legislation at both a national and international level.[45] To this incomplete network of conventions between the American republics must be added the fact that, with the limited exception of the Montevideo Convention, copyright relations with non-American states were confined to bilateral arrangements.

---

[39] Pan-American Convention 1928, art 2. [40] ibid, arts 3 and 6. [41] ibid, art 3.

[42] ibid, art 6.

[43] Costa Rica (1933), Guatemala (1931), Panama (1928), and Nicaragua (1934): Ladas (1938), 648.

[44] Ladas (1938), 649. [45] ibid, 650.

Prior to 1928, the only American republic, apart from Haiti, which had joined the Berne Union was Brazil.

(2) Moves to merge the Berne Union and the Pan-American Conventions

By 1928, two distinct systems of international copyright protection had come into existence: one comprising the countries of the Old World and their colonies, and the other centred on the independent republics of the New World. Nonetheless, the substantive differences between the two systems were not as great as might be supposed. Although the Montevideo Convention and its successors may be seen as an expression of a desire by the American states to 'go it alone', these instruments were still closely modelled on the provisions of the Berne Convention. Moreover, the laws of the various American republics were not greatly at variance with those of most Berne Union countries. Following the adoption of the Berlin Act, the most significant difference was to be found in relation to the question of formalities which were provided for in each of the Pan-American Conventions and remained an important part of the copyright laws of most of the American republics, in particular the USA. Accordingly, the task of bringing the two systems into harmony with each other did not seem an insuperable one and this was a matter that began to preoccupy international copyright experts from the late 1920s on. The impetus for this examination came from the resolutions of several international meetings. The first was a '*voeu*' adopted by the Rome Conference in 1928, at the motion of the French and Brazilian delegations. This read: **18.12**

> The Conference,
>
> In view of the identity of the general guiding principles of, and the ends aimed at by, the Convention of Berne, as revised in Berlin and later in Rome, and the Convention signed by the American States in Buenos Aires in 1910, and later revised in Havana, in February of 1928;
>
> And, in view of the manifest agreement between the majority of provisions of the two Conventions;
>
> Expresses the wish (*voeu*), . . . that, on the one hand, the American Republics which are signatories of a Convention to which non-American States cannot adhere, shall adhere, in accordance with the example set by Brazil, to the Convention of Berne as revised in Rome, and on the other hand, all the interested Governments shall co-operate with a view to preparing a general agreement which shall have as its basis the similar rules of the two Conventions and as its object the world-wide unification of the laws protecting the creations of the spirit.[46]

As one commentator notes, this *voeu* was 'extremely vague' when it came to suggesting solutions to the dilemma posed by the existence of two parallel

[46] *Actes* 1928, 350 (English translation from Ladas (1938), 650).

multilateral copyright conventions.[47] On the one hand, it seemed to suggest that the American republics should adhere to the Rome Act. On the other hand, it envisaged the creation of a new multilateral convention that would be truly universal in scope. These conflicting ideas may explain the different proposals that were put forward in the decade following the Rome Conference. Despite its ambiguity, however, the Rome *voeu* was confirmed by a *voeu* of the Ninth Assembly of the League of Nations on 24 September 1928 in which it instructed that Council of the League, through its organs, to conduct the 'studies and consultations necessary to bring about a general agreement on the international unification of the laws and measures protecting creations of the intellect, in accordance with the *voeu* expressed by the Conference of Rome . . .'.[48] Following these *voeux*, two bodies associated with the League of Nations undertook comparative studies of the Rome and Havana Conventions: the International Institute of Rome for the Unification of Private Law[49] and the International Institute for Intellectual Co-operation (in Paris).[50] Further studies and investigations were carried out by other expert bodies during the remainder of the 1930s on both sides of the Atlantic.[51] Of particular importance were the report and draft conventions prepared in April 1936 by a Committee of Experts appointed by the League of Nations and comprising representatives of the Paris and Rome Institutes and the International Office, as well as relevant authors' organizations (the 'Paris draft').[52] Equally significant were the report and draft convention prepared at the same time by an Inter-American Committee appointed by the seventh Pan-American Conference (the 'Montevideo draft').[53] Unofficial

[47] A Bogsch, 'Co-Existence of the Universal Copyright Convention with the Berne Conventions', in T R Kupferman and M Foner (eds), *Universal Copyright Convention Analyzed* (1955), 141, 143.

[48] *Journal officiel de la Société des Nations*, supplément spécial, no 64, 134 (1928).

[49] *Observations de l'Institut international de Rome pour l'Unification du Droit privé sur les Conventions de Berne et de la Havane pour la protection des oeuvres littéraries et artistiques*, Document UDP, Études V, SdN, 1930 CD, 1930, 'Mémoire rédigé en juillet 1930 a la demande de l'Institut international de Coopération intellectuelle'; also contained in *Documents préliminaires publiés par l'Administration belge et l'Institut international de Coopération intellectuelle*, Fascicule I (1938), 11ff ('*Documents préliminaires*').

[50] R Weiss, 'Vers un droit d'auteur universal' (1931) LVIII *Journal du droit international* 786, 793ff. See also the *Mémoire* of the Institute submitted to the Committee of Experts for the Study of a Universal Copyright Statute, meeting in Paris, 1, 2 and 25 Apr 1936: Institut international de Coopération intellectuelle, Document E 42 (1936) in *Documents préliminaires* (n 49 above), 34.

[51] See the survey of these studies in F Deàk, *Report on the Status of International Copyright Protection and on the Brussels Meeting of the Committee of Experts* (1938), 3ff.

[52] *Avant-Projet de Convention universelle pour la Protection du Droit d'Auteur, élaboré par le Comité d'Experts pour l'Etude d'un Statut universel du Droit d'Auteur réunie à Paris, les 1 er 2 et 25 avril 1936*, in *Documents préliminaires* (n 49 above), 48ff. The authors' organizations represented were the ALAI, *CISAC*, and the *Fédération internationale des Journalistes.*

[53] *Avant-Projet de Convention universelle pour la Protection des Droits d'Auteur, établi par la Commission interaméricaine créeé par la Conférence de Montevideo*, in *Documents préliminaires* (n 49 above), 41ff.

proposals were also put forward by the International Office in Berne.[54] These investigations soon became enmeshed in the preparations for the revision of the Berne Convention that were being made by the Belgian Government. At the request of the Brazilian Government and the League of Nations Committee of Experts, the latter postponed the Conference which was scheduled to be held in Brussels in September 1936. Furthermore, the Belgian Government was asked to

> ... take under advisement the calling, at a later date, of a special conference, to precede and to be wholly distinct from the conference of the signatories of the Berne Convention; the task of this special conference, to which all States of the world would be invited, would be to explore the possibilities of a universal agreement concerning international copyright protection.[55]

Following this, the Belgian Government, in collaboration with the Paris and Rome Institutes, began preparations for a 'world conference' of states to be held in Brussels in early 1939.[56] In May 1938, detailed documentation relating to this (including the work of the various American committees) was communicated to all governments by the Belgian Government[57] which convoked a meeting of a further Committee of Experts prior to the Conference.[58] This met in Brussels in October 1938 and took the Paris draft as the starting point for its discussion. To some extent, this meeting was premature, as many governments had not submitted their observations on the Paris draft, and some of the American states were unprepared to do so until the next Pan-American Conference, scheduled for the end of 1938 in Lima, had considered the matter.[59] Nevertheless, after lengthy discussion, the Committee finalized a report with a number of recommendations for the proposed world conference of states.[60] It was contemplated now that this should be held in September or October 1939, but the outbreak of World War II put an end to these plans.

(a) *The pre-1939 proposals*

As noted above, the ambiguity of the Rome *voeu* may have been responsible for the different proposals that were advanced in the period from 1929 to 1939 for reconciling the Berne and Pan-American Conventions. Essentially, these can be **18.13**

[54] 'L'Unification des Conventions de Berne et de la Havane' [1934] *DA* 50, 61 and 74 and 'Le rapprochement des Conventions de Berne et de la Havane' [1935] *DA* 100, 109 and [1936] *DA* 13 and 24.

[55] Deàk (n 51 above), 6. See also the circular letter of the Belgian Government to diplomatic representatives of the governments of members of the Berne Union, 6 June 1936, in *Documents préliminaires* (n 49 above), 53 and the proposals of the Brazilian Government in ibid, 38.

[56] Deàk (n 51 above), 6–7. [57] *Documents préliminaires* (n 49 above).

[58] See the English translation of the *Final Report of the Committee on its Session in Brussels, October 19–21, 1938,* in Deàk (n 51 above), 81ff.

[59] ibid, 8–9. [60] ibid, 82ff.

grouped into four categories: (i) proposals to achieve a universal convention through the amendment of the Rome Act of the Berne Convention so as to facilitate the accession of the American republics; (ii) proposals for the creation of a new convention that would replace both the Berne and Pan-American Conventions; (iii) proposals for the creation of a 'bridge convention' that would provide a link between both conventions; and (iv) proposals for the creation of a third convention that would embody a number of principles common to both conventions but without affecting the continuance of those conventions. It was the fourth of these approaches that was ultimately to prove successful after World War II, with the adoption of the UCC.

(b) Amendment of the Berne Convention

18.14 As the principal difference between the Berne and Pan-American systems arose over the matter of formalities, several proposals sought to overcome this obstacle by offering concessions to those countries whose laws still required compliance with such formalities as registration, deposit, or notice. Thus, an article published by the Director of the International Office, Fritz Ostertag, in *Le Droit d'Auteur* in 1936, proposed that the Rome Act be amended so as to permit such countries to make a reservation with respect to article 4(2) of that Act and to require that works published in other countries of the Union should be entered in an international register kept by the Berne Office.[61] Another proposal, made by the Brazilian Government in 1938 and based on an analogous solution in the Montevideo draft (see below), suggested that these states should retain the right to subordinate the protection of works from other Union countries to the fulfilment of a single formality such as international registration by the Berne Office or a formal notice of reservation of his rights made on copies of his work by the author.[62]

(c) A new convention to replace the Berne and Pan-American Conventions

18.15 A proposal along these lines was to be found in the Montevideo draft which was based largely on a text prepared by the Brazilian Government. Comprising sixty-six clauses, this incorporated most of the provisions of the Rome Act, with some modifications as well as further additions that took account of proposed amendments that had already been circulated by the Belgian Government in its preparatory documents for the Brussels Revision Conference.[63] In particular, *lex*

[61] 'Le rapprochement des Conventions de Berne et de la Havane' [1936] *DA* 24, 29.

[62] Proposition of the Brazilian Government relating to the revision of the Berne Convention and the convocation of a universal conference in *Propositions, contre-propositions et observations présentées par les Administrations des Pays de l'Union, Documents préliminaires de la Conférence de Bruxelles* (3e Fasc, 1936). See also the Montevideo draft, art 60 in *Documents préliminaires* (n 49 above), 47.

[63] ibid, 41ff.

fori rather than *lex soli* (as under the Havana Convention), was proposed as the source of law for the protection of works under the Convention, thereby bringing unpublished works within its scope.[64] Recognition of public recitation rights and protection of titles of works was also proposed,[65] and the rights of mechanical recording, cinematographic exploitation, and broadcasting were defined with greater precision.[66] With respect to formalities, the basic principle was applied as under the Rome Act, but special provision was made for American countries whose legislation prescribed compliance with formalities to make a reservation on ratification or accession to the Convention.[67] Where such a country made a reservation of this kind, it was further provided that authors from other countries would be able to obtain protection by satisfying the following two requirements: (i) the attachment to their work of a notice reserving their rights, and (ii) international registration, within a year of first publication, in the International Office.[68] Article 66 also contained an interim provision to take account of the fact that a considerable period of time might elapse before the new convention replaced those of Berne and Havana. Until this happened, it was provided that both instruments were to continue in force, but that each country belonging to one of the conventions was to protect works first published in a country belonging to the other convention in accordance with the provisions of the new convention.

(d) A 'bridge' convention

This proposal emanated from the International Office of the Berne Union and was published in *Le Droit d'Auteur* in 1935.[69] This started from the position that any proposal for unifying the Berne and Havana Conventions was 'sheer Utopianism'. As an alternative, the Office proposed the introduction of a new convention 'serving merely as a bridge between the two groups of countries'[70] under which countries in one group would grant national treatment to works first published in one of the countries of the other group but without having any effect on the relations between countries within each group.[71] A complete draft to this effect was prepared by the International Office and this also contained a series of conventional rules relating to such matters as translation rights and rights of reproduction.[72] As for the question of formalities, all that was allowed **18.16**

[64] Montevideo draft, arts 12–13. [65] ibid, arts 33 and 41.
[66] ibid, arts 35–7. [67] ibid, art 60.
[68] The International Office was established in art 45.
[69] See 'Le rapprochement des Conventions de Berne et de la Havane' [1935] *DA* 100, 109 (for draft convention and commentary). See further Ladas (1938), 673ff.
[70] [1937] *DA* 70.
[71] See the *Survey of the Preparatory Work for the Universal Copyright Conference* prepared by the International Institute for Intellectual Co-operation, Paris, 18 Oct 1938 in Deàk (n 51 above), 62.
[72] [1935] *DA* 100ff.

under this draft was the possibility of demanding international registration.[73] It has been suggested that this last limitation made the bridge convention potentially unattractive to the American republics, most of which were committed to some system of formalities under their laws.[74] In addition, the proposed 'bridge' did not appeal to Berne Union countries as the weight was placed mostly on its European pillar.[75] By contrast, the American pillar represented by the Havana Convention comprised only four Central American republics.[76]

(e) A third convention

18.17 If the idea of a bridge convention appeared unrealistic, it did suggest the possibility that a third convention might be created alongside the old conventions and co-exist with them while providing a meeting point for the countries of both systems.[77] This also avoided the difficulties raised by the other proposals in seeking to revise the Berne Convention so as to allow for the accession of the American states or forming a new convention to replace the two existing ones. The idea of a third convention was embodied in the Paris draft prepared by the League of Nations Committee of Experts,[78] but was also consistent with proposals that had been made by the American Institute of International Law,[79] ALAI,[80] and the seventh Pan-American Conference that met in Montevideo in 1933.[81] It was a more limited draft convention of twenty-three articles that provided that each signatory country would grant national treatment to works published in other signatory countries[82] as well as guaranteeing protection of a number of the most basic authors' rights such as those of reproduction, translation, adaptation, mechanical reproduction, broadcasting, and cinematographic presentation[83] as well as moral rights.[84] Provision was also made for the International Office of the Berne Union to centralize and co-ordinate all information relating to the application of the Convention[85] and for the Permanent Court of International Justice to have jurisdiction to resolve disputes between signatory states over the application of the Convention.[86] This draft was modified

[73] ibid, 102. [74] Bogsch (n 47 above), 148. [75] ibid. [76] ibid.

[77] ibid. See also 'La Convention mondiale pour la protection en droit d'auteur' [1938] *DA* 58 (including a draft convention prepared by the eminent German jurist, W Hoffman).

[78] See text in *Documents préliminaires* (n 49 above), 48.

[79] *The Inter-American Protection of Intellectual Property and the Reconciliation of the Conventions of Havana and Rome* (report presented to the Seventh International Congress of American States by the American Institute of International Law), English text in *Documents for the Use of Delegates to the Seventh International Conference of American States* (Montevideo, Uruguay, 3 Dec 1933), no 5, Pan-American Union, Washington, and French translation in *Documents préliminaires* (n 49 above), 17ff).

[80] Deàk (n 51 above), 61. See also [1935] *DA* 72.

[81] *Seventh International Conference of American States, Final Act* (1934), 25ff (text of resolution passed on 16 Dec 1933), French translation in *Documents préliminaires* (n 49 above), 9–10.

[82] Paris draft, art 5. [83] ibid, arts 7, 13, 14, and 18. [84] ibid, art 9.

[85] ibid, art 17. [86] ibid, art 18.

in a number of respects by the meeting of the Committee of Experts in Brussels in October 1938.[87] The latter meeting also was notable for the concern expressed by the Japanese Government over the question of freedom of translation,[88] and by the US Government over the questions of formalities, moral rights, and retrospectivity.[89] While the proposal for a third convention had gathered strong support by 1939, it was clear that these issues needed resolution before such an instrument could be successfully adopted.

(3) Progress after World War II

The quest for a universal copyright convention was suspended while hostilities **18.18** lasted, but shortly afterwards the matter was taken up by the newly constituted UNESCO. The latter took its mandate for concerning itself with the question of international copyright protection from the Universal Declaration of Human Rights which guaranteed the right of each person to 'the protection of the moral and material interests resulting from any scientific, literary or artistic production of which he is the author'.[90] Crucial political support also came from the USA, which was more concerned now than before World War II with the question of international copyright protection, perhaps as a consequence of its newly assumed role in world affairs, and increased export of copyrighted works. Under the auspices of UNESCO, a series of preparatory meetings were held between 1947 and 1951,[91] leading to a diplomatic conference in 1952 at which the new Universal Convention was adopted.[92] It is noteworthy that, even at this stage, the idea of amending the Berne Convention so as to permit accession by the American republics had not been entirely abandoned. Thus, the first meeting of the BUPC in Neuchâtel in 1949 adopted a resolution in which it noted that the

[87] Committee of Experts for Universal Copyright Protection, *Final Report of the Committee on its Session in Brussels*, 19–21 Oct 1938 in Deàk (n 51 above), 81ff (English translation). See further 'La Convention universelle sur le droit d'auteur' [1939] *DA* 13, 25.

[88] Deàk (n 51 above), 85 (Appendix V). See also the statement made by Professor Kenzo Takayanagi at the second session of the Committee of Experts in ibid, 73 (Appendix IV).

[89] ibid, 10ff and 84ff.

[90] Universal Declaration of Human Rights, art 27. See further B Ringer, 'The Role of the United States in International Copyright: Past, Present and Future' (1968) 56 *Georgetown Law Journal* 1050, 1061ff. See also 'Pour la conclusion d'une Convention universelle sur le droit d'auteur' [1947] *DA* 101; 'La première conférence générale de l'UNESCO et le droit d'auteur' [1947] *DA* 4.

[91] For the general background to these meetings, see *Records of the Intergovernmental Conference, Geneva, 1952* (1954), Introduction. The first three comprised experts nominated in their personal capacity and met in Paris in Sept 1947, July 1949, and Oct 1950: *UNESCO Copyright Bulletin*, vol IV, no 3 and vol V, no 1. The reports of the Washington and final Paris meetings are to be found in Kupferman and Foner (n 47 above), 249ff. See further 'Vers une nouvelle Convention internationale pour la protection du droit d'auteur' [1951] *DA* 13; 'Raison dêtre de la Convention universelle' [1951] *DA* 30; J Forns, 'A propos du projet de Convention universelle sur le droit d'auteur' [1952] *DA* 54.

[92] 18 Aug to 6 Sept 1952: *Records of the Intergovernmental Conference* (n 91 above).

'Berne Convention was open to the adhesion of all States' and expressed the opinion that 'the difficulties of new adhesions could be overcome by appropriate amendment of the Convention . . . according to the wishes of the new adherents'.[93] Nonetheless, in the preceding year the Berne Convention had already been revised at Brussels with scant regard to this matter and it seems clear that the 1949 resolution of the BUPC held little attraction to those states that were already preparing the new convention. In the view of G B Crewe, the chief UK delegate at Brussels, this was not a bad thing, as too many amendments would be required for such a proposal to be practical. Furthermore, even if they were practical, he argued that they were undesirable as a matter of principle:

> The Berne Convention must remain as the standard par excellence of copyright protection and our object must be to bring non-member countries into international relationship in the hope that ultimately—it will of course take many years—they will voluntarily accept the Berne standard and both Conventions brought on to the same plane.[94]

In any event, it seems clear that, at this time, events were moving away from the BUPC which soon gave its tacit support to the new universal convention that was being prepared by UNESCO, limiting itself to specific proposals to preserve the operation of the Berne Convention among those Berne countries which acceded to the new convention (see below). What was now envisaged was a third convention, existing independently of the others. Rather than a 'bridge' with uncertain support on one side, the appropriate analogy for this new convention was that of a 'low staircase' to which further steps might be added. Thus, it was not an end in itself, but 'an intermediate step on a rising staircase' that would ultimately lead from the lower levels of protection found in the American republics to the highest level embodied in the Berne Convention.[95]

18.19 Despite the modest level of protection afforded by the new convention, there were still obstacles to be overcome before it could be realized. To adopt another analogy, it was necessary to open a 'difficult double lock' in order to gain access even to this level.[96] In the words of Barbara Ringer, the former US Register of Copyrights:

[93] [1949] *DA* 132 (adopted 30 Sept 1949). For English translation, see *UNESCO Copyright Bulletin*, vol III, nos 3–4, 203.

[94] G B Crewe, 'National Treatment as the Basis for a Universal Copyright Convention', *UNESCO Copyright Bulletin*, vol III, no 1, 6. In fact, it was to be another forty years before the US joined the Berne Convention.

[95] This analogy was made by Judge Charles Wyzanki, one of the US delegates, at the meeting of experts in Paris, 5 July 1949: summary records reprinted in *UNESCO Copyright Bulletin*, vol II, nos 2–3, 186.

[96] B Ringer, 'The Universal Copyright Convention and its Future' [1976] 45 *NIR* 14.

> One part of the lock consisted of the fear of leading members of the Berne Union that the Berne Convention would be undermined and debased by promulgation of another world-wide convention offering a lower level of protection. The second lock to be opened was the insistence, notably on the part of the USA, upon maintaining certain fundamental principles, such as formalities as a condition of copyright and duration based on publication.[97]

After lengthy discussions and concessions on both sides, the two keys to the double lock were fashioned at a meeting of experts in Washington, DC, in 1950[98] and were subsequently enshrined in the new convention. These were the 'Berne Safeguard Clause' and the © notice, both of which are discussed in more detail below. The final shape of the draft convention was settled by a Committee of Experts in Paris in June 1951[99] and this was used as the basis of discussion at the Diplomatic Conference that was held the following year.

(4) The adoption of the UCC

This was done at the Diplomatic Conference held in Geneva from 18 August to **18.20**
6 September 1952. The Conference was attended by delegations from fifty nations, including most of the member states of the Berne Union and American republics, and there were observers from nine intergovernmental organizations and six non-governmental bodies.[100] The text finally adopted consisted of thirty-one articles and three protocols. In brief, the new principal features of the convention were as follows.[101]

(a) Works protected

Unlike the Berne Convention, there was no detailed listing of works to be **18.21**
protected. A more general formula was adopted as follows in article I.

> Each Contracting State undertakes to provide for the adequate and effective protection of the rights of authors and other copyright proprietors in literary, scientific, and artistic works, including writings, musical, dramatic and cinematographic works, and paintings, engravings, and sculpture.[102]

---

[97] ibid, 14–18. See further M James, 'The United States and the movement for Universal Copyright' (1955) 25 *Library Quarterly* 219 and H G Henn, 'The Quest for International Copyright Protection' (1953) 39 *Cornell Law Quarterly* 43.

[98] See James (n 97 above), 231–2.

[99] See Kupferman and Foner (n 47 above), 281ff (report of G H C Bodenhausen, *rapporteur* for the Committee).

[100] *Records of the Intergovernmental Conference* (n 91 above), 69.

[101] For a general comparison of the UCC and Berne Convention, see H Desbois [1955] *DA* 130, 150, 169, 193.

[102] See further Bogsch (n 1 above), 5ff.

(b) The principle of national treatment

18.22 This was adopted in article II and was accorded to the published and unpublished works of nationals of any contracting state and to works first published in that state. In according protection to the 'published works of nationals of any Contracting State', the new text was in advance of the Brussels Act of the Berne Convention which applied only to works of Union nationals first published in a Union country.[103] Article II of the UCC also made provision for a contracting state to assimilate to its own nationals any person domiciled in that state.[104]

(c) Formalities

18.23 This was clearly the most important matter dividing the states of the Berne Union from those of the American continent. The basic compromise contained in article III was the acceptance by those states whose domestic laws required, 'as a condition of copyright, compliance with formalities such as deposit, registration, notice, notarial certificates, payment of fees or manufacture or publication', that these requirements were satisfied with respect to all works entitled to protection under the Convention by the placing on all copies of the published work of a notice comprising the © symbol, followed by the name of the copyright proprietor and year of first publication. This provision did not preclude contracting states from requiring compliance with other formalities with respect to works of their own nationals or works first published in their territory.[105] No formalities, however, could be required with respect to unpublished works that were entitled to protection under the Convention.[106] It will be seen that this provision embodied considerable concessions on both sides. For the American republics, it was a significant breach in the systems of formalities they had long maintained. In particular, for the USA, it represented a considerable sacrifice with respect to its strict requirements of notice, registration, deposit, and domestic manufacture.[107] On the other hand, for Berne Union countries, the acceptance of the © notice requirement was also a considerable concession, in view of the fact that the 'no formalities' provision had been a central part of the Berne Union system for nearly forty years.[108]

---

[103] Brussels Act, art 4(1). [104] UCC, art II(3).

[105] ibid, art III(2). See further W Bappert and E Wagner, 'La mention de reserve dans la Convention universelle sur le droit d'auteur (Art III): Conditions, forme et effets' [1956] *DA* 110, 119, and 157.

[106] UCC, art III(4). [107] Stewart (1989), 134–5.

[108] cf the view of Dr Arpad Bogsch that the Berne Union might have gained the USA as an adherent if, at Brussels, its members had been prepared to make the same concessions as to formalities (as well as duration) which many of the same countries were later prepared to make in Geneva in 1952: A Bogsch, 'The First Hundred Years of the Berne Convention' [1986] *Copyright* 291, 298.

(d) Duration of protection

The requirements here were far less rigorous than those of the Berne Convention. A minimum term of protection of twenty-five years *post mortem auctoris* was adopted in article IV, but there was the possibility of shorter terms of not less than twenty-five years from first publication in the case of certain classes of works.[109] Shorter terms of not less than ten years were also permitted for photographic works and works of art.[110] Provision was further made to accommodate countries such as the USA which did not compute the term of protection upon the basis of the life of the author and a minimum term of twenty-five years from first publication or from registration prior to publication as was specified in such cases.[111] Other provisions dealt with successive terms of protection and the question of simultaneous publication.[112] **18.24**

(e) Rights protected

Unlike the Berne Convention, the UCC dealt expressly with only one right that was to be accorded to authors and copyright proprietors. This was the right of translation[113] and was made subject to a compulsory licence which could be imposed by a contracting state after a period of seven years from first publication in the event that a translation in the national language or languages of that country had not been published in that time.[114] This provision was only arrived at after considerable debate between the delegates, as a significant number (chiefly those from Berne Union countries) felt strongly that translation rights should be fully protected throughout the entire term of copyright.[115] On the other hand, there were many countries which felt that the author's exclusive right in this regard should be limited to a relatively brief time.[116] **18.25**

Indeed, in the preparatory meetings that had taken place before World War II, the Japanese Government had pressed for 'freedom of translation' to be incorporated in the Convention with respect to translations in the relations between countries using ideographic writing and others.[117] At the 1952 Conference, there was also concern by a number of Berne Union countries that had made reservations with respect to translation rights under that Convention that they should be allowed the same facility under the UCC.[118] This last proposal

[109] UCC, art IV(2). [110] ibid, art IV(3). [111] ibid, art IV(2).

[112] ibid, art IV(4)–(6). See further 'La comparison des délais dans la Convention universelle sur le droit d'auteur (interpretation de l'art IV al 4)' [1958] *DA* 12.

[113] UCC, art V(1). [114] ibid, art V(2).

[115] *Records of the Intergovernmental Conference* (n 91 above), 80–1 (Report of Sir John Blake, *rapporteur général*).

[116] ibid. [117] See n 88 above.

[118] *Records of the Intergovernmental Conference* (n 91 above), 82 (Greece, Japan, and Turkey).

was finally defeated and the seven-year regime described above was adopted as a compromise solution.[119]

(f) Other provisions

18.26 A number of miscellaneous matters were dealt with in the remaining provisions of the Convention. The concept of publication under the Convention was dealt with in article VI, while article VII was concerned with the question of retroactivity, declaring the Convention to be inapplicable to works 'permanently in the public domain' in a contracting state at the time of the Convention's entry into force. Provision was made under article XII for the revision of the Convention and under article XV jurisdiction was given to the International Court of Justice to hear disputes between contracting states concerning the interpretation or application of the Convention. Although no union was established under the Convention, under article XI an Intergovernmental Committee comprising twelve contracting states was created, with the following duties:

> (a) to study the problems concerning the application and operation of this Convention;
> (b) to make preparation for periodic revisions of this Convention;
> (c) to study any other problems concerning the international protection of copyright, in co-operation with the various interested international organizations, such as the United Nations Educational, Scientific and Cultural Organisation, the International Union for the Protection of Literary and Artistic Works and the Organization of American States;
> (d) to inform the Contracting States as to its activities.[120]

The procedure for electing the Committee was dealt with in a resolution attached to article XI and the 'wish' was expressed that the secretariat of the Committee be provided by UNESCO[121] (this, indeed, was done by the Copyright Division of UNESCO, which had carried out the preparatory work for the 1952 Conference). The remaining provisions of the Convention dealt with the matters of signature and adhesion (article VIII), entry into force (article IX), giving effect to the Convention (article X), application to non-self-governing territories (article XIII), languages (article XVI), reservations (article XX, under which none was allowed), and the application of the Convention to the works of stateless persons and refugees and certain international organizations (Protocols 1 and 2). Finally, several articles (articles XVII–XIX) dealt with the relations of the UCC to other multilateral conventions and treaties. For our present purposes, the most important of these were article XVII and the Appendix

[119] *Records of the Intergovernmental Conference* (n 91 above), 82. See further W Bappert and E Wagner, 'Le droit de traduction dans la Convention de Berne et dans la Convention universelle' [1958] *DA* 27, 41.

[120] UCC, art XI(1).

[121] ibid (resolution concerning art XI).

Declaration thereto which were concerned with the relations of the UCC to the Berne Convention (the 'Berne Safeguard Clause').

(5) The Berne Safeguard Clause

This was the key to the second part of the double lock that had to be opened in order to assure the success of the UCC. Following its fruitless call of 1949 for revision of the Berne Convention to allow for accession by the American republics, the BUPC had concentrated its efforts on ensuring that the proposed convention did not undermine the existing operation and application of the Berne Convention. Its main concern was to find a device by which the possibility of withdrawals from the Berne Union in favour of the UCC, with its lower level of protection, could be reduced or even eliminated. This was the subject of extended consideration at the meetings of experts that were held in 1950[122] and 1952[123] to prepare for the proposed conference, and a clause to this effect was included in the draft convention that was used as the basis for discussion at the conference.[124] After further changes, this was adopted as article XVII and an Appendix Declaration that was appended thereto. These provided as follows: **18.27**

Article XVII:

1 This Convention shall not in any way affect the provisions of the Berne Convention for the Protection of Literary and Artistic Works or membership in the Union created by that Convention.

2 In application of the foregoing paragraph, a Declaration has been annexed to the present article. This Declaration is an integral part of this Convention for the States bound by the Berne Convention on January 1, 1951, or which have or may become bound to it at a later date. The signature of this Convention by such States shall also constitute signature of the said Declaration, and ratification, acceptance or accession by such States shall include the Declaration as well as the Convention.

Appendix Declaration relating to Article XVII:

The States which are members of the International Union for the Protection of Literary and Artistic Works, and which are signatories to the Universal Copyright Convention,

Desiring to reinforce their mutual relations on the basis of the said Union and to avoid any conflict which might result from the co-existence of the Convention of Berne and the Universal Convention,

---

[122] See the Recommendations of the Committee of Experts (Washington, 23 Oct to 4 Nov 1950): [1951] *DA* 21 and the report of W P J O'Meara in Kupferman and Foner (n 47 above), 249, 256, 258ff.

[123] Report of G H C Bodenhausen, *rapporteur*, for the Committee of Governmental Experts (Paris, 18 to 26 June 1951) in Kupferman and Foner (n 47 above), 281, 285.

[124] ibid, 277–8. See further G Straschnov, 'Rapports entre la Convention de Berne et la Convention universelle' [1953] *DA* 37.

Have, by common agreement, accepted the terms of the following declaration.

(a) Works, which, according to the Berne Convention, have as their country of origin a country which has withdrawn from the International Union created by the said Convention, after January 1, 1951, shall not be protected by the Universal Copyright Convention in the countries of the Berne Union;

(b) the Universal Copyright Convention shall not be applicable to the relationships among countries of the Berne Union insofar as it relates to the protection of works having as their country of origin, within the meaning of the Berne Convention, a country of the International Union created by the said Convention.

These provisions were amended in 1971 to take account of the needs of developing countries. The background to these amendments has already been discussed in Chapter 14 above and their effect is discussed further below. Apart from this, however, the provisions of article XVII and its Appended Declaration remain the same, and can be analysed under the following three heads: (a) the declaration that the UCC is to have no effect on the operation of the Berne Convention; (b) the sanction against withdrawal from the Berne Union by countries belonging to both conventions; and (c) the application of the Berne Convention in the relations of countries that are parties to both conventions. Each of these requires separate examination.

(a) No effect on the Berne Convention

18.28 There was no intention on the part of the delegates at the Geneva Conference to modify or amend the provisions of the Berne Convention. Nor, indeed, was there any power in the delegates to that Conference to do so, as changes to the Berne Convention required the unanimous consent of all members of the Berne Union and the normal method was for this consent to be obtained at its periodic revision conferences.[125] Accordingly, the statements in article XVII(1) that the UCC does not in any way affect the provisions of the Berne Convention or membership in the Berne Union is unnecessary from a legal point of view. In the words of one commentator, their inclusion in the UCC:

> . . . merely shows that some countries of the Berne Union present at the Geneva Conference thought it necessary to emphasize the point that the provisions of the Berne Convention and membership in the Berne Union are an internal affair of the Berne countries.[126]

[125] Berlin, Rome, and Brussels Acts, art 24.

[126] Bogsch (n 47 above), 152. See further Bogsch (n 1 above), 112–13.

(b) Sanction for withdrawal

As the Berne Convention expressly permitted member countries to withdraw from the Union[127] and it was impossible for the Geneva Conference to prohibit this directly, paragraph (a) of the Appendix Declaration contains an indirect sanction against this occurrence. The origins of this are to be found in a resolution of the BUPC that was passed in 1951[128] and was adopted by the Conference with little change.[129] In brief, its effect is that countries which withdraw from the Berne Union are not able to claim the benefit of the UCC in those countries of the Berne Union that are also signatories to the UCC. In other words, countries which denounce the Berne Convention in order to rely on the lower level of protection embodied in the UCC will only gain the benefit of this protection in those countries which are signatories of the UCC alone. A number of points here require further clarification. **18.29**

(c) Countries which may be the subject of sanction

There is some ambiguity here, as it is not completely clear which countries are bound by the Appendix Declaration. The second sentence of article XVII(2) declares that the Declaration is 'an integral part' of the Convention for the following classes of states: (i) those which were bound by the Berne Convention on 1 January 1951; and (ii) those which become bound by it at a later date (whether before or after the date of the UCC). **18.30**

The third sentence, which appears redundant,[130] goes on to state that signature, ratification, acceptance, or accession to the UCC by 'such States' automatically entails signature, ratification, etc, of the Declaration. By negative implication, the provisions of the Declaration do not bind states that are parties to the UCC alone. This may lead to problems in relation to the question of which convention applies in the relations between Berne countries and non-Berne countries that are parties to the UCC (see further para 18.35 below). It also gives rise to the following questions:

(i) States bound by the Berne Convention on 1 January 1951: Is a state that was bound by the Berne Convention on 1 January 1951, but leaves the Berne Union before joining the UCC, bound by the Declaration and therefore subject to the sanction in paragraph (a)? Common sense indicates that this should not be the case, as such a state, in joining the UCC, is moving from a situation in

[127] Brussels Act, art 29.

[128] [1950] *DA* 127, 131. See also the reply of Switzerland to UNESCO's 'Request for Views on a Universal Copyright Convention', *UNESCO Copyright Bulletin*, vol III, no 2, 47.

[129] *Records of the Intergovernmental Conference* (n 91 above), 90 (report of Sir John Blake).

[130] See further Bogsch (n 1 above), 114.

which it has no international copyright relations to one where it does, even if the latter are on a lower level to those which it enjoyed previously under the Berne Convention. On the other hand, the words 'the States bound by the Berne Convention on 1 January 1951' in article XVII(2) can be interpreted as referring to an historical situation only, with the consequence that a state which was bound at this date, retains this status for all time, even if it subsequently withdraws from the Union. The only states not caught by this interpretation would be Liberia and Haiti which denounced the Berne Convention in 1930 and 1943 respectively.[131] Other Berne-denouncing states since 1 January 1951 are Indonesia (1960),[132] Syria (1962),[133] and Upper Volta (1970),[134] but each of these has now rejoined Berne in any event.

(ii) States bound by the Berne Convention after 1 January 1951: The same uncertainty arises in the case of states that become bound by the Berne Convention after 1 January 1951 but denounced it prior to joining the UCC. Do the words 'have or may become bound to it at a later date' in article XVII(2) refer to an historical status that such states continue to possess, whether or not they remain in the Union, or do they mean that these states should still be bound at the time they adhere to the UCC?

In both these cases, the 'common sense' solution suggested in (i) can be supported by reference to the opening words of the Declaration itself: 'The States which are members of the International Union . . . and which are signatories to the Universal Copyright Convention . . .'. The use of the present tense here indicates that it was contemplated that the Declaration was only to apply to those states which are members of the Berne Union at the time they sign, ratify, accept, or accede to the UCC. Thus, in the case of Syria and Indonesia, which denounced the Berne Convention after 1 January 1951 but did not become parties to the UCC, both states would have been free to join the UCC without becoming subject to the sanction in paragraph (a) (this position would have continued until 2004 and 1997, the dates of their respective accessions to Berne). In the case of Upper Volta (now Burkina Faso), it appears that it is not regarded by the Berne Union as having had a break in its membership between its denunciation and rejoining of Berne (see further paras 17.34, 17.59–17.60 above).

(iii) State fulfilling neither of the conditions laid down in article XVII(2): If the above argument is accepted, it follows that a state would not be subject to the sanction in paragraph (a) in the event that it adhered first to the UCC, then to the Berne Convention and later denounced Berne while remaining bound by

---

131 [1929] *DA* and [1942] *DA* 73.
132 [1959] *DA* 79.
133 [1961] *DA* 70.
134 [1969] *Copyright* 235.

the UCC. In such a case, this state would fulfil neither of the conditions laid down in article XVII(2) and would not have been bound by the Berne Convention at the time it signed, ratified, accepted, or acceded to the UCC. This gives rise to the anomalous situation where a state may join and leave the Berne Union at will, if it was a party to the UCC first. While this may have been a relevant consideration at the time of the first edition of this work (1987), when there were only seventy-six Berne members, it is probably now only a matter of academic interest (see further para 18.39 below).

(d) Works affected

These are works of which the country of origin is, according to the Berne Convention, a country which has withdrawn from the Union after 1 January 1951. Under the Paris Act, these comprise the following categories of works: (i) all unpublished works of nationals of that country; (ii) all works first published in that country; (iii) all works of a national of that country first published in a non-Union country; and (iv) all works simultaneously published for the first time in two or more Berne countries or in a Berne and non-Berne country or countries.[135] **18.31**

In the case of works published before the date of withdrawal, as long as they fulfil the criteria referred to in (ii) or (iii), they will continue to be protected after this date on the basis that their country of origin at the time of first publication was still a Berne country. On the other hand, with unpublished works created before the date of withdrawal and works first published in a non-Union country before this date, this would not be the case as their country of origin is no longer a Berne country (see further para 6.70 above).

(e) Countries applying the sanction

The countries required to do this are those Berne Union countries that are parties to the UCC. In 1986, this was only a proportion, albeit a major one, of UCC membership: there were then seventy-five UCC members and only fifty-four of these were also Berne signatories, while by 2005 there were ninety-nine UCC members and all of which were Berne members (there being 159 Berne members in all in 2005). On the other hand, a country which withdraws from the Union will still be required to accord protection under the UCC to works from Berne/UCC countries, as paragraph (a) does not allow the former to restrict protection on a reciprocal basis.[136] In this way, a kind of 'halfway house' **18.32**

---

135 Paris Act, art 5(4).

136 Where several countries withdraw from the Union, their *inter se* relations will become more complex: see here the hypothetical example concerning Greece and Austria given by Dr Bogsch in Bogsch (n 47 above), 156ff.

of protection will apply, so as to prevent countries from leaving the international copyright system altogether.[137]

(f) Meaning of 'withdrawn'

18.33 The usual method by which a country may leave the Berne Union is by the giving of a notice of denunciation which is expressly provided for under article 29 of the Berne Convention. There can be little doubt that a country which denounces the Convention under this article has 'withdrawn' from the Union in the sense that this word is used in paragraph (a). However, there are other ways in which a country may cease to be governed by the Berne Convention and the question which arises in these cases is whether the country in question can be said to have 'withdrawn' from the Union. The following situations require consideration:

1. Where a country, being a former colony or dependent possession to which the Convention was applied, indicates that it no longer regards itself as bound by the Convention following its independence. This has happened in several cases, such as South Korea, Vietnam, and Cambodia (see para 17.61 above).
2. Where a country, being a former colony or dependent possession to which the Convention was applied, fails to indicate one way or other whether it considers itself bound by the Convention.
3. Where a country, having made no indication of its status in relation to the Berne Convention (as in paragraph 2), does something quite inconsistent with continued application of the Convention, such as the adoption of legislation that does not comply with the standards of the Berne Convention.

These examples raise difficult issues of the kinds already traversed in Chapter 17 above although it is difficult to envisage circumstances in which such cases will arise. For the purposes of analysis, however, it is sufficient to distinguish between the matter of membership of the Union and application of the Convention (in a territorial sense). Thus, in the above instances, none of the hypothetical former colonial countries has been a member of the Berne Union in any full sense, although it has obviously been part of the territory of the Union as one of the countries to which the Convention was applied. Accordingly, it does not seem appropriate to describe such countries as having 'withdrawn' from the Union, if the latter is understood as a reference to withdrawal from membership of the

---

[137] See further Bogsch (n 47 above), 158.

Union. None of these countries have been members and therefore there is nothing from which they can withdraw.[138]

(g) Application of the Berne Convention in relations between Berne Union/UCC countries

18.34 The decision to create the UCC as a separate convention rather than as a replacement of the Berne Convention clearly gave rise to the possibility of conflicts arising between the two conventions where a country became bound by both. As Dr Bogsch points out, a number of solutions were theoretically available to resolve these conflict problems. The application of the maxims *lex posterior derogat priori* and *lex specialis derogat generali* provided two possible solutions, while the principle adopted in article 20 of the Berne Convention would have provided that, in the case of conflict, the provision more favourable to the author should prevail.[139] However, the solution adopted in the draft convention that was used as the basis for discussions at the 1952 Conference took a more radical approach. This proposed simply that, in the relations between countries of the UCC that also belonged to the Berne Convention, the UCC should not be applicable so far as concerned 'the protection of works having as their country of origin within the meaning of the Berne Convention, a country of the said Berne Union'.[140] A special conflicts rule was also proposed in the case of works published simultaneously in a country of the Berne Union and in a non-Berne country that was a party to the UCC. In this case, it was provided that the author or copyright proprietor should not be prevented 'from relying on the application of the terms of the Universal Copyright Convention which confer rights greater than those conferred by the Berne Convention'.[141] After considerable debate at the 1952 Conference, this proviso was deleted, chiefly, it seems, because of the ambiguities or difficulties that might arise in practice, particularly in relation to the question of which convention was the more favourable with respect to translation rights in any particular case.[142] As a result, the general rule of non-applicability of the UCC was adopted and was embodied in paragraph (b) of the Appended Declaration to article XVII (now paragraph (c)).

18.35 A precondition for the operation of this provision is that the work in question should have a Berne country as its country of origin 'within the meaning of the Berne Convention'. In the majority of cases, this requirement will not give rise

[138] See further C Masouyé, 'Décolonisation, indépendance et droit d'auteur' (1962) 36 *RIDA* 85.
[139] Bogsch (n 47 above), 119.
[140] Kupferman and Foner (n 47 above), 277–8 (art XV and Protocol of draft Convention).
[141] ibid (para 1(c) of draft Protocol).
[142] *Records of the Intergovernmental Conference* (n 91 above), 90, 92–3 (report of Sir John Blake).

to any problems: the country of origin of a work will be either the country of which the author is a national (in the case of unpublished works) or the country in which the work is first published (whether or not the author is a Berne national, a national of a non-Berne UCC country, or a country that is not party to either convention). As long as these countries are members of the Berne Union, the rule in paragraph (c) will apply where protection for works which have them as their country of origin is sought in other UCC countries that are also members of the Berne Union. This would also be the case where a work is simultaneously published in both a Berne/UCC country and another country (whether or not a member of the UCC). However, the rule in paragraph (c) will not always be applicable where a Berne country remains bound by earlier Acts of that Convention. Under the pre-Stockholm, Paris Acts, where a national of a Union country first published his work in a non-Union country this work was unprotected under the Berne Convention and, in consequence, had no country of origin within the meaning of that Convention. This position was changed in the Stockholm, Paris Acts and such works are now protected, having as their country of origin the country of which the author is a national.[143] Suppose, then, that countries A and B are bound by the Paris Act of the Berne Convention and countries C and D by the Brussels Act and all are members of the UCC. The following situations can be envisaged, although situation (a) will no longer arise as there is no longer any country that is a member of the UCC alone (following the accession of the Russian Federation, most of the South American states, and other important UCC states to Berne in the mid-1990s):

(i) **Situation (a)**: An author who is a national of country B first publishes his work in a non-Berne country that is a party to the UCC (until 1995, the obvious example here was the Russian Federation and former USSR). If the author then seeks protection for the work in country A, this will be accorded under the Paris Act rather than the UCC as a result of the application of paragraph (c) of the Declaration.

(ii) **Situation (b)**: The same facts as in situation (a), except that the author is now a national of country C. As far as country D is concerned, his work will not be entitled to protection under the Berne Convention as it does not have a country of origin within the provisions of the Brussels Act. Accordingly, country D should apply the provisions of the UCC as the precondition for the operation of paragraph (c) of the Declaration is not present.

(iii) **Situation (c)**: The result in situation (b) will also follow with respect to countries A and B if the latter were also bound by the Brussels Act prior to their accession to the Paris Act. However, if countries A and B are bound only by the

---

[143] Stockholm, Paris Acts, art 5(4)(c).

Paris Act, there will be no Act of the Berne Convention in common between them and countries C and D. In consequence, countries A and B would be required to apply the Paris Act in their dealings with countries C and D and to treat the works of an author of country C first published in the non-Berne UCC country as having country C as their country of origin. Paragraph (c) of the Declaration would therefore be applicable in such a case.

(iv) Situation (d): The same facts as in situation (a), except that the first publication occurs in a country that is neither a party to the Berne Convention nor the UCC (there will only be a very limited group of such countries in 2005, for example, Myanmar, Ethiopia, Eritrea, or Nepal). The same result will follow and this will also be the case on the facts given in situation (c). On the facts given in situation (b), the UCC would still be applicable as the latter applies to works of nationals of a UCC country wherever published.

There is a further gloss to paragraph (c) of the Declaration that needs to be considered. This is the statement that the UCC is to be 'inapplicable to the relationships among countries of the Union'. In the examples given in the preceding paragraph, the 'relationships' among the countries in question were between countries of the Union, these being the country of origin of the work and the country where protection was claimed. However, there are also situations (now increasingly unlikely) where a non-Berne country may be involved, for example, where the author of the work is a national of a non-Berne country, such as one of the quartet referred to above, who has first published his work in a Berne country. While the latter is the country of origin of the work for the purposes of the Berne Convention, under the UCC the author can also claim protection in another Berne country on the basis of nationality (article II). The tripartite relationship is illustrated in Figure 18.1. **18.36**

In the relationship between B and C, there is no doubt that, under paragraph (c) of the Declaration, C should apply the Berne Convention as this is a relationship between two Berne countries. In the relationship between A and C, however, only C is a Berne member.

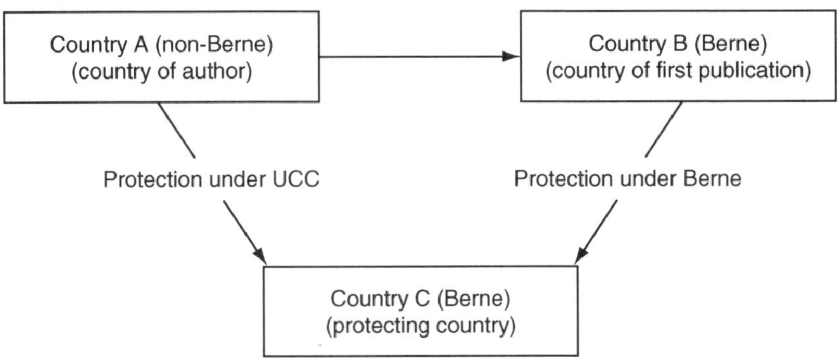

Figure 18.1

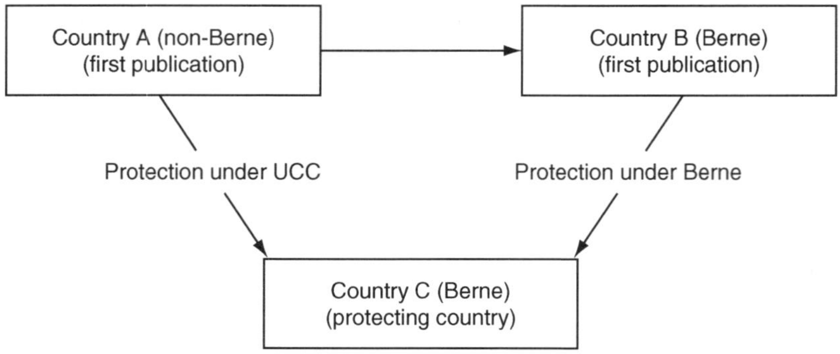

Figure 18.2

A similar situation arises where a work is published simultaneously in countries A and B and protection is sought in country C (see Figure 18.2).

Once again, there are two distinct relationships here: one between two Berne countries (B and C) and one between a Berne and a non-Berne country (A and C). Can country A, in its relations with country C, require that the latter apply the UCC rather than the Berne Convention? The wording of paragraph (c) appears to require this, as the relationship here is not among countries of the Berne Union. Furthermore, the wording of both paragraph (c) and article XVII(2) indicates that the provisions of the Declaration are binding only on Berne Union countries and are applicable only between those countries.[144] On the other hand, it is difficult to see why country A would wish to insist that country C should apply the UCC rather than the Berne Convention to the works of its authors. In most cases, there will be no practical difference as the basic principle of national treatment is the same under both conventions. Nonetheless, the general level of protection offered by the Berne Convention is higher than the UCC and no advantage would be obtained by insisting that the latter is applied.[145] Furthermore, if paragraph (c) does require the application of the UCC in these cases, this would be in contravention of article XVII(1) as it would affect the obligations that country C otherwise has under the Berne Convention in relation to works which have country B as their country of origin (even if their authors are nationals of country A). As such a result cannot have been intended by the delegates at the Geneva Conference, it can be concluded that paragraph (c) does not preclude the application of the Berne Convention in these instances. As noted above, the situations just considered are now almost entirely hypothetical, given the large access to membership of Berne that has occurred since publication of the first edition of this commentary (1987).

[144] See further Bogsch (n 1 above), 123ff.

[145] ibid.

(h) The 1971 Revision of the UCC

The UCC was revised in Paris in July 1971. The background to this revision conference, particularly in relation to the needs of developing countries, and the crucial role of the UCC members in bringing about a resolution to the conflict between these countries and the developed countries, has already been discussed in Chapter 14 above. At the same time as the UCC was revised, the Berne Convention was also revised as part of the 'package deal' agreed in Washington in 1970. The principal amendments made to the UCC concerned the addition of new compulsory licences for the translation and reproduction of works in developing countries (articles V*bis* to V*quater*). Other significant changes were also made, including the specification, in article IV*bis*(1), of the 'basic rights ensuring the author's economic interests' that were to be protected by contracting states. These included the exclusive rights to 'authorize reproduction by any means, public performance and broadcasting'. Although by no means as detailed as the corresponding provisions of the Berne Convention, they were nonetheless an indication that the UCC was fulfilling its initial promise of providing a low staircase that could be steadily raised towards the level of protection offered by the Berne Convention. However, part of the 'package deal' for revision of the two conventions provided for a temporary suspension of the sanction contained in the Appendix Declaration to article XVII in the case of developing countries.[146] At the 1971 Conference itself, a more radical proposal for the complete deletion of the Declaration was made by the Portuguese delegation which argued that the coercion implicit in its provisions was contrary to international custom and did not serve the interests of the Berne Convention.[147] Thus, the countries which were 'not members did not wish to join, and member countries which are not the largest exporters of intellectual works were not at all interested in any increase in protection'.[148] The Portuguese plea for a 'climate of freedom' in which countries could choose which of the conventions they should belong to without fear of the sanction contained in the Berne Safeguard Clause attracted considerable sympathy among a number of delegations,[149] but still faced general opposition, particularly from the developed countries which were concerned that it might imperil the final acceptance of the 'package deal'.[150] The text adopted by the Conference therefore retained the Safeguard Clause in paragraph (a) of the Declaration, but made it subject to the following exception in recognition of 'the temporary need of some States to adjust their level of 18.37

146 UNESCO, *Records of the Conference for the Revision of the Universal Copyright Convention* (1973), 214 (INLA/UCC/3).
147 ibid (INLA/UCC/25).
148 ibid, 153 (Portuguese delegate, Summary Records of the Proceedings).
149 ibid (Czechoslovakia and Brazil).
150 ibid, 153–4 (UK, FRG, France, Kenya, and Spain), 92 (general report of A Kaminstein).

copyright protection in accordance with their stage of cultural, social and economic development'.[151] To this end, a new paragraph (b) was inserted as follows (the former paragraph (b) now becoming paragraph (c)):

> (b) Where a Contracting State is regarded as a developing country in conformity with the established practice of the General Assembly of the United Nations, and has deposited with the Director-General of the United Nations Educational, Scientific and Cultural Organization, at the time of its withdrawal from the Berne Union, a notification to the effect that it regards itself as a developing country, the provisions of paragraph (a) shall not be applicable as long as such State may avail itself of the exceptions provided for in this Convention in accordance with Article V*bis*.

18.38 The conditions under which a country is to be treated as a developing country have already been discussed above (see paras 14.51ff), with respect to the application of the Paris Appendix of the Berne Convention, which is couched in similar terms to V*bis* of the UCC. However, the dispensation provided in paragraph (b) of the revised declaration is subject to certain limitations. First, the notification of developing country status must be made at the time of the withdrawal from the Berne Union. Thus, paragraph (a) will continue to be applicable to a developing country that leaves the Union without giving such a notification.

Second, the dispensation only continues as long as the country is a developing country within the meaning of article V*bis* of the UCC. When this ceases to be so is a matter of some difficulty (see para 14.55 above), but once it has occurred paragraph (a) will then be applicable. At this point, the former developing country will have to reassess its original decision to leave the Berne Union or find that the protection of its authors under the UCC is severely curtailed. Thus, any developing country considering which of the two conventions it should adhere to should logically join the UCC first so as to preserve its complete liberty of choice as to when to adhere to the Berne Convention. At the time of the first edition (1987), this comment was of particular relevance to the Peoples' Republic of China and the Republic of Korea, both of which were in the course of making this decision.[152]

---

[151] Note, however, the declaration by the Portuguese delegate, in withdrawing his proposal, that Portugal continued to oppose the system of coercion implicit in the 'Berne Safeguard Clause' and 'would oppose any future efforts to increase the level of protection under Berne unless they were accompanied by the restoration of a climate of free choice, which he considered essential in international copyright matters': ibid, 92 (Kaminstein report).

[152] As to the PRC, see Gou Shoukang, 'China and the Berne Convention' (1986) 11 *Columbia-VLA Journal of Law and the Arts* 121; as to the Republic of Korea, see Lee Tae-Hee, 'Intellectual Property Laws in Korea', Korean-American Business Institute, Annual Seminar on Doing Business in Korea (Seoul, Korea, 6–7 Nov 1986), 19. Subsequently, the PRC joined the UCC in July 1992 and Berne in Oct 1992, while Korea joined the UCC in July 1987 and Berne in 1996.

(6) The Present Relationship between the Berne Convention and the UCC

(a) The period 1971–86

In the period following the Paris Revision of both conventions, the relations between them remained in relative equilibrium, with no Berne member leaving the Berne Union in order to rely on the protection of the UCC alone, while the number of states adhering to both conventions increased steadily with a growing overlap of membership. Accordingly, in this period the membership of the Berne Union was not affected by the existence of the UCC; indeed, the existence of the latter undoubtedly provided an incentive for those states with few or no previous international copyright relations to enter these on a multilateral level whereas they might have been otherwise unprepared to meet the high standards required by the Berne Convention. On the other hand, the Paris Revision of the UCC saw that convention move closer to the Berne Convention in the matter of substantive protection. The 'low staircase' was raised, although a number of steps were still required for the two conventions to come into harmony (for example, with respect to formalities, duration of protection, and moral rights).[153] The relations between the two conventions in this period could therefore be described as follows. **18.39**

(i) South and Central American countries: While the majority of South and Central American countries were outside the Berne Union, they had now become members of the UCC.[154] This was a significant achievement in view of the fact that an original aim of the UCC was to provide a means of bringing the American republics into international copyright relations with non-American countries, notably those of the Berne Union. On the other hand, the UCC itself had been no more successful than the Pan-American Conventions in providing a common multilateral instrument to which all the American republics were party.[155]

(ii) A meeting point between Berne and non-Berne countries: As a meeting point between Berne Union and non-Berne Union countries, the UCC had not been completely successful in attracting Berne members and, as of 1 January 1986, only fifty-four Berne Union members belonged to the UCC.[156] Despite French membership, most of the francophone countries were outside the UCC,

---

[153] For a useful review of the workings of the two conventions in this period, see H Sandison, 'The Berne Convention and the UCC: The American Experience' (1986) 11 *Columbia-VLA Journal of Law and the Arts* 89.

[154] As of Jan 1987, the following were members of the UCC (Berne Union membership is indicated by the symbol (B)): Argentina (B), Belize, Brazil (B), Chile (B), Colombia, Costa Rica (B), Cuba, Dominican Republic, Ecuador, El Salvador, Guatemala, Haiti, Mexico (B), Nicaragua, Panama, Paraguay, Peru, and Venezuela (B): [1986] *Copyright* 12–13 and *UNESCO Copyright Bulletin*, vol XX, no 1, 38 (1986).

[155] See n 154 above.

[156] [1986] *Copyright* 6, 12.

although they had generally opted for Berne Union membership following their independence.[157] On the other hand, a number of former British possessions that had not continued to apply the Berne Convention post-independence had joined the UCC.[158] This had also been done by a variety of other countries that remained outside the Berne Union.[159]

(iii) The USA: The greatest success or 'prize' of the UCC before 1971 had been the adherence of the USA[160] and the entry of that important country into general international copyright relations. A second important prize post-1971 was the accession of the USSR which joined the UCC in 1973.[161]

(b) The period 1986–2005

18.40 In a general sense, it can be said that the ultimate goal of the UCC was its absorption into the higher-level Berne Convention. In formal terms this has not occurred, as there has not been a further revision of the UCC in this period, and the current texts still remain some distance apart on such important issues as formalities, duration, and the scope of rights to be protected. But a number of significant events have occurred that now point to the ultimate irrelevance of the UCC, beginning with the adherence of the USA to Berne in 1989, China in 1992, and the Russian Federation in 1995. The balance has shifted steadily but inexorably in favour of the Berne Convention, and the significance of the UCC as a 'universal convention' has decreased. From 1987 to 2003, only twenty-three countries acceded to the UCC, leading to a total membership of ninety-nine by November 2003, with only sixty-four having acceded to the 1971 text (the latest listing of contracting states on the UNESCO website). By contrast, accessions to Berne have been more than three times this number, with all the Latin American states, previously UCC stalwarts, and all the previous non-Berne UCC members joining Berne. To extend the analogy of the 'low staircase', these nations have now passed over the top step of the UCC to the higher level of Berne, while a large number of other states that previously had no international copyright relations have simply moved straight on to Berne (a good example being China). UNESCO, as the depository for the Convention and the secretariat for the Intergovernmental Committee, continues its activities with respect to copyright education, particularly with respect to cultural matters and the needs of developing nations. But the significance of the UCC, once so great in

[157] As of Jan 1986, only Cameroon, Morocco, Senegal and Tunisia belonged to the UCC: ibid.

[158] eg Ghana, Kenya, Malawi, Mauritius, Nigeria, and Zambia: ibid.

[159] eg Algeria, Democratic Kampuchea, Liberia, and Laos: ibid.

[160] See Stewart (1989), 135. See further 'La ratification, par les États-unis d'Amériques de la Convention universelle sur le droit d'auteur' [1955] *DA* 63.

[161] ibid. See further P B Maggs, 'New Directions in US–USSR Copyright Relations' (1974) 68 *Am Jo Int Law* 391.

those days when the USA and other great population blocs lay outside Berne, has now subsided, with the consequence that the UCC now looks wholly peripheral to the current international copyright framework. The fact of this irrelevance, however, may underline the ultimate achievement of the UCC as providing an important stepping stone to the Berne Convention for many nations.

19

THE BERNE CONVENTION AND NEIGHBOURING RIGHTS

A. Introduction[1]

It was seen in Chapter 8 above that, although the range of subject matter protected by the Berne Convention has been steadily extended over the past century, there have also been decisions made by successive revision conferences to exclude specific categories of subject matter. These included sound recordings, broadcasts, live performances, and the titles of works. As will be apparent, each of these differs in character and the reason for its exclusion from the umbrella of the Convention has also differed. Thus, in the case of sound recordings the objection was made that these were productions of an 'industrial character' and not capable of constituting literary or artistic creations. In the case of **19.01**

[1] For general background to the protection of neighbouring rights, see S Stewart, *International Copyright and Neighbouring Rights*, 2nd edn (1989), chs 7 and 8; C Masouyé, *Guide to the Berne Convention for the Protection of Literary and Artistic Works* (1978) ('Masouyé (1978)'), 7–13; X Desjeux, *La Convention de Rome (10–26 octobre 1961): Etude de la protection des artistes, interprètes ou exécutants, des producteurs de phonogrammes et des organisms de radiodiffusion* (1966), Titres I and II; 'La protection des droits voisins du droit d'auteur' [1942] *DA* 38, 51, 61, 75, 85, 122. See also J A L Sterling, *Intellectual Property Rights in Sound Recordings, Film & Video* (1992).

broadcasts, these were usually produced by large public organizations and it was difficult to identify their 'author' or 'authors' (the same could also be true of sound recordings). On the other hand, with live performances, there was usually no problem in identifying the person making the performance, but the question which arose was whether the performance or interpretation of another's work was in itself a work and whether a performer could consequently be regarded as an author. Finally with the titles of works, the question of substantiality arose and it was generally felt that their protection lay more appropriately within the scope of unfair competition laws rather than copyright.

19.02 In a general sense, each of the above categories, with the exception of titles of works, is a derivative kind of subject matter that is generally dependent, for its creation, on the use of a pre-existing literary or artistic work. Thus, with the *de minimis* exception of natural and background noises, a sound recording will usually embody the performance of a literary or artistic work. The same is true in the case of broadcasts, although the broadcast of live spectacles or events may provide significant exceptions to this. Finally, the subject of a performer's claim to protection is his performance or interpretation of a particular work: in the event that he creates a work himself in the course of an improvised performance this will be an original work entitled to protection in its own right, subject to the particular requirements of national laws concerning fixation. Nonetheless, their derivative character cannot, by itself, provide the common link in explaining the exclusion of these categories of subject matter from the Berne Convention, as the latter has always accorded protection to a large range of subject matter that is also derivative in character. For example, translations were protected as original works from the time of the Berne Act and successive Acts have extended their protection to adaptations, musical arrangements, and other alterations of literary and artistic works and collections of works. While comparisons are always difficult, the degree of skill required of a translator or adapter is not far different from that required of the maker of a sound recording or a broadcast or a performer. Each applies his or her skill to a pre-existing literary or artistic work and there seems to be little reason to distinguish between the results of their respective endeavours. It can be argued that a difference is to be found in the mechanical or technical nature of the work of the recorder or broadcaster. However, such an argument cannot be applied to performers and, in any event, the technical skills of the recording engineer or broadcaster require considerable artistic sensitivity if a successful recording or broadcast is to be made. Furthermore, the inclusion of photographs and cinematographic films within the scope of the Berne Convention undermines an argument that tries to distinguish the kind of skill applied in the creation of these various subject matters. Thus, the skill of the photographer or cinematographer may be mainly of a mechanical nature, with little that is artistic or literary about it. The truth is that there is no logical reason, based on the need for literary or artistic creation, why each of these subject matters should not be protected under the Berne Convention. Furthermore, this does not mean that every photograph, sound recording, and so on need be protected: the requirement of 'intellectual creation' or originality can be applied so as to exclude the most banal or mechanical of each category. On the same basis, protection could also be accorded to live performances. The logical opposite to this would be to exclude derivative productions completely from the Convention, including those, such as translations and adaptations, which have been traditionally within its scope.

While the exclusion of sound recordings, broadcasts, and performances from the Berne Convention therefore appears arbitrary, a reason of a more practical kind may be found to explain the position of the first two. This has already been alluded to (see para 19.01 above) and concerns the problem of identifying the 'author' or 'authors' of a sound recording and broadcast. While not invariably so, the making of a sound recording or broadcast is usually a collective exercise, carried on by a team of trained personnel employed by a corporate or public enterprise. Although the collective nature of the undertaking cannot, in itself, be an objection to inclusion in article 2(1), as joint and collective authorship are clearly recognized under the Berne Convention,[2] the determination of who should be regarded as an author in the case of a sound recording or broadcast can be a difficult question. For example, with a sound recording of a musical or dramatic work, would the 'authors' include the sound engineer, the record producer, and the various performers or actors who contribute to the making of the final recording? Within the framework of the Berne Convention, the question of authorship has already given rise to great differences in the case of cinematographic films and a wide variety of approaches are adopted by Union countries (see further Chapter 7 above). In consequence, as a purely pragmatic matter, the exclusion of sound recordings and broadcasts prevents further problems of this kind arising.[3] Furthermore, the history of claims for protection of sound recordings and broadcasts shows that these have been advanced by the corporate bodies that underwrite these activities, rather than the individuals concerned. Rather than protection of the kind accorded to authors (including moral rights), what has been sought is protection for the financial investment involved in the making of a recording or broadcast. At the time these claims were first made, the Berne Convention appeared to provide the only relevant international forum in which this could be done. However, this did not mean that the answers to these claims lay necessarily within the framework of that Convention. If it seemed arbitrary that photographs and cinematographic films **19.03**

[2] Paris Act, arts 2(5) and 7*bis*.

[3] See further Stewart (n 1 above), 189 ff.

fell on the right side of the Berne fence while sound recordings and broadcasts did not, there was nothing to prevent the development of forms of protection for the latter that were more closely tailored to the needs and requirements of their makers.

19.04 This, indeed, began to happen at a national level, although in widely differing ways. In the UK and other common law countries, there was little difficulty in according protection to the makers of sound recordings and this, in fact, was achieved through the grant of a separate 'copyright'.[4] However, as this protection was available as much to corporate record makers as to natural persons, this was not an acceptable approach to those countries, such as France, which saw authors' rights as rights accorded to natural persons only.[5] Other countries, while not prepared to grant copyright protection, were prepared to protect rights in sound recordings (or 'phonograms') on the basis that these were rights that were closely connected to or related to the more traditional category of copyright. An early example was to be found in the Italian Law of 1941 which also recognized a similar right in their broadcasts on the part of broadcasting organizations.[6] In the history of intellectual property rights generally, this was a significant development, as it recognized the possibility of a hierarchy of rights: rights in the traditional categories of literary and artistic works which were accorded to 'authors' and rights in other kinds of subject matter that were accorded to persons other than authors, that is, record manufacturers and broadcasting organizations (to give the most obvious claimants). In part, at least, this can be seen as a necessary recognition that technological change, in the form of sound recordings and broadcasts, made the application of traditional concepts of authors' rights more difficult. It can also be seen as an acknowledgement of the problems that had already arisen when other kinds of analogous subject matter such as photographs and cinematographic films had been brought within the ambit of copyright. In addition, it made it easier to accord protection to other categories of creators, without having to grant them the status of author. For our present purposes, the most important of these were performers, although to rank these with record manufacturers and broadcasting organizations appears anomalous. Unlike the latter, performers are invariably natural persons and, as stated above, their skill and creativity does not seem to be qualitatively different from that of other kinds of derivative authors such as translators and adapters. It has been suggested that one reason for the historic refusal to grant performers rights in their performances was the perception that

[4] Copyright Act 1911 (UK), s 19(1) (mechanical instruments), Copyright Act 1956 (UK), ss 12 (sound recordings), 14 (television and sound broadcasts).

[5] Stewart (n 1 above), 189 ff; Desjeux (n 1 above) 19.

[6] Italian Law of 1941, arts 72 and 79. See further Desjeux (n 1 above), 35.

their labour was unproductive.[7] More important, however, must be the fact that, until the beginning of the twentieth century, performers were in little need of protection apart from that provided by the laws of contract and unfair competition: because of the transitory nature of their performances, no one could readily 'steal' them and their audiences were limited by purely physical factors, such as the size of their venue and the number of people in a particular locality. With the advent of phonograms, films, and broadcasting this situation changed rapidly. Particular performances might be fixed on record or film or broadcast to a much wider audience, with the result that the uniqueness of a live performance began to disappear.[8] It was only with the appearance of widespread 'technological unemployment' in their ranks that performers began to seek protection for their performances through rights against unauthorized fixation and dissemination. Too late, and perhaps too weakly organized, to gain protection as authors, their claims came gradually to be recognized in national legislation in a variety of ways: through the grant of a distinctive neighbouring right,[9] the application of laws of unfair competition,[10] and the imposition of criminal sanctions.[11] In this way, the rights of performers came to be grouped with the rights of record manufacturers and broadcasting organizations as rights related to copyright but meriting protection of a different character.

The present chapter, therefore, is concerned with the international agreements that have sought to provide protection to these categories of 'non-authors' whose productions may nevertheless be seen as closely relating to, or neighbouring upon, the traditional categories of authors' rights. It begins with an account of the first major treaty in this area, the International Convention for the Protection of Performers, Producers of Phonograms and Broadcasting Organizations 1961 (the 'Rome Convention'), and then considers the international agreements that have followed in the wake of Rome: the Phonograms Convention, the Satellites Convention, the World Intellectual Property Organization ('WIPO') Performances and Phonograms Treaty (the 'WPPT'), and the relevant provisions of the Agreement on Trade-Related Aspects of Intellectual Property

[7] E Thompson, 'Twenty Years of the Rome Convention' [1981] *Copyright* 270, 274, quoting the views of Adam Smith in *The Wealth of Nations* (1776), Book II, ch III. See further Stewart (n 1 above), 194–5.

[8] Masouyé (1978), 9ff.

[9] eg the Italian Law of 1941, art 80(2). Cf the earlier German Law of 1910, art 2(2), which treated a performance as being analogous to an adaptation. See further Stewart (n 1 above), 181–2.

[10] As in France: see the cases discussed in Desjeux (n 1 above), 13ff and Stewart (n 1 above), 196, notably the *Spedidame* case where the *Cour de Cassation* based its protection on art 1382 of the Civil Code (15 Mar 1977, noted in [1977] *RIDA* 141).

[11] As in the UK: Dramatic and Musical Performers' Protection Acts 1925; Dramatic and Musical Performers' Protection Act 1958; Performers' Protection Act 1963; Performers' Protection Act 1972.

Rights 1994 (the 'TRIPs Agreement'). For the sake of completeness, a number of other agreements touching upon authors' and neighbouring rights are considered at the end of the chapter: as will be seen, some of these have never entered into force or have not yet reached the stage of a final text.

B. The Rome Convention

(1) Origins

19.05 Even prior to the Brussels Conference, there had been attempts to achieve international protection for performers, phonogram producers, and broadcasting organizations. In 1939, Fritz Ostertag, the former Director of the International Office, had drafted a project for an international convention of twelve articles to be 'connected with' the Berne Convention.[12] This dealt with a number of disparate rights which were closely related to copyright, but had, so far, not been brought within the Berne Convention: these included the rights of performers, phonogram producers, and broadcasting organizations, as well as the *droit de suite*, and a separate copyright in private letters, portraits, and press information.[13] This was discussed at a meeting of experts which met in Samaden (Switzerland) in July 1939 and was convened under the auspices of the International Office and the International Institute of Rome for the Unification of Private Law.[14] This meeting finally adopted four separate draft treaties that were intended to be annexes to the Berne Convention, to be adopted at the Brussels Revision Conference scheduled for later in 1939. These dealt with (i) performers and producers of phonograms, (ii) broadcasting organizations, (iii) press information, and (iv) *droit de suite*.[15] The outbreak of World War II prevented any further progress and when the postponed Brussels Conference met in 1948, it did not deal with the proposed annexes, although provision for the protection of *droit de suite* was made in article 14*ter*. In the view of one distinguished commentator, the main reason no further action was taken in relation to the remaining matters was to avoid unnecessary divisiveness between Union members, many of whom had been on opposite sides during the recent war.[16] The Conference therefore contented itself with adopting three resolutions calling on member countries to study the protection of performers, phonograms, and broadcasting organizations.[17]

---

[12] F Ostertag, 'Nouvelles propositions pour la Conférence de Bruxelles' [1939] *DA* 62ff.

[13] ibid, 71–2. [14] See further the note in [1940] *DA* 8–9.

[15] See further 'La Protection internationale des droits voisins du droit d'Auteur (État actuel de la question)' [1940] *DA* 109, 121, 133 and the texts of the draft conventions at 125, 134, 136, and 138.

[16] Stewart (n 1 above), 222.

[17] *Documents de la Conférence réunie à Bruxelles du 5 au 26 juin 1948* (1951), 587.

Following the Brussels Conference, work began on a separate convention dealing with these matters. This came to be done under the auspices of three international organizations: BIRPI, the ILO, and UNESCO. The interest of the first was obvious, and, after the creation of the Universal Copyright Convention ('UCC'), the reason for the involvement of UNESCO was also clear. As for the ILO, this organization had been concerned with the interests of performers, as the victims of technological unemployment, from the mid-1920s.[18] Between 1949 and 1960, the protection of performers, producers of phonograms, and broadcasting organizations was considered separately by each organization and a series of joint meetings of experts and advisory committees was also held. In addition, there was a close involvement in this preparatory work by a number of international non-governmental organizations with direct interests in these matters: the International Federation of Musicians (*FIM*), the International Federation of Actors (*FIA*), the International Federation of Producers of Phonograms (IFPI) and the European Broadcasting Union (EBU).[19] A series of draft conventions was produced: the first in Rome in 1951[20] and a second in Geneva in 1956 by committees of experts convened by the ILO[21] and a third in Monaco in 1957 prepared by a committee of governmental experts convened by UNESCO and the International Office.[22] There were substantial differences between these drafts and a further committee of governmental experts was convened by all three organizations in The Hague in 1960 with the aim of resolving these matters.[23] This meeting produced a fourth draft convention that served as the basis of discussions at the Diplomatic Conference that was held in Rome in the following year (1961) under the auspices of BIRPI, UNESCO, and the ILO.[24] Delegations from forty-four countries attended the Conference[25] and there were observers from three other international organizations[26] and fifteen international non-governmental organizations.[27] In just over two weeks, a final text of the Convention was agreed and this was signed on 26 October 1961 by forty **19.06**

[18] Masouyé (1978), 7ff. [19] Stewart (n 1 above), 224.

[20] [1951] *DA* 137 (including draft convention). See further 'Droit d'auteur et droits voisins' [1952] *DA* 133 and the observations on the draft convention by H Desbois and V de Sanctis in [1954] *DA*, 149, 164.

[21] [1956] *DA* 93, 10–17 July 1956; see also Desjeux (n 1 above), 251 (text of draft convention). See further 'The Performing Artist, The Record Manufacturer, The Broadcaster' [1956] *DA* Apr Supplement (in English) 13; A Bogsch, 'Study Group on so-called "Neighbouring Rights" ' [1956] *DA* May Supplement 49; R Plaisant, 'Le droits sur les phonogrammes' [1956] *DA* Aug and Sept Supplements 61 and 69; 'Quelques conditions prélable pour que soit viables un accord international sur les droits voisins' [1957] *DA* 22.

[22] [1957] *DA* (4–13 Mar 1957); also in Desjeux (n 1 above), 259ff.

[23] [1960] *DA* 161 (9–20 May 1960); see also Desjeux (n 1 above), 263ff.

[24] *Records of the Diplomatic Conference on the International Protection of Performers, Producers of Phonograms and Broadcasting Organizations*, Rome, 10–26 Oct 1961, ILO (Geneva), UNESCO (Paris), and *BIRPI* (Geneva) (1968).

[25] For a list of these states, see ibid, 23ff. [26] ibid, 29–30. [27] ibid, 30–1.

states.[28] It came into force on 18 May 1964 and, as of 4 November 2004, had been ratified or acceded to by seventy-nine states[29]—a marked increase from a membership of only twenty-nine states as of January 1986 (when the first edition of this book was finalized).[30]

(2) Provisions of the Convention[31]

19.07 These provide for the protection, at the international level, of the three principal categories of neighbouring rights: those of performers, producers of phonograms, and broadcasting organizations. From a purist point of view, this conjunction of rights may be criticized, in that there is no obvious common link between the first and the second two. On the other hand, as the adjective 'neighbouring' indicates, each is closely connected to the creation and exploitation of literary and artistic works, as well as being concerned with the prevention of particular kinds of unfair appropriation of the efforts of others. Furthermore, as Masouyé points out, the Rome Convention serves a different purpose to the Berne Convention.[32] The latter was largely the result of a consensus between the national laws of its member countries as to what should be protected and how this should be done. By contrast, the Rome Convention tends more to set out the rights that states should incorporate into their laws.[33] This educational role was also necessary in view of the many differences that existed between states over the protection of neighbouring rights. For this reason, while the Convention contains a certain number of conventional rules (what Masouyé calls the 'basic *table d'hôte*'), it also allows states a considerable degree of latitude as to the way in which they apply them (the '*à la carte* provisions').[34] In brief, the requirements of the Convention are as follows.

(3) Performers

19.08 These are defined as 'actors, singers, musicians, dancers and other persons who act, sing, deliver, declaim, play in, or otherwise perform literary or artistic

[28] *Records* (n 24 above), 19–20.

[29] www.wipo.int. This still remained the number of contracting states as at 29 September 2005.

[30] [1986] *Copyright* 29.

[31] For general commentaries on the Convention, see W Nordemann, K Vinck, and P W Hertin, *Internationales Urheberrecht und Leistungsschutzrecht der deutschsprachigen Länder unter Berücksichtigung auch der Staaten der Europäischen Gemeinschaft, Kommentar* (1977) ('Nordemann et al (1977)'), 337 ff and Stewart (n 1 above), ch 8.

[32] Masouyé (1978), 12. See also Stewart (n 1 above), 224.

[33] Masouyé (1978), 12.

[34] ibid. See further Desjeux (n 1 above); Nordemann et al (1977), 340ff; H Desbois, A Françon, and A Kéréver, *Les Conventions internationales du droit d'auteur et des droits voisins* (1976) ('Desbois et al (1976)'), 320ff; J F Da Costa, 'Some Reflections on the Rome Convention' [1976] *Copyright* 80; G Davies, 'The Rome Convention 1961: A Brief Summary of its Development and Prospect' [1979] *EIPR* 154; Thompson (n 7 above); H von Rauscher auf Weeg, 'The Rome Convention Rights: A Comparative Review of Legislation and International Legal Developments over 12 years' (1974) *Bull Cop Soc USA* 237.

works'.[35] Under article 4, contracting states are required to grant national treatment to performers if any of the following points of attachment are satisfied: the performance has taken place in another contracting state, the performance is incorporated in a phonogram which is protected under the Convention, or is carried by a broadcast which is protected by the Convention. Article 7 then outlines the minimum protection that must be provided for performers under the Convention. This is to 'include the possibility of preventing' the following unauthorized acts: the broadcasting and communication to the public of their live performances; the fixation of their unfixed performance; and the reproduction of a fixation of their performance if the original fixation was made without their consent or the reproduction is made for purposes different from those for which the performers gave their consent. Article 7 is one of the *à la carte* provisions of the Convention as it leaves contracting states complete freedom to decide how they will protect performers against these acts ('include the possibility of preventing'). Apart from the grant of an exclusive right at one end of the spectrum, the 'possibility of preventing' could also be achieved through the law of employment or unfair competition or through the application of criminal sanctions.[36] In addition, under article 12, performers have the possibility of receiving remuneration with respect to the broadcasting and public communication of phonograms (see further para 19.09 below). Latitude is also provided to contracting states to extend the categories of persons who may be regarded as performers for the purposes of protection under the Convention, notably to artists who do not perform literary and artistic works.[37] The obvious examples of such artists are clowns, acrobats, and jugglers.[38] In addition, contracting states may specify, in their domestic laws and regulations, the manner in which groups of performers will be represented in the exercise of their rights in the case of joint performances.[39]

More controversial, however, is article 19 which provides that article 7 is to have no application once a performer has consented to the incorporation of his performance in a visual or audio-visual fixation. In other words, once a performance has been filmed (whether for the cinema, television, or otherwise), she has no further rights under the Convention. This provision was a concession made at Rome to accommodate the concerns of film producers[40] and clearly

[35] Rome Convention, art 3(a). See further C Masouyé, 'Les droits des artistes interprétes ou exécutants dans la Convention de Rome' [1965] *RIDA* 161.

[36] Masouyé (1978), 34. See further *Records of the Diplomatic Conference* (n 24 above), 43 (report of A Kaminstein, *rapporteur général*).

[37] Rome Convention, art 9.

[38] Masouyé (1978), 42.

[39] Rome Convention, art 8.

[40] ibid, 65. See also Desjeux (n 1 above), 144ff.

places performers in a vulnerable position in an area which is of great concern to them.

With respect to the minimum term of protection to be given to performers, this is twenty years from the end of the year in which the performance was incorporated in a phonogram or twenty years from the year in which the performance took place (if unfixed).[41] Exceptions from protection are also allowed and, by analogy with the Berne Convention, may cover the following cases: private use, reporting of current events, ephemeral fixation by broadcasting organizations, and use for the purposes of teaching or scientific research.[42] The same exceptions apply in relation to phonograms and broadcasting organizations and are discussed below (see paras 19.11ff).

(4) **Producers of phonograms**

19.09 Rather than 'sound recording', an expression commonly used in US, UK, and Commonwealth legislation,[43] the Convention refers to 'phonograms' and 'producers of phonograms'.[44] 'Phonogram' is defined as 'any exclusively aural fixation of sounds of a performance or other sounds'.[45] The expression 'or other sounds' would include such things as birdsong and other nature noises, thus making it clear that 'whatever the origin of the sound, the phonogram as such is protected by the Convention'.[46] The expression 'producer of phonograms' is also defined and means 'the person who, or the legal entity which, first fixes the sounds of a performance or other sounds'.[47] The references to 'first fixation' and 'legal entity' make it clear that the emphasis here is on an industrial rather than a personal activity.[48] Each contracting state is required to accord national treatment to producers of phonograms where any of the following points of attachment are met: the producer is a national of another contracting state, the first fixation was made in another contracting state, or the phonogram was first published in another contracting state.[49] However, it is open to a state to declare at the time of accession, ratification, or at any time afterwards, that it will not apply either of the criteria of publication or fixation: such a declaration becomes

[41] Rome Convention, art 14(b).

[42] ibid, art 18.

[43] eg 17 USC § 102(a)(7); Copyright, Designs and Patents Act 1988 (UK), s 5A.

[44] Oddly enough, 'phonogram' does not appear in the *Concise Oxford Dictionary* although the term 'phonograph' does.

[45] Rome Convention, art 3(b).

[46] *Records of the Diplomatic Conference* (n 24 above), 40 (report of Kaminstein).

[47] Rome Convention, art 3(c).

[48] Masouyé (1978), 23.

[49] Rome Convention, art 5(1). A thirty-day rule applies in the case of publication in both a non-contracting and contracting state: art 5(2).

effective six months after deposit with the Secretary General of the United Nations.[50]

The minimum of protection that must be accorded is the right to authorize or prohibit the direct or indirect reproduction of phonograms.[51] 'Direct reproduction' is understood here to mean reproductions made by means of moulding and casting, while 'indirect reproduction' refers to reproductions made by recording the sounds produced by playing a pre-existent phonogram or recording off the air, that is a broadcast (either radio or television) of the sounds produced by playing a phonogram.[52] In the case of secondary uses of phonograms, that is, where they are used directly for broadcasting or for any communication to the public, there is no requirement that these be the subject of an exclusive right, but simply an obligation that the user should pay 'a single equitable remuneration' to the performers, or to the producers of the phonograms, or to both, for that use.[53] In the absence of agreement between these parties, domestic law may lay down the conditions as to the sharing of this remuneration between performers and phonogram producers. This, however, is another *à la carte* provision that contracting states may exclude in whole or in part by way of a reservation upon becoming bound by the Convention.[54] In addition, they have the choice of the party or parties to whom the remuneration should be paid—the performers, the producer of the phonogram, or both.[55] This provision was the result of a compromise between the many interested parties involved, as well as between the different approaches of national legal systems.[56] In part, at least, the requirement to pay equitable remuneration finds an analogy in the compulsory licence provided for in article 11*bis* of the Berne Convention.

With respect to duration of protection, a minimum period of twenty years from the date of fixation is required.[57] Provision is also made for the same exceptions that are allowed in respect of performers[58] (see further para 19.11 below). Finally, although it is assumed that protection of phonograms under the Convention should be provided free of formalities, it is provided that, where the

---

50 Article 5(3). 51 ibid, art 10.

52 *Records of the Diplomatic Conference* (n 24 above), 46 (report of Kaminstein). The reference to 'moulding and casting', presumably appropriate in 1961, seems rather antiquated now in 2005.

53 Rome Convention, art 12. See further Masouyé (1978), 46.

54 Rome Convention, art 16(1)(a). See further Masouyé (1978), 60ff; X Desjeux, " 'The Narrow Gate": Commentary on Article 16(1)(a)(i) Rome Convention' [1965] *Copyright* 151.

55 Rome Convention, art 12. See further Masouyé (1978), 48ff; Stewart (n 1 above), 239ff; Report of the Subcommittee of the Intergovernmental Committee of the Rome Convention on the Implementation of the Rome Convention: [1979] *Copyright* 107 (recommendations on the 'Collection and Distribution of Remuneration').

56 *Records of the Diplomatic Conference* (n 24 above), 48–9 (report of Kaminstein); Masouyé (1978), 46.

57 Rome Convention, art 14(a). 58 ibid, art 18.

latter are required by the law of any contracting state, these requirements will be satisfied by the fixation of a ℗ notice and the date of first publication on each copy.[59]

(5) Broadcasting organizations

19.10 This term is left undefined, but it is clear from the context that 'organization' refers essentially to the legal entity responsible for the making of the broadcast. The term 'broadcasting', however, is defined as meaning the 'transmission by wireless means for the public reception of sounds or of images and sounds',[60] This clearly excludes the various forms of transmission by wire diffusion, such as cable television and it must be doubted whether it would cover encrypted transmissions that require decrypting by recipients, for example, through box-top devices on their television or radio receivers. Each contracting state is required to grant national treatment to broadcasting organizations if either of the following points of attachment is met: the headquarters of the organization is situated in, or the broadcast was transmitted from a transmitter situated in, another contracting state.[61] The minimum rights to be accorded to broadcasting organizations are the rights to authorize or prohibit the rebroadcasting of their broadcasts, their fixation, the reproduction of unauthorized fixations, and the communication to the public of their television broadcasts where this is done in places accessible to the public on payment of an entrance fee.[62] The minimum period of protection is twenty years from the end of the year of the making of the broadcast[63] and the same exceptions to protection may be made as in the case of performers and producers of phonograms.[64]

(6) Exceptions

19.11 So far as possible limitations and exceptions to the above rights are concerned, these are contained in article 15. The latter is permissive in character, in that it enables contracting states to provide for certain kinds of limitations or exceptions to the rights to be protected, but imposes no obligation to do so. Two kinds of limitations and exceptions are allowable under article 15: (i) specific exceptions contained in article 15(1); and (ii) all limitations contained in domestic laws and regulations with respect to the protection of copyright in literary and artistic works (article 15(2)).

[59] Rome Convention, art 11. [60] ibid, art 3(f). [61] ibid, art 6(1).
[62] ibid, art 13. [63] ibid, art 14(c). [64] ibid, art 18.

(a) Private use (article 15(1)(a))

This means a use that is neither public nor for profit,[65] and will be principally relevant to the copying or fixation of performances, phonograms, or broadcasts in the privacy of the recipient's home. Even though 'private', in the sense that such use is neither public nor of a commercial kind, it is possible that these uses may still be detrimental to the interests of the right holder. One commentator, Stewart, suggests that the criteria in article 9(2) of the Berne Convention might be appropriate in testing the validity of any private-copying exception in national law, thereby ruling out such acts as the private copying of phonograms and videograms.[66] On the other hand, there is nothing in the text of article 15(1)(a) that qualifies the adjective 'private' in this way, and the better view must be that it means 'private' as distinct from 'professional' or 'commercial' uses, and that it is inappropriate to go further and consider the effect on the normal exploitation of the work or the legitimate interests of the right holder (as under an article 9(2) approach). At the same time, the cumulative effect of 'private' copying may be such as to make it 'commercial' and hence outside the scope of article 15(1)(a), for example, as in the case of online peer-to-peer copying. **19.12**

(b) Use of short excerpts in connection with the reporting of current events: article 15(1)(b)

This appears to be a counterpart to the news-reporting exception under Berne, but the language is based more closely on the text of article 10*bis* of the Brussels Act, rather than article 10*bis*(1) of the Paris Act. A contrast with the latter is that only 'short excerpts' may be used, and there is no scope for arguing that longer excerpts or the whole of a performance, phonogram, or broadcast could be used 'to the extent justified by the informatory purpose'. **19.13**

(c) Ephemeral fixation by a broadcasting organization by means of its own facilities and for its own broadcasts: article 15(1)(c)

This parallels article 11*bis*(3) of Berne, and allows broadcasting organizations to make ephemeral recordings of phonograms or performances for the purposes of their own broadcasts. The requirement of ephemerality means that any recordings that are made must be destroyed after a reasonable time, although clearly there may be differences between national laws as to the precise times for this.[67] **19.14**

65 See generally Stewart (n 1 above), para 8.41.
66 ibid.
67 See further Stewart (n 1 above), para 8.43, and see also para 13.72 above.

(d) Use solely for the purposes of teaching or scientific research: article 15(1)(d)

19.15 The reference to 'scientific research' goes beyond what is allowed under article 10(2) of Berne, although Professor Nordemann et al comment that 'commercial phonograms and radio and television programs could scarcely offer material for use in scientific research. A greater usefulness may be found in the fields of the cultural and social sciences.'[68] The same authors suggest that care should be taken to ensure that the label of 'science' is not misused here, for example, so as to include such things as popular science broadcasts within the rubric of 'scientific research'. In their view, the latter is a much more restricted concept, being confined to the non-public activity of research: popularization and dissemination of the results of such research is therefore not embraced by this concept.[69] On the other hand, the reference to 'teaching' in article 15(1)(d) must permit the dissemination of such material as part of the instructional function, whether in schools or tertiary institutions.

(e) Limitations contained in domestic laws: article 15(2)

19.16 This is an alternative and parallel set of allowable limitations, where they fall within the boundaries provided by domestic laws with respect to the protection of copyright in literary and artistic works. The latter is also an indirect reference to the Berne Convention, on the basis that such domestic laws will, as a matter of principle, need to be consistent with the provisions of that Convention so far as permissible limitations and exceptions are concerned (under article 23 of the Rome Convention, membership is open to any state that is a member of the Berne Convention or the UCC; as there are now 159 members of Berne, this convention has become almost universal in its application).

The only restriction on the adoption of Berne-type limitations and exceptions with respect to the rights protected under Rome is that these may only provide for compulsory licences 'to the extent to which they are compatible with this [Rome] Convention'. The latter allows for compulsory licences under a number of provisions: article 7(2)(2) (broadcasting of performances); article 12 (broadcasting of phonograms); and article 13(d) (communication to the public of certain broadcasts). Outside of these, no other compulsory licences could be justified by virtue of article 15(2), for example, one that was otherwise justified by reference to a provision of the Berne Convention, such as article 9(2) or 11*bis*(2).[70]

---

68 Nordemann et al (1990), 411. 69 ibid.

70 See further Stewart (n 1 above), para 8.40; Nordemann et al (1990), 411.

(7) Reservations

Unlike the current text of Berne, article 16 of the Rome Convention contains a relatively generous regime as to the reservations that contracting states may make upon becoming parties to the Convention. These provisions, more than anything, reflect the compromises and balances that were struck in the formulation of the Convention. Thus, reservations by way of declarations may be made 'at any time' (not just on accession, ratification, or acceptance) in relation to the following articles. **19.17**

(i) Article 12 (secondary uses of phonograms): The scope of the reservations allowable here are considerable, in that a contracting party may declare that it will not apply the provisions of that article at all, that it will only apply it 'in respect of certain uses', that it will not apply the article to phonograms that have a producer that is not a national of another contracting state, or, in the case of phonograms where the producer is a national of another contracting state, that will limit the protection to the extent to which, and the term to which, the latter state grants protection to phonograms first fixed by a national of that state (a limitation here, however, is that differences as to the beneficiaries or classes of beneficiaries as between such states is not to be considered as a difference to the extent of the protection): article 16(1)(a)(i)–(iv).

(ii) Article 13(d) (communications to the public of television broadcasts where made available in places accessible to members of the public against payment of a fee): Where a contracting state makes a declaration of reservation in relation to this provision, material reciprocity so far as other contracting states applies, ie the latter are not obliged to grant the same right to broadcasting organizations whose headquarters are in the state making the declaration: article 16(1)(b).

(iii) States applying the criterion of fixation alone under article 5: Under article 17, there is a further limitation of protection that may be applied by these states in relation to the criteria specified in article 16(1)(a)(iii) and (iv) (phonograms where the producer is not a national of another contracting state or where the extent or term of protection is shorter). Article 17 provides that where such a state, as at 26 October 1961, applied protection to phonogram producers solely on the basis of fixation, that state may declare that it will only apply the criterion of fixation, instead of the criterion of nationality, in the case of phonograms falling within article 16(1)(a)(iii) and (iv). Unlike the other declarations that may be made under article 16, a declaration under article 17 has to be made at the time of ratification, acceptance, or accession.

(8) Other provisions

19.18 Unlike the Berne Convention, the Rome Convention is non-retroactive.[71] It also is clearly stipulated that the Convention provides merely a minimum of protection and is not to prejudice any protection otherwise secured to the beneficiaries of this protection, whether under national laws, such as those of defamation and unfair competition, or under international law, such as the Phonograms or Satellites Convention.[72] Provision is also made for the revision of the Convention,[73] although this has not occurred, and the International Court of Justice is given jurisdiction to settle disputes between contracting states.[74] Finally, an Intergovernmental Committee is established, with the tasks of studying the application and operation of the Convention and the preparation of proposals for revision conferences.[75] This Committee has met regularly since 1967 (the last meeting being held in June 2001[76]) and, among other things, has adopted a model law on neighbouring rights (1974)[77] as well as detailed guidelines on the application of the Convention (1979),[78] and, more recently, commissioning expert studies on the operation of the Convention and its link to other conventions in the copyright and neighbouring rights area.[79] The secretariat of the Committee is provided jointly by WIPO, the ILO, and UNESCO.[80]

(9) Relationship between the Rome and Berne Conventions

19.19 During the preparations for the Rome Convention, there were fears on the part of authors and authors' societies that the recognition of neighbouring rights would prejudice the rights already secured to them in national legislation and by the Berne Convention. This was a factor that, to a great extent, delayed the final adoption of the Convention.[81] The objections that were made were various. For example, it was argued that the new rights were hardly necessary as contractual solutions could be used to protect the position of the proposed beneficiaries of protection.[82] It was also argued that a convention dealing with these matters was, in any event, premature as many states did not yet protect neighbouring rights at all.[83] As to the first of these, contractual solutions were hardly adequate to deal with unauthorized uses of performances, phonograms, and broadcasts by third parties. As to the second, while it was true that the Rome Convention was

---

[71] Rome Convention, art 20. [72] ibid, art 21. See further Masouyé (1978), 69.
[73] Rome Convention, art 29. [74] ibid, art 30. [75] ibid, art 31.
[76] See www.wipo.int/meetings.
[77] 'Model Law Concerning the Protection of Performers, Producers of Phonograms and Broadcasting Organizations' [1974] *Copyright* 163.
[78] [1979] *Copyright* 107. [79] www.wipo.int/meetings.
[80] Rome Convention, art 32(5). [81] Masouyé (1978), 16ff.
[82] Stewart (n 1 above), 225ff (paras 8.05ff). [83] ibid.

in advance of many national laws, in the years since its adoption it has served as a useful model for national legislation and a large number of countries have adopted some form of protection for one or more neighbouring rights.[84] More substantive fears, however, were expressed by authors' organizations. Thus, it was argued that the new rights owners might use these rights to prohibit uses that authors might otherwise have authorized.[85] For example, a concert pianist might forbid the recording of a performance of a work which the author had already licensed or a broadcasting organization might prohibit the broadcast of a work which the author had permitted. These were, perhaps, cases of marginal importance, as the owners of the copyright and neighbouring rights in a work are usually equally eager to exploit their respective rights and there is a high degree of interdependence here. A more significant objection, however, arose from the fear that the grant of new rights parallel to those already enjoyed by authors, particularly in the case of secondary users of phonograms, would diminish the returns to authors. This was because the same user would be paying both authors and performers and/or producers of phonograms and/or broadcasting organizations and would therefore be unprepared to increase the total amount he expended. Sometimes called the 'cake theory',[86] because of its assumption that there was only one 'cake' to be divided between the increased number of rights owners, this was a difficult question to resolve, although in practice it does not appear that authors' incomes have been reduced following the recognition of neighbouring rights.[87]

Several provisions were inserted in the Rome Convention to take account of **19.20**
the objections described above. The most important of these is article 1 which provides as follows:

> Protection granted under this Convention shall leave intact and shall in no way affect the protection of copyright in literary and artistic works. Consequently, no provision of this Convention may be interpreted as prejudicing such protection.

As a statement of principle, this is clear enough: nothing under the Rome Convention is to be interpreted as affecting the legal situation of copyright owners. In a sense, this may seem superfluous as the Convention, which does not deal with authors' rights, could not affect these rights. Nonetheless, it serves

[84] Thus, in 1979, the Intergovernmental Committee noted that, since 1961, as many as fifty-one countries had given protection to one or more of the beneficiaries of the Convention and twenty-four of these countries had done so for the first time: Report of the Intergovernmental Committee of the Rome Convention 1979, Annexe 1, para 15 of Document ILO/WIPO/UNESCO/ICR/SCI/IMP/5 in [1979] *Copyright* 105. See also WIPO, *Legal Protection of Phonograms, Summary Tables* (1979).

[85] Masouyé (1978), 17; Stewart (n 1 above), 226.

[86] Stewart (n 1 above), 192, 226.

[87] This was the view of the Intergovernmental Committee in the report referred to in n 84 above, at para 28.

as a reminder to national legislation that, in providing for neighbouring rights protection, this should not be done in such a way as to affect the existence of authors' rights.[88] Thus, to quote the general report of Kaminstein to the Rome Conference:

> ... it is clear that whenever, by virtue of the copyright law, the authorization of the author is necessary for the reproduction or other use of his work, the need for this authorization is not affected by the Convention.[89]

On the other hand, it does not appear that article 1 is concerned with the effects of neighbouring rights protection on the economic interests, as distinct from the legal rights, of copyright owners. Thus, the exercise of a neighbouring right may frustrate the exercise of an author's right (as in the example of the concert pianist given above), or, more importantly, it may reduce the remuneration otherwise earned by the copyright owner (the 'cake theory'). This was a strong concern of the French and Italian delegations at the Rome Conference, which proposed that article 1 should be amended so as to state that the protection granted under the Convention should not affect 'the exercise of that right [ie the copyright] over the work performed, recorded or broadcast'.[90] While these delegations stated that their proposal was only to be applied in extreme cases,[91] it was opposed by a number of other delegations which argued that it might render ineffective those provisions of the Convention requiring the authorization of the performer, recorder, or broadcaster.[92] This was on the basis that, under the Franco-Italian amendment, it might be argued that requiring the consent of these other parties could be considered as 'affecting the exercise' of the rights of the copyright owner, as, for example, where a composer had already consented to the recording of his work.[93] Finally, the Franco-Italian amendment was rejected by a decisive margin[94] and the following statement was inserted in the general report to make it clear that both sets of rights were to exist alongside each other:

> ... when, by virtue of this Convention, the consent of the performer, recorder, or broadcaster is necessary, the need for his consent does not disappear because authorization by the author is also necessary.[95]

This, then, acknowledges the possibility that the exercise of rights under the Rome Convention may prejudice the economic interests of copyright owners. On the other hand, it must be stated that the instances where a neighbouring

[88] *Records of the Diplomatic Conference* (n 24 above), 38.
[89] ibid.
[90] ibid, 205 (CDR/15).
[91] ibid, 104 (Puget, France, summary records of the proceedings).
[92] ibid, 102ff (the FRG, the UK, Austria, the Netherlands).
[93] ibid, 38 (report of Kaminstein).
[94] ibid, 106 (rejected by nineteen votes to ten, with five abstentions).
[95] ibid, 38.

right is actually used to block the exercise of an author's right will be rare and of marginal importance. Furthermore, there does not seem to be any evidence supporting the existence of the 'cake theory', persuasive as it may sound in theory.[96] The net effect is that the practical detriment that the recognition of neighbouring rights may have on the economic interests of copyright owners is probably insignificant, although this will always be an area for argument. Furthermore, as both are concerned, in different ways, with the exploitation of literary and artistic works, they have far more in common than not, particularly in the area of enforcement, and co-operation is far more mutually beneficial than competition. In this regard, the period following the adoption of the Rome Convention saw a number of important endeavours by both sets of rights owners to improve and extend the scope and effectiveness of their respective rights.[97] In the 1990s, these efforts culminated in the adoption of a new and separate treaty, the WPPT (see para 19.34 below).

Several other provisions of the Rome Convention provide for a direct link between the signatories to the Rome Convention and the Berne and the Universal Copyright Conventions. These are article 23, which deals with signature and deposit, and article 24, which deals with ratification and accession. The basic position under both provisions is that states that sign, ratify, or accede to the Convention must comply with two cumulative conditions: (i) they must have been invited to the Rome Conference (whether or not they attended) or be a member state of the United Nations, and (ii) must be a party to the UCC or a member of the Berne Union. As to the first of these requirements, the following states were invited to the Conference: members of UNESCO, the ILO, and the Berne Union and parties to the UCC.[98] As to the second requirement, there were two opposing schools of thought at the Conference as to the need for a link with the two copyright conventions. Those states which were against this argued that the Rome Convention should be open to any country whatsoever.[99] However, proponents of the opposite view argued that, as the use of literary and artistic works was usually implied in the work of performers, recorders, and broadcasters, it was logical to establish a link between the two major copyright **19.21**

[96] See n 86 above.

[97] eg the Report of the Group of Experts on Unauthorized Private Copying of Recordings, Broadcasts and Printed Matter (Geneva, 4–8 June 1984): [1984] *Copyright* 280; the WIPO Forum on the Piracy of Broadcasts and the Printed Word (Geneva, 16–18 Mar 1983): [1983] *Copyright* 159; and the Subcommittees of the Executive Committee of the Berne Union, of the Intergovernmental Committee of the UCC and of the Intergovernmental Committee of the Rome Convention on Television by Cable (Geneva, 5–7 Dec 1983), Annotated Principles of Protection of Authors, Performers, Producers of Phonograms and Broadcasting in Connection with the Distribution of Phonograms by Cable: [1984] *Copyright* 131.

[98] *Records of the Diplomatic Conference* (n 24 above), 54 (report of Kaminstein).

[99] ibid.

conventions and a convention on 'neighbouring rights', that is, rights neighbouring on copyright.[100] Thus, it was said that it would be inequitable for performers, recorders, and broadcasters to enjoy international protection by virtue of the new convention, while the works they use might be denied protection in that country because it was not a party to either copyright convention.[101] After further debate,[102] a majority of the Conference voted for the establishment of the link that is now contained in articles 23 and 24.[103]

C. The Phonograms Convention

(1) Background

19.22 One of the striking phenomena of the 1960s was the huge increase in the use of discs and cassettes and the opportunity that this offered for unscrupulous operators to reap huge profits from the clandestine copying and sale of recordings that had been lawfully made.[104] The extent of this piracy differed from country to country, but by the end of the decade was causing large losses to the legitimate phonogram industry. These losses also flowed on to the authors and performers of the works recorded. Damage was further caused to all these parties, either directly or indirectly, through the practice of 'bootlegging' where pirates made their own unauthorized recordings of live performances.[105] Copyright owners had legal protection against these activities under both national laws and the international conventions, although enforcement of these rights was obviously another matter. On the other hand, the legal position of phonogram producers, who were the most directly affected group, was weaker. They were not covered by the copyright conventions and their entitlement to neighbouring rights protection was only slowly being recognized under national legislation. While their right to reproduce their recordings was now enshrined in the Rome Convention, this did not extend to the importation and unauthorized distribution of phonograms which were often the most damaging activities of pirates. Furthermore, the membership of the Rome Convention was slow in growing: by 1971 there were only eleven parties to it and, of these, the UK and Germany (meaning here the FRG) were the only ones with a significant phonographic industry.[106] In addition, as noted above (see para 19.21), the Rome Convention was only open to states which were parties to either the UCC or Berne

[100] ibid, 90 (Czechoslovakia, Cuba, Mauritania: summary records of the proceedings).
[101] ibid, 55 (report of Kaminstein).
[102] ibid. [103] ibid, 55, 90.
[104] See generally G Davies, *Piracy of Phonograms*, 2nd edn (1986).
[105] Stewart (n 1 above), 257. [106] [1971] *Copyright* 12.

Convention. However, the market for phonograms was not confined to these countries and the sources of pirated copies were to be found in many non-Berne and non-UCC countries. As Masouyé points out: 'The fight against record piracy required the collaboration of as many countries as possible on a world-wide scale.'[107] This state of affairs therefore led the phonographic industry to press for the adoption of a new international treaty that was specifically directed at the problem of record piracy. This request was first made at the Committees of Experts that met in 1970 in order to prepare for the revisions of the Berne and Universal Copyright Conventions that took place in 1971.[108] It was sympathetically received and thereafter events moved rapidly. Under the auspices of WIPO and UNESCO, a Committee of Governmental Experts met in Paris in March 1971[109] and produced a draft convention of thirteen articles which was then adopted at a full diplomatic conference held in Geneva in October 1971.[110] The speed with which this was done was exceptional in the area of intellectual property conventions. The new convention entered into force on 18 April 1973 and the number of parties has increased at a steady rate: by the beginning of 1986 (when the first edition of this book was finalized) there were thirty-nine states that were party to it[111] and, as at 15 April 2005, there were seventy-three members. As will be seen below, its provisions have now been largely overshadowed by those contained in the TRIPs Agreement (see paras 19.27ff).

(2) The provisions of the Convention[112]

Although the Convention, as its name indicates, is concerned only with the rights of producers of phonograms, the increased protection which it seeks to **19.23**

[107] C Masouyé, *Guide to the Rome Convention and to the Phonograms Convention* (1981), 93.

[108] [1970] *Copyright* 160.

[109] See report in [1971] *Copyright* 54. See further Stewart (n 1 above), 238.

[110] [1971] *Copyright* 240 and, for the records of proceedings, see WIPO, *Records of the International Conference of States on the Protection of Phonograms, Geneva, 18 to 19 October 1971* (1972).

[111] Argentina, Australia, Austria, Barbados, Brazil, Chile, Costa Rica, Czechoslovakia, Denmark, Ecuador, Egypt, El Salvador, Fiji, Finland, France, the FRG, Guatemala, Holy See, Hungary, India, Israel, Italy, Japan, Kenya, Luxembourg, Mexico, Monaco, New Zealand, Peru, Paraguay, Panama, Norway, Spain, Sweden, the UK, the USA, Uruguay, Venezuela, and Zaire: [1986] *Copyright* 10.

[112] See generally, Masouyé (1978), 94ff; Stewart (n 1 above), ch 9; Davies (n 104 above), 36ff; Nordemann et al (1977), 435ff; Desbois et al (1976), 351ff; V De Sanctis, 'Some General Considerations on the Recent Geneva Convention for the Protection of Phonograms' [1972] *Copyright* 111; A Kaminstein, 'The Phonogram Convention' (1972) *Bull Cop Soc USA* 175; C Masouyé, 'A New International Convention on the Protection of Phonograms' [1972] *EBU Legal Rev* 59; S Stewart, 'The Geneva Convention for the Protection of Phonograms' Copyright' [1973] *Copyright* 100; E Ulmer, 'The Convention for the Protection of Producers of Phonograms' (1972) 3 *IIC* 317.

ensure must inevitably be to the long-term advantage of authors and copyright owners whose works are incorporated in phonograms. In any case, article 7 seeks to underline the fact that the Convention is not intended to affect existing rights by providing that it is to be in no way interpreted 'to limit or prejudice the protection otherwise secured to authors, to performers, to producers of phonograms or to broadcasting organizations under any domestic law or international agreement'. Unlike the older intellectual property conventions, the Phonograms Convention is not based on the principle of national treatment but is centred on one fundamental obligation contained in article 2. Under this, each contracting state is required to protect producers of phonograms who are nationals of other contracting states against 'the making of duplicates without the consent of the producer and against the importation of such duplicates, provided that any such making or importation is for the purpose of distribution to the public, and against the distribution of such duplicates to the public'. The means by which this obligation is to be implemented are left to each contracting state, as long as they include protection by one or more of the following means: the grant of a copyright or other specific right, unfair competition laws, or penal sanctions.[113] The length of this protection is a minimum of twenty years from the end of the year in which the sounds embodied in the phonogram were first fixed or the phonogram was first published.[114] In the event that the domestic law of a contracting state requires compliance with formalities, this is satisfied by the fixation of a ℗ symbol and a notice of the year of first publication and the name of the producer (if not otherwise apparent).[115] Where protection is conferred by the grant of a copyright or other specific right or by means of penal sanctions, similar limitations may be allowed as are permitted in the case of the protection of literary and artistic works.[116] However, the imposition of compulsory licences is permitted only in the case of duplication for use solely for the purpose of teaching or scientific research and is subject to territorial restrictions and an obligation to pay equitable remuneration.[117] No intergovernmental committee is established, as under the Rome Convention, but WIPO carries out the functions of collecting and publishing information relating to the protection of phonograms and carrying out studies and other services related to this question.[118] No provision is made for revision of the Convention, since, as Masouyé says, its object, the elimination of record piracy, is 'permanent'.[119] As it was desired to obtain the adherence of as many states as possible to this object, the

[113] Phonograms Convention, art 3. The words 'other specific right' refer to 'neighbouring right': see further Masouyé (1978), 101.

[114] Phonograms Convention, art 4.

[115] ibid, art 5.

[116] ibid, art 6.

[117] ibid.

[118] ibid, art 8. This is to be done in co-operation with UNESCO and ILO: art 8(3).

[119] Masouyé (1978), 91.

Convention is open to any state to join.[120] In this respect, however, it should be noted the activity of 'bootlegging' lies outside its scope, as do videograms which are now the subject of extensive piracy. However, the exclusion of the latter from the Phonograms Convention is logical, as videograms fall within the category of cinematographic works and therefore within the scope of copyright protection.[121]

D. The Satellites Convention

The protection of literary and artistic works under the Berne Convention when they are transmitted via satellite has already been discussed in Chapter 12 above. During the late 1960s, broadcasting organizations also began to look for protection of their broadcasts when transmitted by satellite.[122] This did not so much involve questions of copyright, as many of the programmes transmitted in this way were not subject to copyright protection but were items such as live sporting events, news reports, and the like. Nonetheless, these were still vulnerable to piracy at the hands of unauthorized parties who received and distributed the signals that had been transmitted. The extent to which such transmissions might receive protection under the Rome Convention was unclear. As under the Berne Convention, the answer to this question depended upon the interpretation which was attached to the word 'broadcasting'. On the narrow view, transmissions via point-to-point and distribution satellites were excluded, as there was no direct reception by the public, although transmissions by direct broadcasting satellites would be included.[123] On the broader view, all transmissions by satellite would be covered, as their ultimate aim or end use is their reception by the public.[124] This uncertain legal situation therefore led the broadcasting industry to seek more explicit protection against the piracy of their satellite transmissions of programmes. Work at an international level was begun by BIRPI which, in 1968, convened a working group of experts.[125] UNESCO also convened a Committee of Governmental Experts for this purpose in 1969,[126] and thereafter both organizations co-ordinated their activities through **19.24**

[120] Phonograms Convention, art 9(2).

[121] See further Stewart (n 1 above), 258.

[122] ibid, 270.

[123] ibid, 270–1. See further G Straschnov, 'The Broadcast-Satellite Service in Private Law' [1977] *EBU Legal Rev* 97; E Ulmer, 'Protection of Authors in Relation to the Transmission via Satellite of Broadcast Programmes' [1977] *RIDA* 4.

[124] ibid.

[125] Working Group on Copyright Problems of Satellite Communications (Geneva, 14–16 Oct 1968): [1968] *Copyright* 230.

[126] [1970] *Copyright* 57.

a series of joint meetings.[127] These culminated in a diplomatic conference that was held in Brussels in 1974.[128] This meeting adopted a new multilateral convention that is usually known as the 'Satellites Convention' or the 'Brussels Convention', its full title being the 'Convention Relating to the Distribution of Programme-Carrying Signals Transmitted by Satellite'.

(1) Provisions of the Convention[129]

19.25 The Convention does not create a new kind of intellectual property right, as is the case with broadcasts under the Rome Convention. Its sole concern is with the protection of programme-carrying signals transmitted via satellite by broadcasting organizations. To this end, the obligation which is cast upon each contracting state is to take adequate measures to prevent the distribution on or from its territory of any programme-carrying signal transmitted by satellite.[130] This obligation exists with respect to the signals of any broadcasting organization which is a national of another contracting state (known as the 'originating organization').[131] The words 'take adequate measures' leave it to each state to determine for itself how it will give effect to this obligation. For example, this could be done by the grant of a specific right, but other means such as administrative measures or penal sanctions are equally possible.[132] The word 'programme' in this context covers both copyright and non-copyright material,[133] while 'signal' means simply 'an electronically-generated carrier capable of transmitting programmes'.[134] The duration of protection is left to national legislation[135] and certain exceptions relating to such matters as educational use, news reporting, and the like are permitted.[136] Transmissions via direct broadcasting satellites are also excluded from the scope of the Convention.[137]

---

[127] The following meetings of Governmental Experts took place under the auspices of WIPO and UNESCO: Lausanne-Duchy, 21–30 Apr 1971 ([1971] *Copyright* 102); Paris, 9–11 May 1972 ([1972] *Copyright* 142); and Nairobi, 2–11 July 1973 ([1973] *Copyright* 147).

[128] [1974] *Copyright* 143. See also the *Actes de la Conférence internationale d'États sur la distribution de signaux porteurs de programmes transmis par satellite, Bruxelles, 6–21 mai 1974* (1977), 31 (also published in English).

[129] See generally Desbois et al (1976), 372ff; Stewart (n 1 above), ch 9; R Dittrich, 'The Brussels Satellite Convention' [1974] *EBU Legal Rev* 60; G Boytha, 'The Draft Convention Adopted at Nairobi Relating to the Distribution of Programme-Carrying Signals Transmitted by Satellite Seen from the Angle of the Protection of Authors' Rights' [1974] *Copyright* 70.

[130] Satellites Convention, art 2(1).

[131] ibid. See also the definition of 'originating organization' in art 1(vi).

[132] [1974] *Copyright* 267, 277 (report of B Ringer, *rapporteur général*, para 79).

[133] Satellites Convention, art 1(ii).

[134] ibid, art 1(i). [135] ibid, art 2(2). [136] ibid, art 4. [137] ibid, art 3.

(2) Relationship to the Berne Convention

In formal terms the protection granted by the Berne Convention to authors cannot be affected by the provisions of the Satellites Convention which is concerned with quite a different subject matter. The same is true of the rights protected by the Rome Convention and this position is confirmed by article 6 of the Satellites Convention, which provides as follows: **19.26**

> This Convention shall in no way be interpreted to limit or prejudice the protection secured to authors, performers, producers of phonograms, or broadcasting organizations, under any domestic law or international agreement.

As with the Rome Convention, however, it is possible to see that conflicts may arise with respect to the exercise of rights under the Berne Convention where the protection accorded under the Satellites Convention is given by means of the grant of an exclusive right. In such a case, it would be necessary for a would-be distributor of any programme-carrying signal to seek two sets of authorizations, with the danger that one may be refused and the other given, or vice versa. In practice, however, such conflicts will probably be of marginal importance only and both right owners will usually share the same concern to exploit and enforce their respective rights. Thus, co-operation rather than rivalry is more likely to be the case. Furthermore, as no intergovernmental organ is established under the Satellites Convention, the progress of the latter is monitored by the Berne Assembly and Executive Committee which encourage ratifications and accessions to the Convention.[138] In addition, the expenses of the Convention are met from the budget of the Berne Union.[139] The Convention entered into force on 25 August 1979, but as at 1 January 1986 (when the first edition of this book was finalized) only eleven states were party to it;[140] by 15 October 2004, this had increased to twenty-six states.[141]

E. The TRIPs Agreement

(1) In general

Chronologically, this is the next stage in the growing protection of neighbouring rights that began with the Rome, Phonograms, and Satellites Conventions. The neighbouring rights obligations in TRIPs are contained in article 14: performers **19.27**

[138] A Bogsch, 'The First Hundred Years of the Berne Convention for the Protection of Literary and Artistic Works' [1986] *Copyright* 291, 326.

[139] ibid.

[140] Austria, the FRG, Italy, Kenya, Mexico, Morocco, Nicaragua, Panama, the USA, and Yugoslavia: [1986] *Copyright* 10.

[141] www.wipo.int/treaties.

(article 14(1)), producers of phonograms (article 14(2)), broadcasting organizations (article 14(3)), rental rights for phonograms (article 14(4)), terms of protection (article 14(5)), and exceptions and limitations (article 14(6)). These provisions build on and supplement those under Rome, but there are no corresponding definitions of terms, for example, 'performer', 'phonogram', 'producer of phonogram', and so on.

(2) **Performers (article 14(1))**

19.28 This is concerned with fixations of performances on phonograms. In the same way as article 7 of the Rome Convention, article 14(1) requires that performers should have the 'possibility of preventing the following acts when undertaken without their authorisation: the fixation of their unfixed performance and the reproduction of such fixation'. It is further provided that performers should have the 'possibility of preventing' certain unauthorized other acts: broadcasting their live performance by wireless means and the communication to the public of their live performance. This covers the same ground as article 7(1)(a), (b), and (c) of the Rome Convention, even to the extent of retaining the Rome formulation of the 'possibility of preventing', an expression which is sufficiently flexible to allow implementation through other laws, such as unfair competition or even criminal sanctions.

(3) **Producers of phonograms (article 14(2))**

19.29 This follows article 10 of the Rome Convention (and article 2 of the Phonograms Convention), in providing that phonogram producers are to have the right to authorize or prohibit the direct or indirect reproduction of their phonograms.

(4) **Broadcasting organizations (article 14(3))**

19.30 This largely follows article 13 of the Rome Convention, in providing that such organizations are to have the right to prohibit the unauthorized fixation, reproduction of fixations, and rebroadcasting by wireless means of broadcasts as well as the communication to the public of television broadcasts of the same. However, there is a qualification to the effect that where a member does not grant such rights to broadcasting organizations, they must provide owners of copyright in the 'subject matter of broadcasts', ie what is broadcast, with 'the possibility of preventing the above acts, subject to the provisions of the Berne Convention (1971)'. Thus, there appears to be no obligation to accord these rights to broadcasting organizations where a member already accords copyright protection to the subject matter broadcast, ie the works and other subject matter broadcast. This might also include any copyright that is given by the member to the broadcast itself, as distinct from rights that are given to the broadcasting organization itself. According to one commentator, article 14(3) is the 'result of a compromise' between those countries which already accorded protection to broadcasting organizations as per article 13 of the Rome Convention, and those which did not.[142] Protection for broadcasting organizations was therefore accorded in this qualified way under the TRIPs Agreement, while the WIPO treaties of 1996 left the question aside. As noted below, since 1996 WIPO has been hosting discussions and meetings on the establishment of a third treaty on the rights of broadcasting organizations.

(5) **Rental rights** (article 14(4))

This applies the commercial rental right accorded under article 11 to computer programs and cinematographic works *mutatis mutandis* to producers of phonograms and any other right holders in phonograms 'as determined in a Member's law'. Thus, if a member's law accords protection to performers with respect to performances fixed in phonograms, they would be entitled to such a commercial rental right under the rubric of 'any other right holder', although presumably the way in which they could exercise this right would be 'as determined' in that member's law. Another group of right holders that would presumably be given such rights would be the copyright owners of works that are embodied in the phonogram, but again whether this is so, and the way in which it occurs, would be a matter for the member's law. **19.31**

The second part of article 14(4) contains a grandfathering clause in favour of countries which, at the time of the entry into force of the TRIPs Agreement (15 April 1994) had in force systems of equitable remuneration of right holders in respect of the rental of phonograms,[143] subject to the requirement that the maintenance of such a system is dependent upon the commercial rental of phonograms not giving rise to the material impairment of the exclusive reproduction rights of the right holders (see further the discussion of 'material impairment' at para 19.59 below).[144]

(6) **Terms of protection** (article 14(5))

The minima here are fifty years for both performers and producers of phonograms: fifty years from the end of the calendar year in which the fixation was made or the performance took place. In the case of the protection given under **19.32**

[142] D Gervais, *The TRIPS Agreement: Drafting History and Analysis*, 2nd edn (2004) ('Gervais (2003)'), 160–1.

[143] An example of such a country is Japan: ibid, 161.

[144] See further ibid, 140.

article 14(3), this is for a minimum of twenty years from the end of the calendar year in which the broadcast took place.

(7) **Exceptions and limitations (article 14(6))**

19.33 There is no obligation under the TRIPs Agreement for members to apply the provisions of the Rome Convention to performers, phonogram producers, and broadcasting organizations: under article 3(1) members are required only to apply rights accorded under the TRIPs Agreement itself. These are contained in article 14(1)–(5): as seen above, these parallel, and in some respects go beyond, the requirements under Rome.

The matter of exceptions and limitations to these rights is dealt with in two places in the TRIPs Agreement, where they are tied to the requirements of Rome as follows:

(a) Article 3(1)

This provision requires national treatment, and specifies that this is 'subject to the exceptions already provided in . . . the Rome Convention . . .'. The reference here is to article 15 of Rome (discussed at paras 19.11ff above).

(b) Article 14(6)

This provision also deals with exceptions as follows:

> Any member may, in relation to the rights conferred under paragraphs 1, 2 and 3 provide for such conditions, limitations, exceptions and reservations to the extent permitted by the Rome Convention . . .

This appears to add nothing to the general obligation in article 3(1), but note the restriction in article 15(2) with respect to compulsory licences (see para 19.16 above).

Accordingly, members can only provide for limitations and exceptions only within the categories listed in article 15(1) and (2) of the Rome Convention.

The second sentence of article 14(6) adopts *mutatis mutandis* the provisions of article 18 of the Berne Convention, with respect to the application of the TRIPs Agreement to the rights of performers and producers of phonograms in phonograms. No reference is made here to protection given to broadcasts and broadcasting organizations under article 14(3). Nor is there any reservation allowed in respect of some rights, as in the case of moral rights of performers under article 5 of the WPPT (see para 19.74 below).

F. The WIPO Performances and Phonograms Treaty

The greatest achievement in the international protection of neighbouring rights thus far is to be found in the WPPT, which entered into force on 20 May 2002 and, as at 17 January 2005, had forty-nine contracting parties. Something of the origins of this treaty has already been recounted in Chapter 4 above (see para 4.30), and detailed accounts of its origins and contents are to be found elsewhere.[145] Accordingly, the following review is intended merely to outline the principal features of the WPPT and to consider its relation to the Berne and Rome Conventions and the WCT. **19.34**

(1) Preliminary matters

(a) Origins

As described above at para 4.18, the proposal for a separate international agreement dealing with performers and phonograms arose from the initial Berne Protocol proposals of 1991. It will be recalled that one of the decisions reached at this stage was to bifurcate the revision process, but to conduct each in parallel, with meetings of the two committees of experts being held back to back. This meant that, while the traditional distinction between authors' and neighbouring rights was maintained, most issues were, in practice, considered together, and the final treaty language proposed for both drafts was very similar so far as many of the substantive obligations that were proposed, as well as with respect to the administrative and final clauses. At the 1996 Diplomatic Conference itself, both sets of treaty provisions were considered by the same committees: Main Committee I in the case of substantive provisions and Main Committee II in the case of the administrative and final clauses, and hence the records of discussions often do not distinguish between those relating to the WPPT as distinct from the WCT. Nonetheless, as the following examination reveals, there are some distinctive, if not unusual, aspects about the WPPT. **19.35**

(b) Title and preamble

In the discussions of the Committee of Experts leading up to the preparation of the draft treaty, it was referred to as the 'Possible Instrument', a term which was thought to be too generic an expression for the official title. Accordingly, the draft treaty submitted to the Diplomatic Conference in December 1996 was entitled 'Treaty for the Protection of the Rights of Performers and Producers **19.36**

[145] M Ficsor, *The Law of Copyright and the Internet* (2001) ('Ficsor (2001)'), ch 8; J Reinbothe and S von Lewinski, *The WIPO Treaties 1996* (2002) ('Reinbothe and von Lewinski (2002)'), pp 232ff.

of Phonograms' on the basis that this was 'an accurate characterisation of the contents of this proposed Treaty'.[146] The present title, which refers simply to the 'WIPO Performances and Phonograms Treaty', derived from a proposal of the then WIPO Director General, Dr Bogsch, and was adopted by the Conference after meeting with consensus during informal consultations with delegates.[147]

The objectives of the Treaty are contained in the preamble as follows:

> *Desiring* to develop and maintain the protection of the rights of performers and producers of phonograms in a manner as effective and uniform as possible,
>
> *Recognizing* the need to introduce new international rules in order to provide adequate solutions to the questions raised by economic, social, cultural and technological developments,
>
> *Recognizing* the profound impact of the development and convergence of information and communication technologies on the production and use of performances and phonograms,
>
> *Recognizing* the need to maintain a balance between the rights of performers and producers of phonograms and the larger public interest, particularly education, research and access to information,
>
> *Have agreed* as follows:

The first three of these are in the same form as in the draft treaty presented to the Diplomatic Conference;[148] the fourth, concerned with the question of balance, was added in a draft prepared by the chairman of Main Committee I (J Liedes) on 12 December 1996 and approved by the Plenary of the Conference with no substantive debate on 20 December 1996.[149]

These objectives will clearly be relevant to the task of treaty interpretation, so the following points can be briefly noted. The first recital reflects the language of the preamble to the Paris Act of the Berne Convention, but applied here to performers and phonogram producers. The adjectives 'effective' and 'uniform' underline the quality of the protection required by the Treaty, while the reference to 'develop and maintain' indicate that this protection should not be at a lower level than that already required under earlier instruments such as the Rome or Phonograms Conventions.[150]

The second recital makes the obvious point that new international rules are required in order to provide 'adequate solutions' having regard to 'manifold developments that call for improved protection in the field covered by the

---

[146] *Records* 1996, vol I, 240 (Document CRNR/DC/5).

[147] ibid, 776, para 984 (summary minutes of Main Committee I); 627 (adoption by Plenary Session).

[148] *Records* 1996, vol I, 240 (DOC CRNR/DC/5).

[149] ibid, 627.

[150] Reinbothe and von Lewinski (2002), 234, para 4.

proposed Treaty'.[151] Reinbothe and von Lewinski also note that, by contrast with the corresponding recital in the WCT preamble, there is no reference here to the need to 'clarify the interpretation of existing rules'.[152] This omission underlines the fact that the WPPT is a free-standing treaty that does not seek, like the WCT or the TRIPs Agreement, to build upon what has gone before in earlier treaties such as Berne. While the WPPT certainly has a subject-matter link to the Rome and Phonograms Conventions, it is self-contained and does not depend upon the earlier instruments.

The third recital calls attention to the wider sphere within which the Treaty is to be applied, namely its connection to the 'evolution of the overall environment of the intellectual property system: the accelerating development and convergence of information and communication technologies'. Thus, the commentary to the draft treaty noted that this evolution extended even to the convergence of industry structures and content provision, and the profound effect that this had on the production and distribution of work by performers and phonogram producers. According to the commentary, the proposed treaty was to be seen as part of a 'series of simultaneously published draft Treaties which could be described as "Global Information Infrastructure Treaties" in the field of copyright and rights related to copyright'.[153] Insofar as the WCT and WPPT were to be seen as the first tranche of this series of treaties, subsequent proposals to fill out the gaps, for example, with respect to databases, audiovisual performances, and broadcasts, have yet to be consummated (see further paras 19.82ff below).

The fourth recital, although only added during the Conference, reflects the same recital in the WCT and acknowledges the now explicit recognition in both treaties that there is a wider public interest to be balanced against the private interests of both performers and phonogram producers. Neither treaty therefore is to be interpreted solely from the perspective of performers and/or phonogram producers. At the same time, this 'balancing' factor will need to be interpreted with reference to the obligations under article 1 (see para 19.37 below).

(c) Relation to other conventions

This is dealt with in article 1, which provides three important rules that will **19.37**
affect its interpretation. First, nothing in the WPPT is to derogate from obligations that contracting parties have to each other under the Rome Convention (article 1(1)). As in the case of the UCC (see paras 18.27ff above), this could be termed the 'Rome Safeguard Clause', although the use of the term 'obligations'

151 *Records* 1996, vol I, 240 (DOC CRNR/DC/5).
152 Reinbothe and von Lewinski (2002), 234, para 6.
153 *Records* 1996, vol I, 240 (DOC CRNR/DC/5).

is nicely nuanced here. It will be recalled that obligations under Rome may be modified or reduced by parties making reservations under articles 16 and 17 of that Convention. But these modified 'obligations' will almost invariably be at a lower level than those required by the WPPT, with the result that, even though the latter may require enhanced levels of protection, it will hardly be possible to say that this represents a 'derogation' of the obligations that Rome contracting parties have towards each other.[154]

Second, protection granted under the WPPT is to 'leave intact and shall in no way affect' the protection of copyright in literary and artistic works' (article 1(2)); in particular, no provision of the Treaty is to be interpreted 'as prejudicing its interpretation'. This provision is amplified by the following agreed statement that was adopted by the Diplomatic Conference at the same time as the Treaty:

> It is understood that Article 1(2) clarifies the relationship between rights in phonograms under this Treaty and copyright in works embodied in the phonograms. In cases where authorization is needed from both the author of a work embodied in the phonogram and a performer or producer owning rights in the phonogram, the need for the authorization of the author does not cease to exist because the authorization of the performer or producer is also required, and vice versa.
>
> It is further understood that nothing in Article 1(2) precludes a Contracting Party from providing exclusive rights to a performer or producer of phonograms beyond those required to be provided under this Treaty.

The first of these paragraphs underlines the separate character of the rights subsisting in a phonogram, namely those of the authors of works embodied therein, those of any performer whose performance of those works is also embodied therein, and those of the phonogram producer itself. None can proceed without the authorization of the other: no primacy is accorded to any one as against the others. The second paragraph underlines the fact that the obligations in the WPPT embody minimum standards of protection and parties are free to accord greater protection if they so desire.

Finally, the WPPT is to have no connection with and is not to prejudice any rights or obligations under any other treaties (article 1(3)). Of particular relevance here would be the Phonograms Convention, but it should be noted that the TRIPs Agreement also has limited provisions dealing with the protection of performers and phonograms (see further paras 19.28–19.29, and 19.31). There might also otherwise be an argument that the WPPT is in some way linked to

[154] Reinbothe and von Lewinski (2002) at 241, para 9, suggest that stronger protection is, in fact, a derogation, but, with respect, this seems a misdescription in that any additional protection required by the WPPT will be an augmentation of the obligations required under Rome, rather than a taking away or detracting from ('derogation').

the WCT, by virtue of their common provisions and common drafting history: such an inference, whatever it might mean, is therefore excluded by the opening words of article 1(3). A further question is whether this paragraph applies to the Rome Convention, but the better view must be that 'any other treaties' must mean 'any other treaties *apart from the Rome Convention*' on the basis that the Rome Convention is already the subject of a specific provision under article 1(1) (see above). If that is so, the consequence also follows that the WPPT can be regarded as a 'special agreement' under article 22 of Rome (this is in similar terms to article 20 of the Berne Convention).[155] This will only have effect among those WPPT members that are Rome members (the WPPT imposes no eligibility requirement in this regard, apart from WIPO membership or acknowledged intergovernmental organization status, as to which see article 26). However, it is difficult to see what such 'special agreement' status under article 22 of Rome will add to the obligation already imposed under article 1(1) of the WPPT: under article 22, any special agreement may grant more extensive rights to performers, phonogram producers, and broadcasting organizations or contain other provisions not contrary to Rome. Nothing in article 22 prevents a special agreement dealing with only one or two of the subject matters dealt with in the Rome Convention: the fact that the WPPT accords greater protection with respect to only some of the subject matter protected under Rome, ie phonograms and audio performances as distinct from audio-visual ones, does not infringe the stipulations in article 22, so long as it does not limit the protection for the categories of subject matter that are excluded.

(2) General provisions

Matters of definition, eligibility for protection, and the obligation to accord national treatment are dealt with in articles 2, 3, and 4 respectively, and, for purposes of exposition, are better dealt with first before we consider the specific obligations applying with respect to performances and phonograms. **19.38**

(a) Definitions

A number of terms used in the WPPT are defined in article 2: 'performers', 'phonograms', 'fixation', 'producer of a phonogram', 'publication' (in relation to a fixed performance or phonogram), 'broadcasting', and 'communication to the public'. During the preparatory stages for the Diplomatic Conference, there was considerable discussion and consideration of definitional issues, beginning in 1993 with those drafted by WIPO for the Committee of Experts.[156] The **19.39**

---

[155] To similar effect, see Ficsor (2001), 591.
[156] INR/CE/1/2, referred to in *Records* 1996, vol I, 244, para 2.01.

draft treaty definitions that were submitted to the Diplomatic Conference, and that were largely adopted unchanged, had their origins in a February 1996 submission by Argentina.[157]

(b) 'Performers'

19.40 This is in similar terms to that in article 3(a) of the Rome Convention (see para 19.08 above), but is not limited to the acting, singing, etc of literary or artistic works alone, extending to 'expressions of folklore'. The latter expression is not defined in the Convention; nor is it the subject of any of the agreed statements appended to the Treaty. However, the protection of expressions of folklore has been a significant area of investigation by WIPO and UNESCO in recent years, together with the more general category of 'traditional knowledge'. As long ago as 1982, both WIPO and UNESCO developed a set of Model Provisions on the Protection of Expressions of Folklore Against Illicit Exploitation and other Prejudicial Actions, and section 2 of these provides that 'expressions of folklore' are understood as productions consisting of characteristic elements of the traditional artistic heritage developed and maintained by a community in the country or by individuals reflecting the traditional artistic expectations of such a community. The following list of illustrative examples of expressions of folklore is also provided:

- Expressions by words ('verbal'), such as folk tales, folk poetry, and riddles;
- Expressions by musical sounds ('musical'), such as folk songs and instrumental music;
- Expressions 'by action' (of the human body), such as 'folk dances, plays and artistic forms of rituals'; and
- Expressions incorporated in a material object ('tangible expressions'), such as 'drawings, paintings, carvings, sculptures, pottery, terra-cotta, mosaic, woodwork, metalware, jewelry, basket weaving, needlework, textiles, carpets, costumes; musical instruments; architectural forms'.

While the last of these categories, with the exception of living works of art (as to which, see further below), may not be relevant in the case of performers, the above definition provides a useful guide as to what may fall within the scope of performances of expressions of folklore for the purposes of the WPPT: certainly, the definition in the Model Provisions has been used as the basis for its work in this area by WIPO, as well as in national laws that have addressed the issue of protection of folklore.[158] It may also be the case that some performances of expressions of folklore will be protected, in any event, as performances of

[157] ibid.

[158] There is a body of useful material stored at the WIPO website: www.wipo.int/tk/en.

literary or artistic works where they have been reduced to some material form and where it is possible to identify clearly the authors.

Nonetheless, there are some possible gaps among the kind of performers that fall within the definition in article 2(a) of the WPPT. Notable among these are circus and variety performers, radio and television announcers, and sports participants. Obviously, each of these categories will be covered if they can be regarded as acting, singing, delivering, declaiming, playing in, interpreting, or otherwise performing literary or artistic works (in the form of a script or choreographic work) or expressions of folklore. In the event, however, that their performances are not so based, they will not be within the article 2(a) definition. In the case of circus and variety performers, this may be a significant omission, and it is worth noting that there is provision for the optional inclusion of such performers where they do not perform literary or artistic works under article 9 of the Rome Convention. In several of the drafts of article 2(a) of the WPPT that were submitted to the Diplomatic Conference, variety or circus performers were included,[159] but these were omitted from the final text that was drafted by the chairman of Main Committee I and submitted for adoption.[160] No specific explanation for this omission appears from the Conference records, but it is clear from this that variety or circus performers do not come within article 2(a) unless they happen to be performing works or expressions of folklore. In the case of radio or television announcers and commentators, the requirement of a script may often be readily met, but *ex tempore* interviews, sports commentaries, and 'chat shows' will not be so scripted, although the 'performance' values may nonetheless be quite high. Sports performances are, of course, in a category of their own, but are highly unlikely ever to involve performance of a literary or artistic work (despite rhapsodic references by commentators to 'poetry in motion' and 'an artist with the ball') or expressions of folklore (except in the highly unusual case of some ancient sporting event, such as Chinese horse archery or re-creations of the Greek Olympiads). In definitional terms, however, sports performances remain outside article 2(a) and would generally be excluded, in any event, from the protection offered by the WPPT which is limited to fixations of sounds.[161]

Some further points to be noted about the definition in article 2(a). First, the definition does not distinguish between individual and group performances. Accordingly, performances by orchestras, choirs, and other ensembles of **19.41**

[159] In particular, there were proposals by Peru and Argentina to this effect: see CRNR/DC/77 (13 Dec 1996) (Peru) (*Records* 1996, vol I, 495) and CRNR/DC/45 (11 Dec 1996) (Argentina) (*Records* 1996, vol I, 495).

[160] CNRN/DC/58 (12 Dec 1996), *Records* 1996, vol I, 451.

[161] A possible class of sports performers who would lose out here would be the 'grunters', 'screamers', and otherwise vocal contenders who are to be found in tennis, golf, and soccer.

performers will be covered, as much as individual performances. Under article 8 of the Rome Convention, however, this was a matter that was left largely to national laws to determine, at least so far as the way in which such joint performers were to be 'represented'.

Second, while it may be unlikely at first blush that an artistic work will be capable of performance, bear in mind that there are such things as 'living sculptures' to be seen in the main streets and public places of many WPPT countries and these can readily well be regarded as instances of acting, interpreting, or otherwise performing an artistic work. Another 'performance type' work that was well known in the late nineteenth century was the *tableau vivant* where groups of persons would dress up and depict themselves in a scene from a well-known painting or sculpture. These, equally, should be capable of being 'performers' within the meaning of article 2(a). On the other hand, they will not fall within the scope of protection offered by the Treaty which is limited to fixation of sounds of performances (see below).

Third, the activities by which performances occur are more extensive under article 2(a) of the WPPT than under the Rome Convention, and include 'interpretation'. However, it may be a moot point as to what this actually adds to the more directly descriptive verbs of acting, singing, declaiming, and playing: each of the foregoing will clearly also involve the activity of 'interpretation' in any event.

Finally, there is no reference here as to whether the performance should take place in front of a live audience or not. Presumably, the definition is apt to cover a performance that takes place when the performer is on his or her own, for example, carrying out a private rehearsal or performing in the privacy of a broadcasting or recording studio.

(c) 'Fixation'

19.42 Although defined in article 2(c), this term is critical in the definition of 'phonogram' in article 2(b) and is considered first. 'Fixation' is defined as the 'embodiment of sounds, or of the representations thereof, from which they can be perceived, reproduced or communicated through a device'. According to the commentary in the Basic Proposal, 'embodiment' refers to the 'material form of the fixation',[162] and the reference to a machine or device was made because this was the only way in which the 'perceiving, reproduction or communication' of the sounds could take place.[163] The Basic Proposal commentary also indicated that this definition was not intended to quantify or qualify the duration of the life of the embodiment necessary to result in fixation, ie there is no requirement

[162] Document CRNR/DC/5, in *Records* 1996, vol I, 246. [163] ibid.

here for permanency or stability and this is a matter left for national law to determine.[164] The limitation to fixations of 'sounds' also underlines the significant restriction on the scope of the WPPT in the exclusion of audio-visual performances—as large a point of difference between delegates to the WPPT Conference as it had been at the time of negotiation of the Rome Conference (see further para 19.08 above).[165]

(d) 'Phonogram'

This is defined in article 2(b) as 'the fixation of the sounds of a performance or of other sounds, or a representation of sounds, other than in the form of a fixation incorporated in a cinematographic or other audiovisual work'. There is also the following agreed statement: 'It is understood that the definition of phonogram in article 2(b) does not suggest that rights in the phonogram are in any way affected through their incorporation into a cinematographic or other audiovisual work.' The following points can be made about this definition, as supplemented by the agreed statement: **19.43**

1. The term 'fixation' is technology-neutral, in that it is not limited to particular forms of fixation such as discs, vinyl records, cylinders, etc—the forms in which phonograms have been historically embodied. In particular, it is apt to cover fixation in digital form.
2. The fixation may be of the sounds (not the images) of a performance or 'other sounds'. Presumably, the latter would cover fixations of sounds from nature (bird sounds, wind, thunder), street sounds and other public events that do not amount to performances, such as street interviews, sports events, a public demonstration or procession.
3. The fixation may also be of 'representations of sounds', ie this covers the case of phonograms produced using digital technology that fixes data that can be used to generate sounds by the use of the appropriate electronic equipment even though no 'real sounds' have yet been produced.[166] An early proposal to include the adjective 'digital' before 'representation' was omitted from the Basic Proposal, as adopted by the Diplomatic Conference, on the basis that this could be 'obsolete as technology evolves'.[167]
4. Cinematographic films and their soundtracks are excluded from the

---

[164] ibid.

[165] Note that the proposed definition in the Basic Proposal, however, left it open as to whether the term 'fixation' should be limited to sounds alone or should extend to 'sounds and images', both being put as alternatives in the draft for the Conference: Document CRNR/DC/5, in *Records* 1996, vol I, 246.

[166] ibid.

[167] ibid. This has been contained in a proposal by Argentina and in earlier versions prepared by WIPO.

definition, which is more explicit in this regard than the definition in article 3(b) of the Rome Convention which refers to 'any exclusively aural fixation of sounds . . .'.

5. At the same time, the agreed statement indicates a legal consequence where a phonogram is incorporated into a cinematographic or other audio-visual work, namely that this does not affect the rights in the phonogram.

(e) 'Producer of a phonogram'

19.44 This is the person or legal entity that 'takes the initiative and has the responsibility for the first fixation of the sounds of a performance or other sounds, or the representations of sounds' (article 2(d)). This is more expansive than the corresponding definition in article 3(c) of the Rome Convention under which the producer is the person or entity which 'first fixes' the sounds of the performance or other sounds. The expression 'takes the initiative and has the responsibility for . . .' indicates that this is the producer, that is, the person or entity that 'takes, the initiative, co-ordinates and assumes economic and other responsibility for the first fixation of a phonogram, regardless of the technology used'.[168] This might suggest that this is really the person or entity that has made the necessary investment or taken the entrepreneurial risk required for the production of the phonogram, but this is probably too narrow an interpretation. Thus, it should be noted that the adjective 'economic' appeared before 'responsibility' in a draft text of the WPPT prepared by the chairman of Main Committee I (J Liedes),[169] but this was deleted in the final text, which suggests that 'other' kinds of responsibility, for example, of a technical and even artistic kind, should be relevant in determining who or what is the 'producer of a phonogram'.[170]

A further point to note about the definition is the reference to 'first fixation' which indicates that work done on subsequent fixations, for example, digitizing or 'remastering' existing fixations of performances will not be a 'first fixation', regardless of the time, effort, and resources expended in 'corrections, noise removal and other such alterations'.[171] This will then remove outside the definition of 'producer' the fixations produced by those skilled individuals who make digital and 'cleaned up' versions of famous early recordings, for example, in the areas of opera, concert performances, and jazz.

(f) 'Publication'

19.45 This, again, is more detailed than the counterpart definition under article 3(d) of the Rome Convention which referred to the offering of copies of a

[168] Document CRNR/DC/58, *Records* 1996, vol I, 251 [169] ibid.

[170] See further Reinbothe and von Lewinski (2002), 251, para 15.

[171] Document CRNR/DC/58, *Records* 1996, vol I, 452.

phonogram to the public 'in reasonable quantity'. Under article 2(e) of the WPPT, publication of a 'fixed performance or of a phonogram' means the offering of copies thereof to the public with the consent of the right holder and provided that copies are 'offered to the public in reasonable quantity'. To this is appended the following agreed statement: 'As used in these Articles, the expressions "copies" and "original and copies" being subject to the right of distribution and the right of rental under the said Articles, refer exclusively to fixed copies that can be put into circulation as tangible objects.' As the opening words of the agreed statement indicate, this is really relevant to articles 8 and 9 and 12 and 13 which deal with distribution and rental rights for performers and phonograms respectively (see further paras 19.57–19.58 and 19.63–19.64 below). For the purposes of defining 'publication' under article 3(d), it underlines the requirement that this must be a making available of tangible or hard copies, as opposed to the making available of electronic or digital versions. Copies that are made available online leave the supplier's server in intangible (digital) form and 'may only later become copies in tangible form, namely at the user's terminal, after having been offered to them'.[172]

In this context, however, it should be noted that, in the Basic Proposal formulation of 'publication' it was proposed that this would include the making available of the fixed performance or phonogram, by wire or wireless means, in such a way that members of the public could access it from a place or at a time individually chosen by them. As a matter of logic, making copies available online can be regarded as a 'publication', even if the copies transmitted are intangible and may not become tangible objects until after receipt. In the notes to the Basic Proposal, it was stated that this extension of the concept of publication would take into account 'the new technological environment in which publication may now take place' and further '. . . that making performances and phonograms available in the online context may be compared to the establishment of a global record shop, offering copies to everyone, everywhere, and still satisfying the condition of "reasonable quantity" because the availability of copies is virtually unlimited'.[173] This proposal, and a corresponding proposal with respect to the WCT (proposed article 3) received support from a number of delegations at the Diplomatic Conference, such as the USA and Australia, as 'recognising the realities of online publication'[174] but also led to concern on the part of others that this might confuse the acts of publication and

172 Reinbothe and von Lewinski (2002), 254, para 48.
173 Document CRNR/DC/5, *Records* 1996, vol I, 252.
174 *Records* 1996, vol II, 680, para 328 (Kushan, USA) and 681, para 330 (Creswell, Australia).

communication,[175] and the present formulation, consistent with those in both the Rome and Berne Conventions, was adopted.

(g) 'Broadcasting'

19.46 This is limited to wireless transmissions for public reception of sounds or of images and sounds of the representations thereof; satellite transmissions are also included; as are transmissions of encrypted signals where the means for decrypting are provided to the public by the broadcasting organization or with its consent' (article 2(f)). This is an expanded version of the definition of broadcasting under article 3(f) of the Rome Convention, and the following points may be noted. First, there are three specific activities outlined in the definition which will be 'broadcasting' for the purposes of the WPPT: 'free to air' broadcasting; satellite transmissions; and encrypted satellite broadcasts.

(i) Free-to-air broadcasting: 'Free to air' is broadcasting of the 'traditional' wireless kind, that first became the focus of the new right in relation to literary and artistic works that was recognized under article 11*bis*(1) of the Berne Convention at the time of the 1928 Revision Conference (see further Chapter 12 above). Under the WPPT definition, this includes 'rebroadcasting', which is not the case under the Rome Convention, where this is defined separately, as 'the simultaneous broadcasting by one broadcasting organisation of the broadcast of another organisation'.[176] According to the notes for the Basic Proposal for the 1996 Diplomatic Conference, the proposed definition of 'broadcasting' (which was adopted unchanged in the final text) is covered by the 'simplified definition' in article 3(f) on the basis that 'rebroadcasting is broadcasting' and there was no need to import the restricted meaning used in the Rome Convention.[177]

(ii) Satellite transmissions: 'Satellite transmissions' would appear to cover the situation where either the transmissions are directly received by members of the public or are retransmitted from an earth receiving station. In either case, such transmissions would be 'for public reception', regardless of the intervening link.[178]

(iii) Encrypted satellite transmissions: 'Encrypted satellite transmissions' captures those transmissions which have been encrypted against piracy by third

---

[175] *Records* 1996, 680, para 327 (Hennessy, Ireland), and 681, para 331 (Govoni, Switzerland), and para 332 (Gyertyaney, Hungary). Note also the problems of applicable law that were raised by the proposal, eg in relation to online service providers: see further *Records* 1996, vol II, 680, paras 325, 328, 332, and 652, and see the discussion by Reinbothe and von Lewinski (2002), 52, para 11.

[176] Rome Convention, art 3(g),

[177] Document CRNR/DC/5, *Records* 1996, vol I, 252.

[178] See further Reinbothe and von Lewinski (2002), 266, para 55, and, accord, Nordemann et al (1977), 369ff.

parties and to which the individual recipient has access through a decoding or decrypting device provided by the broadcaster.

The second obvious point should be made that, for the purposes of the WPPT, 'broadcasting', meaning wireless communications, and 'communication to the public', which includes wired or 'non-wired' transmissions, is treated separately, and this distinction is carefully observed in the formulation of the different exclusive rights to be protected under the Treaty, for example, article 6 (economic rights of performers in their unfixed performances) and article 15 (secondary uses of performances and phonograms for broadcasting and public communication). By contrast, under article 8 of the WCT, wired and wireless communications are subsumed within the one general right, together with the right of making available online which, again, is treated separately under articles 10 and 14 of the WPPT (see further paras 19.60 and 19.66 below).

To be a 'broadcast' within article 2(f) of the WPPT, it must be 'for public reception'; this also applies to 'such transmission by satellite'; and, in the case of encrypted satellite transmissions, there must be provision 'to the public' of the means for decrypting by the broadcasting organization or with its consent. The notion of 'public' is critical to a number of other WPPT provisions, notably in the context of 'communication to the public' and 'making available online', but there is no definition of the concept. Essentially, then, this remains a matter for determination by national laws. However, while the outer limits of the concept may be, at one extreme, transmissions that anyone with the appropriate reception equipment is able to receive (as in the classic free-to-air situation), and, at the other extreme, person-to-person transmissions that are limited to those persons alone, it is clear that there will be points along this spectrum that may well fall within the scope of 'public' rather than 'private' and therefore 'non-public'. Such a possibility is suggested by the reference to encrypted satellite transmissions in the last part of the definition of 'broadcasting' in article 2(f): such transmissions, by their nature, are to a limited audience, but the definition indicates that the means of decrypting are to be made available to the public by the broadcasting organization, ie those members of the public who subscribe to receiving the broadcast in question. This clearly suggests that subscription broadcasting, whether by this means or others, will be within the meaning of 'public', even if it is a narrow segment of the general public, for example, those interested in sports or nature programmes or broadcasts in Serbo-Croat or Turkish (significant language groups in countries such as Australia).

(h) 'Communication to the public'

These are transmissions of sounds of a performance or of the sounds or repre- **19.47**
sentations of sounds fixed in a phonogram to the public by any means otherwise than by broadcasting (article 2(g)). For the purposes of article 15 (see para 19.68

below), this includes the making of sounds or representations of sounds fixed in a phonogram audible to the public as well as any communication over a 'non-wireless medium', for example, telephone cables, cables of a digital network, or cables designed for retransmission of broadcasts or other cable transmissions.[179] However, in view of the fact that 'communication to the public' and 'making available online' are the subject of separate exclusive rights under articles 6 and 10 (performers) and there is a separate 'making available online' right in the case of phonograms under article 14 (see further para 19.61 below), it will be clear that the definition of 'communication to the public' for the purposes of the WPPT will not include 'making available online' as is the case under article 8 of the WCT.

(3) Eligibility for protection

19.48 The basic criterion here for both performers and phonogram producers is nationality of a contracting party, the obligation for each contracting party being to provide the protection provided under the WPPT to 'nationals of other Contracting Parties': article 3(1). There is a link back to the Rome Convention here, in that the term 'nationals of other Contracting Parties' is to be understood to be those who would meet the criteria for eligibility under Rome, but applying the definitions as set out in article 2 of the WPPT (article 3(2)). The latter provision is not happily drafted, but is essentially intended to adapt the Rome criteria to WPPT countries as though the latter were all contracting parties to the Rome Convention (which may or may not actually be the case, as Rome membership is not a requirement for WPPT membership).

So far as the eligibility criteria under Rome are concerned, these are as follows:

(i) **Performers**: The performance must have taken place in another contracting state, be incorporated in a phonogram protected under article 5 of the Rome Convention or, not being fixed on a phonogram, is carried by a broadcast protected by article 6 of Rome: see generally article 4 of the Rome Convention. There is a cumulative effect here between article 3(1) of the WPPT and article 4 of Rome, in that the nationality of the performer is not relevant to the Rome provision, but is relevant to the WPPT in that (i) the performer must be a national of another WPPT country ('Contracting Party'), and (ii) the performance must also meet the criteria specified in article 4 of the Rome Convention. Thus, while under Rome, it would be possible for a performer from a non-Rome country to gain protection in Rome countries generally in respect of a performance taking place in a given Rome country (or fixed in a phonogram or carried in a broadcast under articles 5 and 6 of Rome respectively), under the

[179] See Reinbothe and von Lewinski (2002), 267, para 58.

WPPT the performer would need to be a WPPT national before protection could be claimed in respect of a performance that took place in another WPPT country.

(ii) Producers of phonograms: Nationality, first fixation, and first publication are the alternative criteria provided for in article 5(1) of the Rome Convention, and a thirty-day grace period applies in the case of simultaneous publication in a non-contracting and contracting state under article 5(2). It will also be recalled that it is possible for contracting states under Rome to make reservations concerning the application of the publication or fixation criteria: see article 5(3) and 17 (and see further para 19.17 above). This capacity to make reservations also applies for the purposes of the WPPT by virtue of article 3(2) of the WPPT, but article 3(3) thereof provides that where a WPPT contracting party wishes to avail itself of this possibility it needs to make a notification to the Director General of WIPO, rather than to the Secretary General of the UN as under article 17 of the Rome Convention. In other words, the notification, although done according to the Rome Convention provision, is in fact one for the purposes of the WPPT and would be open to any WPPT contracting party to make, regardless of whether it is also a Rome contracting state.

There are two agreed statements that are relevant to article 3 of the WPPT. The first relates to article 3(2) and states that, for the application of this provision, it is understood that 'fixation' means the finalization of the master tape ('*bande-mère*'). The second, in relation to article 3(3), picks up the possibility that intergovernmental organizations may be WPPT contracting parties (as to which see para 17.97 above) and provides that the references to 'national of another Contracting State' in articles 5(a) and 16(a)(iv) of the Rome Convention are to be understood, when applied to the WPPT, in regard to an intergovernmental organization that is a contracting party, to mean a national of one of the countries that is a member of the intergovernmental organization in question.

(4) National treatment

National treatment requirements vary under each of the conventions considered **19.49**
in this treatise. Thus, article 5(1) of the Berne Convention may be regarded as the widest-ranging, requiring for 'authors . . . in respect of works for which they are protected under this Convention, in countries of the Union other than the country of origin, the rights which their respective laws do now or may hereafter grant to their nationals, as well as the rights specially granted by this Convention'. The scope of this requirement has already been considered at length in Chapter 6 above; for present purposes, it is enough to note that it is a requirement to extend the protection of national law for rights granted both now and in the future, plus the 'rights specially granted by this Convention'

(which, in theory, could be withheld from nationals). This might be described as the 'strong' version of national treatment, although there is, of course, room for considerable debate about the scope of rights and subject matter protected under this formulation.

The national treatment requirement under article 2 of the Rome Convention is somewhat differently worded, being 'the treatment accorded by the domestic law of the contracting state in which protection is claimed . . .' (for performers, phonograms producers, broadcasting organizations, as the case may be), 'subject to the protection specifically guaranteed, and the limitations specifically provided for, in this Convention'. Given that the domestic treatment accorded to these categories of claimants in any given contracting state may be very different or even non-existent, the default position provided by the 'protection specifically guaranteed' under Rome provides only limited comfort, in view of the limitations and reservations with respect to it that are allowable under the Convention (see para 19.17 above). This might be described as a weaker version of the national treatment requirement, although it is understandable that it should have taken this form in Rome which, in 1960, was an agreement entering new and contested areas of protection.

The TRIPs Agreement, again, embodies a different approach to national treatment, requiring in article 3(1) for members to accord 'treatment no less favourable' than that accorded to nationals with respect to the 'protection of intellectual property' (including copyright and neighbouring rights). In this regard, it should noted that 'protection' is defined in a note as including 'matters affecting the availability, acquisition, scope, maintenance and enforcement of intellectual property rights as well as matters affecting the use of intellectual property rights specifically addressed in this Agreement'. This might be described as another stronger version of national treatment.

The formulation of a national treatment obligation under the proposed WPPT was a matter for some controversy between delegates at the Committee of Experts, leading into the Diplomatic Conference.[180] Indeed, in the second last session of Main Committee I, on 20 December 1996, it was described as 'the last obstacle to completion of the work leading to the adoption of Treaty No 2 [the WPPT]'.[181] In brief, it appears that the contending views were between a provision along the lines of article 5(1) of Berne, and a provision that tied the national treatment requirement more precisely to the kind of rights that were to be protected under the proposed instrument. This, in turn, gave rise to uncertainties about whether rights of remuneration that were already granted

[180] For a detailed and careful discussion, see Reinbothe and von Lewinski (2002), 279 ff.
[181] *Records* 1996, vol II, 771, para 947 (Govoni, Switzerland).

under national laws, for example, in relation to private copying, should be included within the scope of the national treatment requirement.[182] Ultimately, it was the second, and more limited, of these approaches that found its way into article 4(1) of the final text, as the result of a compromise text proposed by the Swiss delegation.[183] This provides that each contracting party is to accord to nationals of other contracting parties as defined under article 3(2) the 'treatment it accords to its own nationals with regard to the exclusive rights specifically granted in this Treaty and to the right to equitable remuneration provided for in Article 15 of this Treaty'. It will be seen that this requirement is quite differently formulated from the weaker national treatment requirement under Rome; on the other hand, it does not adopt the wider formulations applied under the Berne Convention or the TRIPs Agreement, where it is necessary to have regard to the whole of the protection accorded to these rights and subject matter under national law. It is an attempt, therefore, to encapsulate the national treatment requirement in more precise and quantifiable terms.

The following further comments may be made about the operation of article 4. **19.50**

(a) Limits

The reference in article 4(1) to 'the exclusive rights specifically granted in this Treaty' sets the limits within which the national treatment requirement is to operate and is intended to be quite specific in this regard, as distinct from the formulation in article 5(1) of the Berne Convention, or article 3(1) of the TRIPs Agreement. The exclusive rights granted in the Treaty are discussed in more detail below, but may be briefly listed here as follows. Performers have the exclusive rights of authorizing:

1. broadcasting and communicating to the public their unfixed performances: article 6(i);
2. fixation of their unfixed performances: article 6(ii);
3. direct or indirect reproduction of performances fixed in phonograms: article 7;
4. distribution of originals or copies of performances fixed in phonograms: article 8;
5. commercial rental of originals or copies of performances fixed in phonograms: article 9;
6. the making available online of fixed performances: article 10.

[182] See in particular the debates in Main Committee I in *Records* 1996, vol II, 725–30 and 770–6.

[183] ibid, 775. This was accepted in preference to a US amendment to extend the obligation in art 4(1) to remuneration systems for private digital copying of phonograms in a digital form, subject to a material reciprocity limitation: the latter was rejected by a vote of sixty to four, with seventeen abstentions: ibid, 776, para 980.

Producers of phonograms have the exclusive rights of authorizing:

1. direct or indirect reproduction of their phonograms: article 11;
2. distribution of originals or copies of their phonograms: article 12;
3. commercial rental of originals or copies of their phonograms: article 13;
4. the making available online of their phonograms: article 14.

(b) Moral rights

A question arises as to whether the moral rights that are given to performers under article 5 are included with the scope of article 4(1). These are not referred to explicitly as 'exclusive rights' in the same way as the various 'economic' rights listed above, and this omission suggests, on *a contrario* basis, that they are not therefore covered by article 4(1). As against this interpretation, Reinbothe and von Lewinski suggest that performers' moral rights under article 5 should be included on the basis that the purpose of article 4(1) was to 'cover all minimum rights as set out in the WPPT'.[184] Given the close involvement of both these authors in the Diplomatic Conference, particularly Dr Reinbothe as the EC delegate, this view must be given considerable weight. On the other hand, for the purposes of treaty interpretation, the written records of the Conference must take precedence and these cast little light on the intentions of the drafters of article 4(1) other than to suggest the choice of 'exclusive' was deliberate and was certainly adopted to differentiate such rights from rights to remuneration (there was considerable controversy over these, particularly with respect to differing views of the US and EC delegations). In truth, the status of the moral rights provision was not directly alluded to in these recorded discussions, and this leaves some uncertainty as to whether these are to be included within the scope of the expression 'exclusive rights' for the purposes of article 4(1).

(c) Extent of the requirement

The reference to 'treatment . . . with regard to . . .' indicates that the national treatment requirement in article 4(1) goes beyond just the recognition of the exclusive rights themselves, but extends to other provisions of the WPPT relating to those rights, for example, as to matters of duration (article 17) and enforcement and related measures (articles 18, 19, and 23) (as to which see further paras 19.71ff below).

(d) Application to a contracting party's own nationals

While the national treatment requirement is limited by reference to the 'treatment [each contracting party] . . . accords to its own nationals with respect to the exclusive rights specifically granted in this Treaty . . .', there is, of course, no

[184] Reinbothe and von Lewinski (2002), 287, n 13.

obligation under the WPPT for contracting parties actually to apply all or any of these exclusive rights to their own nationals. Thus, article 3(1) of the WPPT requires only of contracting parties that they 'accord the protection provided under this Treaty to the performers and producers of phonograms who are nationals of other Contracting Parties'. On the other hand, it is, of course, to be expected that if any contracting party is required to grant these exclusive rights to nationals of other contracting parties, it will extend them to its own nationals as well. On the other hand, if national laws go further than this and accord additional exclusive rights to performers and producers of phonograms, under article 4(1) there will be no national treatment requirement that will apply to these, unlike that under article 5(1), Berne.

(e) Rights of remuneration under national laws

The limitation to exclusive rights in article 4(1) of the WPPT excludes national treatment claims with respect to rights of remuneration that have been accorded under national laws, for example, in relation to private copying. Quite simply, a right to remuneration is not an exclusive right, even though it may be a derivative of, or express limitation on, such a right. This was one of the contentious issues at the Diplomatic Conference, where the USA was keen to include remuneration rights with respect to private copying of phonograms in a digital form, but this was strongly contested by other delegations, leading to the adoption of the present text.[185]

(f) Remuneration right in relation to broadcasting and public communication

The exclusion of remuneration rights is underlined by the express inclusion in article 4(1) of one form of remuneration right, that in relation to broadcasting and public communication of phonograms under article 15: see para 19.68 below.

(g) Limited material reciprocity

A rider to the national treatment obligation under article 4(1) appears in article 4(2), which provides that it does not apply to the extent that another contracting party makes use of the reservations permitted by article 15(3) of the WPPT. This, in effect, allows for an application of limited material reciprocity in these areas (see further the discussion of article 15(3) at para 19.68 below).

(5) Rights of performers

Under the WPPT, performers are given both exclusive moral and economic rights. A critical starting point, however, is to note that these only concern aural performances and those fixed in phonograms: audio-visual performances are **19.51**

[185] See generally the debates in Main Committee I in *Records* 1996, vol I, 776–7.

excluded from its scope. This was a significant issue of difference throughout the preparatory work for the Treaty, and the Basic Proposal prepared for the Diplomatic Conference highlighted this in the alternative formulations it proposed for the definition of 'fixation', namely '*Alternative A*: sounds, *Alternative B:* sounds or images'.[186] A further alternative contained in the Basic Proposal was to allow for a system of reservations for contracting parties under which they could limit the protection of the Treaty to sounds and musical performances only.[187] These differences were then sharply highlighted in statements by protagonists for and against extending protection to audio-visual performances at the seventh session of Main Committee I on 10 December 1996, with the European Community states favouring their inclusion within the one instrument, and the USA and others, notably India, being strongly opposed.[188] In the interests of capitalizing on the agreement that otherwise existed with respect to audio performances, audio-visual performances were omitted and the draft finally presented to Main Committee I was limited to sound performances.[189]

(a) Moral rights

19.52 There is no entitlement to performers' moral rights under Rome, and the genesis of the present obligation under article 5 of the WPPT is to be found in a proposal of the International Office for the first session of the Committee of Experts on a possible new instrument in 1993.[190] This proposed two separate rights: the right to be identified as the performer of his or her performance (the right to claim 'performership' being the analogue of the author's right to claim authorship under article 6*bis* of the Berne Convention) and the right to object to any distortion, mutilation, or other modification thereof. One of the major justifications advanced for these proposals, in particular the second, was the vulnerability of performers to manipulations of their performances with digital technology. During the successive sessions of the Committee of Experts, it appears that there was general support for the proposals, which were modelled on the provision in article 6*bis* of the Berne Convention. This was the form in which they appeared in the Basic Proposal, although two alternatives were advanced with respect to the performances to be covered by the proposed rights: (A) to be limited to 'musical performances' and (B) not to be so limited.[191] At the Diplomatic Conference, there were no alternative proposals put forward,

---

[186] Document CRNR/DC/5, *Records* 1996, vol I, 246ff and note the commentary herein of the history of this question through the successive sessions of the Committee of Experts.

[187] 'Alternative C' in art 25 of Document CRNR/DC/5, *Records* 1996, vol I, 327ff.

[188] See the lengthy statements by the USA, European Union, and India in Main Committee I, 10 Dec 1996: *Records* 1996, vol II, 699 ff.

[189] Document CRNR/DC/84 Prov, *Records* 1996, vol I, 517ff.

[190] [1993] *Copyright* 142, 148.

[191] Document CRNR/DC/5, in *Records* 1996, vol I, 246, 262 ff.

apart from a proposal for deletion from Singapore[192] and a more elaborate amendment concerning the way in which the requirement of identification might be satisfied.[193] In the discussions in Main Committee I, Singapore explained its opposition to performers' moral rights on the basis that, although modelled on the Berne article 6*bis* provision, it was not a requirement under the TRIPs Agreement and that there was no such requirement under Rome.[194] Several other delegations, including the USA and UK, spoke of their reservations concerning moral rights for performers. Thus, the UK delegation stated that, while in favour of performers achieving appropriate recognition for their performances, it felt that it could be better guaranteed through the exercise of the economic rights and through contractual arrangements, and that specific recognition of moral rights in the proposed treaty was therefore unnecessary.[195] On the other hand, there was a strong body of opinion among delegates in favour of such protection (and for the Basic Proposal Alternative B),[196] particularly from European and South and Central American delegates.[197] Following further informal discussion among delegates, a slightly amended version, still with the option of limiting it to musical performances, was put before Main Committee I,[198] where the UK delegation, supported by the USA, stated that it was prepared to lift its reservation on article 5 in view of its understanding of the 'strong desire of other delegations to see an international treaty for the first time provide for the moral rights of performers' and 'in a spirit of compromise'. This compromise was subject to the following amendment to article 5(1), namely the removal of the adjective 'musical' in front of 'performance' (as in Alternative A) and its replacement by the words 'live aural performances or performances fixed in phonograms'.[199] In addition, the UK/US compromise was premised on acceptance of an amendment proposed by Canada to article 26 (finally article 22) which dealt with the application in time of the proposed treaty: under the Canadian proposal, it would be possible for contracting parties to apply article 5 prospectively only, ie to performances taking place after the WPPT entered into force.[200] However, a more expansive proposal by the German delegation to

---

192 Document CRNR/DC/12, in ibid, 397.

193 Document CRNR/DC/30, in ibid, 413–14.

194 *Records* 1996, vol I, 694–5.

195 ibid, vol II, 692, para 409 (Startup, for the UK); note also the similar views expressed by the Australian delegate, Creswell, at 695, para 434, USA at para 408, as well as Thailand which was 'strongly opposed', at para 417.

196 'Broad support', in the words of the chairman of Main Committee I: ibid, 697, para 451.

197 eg Germany, Sweden, Finland, France, Italy, Denmark, Spain, Netherlands, Belgium, Peru, Bolivia, Colombia, Argentina, Chile, Venezuela, and Costa Rica: ibid, 691–8. Other strong supporters were China, Hungary (speaking also for Albania, Bulgaria, the Czech Republic, Croatia, The Former Yugoslav Republic of Macedonia, Latvia, Slovenia and Romani, Cote d'Ivoire. Senegal, Nigeria, and the Philippines.

198 CRNR/DC/84 Prov, *Records* 1996, vol II, 522.

199 ibid, 765, para 894 (Startup for the UK).

200 Document CRNR/DC/44 (11 Dec 1996), *Records* 1996, vol I, 425.

reopen debate on article 5 so as to add a provision making the moral rights guaranteed under that article available to performers regardless of nationality was rejected by a majority of Main Committee I.[201]

19.53 As finally adopted by the Diplomatic Conference, article 5 of the WPPT, provides as follows:

> (1) Independently of a performer's economic rights, and even after the transfer of those rights, the performer shall, as regards his live aural performances or performances fixed in phonograms, have the right to claim to be identified as the performer of his performances, except where omission is dictated by the manner of the use of the performance, and to object to any distortion, mutilation or other modification of his performances that would be prejudicial to his reputation.
>
> (2) The rights granted to a performer in accordance with paragraph (1) shall, after his death, be maintained, at least until the expiry of the economic rights, and shall be exercisable by the persons or institutions authorized by the legislation of the Contracting Party where protection is claimed. However, those Contracting Parties whose legislation, at the moment of their ratification of or accession to this Treaty, does not provide for protection after the death of the performer of all rights set out in the preceding paragraph may provide that some of these rights will, after his death, cease to be maintained.
>
> (3) The means of redress for safeguarding the rights granted under this Article shall be governed by the legislation of the Contracting Party where protection is claimed.

It will be seen that this follows the same basic format as article 6*bis* of the Berne Convention; accordingly, the commentary on this article that appears in Chapter 10 above is equally applicable to interpretation of article 5 of the WPPT. However, at the risk of some repetition, the following general points about the latter may be noted.

(i) The independence of moral rights: Moral rights for performers are independent of economic rights and remain so, even after the latter have been transferred. But, as discussed earlier (see para 10.15 above), the Berne Convention does not mandate the inalienability of moral rights (though member states may choose to prohibit or limit their transfer or waiver). It follows that performers' moral rights should be alienable, or waivable, to the same extent as are authors' moral rights.[202] This was also the position taken

[201] *Records* 1996, 766.

[202] See Explanatory Notes added to draft art 5 of the Basic Proposal, *Records of the Diplomatic Conference*, 264, para 5.07, WIPO Publication No 348(E) (Geneva 1999) (waivers permitted under WPPT, art 5). By contrast, the Explanatory Notes take a more limited view of assignability of moral rights that that offered in this treatise (see the earlier discussion at para 10.15 above): 'The position of a performer as the performer of a given performance cannot, of course, be

during the discussions of the WIPO Committee of Experts on a Possible New Instrument,[203] and the delegates to the Diplomatic Conference determined not to insert specific text addressing the transferability or waivability of moral rights.[204] The principal difference between the two texts concerns the subject matter and scope of protection: as we will see, performers have fewer moral rights to transfer or waive (see the further discussion below).

(ii) Persons protected: All performers who present any kind of 'aural' work live before an audience, or live in a recording studio, are covered. Thus, the text does not limit its coverage to performers of musical works. For example, oral deliveries of poetry, stories, or dramatic works also come under the aegis of article 5(1). One might further inquire whether deliveries of public lectures and speeches also enjoy rights of attribution and integrity. The delivery is a 'performance' under traditional notions of public performance (see Chapter 12 above), but is the speaker a 'performer?' Article 2(a) of the WPPT defines 'performers,' as

> actors, singers, musicians, dancers, and other persons who act, sing, deliver, declaim, play in, interpret, or otherwise perform literary or artistic works or expressions of folklore.

This definition does not require the performer to be a professional, nor is it limited to traditional forms of entertainment. The principal criterion is that the object of the performance be a 'literary or artistic work or expression . . . of folklore'. This category is broad enough to cover lectures and speeches, and this conclusion is reinforced by the inclusion of 'deliver' and 'declaim' on the list of acts of performance. Coverage of any of these performances, however extends only to their 'aural' component. To the extent that the performance also has a visual dimension, this portion does not enjoy the protection of article 5(1). As a result, were an actor's performance telecast without sound, this might be a distortion of the performance, but member states would have no obligation under article 5 to grant the actor a right of action to vindicate the integrity of her performance (depending on the facts, the actor could, however, have an economic rights claim for unauthorized broadcast under article 6 of the WPPT, as that article is not limited to 'aural' performances).

(iii) Subject matter: Performers' moral rights apply with respect to 'live aural

---

transferred: no one can step into his shoes in this sense.' Ibid. The performer, however, would be transferring the right to claim to be identified as the performer, presumably in the audio equivalent ('lip-synching') of ghostwriting.

[203] See WIPO Document BCP/CE/V/9-INR/CE/IV/8, paras 140–2 (report on fourth session of Committee of Experts); WIPO Document BCP/CE/CI/16-INR/CE/V/14, para 144 (report on fifth session of Committee of Experts).

[204] See Reinbothe and von Lewinski (2002), 293, who characterize the absence of specific text as a 'compromise solution . . . not to deal with this topic in the text of the provision'.

performances', not audio-visual performances, and to performances fixed in phonograms. Accordingly, it would equally be a breach of the right of identification/attribution of a performer to broadcast the performance without acknowledgement of the identity of the performer as it would be to broadcast or sell a copy of a phonogram of that performance without the appropriate identification. However, the fixation of sounds together with images is not a phonogram, and the performer does not enjoy protection of her attribution and integrity interests in the audio-visual fixation. As a result, a mangled soundtrack accompanying a motion picture or music video will breach no moral rights of the performer whose voice or instrumental accompaniment was recorded onto the soundtrack. The same mangling done to the same soundtrack, when the sounds are decoupled from the visual portion, and the soundtrack is made available as a phonogram, however, would be actionable under article 5 because the fixation of the recorded music would no longer be 'incorporated in a cinematographic or other audiovisual work'.

(iv) Scope of rights protected: divulgation right: Article 5 labels as 'moral rights' the rights to claim to be identified as the performer, and the right to object to any distortion, etc that would be prejudicial to the performer's reputation. Article 5 does not include the right of divulgation. However, although it designates it an 'economic right', article 6 recognizes rights of fixation; in addition, article 8 enunciates a right of distribution, and article 10 a right of making available of fixed performances. Together, these may cover the performer's divulgation interests.

(v) Attribution right: Article 5(1) of the WPPT entitles the performer 'to claim to be identified as the performer'. The text does not specify the manner of attribution, though it does allow for occasions of non-attribution (see immediately below). Given the parallelism with article $6^{bis}(1)$ of the Berne Convention, one may infer that the level of prominence there anticipated for the author's name or pseudonym (see the earlier discussion at para 10.16 above) would guide interpretation of the appropriate kinds of attribution of the names of performers under the WPPT. Some attribution issues, however, may be specific to, or at least more prevalent in the case of, performers: some kinds of performances may emanate from a greater multiplicity of performers than is likely in the case of jointly authored works. For example, a symphony orchestra may be composed of over 100 players. The circumstances under which some performers may not enjoy a right to claim identification are explored immediately below. Like article $6^{bis}(1)$ of the Berne Convention (see the earlier discussion at para 10.19 above), article 5(1) of the WPPT does not include a right to prevent false attributions.

(vi) Limitation on the attribution right: Unlike article 6bis of Berne where it may be necessary to imply a condition of reasonableness into the exercise of the right of identification, in article 5(1) of the WPPT, a qualification is expressly made, namely where the 'omission is dictated by the manner of the use of the performance'. This qualification appears to have come originally from an Argentinian proposal[205] and was incorporated in the draft provision prepared by the chair of Main Committee I after informal consultations.[206] This provides some flexibility for national legislators to provide for cases where identification may be difficult or impracticable, and therefore not required. To return to the example of the symphony orchestra, the contexts in which attribution difficulties may arise may be more frequent in the case of performers than of authors. On the other hand, the 'dictated by' standard appears more stringent than a standard of 'usual practice', or 'customary in the industry'.[207] Moreover, the structure of the text, making the 'dictated by' context an exception, suggests that the burden is on the person exploiting the performance to demonstrate that the manner of use required omission of the performer's name. That said, it remains to be seen what 'dictated by' in fact means. For example, suppose a radio broadcast of a performance of a popular song with lead singers and back-up singers, and lead instrumentalists and background instrumentalists. It may not be customary practice to identify all the back-up singers and instrumentalists, but do the demands of air time 'dictate' the omission of some or all of their names?[208] At the least, if the omission is not reasonable in context, it is unlikely to be 'dictated by' the manner of the use. Thus, whether or not a use for broadcasting dictates the omission of some performers' names, it should be much more difficult for the exploiter to justify the omission from printed matter accompanying a live performance or distributed copies of the phonograms. The omission would be even less likely to have been 'dictated by' the manner of the use if the use is in a digital format permitting reference to a complete list of the performers, for example, by a link within the phonogram, or to another source.

(vii) Integrity right: To the extent that the language of article 5(1) of the WPPT tracks article 6*bis*(1) of the Berne Convention, the analyses offered with respect to authors' moral rights (see the earlier discussion at paras 10.20–10.22 above) of the terms 'distortion, mutilation or other modification' should apply here as well. Phonogram-specific examples of distortions, etc would include alterations to the speed, timbre, or pitch of the recording, as well, potentially, as

205 Document CRNR/DC/31 (10 Dec 1996), *Records* 1996, 413.

206 Document CRNR/DC/84 Prov (18 Dec 1996), *Records* 1996, 522.

207 See Reinbothe and von Lewinski (2002), 297 (WPPT drafters rejected 'in a customary way' and 'as far as practical' on the ground that those wordings 'might have limited the performer's right too strongly, particularly since they were seen as being too vague and leaving too much leeway to those obliged to identify the performers').

208 The *Records of the Diplomatic Conference* suggest an affirmative answer to this hypothetical; see *Records*, 1996, 692, para 409.

sampling.[209] In addition, it may be inferred that, like article $6^{bis}(1)$ of the Berne Convention (see the earlier discussion at para 10.26 above), article 5(1) of the WPPT does not include a right to prevent the destruction of copies, including the master copy, of recorded performances. However, the WPPT also departs in certain respects from article $6^{bis}(1)$. First, it omits the phrase 'or other derogatory action in relation to'. This suggests that the kinds of juxtapositions or changes of artistic context that might be found to constitute a derogatory action in relation to a work, even though the work itself is not altered, would not require redress under article 5 of the WPPT. For example, while the display of an artwork in a pornographic context might constitute a 'derogatory action' under article 6bis of the Berne Convention (see the earlier discussion at paras 10.23–10.24 above), it would appear that, for example, the playing during a striptease of a recorded performance by a singer known for her wholesome repertoire and style would not be actionable under article 5. In addition, no reference to 'honour' is made in the case of the right of integrity, which may make the right more accessible for common law systems that are used to protecting reputational interests through such actions as defamation and passing off/unfair competition. This might therefore suggest that, unlike article 6bis, the assessment of prejudice is a more objective one, looking to the effect on the performer's reputation with their public rather than taking into account the way the performer him- or herself may regard the allegedly distorting action. It is therefore arguable that the scope of the integrity right under article 5 is narrower than under article 6bis.

(viii) Duration of performers' moral rights: Article 5(2) tracks closely the wording of article $6^{bis}(2)$, and accordingly allows a window of opportunity for contracting parties to limit the term of protection for the different performers' moral rights if they satisfy the requirements of the provision.[210] Performers' rights, however, present a peculiarity generally not present in the case of authors' rights. Pursuant to article 7 of the Berne Convention, authors' economic rights last for a minimum of fifty years *post mortem auctoris* (with the possible exception of cinematographic and photographic works, and works of applied art; see the earlier discussion at para 10.35 above); thus, if authors' moral rights are tied to the duration of economic rights, they will endure past the death of the author. By contrast, under article 17(1) of the WPPT, the term of protection of economic rights is fifty years from fixation. For performers who began their careers young, and lived to a ripe old age, it is entirely possible that their economic rights will expire before they do. Thus, although the text of article 5(2) of the WPPT appears to assume that performers' moral rights will

[209] For more examples, see Reinbothe and von Lewinski (2002), 298–9.

[210] For an extensive critique of WPPT, art 5(2)'s reiteration, *mutatis mutandis*, of Berne Convention, art $6^{bis}(2)$, see Reinbothe and von Lewinski (2002), 301–2.

endure at least until the performer's death (if not indeed for some period *post mortem*), this will not be the case unless, notwithstanding article 17(1), article 5(2) is interpreted to require that, in the event that the performer survives the period of protection of the economic rights, the minimum period of protection shall be the life of the performer.[211]

(ix) Enforcement of performers' moral rights: The same is true of article 5(3), which again tracks article $6^{bis}(3)$ so far as issues of enforcement of moral rights at the national level is concerned.

(x) Transitional measures: Finally, article 22(2) should be noted: this allows contracting parties to apply article 5 only to performances occurring after the WPPT enters into force (this was part of the compromise that made performers' moral rights acceptable for certain delegations at the Diplomatic Conference: see para 19.52 above).

(b) Economic rights

The exclusive rights the WPPT requires to be granted to performers have already been referred to above (see para 19.46), and are treated in more detail below. **19.54**

(i) Unfixed performances (article 6): In respect of these, article 6 gives performers the exclusive right of authorizing the following acts: (i) broadcasting and communication to the public, except where the performance is already a broadcast performance; and (ii) fixation of their unfixed performances. The following comments can be made about this provision. **19.55**

First, this is a clear advance on the protection offered under article 7(1)(a) and (b) of the Rome Convention, where, rather than an exclusive right, all that is required is the 'possibility of preventing' the specified activities.

Second, insofar as the exclusive right under article 6(i) of the WPPT applies to broadcasting, this is the one instance under the WPPT where audio-visual performances are to be protected (note the definition of 'broadcasting' in article 2(f) which includes 'sounds' and 'sounds and images'). Communication to the public, however, is limited to sounds alone, meaning that an original wired transmission of an unfixed audio-visual performance would not be caught, so far as the images are concerned. Communication to the public would also occur where the live performance is conveyed to the public through loudspeakers. Likewise, transmission of a live performance over the Internet would be covered, as a communication to the public, as would a satellite transmission (this being a 'broadcast' within the meaning of article 2(f)).

[211] Reinbothe and von Lewinski (2002), 301, advocate this solution.

The third comment to make about this provision is that broadcast performances, however, are excluded, meaning that a rebroadcast or wired transmission of a broadcast of an unfixed performance will not be within the scope of the right. Where a performance fixed in a phonogram is broadcast or communicated to the public, this will come within the remuneration right provided under article 15 (as to which, see para 19.68 below).

Finally, the right of 'fixation' under article 6(ii) clearly covers traditional 'bootlegging' activities where unauthorized recordings are made of live performances. Unlike the broadcasting right in article 6(i), this is limited to fixations of sounds and representations of sounds (as per the definition of 'fixation' in article 2(c) of the WPPT).

19.56 **(ii) Reproduction (article 7):** The exclusive right here is to authorize the 'direct or indirect reproduction of their performances fixed in phonograms in any manner or form'. An agreed statement (which also applies to the reproduction right with respect to phonograms) provides as follows:

> The reproduction right, as set out in Articles 7 and 11, and the exceptions permitted thereunder through Article 16, fully apply in the digital environment, in particular to the use of performances and phonograms in digital form. It is understood that the storage of a protected performance or phonogram in digital form in an electronic medium constitutes a reproduction within the meaning of these Articles.

This is clearly a stronger right than article 7(1)(c) of the Rome Convention, which refers rather limply to the 'possibility [for performers] of preventing . . . the reproduction, without their consent, of a fixation of their performance . . .' (see further para 19.08 above). The following points may be made about its scope.

Limits on the right: The exclusive right is limited to reproductions of the *fixation* of the performance in a phonogram. This must mean the actual sounds of the performance: hence, there will be no relevant act of reproduction where another party simply recreates a performance that is fixed on a phonogram, ie by making a 'soundalike' recording, such as an Elvis Presley or Marlene Dietrich impersonation. In the case of a literary or artistic work, such acts of recreation could well be reproductions if the resultant work is sufficiently like the original, for example, where the plot of a play is taken but without the actual words.

Meaning of 'direct' and 'indirect': 'Direct' and 'indirect' are not defined, but they indicate that it should matter whether the unauthorized party simply makes a copy of the fixation of the performance, for example, through pressing a copy, or whether this is done at more of a remove, for example, by recording a broadcast or other public communication of the fixation.[212] In the commentary in the Basic Proposal, the International Office stated that: 'Any form of remote copying that is made possible by a communication network between the original and the copy is intended to come within the reach of this provision.'[213]

Digital copies: The words 'in any manner or form', as amplified by the agreed statement, make it clear that making a digital copy of a fixation will be a reproduction. This would occur, for instance, where a copy is downloaded over the Internet.

Temporary reproduction: The issue of temporary reproduction is not directly addressed in the article, although the text in the Basic Proposal referred expressly to 'authorizing the direct or indirect reproduction, *whether permanent or temporary*', in line with a proposal to the May 1996 session of the Committee of Experts from the European Communities to include a statement in the Conference records or the general report to the following effect: 'Contracting Parties confirm that the permanent or temporary storage of a protected fixed performance in any electronic medium constitutes a reproduction. This includes acts such as uploading and downloading of a fixed performance to or from the memory of a computer.'[214] A further paragraph was included in the Basic Proposal to permit contracting parties to limit the right of reproduction in cases of temporary reproduction where this had the sole purpose of making the fixed performance perceptible or 'where the reproduction was of a transient or incidental nature, provided that such reproduction takes place in the course of use of the fixed performance that is authorized by the performer or permitted by law.'[215] There was considerable debate about these provisions in Main Committee I where they were also considered together with the proposed article 7of the WCT.[216] There were deep divisions among delegates as to the need for, and the effect of, the proposed article 7(2) and its interaction with the three-step tests contained in article 9(2) of Berne as well as in proposed article 16 of the WPPT (see para 19.69 below). After further consultations, and in light of the decision of Main Committee I to delete proposed article 7 on the right of reproduction from the WCT (see para 11.74 above), on the proposal of the South African and US delegations, the words 'whether permanent or temporary' were deleted from article 7(1) of the WPPT, and draft article 7(2) was deleted altogether. This was done by consensus; likewise, no agreed statement on the matter of temporary reproduction was included in the

[212] To similar effect, see ibid, 314, para 144.

[213] Document CRNR/DC/5, *Records* 1996, vol I, 268, para 7.06.

[214] Set out in ibid, 270, para 7.10. [215] ibid, 271. [216] ibid, vol II, 667–75.

Conference records.[217] Accordingly, the status of temporary or transient/incidental reproductions of fixed performances is not explicitly addressed in article 7, as finally adopted. However, it may be thought that the words 'in any manner or form' are still apt to cover such reproductions, and it will therefore remain a matter for application of the three-step test (as to which see article 16 and para 16.69 below) as to whether any exceptions covering these reproductions will be permitted under national laws. This clearly defers making judgements as to what is allowable or not, but the debates in Main Committee I indicate the difficulties that delegates saw about trying to provide a more specific regime directly in the WPPT itself.

Altered or manipulated versions: A further question is the extent to which the right of reproduction will cover the making of altered or manipulated versions of a performance that has been fixed in a phonogram, a possibility that becomes all the more common with digital fixation. In this regard, it is worth noting that, in the Basic Proposal prepared for the Diplomatic Conference, there was a proposal for an exclusive right of 'modification' of performances fixed in phonograms or any medium.[218] A similar proposal was also put forward with respect to producers of phonograms.[219] The proposed articles had their origins in proposals made by Argentina, the USA, and Uruguay (the last two proposals used 'adaptation' and 'alteration' rather than 'modification'). The reason for the proposal was that it would cover 'any possible situation in which digital or other technological manipulation might be used to circumvent traditional notions of reproduction'.[220] However, objections were made in the preceding sessions of the Committee of Experts that the proposed right was unnecessary, in that any alteration or modification of a performance or a phonogram would involve the reproduction of a fixation of the performance or phonogram. These objections were maintained in Main Committee I at the Diplomatic Conference,[221] although there were some strong expressions of opinion in favour of the proposed right.[222] Ultimately, the proposed articles 8 and 15 were dropped, with the following 'agreed understanding' being noted in the minutes of Main Committee I as to the relationship between the right of modification and the right of reproduction, namely that 'the right of reproduction met the need for protection in that respect'.[223] While this 'understanding' was not formally recorded as a separate statement attached to the WPPT, it nonetheless should

[217] *Records* 1996, vol II, 767.
[218] Proposed art 8, Basic Proposal, Document CRNR/DC/5, *Records* 1996, vol I, 277.
[219] ibid, 301 (proposed art 15). [220] ibid, 300 (notes to art 11).
[221] eg Senegal, Korea, Singapore, UK, and Australia: ibid, vol II, 664–5.
[222] eg France, Germany, Belgium, Sweden, Spain, and Norway: ibid, vol II, 665–6.
[223] ibid, vol II, 768, para 920 (statement of chairman, J Liedes).

enjoy equal status for the purposes of interpretation of the reproduction right, as part of the 'context' of the Treaty pursuant to article 31(2)(a) of the Vienna Convention on the Law of Treaties.

(iii) **Right of distribution** (article 8): This exclusive right replicates the language of article 6 of the WCT, and readers are referred to the commentary on the latter article (see paras 11.89ff above). There is a similar agreed statement that applies to article 8, as well as to articles 9 (see below) and 2(e) (see above) that states: **19.57**

> As used in these Articles, the expressions 'copies' and 'original and copies,' being subject to the right of distribution and the right of rental under the said Articles, refer exclusively to fixed copies that can be put into circulation as tangible objects.

As with article 6(2) of the WCT, article 8(2) of the WPPT provides contracting parties with the facility to limit the right of distribution to the first authorized sale or other transfer of ownership.

(iv) **Right of rental** (article 9): Under article 9(1), performers are to have the exclusive right of 'authorizing the commercial rental to the public of the original and copies of their performances fixed in phonograms as determined in the national law of Contracting Parties, even after distribution of them by, or pursuant to, authorization by the performer'. The same agreed statement for article 8 (see above) applies here as well. The following five comments about article 9 can be made here. First, it is limited to 'commercial rental', as distinct from lending generally, such as might occur through a public library that charges no fees to its borrowers. There is no further interpretation of 'commercial' provided in the Treaty, but presumably this would extend to cases where rental occurs for money's worth, ie for goods or services rather than for money. **19.58**

Second, the term 'to the public' is left undefined, and is therefore a matter for national laws to determine. There is a spectrum of meanings that may be attached to this term, but it will be noted that the same expression is used in article 10 with respect to the making available right and the issue of what is the 'public' is explored in more detail there (see para 19.60 below).

Third, the right applies even after the original and copies have been distributed by, or with the authorization of the performer.

Fourth, as the agreed statement makes clear, it is limited to the tangible copies of the fixation in a phonogram.

Finally, the right is qualified significantly by the requirement that it is as 'determined in the national law of Contracting Parties'. This is similar to the requirement in article 14(4) of the TRIPs Agreement ('as determined in Member's law') as well as in article 7 of the WCT. In this regard, the following agreed statement that is attached to article 7 of the WCT, but not to article 9 of the WPPT, should be noted: 'It is understood that the obligation under article 7(1) does not require a Contracting Party to provide an exclusive right of commercial rental to authors who, under that Contracting Party's law, are not granted rights in respect of phonograms. It is understood that this obligation is consistent with Article 14(4) of the TRIPS Agreement.' Reinbothe and von Lewinski suggest that article 9(1) of the WPPT is to be interpreted in the same way, so that if a given national law grants performers rights in performances fixed in phonograms it must also grant them rental rights; on the other hand, there is no requirement to grant commercial rental rights if no rights are otherwise granted in performances fixed in phonograms.[224]

19.59 There is a further paragraph to article 9, which is a kind of 'grandfathering provision' and is concerned with contracting parties that had systems of equitable remuneration in place for performers for the rental of copies of their performances fixed in phonograms prior to 15 April 1994 (the date of the TRIPs Agreement). Article 9(2) therefore allows such countries to maintain these systems, rather than introduce exclusive rights, provided that the commercial rental of phonograms is not giving rise to 'the material impairment of the exclusive right of reproduction of performers'. This, again, is similar to article 7 of the WCT, and article 14(4) of the TRIPs Agreement. The 'material impairment' test in TRIPs arises also in article 11, in relation to rental rights for cinematographic works.[225] In practice, it may be difficult to apply, and invites an interesting comparison with the criteria established by the three-step test in relation to exceptions and limitations. Would a 'material impairment' require something more than a 'conflict with a normal exploitation' of the performers' right of reproduction? Given that performers under such a system would already be receiving remuneration, at what point does the commercial rental of phonograms cross the boundary of 'material impairment'?

19.60 (v) **Right of making available of fixed phonograms (article 10):** Under article 10 of the WPPT, performers also have the exclusive right of authorizing the 'making available to the public of their performances fixed in phonograms, by wire or wireless means, in such a way that members of the public may access them from a place and at a time individually chosen by them'. This is in the same form as in the Basic Proposal, except that the latter provided the alternative of limiting it to 'musical performances' rather than performances generally.[226] This was a new right that was proposed by the European

[224] Reinbothe and von Lewinski (2002), 329, para 13.

[225] See further the discussion by Gervais (2003), 139–40.

[226] Basic Proposal, art 11, Document CRNR/DC/5, *Records* 1996, vol I, 284.

Community and its member states in May 1996. The following comments can be made about the provision.

First, the provision stands in contradistinction from the distribution right in article 8 which is concerned with the distribution of copies of fixed performances in tangible form. Under article 10, the fixations are made available through wired or wireless transmission.

Second, according to the Basic Proposal, the availability is 'based on interactivity and on "on-demand access", ie the fixations are made available in such a way that members of the public may access them from a place and at a time individually chosen by them'.[227] In the Basic Proposal, a distinction was drawn between access available online to members of the public without restriction, and access that may only be available on the payment of a subscription. Whether the latter is caught within the scope of the article must ultimately depend upon how national laws will interpret the expression 'to the public'. In some laws, this may mean everyone but the immediate family circle, on the basis that this is all legitimately part of the rights owner's 'audience'. On another view, however, the word 'public' may have a spatial connotation, referring to places open to public access and therefore not encompassing the privacy of the home. In the present context, guidance is provided by the closing words that access is to be available to members of the public 'from a place and at a time individually chosen by them', which indicates clearly that there may still be a making available to the public where the fixed performance is viewed by a single individual in the privacy of his or her home. Under this view, open access and access by subscription would be equally covered, and the only exception would be in relation to dedicated person-to-person communications.

(6) Rights of producers of phonograms

Given that these may be bodies corporate rather than individuals there is no conferring of moral rights with respect to phonograms. However, it should be noted that the proposed right of modification had a kind of moral rights overtone, being directed at manipulations of fixed performances and phonograms that are made possible in the digital environment (see para 19.52 above in relation to performers). **19.61**

However, the exclusive economic rights closely parallel those already outlined above in relation to performers. As with performers, they represent a much firmer corpus of rights than are available under the Rome Convention.

[227] ibid.

(a) Right of reproduction (article 11)

19.62 This is in identical terms to article 7 in relation to performers, although obviously directed, in this context, to the phonogram itself. The same agreed statement to article 7 with respect the digital environment also applies here. Accordingly, the comments made above (see para 19.56) with respect to article 7 apply equally here.

(b) Right of distribution (article 12)

19.63 This, again, is in identical terms (with necessary modifications) to article 8, and is subject to the same first sale limitation and the same agreed statement concerning 'fixed copies that be put into circulation as tangible object'. The comments made above (see para 19.57) are equally applicable here.

(c) Right of commercial rental (article 13)

19.64 Article 13(1) is in similar terms as article 9(1) with respect to performers, but without the reference to national law. Accordingly, contracting parties are required to accord an exclusive commercial rental right to phonogram producers, and this must continue to apply even after the original and copies (which must be hard copies or 'tangible objects' pursuant to the agreed statement that also applies to articles 8, 9, and 12) have been distributed by or with the authorization of the producer.

19.65 Article 13(2) also contains a similar 'grandfathering' clause in relation to contracting parties which, prior to 15 April 1994, had in force a system of equitable remuneration of producers of phonograms for the rental of their phonograms. These systems may be retained, provided that the commercial rental of phonograms is not giving rise to a 'material impairment' of the exclusive reproduction right of the phonogram producer. The difficulties of determining how this test of 'material impairment' is to be applied in practice is discussed above (see para 19.59).

(d) Right of making available of phonograms (article 14)

19.66 This is in identical terms to that given to performers with respect to the making available to the public fixations of their performances in phonograms under article 10 and the comments made above (see para 19.60) apply equally here.

(7) **Common provisions**

19.67 Chapter IV of the WPPT contains a series of provision that are described as 'common provisions' equally applicable to both performers and phonogram producers. These deal with the following topics:

- right to remuneration for broadcasting and communication to the public: article 15;

- limitations and exceptions: article 16;
- term of protection: article 17;
- obligations concerning technological measures: article 18;
- obligations concerning rights management information: article 19;
- formalities: article 20;
- reservations: article 21;
- application in time: article 22; and
- enforcement of rights: article 23.

For the most part, these matters have already been commented upon in earlier sections of this treatise and it is unnecessary to cover the same ground again. However, the following points about each may be briefly noted.

(a) Right to remuneration (article 15)

This is similar to article 12 of the Rome Convention (see para 19.08 above), but goes further in its area of application. The fundamental right contained in article 15(1) of the WPPT applies to both performers and producers of phonograms, who shall 'enjoy the right to a single equitable remuneration for the direct or indirect use of phonograms published for commercial purposes for broadcasting or for any communication to the public'. It goes without saying that, so far as performers are concerned, it must be their performances that are fixed in the phonogram in question. It should also be noted that the rights of producers of phonograms are more limited in the areas of broadcasting and public communication than those of performers in relation to their unfixed performances under article 6 of the WPPT. Phonogram producers only acquire any rights by virtue of the WPPT once fixation has occurred, this being logically the point at which their contribution of resources and skills is crystallized. Following this point, while most of the rights of phonogram producers in respect of their fixations are framed as exclusive rights, for example, reproduction, rental, etc, the significant limitation under the WPPT in relation to broadcasting and communication to the public is that contracting parties are at liberty to treat this as subject to a right to remuneration only (they could of course go further than this by virtue of article 1(2) and the agreed statement thereto). Article 15 is therefore something of a compromise position between conflicting interests, and, by and large, indicates that the position already reached under article 12 of Rome, could not be advanced any further in the context of the WPPT.[228] The following comments may therefore be made about the operation of article 15, WPPT. **19.68**

[228] For the history of the proposal through the successive sessions of the Committee of Experts from 1993 on, as well as at the Diplomatic Conference, see Reinbothe and von Lewisnki (2002), 375–80.

(i) **Direct and indirect use**: Unlike article 12 of the Rome Convention, article 15(1) applies to both the 'direct' and 'indirect use' of phonograms. The term 'direct' poses no particular problems, covering the case where the broadcast or public communication is made directly from the phonogram itself or a copy thereof, for example, in a free-to-air broadcast, through playing the phonogram in a public place, transmission over a cable network. 'Indirect', however, would cover the case where the phonogram is transmitted over a closed network prior to broadcasting or communication to the public.

(ii) **Commercial purposes**: The phonogram must have been 'published for commercial purposes', which appears to be a gloss on the definition of 'publication' in article 2(e) where the principal criterion is that copies should be offered to the public, with the authority of the right holder, and that this should be in 'reasonable quantity'. Under that definition, publication could take place through the means of a gratuitous distribution or 'giveaway', whereas the qualifying phrase 'for commercial purposes' implies that some pecuniary benefit, whether or not in terms of money, should be intended. Article 15(4) of the WPPT, however, provides an interpretation of 'for commercial purposes' that indicates that this expression is to be more broadly interpreted:

> For the purposes of this Article, phonograms made available to the public by wire or wireless means in such a way that members of the public may access them from a place and at a time individually chosen by them shall be considered as if they had been published for commercial purposes.

(iii) **Meaning of 'equitable remuneration'**: No guidance is provided as to the meaning of 'equitable remuneration', a matter that will therefore remain for determination under national laws. However, the remuneration must be 'single', indicating that the use of the phonogram as a whole is to be valued here, rather than undertaking a separate valuation of each input, ie that of the performer and that of the phonogram producer. Article 15(2) confirms this, by providing that national laws may establish how the single equitable remuneration is to be claimed, for example, whether by the performer, phonogram producer, or by both, and the terms on which it is to be shared (in the absence of agreement between the performer and phonogram producer). The language of article 15(2), however, indicates that the setting of terms by national legislation should only occur after the performer and phonogram producer have failed to reach agreement. In other words, contractual solutions between the parties have priority, with national legislation providing the default machinery that is to come into operation in the absence of agreement. As noted in the context of article 11*bis*(2), 'equitable remuneration may mean something less than market value', given that the existence of the default machinery means that the parties will not be negotiating in a free-market environment (see further paras 13.67ff above).

(iv) Reservations: Article 15 presents no advance on article 12 of the Rome Convention, so far as the matter of reservations is concerned. Thus, under article 15(3), any contracting party may, on deposit of notification with the Director General of WIPO, make the following declarations: (i) that it will apply the provisions of paragraph (1) only in respect of certain uses; (ii) that it will limit their application in some other way; or (iii) that it will not apply these provisions at all. Accordingly, the path is prepared for a wide variety of national applications (or even non-applications) of the single equitable remuneration regime provided for in article 15(1).

(v) Agreed statement: The fact of lack of consensus between delegates at the Diplomatic Conference on these matters is explicitly reflected in the following agreed statement which is very open about the issue:

> *Agreed statement concerning Article 15:* It is understood that Article 15 does not represent a complete resolution of the level of rights of broadcasting and communication to the public that should be enjoyed by performers and phonogram producers in the digital age. Delegations were unable to achieve consensus on differing proposals for aspects of exclusivity to be provided in certain circumstances or for rights to be provided without the possibility of reservations, and have therefore left the issue to future resolution.

(vi) Further agreed statement: A further agreed statement is concerned with performers of folklore and producers of phonograms recording folklore and provides:

> *Agreed statement concerning Article 15:* It is understood that Article 15 does not prevent the granting of the right conferred by this Article to performers of folklore and producers of phonograms recording folklore where such phonograms have not been published for commercial gain.

This has no effect so far as the interpretation of article 15 is concerned: it simply draws the attention of national legislators to the fact that they may exceed their obligations under the article in relation to this category of performers and phonograms.

(b) Limitations and exceptions (article 16)

This provision draws partly on the model provided in article 15(2) of Rome, but **19.69**
also continues the transplantation of the three-step test away from its original home in article 9(2) of the Berne Convention, and into the area of neighbouring rights. Thus, under article 16(1), contracting parties in their national legislation may provide for the same kinds of limitations and exceptions with regard to the protection of performers and producers of phonograms as 'they provide for, in their national legislation, in connection with the protection of copyright in literary and artistic works'. These 'equivalents with copyright' will presumably be Berne-consistent in any event (on the assumption that all WPPT parties will

inevitably now be Berne members as well), but the effect is to provide contracting parties with a ready template to apply to limitations and exceptions with respect to the rights of performers and producers of phonograms (see further the discussion at para 19.16 above). It should be noted, however, that article 16(2) does not contain the proviso to article 15(2) of the Rome Convention, namely that 'compulsory licences may be provided for only to the extent to which they are compatible with this Convention [Rome]'. Subject to article 16(2) (see below), this omission would mean that national laws could provide for compulsory licences to the extent that they would otherwise be permissible under the relevant provisions of Berne in respect of literary and artistic works, for example, under article 11*bis*(2) and 13.

Article 16(1) applies generally to national laws pertaining to the 'protection of performers and producers of phonograms'. However, article 16(2) introduces the three-step test as setting the boundaries within which 'any limitations of or exceptions to rights provided for in this Treaty'. As adapted for this purpose, article 16(2) reads as follows:

> Contracting Parties shall confine any limitations of or exceptions to rights provided for in this Treaty to certain special cases which do not conflict with a normal exploitation of the performance or phonogram and do not unreasonably prejudice the legitimate interests of the performer or of the producer of the phonogram.

Agreed statements in similar form to those attached to article 10 of the WCT, are also appended:

> The reproduction right, as set out in Articles 7 and 11, and the exceptions permitted thereunder through Article 16, fully apply in the digital environment, in particular to the use of performances and phonograms in digital form. It is understood that the storage of a protected performance or phonogram in digital form in an electronic medium constitutes a reproduction within the meaning of these Articles.
>
> The agreed statement concerning Article 10 (on Limitations and Exceptions) of the WIPO Copyright Treaty is applicable *mutatis mutandis* also to Article 16 (on Limitations and Exceptions) of the WIPO Performances and Phonograms Treaty. [The text of the agreed statement concerning article 10 of the WCT reads as follows: 'It is understood that the provisions of Article 10 permit Contracting Parties to carry forward and appropriately extend into the digital environment limitations and exceptions in their national laws which have been considered acceptable under the Berne Convention. Similarly, these provisions should be understood to permit Contracting Parties to devise new exceptions and limitations that are appropriate in the digital network environment.
>
> It is also understood that Article 10(2) neither reduces nor extends the scope of applicability of the limitations and exceptions permitted by the Berne Convention.']

See further the commentary at paras 13.03–13.37 and 13.116–13.128.

(c) Term of protection (article 17)

The minima provided for here are considerably greater than the twenty-year norm contained in article 14 of the Rome Convention. Under article 17 of the WPPT, the minima are: **19.70**

- *performers*: at least fifty years from the end of the year in which the performance was fixed in a phonogram (article 17(1)); and
- *producers of phonograms*: at least fifty years from the end of the year in which the phonogram was published, or failing such publication within fifty years from fixation, fifty years from the end of the year in which the fixation was made (article 17(2)).

The fifty-year term was contained in the Basic Proposal presented to the Diplomatic Conference,[229] and was originally proposed by the International Office in its memoranda to the first session of the Committee of Experts in 1993 and to the third session in 1994.[230] In the notes to the Basic Proposal, it was stated that the reasons for increasing the term to fifty years are 'obvious', although no reason was actually advanced apart from repeating the common mantra advanced for increases in terms of protection, namely 'There is a clear trend towards a fifty-year term of protection for performers and for producers of phonograms.'[231] However, a more compelling influence not mentioned in the Basic Proposal must have been article 14(5) of the TRIPs Agreement which stipulates a fifty-year minimum term of protection for performers and phonogram producers from the date of fixation or performance, as well as articles 3 of the EU Term Directive.[232]

(8) Obligations concerning technological measures (article 18)

This is in identical terms to article 11 of the WCT, and was discussed together with that article in the Diplomatic Conference.[233] The requirements of these provisions are considered in detail in Chapter 15 above (paras 15.10–15.25). **19.71**

(9) Obligations concerning rights management information (article 19)

This is in identical terms to article 12 of the WCT, and was also discussed together with that article in the Diplomatic Conference.[234] The requirements of these provisions are considered in detail in Chapter 15 above (paras 15.30–15.40). **19.72**

229 Documents CRNR/DC/5, *Records* 1996, vol I, 319. 230 ibid, 318. 231 ibid.

232 Council Directive (EEC) No 93/98 of 29 Oct 1993 harmonizing the term of protection of copyright and certain related rights.

233 *Records* 1996, vol II, 709–16 (Main Committee). 234 ibid.

(10) Formalities (article 20)

19.73 As in the Berne Convention, the enjoyment and exercise of the rights provided under the WPPT are not to be subject to any formality, and is in contrast to the (P) symbol that is provided for in article 11 of the Rome Convention. There was no substantive discussion of this provision during the Diplomatic Conference, but it is clear from the notes to the Basic Proposal that it is based on the model of the Berne Convention and is to be interpreted 'in an equivalent manner'[235] (see further the discussion of article 5(2) of Berne at paras 6.101ff above). There is no corresponding 'no formalities' rule in the WCT, presumably because any imposition of formalities would be contrary to article 20 of Berne in any event.

(11) Reservations (article 21)

19.74 There are no reservations allowed, other than those permitted under article 15(3) with respect to the remuneration right for broadcasts and public communications of performances fixed in phonograms and phonograms.

(12) Application in time (article 22)

19.75 The requirement is that contracting parties are to apply the provisions of article 18 of Berne *mutatis mutandis* to the rights of performers and phonogram producers provided under the Treaty: article 22(1) (and see further the commentary at paras 6.112ff above). However, in the case of performances, it is possible for contracting parties to limit the application of article 5 of the Treaty (moral rights) to performances occurring after the entry into force of the Treaty: article 22(2). According to Reinbothe and von Lewinski, the purpose of article 22(2) is to 'facilitate accession for those countries—in particular countries adhering to the "copyright system"—which do not know a tradition of moral rights, particularly for performers'.[236]

(13) Enforcement of rights (article 23)

19.76 This is identical to article 14 of the WCT (see further the commentary at para 15.41).

(14) Administrative and final clauses (articles 24–33)

19.77 These are identical to those in articles 15 to 25 of the WCT, and have been dealt with above (see paras 16.50ff and 17.94ff above)

---

235 Document CRNR/DC/5, *Records* 1996, vol I, 324.

236 Reinbothe and von Lewinski (2002), 445, para 16.

G. Other Relevant Agreements: Past, Present, and Proposed

Passing mention has already been made above of other kinds of neighbouring rights and topics relating to the protection of authors' and neighbouring rights. Thus far, we have considered treaties that have been negotiated and have come into effect: Berne, Rome, WCT, WPPT, and the TRIPs Agreement. However, there are other projects for treaties that have been undertaken and even taken to completion, but now seem to have fallen by the wayside or to have become diminished in significance: examples are the Satellites Convention (see para 19.24 above), the Madrid Convention for the Avoidance of Double Taxation of Copyright Royalties, the 1960 Hague Act of the Hague Agreement Concerning the International Deposit of Industrial Designs, the Vienna Agreement for the Protection of Typefaces and their International Deposit, and the Film Register Treaty. Since the adoption of the WIPO treaties in 1996, there have been projects for three other treaties, none of which has yet been adopted: a database treaty, an audio-visual performers' treaty, and a treaty on the rights of broadcasting organizations. These last three are part of what Dr Ficsor has called the 'unfinished work' of the 1996 Diplomatic Conference,[237] but, as will be seen below, these are projects that are far from being launched as fully fledged instruments. For the sake of completeness, these agreements, both actual and proposed, are described briefly below. **19.78**

(1) The Madrid Convention for the Avoidance of Double Taxation of Copyright Royalties

This Convention, which has never come into force, was concerned with a matter of considerable importance to authors, although not in any way directly concerned with the creation and subsistence of their rights. This is the avoidance of double taxation of copyright royalties where an author becomes liable to taxation of his royalties not only in the country where the royalties are earned but in his own country. After preparatory work by WIPO and UNESCO on this matter,[238] a diplomatic conference attended by forty-four states was held in Madrid in 1979 and a final text was adopted.[239] By January 1986 only four states adhered to it,[240] and the treaty never came into force. Nonetheless, its principal features deserve a brief mention in this present overview of 'other relevant agreements'. **19.79**

[237] Ficsor (2001), 665.

[238] Meetings of Committees of Governmental Experts in Paris, 3–10 Nov 1975 and Paris, 8–16 Dec 1976: [1977] *Copyright* 42; 19–30 June 1978: [1978] *Copyright* 270.

[239] [1980] *Copyright* 12.

[240] Czechoslovakia, Egypt, India, and Iraq: [1986] *Copyright* 11.

The basic obligation imposed under the Convention was that each contracting state would undertake to make every possible effort, in accordance with its constitution and the 'guiding principles' set out in the Convention, to avoid the double taxation of copyright royalties where possible, and, should it subsist, to eliminate it or reduce its effect.[241] This action was to be carried out by means of bilateral agreements or through domestic measures.[242] The remaining articles of the Convention contained definitions of particular terms[243] as well as the 'guiding principles' for action against double taxation.[244] A model bilateral agreement, which was not part of the Convention, was appended to act as a guide to member states in reaching arrangements with each other. Given that the requirements of the Convention were exhortatory rather than mandatory, this may be the reason for so few states ratifying or acceding to it; nonetheless, it may remain a useful starting point for any further international agreements in this difficult area.

(2) The 1960 Hague Act of the Hague Agreement Concerning the International Deposit of Industrial Designs

19.80 The original Hague Agreement was concluded in 1925 as a 'special agreement' under the Paris Convention for the Protection of Industrial Property rather than the Berne Convention. Nonetheless, when this Agreement was revised in 1960, the BUPC sought to ensure that the formalities required for protection under industrial property laws should not intrude into protection accorded by copyright laws.[245] To this end, article 14 of the Hague Act of 1960 provides that, in relation to the international design notice provided for under that article, the 'mere appearance' of that notice on an article is not to be interpreted 'as implying a waiver of protection by virtue of copyright or any other grounds, whenever, in the absence of such notice, such protection may be claimed'. In addition, article 18 stipulates that the provisions of the Agreement are not to preclude:

> . . . the making of a claim to the benefit of any greater protection which may be granted by domestic legislation in a Contracting State, nor shall they affect in any way the protection accorded to works of art and works of applied art by international copyright treaties and conventions.

By 17 January 2005, there were thirty-one states that were party to this Act of the Agreement.[246]

---

[241] Madrid Convention, art 8(1). [242] ibid. [243] ibid, arts 1–4.
[244] ibid, arts 5–7.
[245] [1959] *DA* 188 (seventh ordinary session, Geneva) and [1959] *DA* 206 (eighth ordinary session, Munich).
[246] www.wipo.int/treaties.

(3) The Vienna Agreement for the Protection of Typefaces and their International Deposit and the Film Register Treaty

The first of these, negotiated in 1973 and open to Paris, Berne, and UCC members, constituted a union for the protection of typefaces which were defined as sets of designs of letters and alphabets, together with accents and punctuation, numerals and other signs and symbols, and ornaments such as borders, fleurons, and vignettes which are intended to provide means for composing texts by any graphic technique.[247] By January 1986, only two states had ratified the Agreement, and it appears never to have entered into force.[248] The second, adopted in 1989, provides in articles 3 and 4 for an international register situated in Vienna to provide rebuttable (and 'Berne-compliant') evidence of entitlements and transactions in relation to audiovisual works. It had thirteen members as at 15 April 2005.[249] **19.81**

(4) Audio-visual performers

While the WPPT ultimately is mainly concerned with audio performances, proposals to include audio-visual performances were part of the original programme formulated by the Committee of Experts in its preparatory work and remained on the table as options even as the Diplomatic Conference got under way in December 1996. While logic and principle would suggest that the two kinds of performances should be treated alike, in practice there have been considerable and continuing differences between the audio and audio-visual industries, particularly in relation to contractual arrangements where national approaches vary widely. This led to significant division at the Conference, notably between those countries such as the US and India that have large film industries where manifold contributions, including those of performers both local and foreign, are brought together, and those countries which had less difficulty in accepting the logic of treating audio-visual and audio performers in the same way.[250] Despite a number of compromise proposals that sought to provide a meeting point between the two perspectives, including a system of reservations, no agreement could be reached and, as noted above (see para 19.51), proposals for the inclusion of audio-visual performers were jettisoned from the final act of the WPPT. **19.82**

Some hint of the frustrations that had arisen over these matters, mainly through the course of informal negotiations between delegates, during the course of the

[247] Vienna Agreement, art 2(i) (text contained in [1973] *Copyright* 132ff).

[248] [1986] *Copyright* 11 (France and Germany).

[249] www.wipo.int/treaties (text and status).

[250] See the excellent treatment of the course of these discussions in Reinbothe and von Lewinski (2002), 478–85. See further Ficsor (2001), 668ff (paras 10.06ff).

Diplomatic Conference, is reflected in the following resolution that was adopted by the last plenary session of the Conference on 20 December 1996:[251]

> The Delegations participating in the Diplomatic Conference on Certain Copyright and Neighboring Rights Questions in Geneva,
>
> *Noting* that the development of technologies will allow for a rapid growth of audiovisual services and that this will increase the opportunities for performing artists to exploit their audiovisual performances that will be transmitted by these services;
>
> *Recognizing* the great importance of ensuring an adequate level of protection for these performances, in particular when they are exploited in the new digital environment, and that sound and audiovisual performances are increasingly related;
>
> *Stressing* the urgent need to agree on new norms for the adequate legal international protection of audiovisual performances;
>
> *Regretting* that, in spite of the efforts of most Delegations, the WIPO Performances and Phonograms Treaty does not cover the rights of performers in the audiovisual fixations of their performance;
>
> *Call* for the convocation of an extraordinary session of the competent WIPO Governing Bodies during the first quarter of 1997 to decide on the schedule of the preparatory work on a protocol to the WIPO Performances and Phonograms Treaty, concerning audiovisual performances, with a view to the adoption of such a protocol not later than in 1998.[252]

19.83 The WIPO assemblies of member states and the unions administered by WIPO duly decided in their March 1997 sessions to establish a committee of experts on a Protocol concerning Audiovisual Performances (Document AB/XXX/4 Rev), following which the Director General of WIPO convened the Committee of Experts in two sessions, the first in September 1997 and the second in June 1998. This body was then replaced by the Standing Committee on Copyright and Related Rights ('SCCR') as part of the restructuring of its system of committees of experts by WIPO in early 1998 (see para 16.10 (viii) above), and consideration of the audio-visual issue was then carried forward by the SCCR in a series of sessions held in November 1998, May 1999, November 1999, and April 2000.[253] Regional consultations were also conducted by WIPO before several sessions of these Committee meetings, as well as inquiries into relevant national legislation on audio-visual performances and contractual practices. Following recommendations of the SCCR, WIPO member states as well as the EC, were then invited to provide proposals in possible treaty language, and the

---

251 *Records* 1996, vol II, 630, para 516.

252 ibid, vol I, 93.

253 See the background given in Document IAVP/DC/3 ORIGINAL, 1 Aug, 2000, entitled 'Basic Proposal for the Substantive Provisions of an Instrument on the Protection of Audiovisual Performances to be Considered by the Diplomatic Conference' (the 'Basic Proposal'), 3–5, available at www.wipo.int.

fourth session of the SCCR in April 2000 recommended that preparations were now sufficiently advanced for the holding of a diplomatic conference to adopt a new instrument by the end of 2000. This was duly approved by the WIPO General Assembly on 13 and 14 April 2000, and a Basic Proposal and commentary was prepared by the International Office. Further regional consultations occurred, and the proposed diplomatic conference was held from 7–20 December 2000. There were 119 states represented at the Conference,[254] together with a 'special delegation' from the European Community and two observer delegations (Djibouti and Iran), some nine intergovernmental organizations,[255] and fifty-seven non-governmental organizations.[256]

The Basic Proposal put before the Diplomatic Conference followed the model provided by the WPPT with similar or identical provisions for the protection of moral rights (article 5) and exclusive rights in respect of unfixed performance (article 6), reproduction (article 7), distribution (article 8), rental (article 9), making available online of fixed performances (article 10), and broadcasting and communication to the public (article 11). Corresponding provisions on limitations and exceptions (article 13), term of protection (article 14), technological protection measures (article 15), rights management information (article 16), and the prohibition of formalities (article 17) were also included, as well as agreed statements similar to those applying to the WPPT. There were uncertainties about the form that the new instrument should take, whether as a protocol to the WPPT, a free-standing instrument or as a special agreement, but these were not of critical importance. Another point of difference, as in the case of the WPPT, was the scope of the proposed principle of national treatment and whether this would apply to remuneration rights (article 4). **19.84**

However, while agreement and/or compromise was ultimately reached on all these issues,[257] the real point of dissension between delegates was over proposed

[254] Document IAVP/DC/INF/1, available at www.wipo.int. These included all the larger Berne member states, such as the USA, China, the Russian Federation, and EC members, India, Indonesia, Korea, and Japan. For a general review of the work of the Conference, see S von Lewinski, 'WIPO Diplomatic Conference on Audiovisual Performances: A First Resume' [2001] *European Intellectual Property Review* 333.

[255] Including the ILO, UNESCO, ITU, WTO, League of Arab States, Organisation of the Islamic Conference, Organisation of African Unity, Arab States Broadcasting Union, and Organisation internationale de la Francophonie: ibid.

[256] Noteworthy here were large delegations from the International Federation of Actors, the International Federation of the Phonographic Industry, the International Federation of Film Producers Associations, International Federation of Musicians, and the Copyright Research and Information Centre, Japan: ibid.

[257] Thus, the minutes of Main Committee I report at para 415 that: 'Main Committee I adopted, by consensus, the Preamble and Articless 2, 3, 5(2) and (3), 6, 7, 8, 9(1), 10, 13, 15, 16, 17 and 20, as contained in document IAVP/DC/33, with the corrections indicated by the President of the Committee and the Title and Arts 1, 9(2), 11, 14, 18 and 19, as contained in

article 12(2) concerning transfer of rights. This was a matter of particular importance to delegations such as the USA which wished to preserve transfers as a matter for one national law, preferably that of the producer's country where all the disparate components for an audio-visual production could be brought together and exploited by reference to one law. It will be recalled that there had been an attempt to deal with these issues in relation to cinematographic works under article 14*bis* of the Berne Convention (see paras 7.31ff above), and a number of formulations were proposed to apply to audio-visual performers as part of article 12 of the Basic Proposal. These included a deemed transfer of all rights in a particular fixation to the producer by a performer once he or she had consented to the incorporation, subject to written contractual clauses to the contrary ('Alternative E'); a less sweeping deemed entitlement for the producer in such a case to 'exercise the exclusive rights of authorization' of the performer with respect to that particular fixation, subject to written contractual clauses to the contrary ('Alternative F'); and a proposed choice of law rule that, '[I]in the absence of any contractual clauses to the contrary, a transfer to the producer of an audiovisual fixation of a performance, by agreement or operation of law, of any of the exclusive rights of authorization granted under this Treaty, shall be governed by the law of the country most closely connected with the particular audiovisual fixation', followed by a list of factors relevant to determining the 'country most closely connected' ('Alternative G'). A final proposal ('Alternative H') proposed that there should be no provision, leaving it as a matter for legislation in the contracting parties whether or not to provide for a transfer of rights and to determine its nature and scope.

The extreme positions here were represented by the large audio-visual producer countries, such as the USA and India,[258] which argued for one clear law to govern the transfer and exercise of performers' rights by the producer upon the first incorporation into an audio-visual production, and the EC countries which

---

document IAVP/DC/34 with the corresponding agreed statements.' (Document IAVP/DC/37, Summary Minutes, Main Committee I). Another controversial issues concerning national treatment (art 4) was adopted subject to the following declaration by the President of Main Committee I: '. . . during the work of Main Committee I, a proposal was made to include in the Treaty a provision stating that no Contracting Party should allow collection of remuneration in respect of performances of nationals of another Contracting Party, unless distribution of such remuneration is made to those nationals. Such rules have not been taken to the text of the Treaty. It is understood that there is no legal basis for collection of remuneration in a Contracting Party in respect of nationals of another Contracting Party for rights that it does not accord to those nationals. Collections in such circumstances would be inappropriate and without legal authority. Therefore all those from whom such remuneration is claimed should have legal remedies against the payment. Where remuneration is collected, on the basis of proper mandates, in a Contracting Party for rights that it accords to the nationals of another Contracting Party, but not distributed to them, those nationals should have legal means to ensure that they received the remuneration collected on their behalf.'

[258] India's film industry, based in Bombay, is sometimes referred to as 'Bollywood'.

took the position that private international law questions essentially belonged outside a treaty such as this one which should be confined to establishing and recognizing the basic norms of protection for this new category of rights.[259] As we have already seen above in Chapter 7, in relation to cinematographic works, attempts to deal with choice of law questions in Berne have been generally only of limited value, and the discussions in the 2000 Diplomatic Conference in relation to audio-visual performances proved equally so. After extensive discussions, both formally and informally, where both blocs moved some way towards each other on this 'thorny issue',[260] it proved ultimately impossible within the allotted time to reach an acceptable compromise position. Thus, although agreement was possible on everything else, choice of law issues addressed by proposed article 12(2) was the stumbling block,[261] and no Final Act could be signed.[262] The president of the Conference summarized the results of the discussions that had occurred in the following statement adopted by the delegates:

> The Diplomatic Conference
>
> (i) notes that a provisional agreement has been achieved on 19 Articles;
>
> (ii) recommends to the Assemblies of Member States of WIPO, in their September 2001 session, that they reconvene the Diplomatic Conference for the purpose of reaching agreement on outstanding issues.

To the time of writing, there has been no such reconvening of the Diplomatic Conference, although this remains open. However, it does not seem that it has been possible to achieve the necessary consensus on the sticking point or 'last hurdle'[263] of choice of law issues. Thus, while the Diplomatic Conference recommendation was duly reported to the 2001 WIPO Assembly, statements by the principal protagonists made it clear that more work was needed before the Conference could be reconvened, and the issue was therefore placed as a standing item on the annual WIPO Assembly agendas while more informal negotiations and consultations continued, including studies of national laws. At the time of writing, this still appears to be the case and the differences between delegates, particularly on the choice of law issue, have not yet been resolved. In view of this, it has been thought unhelpful simply to adopt an instrument

[259] The most concise statements of the differing positions are to be found in the Summary Minutes of Main Committee I, at para 442 (Reinbothe, EC) and para 444 (Keplinger, USA).

[260] Ficsor (2001), 700.

[261] This read as follows: '(2) Without prejudice to international obligations and to public or private international law a transfer by agreement of exclusive rights of authorization granted under this Treaty, or [an agreement to exercise such rights] [an entitlement to exercise such rights based on the consent of the performer to the fixation], shall be governed by the law of the country chosen by the parties or, to the extent that the law applicable to the agreement between the performer and the producer has not been chosen, by the law of the country with which the agreement is most closely connected.' (Document IAVP/DC/34.)

[262] See further von Lewinski, (n 254 above).

[263] Ficsor (2001), 698.

dealing with those matters in which there is consensus and to defer the reconvening of the Diplomatic Conference. Thus, at the 2004 WIPO Assembly meeting, the following minutes appear in the report of the meeting and provide some insight into the interests and passions at play:

> 37. The Chair of the General Assembly expressed his appreciation for the work done on the issue of the protection of audiovisual performances, and notably to Deputy Director General, Mrs. Rita Hayes. He noted the previous intervention by the Egyptian Delegation on the expectations of African performers, and recalled the presentation by the performer, Mr. Gerard Essomba, at the *ad hoc* Informal Meeting on the Protection of Audiovisual Performances. On that occasion, Mr. Essomba strongly appealed to States to pursue their efforts to achieve international protection for audiovisual performers. It was interesting to note that, during the discussion by the General Assembly, not a single delegation had requested that the issue of the protection of audiovisual performers be removed from the agenda of the General Assembly. However, convening of a Diplomatic Conference would be premature, as such a course could extinguish future possibilities for resolution of outstanding questions. Neither was it possible to accept only the articles that were agreed and exclude the issues where differences remain. The only solution at present was to continue the existing efforts, seeking new means to implement international protection by reconciling different concepts and views. It was therefore necessary that delegates as well as stakeholders from the private sector avail themselves of every occasion for exchange and dialogue so that, at the next General Assembly, a decision could be taken on the matter.

As with so much in the area of international copyright and related rights, this is a 'work in progress' where the logic and appeal of principle (protection for all categories of performers) has to accommodate the realities of industry practice and national sensitivities.

(5) **Databases**

19.85 Another claimant for neighbouring rights protection has been non-original databases, ie compilations of data that will not qualify for protection as literary works under the Berne Convention and the WCT. This has long been an area of concern in a number of countries, particularly in the USA and EC, and led to specific proposals for their protection in the Committee of Experts on a possible protocol to the Berne Convention. Thus, at the fourth session in 1995, there was a consensus that this should be a matter included in the proposed protocol or should even be the subject of a separate new instrument.[264] More specific proposals were presented by the EC and then the USA at subsequent sessions,[265] and a separate Basic Proposal for the Substantive Provisions of the Treaty on Intellectual Property in Respect of Databases which drew on both the US and

---

[264] Report of the fourth session: [1995] *Industrial Property and Copyright* 107, 109.
[265] See generally Reinbothe and von Lewinski (2002), 486–7; Ficsor (2001), 69–70.

EC proposals was approved for presentation to the Diplomatic Conference in December 1996.[266] Essentially, this was based on the notion that there should be protection for databases that represented a 'substantial investment in the collection, assembly, verification, organisation or presentation of the contents of the database'.[267] This protection was to apply regardless of the form or medium in which the database was embodied or whether or not it was made available to the public,[268] and irrespective of any protection that might be available under copyright.[269] The right conferred was to be the right to authorize or prohibit the extraction or utilization of its contents,[270] and was to be owned by the maker of the database.[271] Provision was made for exceptions and limitations to be subject to the three-step test.[272] The principles of national treatment and independence of protection were to apply,[273] with alternative proposed terms of twenty-five or fifteen years.[274] Protection was not to be subject to formalities,[275] and there were to be obligations with respect to technological measures[276] and enforcement.[277]

By the time of the Diplomatic Conference, however, it was clear that there would not be the time or space within the Conference programme to deal with this third treaty, and it was therefore not considered, being left on the 'back burner'.[278] Reinbothe and von Lewinski also suggest that another, and perhaps more substantive, reason for not proceeding was that there were doubts by the USA as to the appropriateness of the protection proposed, and that more time was needed for discussion.[279] The formal decision of the Conference therefore was a recommendation adopted at its final plenary session: **19.86**

> The Delegates participating in the Diplomatic Conference on Certain Copyright and Neighbouring Rights Questions in Geneva,
>
> *Recognising* that databases are a vital element in the development of a global information infrastructure;
>
> *Conscious* of the importance of encouraging further development of databases;
>
> *Aware* of the need to strike a balance between the interests of the producers of databases in protection from unfair copying and the interests of users in having appropriate access to the benefits of a global information infrastructure;
>
> *Expressing interest* in examining further the possible implications and benefits of a *sui generis* system of protection of databases at the international level;
>
> *Noting* that a treaty on such a *sui generis* system was not negotiated or adopted at the Conference;
>
> *Recommend* the convocation of an extraordinary session of the competent WIPO Governing Bodies during the first quarter of 1997 to decide on the schedule of

[266] Document CRNR/DC/6 at *Records* 1996, vol I, 336 and following ('Basic Proposal').
[267] ibid, art 1(1). [268] Article 1(2). [269] Article 1(3). [270] Article 3(1).
[271] Article 4(1). [272] Article 5(1). [273] Article 7. [274] Article 8.
[275] Article 9. [276] Article 10. [277] Article 13. [278] Ficsor (2001), 69.
[279] Reinbothe and von Lewinski (2002), 488, para 57.

further preparatory work on a Treaty on Intellectual Property in Respect of Databases.

The history since the Diplomatic Conference suggests that the proposed treaty was certainly premature, with a definite lack of consensus among nations as to how to proceed. Thus, the extraordinary session of WIPO governing bodies foreshadowed in the Conference recommendation did not take place, and the subject of databases has been an item on the agenda of a number of meetings of the SCCR and has been the focus of regional consultations and meetings since 1997, but no clear agreement on the form of a treaty has yet emerged.[280] Significant issues of policy are raised by proposals for the protection of non-original databases, and there are difficult questions as how to balance the competing interests involved. Furthermore, there are strong differences as to the appropriate form of such protection: whether this should be an exclusive right against unauthorized extraction as a protection for investment, should it be based on an unfair competition rationale, or something else again.[281] These issues are far from settled at the level of national and regional law,[282] so it is unsurprising that the necessary consensus on international norms has not yet emerged.

(6) Broadcasting organizations

19.87 The latest claimants for international protection of its interests have been broadcasting organizations,[283] although it will be recalled that these were one leg of the somewhat flimsy three-legged stool erected under Rome. More recently,

---

[280] For a list of regional roundtable meetings that have occurred since 1999, see the list at www.wipo.int/meetings/en/topic.jsp?group_id=229. Valuable national and comparative surveys and other reports are to be found in the papers prepared for these and other expert meetings, see eg those prepared for the WIPO International Conference on Electronic Commerce and Intellectual Property, Geneva, 14–16 Sept 1999, in particular those by Reinbothe (Document WIPO/EC/CONF/99/SPK/22-A), Glazier (Document WIPO/EC/CONF/99/SPK/22-B), and Mille (Document WIPO/EC/CONF/99/SPK/22-C/e). Note also the obvious awareness of WIPO of the wider economic and social significance of according protection in this area, as indicated by the meeting of the Working Group on the Economic Impact of the Intellectual Property Protection of Databases, 29–31 Jan 2002, Geneva, Switzerland.

[281] See the discussion by Reinbothe and von Lewinski (2002), 492–4, and see further M Davison, *The Legal Protection of Databases* (2003).

[282] In this regard, see Directive 96/9/EC of the European Parliament and of the Council of 11 Mar 1996 on the legal protection of databases, and note the different proposals that have been introduced into the US Congress over this period: see A Perkins, 'United States Still No Closer to Database Legislation' [2000] *EIPR* 366. Note also that, in some Commonwealth common law countries such as Australia, protection for 'non-original' databases is effectively applied through a lower requirement generally for originality in relation to literary works: see *Desktop Marketing Systems Pty Ltd v Telstra Corporation Ltd* (2001) 51 IPR 257 (Full Court, Federal Court of Australia).

[283] Colourfully described by Dr Ficsor as the 'orphans of Rome' (Ficsor (2001), 74), although the authors of this commentary have yet to come across any broadcasting organizations that are still looking for their parents!

the question of protection of the rights of broadcasting organizations has been part of the agenda of the SCCR, beginning at its first session in November 1998. At this time, governments and the EC were invited to submit proposals on the issue, and a considerable number of these were duly received.[284] The WIPO secretariat then prepared various documents to guide consideration by the SCCR, including a working paper on terminology and concepts[285] and a comparison of the various proposals, the latest version being considered by the tenth session of the SCCR in September 2003.[286] At that session, the SCCR requested its chair, together with the WIPO secretariat, to prepare a consolidated draft of proposals for consideration at its next session, with a view to determining whether to recommend to the WIPO General Assembly that a diplomatic conference be convened for the adoption of a formal treaty. This, indeed, is what happened at the eleventh session of the SCCR, which recommended that the next session of the WIPO General Assembly consider the 'possibility of convening, at an appropriate time, a diplomatic conference on the protection of broadcasting organizations'. At the same time, the SCCR clearly recognized that it needed to do more work on preparing a revised consolidated text, including the preparation of a 'basic proposal', so at this stage the General Assembly was really being asked for approval in principle of the 'convening of a diplomatic conference on the protection of broadcasting organizations to be organized at an appropriate time'.[287] The General Assembly duly accepted this recommendation, and 'requested the SCCR to accelerate its work on the protection of broadcasting organizations with a view to approving the convening of a diplomatic conference by the WIPO General Assembly in 2005'.[288]

Notwithstanding the apparent optimism of the language used, it was soon apparent that the conditions for convening of a diplomatic conference were hardly present: to adopt the language of Mark Antony, this was not 'a tide in the affairs of men which, taken at the flood, leads on to fortune'[289] let alone the formulation of a new international instrument on the rights of broadcasters. Even at the General Assembly, strong reservations about proceeding so rapidly **19.88**

[284] A list of some seventeen proposals from a wide range of states, as well as the EC, that had been received up to Sept 2003 is set out in Document SCCR/12/2 (Revised Consolidated Text for a Treaty on the Protection of Broadcasting Organizations), paras 15–17 (4 Oct 2004).

[285] 'Protection of Broadcasting Organizations: Terms and Concepts', Document SCCR/8/INF/1, requested by the seventh session of the SCCR in May 2002 for its eighth session of 13–17 May 2002.

[286] SCCR/10/3, 15 Sept 2003.

[287] As noted in Document WO/GA/31/15, para 40 (report of thirty-first session, fifteenth extraordinary session, WIPO General Assembly, 27 Sept–5 Oct 2004). The relevant document setting out the views of the SCCR was Document WO/GA/31/7, all available on www.wipo.int.

[288] Document WO/GA/31/15, para 40.

[289] Shakespeare, *Julius Caesar*, iii, 215.

had been expressed by several delegations,[290] and these doubts and criticisms came more readily to the surface when the twelfth session of the SCCR met in November 2004. The revised 'Consolidated Text for the WIPO Treaty on the Protection of Broadcasting Organizations' was formulated in treaty language, but with various alternative proposals for different articles.[291] In keeping with the format adopted under the WCT and WPPT, this proposed the grant of a broad palette of exclusive rights for broadcasting organizations, namely with respect to retransmission (article 6), communication to the public (article 7), right of fixation (article 8), reproduction of fixations (article 9), distribution of fixations (article 10), transmission following fixation (article 11), and making available of fixed broadcasts (article 12). Corresponding obligations with respect to technological measures (article 16) and rights management information (article 17) were included, with the inevitable proposal for exceptions and limitations to be subject to the three-step test (article 14), alternative terms of twenty and fifty years (article 15), and a no-formalities requirement (article 18). A further requirement was to accord broadcasting organizations 'adequate and effective legal protection against any acts referred to in Article 6 to 12 of this Treaty in relation to their signals prior to broadcasting'.

19.89 While the proposed text was comprehensive in the framework of protection proposed, there were many issues on which there was no consensus among delegates (and observers) at the twelfth session of the SCCR. These included:

---

[290] See eg the comments by the Indian delegation at Document WO/GA/31/15, para 41:

> The Delegation of India noted that Article 14 of the Agreement on Trade-Related Aspects of Intellectual Property Rights (the TRIPS Agreement) provided protection for broadcasting organizations. Many Member States, including India, had modified their legislation to extend protection to broadcasting organizations as mandated under the TRIPS Agreement. The proposed new treaty would provide for a TRIPS-plus level of protection, at a moment where most developing countries were still in the process of understanding and complying with that Agreement. At the same time, the obligation mandated under Article 7 of the TRIPS regarding promotion of technological innovations and dissemination of technological innovations and transfer of technology to the mutual advantage of producers and users of technological knowledge remained a thought. No consensus existed on the broad parameters for developing a new treaty, and further discussions were needed in the SCCR, on the basis of a new consolidated text. It was necessary to fully take into account the interests of developing nations, the implications of technologies, the interests of content creators and of society at large before moving towards a diplomatic conference. The Delegation had taken due note of the information contained in document WO/GA/31/7, but it was unclear what it was that the Assembly was asked to approve. The decision should be amended in line with what had been proposed for audiovisual performers in document WO/GA/31/4. The item would have to remain on the agenda of the next WIPO General Assembly in 2005. Such decision would preserve the functioning of the General Assembly. Issues should be brought to the General Assembly only when ripe enough, and that stage had not yet been reached.

[291] Document SCCR/12/2, Revised Consolidated Text for the WIPO Treaty on the Protection of Broadcasting Organizations, available at www.wipo.int. The accompanying commentary and notes on the proposed articles provide considerable assistance as to the background for the proposals and will clearly form an important part of the 'preparatory work' for any treaty that is ultimately negotiated.

- the kinds of broadcasts to be protected, in particular whether it was to be limited to 'traditional' (free to air) broadcasting, or would extend to cablecasting, as well as the communications over the Internet ('webcasting');
- the relationship between the rights of broadcasting organizations and those of 'content providers', ie the rights of authors, phonogram producers, and performers;
- the scope of national treatment requirements;
- the form of protection to be offered, ie whether these should be all exclusive rights or all or some subject to rights of remuneration only; and
- the scope for exceptions and limitations, having regard to national, cultural, and developmental sensitivities.

The differences between delegates also seemed to reflect both regional and developing/developed country divides, essentially with the more developed states pushing for a wider form of protection and the developing countries expressing clear reservations. The general impression from the draft report of the session is that it was 'all too much, too soon', with divisions even arising as to the 'conclusions' formulated by the chair of the SCCR, a point that may have future significance for the purposes of treaty development and interpretation.[292] Unusually, the 'conclusions' of the chair, summing up the discussions, were not accepted by consensus, with several delegations noting their dissent.[293] These conclusions called for the preparation of a 'second revised version of the Consolidated Text' by the chair of the present session of the SCCR (Finland) and a working paper on alternative non-mandatory solutions to the protection of webcasting organizations, including simulcasting organizations, as well as the holding of regional consultations and other types of informal consultations to be organized by WIPO as requested by member states. So far as the next (thirteenth) session of the SCCR was concerned, it was proposed that:

[292] Thus, concluding comments by the chair of such a committee may provide an authoritative guide to what delegates had in mind in their discussions of a particular matter and may also operate as an authoritative, even binding, direction for future meetings. In the context of a full diplomatic conference, such statements may also take their place as 'agreements made between all the parties in connexion with the conclusion of the treaty' within the meaning of art 31(2)(a) of the Vienna Convention on the Law of Treaties (so long, of course, as the interpretation is 'uncontested').

[293] Notably Argentina, Brazil, Egypt, India, and the Islamic Republic of Iran: Document SCCR/12/4 (draft report, twelfth session, SCCR, 17–19 Nov 2004, Geneva), para 275. The chair is recorded further as stating that: 'A substantial majority of Members indicated their support of the conclusions of the Chairman. The Chairman noted that the Committee had to respect the opinion of the majority and, as consensus could not be reached on any set of conclusions within the time available, the conclusions of the Chairman would be included in the report. The Chairman expressed deep regret at the spirit in which the Committee's discussions ended, particularly in view of the flexibility and willingness shown by its Members to reach agreement on the substantive issues.'

- the next session of the Standing Committee will take into account the progress made in the regional consultations and other types of informal consultation meetings;
- the Committee will, in light of the results of the regional consultations and other types of informal consultations, consider the second revised version of the Consolidated Text, and examine the working paper on alternative solutions on the protection of webcasting organizations.

These 'conclusions' are a considerable step backwards from the General Assembly recommendation for 'accelerated action' in relation to a treaty and diplomatic conference. This is still clearly a project in its early stages, a true 'work in progress', and the possibility of formulating a new treaty in this area has disappeared, at least for the immediate future.

H. Concluding Comments

19.90 This chapter has demonstrated, albeit in truncated form, the significant developments that have occurred outside the scope of the Berne Convention in the years since the adoption of the Rome Convention in 1960. It has been an uneven history, with some notable achievements in the adoption of free-standing treaties (Rome and the WPPT), some important ancillary provisions (as in the case of the TRIPs Agreement), and some equally notable failures, at least to date (satellites, databases, audio-visual performances, and broadcasting organizations). Activity in the sphere of 'norm creation' has intensified, particularly since the successful negotiation of the 1996 treaties, but the developments noted in the last section may indicate that more time and reflection will now be required before treaties in these other areas can or will be concluded. In truth, these are matters that are still contested and far from resolution at both the national and regional levels, so it is unsurprising that international solutions have not yet been reached. The advent of digital technologies and networked communications have created an entirely new environment for rights owners and users, meaning that issues relating to the formulation of rights, the kinds of exceptions and limitations to be allowed, and the relations between different groups of rights owners have become far more difficult to negotiate. Consensus at national and regional levels will be necessary before more formal agreements at the international level can be reached, and it may be that WIPO will now find its role returning to the one that it fulfilled in the years of 'guided development' following the Stockholm and Paris Revision Conferences of 1967 to 1971 (see further Chapter 4 above).

I. Comparative Table of Neighbouring Rights

19.91

Subject matter not covered by Berne Convention (coverage rejected)	1961 Rome Convention	1971 Phonograms Convention	TRIPs Agreement	WPPT	Gaps and ambiguities
Broadcasts	article 13 (right of broadcasting organization to control rebroadcasting, fixation, and certain reproductions of their broadcasts)		article 14(3) but member states need not recognize rights in broadcasting organizations if copyright owners of broadcast content can control fixation, reproduction, wireless rebroadcast of the broadcast, and communication to the public of television broadcasts	nil	Rome: reservations allowable under article 16(2)
Sound recordings	article 11 (phonogram producers' rights of reproduction); article 12 (equitable remuneration for communication to the public of commercially published phonograms)	article 2 (duplication and public distribution of phonogram)	article 14(2) (direct or indirect reproduction of phonograms); article 11 (rental rights, subject to equitable remuneration with respect to pre-May 1994 rental schemes under article 14(4)	article 11 (reproduction), article 12 (distribution), article 13 (rental), article 14 (making available), article 15 (single equitable remuneration for direct or indirect use of commercially published phonograms for broadcasting or public communication)	Rome: reservations allowable under article 16(1) and 17; WPPT: reservations allowable under article 15(3)

Continued overleaf

Comparative Table of Neighbouring Rights (*cont.*)

Subject matter not covered by Berne Convention (coverage rejected)	1961 Rome Convention	1971 Phonograms Convention	TRIPs Agreement	WPPT	Gaps and ambiguities
Interpretations of performing artists	article 7 (the 'possibility of preventing' certain acts, ie broadcasting and public communication of performances, fixation of unfixed performances, and reproduction of such fixations); article 12 (equitable remuneration for communication to the public of commercially published phonograms of performances)		article 14(1) ('possibility of preventing' fixation of unfixed performances on phonograms and reproduction of such fixations; broadcasting and public communication of live performances)	article 5 (moral rights), article 6 (broadcasting, communication and fixation of unfixed performances), article 7 (reproduction), article 8 (distribution), article 9 (rental), article 10 (making available of fixed performances), article 15 (single equitable remuneration for direct or indirect use of commercially published phonograms for broadcasting or public communication)	WPPT limited to audio performances (except for article 6)

Part V

PRIVATE INTERNATIONAL LAW ASPECTS OF INTERNATIONAL COPYRIGHT AND NEIGHBOURING RIGHTS PROTECTION

20

PRIVATE INTERNATIONAL LAW MATTERS: JURISDICTION AND APPLICABLE LAW

A. Introduction

20.01 At several points throughout this treatise, we have seen that the Berne Convention and related subsequent agreements do not always impose a substantive rule to resolve a variety of issues, from protectable subject matter, to authorship and ownership, to scope of rights. Arguably, for some of these questions, the Convention instead designates the applicable domestic law to resolve the issue, but the extent to which Berne creates choice of law rules is controversial.[1] The less Berne leaves to national law, including domestic private international law, the less uncertainty in the international copyright system. But, even after the Agreement on Trade-Related Aspects of Intellectual Property Rights 1994 ('the TRIPs Agreement'), Berne operates as a supranational copyright code only at a rather high level of abstraction. Moreover, in some member states, its text is not directly applicable, but must be implemented by national law.[2] Thus, deriving from the Berne text supranational choice of law rules is a delicate, if not improbable, operation. This chapter will consider the extent to which Berne does require or permit extrapolation of a supranational set of choice of law rules. In the absence of a Berne rule on legislative competence (jurisdiction to prescribe[3]), the chapter will next address general principles of private international law to inquire whether a *de facto* or customary set of choice of law rules applied by national courts exists or is in prospect. First, however, this chapter will take up the predicate question of judicial competence (jurisdiction to adjudicate[4]): when does a national court have power to hear claims alleging infringement of copyright in other countries? This inquiry is of considerable practical importance for two reasons. First, effective enforcement (or defence) of copyright claims may turn on the ability to resolve a broad range of territorial infringements in a single action. Second, in the absence of a supranational rule on jurisdiction to prescribe, the forum will apply its own choice of law rules. If different forums have different choice of law rules, the determination of judicial jurisdiction may affect, or dispose of, the outcome in the case.

---

[1] See generally Mireille van Eechoud, *Choice of Law in Copyright and Related Rights: Alternatives to the Lex Protectionis* (2003), 95–127.

[2] See eg the US Berne Convention Implementation Act of 1988 (Public Law 100–568) (codified at 17 USC §§ 101, 104, 116, 301, 401–2, 404–8, 801 (1988)). 'The Convention for the Protection of Literary and Artistic Works, signed at Berne, Switzerland, on September 9, 1886, and all acts, protocols, and revisions thereto . . . are not self-executing under the Constitution and laws of the United States' (ibid, § 2(1)).

[3] The terminology is that of the American Law Institute Restatement of the Law, 3d, Foreign Relations Law of the United States, § 401(a).

[4] See ibid, § 401(b).

B. Jurisdiction to Adjudicate

Does the Berne Convention have anything to say about judicial competence? Article 5(2) refers to 'the country where protection is claimed' as the country whose laws 'exclusively' govern 'the extent of protection, as well as the means of redress afforded to the author to protect his rights'. This may more resemble a choice of law provision than one pertaining to the competence of a forum. But the phrase 'where protection is claimed' may imply that the forum will be one in which an alleged infringement has occurred. If that country's laws are to govern the claim, it would follow that they have some relationship to the claim, for example, because the harmful act occurred in that territory. Basing judicial competence on the occurrence of a wrongful act in the territory would be consistent with general principles of jurisdiction recognizing the competence of the place of the harm.[5] **20.02**

There are several problems with this analysis, however. First, it makes jurisdiction, normally the predicate question, turn on determination of the applicable law. While this approach is not unknown in some jurisdictions, notably those adhering to the old Commonwealth rule of non-justiciability of foreign copyright claims,[6] analytically, it puts the cart before the horse. Second, the country 'where' protection is claimed is not necessarily the country where the infringement occurred. A copyright owner may choose to pursue a defendant in her country of residence, even though the infringing acts may have occurred elsewhere, because in the country of the infringement she may not have sufficient assets to satisfy a judgment.[7] If the country of her residence is otherwise unrelated to the claim, the application of its substantive law seems questionable. Third, the problem of applying a law unrelated to the claim might be resolved if one understood article 5(2) as a direction to apply the conflicts law (rather than the substantive law) of the country 'where' protection is claimed (on the theory that the national conflicts law would designate the application of the law of the country of the harm), but then the term 'country where protection is claimed'

[5] See eg Council Regulation (EC) No 44/2001 of 22 Dec 2000 on jurisdiction and the recognition and enforcement of judgments in civil and commercial matters, *Official Journal* L 012, 16/01/2001 P 0001–0023 ('Brussels Regulation'), art 5(3); NYCPLR § 302(a)(2)(3) (New York 'long arm' jurisdiction statute).

[6] See eg *Tyburn Prods Ltd* v *Conan Doyle* [1991] Ch 75; [1990] RPC 185; *Potter* v *Broken Hill Proprietary Co* (1906) 3 CLR 479, 492 (Australia) (courts do not have jurisdiction over claims requiring application of a foreign copyright law). The rule has, however, been criticized, see eg *Griggs Group Ltd* v *Evans (No 2)* [2004] FSR 48 (Prescott, QC, deputy judge); appeal (on other grounds) dismissed [2005] EWCA Civ 11.

[7] See eg C Masouyé, *Guide to the Berne Convention for the Protection of Literary and Artistic Works* (1978) ('Masouyé (1978)'), para 5.7.

would no longer offer much guidance as to what country that is supposed to be.[8] In other words, article 5(2) might direct the application of the forum's conflicts law (or even its substantive law), but it does not tell us the basis on which the forum became the forum. The answer may lie in the application of general principles of jurisdiction, but in that case, article 5(2) will not have added anything to the determination of judicial competence.

20.03 The likely conclusion, therefore, is that the Berne Convention does not supply a rule designating a forum for copyright actions. The question thus will be left to member state law. Where Berne member states are also party to a multilateral instrument on jurisdiction, such as the European Union Brussels Regulation, its general rules (or specific rules, if any[9]) will determine the competent forum or forums. It is not the aim of this treatise to review the domestic laws of judicial competence in the Berne member states.[10] But a few general observations may be ventured. First, judicial competence covers two distinct issues, personal (or *in personam*) jurisdiction, including the power of the court to hear claims concerning foreign defendants; and subject-matter jurisdiction (or justiciability), the power of the court to hear certain kinds of claims. A court may have personal jurisdiction, for example, because the defendant is a forum resident, yet lack subject-matter jurisdiction, for example, because the claim alleges infringement of a foreign copyright, and in that country, such claims are considered non-justiciable. We will first consider rules of personal jurisdiction, and then will turn to subject-matter jurisdiction.

(1) Judicial power over foreign defendants

20.04 The following discussion is based on the rules of the Brussels Regulation, but those rules are likely to be generally compatible with jurisdictional principles applicable elsewhere. First, a defendant is amenable to suit in the country of her residence.[11] Second, she may be sued in the country 'where the harmful event [the infringement] occurred'.[12] This event may transpire in either, or both, the

[8] cf Graeme B Dinwoodie, 'Conflicts and International Copyright Litigation: The Role of International Norms', in Jurgen Basedow, Josef Drexl, Annete Kur, and Axel Metzger (eds), *Intellectual Property in the Conflict of Laws* (2005), 195, 201 (in related context of applicable law, 'the national treatment obligation of the Berne Convention . . . suggests that some notion of "place" . . . should be controlling. But . . . it is not clear which "place" is the most relevant').

[9] The Brussels Regulation (n 5 above), art 22(4), provides for exclusive jurisdiction over claims of invalidity of registered rights in the courts of the country of registration, but copyrights (whether or not registered) are not registered rights within the meaning of this article.

[10] For a helpful distillation of general principles of jurisdiction applicable in Western Europe (written primarily for US readers), see ch 5 ('Jurisdiction: The Power of European Civil Courts') of Mathias Reimann, *Conflict of Laws in Western Europe* (1995), 65–85.

[11] See Brussels Regulation (n 5 above), art 2 (domicile).

[12] ibid, art 5(3).

country whence the harm originated, or the country or countries where the harm impacted.[13] Because transborder communications, for example, by cable, satellite, or the Internet, may frequently occasion copyright infringements, the recognition that the courts of both the country of emission and the country or countries of receipt are competent has considerable practical significance.

(2) Scope of claims adjudicable against foreign defendants

Once the forum can compel a foreign defendant to appear before it, against what claims will she have to defend? As a general matter, if the court has exercised jurisdiction on the basis of a harmful act committed in the forum, the forum's competence should be limited to those claims. For example, if a French defendant is alleged to have distributed copies of an infringing work in the UK, Germany, and the Netherlands, a UK court may adjudicate those infringement claims arising out of the distribution of copies in the UK, but not those arising out of the distribution of copies in Germany and the Netherlands.[14] If, however, the defendant published the copies in Belgium, from which she then sent them to the UK, Germany, and the Netherlands, then the courts of Belgium, as the place of origination of the harm, may be competent to hear claims arising out of the original publication, including claims relating to foreign territories to which the copies were sent (what laws apply is another matter; see the further discussion at paras 20.08ff below).[15] **20.05**

A copyright owner thus would have a choice of forums when the infringing copies are distributed or infringing transmissions are received in multiple territories. The copyright owner may sue at the source of the infringement—the place of physical origination, or the headquarters of the party that has initiated the infringing acts; or it may sue in each country where the infringement culminated. But only the former forums (assuming the place of physical origination is elsewhere than the headquarters) will be competent to take into account the full panoply of infringing acts. When the infringements are thus globally scattered, and especially if they are not heavily concentrated in a few jurisdictions, the author or her successor will need to proceed either in multiple countries of receipt, or in a single action at the defendant's headquarters, in order to secure meaningful relief. Fragmentation of litigation (and considerable augmentation of enforcement and defence costs) may thus result: if the country from **20.06**

[13] See eg *Shevill and Others* v *Presse Alliance SA*, Case 68/93 [1995] ECR 415 (defamation claim; defendant newspaper amenable to suit in countries where newspaper was sold, or the country where it was published).

[14] This example transposes *Shevill* from its original libel context to an infringement context.

[15] This, too, is a transposition of *Shevill*, in which the European Court of Justice held that the courts of the country of the libel's publication were competent to hear claims alleging harm to reputation in the countries to which the newspaper was distributed.

which the infringement departed is a 'copyright haven' (that is, a propitious country in which to locate an infringing business, either because of the laxness of its laws or the slowness of its judicial process, or both), there will be no point in litigating in the one forum that is competent to hear the entire claim. The author will have to seek redress *seriatim*, by resort to as many national courts as there are countries of receipt.[16]

(3) Justiciability of foreign copyright claims

20.07 As a general rule, a forum-resident defendant is amenable to suit on any claim, whether or not it arises in the forum.[17] In countries bound by the Brussels Regulation, a court cannot decline to hear a claim against a local defendant alleging the commission of a copyright infringement in another country.[18] Outside the ambit of the Brussels Regulation, and particularly in common law countries, the justiciability of foreign copyright claims may turn on the characterization of the claim as a 'local action' or as a 'transitory action'.[19] In the latter event, as appears to be the case in the USA,[20] the court will treat a claim for copyright infringement like any other tort action, and, assuming it otherwise has subject-matter jurisdiction,[21] will hear the claim. In at least some Commonwealth countries, however, courts have expanded a common law rule barring the adjudication of claims to land situated abroad (the quintessential

[16] See, for this criticism, Gabrielle Kaufmann-Kohler, 'Internet: Mondialisation de la communication: mondialisation de la résolution des litiges?', in Catherine Kessedjian and Katharina Boele-Woelki (eds), *Internet, Which Court Decides, Which Law Applies?* (1989), 89, 115–18. See also France, Conseil d'Etat, *Internet et les réseaux numériques* (1998), 151 (suggesting, in light of the problem of serial litigation, that a national court, additional to that of the country of origin of the infringement, should be competent to remedy worldwide damage).

[17] See eg Brussels Regulation (n 5 above), art 2.

[18] See eg *Pearce* v *Ove Arup Partnership, Ltd* [1999] 1 All ER 769, [1999] FSR 525 (Court of Appeal) (suit alleging infringement of plaintiff's architectural plans by English architecture firm's construction of a building in Rotterdam, NL). The Brussels Regulation (n 5 above) appears to require the defendant's forum to adjudicate claims regarding foreign copyrights when the defendant is an EU domiciliary (it is not necessary that plaintiff also be domiciled in an EU member state), *Group Jose Reinsurance Co SA* v *Universal General Insurance Co*, Case C-412/98 [2000] ECR I-5925 (Brussels Convention, predecessor to Brussels Regulation, is claimant-blind); *Owusu* v *Jackson (t/a Villa Holidays Bal Inn Villas)*, Case C-281/02 (ECJ) (1 Mar 2005), (2005/C 105/02) OJ of 30.04.2005.

[19] For a comparison of US and UK approaches, see eg Paul Goldstein, *International Copyright: Principles, Law, and Practice* (2001), 91–4; see also ibid, 95–7 (comparing approaches to *forum non conveniens* dismissals).

[20] See eg *London Film Prods Ltd* v *Intercontinental Communications, Inc*, 580 F Supp 47 (SDNY 1984); Paul Goldstein, *Copyright: Principles, Law & Practice*, 2nd edn (1996), § 16.2.

[21] If the claim pits a foreign citizen against a US citizen, a federal court has jurisdiction by virtue of the 'diversity' of the parties. See 28 USC § 1332(a)(2) (1994). If the plaintiff and defendant are both foreigners, then there is no diversity, but a federal court's jurisdiction over the action would be 'supplemental' to the claim arising under US copyright law (assuming a US-law claim is pleaded). Ibid, § 1367.

local action)[22] into a broader prohibition on adjudicating claims of infringement of foreign intellectual property rights.[23] As a result, fragmentation of a multiterritorial copyright litigation may be inevitable: under the rules addressed above, the only forum in which all territorial claims might be concentrated may be that of the defendant's domicile; if the defendant's domicile rejects the justiciability of foreign copyright claims, then the author will be obliged to litigate, and the alleged infringer to defend, copyright actions around the world (unless the defendant consents to jurisdiction[24] in a forum competent to hear foreign copyright claims).

C. Applicable Law

(1) Introduction: national treatment and choice of law

(a) Berne Convention, article 5(1) and (2): a choice of law rule?

From its inception, the Berne Convention has combined two different techniques: substantive supranational minimum rules, and national treatment.[25] **20.08** Under the former approach, the Convention supplies the substantive rule, though member states may enjoy some room for interpretation, and may also provide for greater protection. In that event, or with respect to matters for which the Convention does not supply a substantive rule, what law applies? Under the rule of national treatment, as set out in article 5(1), a foreign Berne author is assimilated to a local author, and receives the same rights as the laws of that country would grant a local. (The scope of the rights the rule of national treatment requires member states to extend is discussed in greater detail at paras 6.93ff above.) This seems to mean that each country of the Union will apply its

---

22 See *British South Africa Co* v *Companhia de Moçambique* [1893] AC 602, HL. Where immovable property is concerned, the Brussels Regulation (n 5 above) confers exclusive jurisdiction on the courts of that country, see art 22(1).

23 See eg *Atkinson Footwear Ltd* v *Hodgskin International Services Ltd* (1994) 31 IPR 186 (NZ HC) (copyright); *Tritech Technology Pty Ltd* v *Gordon* (2000) 48 IPR 52 at 58 (Finkelstein J) (patents); *Potter* v *Broken Hill Proprietary Co* (n 6 above), 492 (Australia) (patents); *Tyburn Prods Ltd* v *Conan Doyle* (n 6 above) (copyright). See generally G W Austin, 'The Infringement of Foreign Intellectual Property Rights' (1997) 113 *Law Quarterly Review* 321.

24 It is generally recognized that a defendant may consent to the court's jurisdiction by entering an appearance and not contesting jurisdiction. See eg Brussels Regulation (n 5 above), art 24.

25 See eg Roberto Mastroianni, *Diritto Internationale e Diritto d'Autore* (1997), 89 (describing national treatment and substantive treaty minima—*jus conventionis*, as the two 'pillars' on which the Berne Convention rests).

Reciprocity is a third technique, but its domain is confined to specific, and, apart from duration (where, under art 7.8's rule of the shorter term, only partial reciprocity applies), somewhat marginal, situations. See arts 2(7) (works of applied art); 14*ter* (*droit de suite*).

substantive law to works of foreign Union authors.[26] In other words, the principle of national treatment would supply a choice of law rule directing application of the substantive law of the countries in which the author seeks to enforce her rights.[27]

20.09 Article 5(2) appears to reinforce this conclusion. Under art 5(2) of the Berne Convention,

> the extent of protection, as well as the means of redress afforded to the author to protect his rights, shall be governed exclusively by the laws of the country where protection is claimed.

There is in fact some dispute as to whether this text announces a choice of law rule, or simply a non-discrimination rule.[28] But the latter characterization begs the question, 'non-discrimination as to what?' As to the substantive rules governing the claims of local and of foreign authors? Or as to the choice of law rule to determine the law governing local and foreign authors' claims? In the latter event, the 'country where protection is claimed' need not apply its own law to a Unionist author, so long as it would apply the same choice of law rule to a local author in the same circumstances. (A similar effect would be achieved were article 5(2) considered a choice of law rule, but one designating the whole law, including the conflicts law, of the country 'where protection is claimed'.) This approach leads to considerable unpredictability, because its consequences for actual equality of treatment will depend on what the local choice of law rule is. Suppose the local choice of law rule directed application of the law of the country where the infringement occurred, and that the infringement occurred in a country other than the forum. In that case, the same law—the law of that other country—would apply to local and to foreign works. But suppose the local choice of law rule selected the law of the country of origin. In that case, local law would determine the infringement of local works, but foreign laws would govern the infringement of foreign works. This, in turn, could lead to different outcomes for domestic and for foreign works. Thus, if the forum applied the same choice of law rule to the infringement of domestic and foreign works, this could result in a denial of substantive national treatment. It seems reasonable to conclude, therefore, that the principle of non-discrimination calls for the application of the same substantive rules to local and to foreign authors.

---

[26] Some have contended, however, that the national treatment requirement simply entitles the foreign claimant to the same choice of law rule as the forum would apply to its own authors. See eg Michael Walter, 'Contractual Freedom in the Field of Copyright and Conflict of Laws' (1976) 87 *RIDA* 44, 46. This may lead to application of the same substantive law to foreign and local authors (particularly if the infringement has allegedly occurred in the forum), but it may not.

[27] See eg van Eechoud (n 1 above), 107 and authorities cited at n 300.

[28] See generally ibid at 95–127; James J Fawcett and Paul Torremans, *Intellectual Property and Private International Law* (1998), 466–75 (reviewing various interpretations of article 5(2)).

But does article 5(2) express not only a principle of non-discrimination, but also a choice of (substantive) law rule? Certainly the language 'shall be governed exclusively by the laws of the country where protection is claimed' *looks* like a rule of legislative competence, directing application of the law of the territory on which the alleged infringement occurred. But there are at least two problems. First, the text states 'country *where* protection is claimed', rather than 'country *for which* protection is claimed'. If this is a choice of law rule, then it looks like a direction to apply the *lex fori*. As we have seen earlier (see para 20.02 above), however, the forum is not necessarily the place of the infringement. (Although the drafters of article 5(2) may have assumed that the place of litigation and the place of the harm would coincide in practice, and this might have been a reasonable factual assumption at the time the rule was formulated.[29]) Applying the *lex fori* may result in a disjunction between the law applied to the claim and the law that governs in the place where the infringement occurred; that in turn may mean that the author does not receive the same level of protection as do authors in the country of infringement. As Roberto Mastroianni has emphasized, this outcome is inconsistent with the general Berne Convention goal of ensuring that authors be protected in as uniform a manner as possible.[30] As a result, many commentators have interpreted article 5(2) to mean 'country, or countries, *for which* protection is claimed'.[31] Second, even if article 5(2) announces a choice of law rule, it does not purport to cover all issues of international copyright.[32] Notably, questions of authorship, initial ownership, and transfers of ownership remain unaddressed. **20.10**

At most, then, article 5(1) and (2) anticipate that the law of the territories on which alleged infringements occur will determine most questions regarding the existence of protection, its scope, and the available remedies. This falls short of a fully territorial approach in two ways. First, as noted above, there are the matters left off the article 5(2) list. Second, at various points, the Convention designates application of a law other than that of the country of protection to determine the existence or scope of protection; this is the case in relation to duration, as well as to the protection of works of applied art and of the *droit de suite*.[33] These are all variations on the rule of reciprocity, an approach generally spurned by the **20.11**

[29] See van Eechoud (n 1 above), 108; Eugen Ulmer, *Intellectual Property Rights and the Conflict of Laws* (1978), 10 (in practice forum will most often be the place of infringement).

[30] Mastroianni (n 25 above), 92.

[31] See eg A Lucas and H-J Lucas, *Traité de la propriété littéraire et artistique*, 2nd edn (2001), paras 1088–90 (2001); H Desbois, A Françon, and A Kérever, *Les Conventions internationales du droit d'auteur et des droits voisins* (1976) ('Desbois et al (1976)'), paras 135–9; Stefania Bariatti, 'Internet e il diritto internazionale privato: aspetti relativi all a disciplina del diritto d'autore' (1996) *AIDA* 59, 70.

[32] See eg Goldstein (n 19 above), 89; Ulmer (n 29 above), 9.

[33] See Berne Convention, arts 2(7), 7(8), 14*ter*.

Convention (see the earlier discussion at paras 6.74ff above). Nonetheless, these derogations from the rule of national treatment make the law of the work's country of origin applicable to determine the existence or scope of protection in certain—admittedly limited—situations, thus undercutting the primacy of the law of the country of protection.

(b) Inferences to draw from article 14bis(2)(a)

20.12 Outside of article 5(2), there is one instance in which the Berne Convention both addresses questions of ownership and designates the applicable law. Article 14bis(2)(a) provides:

> Ownership of copyright in a cinematographic work shall be a matter for legislation in the country where protection is claimed.

Assuming this is not a direction to apply the conflicts law of the country 'where' (for which?) protection is claimed, article 14bis(2)(a) makes the law of each country of exploitation competent to determine ownership of rights in cinematographic works, subject to a complex set of presumptions of transfers of ownership set out in subsections (b)–(e). The earlier discussion (see paras 7.31–7.41 above) has queried whether the resulting system makes any sense.[34] For present purposes, the question is whether this rule should be understood to reflect a choice of law principle applicable generally to questions of copyright ownership, or indeed to all questions in contention in a copyright dispute. Or should the opposite inference be drawn? If the law of the country of protection was singled out in this instance, is that because it is a special case, and in any other matter of ownership, some other law will apply (for contending candidates, see the further discussion at para 20.39 below)? Indeed, pushing the negative inference to the extreme, some other law, perhaps that of the country of origin, might be the residually applicable law, from which articles 5(2) and 14bis(2)(a) derogate.[35] It is not necessary to choose between these competing default positions; the point is that the plausibility of either one further underscores the Berne Convention's failure to create a general structure for identifying applicable law.

20.13 In the absence of a fully articulated system of Treaty-mandated choice of law rules, we turn next to general principles of private international law to consider

[34] Desbois, Françon and Kérever contended that the treaty's ambiguity reflects an awkward attempt to compromise between countries vesting film producers with initial copyright and those reposing rights initially in actual authors. They charged that where the Berne Convention should have supplied a substantive supranational rule, or at least a single conflicts rule, it has simply introduced confusion. See Desbois et al (1976), 216–21.

[35] See eg Georges Koumantos, 'Private International Law and the Berne Convention' [1988] *Copyright* 415; Georges Koumantos, 'Copyright and Private International Law in the Face of the International Diffusion of Works', in *WIPO Worldwide Symposium on the Future of Copyright and the Neighboring Rights* (1994) (WIPO publication no 731(E)), 233.

what might be the laws applicable, first, to the existence and scope of protection, and second to matters of authorship and ownership.

(2) Existence and scope of protection

Given article 5(2)'s designation of the law of the country 'where' protection is claimed to 'govern' the 'extent of protection', one might conclude that the Convention at least tells us that the law of the country of protection (*lex protectionis*) applies to determine whether and to what extent a work is protected. But the matter is more complicated than first appears. We have already discussed the question whether article 5(2)'s use of the term 'where' evidences an intent that the substantive law of the forum should apply (see the earlier discussion at para 20.10 above). It may be reasonable to conclude that the drafters either did not anticipate that the country 'where' protection was claimed would not also be the country where the infringement occurred, or assumed that the forum's choice of law rules would lead to the application of the law of the place of infringement. In either event, whether by designating a national substantive law, or a national conflicts rule whose outcome could be predicted, article 5(2) would have led to the ultimate application of a law consistent with the basic notions of territoriality implicit in that article's formulation. But territoriality offers insufficient comfort if the alleged infringement is occurring in many places at once. **20.14**

(a) Territoriality and the problem of a multiplicity of possible laws

Particularly in the context of digital media, the infringement may take place pervasively, in the country from which the alleged infringement originated, as well as in the countries to which the infringement was communicated. Does the Berne Convention require a strictly territorial approach, applying successively the law of each country of receipt, or will it suffice to apply a single law, for example, that of the country of initiation of the infringement?[36] **20.15**

Applying the law of each country of receipt would be consistent with a widely held concept of international copyright law: that there is no international copyright law as such, but rather a collection of national copyright laws, bound by the Berne Convention into a multilateral non-discrimination (national treatment)

[36] cf P-Y Gautier, 'Du droit applicable dans le "village planétaire", au titre de l'usage immatériel des oeuvres' [1996] *D* 131 (recommending distributive application of law of countries of receipt), with A Kéréver, 'Droit d'auteur et satellites spaciaux' (1984) 121 *RIDA* 27, 51–3 (urging application of law of country of the uplink in cases of infringement via satellite) and Lucas and Lucas (n 31 above), para 1089 (stating that it is consistent with art 5(2) to generalize to multiterritorial infringement claims the competence of the law of the country where act initiating the infringement—'*fait générateur*'—occurred); see also ibid, para 991 (advocating application of the law of the place of initiation as a matter of French private international law).

accord.[37] Thus, the author of a work first published in France is not only the French copyright owner, but, by virtue of the Berne Convention, the UK copyright owner, the US copyright owner, the Japanese copyright owner, and so forth. Each national market for copyrighted works is distinct, and—within the constraints of Berne minima—defines the contours of local protection. Thus, to apply anything less than the laws of all the countries where the alleged infringement occurred would be to disregard the basic nature of international copyright under the Berne Convention.[38]

20.16 But, applying such a territorial approach to the pervasive and simultaneous infringements that modern means of communication enable seems to render the task of adjudicating a multiterritorial infringement claim quite daunting. Hence the impetus to attach another meaning to 'country where protection is sought'. If we consider the country from which the alleged infringement originated as the country contemplated by article 5(2) of the Berne Convention, then the task appears somewhat simpler. As Professor Dinwoodie has observed, 'one can conform to the basic principle of territoriality *and* effectuate the objective of applying a single law to a worldwide dispute by designating a single point as the relevant "place". That is, the localization sub-rule allows us to get the practical benefits of a single law without nominally departing from territoriality.'[39] This approach has some support in positive law. In the context of satellite transmissions, the European Commission determined that the country from which the copyright-relevant act of 'communication to the public' occurs is the EU country from which the satellite signal was uplinked.[40] This definitional technique removed the other EU countries of receipt from the realm of countries from which to seek protection. In effect, the Satellite Directive characterizes the 'country where protection is sought' as the country from which a multiterritorial

[37] See eg Jon Baumgarten, 'Primer on the Principles of International Copyright', in *Fourth Annual US Copyright Office Speaks: Contemporary Copyright and Intellectual Property Issues* (1992), 470, 471. But see Jane Ginsburg, 'International Copyright: From a "Bundle" of National Copyright Laws to a Supranational Code?' (2000) 47 *Journal of the Copyright Society of the USA* 265.

[38] See eg Graeme W Austin, 'Domestic Laws and Foreign Rights: Choice of Law in Transnational Copyright Infringement Litigation' (1999) 23 *Colum-VLA JL & Arts* 1, 22–8. The so-called 'Bogsch theory', which called for the application of the national laws of each country of receipt within a satellite's 'footprint', is one expression of this principle (although it was also characterized in terms of national treatment). See WIPO/UNESCO Group of Experts on the Copyright Aspects of Direct Broadcasting by Satellite: [1985] *Copyright* 181, discussed in Mihàly Ficsor, *The Law of Copyright and the Internet* (2002), 172–3.

[39] Dinwoodie (n 8 above), 203.

[40] See Council Directive 93/83/EEC of 27 Sept 1993 on the coordination of certain rules concerning copyright and rights related to copyright applicable to satellite broadcasting and cable retransmissions, OJ L 248/15, art 2(b) (the 'Satellite Directive'). This Directive localizes the act of communication 'solely in the Member State where, under the control and responsibility of the broadcasting organization, the programme-carrying signals are introduced into an uninterrupted chain of communication . . .'.

communication originates. The localization technique has the advantage of considerably simplifying the inquiry into both licensing and infringement. But the object of the choice of law is not simply to reduce the number of potentially applicable laws; it is, or should be, to identify the rule that will designate the country which is best placed to accord an effective international remedy (or, from a defendant's point of view, to settle definitively her lack of liability).[41] That goal should guide analysis of alternatives to (or recharacterizations of) territoriality.[42]

(b) Alternatives to territoriality: law of the country of the initiating act

As indicated above (see para 20.16), a choice of law rule that looks to the country of the initiating act, rather than to the multiple countries of receipt or impact, does not fully reject the territorial approach, rather, it confines it. The sole territory to take into account, under this approach, is the one from which the infringement originated.[43] In the positive law of Berne member states, there are two variations on this theme, one based on localizing the distribution of copies, the other on localizing the origin of a communication to the public. **20.17**

(c) The US 'root copy' approach

In a series of decisions dating back to 1939, the US Court of Appeals for the Second Circuit has upheld the application of US law to distribution of copies abroad, when the foreign copies were further reproductions of an initial infringing reproduction committed in the United States.[44] Other US courts have also applied this master copy, or root copy, approach to the extraterritorial **12.18**

[41] See eg Paul Edward Geller, 'Conflict of Laws in Cyberspace: Rethinking International Copyright in a Digitally Networked World' (1996) 20 *Colum-VLA JL & Arts* 571, 597 (making a similar argument, in the context of infringements for which a point of origin cannot easily be identified); Michel Vivant, 'Cybermonde: Droit et droits des reseaux' [1996] *JCP* I, 3969, § 6 (arguing that the country whose law should apply may be the forum country when the forum is also the headquarters of the originator of the digital communication).

[42] A more radical approach would abandon the search for a choice of law rule that leads to the most competent national law, and would instead devise appropriate substantive international copyright rules for a given dispute. See Graeme B Dinwoodie, 'A New Copyright Order: Why National Courts Should Create Global Norms' (2000) 149 *U Pa L Rev* 469.

[43] See Satellite Directive (n 40 above), art 2(b).

[44] See eg *Sheldon* v *Metro-Goldwyn Pictures, Corp*, 106 F 2d 45 (2d Cir 1939), aff'd, 309 US 390 (1940) (distribution in Canada of motion picture held to infringe plaintiff's play); *Update Art Inc* v *Modiin Publ'g Ltd*, 843 F 2d 67 (2d Cir 1988) (publication in Israel of photograph of poster; initial copy of photograph allegedly made in USA and sent to Israel for further copying and distribution); *Famous Music Corp* v *Seeco Records, Inc*, 201 F Supp 560 (SDNY 1961) (pirate records sold in Europe allegedly made from illicit US master tape); see also *Fun-Damental Too, Ltd* v *Gemmy Indus Corp*, 41 USPQ 2d 1427 (SDNY 1996) (dismissing copyright infringement claim because plaintiff 'failed to allege an infringement within the United States that led to extraterritorial infringement').

extension of US copyright law.[45] US courts have generally, however, distinguished the root copy cases when a plaintiff sought recovery for offshore *performances* of copyrighted works. When an unauthorized performance culminated abroad, the material connection to the USA provided by an initial unauthorized reproduction was considered lacking.[46] Thus, a public performance initiated in the USA but culminating outside the USA had been considered outside the scope of US law.[47] (At the same time, US courts continue to

---

[45] See *P & D Int'l* v *Halsey Publ'g Co*, 672 F Supp 1429 (SD Fla 1987) (unauthorized exhibition on cruise ship of film print made without authorization in Miami).

[46] See *Robert Stigwood Group Ltd* v *O'Reilly*, 530 F 2d 1096, 1100 (2d Cir 1976) (distinguishing *Sheldon*, 106 F 2d 45, on the ground that case involved a US reproduction further reproduced in Canada, while case at bar concerned live performances in Canada); *Gasté* v *Kaiserman*, 683 F Supp 63, 65 (SDNY), aff'd, 863 F 2d 1061 (2d Cir 1988) (no recovery for infringing performances abroad, unless plaintiff can show that these performances 'resulted from the reproduction of recordings originally made in the United States'). Accord, *Allarcom Pay TV Ltd* v *General Instrument Corp*, 69 F 3d 381, 387 (9th Cir 1995) (in a controversy concerning diversion of cable signal to Canadian viewers, held that it made no difference whether the US defendant had authorized Canadians to appropriate the signal, or had instead itself broadcast the signal from the USA to Canada. 'In either case, the potential infringement was only completed in Canada once the signal was received and viewed.'); *LA News Serv* v *Reuters Television*, 149 F 3d 987 (9th Cir 1998), in which the Ninth Circuit indicated that the unauthorized transmission of film footage from New York to Europe and Africa would violate no rights under US law because those transmissions would not constitute 'completed act of infringement' within the USA (ibid at 991) (the Ninth Circuit nonetheless awarded damages for the extraterritorial transmissions because those transmissions were made from unauthorized copies of the footage that had been made in New York, following an unauthorized transmission of the film from Los Angeles to New York; these acts did 'complete' infringements within the USA).

[47] A 2000 decision of the Second Circuit Court of Appeals appears to reject, or at least substantially modify that approach. In *National Football League* v *PrimeTime* 24, 211 F 3d 10 (2d Cir 2000), a case involving the diversion of satellite signals from the USA to Canada, the defendant asserted that no 'public performance' occurred in the USA when the signals were received in Canada. The Second Circuit disagreed with the geographic characterization of defendant's acts. Reviewing US cases on cable and satellite retransmission (albeit not involving extraterritorial diversion of the signals), the court observed that 'a transmission need not be made directly to the public in order for there to be a public performance or display . . . Congress intended the definitions of "public" and "performance" to encompass each step in the process by which a protected work wends its way to its audience. . . . [T]he definition of transmit is broad enough to include all conceivable forms and combinations of wired or wireless communications media. . . . Under that analysis, it is clear that [the] uplink transmission of signals captured in the United States is a step in the process by which [a] protected work wends its way to a public audience.' Ibid at 12–13, citing *David* v *Showtime/The Movie Channel, Inc* 697 F Supp 752, 759 (SDNY 1988). Under this approach, then, initiating, or perhaps simply relaying, transmissions from or through the USA constitutes a public performance in the USA that is subject to US law, even though the 'public audience' is not located in the USA. This holding is potentially significant because the communication of works from the USA to points offshore, whence they are received by a public audience, would require the US copyright owner's authorization. With respect to digital network transmissions, the implications could be even more striking. Because of the architecture of the Internet, a digital communication may transit through US servers without reaching a US public, and without initiation from the USA. If one takes literally the Second Circuit's 'each step of the process' standard, then even these communications would come within the scope of the US Copyright Act. When one recalls the context of the decision, however, it becomes possible to limit

characterize communications originating outside the USA, but culminating within, as acts of public performance arising under US law.[48])

20.19 The distinction between distribution of copies (justifying application of US copyright law to acts culminating abroad) and public performance (non-application of US law to communications received abroad) may seem rather artificial, particularly when digital media blur the borders between distribution of copies and communication to the public. Worse, an approach that holds that the public performance right is not infringed in the USA unless the performance is received in the USA seems in some tension with the European Commission's determination that the copyright-affecting act of communication to the public is completed when the work is make available (at least by satellite[49]), not when it is in fact received. If one puts the two doctrines together, it is possible that an unauthorized transmission originating in the USA but received in Europe would violate no rights, because the law of the country of departure considers that no copyright-triggering act has occurred within its borders, and the laws of the countries of receipt do not apply to reception of the transmission.

20.20 The Internet may avoid this impasse, because any transmission also involves the creation of copies in the computers of the recipients (though this may seem somewhat arbitrary, simply a consequence of the technology). Moreover, with respect to a US website, even if the only users who download the work are located outside the USA, the presence of an unauthorized copy of the work on a server located in the USA could suffice to constitute a root copy infringement. With respect to peer-to-peer or other transmissions of copies from computers located in the USA, the transit of temporary copies from US servers might provide a point of attachment for a root copy approach.[50] (Whether this approach can be generalized to other countries may depend on whether the country from which the copies departed credits the RAM-copying doctrine.) More importantly, localization of root copies is ultimately a rather formalistic way of identifying domestic acts of planning and implementing a multiterritorial dissemination in a way that makes it appropriate to consider that country a

the reach of the court's holding to communications intentionally initiated from the USA. As a result, the automatic transiting of communications through computers located in the USA should not, standing alone, constitute a public performance in the USA. The broader implications of the decision have not since been realized.

[48] See eg *Twentieth Century Fox Film Corp* v *iCraveTV*, No 00–121 (WD Pa, filed 20 Jan 2000); *National Football League* v *TV Radio Now Corp d/b/a iCraveTV*, No 00–120 (WD Pa, filed 20 Jan 2000) (case settled 28 Jan 2000) (webcasting digitized television signals from Canada to the USA; the court found for choice of law purposes that the alleged infringement occurred in the USA when US citizens 'received and viewed defendants' streaming of the copyrighted materials.).

[49] See Satellite Directive (n 40 above), art 2(b).

[50] See *NFL* v *Primetime* (n 47 above), 24.

'nerve centre' for communications to offshore sites. What should matter is not simply that an initial copy is made within the USA (or other country adopting this approach), but that, in this view, the nerve centre country is the one with the 'closest relationship' to the resulting harm.[51]

(d) Objections to the 'root copy' doctrine

20.21 Some authors, notably Professor Austin, have forcefully criticized the root copy approach and its consequences. US law should be confined to US borders; copies or transmissions received outside the US should be judged by the laws of the countries of receipt, he claims.[52] Similarly, Professor Bradley has contended that application of US copyright laws to acts occurring outside the USA undermines the Berne Convention system of tolerating international divergence in copyright regimes (subject to the conventional minima): the 'unilateral imposition of one country's laws into another country's territory' in effect 'override[s] the [Berne Convention's] choice' to allow for some diversity among national copyright laws.[53] There is another objection to the US 'root copy' or initiating act point of attachment: US courts do not treat it as a genuine, bilateral, choice of law rule. Rather, they appear to apply it primarily when it justifies the application of US law by US courts.[54] US courts seem considerably more territorially inclined when applying the law of the country of the initiating act would lead to the application by a US court of a *foreign* law that would exculpate an act which US law would hold infringing.[55]

(e) Communication to the public: the European Union's 'initiating act' approach

20.22 The US is not alone in short-circuiting the inquiry into territorially competent laws. In the case of the Satellite Directive, the *only* copyright-engaging act is the uplink; receipt of the signal does not implicate the right of communication to

[51] cf Conseil d'Etat (France), *Internet et les réseaux numériques* (1998) (n 16 above), 148–51 (the law competent to govern the entire infringement claim is that of the law with the 'closest relationship to the harm'; this country is presumed to be the country of residence/principal place of the uploading entity when that country is a member of the European Union; one might extend this principle beyond the EU to countries with a similarly high level of copyright protection).

[52] For extensive elaboration of this argument, see Austin (n 38 above), 1, and esp 46–8.

[53] Curtis Bradley, 'Territorial Intellectual Property Rights in an Age of Globalism' (1997) 37 *Virginia Journal of International Law* 505, 549.

[54] An exception may be *Creative Technology* v *Aztech Sys*, 61 F 3d 696 (9th Cir 1996), in which a Singaporean software producer charged another Singaporean producer with reverse engineering its program in Singapore, and distributing the result in the USA. While US law applied to US distributions, a majority of the Ninth Circuit panel dismissed the claim on grounds of *forum non conveniens*, asserting that the case would be better pressed in the country where the acts that culminated in the US distribution were initiated.

[55] cf *Playboy Ents* v *Chuckleberry*, 939 F Supp 1032 (SDNY 1996) (applying US law, not Italian law, to US receipt of webpage located on server in Italy; Italian court had previously, and contrary to determination in US proceeding under US law, held use of 'Playmen' for 'adult' magazine not to infringe Playboy's trade mark).

the public. The impetus for the Satellite Directive's approach was to simplify rights-clearing by the satellite transmitter.[56] The same concern might equally well apply to other transnational modes of communication. For example, the point of initiation approach would assist the exploiter of digital media who seeks to organize its website business and predict what its liabilities may be.[57] This, however, may appear solicitous of digital entrepreneurs at the cost of authors and copyright owners. Certainly, applying the law of the country of initiation would not yield effective relief to copyright owners if the originator of the transmission had opportunistically relocated its business to a country with underprotective copyright laws, or to one of the few remaining countries outside any international copyright treaties.[58] There are other considerations that might also counsel in favour of application of the laws of the countries of receipt, rather than of the source country.[59] For example, one might contend that the point of origin approach makes sense where, as in satellite transmissions, there is a single point of origin; but in digital communications there may be many points of origin.[60] Moreover, in digital communications, the location of servers may be irrelevant, and often fortuitous in the chain of digital transmissions; by contrast, the effects of an unauthorized communication are felt in the countries of receipt.[61]

Furthermore, if a digital communication may become available from more than one point, it might follow that a choice of law rule making the place of initiation the point of attachment proves scarcely more workable than designating the laws of the countries of receipt. The problem of a multiplicity of points of origin in fact reveals the potential multiplicity of defendants. Some of these may be websites whose communications with end-users are straightforward point-to-point transactions. Here, each website is making the work available to the public, and may be fairly readily identified and pursued. But other forms of **20.23**

[56] See Satellite Directive (n 40 above), recitals 5–7, 13–15.

[57] Accord, Lucas and Lucas (n 31 above), para 991 ('one of the essential justifications of the *lex loci delicti* in copyright cases points logically in favor of the law of the place of origin of the infringement, because it is in the country in which he carries on his activities that the exploiter should be able to organize his exploitation').

[58] In its communication following up on the Green Paper on *Copyright and Related Rights in the Information Society*, the European Commission expressed some doubt about transposing the approach of the Satellite Directive (n 40 above) to the Internet context. The Commission indicated that, on the one hand, it may be difficult to identify a single point of origin of the transmission, and, on the other hand, the point of origin could be in a country which denies any effective protection. COM(96) 568 final, 20 Nov 1996 at 23–4 and n 35.

[59] For a fuller discussion, see eg Peter Schønning, 'Applicable Law in Transfrontier On-Line Transmissions' (1996) 170 *RIDA* 21; Gautier (n 36 above).

[60] See Schønning (n 59 above), 37.

[61] See ibid, 47. The location of the server may, however, be significant, eg when the host server is also the website operator.

digital transactions involve much more complicated chains of communication, in which there may be a vast number of participants, but no clearly identifiable point of origin. This may be the case with peer-to-peer file exchanges. Particularly if the work in question is broken up into separate packets emanating from different sources,[62] the path of the uploading communications may implicate as many countries as those of the downloads. In this situation, there will be considerable impetus to seek out the services through which infringing websites become accessible, or which enable end-users to copy files from each other in a peer-to-peer network. These actors, moreover, are more likely than individuals to be subject to personal jurisdiction in forums other than their domiciles.[63] If one adapts the country of initiation approach to cover entities that facilitate online copying, then simplification of choice of law remains possible, at least if the forum applies the domestic law of the facilitating entity, rather than the laws of the various countries in which the infringing acts were facilitated. That in turn may depend on whether the act of facilitation is independently wrongful, for example, as an illicit 'authorization' of infringement. Whether, from the author's point of view, this is a desirable strategy will largely depend on whether the domestic law of the country of facilitation would find liability, for example, on the ground that the facilitating service has knowledge of or control over the activities of the infringers.[64] Where the author seeks to enjoin the communication of the work from a website, her relief will be most effective if the communication

[62] See eg Clive Thompson, 'The Bit Torrent Effect', *Wired*, issue 13.01 (Jan 2005), 151–9, www.wired.com/wired/archive; Konstantinos Karagiannis, 'Spyware-Free P2P: For Free', *PC Magazine*, 2 Mar 2004, 79.

[63] See eg *MGM* v *Grokster*, 234 F Supp 2d 1073 (CD Cal 2003) (upholding jurisdiction over Australian-Vanuatan defendant alleged to have facilitated unauthorized downloading of motion pictures in California).

[64] The extent to which online services who do not themselves originate the content that they communicate are liable for making that content available to the public has been resolved in part in the USA by the Digital Millennium Copyright Act, 17 USC § 512(a)–(d), which provides certain 'safe harbors' from liability if the service complies with the conditions set out in the Act. The DMCA, however, preserves the copyright liability of online service providers who have knowledge that the material they host is infringing, or who derive a direct financial benefit from hosting the material and who have the right and ability to control the website's content. See 17 USC § 512(c)(1). Where these 'safe harbors' do not apply, the scope of derivative liability for facilitating copyright infringement remains uncertain. The US Supreme Court has held that 'active inducement' of infringement will give rise to liability; see *Metro-Goldwyn-Mayer Studios, Inc* v *Grokster, Ltd*, US 125 S. Ct 2764 (2005), but it is not clear whether one who supplies the means to infringe, but who is not proved to have intended to promote infringement, will also be subject to liability. For pre-DMCA decisions involving websites, compare *Playboy* v *Frena*, 839 F Supp 1552 (MD Fla 1993) (retaining direct liability of operator of bulletin board service for the communication of photographs scanned by BBS subscribers without permission from *Playboy* magazine) with *Religious Technology Center* v *Netcom On-Line Communications*, 907 F Supp 1361 (ND Cal 1995) (rejecting direct liability of online service for mere transiting of content uploaded by subscribers, but retaining possibility of liability for contributory infringement if, once notified of the unauthorized communication, the online service failed to remove it from the server).

can be stopped at its source (particularly, at the location of the server); this is not likely to occur unless the law of the source applies (and, of course, if the communication is illicit under that law). But the more widely 'distributed' the path of the allegedly illicit communications, the less likely one may locate a 'source' from which the communications may be cut off. That may depend on the extent of the control the alleged facilitator in fact may exercise over the network.[65]

In addition, there remains the 'applicable law shopping' problem: even if one can identify the country from which the infringing or facilitating acts originated, what if that country provides for a very low level of copyright protection? Will the prospect of denying protection through application of foreign law, where local law would have granted protection, deter the local court from applying foreign law, especially if the forum is the plaintiff's home? Any choice of law rule must tolerate divergent outcomes, but the rule is sorely strained if it ends up promoting the manipulation of connecting factors so that the least protective result (or, for that matter, the most protective result) is always reached. In the context of a choice of law rule designating the application of the law of the country of initiation, this means that the rule will be problematic if it leads to the dissemination (whether by satellite or digital media) of works from 'copyright havens', that is, from countries affording little or no copyright protection.[66] This problem is not new to digital transmissions. Faced with similar concerns, the Satellite Directive recognizes that the point of origin approach will work only if the participating countries share an adequate level of copyright protection. The Directive therefore provides an alternative point of attachment when the physical location of the uplink is outside the EU, but the headquarters of the uplinking entity is located within a member state.[67] Analogizing this principle to digital transmissions, the initiating act would be deemed to take place at the location of the server that hosts the infringing website. But if that server is located in a copyright haven, then the initiating act would be deemed to take place at the defendant's residence or principal place of business. If, however, both of these places are copyright havens, then the 'initiating act' point of attachment would not apply. **20.24**

[65] See, e.g., *Universal Music Australia Pty Ltd* v *Sharman License Holdings Ltd*, [2005] FCA 1242 (holding distributor of P2P software liable for 'authorizing' end-users' infringements when distributor persistently failed to take measures to curtail infringement). See also *Universal Music Australia Pty Ltd* v *Cooper* [2005] FCA 972 (liability of aggregator of links to sites offering unauthorized copies of recorded music).

[66] See European Commission, *Proposal for a Council Directive concerning cable and satellite transmissions, Explanatory Memorandum*, COM(91) 276 final at 4.

[67] See ibid.

(f) Inferences to draw from WCT, article 8 ('making available to the public')

20.25 There may be an additional problem with the initiating act and root copy approaches. Article 8 of the World Intellectual Property Organization ('WIPO') Copyright Treaty ('WCT') states the right of communication to the public as 'including the making available to the public of their works in such a way that members of the public may access these works from a place and at a time individually chosen by them'. The focus of the 'making available' right seems to train on the individual members of the public who access the work. As a result, it would seem that the right is exercised when the work is made available *to* the place where the accessing individual is located, rather than *from* the country from which the communication departed. In other words, the copyright-triggering act would be accessing the work. If this characterization of the WCT right is correct, then the WCT would limit legislative competence over claims involving the 'making available' right to the laws of the countries of receipt.[68] In that case, one should next ask whether the choice of law rule the WCT implicitly applies to interactive communications to the public does or should also apply to any kind of communication to the public.[69] At first blush, it may not make sense to apply the laws of the countries of receipt to on-demand communications, while applying the laws of the countries of emission to communications simultaneously made to multiple recipients. But the distinction between the laws applicable to on-demand and other communications might be justified on the ground that in the case of 'pull' technologies, the initiating act—requesting the communication of the work—emanates from the recipient, while in the case of 'push' technologies, the communications are at the initiative of the transmitting entity. Thus, paradoxically, in the case of on-demand transmissions, the country of the initiating act and of the receipt of the communication would be the same. As a result, if the law of that country applies, its competence could be either on the basis of the initiation or of the culmination of the communication. Ultimately, then, article 8 of the WCT does not answer the question whether the Berne and WIPO conventions designate which law applies to a communication to the public.

(g) Alternative points of attachment: author's residence

20.26 Let us return to the formula in article 5(2) of the Berne Convention, 'the law of the country where protection is claimed'. In the previous section, we treated this

[68] Arguably, the on-demand user might be seen as 'going to' the place from which the digital communication emanates in order to receive the communication, but this is probably too strained a recharacterization. See eg *Playboy* v *Chuckleberry Pubs* (n 55 above).

[69] One might note that an inference that the WCT, and through it, the Berne Convention, implicitly require application of the laws of the countries of receipt for communications to the public in general, would set the EU Satellite Directive (n 40 above) in tension with the inferred Conventional rule.

expression as a variation of the tort law choice of law rule that designates the place of the harm, but we characterized that place as the country of initiation, rather than of impact, of the harm. Now let us consider the opposite characterization: the *lex loci delicti* in the sense of the place where the harm was felt. We earlier raised the concern that this approach leads to excessive complexity, because, if the author is harmed in each national market for the work, there may be too many places of impact. But there is another way of viewing the impact of the infringement: the harm goes to the author's personality (violation of moral rights), and to her pocket (violation of economic rights). Those harms are felt where the author resides (or, if the copyright holder is a juridical person, at its principal business establishment).[70]

This solution certainly enjoys the virtue of simplicity, but it may be *too* simple.[71] **20.27** It tends to undermine the role of a choice of law rule in enabling potential defendant business actors to predict their liabilities. Moreover, it may be in tension with the law of a forum that has exercised jurisdiction on the basis of a territorial connection between the forum and the claim. On the one hand, the author is asking the forum to exercise jurisdiction over the defendant because the defendant sent the work from or made the work available to the forum. The author will also be asking the court to forbid dissemination of the work from or into the forum, and to award damages for any copies already disseminated. But on the other hand, the author would not be asking the court to determine whether the defendant's act was *wrongful* under the forum's law if the forum is not that of the author's residence.

An obvious response to this objection is: that is what private international law is **20.28** all about—applying a law other than the forum's. But, in this instance, the author's law may clash with the forum's. Arguably, one might still designate the law of the author's residence as the generally applicable law, but recognize that certain forums might determine that the consequences of applying that law violate strongly held public policies of those places. These forums would therefore end up applying local law, at least to that portion of the multiterritorial claim that can be localized in the forum. This is a possibility, particularly when the author's residence is either notably less vigorous than the forum in enforcing

[70] See François Dessemontet, 'Internet, la propriété intellectuelle et le droit international privé', in Kessedjian and Boele-Woelki (n 16 above), 47 (arguing in support of this point of attachment); see Bariatti (n 31 above), 80–1. Cf Conseil d'Etat (France), *Internet et les réseaux numériques* (1998) (n 16 above), 151 (advocating application of the law of the country of upload, if that country is within the European Union, otherwise, the law of the country with the 'most significant relationship' to the harm; that country is presumed to be the law of the author's residence).

[71] Except where the work has a multiplicity of authors who reside in different countries, a situation quite foreseeable as the Internet makes increasingly possible the creation of works by far-flung collaborators. (See the Preface to this new edition.)

moral rights and other author-protective prerogatives or, on the contrary, is far more author (or copyright-owner) protective than a more consumer-oriented forum. One should therefore acknowledge that a choice of law rule that is likely to encounter frequent overrides in the name of local public policy is a rule that warrants reconsideration.

(h) Multiple points of attachment

20.29 Part of the difficulty in identifying a satisfactory choice of rule may lie in the attempt to select a *single* point of attachment. The 'author's residence' point of attachment may oversimplify the problem, notably paying insufficient heed to local cultural policies, and to defendants' need to organize their business affairs subject to predictable standards of liability. The 'initiating act' point of attachment may be too easily manipulated. Perhaps the advantages, in predictability for defendants, of applying the defendant's law, might be preserved, and the undesirable consequences of manipulating the point of attachment avoided, were the choice of law rule to designate alternative points of attachment, of which the defendant's residence/principal place of business would be one.[72]

20.30 The conflicts approach that designates the law of the country with the 'most significant relationship' to the harm also identifies a variety of potentially applicable national laws.[73] Several writers have offered proposals of 'cascading points of attachment' to resolve the law applicable to infringements committed over the Internet.[74] For example, Andreas Reindl has proposed designating the defendant's place of business as the primary point of attachment, but offering the plaintiff the option of applying the laws of the countries of receipt, when the defendant's use was for commercial purposes in those places. Where the use was non-commercial, the plaintiff would have the option of applying the laws only of the countries where the harm to its economic interest was 'substantial'. In either event, the plaintiff's option is conditioned upon the foreseeability of the harm in the countries whose laws the plaintiff seeks to apply.[75] With respect to

[72] The technique of designating a principal point of attachment, with alternative criteria, is not novel. See eg Hague Conference on International Law, *Collection of Conventions (1951–1996)*, No XIX, Convention on the Law Applicable to Traffic Accidents, arts 3 (dominant point of attachment is the state where the accident occurred) and 4 (alternative points of attachment that override state of occurrence of accident); ibid, No XX, Convention on the Law Applicable to Products Liability, arts 4–6 (articulating combinations of points of attachment).

[73] See American Law Institute, Restatement (Second) of Conflict of Laws, ch 7 145 (1988).

[74] See eg François Dessemontet, 'Internet: le droit d'auteur et le droit international privé (1996) 92 *SJZ* (Nr 15) 285–94 (law of author's residence, combined with other criteria); Jane Ginsburg, 'Global Use/Territorial Rights: Private International Law Questions of the Global Information Infrastructure' (1995) 42 *Journal of the Copyright Society of the USA* 318, 337–8 (law of the forum, if it is also the law of defendant's residence/place of business or of the country of the initiation of the infringement).

[75] See Andreas Reindl, 'Choosing Law in Cyberspace: Copyright Conflicts on Global Networks' (1998) 19 *Mich J Int'l L* 799, 852.

service providers whose servers host the infringing website, but do not directly participate in or financially benefit from the selection of the content, only their law will apply, because the foreseeability criterion probably will not be met. This result has the merit of simplicity, but its adequacy will depend on the content of the service provider's domestic law. As to website operators who post the alleged infringements, the copyright owner may often have a choice between the law of the defendant, and those of the countries of receipt/substantial economic harm. Where the defendant's law offers a sufficient level of protection, the copyright owner may prefer to apply that law, both because it makes the court's task simpler (particularly if the forum is also the defendant's), and also because, in some cases, that law may in fact be *more* protective than the law of some of the countries of receipt. This last feature makes Reindl's proposal attractive to copyright plaintiffs. Is it fair to copyright defendants? One might argue that defendants have, in effect, already engaged in applicable-law-shopping, by locating their residences or business operations in a particular country. If a defendant wished to be subject to a weaker law, it could have moved to that country. So it cannot be unfair to subject a defendant to the worldwide application of a law that was of its own choosing.[76]

On the other hand, this approach abandons the basic premise of territoriality that underlies article 5(2) of the Berne Convention. It ignores the interest that sovereign nations may have in seeing their law apply to infringements that can be localized on their territories. Arguably, article 5(2) is sufficiently malleable that the territoriality principle may yield to achievement of another principal goal of the Berne Convention: effective enforcement of author's rights. The simpler the action, the more likely the author may be to realize that goal. On the other hand, effective enforcement of the author's rights presumes that the author *enjoys* those rights in each territory for which enforcement is sought. Territoriality remains a powerful intuition. It is difficult to accept the proposition that an act unlawful in one territory should give rise to liability in another territory in which the same act is not wrongful. Territoriality therefore remains a nagging presence provoking some unease even with solutions that, by applying alternative points of attachment, can at least some of the time achieve results that offer meaningful relief to copyright owners, while preserving fairness to defendants. **20.31**

(i) Territoriality bis *presumption that* lex fori *applies:*

Let us therefore reconsider the territorialist interpretation of article 5(2) of the Berne Convention. It has the advantage of maintaining consistency with the **20.32**

[76] A possible unintended consequence of this argument is to hasten flight to copyright havens.

rule of national treatment, and of respecting national sovereignty in defining the contours of each national copyright market. Its disadvantage is its potential complexity in application. But perhaps that complexity may be reduced. Recall that, in addition to requiring non-discrimination, the Berne Convention imposes certain substantive minima as to protected subject matter and rights. Moreover, 159 countries are now members of the Berne Convention (as of September 2005), several more are members of the World Trade Organization ('WTO') (membership in which requires adherence to the TRIPs Agreement, which, in turn incorporates Berne minima[77]). The laws of these countries therefore—at least formally—conform to these minima. The shared threshold of protection is further lifted by the standards set forth in the WCT, which has now entered into force.[78] Thus, one way to alleviate the difficulty of distributive application of the laws of the countries of receipt of infringing communications or distributions might be to presume that the laws of all these countries have assimilated Berne Convention and TRIPs minima, and, where the countries concerned have ratified the WIPO treaties, WCT minima, and leave proof to the contrary to the defendant.[79]

20.33 In sum, were the forum to depart from a strictly territorial application of governing laws, an approach that appears to respect the principle of territoriality, yet diminishes complexity, would be to apply the *lex fori* (when the forum is a Berne Convention or WTO country), subject to proof of specific territorial divergences. This interpretation is consistent both with the words of article 5(2) Berne Convention ('country *where* protection is claimed') and with the *lex protectionis*, since we are presuming that the content of the forum's law is consistent with that of all the countries for which protection is sought. Moreover, given the bases of judicial competence (discussed earlier at paras 20.02–20.07 above), the forum will likely be either the place of initiation of the harm, or a place of impact.

---

[77] Agreement on Trade-Related Aspects of Intellectual Property Rights, Including Trade in Counterfeit Goods, MTN/FA II-A1C. The TRIPs Agreement does not, however, incorporate Berne, art 6*bis* (moral rights protection).

[78] WIPO Copyright Treaty, adopted by the Diplomatic Conference on 20 Dec 1996, CRNR/DC/89; WIPO Performances and Phonograms Treaty, adopted by the Diplomatic Conference on 20 Dec 1996. As of 28 July 2005, fifty-four states were contracting parties to the WCT, see http://www.wipo.int/treaties/en/documents/word/s-wct.doc; and (as of 2 September 2005) fifty-three to the WIPO Performers and Phonograms Treaty, see http://www.wipo.int/treaties/en/documents/word/s-wppt.doc.

[79] cf *Pearce* v *Ove Arup* [1997] 3 All ER 31 (Ch) (presuming similarity of Dutch copyright law with English copyright law) aff'd [1999] 1 All ER 769, [1999] FSR 525 (Court of Appeal); Richard Fentiman, *Foreign Law: Pleading and Proof* (1998), 147–53 (discussing English courts' presumption that the content of foreign law is the same as that of English law).

(3) Copyright ownership

(a) Authorship and ownership under the Berne Convention in general

As we have seen in Chapter 7 (see paras 7.02–7.16, 7.41–7.45 above), the Berne Convention, the TRIPs Agreement, and the WCT primarily address *how* a work shall be protected; they offer little guidance as to *who* is protected. In general, the Berne Convention sets forth neither substantive nor choice of law rules to determine copyright ownership. While, under article 5(2) of the Berne Convention, the law applicable to determine the 'extent of protection as well as the means of redress' is the law of the country where protection is claimed, this provision covers infringement actions, not ownership claims.[80] The Berne Convention affords insufficient guidance as to the law applicable to contracts of transfer of rights under copyright,[81] and particularly, to designation of initial copyright ownership and authorship status.[82] **20.34**

The Berne Convention's allocation of initial ownership rights is ambiguous, as is its identification of the 'author'. The treaty states a general presumption that the 'author' is the person under whose name the work is disseminated.[83] Because this person has standing to sue for infringement, then, implicitly, this person is the copyright owner (entitlement to sue depends on having rights to assert). This presumption, however, is not only rebuttable, it does not seem to fit every type of work of authorship. First, the presumption appears to anticipate works created by only one author (or at any rate, very few), such as traditional works of literature, music, or the visual arts. By contrast, audio-visual works—and particularly multimedia works—have many creative contributors, as do (or will) literary or graphic works created through multiple collaborations over digital networks. Secondly, authorship and ownership of audio-visual works and multimedia products may not even be subject to this presumption: the Berne **20.35**

---

[80] Similarly, Berne Convention, art 5(2) provides that the 'enjoyment' and 'exercise' of protection 'shall be independent of the existence of protection in the country of origin.' The text does not say 'independent of the *ownership of rights* in the country of origin'.

[81] Several scholars have discussed the failure of the conventions to resolve questions of contract validity and transfer. See eg M B Nimmer, 'Who is the Copyright Owner When the Laws Conflict?' (1974) 5 *IIC* 62, 63 ('neither Convention tells us who may qualify as the author's successor in title, or as the copyright proprietor in place of the author'); A Françon, 'Les droits sur les films en droit international privé', in *Travaux du comité français de droit international privé* (1971–3), 39, 53 (contracts concerning the exploitation of films—ie the relationship between producers, distributors, and theatres—are not at all governed by the international copyright conventions). See also Ulmer (n 29 above) (study prepared for the EEC including a proposed international treaty supplying conflicts rules regarding initial title to and transfers of ownership of rights under copyright).

[82] cf Jane Ginsburg, 'Les conflits de lois relatifs au titulaire initial du droit d'auteur' (1986) 5 *Revue du droit de la propriété industrielle* 26, 27–9 (treaties inadequately address designation of initial titleholder of copyright).

[83] Berne Convention, art 15(1) (see para 7.16 above).

Convention establishes a special rule for 'cinematographic works'. According to this rule, 'the person or body corporate whose name appears on a cinematographic work in the usual manner shall, in the absence of proof to the contrary, be presumed to be the maker of said work'.[84] Given the increasing prominence of audio-visual and multimedia works in the digital era, the special rule on ownership of cinematographic works may significantly constrict the reach of the general presumption on authorship/ownership.

On the other hand, while it is true that the Convention permits those signatories (particularly, the UK and the USA) which vest initial ownership in audio-visual producers to maintain that designation, a different provision of the Berne Convention makes ownership of copyright in cinematographic works a matter for the *lex protectionis*.[85] Thus, copyright ownership of these works will vary depending on the country of protection. If member countries are free to deem 'makers' of audio-visual and multimedia works initial copyright *owners*, are they also free to deem 'makers' '*authors*'? Just as the Convention does not require that other member countries accept the country of origin's ownership designation, it seems that other members need not adhere to the country of origin's identification of authorship. Indeed, the drafters of the cinematographic works provisions believed that it was so clear that each member nation was free to deem 'makers' 'authors' or not, a specific statement to that effect was 'unnecessary'.[86]

20.36 The Berne Convention thus spawns several, somewhat divergent, interpretations as to authorship status and initial ownership of rights.

(i) As to authorship status: It is not clear that an 'author' must be a work's actual creator. This is particularly true with respect to the category of 'cinematographic works', a category that multimedia works may greatly expand. The law of the country where protection is sought may determine who enjoys authorship status. The 'author', therefore may be a different person or entity, depending on where a claim is pursued. As a result, the rights and status of creators could vary with each Union country of exploitation.

(ii) With respect to economic rights in works other than cinematographic works: Although article $14^{bis}(2)(a)$ designates the competence of the *lex protectionis* for cinematographic works, the treaty supplies no explicit rule for initial ownership of other kinds of works. By negative inference, the *lex protectionis* would not determine initial ownership of works that are not 'cinematographic

84 Berne Convention, art 15(2) (see para 7.17 above).

85 ibid, art $14^{bis}(2)(a)$. See Desbois et al (1976), 216–21, n 34 above, and para 7.41 above.

86 See Bureau International pour la Protection de la Propriété Intellectuelle ('BIRPI'), Intellectual Property Conference of Stockholm, 1967, *Proposals for Revision of the Substantive Copyright Provisions* (1966), 58.

works'. Each Berne Union forum would be free to apply its conflicts rules to determine initial ownership.

(iii) With respect to both authorship and economic rights ownership: 'Authors' and initial copyright owners are separate concepts. The Berne Convention supplies no clear supranational substantive definition of either; while it provides a choice of law rule regarding initial ownership for cinematographic works, it fails to designate which law governs determination of authorship status of these or any other kind of work. Moreover, article 15(1) sets out the equation between authors and copyright owners as a mere, rebuttable, presumption, and offers no choice of law rule as to what law governs the disproof of authorship status.

In view of this uncertainty, perhaps the rule in article 5(2) of the Berne Convention, designating the law of the country of protection to govern infringement claims, should be construed more broadly, making it the residual choice of law rule for all copyright issues, including authorship and ownership. This would be consistent with a highly territorialist view of international copyright. It would also be consistent with a broad reading of the national treatment provision of article 5(1), which extends to foreign Berne authors 'the rights which [the] respective laws [of the countries of protection] do now or may hereafter grant to their nationals'. Broadly construed, the 'rights' might cover the determination of who is an author (although this may be circular), as well as rights of ownership, including authors' rights vis-à-vis their grantees, as well as substantive exclusive rights. But there is ample evidence from the Berne Convention itself that rigorous territoriality is not the general rule. The Berne Convention in fact abandons or loosens the principle of territoriality with respect to a few provisions that establish several supranational obligations or designate the application of the law of the country of origin.[87] Thus, if it is generally true that the Berne Convention does not resolve the question of the law applicable to copyright ownership, it is also true that the treaty as a whole does not support the radical territoriality that would equate the law applicable to the scope of protection with that applicable to the determination of ownership.[88] **20.37**

[87] For supranational rules, see eg Berne Convention, arts 2(1), 2(3), 2(5), 2(6), 2bis(3), 5(2) al 1, 6bis(1), 6bis(2), 7(1), 7(3), 7(4).2, 7(5), 8, 9(1), 9(2).2, 9(3), 10(1), 10(3), 10bis(1) al 2, 11, 11bis(1), 11bis(2).2, 11bis(3).1, 11ter, 12, 14, 14bis(1), 15(1), 15(2), 15(3), 16(1), 16(2). For application of the law of the country of origin, see eg Berne Convention, arts 2(7).2, 7(8), 18(1). For discussion of the significance of the country of origin in the Berne Convention, see eg Koumantos (1988) and Koumantos (1994) (both n 35 above).

[88] See also Muriel Josselin-Gall, *Les Contrats d'Exploitation de Droit de Propriété Littéraire et Artistique* (1995), 231–63 (for an extensive discussion of the 'inaptitude of the international conventions to resolve the conflict of laws concerning the initial owner of the exclusive right of exploitation').

(b) Private international law choice of law rules

20.38 In the absence of a treaty choice of law rule, issues of authorship and ownership are remitted to the choice of law rules of the member countries. Potentially applicable conflicts rules of treaty member nations may vary depending on the issue to be determined. For example, local choice of law rules may identify one point of attachment for the law governing initial copyright ownership, and another for transfers of ownership.

20.39 With respect to the law applicable to determine the initial allocation of copyright ownership when the creators are employees, any of the following laws might be competent:

1. the personal law (residence, nationality, or domicile) of the actual, human, creator(s);
2. the personal law of the employer (residence, nationality, domicile, principal place of business—if the employer is a corporate entity);
3. the law governing the employment contract (if the contract effects a choice of law; or the law of the country in which the contract is 'localized');
4. the law of the country of origin (first publication);
5. for works of art or architecture that are 'immovable', the law of the place of the immovable work; or
6. the law of the forum as a generally residual choice of law designation.

Concerning transfers of copyright ownership, potentially applicable choice of law rules include:

1. if the forum characterizes questions of transfer to be matters of substantive copyright law, the *lex protectionis*;
2. if the forum characterizes questions of transfers to be matters of contract law, the *lex contractus*; this will be: (i) the law chosen by the parties to the contract; or (ii) the law of the country in which the contract can be localized.[89]

20.40 National laws may offer divergent determinations not only with respect to the authorship status and initial copyright ownership of employed creators, but also regarding the characterization of a work as 'joint', or as consisting of separate independent works. A joint work has two or more authors, all of whom share ownership; duration is calculated by reference to the death of the last surviving author. In the case of joint works, in some countries, rights may not be licensed

---

[89] Or, where the Rome Convention applies, the law of the residence of the party owing the 'Characteristic performance', Treaty 80/934 of 19 June 1980 on the Law Applicable to Contractual Obligations, 1980 OJ L 266/1.

without the accord of all co-authors,[90] while in others, any co-author may grant non-exclusive rights, with only a duty to account to the co-authors.[91] If a work combining two or more contributions is not 'joint', each contribution is initially owned separately, and the duration of each component is calculated by reference to the death of its author. But the same work may be characterized as a joint work in some countries, and a composite work in others (with correspondingly varied dates of expiration of copyright protection), because in some countries the contributions forming a joint work must be inseparable,[92] while in others the contributions may be separable but interdependent:[93] music and lyrics comprising a song are a notable example. When such a work is exploited in countries whose domestic laws on 'joint' works differ, whose law applies to determine whether there is one work or two (or more), and, in the event that the 'joint' characterization applies, whether or not the co-authors must exercise their rights by common accord? Likely candidates include:

1. the personal law (residence, nationality, or domicile) of the actual, human, creators, when all reside in or are nationals or domiciliaries of the same country;
2. when the creators do not share a personal law, the law of the country in which a majority of the creators reside (or are nationals or domiciliaries);
3. the law of the country the creators designate by contract (if one exists);

[90] See eg France, Code de la propriété intellectuelle, art L 113–3(2); Germany, Copyright Act of 1965, art 8 (requires consent of all authors, but consent cannot be unreasonably withheld); UK Copyright, Designs and Patents Act 1988, s 173(2); *Lauri* v *Renad* [1892] 3 Ch 402; *Powell* v *Head* (1879) 12 Ch D 686; *Cescinsky* v *Routledge* [1916] 2 KB 325, 330.

[91] See eg for the US, *Thomson* v *Larson*, 147 F 3d 195, 199 (2d Cir 1998); *CCNV* v *Reid*, 846 F 2d 1489, 1498 (DC Cir 1988), aff'd without consideration on this point, 490 US 730 (1989).

[92] See eg Italy, 1941 Copyright Act, art 10 (indistinguishable and inseparable contributions); UK Copyight, Designs and Patents Act 1988, s 10(1) (contributions of authors not distinct from each other); Germany, Copyright Act of 1965, art 8(1) (joint authors if 'their respective contributions cannot be separately exploited'); Canada, Copyright Act 1985, s 2 (as amended through 1994) (contributions of authors not distinct from each other); Belize, Copyright Act Chapter 252, revised through 2000, art 3(1) (contributions not separate from one another); Ireland, Copyright and Related Rights Act 2000, s 22(1) (contributions 'not distinct').

[93] See eg 17 USC § 101 (defining joint works as composed of contributions that are either 'inseparable or interdependent parts of a unitary whole'); France, Code de la propriété intellectuelle, art L 113–2(2) (work of collaboration; inseparability not required); L 113–2(3) explicitly contemplates that contributions may 'be of different genres' and thus separable; Spain, Consolidated Text of the Law on Intellectual Property, regularizing, clarifying, and harmonizing the applicable statutory provisions approved by Royal Legislative Decree 1/1996 of 12 Apr 1996, and amended by Law 5/1998 of 6 Mar 1998, incorporating Directive 96/9/EC of the European Parliament and of the Council of 11 Mar 1996 on the Legal Protection of Databases, s 7(1) (defining a work of joint authorship as 'a work that is the unitary result of the collaboration of two or more authors'); Portugal, Code of Copyright and Related Rights (No 45/85 of 17 Sept 1985, as last amended by Law No 114/91 of 3 Sept 1991), art 16(1) (a work is a work of joint authorship if 'it has been disclosed or published in the names of all or some of the coauthors, whether or not it is possible to distinguish their individual contributions').

4. the law of the country of origin (first publication); or
5. the law of the forum as a generally residual choice of law designation.

(c) Initial ownership of copyright

20.41 The adoption of a choice of law rule for copyright ownership should further an overall goal of the Berne Convention, to promote the international dissemination of works of authorship.[94] Application of a rule of strict territoriality could result in a multiplicity of laws governing copyright ownership; this might so disrupt international commerce in copyrighted works as to defeat one of the principal purposes of the treaty. Moreover, while it has long been recognized that 'international copyright' is more accurately understood as a collection of national copyrights conferred on the author (or initial copyright holder) by virtue of bilateral and multilateral treaties,[95] that characterization better fits the determination of protectable subject matter and scope of rights than ownership of rights. It makes more sense to conceive of copyright as germinating in a work's source country, subsequently to flower in all other countries in which the work is protected. The countries that later host the work tend to its growth, but the welcome they extend to the work does not uproot it from its source. The work's source country (country of first publication, or residence, or domicile, or nationality of the author, or, where relevant, the country where the immovable work is located) thus should determine who is the initial titleholder. In the case of works composed of interrelated contributions, the source country should determine whether the work is 'joint', and, if so, whether any co-author may contract separately, or all co-authors must together license rights. Instead of seeking alternative points of attachment for identifying the law competent to designate copyright ownership, 'it is simpler and more just simply to refer to the substantive rule as set forth in the national law under whose aegis the work was born'.[96]

20.42 But why is it 'simpler and more just' to adopt the law of the country of origin to govern initial copyright ownership? Because that choice of law rule ensures that the work will not change initial owners by operation of law each time the work crosses an international boundary. By the same token, licensees in all countries will know that they have acquired rights from their owner. This does not mean that local law cannot modify or even disrupt the ownership allocation

---

[94] See eg Masouyé (1978), 5.

[95] See eg Baumgarten (n 37 above), 470, 471: 'The term "international copyright" is something of a misnomer, for neither a single code governing copyright protection across national borders, nor a unitary multi-national property right, exists. What does exist is a complex of copyright *relations* among sovereign states, each having its own copyright law applicable to acts within its territory.' (emphasis in original).

[96] Judgment of 29 Apr 1970, Cass civ (*Soc Lancio* v *Soc Editirice Fotoromanzi Internazionali*) (1971) *Rev Crit Dr Int Pr* 270, note H Batiffol.

established in the source country, for example, by applying the host country's public policy (*ordre public*) exception, or by making the relevant provisions of the local copyright law of mandatory application to all authors, local and foreign.[97] Nonetheless, in principle, resort to the law of the source country reinforces the security of international contracts, and therefore would seem to promote the international exchange of copyrighted works.

In the context of employment relationships, moreover, the source country will **20.43**
often also correspond to at least one of the other points of attachment indicated above. The country of first publication is usually also the country where the employer/publisher has its principal place of business; it may also be the country of residence or nationality of the employees. If one of these additional points of attachment applies, the source country is likely to be the country in which the employment contract is localized as well. In other words the source country is likely to be the country with the 'most significant relationship' to the work.[98]

[97] See eg German Law of 1965, as amended by the Mar 2002 Law on Strengthening the Contractual Position of Authors and Performers, ss 32, 32a, and 32b (making authors' remuneration mandatory for all authors whose works are exploited in Germany), discussed in William R Cornish, 'The Author as Risk-Sharer' (2002) 26 *Colum J L & the Arts* 1, 8–11; Wilhelm Nordemann, 'New Imperative Contract Rules Implemented Into the German Copyright Law', in *Mélanges Victor Nabhan* (2004), 309.

[98] An amendment to the US Copyright Act adopts the 'source country' approach. Section 104A, added to implement US obligations under the TRIPs Agreement, restores copyright protection in qualifying foreign works. Section 104A(b) provides: 'Ownership of Restored Copyright. A restored work vests initially in the author or initial rightholder of the work as determined by the law of the source country of the work.' Thus, in reinstating copyright protection for foreign works whose copyrights had been lost, US courts and the Copyright Office will look to the person or entity that the law of the treaty country of first publication designates as the copyright holder. Where there is more than one treaty country of first publication, the source country is the one with the 'most significant contacts with the work'. In the case of employee-created or commissioned works, that country will likely be the country in which the employment or commissioned work contract is localized.

The US Court of Appeals for the Second Circuit has since ruled that section 104A reflects the general US approach to conflict of laws regarding copyright ownership. In *Itar-Tass Russian News Agency* v *Russian Kurier, Inc*, 153 F 3d 82 (2d Cir 1988), the first appellate decision squarely to confront the question of which country's law applies to determine initial title to copyright, the court held that US courts would look to the allocation of ownership rights in the country with the 'most significant relationship' to the work. In that case, that country was the country of first publication, which was also the country of residence of the authors and publishers of the works at issue. The copyright ownership rule in the country of origin also differed from the US rule: while the copyright in employee-created US works belongs to the employer, under Russian copyright law, according to the court, the employee journalists retain their copyrights. Application of the source country's rule meant the Russian publisher did not automatically own the rights it was asserting in the USA. See also *Silberman* v *Innovation Luggage, Inc*, 67 USPQ 2d (BNA) 1489 (SDNY 2003) (applying Swiss law to determine copyright ownership of work first published in Switzerland).

20.44 Suppose that interrogation of the source country's law reveals that it *does* allocate to the plaintiff the rights that the claimant is asserting in a foreign forum. Is that the end of the inquiry? Or does the law of the country of exploitation also determine ownership rights for its territory? For example, suppose a US employer for hire, who, by virtue of its domestic law is the initial owner of the full copyright in the work, seeks to exploit the work in a country where employers are not initial copyright holders. Consider the analysis of Professor Ulmer. In his influential monograph on conflicts of law and intellectual property, the eminent German copyright scholar opined: 'if for example a work made for hire in the USA is to be exploited in Germany, the principle is that the copyright belongs to the employer. In Germany, however, the acquisition of copyright can only be interpreted as an agreement [as opposed to occurring automatically by operation of law]. It is therefore effective only within the limits in which a grant of rights of use is permissible according to German law: the author's moral right and the rights relating to types of uses which were still unknown at the time of conclusion of the contract remain the property of the author.'[99] In other words, the US-law characterization of the employer as initial copyright owner gives it standing to assert copyright ownership in Germany, but German law defines the scope of what is owned. The employer's 'ownership' bundle in Germany would include neither moral rights, nor forms of exploitation unknown at the time of contracting with the director. The Ulmer approach implies a 'double ownership rule':[100]

1. The claimant must have been the copyright owner in the source country of the work; and
2. The claimant would also have been the copyright owner in the country where protection is sought.

This approach does not seem to favour the smooth international commerce in copyrighted works. Nonetheless, as we shall see (at para 20.51 below), if the second element of the double ownership rule imposes a troublesome criterion for discovering who is the copyright owner, some local limitations on copyright ownership may recur as part of the inquiry into public-policy objections to applying the otherwise competent law. In other words, the second element incorporates the public-policy issues upfront.

---

99 Ulmer (n 29 above), 39.

100 The term is inspired by the now-abandoned English 'double actionability rule', under which a claim concerning an alleged tort committed outside the UK will be actionable in the English courts only if the conduct was tortious both under the law of the country where the act was committed, and under English law. See W R Cornish, 'Intellectual Property Infringement and Private International Law: Changing the Common Law Approach' [1996] *GRUR Int* 285. See also Graeme W Austin, 'The Infringement of Foreign Intellectual Property Rights' (1997) 113 *LQ Rev* 321.

(d) Transfers of ownership: basic principle lex contractus

The law of the source country also affords an appropriate starting point for considering what law applies to transfers of copyright. Suppose the source country's law does not effect a general transfer to the employer, but the employer (or its local licensee) claims to have acquired the pertinent rights by transfer. The court should first inquire if a specific statutory provision in the source country allocates the particular rights that the publisher is claiming. For example, the source country's law may provide for more or less limited presumptions of transfer of rights. By contrast, a compulsory licence should not have extraterritorial effect; the beneficiary of a compulsory licence from country A should not be able to claim rights by virtue of that licence in country B.[101] Unlike the beneficiaries of presumptions of transfer, who have a contractual—employment or commissioned work—relationship with the creator, compulsory licensees are strangers to the copyright owner; the compulsory licence dispenses them from entering into a contract with the copyright owner.[102] **20.45**

Assuming the rights were legitimately acquired in the source country, the next question is what law governs the licensor's grant of rights for a foreign territory. The *lex contractus*, or the *lex protectionis* (bearing in mind that for a contract covering multiple territories, as would be the case for digital network dissemination, there may be many *leges protectionum*)? Where national laws differ significantly with respect to the rights that authors may alienate, and to the means of making a valid transfer, the question of applicable law can become very fraught, as the so-far unsuccessful endeavour to devise a treaty on the rights of audio-visual performers illustrates (see the earlier discussion at paras 19.82ff above). Arguably, in forums that characterize the scope of the grant as a matter of substantive copyright law, the *lex protectionis* would control the scope (see further the discussion at para 20.49 below). But the *lex protectionis* should not effect a *broader* transfer than that made under the *lex contractus*. Thus, even with respect to the substance of the grant, the court should *first* consult the *lex contractus*, and then ask whether the *lex protectionis* requires *narrowing* the scope **20.46**

[101] The Berne Convention does permit member countries to impose compulsory licences for the making of phonograms, see art 13, but this means that Berne country A may subject a musical composition from Berne country B to the licence for the making and distribution of phonograms on A's territory. In effect, national treatment applies to compulsory licences: if A's musical compositions are subject to domestic compulsory licenses, so—on A's territory—may be B's. But art 13 does not permit reliance on country A's compulsory licence to disseminate the licensed phonograms abroad. See also, to similar effect, art 11*bis*(2), limiting to the country prescribing the licence the territorial effect of compulsory licences for certain communications to the public.

[102] See eg 17 USC § 115 (compulsory licence for making and distributing phonograms; the licence is obtained from the Copyright Office).

of the grant. For example, suppose a publishing contract granting rights for print media was submitted to the law of a 'purpose of the grant' jurisdiction,[103] in which electronic rights were considered not to come within the scope of the grant.[104] If the publisher now seeks to license digital media rights in a foreign jurisdiction and the author objects, the court in the foreign territory should first look to the law of the author's contract to determine if digital media rights should be deemed included.

20.47 What is the *lex contractus*? It is the law chosen by the parties, or, in the absence of a choice of law clause, the law ascertained by 'localizing' the contract. In the USA, a court would seek the jurisdiction with which the contract has the 'most significant relationship', for example, the country of the parties' residence, or the place of formation or execution of the contract.[105] Commonwealth countries would look first to the parties' intention, express or implied, and, in the absence of certainty here, to the 'proper law' of the contract which, in turn, would be the law of the country with the closest relationship to the contract.[106] In the European Union, the Rome Convention concerning the law applicable to contractual obligations similarly designates (in the absence of a law selected by the parties) the law of the country with which the contract 'is most closely connected'. This, in turn, is presumed to be the country where the party effecting the 'characteristic performance' has its habitual residence.[107] In the context of copyright transfers, it is not always apparent who owes the 'characteristic performance', particularly where a contract for Internet dissemination is concerned.[108] Nonetheless, we will consider that the characteristic performer is the party who exploits the work, because that party's actions will 'produce receipts for the author'.[109] The law of the contract then would be that of the exploiter's habitual residence. That law will also determine the formal requirements for the

---

[103] See eg art 31(5) of the German Copyright Act of 9 Sept 1965 discussed in P Bernt Hugenholtz, 'Comment: Electronic Rights and Wrongs in Germany and the Netherlands' (1988) 22 *Colum-VLA JL & Arts* 151.

[104] See eg Amsterdam District Court, decision of 24 Sept 1997 (*Heg, Mulder and Stam* v *De Volkskrant*) (English translation at (1998) 22 *Colum-VLA JL & Arts* 181); Brussels Court of Appeals, decision of 28 Oct 1997 and Brussels High Court, decision of 10 Oct 1996 (*Association générale des journalistes professionels de Belgique* v *SCRL Central Station*) (English translations at (1998) 22 *Colum-VLA JL & Arts* 195, 191); Strasbourg tribunal of grand instance, decision of 3 Feb 1998 (*Union of French journalists* v *SDV Pluirmedia*) (English translation at (1998) 22 *Colum-VLA JL & Arts* 199) (all holding online and CD-Rom exploitations of articles written for print periodicals to exceed the scope of any implied licence from the journalists to the newspapers).

[105] See eg Restatement (Second) of the Law of Conflicts of Law § 188(2).

[106] See eg Dicey and Morris, *The Conflict of Laws*, 13th edn (2000), rule 146.

[107] Rome Convention, arts 4(1)(2).

[108] See eg Mario Fabiani, 'Conflicts of Law in International Copyright Assignments' [1998] *Entertainment Law Review* 157, 161; Pierre-Yves Gautier, 'Private International Law Aspects: France', in *ALAI Study Days: Copyright in Cyberspace* (1996), 298–9.

[109] Fabiani (n 108 above).

contract, for example, whether the contract must be in writing and signed by the author, as well as the substance of the grant.[110]

(e) Derogations from the lex contractus

There are two principal circumstances under which a local court would look to a law other than that of the contract. First, under local choice of law rules, transferability in general may be considered a matter of substantive copyright law governed by the *lex protectionis*. More modestly, certain kinds of transfers, or even certain matters going to the form of the transfer (such as whether it must be in writing),[111] might be deemed controlled by substantive copyright rules. Second, even where the law of the contract normally controls, the country of exploitation may also interpose its law when, under the law of the host country (*lex protectionis*), the result of applying the foreign law would conflict with a strongly held local public policy (*ordre public*), such as the inalienability of moral rights. As a variant on this public-policy theme, some local prohibitions might be considered automatically to apply to all contracts as mandatory rules, without regard to what law otherwise governs the contract.[112] For example, if local law provides that a right may not be assigned, then any assignment for that territory will be invalid, whatever the law that governs the contract.[113] In all these circumstances, then, while the law of the source country governs what an author may *grant*, the law of the host country may also determine what the grantee may *receive* in that jurisdiction. **20.48**

[110] See Rome Convention, art 9. In the case of copyright transfers, the distinction between the form of a contract, and the substance of the grant, may not always be apparent, as questions of form (particularly requirements that transfers be in writing and signed by the author) may be characterized as copyright-specific, rather than merely contractual. See eg André Lucas, 'La loi applicable aux contrats d'exploitation des droits d'auteur et des droits voisins', in *Mélanges Victor Nabhan* (2004), 289, 306–8.

[111] For an example of the application of the *lex protectionis* to the form of a grant, see *Corcovado Music Pub* v *Hollis Music, Inc*, 981 F 2d 679 (2d Cir 1993). In that case, a Brazilian-law contract between a Brazilian composer and a Brazilian publisher granted worldwide rights for the duration of the copyright. The composer nonetheless terminated the Brazilian publisher's US rights at the conclusion of the first term of copyright, and granted the US renewal term rights to a US publisher. The Brazilian publisher objected that Brazilian law governed the grant of rights, and that under Brazilian law, the composer had no rights left to grant to another publisher. The Second Circuit acknowledged that Brazilian law governed the contract, but characterized the issue of the form of the grant of renewal rights as determined by US copyright law. Because the Brazilian contract did not contain the requisite language, it was ineffective to transfer rights in the US renewal term.

[112] This approach treats the local prohibition like a 'law of immediate application' or *loi de police*, a local law that the forum applies without even inquiring into what foreign law might govern. See eg F. Juenger, *General Course on Private International Law* (1983), 201–2 (extract from (1985-IV) 193 *Recueil des Cours*).

[113] See eg 17 USC § 203(a)(5) (right to terminate grants of exclusive rights under copyright thirty-five years following contract's conclusion may not be assigned or waived in advance).

(f) Transferability characterized as matter of substantive copyright law, rather than contract law

20.49 Suppose interrogation of the source country's law reveals that the claimant has there acquired the rights it is asserting abroad. But suppose also that the claimant may acquire *more* rights from authors in the source country than the claimant could acquire under the law of the country of exploitation. Applying the principle of national treatment, under which the 'extent of protection . . . afforded to the author to protect his rights'[114] is governed by the copyright law of the country in which protection is sought, some countries treat the scope of the grant as a matter of substantive copyright law; the scope of the grant would therefore be limited to that allowed under local law.[115] Thus, for example, a 1950 US-law contract that transferred exploitation rights 'in all media now known, or later developed' would be valid in the USA,[116] but invalid in Germany as to media unknown in 1950.[117] Assume that online media were unknown in 1950. If only the law of the contract governs, then the grantee may offer the work online throughout the world, including to German users. If German law applies to German exploitations, then the author (or her heirs) may contest the grantee's offering the work on line to users in Germany.

20.50 Characterizing issues of transferability and scope as systematically governed by the *lex protectionis* is consistent with a view of international copyright as a bundle of territorially discrete rights. Under this view, the rule of national treatment means that a Berne Union (or WTO) author is protected to the same extent as a local author in each country of the Union. Thus, when an author assigns her copyright for the whole world, she is in fact assigning whatever rights each Berne Union or WTO country will permit her to assign. If, however, one interprets the national treatment principle as addressing the scope of exclusive rights under copyright vis-à-vis infringers, rather than vis-à-vis grantees, then it is possible to avoid the disruption to the international dissemination of works of authorship that the highly territorialist approach discussed above would provoke, because the entire grant might instead be subject to one country's law.

(g) Public-policy exceptions

20.51 Even where another country's law normally would govern, the host country's law may, as a matter of domestic copyright law, prohibit the transfer of certain kinds of rights. For example, in Germany, a contract may not grant rights in

---

[114] Berne Convention, art 5(2). [115] See eg Ulmer (n 29 above).

[116] See eg *Platinum Records Co* v *Lucasfilm, Ltd*, 566 F Supp 216 (DNJ 1983); *Rooney* v *Columbia Pictures, Inc*, 538 F Supp 211 (SDNY), aff'd, 714 F 2d 117 (2d Cir 1982).

[117] German Copyright Law, art 31(4).

new modes of exploitation unknown at the time of contracting,[118] and in France, moral rights are inalienable.[119] Host country courts may consider these prohibitions to be of such local public-policy significance, that they control on local territory, regardless of the international character of the contract, or the foreign origin of the work. Thus, the French courts have rejected claims by a US motion picture producer that the US film director's contractual waiver of moral rights should bar the director's invocation in France of the moral right of integrity against the French broadcast of a colorized version of the film.[120] On the other hand, French courts have also declined to apply the *ordre public* exception to a claim of right of attribution by a French author bound by a US-law ghostwriter contract when the book under contention was written in the USA and distributed in several countries, including the USA, and the contract specified the application of US law.[121]

[118] ibid. [119] France, Code de la propriété intellectuelle, art L 121–1(3).

[120] See Judgment of 28 May 1991 (*Turner Ent* v *Huston*), Cass Civ 1re, 1991 JCP.II.21731, note A Françon; Judgment of 19 Dec 1994, Cour d'appel de Versailles, combined civil chambers (1995) 164 *RIDA* 389. See also Judgment of 30 May 1984 (*Marius Constant* v *Ste Warner Bros*), Trib Grde Instance de Paris, (1984) 122 *RIDA* 220 (upholding French film composer's attribution right in US film when the film was distributed in France).

[121] See Judgment of 1 Feb 1989 (*Bragance* v *de Grèce*), Court of Appeals of Paris (1989) 142 *RIDA* 301, 307, note Sirinielli.

Appendices

APPENDIX 1

Latest text of Berne Convention (1971 Paris Act plus Appendix)

Berne Convention for the Protection of Literary and Artistic Works

of September 9, 1886, completed at PARIS on May 4, 1896, revised at BERLIN on November 13, 1908, completed at BERNE on March 20, 1914, and revised at ROME on June 2, 1928, at BRUSSELS on June 26, 1948, at STOCKHOLM on July 14, 1967, and at PARIS on July 24, 1971

The countries of the Union, being equally animated by the desire to protect, in as effective and uniform a manner as possible, the rights of authors in their literary and artistic works,

Recognising the importance of the work of the Revision Conference held at Stockholm in 1967,

Having resolved to revise the Act adopted by the Stockholm Conference, while maintaining without change Articles 1 to 20 and 22 to 26 of that Act.

Consequently, the undersigned Plenipotentiaries, having presented their full powers, recognised as in good and due form, have agreed as follows:

Article 1

The countries to which this Convention applies constitute a Union for the protection of the rights of authors in their literary and artistic works.

Article 2

(1) The expression 'literary and artistic works' shall include every production in the literary, scientific and artistic domain, whatever may be the mode or form of its expression, such as books, pamphlets and other writings; lectures, addresses, sermons and other works of the same nature; dramatic or dramatico-musical works; choreographic works and entertainments in dumb show; musical compositions with or without words; cinematographic works to which are assimilated works expressed by a process analogous to cinematography; works of drawing, painting, architecture, sculpture, engraving and lithography; photographic works to which are assimilated works expressed by a process analogous to photography; works of applied art; illustrations, maps, plans, sketches and three-dimensional works relative to geography, topography, architecture or science.

(2) It shall, however, be a matter for legislation in the countries of the Union to prescribe that works in general or any specified categories of works shall not be protected unless they have been fixed in some material form.

(3) Translations, adaptations, arrangements of music and other alterations of a literary or artistic work shall be protected as original works without prejudice to the copyright in the original work.

(4) It shall be a matter for legislation in the countries of the Union to determine the protection to be granted to official texts of a legislative, administrative and legal nature, and to official translations of such texts.

(5) Collections of literary or artistic works such as encyclopaedias and anthologies which, by reason of the selection and arrangement of their contents, constitute intellectual creations shall be protected as such, without prejudice to the copyright in each of the works forming part of such collections.

(6) The works mentioned in this Article shall enjoy protection in all countries of the Union. This protection shall operate for the benefit of the author and his successors in title.

(7) Subject to the provisions of Article 7(4) of this Convention, it shall be a matter for legislation in the countries of the Union to determine the extent of the application of their laws to works of applied art and industrial designs and models, as well as the conditions under which such works, designs and models shall be protected. Works protected in the country of origin solely as designs and models shall be entitled in another country of the Union only to such special protection as is granted in that country to designs and models; however, if no such special protection is granted in that country, such works shall be protected as artistic works.

(8) The protection of this Convention shall not apply to news of the day or to miscellaneous facts having the character of mere items of press information.

Article 2bis

(1) It shall be a matter for legislation in the countries of the Union to exclude, wholly or in part, from the protection provided by the preceding Article political speeches and speeches delivered in the course of legal proceedings.

(2) It shall also be a matter for legislation in the countries of the Union to determine the conditions under which lectures, addresses and other works of the same nature which are delivered in public may be reproduced by the press, broadcast, communicated to the public by wire and made the subject of public communication as envisaged in Article 11*bis*(1) of this Convention, when such use is justified by the informatory purpose.

(3) Nevertheless, the author shall enjoy the exclusive right of making a collection of his works mentioned in the preceding paragraphs.

Article 3

(1) The protection of this Convention shall apply to:

(a) authors who are nationals of one of the countries of the Union, for their works, whether published or not;

(b) authors who are not nationals of one of the countries of the Union, for their works first published in one of those countries, or simultaneously in a country outside the Union and in a country of the Union.

(2) Authors who are not nationals of one of the countries of the Union but who have their habitual residence in one of them shall, for the purposes of this Convention, be assimilated to nationals of that country.

(3) The expression 'published works' means works published with the consent of their authors, whatever may be the means of manufacture of the copies, provided that the availability of such copies has been such as to satisfy the reasonable requirements of the public, having regard to the nature of the work. The performance of a dramatic, dramatico-musical, cinematographic or musical work, the public recitation of a literary work, the communication by wire or the broadcasting of literary or artistic works, the exhibition of a work of art and the construction of a work of architecture shall not constitute publication.

(4) A work shall be considered as having been published simultaneously in several countries if it has been published in two or more countries within thirty days of its first publication.

Article 4

The protection of this Convention shall apply, even if the conditions of Article 3 are not fulfilled, to:

(a) authors of cinematographic works the maker of which has his headquarters or habitual residence in one of the countries of the Union;

(b) authors of works of architecture erected in a country of the Union or of other artistic works incorporated in a building or other structure located in a country of the Union.

Article 5

(1) Authors shall enjoy, in respect of works for which they are protected under this Convention, in countries of the Union other than the country of origin, the rights which their respective laws do now or may hereafter grant to their nationals, as well as the rights specially granted by this Convention.

(2) The enjoyment and the exercise of these rights shall not be subject to any formality; such enjoyment and such exercise shall be independent of the existence of protection in the country of origin of the work. Consequently, apart from the provisions of this Convention, the extent of protection, as well as the means of redress afforded to the author to protect his rights, shall be governed exclusively by the laws of the country where protection is claimed.

(3) Protection in the country of origin is governed by domestic law. However, when the author is not a national of the country of origin of the work for which he is protected under this Convention, he shall enjoy in that country the same rights as national authors.

(4) The country of origin shall be considered to be:

(a) in the case of works first published in a country of the Union, that country; in the case of works published simultaneously in several countries of the Union which grant different terms of protection, the country whose legislation grants the shortest term of protection;

(b) in the case of works published simultaneously in a country outside the Union and in a country of the Union, the latter country;

(c) in the case of unpublished works or of works first published in a country outside the Union, without simultaneous publication in a country of the Union, the country of the Union of which the author is a national, provided that:

 (i) when these are cinematographic works the maker of which has his headquarters or his habitual residence in a country of the Union, the country of origin shall be that country, and

 (ii) when these are works of architecture erected in a country of the Union or other artistic works incorporated in a building or other structure located in a country of the Union, the country of origin shall be that country.

Article 6

(1) Where any country outside the Union fails to protect in an adequate manner the works of authors who are nationals of one of the countries of the Union, the latter country may restrict the protection given to the works of authors who are, at the date of the first publication thereof, nationals of the other country and are not habitually resident in one of the countries of the Union. If the country of first publication avails itself of this right, the other countries of the Union shall not be required to grant to works thus subjected to special treatment a wider protection than that granted to them in the country of first publication.

(2) No restrictions introduced by virtue of the preceding paragraph shall affect the rights which an author may have acquired in respect of a work published in a country of the Union before such restrictions were put into force.

(3) The countries of the Union which restrict the grant of copyright in accordance with this Article shall give notice thereof to the Director General of the World Intellectual Property Organisation (hereinafter designated as 'the Director General') by a written declaration specifying the countries in regard to which protection is restricted, and the restrictions to which rights of authors who are nationals of those countries are subjected. The Director General shall immediately communicate this declaration to all the countries of the Union.

Article 6bis

(1) Independently of the author's economic rights, and even after the transfer of the said rights, the author shall have the right to claim authorship of the work and to object to any

distortion, mutilation or other modification of, or other derogatory action in relation to, the said work, which would be prejudicial to his honour or reputation.

(2) The rights granted to the author in accordance with the preceding paragraph shall, after his death, be maintained, at least until the expiry of the economic rights, and shall be exercisable by the persons or institutions authorised by the legislation of the country where protection is claimed. However, those countries whose legislation, at the moment of their ratification of or accession to this Act, does not provide for the protection after the death of the author of all the rights set out in the preceding paragraph may provide that some of these rights may, after his death, cease to be maintained.

(3) The means of redress for safeguarding the rights granted by this Article shall be governed by the legislation of the country where protection is claimed.

Article 7

(1) The term of protection granted by this Convention shall be the life of the author and fifty years after his death.

(2) However, in the case of cinematographic works, the countries of the Union may provide that the term of protection shall expire fifty years after the work has been made available to the public with the consent of the author, or, failing such an event within fifty years from the making of such a work, fifty years after the making.

(3) In the case of anonymous or pseudonymous works, the terms of protection granted by this Convention shall expire fifty years after the work has been lawfully made available to the public. However, when the pseudonym adopted by the author leaves no doubt as to his identity, the term of protection shall be that provided in paragraph (1). If the author of an anonymous or pseudonymous work discloses his identity during the above-mentioned period, the term of protection applicable shall be that provided in paragraph (1). The countries of the Union shall not be required to protect anonymous or pseudonymous works in respect of which it is reasonable to presume that their author has been dead for fifty years.

(4) It shall be a matter for legislation in the countries of the Union to determine the term of protection of photographic works and that of works of applied art in so far as they are protected as artistic works; however, this term shall last at least until the end of a period of twenty-five years from the making of such a work.

(5) The term of protection subsequent to the death of the author and the terms provided by paragraphs (2), (3) and (4) shall run from the date of death or of the event referred to in those paragraphs, but such terms shall always be deemed to begin on the first of January of the year following the death or such event.

(6) The countries of the Union may grant a term of protection in excess of those provided by the preceding paragraphs.

(7) Those countries of the Union bound by the Rome Act of this Convention which grant, in their national legislation in force at the time of signature of the present Act, shorter terms of protection than those provided for in the preceding paragraphs shall have the right to maintain such terms when ratifying or acceding to the present Act.

(8) In any case, the term shall be governed by the legislation of the country where protection is claimed; however, unless the legislation of that country otherwise provides, the term shall not exceed the term fixed in the country of origin of the work.

Article 7bis

The provisions of the preceding Article shall also apply in the case of a work of joint authorship, provided that the terms measured from the death of the author shall be calculated from the death of the last surviving author.

Article 8

Authors of literary and artistic works protected by this Convention shall enjoy the exclusive right of making and of authorising the translation of their works throughout the term of protection of their rights in the original works.

Article 9

(1) Authors of literary and artistic works protected by this Convention shall have the exclusive right of authorising the reproduction of these works, in any manner or form.

(2) It shall be a matter for legislation in the countries of the Union to permit the reproduction of such works in certain special cases, provided that such reproduction does not conflict with a normal exploitation of the work and does not unreasonably prejudice the legitimate interests of the author.

(3) Any sound or visual recording shall be considered as a reproduction for the purposes of this Convention.

Article 10

(1) It shall be permissible to make quotations from a work which has already been lawfully made available to the public, provided that their making is compatible with fair practice, and their extent does not exceed that justified by the purpose, including quotations from newspaper articles and periodicals in the form of press summaries.

(2) It shall be a matter for legislation in the countries of the Union, and for special agreements existing or to be concluded between them, to permit the utilisation, to the extent justified by the purpose, of literary or artistic works by way of illustration in publications, broadcasts or sound or visual recordings for teaching, provided such utilisation is compatible with fair practice.

(3) Where use is made of works in accordance with the preceding paragraphs of this Article, mention shall be made of the source, and of the name of the author if it appears thereon.

Article 10bis

(1) It shall be a matter for legislation in the countries of the Union to permit the reproduction by the press, the broadcasting or the communication to the public by wire of articles published in newspapers or periodicals on current economic, political or religious topics, and of broadcast works of the same character, in cases in which the reproduction, broadcasting or such communication thereof is not expressly reserved. Nevertheless, the source must always be clearly indicated; the legal consequences of a breach of this obligation shall be determined by the legislation of the country where protection is claimed.

(2) It shall also be a matter for legislation in the countries of the Union to determine the conditions under which, for the purpose of reporting current events by means of photography, cinematography, broadcasting or communication to the public by wire, literary or artistic works seen or heard in the course of the event may, to the extent justified by the informatory purpose, be reproduced and made available to the public.

Article 11

(1) Authors of dramatic, dramatico-musical and musical works shall enjoy the exclusive right of authorising:

(i) the public performance of their works, including such public performance by any means or process;
(ii) any communication to the public of the performance of their works.

(2) Authors of dramatic or dramatico-musical works shall enjoy, during the full term of their rights in the original works, the same rights with respect to translations thereof.

Article 11bis

(1) Authors of literary and artistic works shall enjoy the exclusive right of authorising:

(i) the broadcasting of their works or the communication thereof to the public by any other means of wireless diffusion of signs, sounds or images;
(ii) any communication to the public by wire or by rebroadcasting of the broadcast of the work, when this communication is made by an organisation other than the original one;

(iii) the public communication by loudspeaker or any other analogous instrument transmitting, by signs, sounds or images, the broadcast of the work.

(2) It shall be a matter for legislation in the countries of the Union to determine the conditions under which the rights mentioned in the preceding paragraph may be exercised, but these conditions shall apply only in the countries where they have been prescribed. They shall not in any circumstances be prejudicial to the moral rights of the author, nor to his right to obtain equitable remuneration which, in the absence of agreement, shall be fixed by competent authority.

(3) In the absence of any contrary stipulation, permission granted in accordance with paragraph (1) of this Article shall not imply permission to record, by means of instruments recording sounds or images, the work broadcast. It shall, however, be a matter for legislation in the countries of the Union to determine the regulations for ephemeral recordings made by a broadcasting organisation by means of its own facilities and used for its own broadcasts. The preservation of these recordings in official archives may, on the ground of their exceptional documentary character, be authorised by such legislation.

Article 11ter

(1) Authors of literary works shall enjoy the exclusive right of authorising:

(i) the public recitation of their words, including such public recitation by any means or process;
(ii) any communication to the public of the recitation of their works.

(2) Authors of literary works shall enjoy, during the full term of their rights in the original works, the same rights with respect to translations thereof.

Article 12

Authors of literary or artistic works shall enjoy the exclusive right of authorising adaptations, arrangements and other alterations of their works.

Article 13

(1) Each country of the Union may impose for itself reservations and conditions on the exclusive right granted to the author of a musical work and to the author of any words, the recording of which together with the musical work has already been authorised by the latter, to authorise the sound recording of that musical work, together with such words, if any; but all such reservations and conditions shall apply only in the countries which have imposed them and shall not, in any circumstances, be prejudicial to the rights of these authors to obtain equitable remuneration which, in the absence of agreement, shall be fixed by competent authority.

(2) Recordings of musical works made in a country of the Union in accordance with Article 13(3) of the Conventions signed at Rome on 2 June 1928, and at Brussels on 26 June 1948, may be reproduced in that country without the permission of the author of the musical work until a date two years after that country becomes bound by this Act.

(3) Recordings made in accordance with paragraphs (1) and (2) of this Article and imported without permission from the parties concerned into a country where they are treated as infringing recordings shall be liable to seizure.

Article 14

(1) Authors of literary or artistic works shall have the exclusive right of authorising:

(i) the cinematographic adaptation and reproduction of these works, and the distribution of the works thus adapted or reproduced;
(ii) the public performance and communication to the public by wire of the works thus adapted or reproduced.

(2) The adaptation into any other artistic form of a cinematographic production derived from literary or artistic works shall, without prejudice to the authorisation of the author of the cinematographic production, remain subject to the authorisation of the authors of the original works.

(3) The provisions of Article 13(1) shall not apply.

Article 14bis

(1) Without prejudice to the copyright in any work which may have been adapted or reproduced, a cinematographic work shall be protected as an original work. The owner of copyright in a cinematographic work shall enjoy the same rights as the author of an original work, including the rights referred to in the preceding Article.

(2) (a) Ownership of copyright in a cinematographic work shall be a matter for legislation in a country where protection is claimed.

(b) However, in the countries of the Union which, by legislation, include among the owners of copyright in a cinematographic work authors who have brought contributions to the making of the work, such authors, if they have undertaken to bring such contributions, may not, in the absence of any contrary or special stipulation, object to the reproduction, distribution, public performance, communication to the public by wire, broadcasting or any other communication to the public, or to the subtitling or dubbing of texts, of the work.

(c) The question whether or not the form of the undertaking referred to above should, for the application of the preceding subparagraph (b), be in a written agreement or a written act of the same effect shall be a matter for the legislation of the country where the maker of the cinematographic work has his headquarters or habitual residence. However, it shall be a matter for the legislation of the country of the Union where protection is claimed to provide that the said undertaking shall be in a written agreement or a written act of the same effect. The countries whose legislation so provides shall notify the Director General by means of a written declaration, which will be immediately communicated by him to all the other countries of the Union.

(d) By 'contrary or special stipulation' is meant any restrictive condition which is relevant to the aforesaid undertaking.

(3) Unless the national legislation provides to the contrary, the provisions of paragraph (2)(b) above shall not be applicable to authors of scenarios, dialogues and musical works created for the making of the cinematographic work, or to the principal director thereof. However, those countries of the Union whose legislation does not contain rules providing for the application of the said paragraph (2)(b) to such director shall notify the Director General by means of a written declaration, which will be immediately communicated by him to all the other countries of the Union.

Article 14ter

(1) The author, or after his death the persons or institutions authorised by national legislation, shall, with respect to original works of art and original manuscripts of writers and composers, enjoy the inalienable right to an interest in any sale of the work subsequent to the first transfer by the author of the work.

(2) The protection provided by the preceding paragraph may be claimed in a country of the Union only if legislation in the country to which the author belongs so permits, and to the extent permitted by the country where this protection is claimed.

(3) The procedure for collection and the amounts shall be matters for determination by national legislation.

Article 15

(1) In order that the author of a literary or artistic work protected by this Convention shall, in the absence of proof to the contrary, be regarded as such, and consequently be entitled to institute infringement proceedings in the countries of the Union, it shall be sufficient for his name to appear on the work in the usual manner. This paragraph shall be applicable even if this name is a pseudonym, where the pseudonym adopted by the author leaves no doubt as to his identity.

(2) The person or body corporate whose name appears on a cinematographic work in the usual manner shall, in the absence of proof to the contrary, be presumed to be the maker of the said work.

(3) In the case of anonymous and pseudonymous works, other than those referred to in paragraph (1) above, the publisher whose name appears on the work shall, in the absence of proof to the contrary, be deemed to represent the author, and in this capacity he shall be entitled to protect and enforce the author's rights. The provisions of this paragraph shall cease to apply when the author reveals his identity and establishes his claim to authorship of the work.

(4) (a) In the case of unpublished works where the identity of the author is unknown, but where there is every ground to presume that he is a national of a country of the Union, it shall be a matter for legislation in that country to designate the competent authority which shall represent the author and shall be entitled to protect and enforce his rights in the countries of the Union.

(b) Countries of the Union which makes such designation under the terms of this provision shall notify the Director General by means of a written declaration giving full information concerning the authority thus designated. The Director General shall at once communicate this declaration to all other countries of the Union.

Article 16

(1) Infringing copies of a work shall be liable to seizure in any country of the Union where the work enjoys legal protection.

(2) The provisions of the preceding paragraph shall also apply to reproductions coming from a country where the work is not protected, or has ceased to be protected.

(3) The seizure shall take place in accordance with the legislation of each country.

Article 17

The provisions of this Convention cannot in any way affect the right of the Government of each country of the Union to permit, to control, or to prohibit, by legislation or regulation, the circulation, presentation, or exhibition of any work or production in regard to which the competent authority may find it necessary to exercise that right.

Article 18

(1) This Convention shall apply to all works which, at the moment of its coming into force, have not yet fallen into the public domain in the country of origin through the expiry of the term of protection.

(2) If, however, through the expiry of the term of protection which was previously granted, a work has fallen into the public domain of the country where protection is claimed, that work shall not be protected anew.

(3) The application of this principle shall be subject to any provisions contained in special conventions to that effect existing or to be concluded between countries of the Union. In the absence of such provisions, the respective countries shall determine, each in so far as it is concerned, the conditions of application of this principle.

(4) The preceding provisions shall also apply in the case of new accessions to the Union and to cases in which protection is extended by the application of Article 7 or by the abandonment of reservations.

Article 19

The provisions of this Convention shall not preclude the making of a claim to the benefit of any greater protection which may be granted by legislation in a country of the Union.

Article 20

The Governments of the countries of the Union reserve the right to enter into special agreements among themselves, in so far as such agreements grant to authors more extensive rights than those granted by the Convention, or contain other provisions not contrary to this Convention. The provisions of existing agreements which satisfy these conditions shall remain applicable.

Article 21

(1) Special provisions regarding developing countries are included in the Appendix.

(2) Subject to the provisions of Article 28(1)(b), the Appendix forms an integral part of this Act.

Article 22

(1) (a) The Union shall have an Assembly consisting of those countries of the Union which are bound by Articles 22 to 26.

(b) The Government of each country shall be represented by one delegate, who may be assisted by alternate delegates, advisers, and experts.

(c) The expenses of each delegation shall be borne by the Government which has appointed it.

(2) (a) The Assembly shall:

(i) deal with all matters concerning the maintenance and development of the Union and the implementation of this Convention;
(ii) give directions concerning the preparation for conferences of revision to the International Bureau of Intellectual Property (hereinafter designated as 'the International Bureau') referred to in the Convention Establishing the World Intellectual Property Organisation (hereinafter designed as 'the Organisation'), due account being taken of any comments made by those countries of the Union which are not bound by Articles 22 to 26;
(iii) review and approve the reports and activities of the Director General of the Organisation concerning the Union, and give him all necessary instructions concerning matters within the competence of the Union;
(iv) elect the members of the Executive Committee of the Assembly;
(v) review and approve the reports and activities of its Executive Committee, and give instructions to such Committee;
(vi) determine the programme and adopt the [triennial]* biennial** budget of the Union, and approve its final accounts;
(vii) adopt the financial regulations of the Union;
(viii) establish such committees of experts and working groups as may be necessary for the work of the Union;
(ix) determine which countries not members of the Union and which intergovernmental and international non-governmental organisations shall be admitted to its meetings as observers;
(x) adopt amendments to Articles 22 to 26;
(xi) take any other appropriate action designed to further the objectives of the Union;
(xii) exercise such other functions as are appropriate under this Convention;
(xiii) subject to its acceptance, exercise such rights as are given to it in the Convention establishing the Organisation.

(b) With respect to matters which are of interest also to other Unions administered by the Organisation, the Assembly shall make its decisions after having heard the advice of the Coordination Committee of the Organisation.

(3) (a) Each country member of the Assembly shall have one vote.

(b) One-half of the countries members of the Assembly shall constitute a quorum.

(c) Notwithstanding the provisions of subparagraph (b), if, in any session, the number of countries represented is less than one-half but equal to or more than one-third of the countries members of the Assembly, the Assembly may make decisions but, with the exception of decisions concerning its own procedure, all such decisions shall take effect only if the following conditions are fulfilled. The International Bureau shall communicate the said decisions to the countries members of the Assembly which were not represented and shall invite them to express in writing their vote or abstention within a period of three months from the date of the communication. If, at the expiration of this period, the number of countries having thus expressed their vote or abstention attains the number of countries which was lacking for attaining the quorum in the session itself, such decisions shall take effect provided that at the same time the required majority still obtains.

(d) Subject to the provisions of Article 26(2), the decisions of the Assembly shall require two-thirds of the votes cast.

(e) Abstentions shall not be considered as votes.

(f) A delegate may represent, and vote in the name of, one country only.

(g) Countries of the Union not members of the Assembly shall be admitted to its meetings as observers.

(4) (a) The Assembly shall meet once in every [third]* second** calendar year in ordinary session upon convocation by the Director General and, in the absence of exceptional circumstances, during the same period and at the same place as the General Assembly of the Organisation.

(b) The Assembly shall meet in extraordinary session upon convocation by the Director General, at the request of the Executive Committee or at the request of one-fourth of the countries members of the Assembly.

(5) The Assembly shall adopt its own rules of procedure.

Article 23

(1) The Assembly shall have an Executive Committee.

(2) (a) The Executive Committee shall consist of countries elected by the Assembly from among countries members of the Assembly. Furthermore, the country on whose territory the Organisation has its headquarters shall, subject to the provisions of Article 25(7)(b), have an *ex officio* seat on the Committee.

(b) The Government of each country member of the Executive Committee shall be represented by one delegate, who may be assisted by alternate delegates, advisers, and experts.

(c) The expenses of each delegation shall be borne by the Government which has appointed it.

(3) The number of countries members of the Executive Committee shall correspond to one-fourth of the number of countries members of the Assembly. In establishing the number of seats to be filled, remainders after division by four shall be disregarded.

(4) In electing the members of the Executive Committee, the Assembly shall have due regard to an equitable geographical distribution and to the need for countries party to the Special Agreements which might be established in relation with the Union to be among the countries constituting the Executive Committee.

(5) (a) Each member of the Executive Committee shall serve from the close of the session of the Assembly which elected it to the close of the next ordinary session of the Assembly.

(b) Members of the Executive Committee may be re-elected, but not more than two-thirds of them.

(c) The Assembly shall establish the details of the rules governing the election and possible re-election of the members of the Executive Committee.

(6) (a) The Executive Committee shall:

(i) prepare the draft agenda of the Assembly

(ii) submit proposals to the Assembly respecting the draft programme and [triennial]* biennial** budget of the Union prepared by the Director General;

[(iii) approve, within the limits of the programme and the triennial budget, the specific yearly budgets and programmes prepared by the Director General;]***

(iv) submit, with appropriate comments, to the Assembly the periodical reports of the Director General and the yearly audit reports of the accounts;

(v) in accordance with the decisions of the Assembly and having regard to circumstances arising between two ordinary sessions of the Assembly, take all necessary measures to ensure the execution of the program of the Union by the Director General;

(vi) perform such other functions as are allocated to it under this Convention.

(b) With respect to matters which are of interest also to other Unions administered by the

Organisation, the Executive Committee shall make its decisions after having heard the advice of the Coordination Committee of the Organisation.

(7) (a) The Executive Committee shall meet once a year in ordinary session upon convocation by the Director General, preferably during the same period and at the same place as the Coordination Committee of the Organisation.

(b) The Executive Committee shall meet in extraordinary session upon convocation by the Director General, either on his own initiative, or at the request of its Chairman or one-fourth of its members.

(8) (a) Each country member of the Executive Committee shall have one vote.

(b) One-half of the members of the Executive Committee shall constitute a quorum.

(c) Decisions shall be made by a simple majority of the votes cast.

(d) Abstentions shall not be considered as votes.

(e) A delegate may represent, and vote in the name of, one country only.

(9) Countries of the Union not members of the Executive Committee shall be admitted to its meetings as observers.

(10) The Executive Committee shall adopt its own rules of procedure.

Article 24

(1) (a) The administrative tasks with respect to the Union shall be performed by the International Bureau, which is a continuation of the Bureau of the Union united with the Bureau of the Union established by the International Convention for the Protection of Industrial Property.

(b) In particular, the International Bureau shall provide the secretariat of the various organs of the Union.

(c) The Director General of the Organisation shall be the chief executive of the Union and shall represent the Union.

(2) The International Bureau shall assemble and publish information concerning the protection of copyright. Each country of the Union shall promptly communicate to the International Bureau all new laws and official texts concerning the protection of copyright.

(3) The International Bureau shall publish a monthly periodical.

(4) The International Bureau shall, on request, furnish information to any country of the Union on matters concerning the protection of copyright.

(5) The International Bureau shall conduct studies, and shall provide services, designed to facilitate the protection of copyright.

(6) The Director General and any staff member designated by him shall participate, without the right to vote, in all meetings of the Assembly, the Executive Committee and any other committee of experts or working group. The Director General, or a staff member designated by him, shall be *ex officio* secretary of these bodies.

(7) (a) The International Bureau shall, in accordance with the directions of the Assembly and in cooperation with the Executive Committee, make the preparations for the conferences of revision of the provisions of the Convention other than Articles 22 to 26.

(b) The International Bureau may consult with inter-governmental and international non-governmental organisations concerning preparations for conferences of revision.

(c) The Director General and persons designated by him shall take part, without the right to vote, in the discussions at these conferences.

(8) The International Bureau shall carry out any other tasks assigned to it.

Article 25

(1) (a) The Union shall have a budget.

(b) The budget of the Union shall include the income and expenses proper to the Union, its contribution to the budget of expenses common to the Unions, and, where applicable, the sum made available to the budget of the Conference of the Organisation.

(c) Expenses not attributable exclusively to the Union but also to one or more other Unions administered by the Organisation shall be considered as expenses common to the Unions. The share of the Union in such common expenses shall be in proportion to the interest the Union has in them.

(2) The budget of the Union shall be established with due regard to the requirements of coordination with the budgets of the other Unions administered by the Organisation.

(3) The budget of the Union shall be financed from the following sources:

- (i) contributions of the countries of the Union;
- (ii) fees and charges due for services performed by the International Bureau in relation to the Union;
- (iii) sale of, or royalties on, the publications of the International Bureau concerning the Union;
- (iv) gifts, bequests, and subventions;
- (v) rents, interests, and other miscellaneous income.

(4) (a) For the purpose of establishing its contribution towards the budget, each country of the Union shall belong to a class, and shall pay its annual contributions on the basis of a number of units fixed as follows:

Class I	25
Class II	20
Class III	15
Class IV	10
Class V	5
Class VI	3
Class VII	1

(b) Unless it has already done so, each country shall indicate, concurrently with depositing its instrument of ratification or accession, the class to which it wishes to belong. Any country may change class. If it chooses a lower class, the country must announce it to the Assembly at one of its ordinary sessions. Any such change shall take effect at the beginning of the calendar year following the session.

(c) The annual contribution of each country shall be an amount in the same proportion to the total sum to be contributed to the annual budget of the Union by all countries as the number of its units is to the total of the units of all contributing countries.

(d) Contributions shall become due on the first of January of each year.

(e) A country which is in arrears in the payment of its contributions shall have no vote in any of the organs of the Union of which it is a member if the amount of its arrears equals or exceeds the amount of the contributions due from it for the preceding two full years. However, any organ of the Union may allow such a country to continue to exercise its vote in that organ if, and as long as, it is satisfied that the delay in payment is due to exceptional and unavoidable circumstances.

(f) If the budget is not adopted before the beginning of a new financial period, it shall be at the same level as the budget of the previous year, in accordance with the financial regulations.

(5) The amount of the fees and charges due for services rendered by the International Bureau in relation to the Union shall be established, and shall be reported to the Assembly and the Executive Committee, by the Director General.

(6) (a) The Union shall have a working capital fund which shall be constituted by a single payment made by each country of the Union. If the fund becomes insufficient, an increase shall be decided by the Assembly.

(b) The amount of the initial payment of each country to the said fund or of its participation in the increase thereof shall be a proportion of the contribution of that country for the year in which the fund is established or the increase decided.

(c) The proportion and the terms of payment shall be fixed by the Assembly on the proposal of the Director General and after it has heard the advice of the Coordination Committee of the Organisation.

(7) (a) In the headquarters agreement con-

cluded with the country on the territory of which the Organisation has its headquarters, it shall be provided that, whenever the working capital fund is insufficient, such country shall grant advances. The amount of these advances and the conditions on which they are granted shall be the subject of separate agreements, in each case, between such country and the Organisation. As long as it remains under the obligation to grant advances, such country shall have an *ex officio* seat on the Executive Committee.

(b) The country referred to in subparagraph (a) and the Organisation shall each have the right to denounce the obligation to grant advances, by written notification. Denunciation shall take effect three years after the end of the year in which it has been notified.

(8) The auditing of the accounts shall be effected by one or more of the countries of the Union or by external auditors, as provided in the financial regulations. They shall be designated, with their agreement, by the Assembly.

Article 26

(1) Proposals for the amendment of Articles 22, 23, 24, 25, and the present Article, may be initiated by any country member of the Assembly, by the Executive Committee, or by the Director General. Such proposals shall be communicated by the Director General to the member countries of the Assembly at least six months in advance of their consideration by the Assembly.

(2) Amendments to the Articles referred to in paragraph (1) shall be adopted by the Assembly. Adoption shall require three-fourths of the votes cast, provided that any amendment of Article 22, and of the present paragraph, shall require four-fifths of the votes cast.

(3) Any amendment to the Articles referred to in paragraph (1) shall enter into force one month after written notifications of acceptance, effected in accordance with their respective constitutional processes, have been received by the Director General from three-fourths of the countries members of the Assembly at the time it adopted the amendment. Any amendment to the said Articles thus accepted shall bind all the countries which are members of the Assembly at the time the amendment enters into force, or which become members thereof at a subsequent date, provided that any amendment increasing the financial obligations of countries of the Union shall bind only those countries which have notified their acceptance of such amendment.

Article 27

(1) This Convention shall be submitted to revision with a view to the introduction of amendments designed to improve the system of the Union.

(2) For this purpose, conferences shall be held successively in one of the countries of the Union among the delegates of the said countries.

(3) Subject to the provisions of Article 26 which apply to the amendment of Articles 22 to 26, any revision of this Act, including the Appendix, shall require the unanimity of the votes cast.

Article 28

(1) (a) Any country of the Union which has signed this Act may ratify it, and, if it has not signed it, may accede to it. Instruments of ratification or accession shall be deposited with the Director General.

(b) Any country of the Union may declare in its instrument of ratification or accession that its ratification or accession shall not apply to Articles 1 to 21 and the Appendix, provided that, if such country has previously made a declaration under Article VI(1) of the Appendix, then it may declare in the said instrument only that its ratification or accession shall not apply to Articles 1 to 20.

(c) Any country of the Union which, in accordance with subparagraph (b), has excluded provisions therein referred to from the effects of its ratification or accession may at any later time declare that it extends the effects of its ratification or accession to those provisions. Such declaration shall be deposited with the Director General.

(2) (a) Articles 1 to 21 and the Appendix shall enter into force three months after both of the following two conditions are fulfilled:

(i) at least five countries of the Union have ratified or acceded to this Act without making a declaration under paragraph (1)(b),

(ii) France, Spain, the United Kingdom of Great Britain and Northern Ireland, and the United States of America, have become bound by the Universal Copyright Convention as revised at Paris on July 24, 1971.

(b) The entry into force referred to in subparagraph (a) shall apply to those countries of the Union which, at least three months before the said entry into force, have deposited instruments of ratification or accession not containing a declaration under paragraph (1)(b).

(c) With respect to any country of the Union not covered by subparagraph (b) and which ratifies or accedes to this Act without making a declaration under paragraph (1)(b), Articles 1 to 21 and the Appendix shall enter into force three months after the date on which the Director General has notified the deposit of the relevant instrument of ratification or accession, unless a subsequent date has been indicated in the instrument deposited. In the latter case, Articles 1 to 21 and the Appendix shall enter into force with respect to that country on the date thus indicated.

(d) The provisions of subparagraphs (a) to (c) do not affect the application of Article VI of the Appendix.

(3) With respect to any country of the Union which ratifies or accedes to this Act with or without a declaration made under paragraph (1)(b), Articles 22 to 38 shall enter into force three months after the date on which the Director General has notified the deposit of the relevant instrument of ratification or accession, unless a subsequent date has been indicated in the instrument deposited. In the latter case, Articles 22 to 38 shall enter into force with respect to that country on the date thus indicated.

Article 29

(1) Any country outside the Union may accede to this Act and thereby become party to this Convention and a member of the Union. Instruments of accession shall be deposited with the Director General.

(2) (a) Subject to subparagraph (b), this Convention shall enter into force with respect to any country outside the Union three months after the date on which the Director General has notified the deposit of its instrument of accession, unless a subsequent date has been indicated in the instrument deposited. In the latter case, this Convention shall enter into force with respect to that country on the date thus indicated.

(b) If the entry into force according to subparagraph (a) precedes the entry into force of Articles 1 to 21 and the Appendix according to Article 28(2)(a), the said country shall, in the meantime, be bound, instead of by Articles 1 to 21 and the Appendix, by Articles 1 to 20 of the Brussels Act of this Convention.

Article 29bis

Ratification of or accession to this Act by any country not bound by Articles 22 to 38 of the Stockholm Act of this Convention shall, for the sole purposes of Article 14(2) of the Convention establishing the Organisation, amount to ratification of or accession to the said Stockholm Act with the limitation set forth in Article 28(1)(b)(i) thereof.

Article 30

(1) Subject to the exceptions permitted by paragraph (2) of this Article, by Article 28(1)(b), by Article 33(2), and by the Appendix, ratification or accession shall automatically entail acceptance of all the provisions and admission to all the advantages of this Convention.

(2) (a) Any country of the Union ratifying or acceding to this Act may, subject to Article V(2) of the Appendix, retain the benefit of the reservations it has previously formulated on condition that it makes a declaration to that effect at the time of the deposit of its instrument of ratification or accession.

(b) Any country outside the Union may declare, in acceding to this Convention and subject to Article V(2) of the Appendix, that it intends to substitute, temporarily at least, for Article 8 of this Act concerning the right of translation, the provisions of Article 5 of the Union Convention of 1886, as completed at Paris in 1896, on the clear understanding that the said provisions are applicable only to translations into a language in general use in the said country. Subject to Article I(6)(b) of the Appendix, any country has the right to apply, in relation to the right of translation of works whose country of origin is a country availing itself of such a reservation, a protection which is equivalent to the protection granted by the latter country.

(c) Any country may withdraw such reservations at any time by notification addressed to the Director General.

Article 31

(1) Any country may declare in its instrument of ratification or accession, or may inform the Director General by written notification at any time thereafter, that this Convention shall be applicable to all or part of those territories, designated in the declaration or notification, for the external relations of which it is responsible.

(2) Any country which has made such a declaration or given such a notification may, at any time, notify the Director General that this Convention shall cease to be applicable to all or part of such territories.

(3) (a) Any declaration made under paragraph (1) shall take effect on the same date as the ratification or accession in which it was included, and any notification given under that paragraph shall take effect three months after its notification by the Director General.

(b) Any notification given under paragraph (2) shall take effect twelve months after its receipt by the Director General.

(4) This Article shall in no way be understood as implying the recognition or tacit acceptance by a country of the Union of the factual situation concerning a territory to which this Convention is made applicable by another country of the Union by virtue of a declaration under paragraph (1).

Article 32

(1) This Act shall, as regards relations between the countries of the Union, and to the extent that it applies, replace the Berne Convention of 9 September 1886, and the subsequent Acts of revision. The Acts previously in force shall continue to be applicable, in their entirety or to the extent that this Act does not replace them by virtue of the preceding sentence, in relations with countries of the Union which do not ratify or accede to this Act.

(2) Countries outside the Union which become party to this Act shall, subject to paragraph (3), apply it with respect to any country of the Union not bound by this Act or which, although bound by this Act, has made a declaration pursuant to Article 28(1)(b). Such countries recognise that the said country of the Union, in its relations with them:

(i) may apply the provisions of the most recent Act by which it is bound, and
(ii) subject to Article I(6) of the Appendix, has the right to adapt the protection to the level provided for by this Act.

(3) Any country which has availed itself of any of the faculties provided for in the Appendix may apply the provisions of the Appendix relating to the faculty or faculties of which it has availed itself in its relations with any other country of the Union which is not bound by this Act, provided that the latter country has accepted the application of the said provisions.

Article 33

(1) Any dispute between two or more countries of the Union concerning the interpretation or application of this Convention, not settled by negotiation, may, by any one of the countries concerned, be brought before the International Court of Justice by application in conformity with the Statute of the Court, unless the countries concerned agree on some other method of settlement. The country bringing the dispute before the Court shall inform the International Bureau; the International

Bureau shall bring the matter to the attention of the other countries of the Union.

(2) Each country may, at the time it signs this Act or deposits its instrument of ratification or accession, declare that it does not consider itself bound by the provisions of paragraph (1). With regard to any dispute between such country and any other country of the Union, the provisions of paragraph (1) shall not apply.

(3) Any country having made a declaration in accordance with the provisions of paragraph (2) may, at any time, withdraw its declaration by notification addressed to the Director General.

Article 34

(1) Subject to Article 29 *bis*, no country may ratify or accede to earlier Acts of this Convention once Articles 1 to 21 and the Appendix have entered into force.

(2) Once Articles 1 to 21 and the Appendix have entered into force, no country may make a declaration under Article 5 of the Protocol Regarding Developing Countries attached to the Stockholm Act.

Article 35

(1) This Convention shall remain in force without limitation as to time.

(2) Any country may denounce this Act by notification addressed to the Director General. Such denunciation shall constitute also denunciation of all earlier Acts and shall affect only the country making it, the Convention remaining in full force and effect as regards the other countries of the Union.

(3) Denunciation shall take effect one year after the day on which the Director General has received the notification.

(4) The right of denunciation provided by this Article shall not be exercised by any country before the expiration of five years from the date upon which it becomes a member of the Union.

Article 36

(1) Any country party to this Convention undertakes to adopt, in accordance with its constitution, the measures necessary to ensure the application of this Convention.

(2) It is understood that, at the time a country becomes bound by this Convention, it will be in a position under its domestic law to give effect to the provisions of this Convention.

Article 37

(1) (a) This Act shall be signed in a single copy in the French and English languages and, subject to paragraph (2), shall be deposited with the Director General.

(b) Official texts shall be established by the Director General, after consultation with the interested Governments, in the Arabic, German, Italian, Portuguese and Spanish languages, and such other languages as the Assembly may designate.

(c) In case of differences of opinion on the interpretation of the various texts, the French text shall prevail.

(2) This Act shall remain open for signature until 31 January 1972. Until that date, the copy referred to in paragraph (1)(a) shall be deposited with the Government of the French Republic.

(3) The Director General shall certify and transmit two copies of the signed text of this Act to the Governments of all countries of the Union and, on request, to the Government of any other country.

(4) The Director General shall register this Act with the Secretariat of the United Nations.

(5) The Director General shall notify the Governments of all countries of the Union of signatures, deposits of instruments of ratification or accession and any declarations included in such instruments or made pursuant to Articles 28(1)(c), 30(2)(a) and (b), and 33(2), entry into force of any provisions of this Act, notifications of denunciation, and notifications pursuant to Articles 30(2)(c), 31(1) and (2), 33(3), and 38(1), as well as the Appendix.

Article 38

(1) Countries of the Union which have not ratified or acceded to this Act and which are not bound by Articles 22 to 26 of the Stockholm Act of this Convention may, until 26 April 1975, exercise, if they so desire, the rights provided under the said Articles as if they were bound by them. Any country desiring to exercise such rights shall give written notification to this effect to the Director General; this notification shall be effective on the date of its receipt. Such countries shall be deemed to be members of the Assembly until the said date.

(2) As long as all the countries of the Union have not become Members of the Organisation, the International Bureau of the Organisation shall also function as the Bureau of the Union, and the Director General as the Director of the said Bureau.

(3) Once all the countries of the Union have become Members of the Organisation, the rights, obligations, and property, of the Bureau of the Union shall devolve on the International Bureau of the Organisation.

Appendix

Article I

(1) Any country regarded as a developing country in conformity with the established practice of the General Assembly of the United Nations which ratifies or accedes to this Act, of which this Appendix forms an integral part, and which, having regard to its economic situation and its social or cultural needs, does not consider itself immediately in a position to make provision for the protection of all the rights as provided for in this Act, may, by a notification deposited with the Director General at the time of depositing its instrument of ratification or accession or, subject to Article V(1)(c), at any time thereafter, declare that it will avail itself of the faculty provided for in Article II, or of the faculty provided for in Article III, or of both of those faculties. It may, instead of availing itself of the faculty provided for in Article II, make a declaration according to Article V(1)(a).

(2) (a) Any declaration under paragraph (1) notified before the expiration of the period of ten years from the entry into force of Articles 1 to 21 and this Appendix according to Article 28(2) shall be effective until the expiration of the said period. Any such declaration may be renewed in whole or in part for periods of ten years each by a notification deposited with the Director General not more than fifteen months and not less than three months before the expiration of the ten-year period then running.

(b) Any declaration under paragraph (1) notified after the expiration of the period of ten years from the entry into force of Articles 1 to 21 and this Appendix according to Article 28(2) shall be effective until the expiration of the ten-year period then running. Any such declaration may be renewed as provided for in the second sentence of subparagraph (a).

(3) Any country of the Union which has ceased to be regarded as a developing country as referred to in paragraph (1) shall no longer be entitled to renew its declaration as provided in paragraph (2), and, whether or not in formally withdraws its declaration, such country shall be precluded from availing itself of the facilities referred to in paragraph (1) from the expiration of the ten-year period then running or from the expiration of a period of three years after it has ceased to be regarded as a developing country, whichever period expires later.

(4) Where, at the time when the declaration made under paragraph (1) or (2) ceases to be effective, there are copies in stock which were made under a licence granted by virtue of this Appendix, such copies may continue to be distributed until their stock is exhausted.

(5) Any country which is bound by the provisions of this Act and which has deposited a declaration or a notification in accordance with Article 31(1) with respect to the application of this Act to a particular territory, the situation of which can be regarded as analogous to that of the countries referred to in paragraph (1), may, in respect of such territory, make the declaration referred to in paragraph (1) and the notification of renewal referred to in paragraph (2). As long as such declaration or notification remains in effect, the provisions of this

Appendix shall be applicable to the territory in respect of which it was made.

(6) (a) The fact that a country avails itself of any of the faculties referred to in paragraph (1) does not permit another country to give less protection to works of which the country of origin is the former country than it is obliged to grant under Articles 1 to 20.

(b) The right to apply reciprocal treatment provided for in Article 30(2)(b), second sentence, shall not, until the date on which the period applicable under Article I(3) expires, be exercised in respect of works the country of origin of which is a country which has made a declaration according to Article V(1)(a).

Article II

(1) Any country which has declared that it will avail itself of the faculty provided for in this Article shall be entitled, so far as works published in printed or analogous forms of reproduction are concerned, to substitute for the exclusive right of translation provided for in Article 8 a system of non-exclusive and non-transferable licences, granted by the competent authority under the following conditions and subject to Article IV.

(2) (a) Subject to paragraph (3), if, after the expiration of a period of three years, or of any longer period determined by the national legislation of the said country, commencing on the date of the first publication of the work, a translation of such work has not been published in a language in general use in that country by the owner of the right of translation, or with his authorisation, any national of such country may obtain a licence to make a translation of the work in the said language and publish the translation in printed or analogous forms of reproduction.

(b) A licence under the conditions provided for in this Article may also be granted if all the editions of the translation published in the language concerned are out of print.

(3) (a) In the case of translations into a language which is not in general use in one or more developed countries which are members of the Union, a period of one year shall be substituted for the period of three years referred to in paragraph (2)(a).

(b) Any country referred to in paragraph (1) may, with the unanimous agreement of the developed countries which are members of the Union and in which the same language is in general use, substitute, in the case of translations into that language, for the period of three years referred to in paragraph (2)(a) a shorter period as determined by such agreement but not less than one year. However, the provisions of the foregoing sentence shall not apply where the language in question is English, French or Spanish. The Director General shall be notified of any such agreement by the Governments which have concluded it.

(4) (a) No licence obtainable after three years shall be granted under this Article until a further period of six months has elapsed, and no licence obtainable after one year shall be granted under this Article until a further period of nine months has elapsed

(i) from the date on which the applicant complies with the requirements mentioned in Article IV(1), or

(ii) where the identity or the address of the owner of the right of translation is unknown, from the date on which the applicant sends, as provided for in Article IV(2), copies of his application submitted to the authority competent to grant the licence.

(b) If, during the said period of six or nine months, a translation in the language in respect of which the application was made is published by the owner of the right of translation or with his authorisation, no licence under this Article shall be granted.

(5) Any licence under this Article shall be granted only for the purpose of teaching, scholarship or research.

(6) If a translation of a work is published by the owner of the right of translation or with his authorisation at a price reasonably related to that normally charged in the country for comparable works, any licence granted under this Article shall terminate if such translation is in the same language and with substantially

the same content as the translation published under the licence. Any copies already made before the licence terminates may continue to be distributed until their stock is exhausted.

(7) For works which are composed mainly of illustrations, a licence to make and publish a translation of the text and to reproduce and publish the illustrations may be granted only if the conditions of Article III are also fulfilled.

(8) No licence shall be granted under this Article when the author has withdrawn from circulation all copies of his work.

(9) (a) A licence to make a translation of a work which has been published in printed or analogous forms of reproduction may also be granted to any broadcasting organisation having its headquarters in a country referred to in paragraph (1), upon an application made to the competent authority of that country by the said organisation, provided that all of the following conditions are met:

(i) the translation is made from a copy made and acquired in accordance with the laws of the said country;
(ii) the translation is only for use in broadcasts intended exclusively for teaching or for the dissemination of the results of specialised technical or scientific research to experts in a particular profession;
(iii) the translation is used exclusively for the purposes referred to in condition (ii) through broadcasts made lawfully and intended for recipients on the territory of the said country, including broadcasts made through the medium of sound or visual recordings lawfully and exclusively made for the purpose of such broadcasts;
(iv) all uses made of the translation are without any commercial purpose.

(b) Sound or visual recordings of a translation which was made by a broadcasting organisation under a licence granted by virtue of this paragraph may, for the purposes and subject to the conditions referred to in subparagraph (a) and with the agreement of that organisation, also be used by any other broadcasting organisation having its headquarters in the country whose competent authority granted the licence in question.

(c) Provided that all of the criteria and conditions set out in subparagraph (a) are met, a licence may also be granted to a broadcasting organisation to translate any text incorporated in an audio-visual fixation where such fixation was itself prepared and published for the sole purpose of being used in connection with systematic instructional activities.

(d) Subject to subparagraphs (a) to (c), the provisions of the preceding paragraphs shall apply to the grant and exercise of any licence granted under this paragraph.

Article III

(1) Any country which has declared that it will avail itself of the faculty provided for in this Article shall be entitled to substitute for the exclusive right of reproduction provided for in Article 9 a system of non-exclusive and non-transferable licences, granted by the competent authority under the following conditions and subject to Article IV.

(2) (a) If, in relation to a work to which this Article applies by virtue of paragraph (7), after the expiration of

(i) the relevant period specified in paragraph (3), commencing on the date of first publication of a particular edition of the work, or
(ii) any longer period determined by national legislation of the country referred to in paragraph (1), commencing on the same date,

copies of such edition have not been distributed in that country to the general public or in connection with systematic instructional activities, by the owner of the right of reproduction or with his authorisation, at a price reasonably related to that normally charged in the country for comparable works, any national of such country may obtain a licence to reproduce and publish such edition at that or a lower price for use in connection with systematic instructional activities.

(b) A licence to reproduce and publish an edition which has been distributed as described in subparagraph (a) may also be granted under the conditions provided for in this Article if, after the expiration of the applicable period, no authorised copies of that edition have been on sale for a period of six months in the country concerned to the general public or in connection with systematic instructional activities at a price reasonably related to that normally charged in the country for comparable works.

(3) The period referred to in paragraph (2)(a)(i) shall be five years, except that

(i) for works of the natural and physical sciences, including mathematics, and of technology, the period shall be three years;
(ii) for works of fiction, poetry, drama and music, and for art books, the period shall be seven years.

(4) (a) No licence obtainable after three years shall be granted under this Article until a period of six months has elapsed.

(i) from the date on which the applicant complies with the requirements mentioned in Article IV(1), or
(ii) where the identity or the address of the owner of the right of reproduction is unknown, from the date on which the applicant sends, as provided for in Article IV(2), copies of his application submitted to the authority competent to grant the licence.

(b) Where licences are obtainable after other periods and Article IV(2) is applicable, no licence shall be granted until a period of three months has elapsed from the date of the dispatch of the copies of the application.

(c) If, during the period of six or three months referred to in subparagraphs (a) and (b), a distribution as described in paragraph (2)(a) has taken place, no licence shall be granted under this Article.

(d) No licence shall be granted if the author has withdrawn from circulation all copies of the edition for the reproduction and publication of which the licence has been applied for.

(5) A licence to reproduce and publish a translation of a work shall not be granted under this Article in the following cases:

(i) where the translation was not published by the owner of the right of translation or with this authorisation, or
(ii) where the translation is not in a language in general use in the country in which the licence is applied for.

(6) If copies of an edition of a work are distributed in the country referred to in paragraph (1) to the general public or in connection with systematic instructional activities, by the owner of the right of reproduction or with his authorisation, at a price reasonably related to that normally charged in the country for comparable works, any licence granted under this Article shall terminate if such edition is in the same language and with substantially the same content as the edition which was published under the said licence. Any copies already made before the licence terminates may continue to be distributed until their stock is exhausted.

(7) (a) Subject to subparagraph (b), the works to which this Article applies shall be limited to works published in printed or analogous forms of reproduction.

(b) This Article shall also apply to the reproduction in audio-visual form of lawfully made audio-visual fixations including any protected works incorporated therein and to the translation of any incorporated text into a language in general use in the country in which the licence is applied for, always provided that the audio-visual fixations in question were prepared and published for the sole purpose of being used in connection with systematic instructional activities.

Article IV

(1) A licence under Article II or Article III may be granted only if the applicant, in accordance with the procedure of the country concerned, establishes either that he has requested, and has been denied, authorisation by the owner of the right to make and publish the translation or to reproduce and publish the edition, as the case may be, or that, after due diligence on his part, he was unable to find the owner of the right. At the same time as making the request, the applicant shall inform any national or international information centre referred to in paragraph (2).

(2) If the owner of the right cannot be found, the applicant for a licence shall send, by regis-

tered airmail, copies of his application, submitted to the authority competent to grant the licence, to the publisher whose name appears on the work and to any national or international information centre which may have been designated, in a notification to that effect deposited with the Director General, by the Government of the country in which the publisher is believed to have his principal place of business.

(3) The name of the author shall be indicated on all copies of the translation or reproduction published under a licence granted under Article II or Article III. The title of the work shall appear on all such copies. In the case of a translation, the original title of the work shall appear in any case on all the said copies.

(4) (a) No licence granted under Article II or Article III shall extend to the export of copies, and any such licence shall be valid only for publication of the translation or of the reproduction, as the case may be, in the territory of the country in which it has been applied for.

(b) For the purposes of subparagraph (a), the notion of export shall include the sending of copies from any territory to the country which, in respect of that territory, has made a declaration under Article I(5).

(c) Where a governmental or other public entity of a country which has granted a licence to make a translation under Article II into a language other than English, French or Spanish sends copies of a translation published under such licence to another country, such sending of copies shall not, for the purposes of subparagraph(a), be considered to constitute export if all of the following conditions are met:

(i) the recipients are individuals who are nationals of the country whose competent authority has granted the licence, or organisations grouping such individuals;
(ii) the copies are to be used only for the purpose of teaching, scholarship or research;
(iii) the sending of the copies and their subsequent distribution to recipients is without any commercial purpose; and
(iv) the country to which the copies have been sent has agreed with the country whose competent authority has granted the licence to allow the receipt, or distribution, or both, and the Director General has been notified of the agreement by the Government of the country in which the license has been granted.

(5) All copies published under a licence granted by virtue of Article II or Article III shall bear a notice in the appropriate language stating that the copies are available for distribution only in the country or territory to which the said licence applies.

(6) (a) Due provision shall be made at the national level to ensure

(i) that the licence provides, in favour of the owner of the right of translation or of reproduction, as the case may be, for just compensation that is consistent with standards of royalties normally operating on licences freely negotiated between persons in the two countries concerned, and
(ii) payment and transmittal of the compensation: should national currency regulations intervene, the competent authority shall make all efforts, by the use of international machinery, to ensure transmittal in internationally convertible currency or its equivalent.

(b) Due provision shall be made by national legislation to ensure a correct translation of the work, or an accurate reproduction of the particular edition, as the case may be.

Article V

(1) (a) Any country entitled to make a declaration that it will avail itself of the faculty provided for in Article II may, instead, at the time of ratifying or acceding to this Act:

(i) if it is a country to which Article 30(2)(a) applies, make a declaration under that provision as far as the right of translation is concerned;
(ii) if it is a country to which Article 30(2)(a) does not apply, and even if it is not a country outside the Union, make a declaration as provided for in Article 30(2)(b), first sentence.

(b) In the case of a country which ceases to be regarded as a developing country as referred to in Article I(1), a declaration made according to this paragraph shall be effective until the date on which the period applicable under Article I(3) expires.

(c) Any country which has made a declaration according to this paragraph may not subsequently avail itself of the faculty provided for in Article II even if it withdraws the said declaration.

(2) Subject to paragraph (3), any country which has availed itself of the faculty provided for in Article II may not subsequently make a declaration according to paragraph (1).

(3) Any country which has ceased to be regarded as a developing country as referred to in Article I(1) may, not later than two years prior to the expiration of the period applicable under Article I(3), make a declaration to the effect provided for in Article 30(2)(b), first sentence, notwithstanding the fact that it is not a country outside the Union. Such declaration shall take effect at the date on which the period applicable under Article I(3) expires.

Article VI

(1) Any country of the Union may declare, as from the date of this Act, and at any time before becoming bound by Articles 1 to 21 and this Appendix:

(i) if it is a country which, were it bound by Articles 1 to 21 and this Appendix, would be entitled to avail itself of the faculties referred to in Article I(1), that it will apply the provisions of Article II or of Article III or of both to works whose country of origin is a country which, pursuant to (ii) below, admits the application of those Articles to such works, or which is bound by Articles 1 to 21 and this Appendix; such declaration may, instead of referring to Article II, refer to Article V;

(ii) that it admits the application of this Appendix to works of which it is the country of origin by countries which have made a declaration under (i) above or a notification under Article I.

(2) Any declaration made under paragraph (1) shall be in writing and shall be deposited with the Director General. The declaration shall become effective from the date of its deposit.

Note: Amendments to articles 22 and 25 were adopted by the Berne Assembly at its meeting in 2003 but have not yet come into force. See further para 16.49 of the principal text.

APPENDIX 2

Miscellaneous Documents relating to the Origins of the Berne Convention and its development

(a) Resolutions of the *Congrès de la propriété littéraire et artistique* held in Brussels, 27–30 September 1858 (original French text)

I Droit international

1 Le Congrès estime que le principe de la reconnaissance internationale de la propriété des œuvres littéraires et artistiques en faveur de leurs auteurs doit prendre place dans la législation de tous les peuples civilisés.

2 Ce principe doit être admis de pays à pays, même en l'absence de réciprocité.

3 L'assimilation des auteurs étrangers aux auteurs nationaux doit être absolue et complète.

4 Il n'y a pas lieu d'astreindre les auteurs étrangers à des formalités particulières, afin qu'ils soient admis à invoquer et à poursuivre le droit de propriété. Il doit suffire, pour que ce droit leur appartienne, qu'ils aient rempli les formalités requises par la loi du pays où la publication originale a vu le jour.

5 Il est désirable que tous les pays adoptent pour la propriété des ouvrages de littérature et d'art une législation reposant sur des bases uniformes.

II Propriété des ouvrages de litterature et d'art en général

1 Les auteurs d'œuvres de littérature et d'art doivent jouir, durant leur vie entière, du droit exclusif de publier et de reproduire leurs ouvrages, de les vendre, faire vendre ou distribuer, et d'en céder, en tout ou en partie, la propriété ou le droit de reproduction. Le conjoint survivant doit conserver les mèmes droits, également durant toute sa vie, et les héritiers ou ayants droit de l'auteur doivent en jouir pendant cinquante ans à partir soit du décès de l'autre, soit de l'extinction des droits du conjoint.

2 Il n'y a pas lieu de distinguer, pour l'application de ces droits, entre les diverses catégories d'ouvrages de littérature et d'art, œuvres littéraires, compositions musicales, production des arts du dessin. Il n'y a pas de distinction à faire entre les œuvres pseudonymes et les œuvres signées du nom de l'auteur. Il ne doit pas être non plus établi de distinction, pour la durée des droits, d'après la qualité des ayants cause, enfants, héritiers, donataires ou cessionnaires.

3 La durée du droit du premier éditeur sur un ouvrage anonyme doit être de trente ans à partir de la publication. Si l'auteur se fait connaître avant l'expiration du terme légal, il doit rentrer dans les droits qui lui auraient appartenu, si l'ouvrage avait paru dès l'origine sous son nom.

4 En ce qui concerne les œuvres posthumes, si les droits du conjoint de l'auteur et de ses héritiers ou ayants cause ne sont pas éteints, l'ouvrage posthume doit leur appartenir pendant une durée égale à celle qui leur est accordée par la loi. Si ces droits sont éteints, le propriétaire d'un ouvrage posthume doit avoir un droit exclusif, dont la durée doit être de trente ans à partir de la publication.

5 Le droit exclusif de l'auteur doit être garanti pour la publication des cours publics, sermons et autres discours prononcés publiquement, lequels ne peuvent être publiés isolément, ni en corps d'ouvrage, sans le consentement des auteurs ou de leurs représentants. A l'égard des plaidoyers et des discours prononcés dans les assemblées politiques, ce consentement ne doit être nécessaire que pour leur publication en recueil d'auteur.

6 Le droit de l'auteur sur la reproduction de son œuvre originale doit emporter le droit de traduction, avec la restriction suivante. L'auteur sera pendant dix ans, à partir de la publication de la traduction, le droit exclusif de traduire ou de faire traduire son œuvre dans toute les langues, à la condition d'exercer ce droit avant l'expiration de la troisième année de la publication de l'œuvre originale. Si, à l'expiration de la troisième année, l'auteur n'a pas fait usage de ce droit, chacun pourra l'exercer concurremment, excepté dans le pays d'origine. Après l'expiration des dix années, quoique l'auteur ait usé de son droit, chacun pourra traduire l'œuvre originale et la vendre dans tous les pays, excepté dans le pays d'origine.

7 Il n'y a pas lieu d'astreindre les auteurs d'ouvrages de littérature ou d'art à certaines formalités, à raison de leur droit. Si des formalités particulières peuvent être utiles, soit comme mesure d'administration et d'ordre, soit comme moyen de constater et de prouver le droit de propriété; s'il convient d'assurer l'accomplissement de ces formalités par une sanction quelconque, leur inobservation ne peut et ne doit jamais entrainer la déchéance du droit. Il importe de rendre ces formalités aussi simples que possible; l'enregistrement et le dépôt d'un ou plusieurs exemplaires de l'ouvrage, entre les mains d'une autorité publique constitutée à cet effet, paraissent le mode le plus avantageux.

III Œuvres dramatiques et musicales

1 Le droit de représentation des œuvres dramatiques ou musicales doit être indépendant du droit exclusif de reproduction.

2 Il n'y a pas lieu de faire de distinction entre les deux droits pour la durée de la jouissance.

3 Le droit de propriété des compositions de musique doit mettre obstacles à l'exécution publique de toute partie de l'œuvre musicale sans le contentement de l'auteur, quelle que soit l'importance de l'ouvrage, et quel que soit le mode d'exécution. On ne peut invoquer le droit de l'auteur pour soumettre à des entraves les séances musicales, particulières ou publiques, où aucun but de spéculation ne se mêle à l'intérêt de l'art.

4 Le droit de propriété des compositions musicales doit comprendre le droit de faire des arrangements sur les motifs de l'œuvre originale.

IV Arts du dessin

1 L'auteur d'un dessin, d'un tableau, d'une œuvre de sculpture, d'architecture ou de toute autre œuvre artistique doit avoir seul le droit de la reproduire ou d'en autoriser la reproduction par un art semblable ou distinct, et sur une échelle analogue ou différente.

2 Le reproducteur non authorisé doit être passible des peines du contrefacteur, lorsqu'il y a usurpation du nom, sans préjudice des peines contre le faux en écriture privée, si la contrefaçon descend jusq'à l'imitation de la signature.

3 Le droit de propriété sur les créations des arts du dessin doit embrasser aussi les applications qui seraient faites de ces créations par l'industrie.

4 Des formalités particulières ne doivent pas être exigées pour les œuvres d'art, non plus que pour les productions littéraires, comme condition absolue de l'acquisition et de la conservation de la propriété, cependant, dans un cas comme dans l'autre, des formalités peuvent être désirables comme mesure d'ordre et pour faciliter l'exercice régulier du droit. Les ouvrages pourraient être enregistrés, et le certificat d'enregistrement qui serait délivré à l'artiste permettrait à celui-ci de faire reconnaître, entre ses mains et entre celles de ses cessionnaires, l'authenticité de l'œuvre, et, le cas échéant, celle des copies.

V Questions économiques

Le Congrès demande:

1 L'abolition des droits de douane sur les livres et les œuvres d'art, ou du moins la réduction de ces droits au taux le plus modéré, et leur simplification là où le tarif établit des droits différents par catégorie pour les productions littéraires et des beaux-arts;

2 La faculté de faire rentrer librement les ouvrages non vendus en voyés en commission à l'étranger;

3 L'abaissement des taxes postales aux dernières limites possibles, sur toutes les voies, et l'augmentation des facilités pour le transport et la circulation des imprimés, des gravures et autres articles susceptibles d'être transportés par la voie postale;

4 L'assimilation des épreuves avec corrections aux imprimés, dans les pays où les règlements établissent une différence;

5 La suppression de toutes les formalités qui entravent le commerce de la librairie.

[Source: *Annales de la Propriété Industrielle, Artistique et Littéraire* (1858), 452–4.]

(b) ALAI draft convention (1883) (original French text)

PROJET DE CONVENTION pour constituer une Union générale pour la protection des droits des auteurs sur leurs œuvres littéraires et artistiques

Art. 1er Les auteurs d'œuvres littéraires et artistiques parues, représentées ou exécutées dans l'un des Etats contractants, à la seule condition d'accomplir les formalités exigées par la loi de ce pays, jouiront pour la protection de leurs œuvres dans les autres Etats de l'Union, quelle que soit d'ailleurs leur nationalité, des mêmes droits que les nationaux.

Art. 2 L'expression «œuvres littéraires et artistiques» comprend: les livres, brochures ou tous les autres écrits; les œuvres dramatiques et dramatico-musicales, les compositions musicales avec ou sans paroles et les arrangements de musique; les œuvres de dessin, de peinture, de sculpture, de gravure, les lithographies, les cartes géographiques, les plans, les croquis scientifiques et en général toute œuvre quelconque, littéraire, scientifique et artistique, qui pourrait être publiée par n'importe quel système d'impression ou de reproduction.

Art. 3 Le droit des auteurs s'exerce également sur les œuvres manuscrites ou inédites.

Art. 4 Les mandataires légaux ou ayants cause des auteurs jouiront, à tous égards, des mêmes droits que ceux accordés par la présente convention aux auteurs eux-mêmes.

Art. 5 Les auteurs ressortissant à l'un des Etats contractants jouiront, dans tous les autres Etats de l'Union, du droit exclusif de traduction pendant toute la durée de leur droit sur leurs œuvres originales.

Ce droit comprend les droits de publication, de représentation ou d'exécution.

Art. 6 La traduction autorisee est protégée au même titre que l'œuvre originale. Lorsqu'il s'agit de la traduction d'une œuvre tombée dans le domaine public, la traducteur ne peut pas s'opposer à ce que la même œuvre soit traduit par d'autres écrivains.

Art. 7 En cas d'infraction aux prescriptions qui précèdent, les tribunaux compétents appliqueront les dispositions, tant civiles que pénales, édictées par les législations respectives, comme si l'infraction avait été commise au préjudice d'un national.

L'adaptation sera considérée comme contrefaçon et poursuivie de la même manière.

Art. 8 La presente convention s'applique à toutes les œuvres non encore tombées dans le domaine public dans le pays d'origine de l'œuvre au moment où ladite convention entrera en vigueur.

Art. 9 Il est entendu que les Etats de l'Union se réservent respectivement le droit de prendre séparément entre eux des arrangements particuliers pour la protection des œuvres littéraires et artistiques, en tant que ces arrangements particuliers ne contreviendraient point aux dispositions de la présente convention.

Art. 10 Il sera établi un Bureau central et international auquel seront déposés, par les soins des Gouvernements des Etats de l'Union, les lois, décrets et règlements déjà promulgués, ou qui le seraient ultérieurement, concernant les droits des auteurs.

Ce Bureau les réunira et publiera une feuille périodique rédigée en langue française, où seront contenus tous les documents et renseignements utiles à faire connaître aux intéressés.

[Source: *Actes* 1884, 7–8.]

(c) Swiss Federal Council Programme for the Diplomatic Conference of 1884 (original French text)

Convention

1 Les Etats contractants (énumération) sont constitués à l'état d'union pour la protection des droits des auteurs sur leurs œuvres littéraires et artistiques.

2 Les sujets ou citoyens de chacun des Etats contractants jouiront dans tous les autres Etats de l'Union, en ce qui concerne la protection des droits des auteurs sur leurs œuvres littéraires et artistiques, des advantages que les lois respectives accordent actuellement ou accorderont par la suite aux nationaux. En conséquence, ils auront la même protection que ceux-ci et le même recours légal contre toute atteinte portée à leurs droits, sous réserve de l'accomplissement des formalités et des conditions prescrites par la législation du pays d'origine de l'œuvre.

3 Sont assimilés aux sujets ou citoyens des Etats contractants les sujets ou citoyens des Etats ne faisant pas partie de l'Union, qui sont domiciliés ou ont fait éditer leur œuvre sur le territoire de l'un des Etats de l'Union.

4 L'expression «œuvres littéraires ou artistiques» comprend les livres, brochures ou tous autres écrits; les œuvres dramatiques ou dramatico-musicales, les compositions musicales avec ou sans paroles et les arrangements de musique; les œuvres de dessin, de peinture, de sculpture, de gravure, les lithographies, les cartes géographiques, les plans, les croquis scientifiques, et en général toute œuvre quelconque, littéraire, scientifique, et artistique, qui pourrait être publiée par n'importe quel système d'impression ou de reproduction.

5 Le droit des auteurs s'exerce également sur les œuvres manuscrites ou inédites.

6 Les mandataires légaux ou ayants cause des auteurs jouiront, à tous égards, des mêmes droits que ceux accordés par la présente convention aux auteurs eux-mêmes.

7 Les auteurs ressortissant à l'un des Etats contractants jouiront, dans tous les autres Etats de l'Union, du droit exclusif de traduction pendant toute la durée de leur droit sur leurs œuvres originales. (Eventuellement, ajouter: «s'ils ont fait usage de ce droit dans un délai de dix ans.»)

Ce droit comprend les droits de publication, de représentation ou d'exécution.

8 La traduction autorisée est protégé au même titre que l'œuvre originale.

Lorsqu'il s'agit de la traduction d'une œuvre tombée dans le domaine public, le traducteur ne peut pas s'opposer à ce que la même œuvre soit traduite par d'autres écrivains.

9 Toute œuvre contrefaite pourra être saisie à l'importation dans ceux des Etats de l'Union dans lesquels l'œuvre a droit à la protection légale.

La saisie aura lieu à la requête soit du ministère public, soit de la partie intéressée, conformément à la législation intérieure de chaque Etat.

10 L'adaptation sera considérée comme contrefaçon et poursuivie de la même manière.

11 La présente convention s'applique à toutes les œuvres non encore tombées dans le domaine public dans le pays d'origine de l'œuvre au moment où cette convention entrera en vigueur.

12 Il est entendu que les Hautes Parties contractantes se réservent respectivement le droit de prendre séparément, entre elles, des arrangements particuliers pour la protection des œuvres littéraires et artistiques, en tant que ces arrangements ne contreviendraient point aux dispositions de la présente convention.

13 Un office international sera organisé sous le nom de Bureau International de l'Union pour la protection des œuvres littéraires et artistiques.

Ce bureau, dont les frais seront supportés par les administrations de tous les Etats contractants, sera placé sous la haute autorité de . . . et fonctionnera sous sa surveillance. Les attributions en seront déterminées d'un commun accord entre les Etats de l'Union.

14 La présente convention sera soumise à des révisions périodiques, en vue d'y introduire les améliorations de nature à perfectionner le système de l'Union.

A cet effet, des Conférences auront lieu successivement dans l'un des Etats contractants entre les délégués de ces Etats.

La prochaine réunion aura lieu en . . ., à . . .

15 Les Etats qui n'ont point pris part à la prèsente convention seront admis à y adhérer sur leur demande.

Cette adhésion sera notifiée par écrit au Gouvernement de . . ., et par celui-ci à tous les autres.

Elle emportera, de plein droit, accession à toutes les clauses et admission à tous les advantages stipulés par la présente convention.

16 L'exécution des engagements réciproques contenus dans la présente convention est subordonnée, en tant que de besoin, à l'accomplissement des formalités et règles établies par les lois constitutionnelles de celles des Hautes Parties contractantes qui sont tenues d'eu proposer l'application, ce qu'elles s'engagent à faire dans le plus bref délai possible.

17 La présente convention sera mise à exécution à partir du . . ., et demeurera en vigueur pendant un temps indéterminé, jusqu'à l'expiration d'une année à partir du jour où la dénonciation en sera faite.

Cette dénonciation sera adressée au Gouvernement chargé de recevoir les adhésions. Elle ne produira son effet qu'à l'égard de l'Etat qui l'aura faite, la convention restant exécutoire pour les autres Parties contractantes.

18 La présente convention sera ratifiée, et les ratifications en seront échangées à . . . dans le délai d'un an au plus tard.

Disposition transitoire

Les conventions actuellement en vigueur entre les Etats contractants, qui dérogeraient à la présente convention sur un point ou l'autre, pourrent néanmoins demeurer exécutoires jusqu'à l'échéance qu'elles, prévoient. Dans ce cas, les sujets ou citoyens des Etats de l'Union non liés par ces conventions seront mis de plein droit, dans les Etats respectifs, au bénéfice du traitement de la nation la plus favorisée pour la protection de leurs droits d'auteur.

Protocole de clôture

Au moment de procéder à la signature de la convention conclue à la date de ce jour, les Plénipotentiaires soussignés sont convenus de ce qui suit:

1 Il est entendu que la disposition finale de l'article 2 de la convention ne porte aucune atteinte à la législation de chacun des Etats contractants, en ce qui concerne la procédure suivie devant les tribunaux et la compétence de ces tribunaux.

2 Définir que les mots *arrangements de musique* (article 4 de la convention) ne s'appliquent pas aux morceaux reproduits par des instruments automatiques, tels que pianos électriques, boites à musique, orgues de Barbarie, etc.

3 Définir le sens exact du mot *adaptation.*

4 Organisation du Bureau international; son budget et contributions des Etats de l'Union.

Attributions. Le Bureau international centralisera les renseignements de toute nature relatifs à la protection des droits des auteurs sur les œuvres littéraires et artistiques et les réunira en une statistique générale qui sera distribuée à toutes les administrations. Il recevra de chaque administration la liste des œuvres enregistrées par elle et la communiquera à toutes les administrations. Il procédera aux études d'utilité commune intéressant l'Union et rédigera, à l'aide des documents qui seront mis à sa disposition par les diverse administrations, une feuille périodique, en langue française, sur les questions concernant l'objet de l'Union.

Mode de distribution de cette feuille.

Le Bureau international devra se tenir en tout temps à la disposition des membres de l'Union, pour leur fournir, sur les questions relatives à la protection des œuvres littéraires et artistiques, les renseignements spéciaux dont ils pourraient avoir besoin.

L'administration du pays où doit siéger la prochaine Conférence préparera, avec le concours du Bureau international, les travaux de cette Conférence.

Le directeur de Bureau international assistera aux séances des Conférences et prendra part aux discussions sans voix délibérative. Il fera sur sa gestion un rapport annuel qui sera communiqué à tous les membres de l'Union.

La langue officielle du Bureau international sera la langue française.

Le présent protocole de clôture, qui sera ratifié en même temps que la convention conclue à la date de ce jour, sera considéré comme faisant partie intégrante de cette convention et aura même force, valeur et durée.

[Source: *Actes* 1884, 11–13.]

(d) Draft convention respecting the formation of a General Union for the Protection of the Rights of Authors formulated by the 1884 Diplomatic Conference at Berne (original French text)

(Énumération des Hautes Parties Contractantes)

* * * * * *

également animés du désir de protéger d'une manière efficace et aussi uniforme que possible les droits d'auteur sur les œuvres littéraires et artistiques,

Ont résolu de conclure une Convention à cet effet, et ont nommé pour leurs Plénipotentiaires, savoir:

Lesquels, après s'être communiqué leurs pleins pouvoirs respectifs, trouvés en bonne et due forme, sont convenus des Articles suivants:

Article I

Les Pays Contractants sont constitués à l'état d'Union pour la protection des droits d'auteur sur les œuvres littéraires et artistiques.

Article II

Les auteurs ressortissant à l'un des Pays Contractants jouiront, dans tout les autres pays de l'Union, pour leurs œuvres, soit manuscrites ou inédites, soit publiées dans un de ces pays, des avantages que les lois respectives accordent actuellement ou accorderont par la suite aux nationaux.

Toutefois, ces advantages ne leur seront réciproquement assurés que pendant l'existence de leurs droits dans leur pays d'origine.

Cette jouissance est subordonnée à l'accomplissement des formalités et des conditions prescrites par la législation du pays d'origine de l'œuvre ou, lorsqu'il s'agit d'une œuvre manuscrite ou inédite, par la législation du pays auquel appartient l'auteur.

Article III

Les stipulations de l'Article II s'appliquent également aux éditeurs d'œuvres littéraires ou artistiques publiées dans un des pays de l'Union, et dont l'auteur appartient à un pays qui n'en fait pas partie.

Article IV

L'expression 'œuvres littéraires ou artistiques' comprend les livres, brochures ou tous autres écrits; les œuvres dramatiques ou dramatico-musicales, les compositions musicales avec ou sans paroles; les œuvres de dessin, de peinture, de sculpture, de gravure; les lithographies, les illustrations, les cartes géographiques; les plans, croquis et ouvrages plastiques, relatifs à la géographie, à la topographie, à l'architecture, ou aux sciences en général; enfin, toute production quelconque, du domaine littéraire, scientifique, ou artistique, qui pourrait être publiée par n'importe quel mode d'impression ou de reproduction.

Article V

Les mandataires légaux ou ayants cause des auteurs ou, dans le cas prévu à l'Article III, des éditeurs, jouiront à tous égards des mêmes droits que ceux accordés par la présente Convention aux auteurs ou editeurs eux-mêmes.

Article VI

Les auteurs ressortissant à l'un des pays de l'Union jouiront dans tous les autres pays de l'Union du droit exclusif de traduction sur leurs ouvrages pendant dix années après la publication, dans l'un des pays de l'Union, de la traduction de leur ouvrage autorisée par eux.

Pour jouir du bénéfice de cette disposition, la dite traduction autorisée devra paraître en totalité dans le délai de trois années à compter de la publication de l'ouvrage original.

Pour les ouvrages publiés par livraisons, le terme de trois années stipulé au paragraphe précédent ne commencera à courir qu'à dater de la publication de la dernière livraison de l'ouvrage original.

Dans le cas où la traduction d'un ouvrage paraîtrait par livraisons, le terme de dix années stipulé au paragraphe 1er, ne commencera également à courir qu'à dater de la dernière livraison de la traduction.

Pour les œuvres composées de plusieurs volumes publiés par intervalles, ainsi que pour les bulletins ou cahiers publiés par des Sociétés littéraires ou savantes ou par des particuliers, chaque volume, bulletin, ou cahier sera, en ce qui concerne les termes de dix années et de trois années, considéré comme ouvrage séparé.

Il est entendu que le droit exclusif de traduction ne s'étend qu'à la langue ou aux langues dans laquelle ou lesquelles une traduction autorisée aura paru.

Article VII

Les traductions sont expressément assimilées aux ouvrages originaux. Elles jouiront à ce titre de la protection stipulée aux Articles II et III en ce qui concerne leur reproduction non autorisée dans les pays de l'Union.

Lorsqu'il s'agit d'une œuvre pour laquelle le droit de traduction est dans le domaine public, le traducteur ne peut pas s'opposer à ce que la même œuvre soit traduite par d'autres écrivains.

Article VIII

Sera réciproquement licite la publication, dans l'un des pays de l'Union, d'extraits, de fragments ou de morceaux entiers d'un ouvrage littéraire ou artistique ayant paru pour la première fois dans un autre pays de l'Union, pourvu que cette publication soit spécialement appropriée et adaptée à l'enseignement, ou qu'elle ait un caractère scientifique.

Sera également licite la publication réciproque de chrestomathies composées de fragments d'ouvrages de divers auteurs, ainsi que l'insertion, dans une chrestomathie ou dans un ouvrage original publié dans l'un des pays de l'Union, d'un écrit entier de peu d'étendue publié dans un autre pays de l'Union.

Il est entendu qu'il devra toujours être fait mention du nom de l'auteur ou de la source à laquelle seront empruntés les extraits, morceaux, fragments ou écrits dont il s'agit dans les deux paragraphes précédents.

Sera toutefois considérée comme reproduction illicite l'insertion de compositions musicales dans les recueils destinés à des écoles de musique.

Article IX

Les articles extraits de journaux ou de recueils périodiques publiés dans l'un des pays de l'Union pourront être reproduits, en original ou en traduction, dans les autres pays de l'Union.

Mais cette faculté ne s'étendra pas à la reproduction, en original ou en traduction, des romans-feuilletons ou des articles de science ou d'art. Il en sera de même pour les autres articles de quelque étendue, extraits de journaux ou de recueils périodiques, lorsque les auteurs ou éditeurs auront expressément déclaré, dans le journal ou le recueil même où ils les auront fait paraître, qu'ils en interdisent la reproduction.

En aucun cas l'interdiction stipulée au paragraphe précédent ne s'appliquera aux articles de discussion politique.

Article X

Le droit de protection des œuvres musicales entraîne l'interdiction des morcaux dits arrangements de musique, ainsi que d'autres morceaux qui, sans le consentement de l'auteur, sont composés sur des motifs extraits des dites œuvres, ou reproduisent l'œuvre originale avec des mofications, des réductions, ou des additions.

Il est entendu que les contestations qui s'élèveraient sur l'application de cette clause demeureront réservées à l'appréciation des Tribunaux respectifs, conformément à la législation de chacun des pays de l'Union.

Article XI

Les stipulations de l'Article II s'appliqueront à la représentation publique des œuvres dramatiques ou dramatico-musicales, que ces œuvres soient publiées ou non.

Les auteurs d'œuvres dramatiques on dramatico-musicales seront, pendant la durée de leur droit exclusif de traduction, réciproquement protégés contre la représentation publique non autorisée de la traduction de leurs ouvrages.

Les stipulations de l'Article II s'appliqueront également à l'exécution publique des œuvres musicales non publiées ou de celles publiées, mais dont l'auteur aura expressément déclaré sur le titre ou en tête de l'ouvrage qu'il en interdit l'exécution publique.

Article XII

Pour assurer à tous les ouvrages de littérature ou d'art la protection stipulée à l'Article II, et pour que les auteurs des dits ouvrages soient, jusqu'à preuve contraire, considérés comme tels et admis, en conséquence, devant les Tribunaux des divers pays de l'Union à exercer des poursuites contre les contrefaçons, il suffira que leur nom soit indiqué sur le titre de l'ouvrage, au bas de la dédicace ou de la préface, ou à la fin de l'ouvrage.

Pour les œuvres anonymes ou pseudonymes, l'éditeur dont le nom est indiqué sur l'ouvrage est fondé à sauvegarder les droits appartenant à l'auteur. Il est, sans autres preuves, réputé ayant droit de l'auteur anonyme ou pseudonyme.

Article XIII

Toute œuvre contrefaite pourra être saisie à l'importation dans ceux des pays de l'Union où l'œuvre originale a droit à la protection légale.

La saisie aura lieu à la requête soit du Ministère Public, soit de la partie intéressée, conformément à législation intérieure de chaque pays.

Article XIV

Il est entendu que les dispositions de la présente Convention ne pourront porter préjudice, en quoi que ce soit, au droit qui appartient au Gouvernement de chacun des pays de l'Union de permettre, de surveiller, d'interdire, par des mesures de législation ou de police intérieure, la circulation, la représentation, l'exposition de tout ouvrage ou production à l'égard desquels l'autorité compétente aurait à exercer ce droit.

Article XV

La présente Convention, sous les réserves et conditions à déterminer d'un commun accord, s'applique à toutes les œuvres qui, au moment de son entrée en vigueur, ne sont pas encore tombées dans le domaine public dans leur pays d'origine ou, lorsqu'il s'agit d'une œuvre manuscrite ou inédite, dans le pays auquel appartient l'auteur.

Article XVI

Il est entendu que les Gouvernements des pays de l'Union se réservent respectivement le droit de prendre séparément, entre eux, des arrangements particuliers, en tant que ces arrangements conféreraient aux auteurs ou à leurs ayants cause des droits plus étendus que ceux accordés par l'Union, ou qu'ils renfermeraient d'autres stipulations non contraires à la présente Convention.

Article XVII

Un office international sera organisé sous le nom de 'Bureau International de l'Union pour la Protection des Droits d'Auteur'.

Ce bureau, dont les frais seront supportés par les Administrations de tous les pays de l'Union, sera placé sous la haute autorité de . . ., et fonctionnera sous sa surveillance. Les attributions en seront déterminées d'un commun accord entre les pays de l'Union.

Article XVIII

La présente Convention pourra être soumise à révisions en vue d'y introduire les améliorations de nature à perfectionner le système de l'Union.

Les questions de cette nature, ainsi que celles qui intéressent à d'autres points de vue le développement de l'Union, seront traitées dans des Conférences qui auront lieu successivement dans les pays de l'Union entre les Délégués des dits pays.

Article XIX

Les pays qui n'ont point pris part à la présente Convention et qui assurent chez eux la protection légale contre la violation des droits d'auteur faisant l'object de cette Convention, seront admis à y accéder sur leur demande.

Cette accession sera notifiée par écrit au Gouvernement de . . ., et par celui-ci à tous les autres.

Elle emportera, de plein droit, adhésion à toutes les clauses et admission à tous les avantages stipulés dans la présente Convention.

Article XX

La présente Convention sera mise à exécution trois mois après l'échange des ratifications, et demeurera en vigueur pendant un temps indéterminé, jusqu' à l'expiration d'une année à partir du jour où la dénonciation en aura été faite.

Cette dénonciation sera adressée au Gouvernment chargé de recevoir les accessions. Elle ne produira son effet qu' à l'égard du pays qui l'aura faite, la Convention restant exécutoire pour les autres pays de l'Union.

Article XXI

La présente Convention sera ratifiée, et les ratifications en seront échangées à dans le délai d'un an au plus tard.

En foi du quoi, &c.

Fait à . . ., le. . . .

Projet d'Article Additionnel à la Convention concernant la Création d'une Union Générale pour la Protection des Droits d'Auteur

La Convention conclue à la date de ce jour n'affecte en rien le maintien des Conventions actuellement existantes entre les Pays Contractants, en tant que ces Conventions confèrent aux auteurs ou à leurs ayants cause des droits plus étendus que ceux accordés par l'Union, ou qu'elles renferment d'autres stipulations qui ne sont pas contraires à cette Convention.

Fait à . . ., le . . .

Projet de Protocole de Clôture

Au moment de procéder à la signature de la Convention conclue à la date de ce jour, les Plénipotentiaires soussignés ont déclaré et stipulé ce qui suit:

1 L'accord commun prévu à l'Article XV de la Convention est déterminé ainsi qu'il suit:

L'application de la Convention aux œuvres non tombées dans le domaine public, au moment de sa mise en vigueur, aura lieu suivant les stipulations y relatives contenues dans les Conventions spéciales existantes ou à conclure à cet effet.

A défaut de semblables stipulations entre pays de l'Union, les pays respectifs régleront, chacun pour ce qui le concerne, par la législation intérieure, les modalités relatives à l'application du principe contenu à l'Article XV.

2 Il est entendu que la fabrication et la vente des instruments servant à reproduire mécaniquement des airs de musique qui sont du domaine privé ne sera pas considérée comme constituant le fait de contrefaçon musicale.

3 L'attention des Plénipotentiaires a été attirée par plusieurs d'entre eux sur la question de savoir s'il n'y a pas lieu de défendre expressément certaines catégories d'appropriation indirecte non autorisée et notamment celle que plusieurs Conventions en vigueur désignent sous le nom 'd'adaptation'.

Les Plénipotentiaires ont été d'accord pour reconnaître que la contrefaçon comprend tous les genres d'atteinte illicite portée aux droits d'auteur, mais ils ont été d'avis qu'au lieu de les énumérer et de les définir, il est préférable de s'en remettre aux Tribunaux chargés d'apprécier, dans chaque cas spécial, le préjudice résultant d'une forme quelconque de contrefaçon.

4 La législation de plusieurs des pays de l'Union ne permettant pas de comprendre les œuvres photographiques au nombre des ouvrages auxquels s'applique la Convention conclue en date de ce jour, les Gouvernements des pays de l'Union se réservent de s'entendre ultérieurement sur les dispositions spéciales à prendre, d'un commun accord, à l'effet d'assurer réciproquement dans les pays de l'Union la protection des dites œuvres photographiques.

5 L'organisation du Bureau International prévu à l'Article XVII de la Convention sera fixée par un Règlement que le Gouvernement de . . . est chargé d'élaborer.

La langue officielle du Bureau International sera la langue Française.

Le Bureau International centralisera les renseignements de toute nature relatifs à la protection des droits d'auteur sur les œuvres littéraires et artistiques. Il les coordonnera et les publiera. Il procédera aux études d'utilité commune intéressant l'Union et rédigera, à l'aide des documents qui seront mis à sa disposition par les diverses Administrations, une feuille périodique, en langue Française, sur les questions concernant l'objet de l'Union. Les Gouvernements des pays de l'Union se réservent d'autoriser d'un commun accord le Bureau à publier une édition dans une ou plusieurs autres langues pour le cas où l'expérience en aurait démontré le besoin.

Le Bureau International devra se tenir en tout temps à la disposition des membres de l'Union pour leur fournir sur les questions relatives à la protection des œuvres littéraires et artistiques les renseignements spéciaux dont ils pourraient avoir besoin.

L'Administration de . . . préparera le budget du Bureau et en avec le concours du Bureau International, les travaux de cette Conférence.

Le Directeur du Bureau International assistera aux séances des Conférences et prendra part aux discussions sans voix délibérative. Il fera sur sa gestion un Rapport annuel qui sera communiqué à tous les membres de l'Union.

Les dépenses du Bureau International qui, jusqu'à nouvelle décision, ne pourront pas dépasser le somme de . . . par année, seront supportées en commun par les Pays Contractants, au prorata du chiffre de leur population respective.

L'Administration de . . . préparera le budget du Bureau et en surveillera les dépenses, fera les avances nécessaires et établira le compte annuel qui sera communiqué à toutes les autres Administrations.

6 La prochaine Conférence aura lieu à . . ., en . . .

7 Il est convenu que, pour l'échange des ratifications prévu à l'Article XXI, chaque Partie Contractante remettra un seul instrument, qui sera déposé, avec ceux des autres pays, aux archives du Gouvernement de . . . Chaque parties recevra en retour un exemplaire du procès-verbal d'échange des ratifications, signé par les Plénipotentiaires qui y auront pris part.

Le présent Protocole de Clôture, qui sera ratifié en même temps que la Convention conclue à la date de ce jour, sera considéré comme faisant partie intégrante de cette Convention, et aura même force, valeur, et durée.

En foi de quoi, &c.

Fait à . . ., le . . .

Principes recommandés pour une Unification ultérieure

La Conférence Internationale pour la protection des droits d'auteur,

Vu la diversité des dispositions en vigueur dans les différents pays relativement à plusieurs points importants de la législation sur la protection des droits d'auteurs,

Considérant que, si désirable que soit l'unification des principes qui régissent la matière, une Convention réglant ces points d'une manière uniforme ne rencontrerait peut-être pas en ce moment l'adhésion d'un certain nombre de pays,

Considérant toutefois qu'une codification internationale est dans la force des choses et s'imposera tôt ou tard, et qu'il y a lieu d'y préparer les voies en indiquant dès maintenant, sur quelques points essentials, le sens dans lequel il est désirable que cette codification se fasse,

Croit devoir soumettre aux Gouvernements de tous les pays les vœux suivants:

1 La protection accordée aux auteurs d'œuvres littéraires ou artistiques devrait durer leur vie entière et, après leur mort, un nombre d'années qui ne serait pas inférieur à trente.

2 Il y aurait lieu de favoriser autant que possible la tendance vers l'assimilation complète du droit de traduction au droit de reproduction en général.

Procès-verbal Final de la Conférence Internationale pour la Protection des Droits d'Auteur

Les Soussignés, Délégués à la Conférence Internationale pour la Protection des Droits d'Auteur, se sont convaincus, après l'examen approfondi auquel ils se sont livrés, qu'il serait dans l'intérêt général d'unifier autant que possible les principes régissant la matière dans les différents pays, et qu'il y aurait lieu à cet effet de constituer une Union semblable à celles qui existent pour d'autres objets de nature éminemment internationale. En conséquence, ils sont tombés d'accord pour soumettre à l'examen de leurs Gouvernements respectifs un projet de Convention stipulant le minimum de droits que, de l'avis de la Conférence, les Pays Contractants pourraient réciproquement garantir aux auteurs d'œuvres littéraires ou artistiques.

La Conférence a cru devoir également consigner dans une pièce annexe l'expression de ses vœux quant à deux points essentials qu'il ne lui a pas paru possible de régler d'une manière uniforme, pour le moment.

Les Délégués s'empresseront de remettre à leurs Gouvernements le résultat de leurs délibérations contenu dans les projets ci-annexés et prient le Conseil Fédéral Suisse de le transmettre également aux Gouvernments qui n'ont pas pris part à la Conférence, ainsi que de continuer d'ailleurs les démarches nécessaires en vue de la conclusion de l'entente dont il a pris l'initiative.

Fait à Berne, le 18 Septembre 1884, en un seul exemplaire, qui sera déposé aux archives de la Conféderation Suisse.

(Signé) REICHARDT.
MEYER.
DAMBACH.
EMIL STEINBACH.
JULES ZAÁDOR.
G. ERREMBAULT DE DUDZEELE.
Dr. R. THURMANN.
EMMANUEL ARAGO.
LOUIS ULBACH.
RENé LAVOLLËE.
F. O. ADAMS.
LOUIS JOSEPH JANVIER.
B. L. VERWEY.
A. LAGERHEIM.
F. BÆTZMANN.
L. RUCHONNET.
DROZ.
A. D'ORELLI

[Source: *Actes* 1884, 76–88.]

(e) Resolutions of the 1896 Diplomatic Conference at Paris (original French text)

Il est désirable:

I Que, dans tous les pays de l'Union, la loi protège les œuvres photographiques ou les œuvres obtenues par des procédés analogues, et que la durée de la protection soit de quinze ans au moins.

II Que les législations des pays de l'Union fixent les limites dans lesquelles la prochaine Conférence pourrait adopter le principe que les œuvres musicales publiées doivent être protégées contre l'exécution non autorisée, sans que l'auteur soit astreint à la mention de réserve.

III Que les Conventions spéciales conclues entre des pays faisant partie de l'Union soient examinées par les Parties Contractantes respectives en vue de déterminer les clauses pouvant être considérées comme restées en vigueur conformément à l'Article Additionnel de la Convention de Berne; que le résultat de cet examen soit consacré par un Acte authentique et porté à la connaissance des pays de l'Union par l'intermédiaire du Bureau International, avant la réunion de la prochaine Conférence.

IV Que des dispositions pénales soient insérées dans les législations nationales afin de réprimer l'usurpation des noms, signatures ou signes des auteurs en matière d'œuvres littéraires et artistiques.

V Que des déliberations de la prochaine Conférence sorte un texte unique de Convention.

[Source: *Actes* 1896, 229.]

(f) Resolutions of the 1928 Diplomatic Conference at Rome (original French text)

VŒU I
relatif à la sauvegarde du droit moral après la mort de l'auteur
(Proposition de la Délégation italienne)

La Conférence émet le vœu que les Pays de l'Union envisagent la possibilité d'introduire dans les législations respectives, qui ne contiendraient pas de dispositions à cet égard, des règles propres à empêcher qu'après la mort de l'auteur son œuvre ne soit déformée, mutilée ou autrement modifiée au préjudice de la renommée de l'auteur et des intérêts de la littérature, de la science et des arts.

VŒU II
relatif aux emprunts licites
(Proposition de la Délégation norvégienne)

La Conférence émet le vœu que chaque législation précise clairement les limites du droit d'emprunt.

VŒU III
relatif au «droit de suite»
(Proposition des Délégations belge, française et italienne)

La Conférence émet le vœu que ceux des Pays de l'Union, qui n'ont pas encore adopté de dispositions législatives consacrant au profit des artistes un droit inaliénable à une participation dans le produit des transmissions successives de leurs œuvres originales passant en vente publique, prennent en considération la possibilité de mettre à l'étude de telles dispositions.

VŒU IV
concernant un système de preuve de la date de création des œuvres littéraires, artistiques et scientifiques
(Proposition de la Délégation française)

La Conférence émet la vœu que les Pays de l'Union envisagent des mesures qui, sans imposer aux auteurs aucune formalité obligatoire, leur ouvrent la faculté d'établir soit la date de leurs créations littéraires, artistiques ou scientifiques, par exemple suivant le système de l'enveloppe double dite enveloppe Soleau, soit leur qualité de ressortissants de l'un des Pays de l'Union.

VŒU V
relatif à la protection des droits des artistes exécutants
(Proposition de la Délégation italienne)

La Conférence émet la vœu que les Gouvernements qui ont participé aux travaux de la Conférence envisagent la possibilité de mesures destinées à sauvegarder les droits des artistes exécutants.

VŒU VI
relatif à l'unification des Conventions d'Union de Berne et de Buenos-Ayres, revisée à la Havane
(Proposition des Délégations brésilienne et française)

La Conférence,

Considérant l'identité des principes généraux qui dominent et des buts vers lesquels tendent la Convention de Berne, revisée à Berlin puis à Rome, et la Convention signée par les États américains à Buenos-Ayres en 1910 puis revisée à La Havane en février 1928;

Constatant la concordance du plus grand nombre des dispositions de l'une et l'autre Convention;

Émet le vœu, conformément aux suggestions émises par la Délégation du Brésil et la Délégation française, que, d'une part, les Républiques américaines signataires d'une Convention à laquelle les États non américains n'ont pas la possibilité d'adhérer, viennent, à l'exemple du Brésil, accéder à la Convention de Berne revisée à Rome, et que, d'autre part, tous les Gouvernments intéressés se concertent en vue de préparer une entente générale ayant pour base les règles similaires des deux Conventions et pour objet l'unification mondiale des lois protégeant les créations de l'esprit.

[Source: *Actes* 1928, 349–50.]

(g) Resolution and 'vœux' of the 1948 Diplomatic Conference at Brussels (original French text)

RÉSOLUTION
Création d'un Comité près le Bureau de l'Union

En vue d'assurer un fonctionnement toujours plus satisfaisant de l'Union internationale pour la protection des œuvres littéraires et artistiques, la Conférence de Bruxelles a convenu les dispositions suivantes:

Afin d'assister le Bureau de l'Union dans la tâche qui lui est confiée par l'article 21, paragraphe 2, de la Convention signée à Bruxelles, en date de ce jour, il est créé un Comité composé de douze membres appartenant à douze Pays de l'Union choisis en tenant compte d'une représentation équitable des diverses parties du monde. Le Comité est renouvelable pour un tiers, de trois en trois ans, selon les modalités qu'il établira en s'inspirant du même principe. Les membres sortants ne sont pas immédiatement rééligibles. Les fonctions de membre du Comité sont honorifiques.

La Conférence de Bruxelles désigne les Pays suivants appelés à se faire représenter dans le Comité pour la première période: Brésil, Canada, France, Grande-Bretagne, Hongrie, Inde, Italie, Norvège, Pays-Bas, Portugal, Suisse, Tchécoslovaquie.

B VŒUX
I
Reconnaissance plus complète et plus générale des droits des travailleurs intellectuels

Le Conférence,

considérant que, si la reconnaissance plus complète et plus large des droits imprescriptibles du travail manuel est un progrès social de notre époque, il serait infiniment regrettable que les droits du travail de l'esprit, les droits des auteurs sur leurs œuvres, ne fussent pas également reconnus,

émet le vœu que l'opinion publique soit mieux informée au sujet des droits d'auteur; que s'emploinent à l'èclairer davantage: les autorités, les hommes influents, les puissances d'opinion, les auteurs eux-mêmes; et que ladite opinion publique soit également attentive, dans tous les pays, à la juste répartition des droits revenant aux auteurs.

II
Protection universelle du droit d'auteur

La Conférence émet la vœu de voir se réaliser sans retard une entente entre États, tendant à instituer la protection universelle du droit d'auteur.

III
Protection des œuvres littéraires ou artistiques en vue d'éviter la destruction de celles-ci

Constant que l'article 6 *bis* de la Convention, s'il permet à l'auteur de s'opposer à toute déformation, mutilation ou autre modification de son œuvre, ou à toute autre atteinte à la même œuvre qui serait préjudiciable à son honneur ou à sa réputation, n'interdit pas en termes exprès la destruction des œuvres, la Conférence émet le vœu que les Pays de l'Union introduisent, dans leur législation interne, des dispositions prohibant la destruction des œuvres littéraires et artistiques.

IV
Domaine public payant et caisses de prévoyance ou d'assistance institutées en faveur des auteurs

La Conférence,

reconnaissant l'intérèt que peut présenter, au point de vue de l'amélioration des conditions d'existence et des moyens de travail des auteurs contemporains d'œuvres littéraires ou artistiques, l'obtention et l'affectation éventuelle à des caisses de prévoyance ou d'assistance de ressources nouvelles provenant d'un droit modique sur l'exploitation lucrative des œuvres de cette nature comprises dans le domaine public,

rendant hommage aux initiatives publiques et privées déjà prises en ce sens dans divers pays, émet le vœu de voir mettre à l'étude dans tous les Pays dont les institutions se prêtent à l'adoption d'une telle mesure, la possibilité de réaliser le domaine public payant suivant les modalités convenant à chacun d'eux.

V
Double imposition des auteurs

La Conférence émet le vœu que, dans le plus bref délai, soient conclus, entre les Pays de l'Union, des accords aux termes desquels les auteurs d'œuvres littéraires ou artistiques ne pourront être assujettis à une double imposition en raison des revenus provenant de l'exercice du droit d'auteur dans un des Pays de l'Union.

VI
Protection des fabricants de phonogrammes

La Conférence émet le vœu que les Gouvernements des Pays de l'Union étudient les moyens d'assurer la protection des fabricants d'instruments servant à reproduire mécaniquement les œuvres musicales, sans qu'il soit porté atteinte aux droits des auteurs.

VII
Protection des radioémissions

La Conférence émet le vœu que les Gouvernements des Pays de l'Union étudient les moyens d'assurer la protection des émissions réalisées par les organes de radiodiffusion afin d'éviter toute utilisation non autorisée de celles-ci, sans qu'il soit porté atteinte aux droits des auteurs.

VIII
Droits voisins du droit d'auteur et notamment protection des artistes exécutants

Considérant que les interprétations des exécutants ont un caractère artistique, la Conférence émet le vœu que des études soient activement poursuivies en ce qui concerne les droits voisins du droit d'auteur et notamment la protection des artistes exécutants.

IX
Statut du Bureau international pour la protection des œuvres littéraires et artistiques (Bureau de Berne)

Considérant qu'il importe au bon fonctionnement du Bureau international pour la protection des œuvres littéraires et artistiques (Bureau de Berne) que cet Organisme et ses fonctionnaires soient, notamment en ce qui concerne les statut et les conditions d'emploi, traités selon des normes semblables à celles qui sont appliquées aux autres Unions internationales de caractère universel, dont le siège se trouve en Suisse, la Conférence émet le vœu que le Gouvernement suisse prenne, en tant qu'Autorité de surveillance, toutes mesures utiles à cette fin.

[Source: *Documents 1948* (1951), 425–9, reproduced with permission of WIPO.]

(h) Recommendations of the Stockholm Conference 1967

RECOMMENDATIONS ADOPTED IN THE FIELD OF COPYRIGHT

I Duration of Protection

The Countries members of the Berne Union for the Protection of Literary and Artistic Works,

In a Conference assembled at Stockholm from 12 June to 14 July 1967,

Considering that certain countries have expressed a desire for the general term of protection of literary and artistic works to be extended,

that certain countries already grant a term of protection in excess of fifty years after the death of the author,

that, moreover, several countries of the Union have extended the term of protection, for reasons resulting from the war,

that negotiations have already taken place at the international level with the object of providing for an extension of the term of protection by a special agreement,

that, in addition, bilateral agreements have already been concluded between certain countries for the reciprocal application of extensions of terms of protection, for reasons resulting from the war,

Express the wish that negotiations be pursued between the countries concerned for the conclusion of a multilateral agreement on the extension of the term of protection in countries parties to that agreement.

II Original Musical Scores

The Countries members of the Berne Union for the Protection of Literary and Artistic Works,

In a Conference assembled at Stockholm from 12 June to 14 July 1967,

Having before them proposals to insert in the Berne Convention provisions under which

(i) the publisher of a literary, dramatico-musical or musical work published in a country of the Union should be under an obligation to deposit with the national library of that country, or with some other similar establishment, a facsimile of the earliest and most authentic copy of such work in the form approved by its author;

(ii) it should be a matter for the legislation of the countries of the Union to provide that, where a dramatico-musical or musical work has been made available to the public with the consent of the author thereof, the graphic copies of the said work should also be made accessible to the public without restrictions contrary to fair practice;

Consider sympathetically the spirit and purpose of these proposals, subject always to the protection of the rights of authors of such works; and

Express the wish that the International Bureau undertake a study of the above questions, in order that consideration may be given to the possibility of including provisions relating to them in a future revision of the Convention.

III Developing Countries

The countries members of the Berne Union for the Protection of Literary and Artistic Works,

In a Conference assembled at Stockholm from 12 June to 14 July 1967,

Recognising the special economic and cultural needs of developing countries,

Desirous of enabling developing countries to have access to works protected by copyright for their educational requirements,

Having for this purpose adopted the Protocol Regarding Developing Countries,

Recommend the International Bureau to undertake in association with other governmental and non-governmental organisations a study of ways and means of creating financial machinery to ensure a fair and just return to authors.

[Source: *Records* 1967, 1502, reproduced with permission of WIPO.]

APPENDIX 3

Universal Copyright Convention, 1971 text

Universal Copyright Convention as revised at Paris on 24 July 1971, with Appendix Declaration relating to Article XVII and Resolution concerning Article XI

Paris, 24 July 1971

The Contracting States,

Moved by the desire to ensure in all countries copyright protection of literary, scientific and artistic works,

Convinced that a system of copyright protection appropriate to all nations of the world and expressed in a universal convention, additional to, and without impairing international systems already in force, will, ensure respect for the rights of the individual and encourage the development of literature, the sciences and the arts,

Persuaded that such a universal copyright system will facilitate a wider dissemination of works of the human mind and increase international understanding,

Have resolved to revise the Universal Copyright Convention as signed at Geneva on 6 September 1952 (hereinafter called 'the 1952 Convention'), and consequently,

Have agreed as follows:

Article I

Each Contracting State undertakes to provide for the adequate and effective protection of the rights of authors and other copyright proprietors in literary, scientific and artistic works, including writings, musical, dramatic and cinematographic works, and paintings, engravings and sculpture.

Article II

1. Published works of nationals of any Contracting State and works first published in that State shall enjoy in each other Contracting State the same protection as that other State accords to works of its nationals first published in its own territory, as well as the protection specially granted by this Convention.

2. Unpublished works of nationals of each Contracting State shall enjoy in each other Contracting State the same protection as that other State accords to unpublished works of its own nationals, as well as the protection specially granted by this Convention.

3. For the purpose of this Convention any Contracting State may, by domestic legislation, assimilate to its own nationals any person domiciled in that State.

Article III

1. Any Contracting 'State which, under its domestic law, requires as a condition of copyright, compliance with formalities such as deposit, registration, notice, notarial certificates, payment of fees or manufacture or publication in that Contracting State, shall regard these requirements as satisfied with respect to all works protected in accordance with this Convention and first published

outside its territory and the author of which is not one of its nationals, if from the time of the first publication all the copies of the work published with the authority of the author or other copyright proprietor bear the symbol © accompanied by the name of the copyright proprietor and the year of first publication placed in such manner and location as to give reasonable notice of claim of copyright.

2. The provisions of paragraph 1 shall not preclude any Contracting State from requiring formalities or other conditions for the acquisition and enjoyment of copyright in respect of works first published in its territory or works of its nationals wherever published.

3. The provisions of paragraph 1 shall not preclude any Contracting State from providing that a person seeking judicial relief must, in bringing the action, comply with procedural requirements, such as that the complainant must appear through domestic counsel or that the complainant must deposit with the court or an administrative office, or both, a copy of the work involved in the litigation; provided that failure to comply with such requirements shall not affect the validity of the copyright, nor shall any such requirement be imposed upon a national of another Contracting State if such requirement is not imposed on nationals of the State in which protection is claimed.

4. In each Contracting State there shall be legal means of protecting without formalities the unpublished works of nationals of other Contracting States.

5. If a Contracting State grants protection for more than one term of copyright and the first term is for a period longer than one of the minimum periods prescribed in Article IV, such State shall not be required to comply with the provisions of paragraph 1 of this Article in respect of the second or any subsequent term of copyright.

Article IV

1. The duration of protection of a work shall be governed, in accordance with the provisions of Article II and this Article, by the law of the Contracting State in which protection is claimed.

2. (a) The term of protection for works protected under this Convention shall not be less than the life of the author and twenty-five years after his death. However, any Contracting State which, on the effective date of this Convention in that State, has limited this term for certain classes of works to a period computed from the first publication of the work, shall be entitled to maintain these exceptions and to extend them to other classes of works. For all these classes the term of protection shall not be less than twenty-five years from the date of first publication.

(b) Any Contracting State which, upon the effective date of this Convention in that State, does not compute the term of protection upon the basis of the life of the author, shall be entitled to compute the term of protection from the date of the first publication of the work or from its registration prior to publication, as the case may be, provided the term of protection shall not be less than twenty-five years from the date of first publication or from its registration prior to publication, as the case may be.

(c) If the legislation of a Contracting State grants two or more successive terms of protection, the duration of the first term shall not be less than one of the minimum periods specified in sub-paragraphs (a) and (b).

3. The provisions of paragraph 2 shall not apply to photographic works or to works of applied art; provided, however, that the term of protection in those Contracting States which protect photographic works, or works of applied art in so far as they are protected as artistic works, shall not be less than ten years for each of said classes of works.

4. (a) No Contracting State shall be obliged to grant protection to a work for a period longer than that fixed for the class of works to which the work in question belongs, in the case of unpublished works by the law of the Contracting State of which the author is a national, and in the case of published works by the law of the Contracting State in which the work has been first published.

(b) For the purposes of the application of sub-paragraph (a), if the law of any Contracting

State grants two or more successive terms of protection, the period of protection of that State shall be considered to be the aggregate of those terms. However, if a specified work is not protected by such State during the second or any subsequent term for any reason, the other Contracting States shall not be obliged to protect it during the second or any subsequent term.

5. For the purposes of the application of paragraph 4, the work of a national of a Contracting State, first published in a non-Contracting State, shall be treated as though first published in the Contracting State of which the author is a national.

6. For the purposes of the application of paragraph 4, in case of simultaneous publication in two or more Contracting States, the work shall be treated as though first published in the State which affords the shortest term; any work published in two or more Contracting States within thirty days of its first publication shall be considered as having been published simultaneously in said Contracting States.

Article IVbis

1. The rights referred to in Article I shall include the basic rights ensuring the author's economic interests, including the exclusive-right to authorize reproduction by any means, public performance and broadcasting. The provisions of this Article shall extend to works protected under this Convention either in their original form or in any form recognizably derived from the original.

2. However, any Contracting State may, by its domestic legislation, make exceptions that do not conflict with the spirit and provisions of this Convention, to the rights mentioned in paragraph 1 of this Article. Any State whose legislation so provides, shall nevertheless accord a reasonable degree of effective protection to each of the rights to which exception has been made.

Article V

1. The rights referred to in Article I shall include the exclusive right of the author to make, publish and authorize the making and publication of translations of works protected under this Convention.

2. However, any Contracting State may, by its domestic legislation, restrict the right of translation of writings, but only subject to the following provisions:

(a) If, after the expiration of a period of seven years from the date of the first publication of a writing, a translation of such writing has not been published in a language in general use in the Contracting State, by the owner of the right of translation or with his authorization, any national of such Contracting State may obtain a non-exclusive licence from the competent authority thereof to translate the work into that language and publish the work so translated.

(b) Such national shall in accordance with the procedure of the State concerned, establish either that he has requested, and been denied, authorization by the proprietor of the right to make and publish the translation, or that, after due diligence on his part, he was unable to find the owner of the right. A licence may also be granted on the same conditions if all previous editions of a translation in a language in general use in the Contracting State are out of print.

(c) If the owner of the right of translation cannot be found, then the applicant for a licence shall send copies of his application to the publisher whose name appears on the work and, if the nationality of the owner of the right of translation is known, to the diplomatic or consular representative of the State of which such owner is a national, or to the organization which may have been designated by the government of that State. The licence shall not be granted before the expiration of a period of two months from the date of the dispatch of the copies of the application.

(d) Due provision shall be made by domestic legislation to ensure to the owner of the right of translation a compensation which is just and conforms to international standards, to ensure payment and transmittal of such compensation, and to ensure a correct translation of the work.

(e) The original title and the name of the author of the work shall be printed on all copies of the published translation. The licence shall be valid only for publication of the translation in the territory of the Contracting State where it has been applied for. Copies so published may be imported and sold in another Contracting State if a language in general use in such other State is the same language as that into which the work has been so translated, and if the domestic law in such other State makes provision for such licences and does not prohibit such importation and sale. Where the foregoing conditions do not exist, the importation and sale of such copies in a Contracting State shall be governed by its domestic law and its agreements. The licence shall not be transferred by the licensee.

(f) The licence shall not be granted when the author has withdrawn from. circulation all copies of the work.

Article Vbis

1. Any Contracting State regarded as a developing country in conformity with the established practice of the General Assembly of the United Nations may, by a notification deposited with the Director-General of the United Nations Educational, Scientific and Cultural Organization (hereinafter called 'the Director-General') at the time of this ratification, acceptance or accession or thereafter, avail itself of any or all of the exceptions provided for in Articles Vter and Vquater.

2. Any such notification shall be effective for ten years from the date of coming into force of this Convention, or for such part of that ten-year period as remains at the date of deposit of the notification, and may be renewed in whole or in part for further periods of ten years each if, not more than fifteen or less than three months before the expiration of the relevant ten-year period, the Contracting State deposits a further notification with the Director-General. Initial notifications may also be made during these further periods of ten years in accordance with the provisions of this Article.

3. Notwithstanding the provisions of paragraph 2, a Contracting State that has ceased to be regarded as a developing country as referred to in paragraph 1 shall no longer be entitled to renew its notification made under the provisions of paragraph 1 or 2, and whether or not it formally withdraws the notification such State shall be precluded from availing itself of the exceptions provided for in Articles Vter and Vquater at the end of the current ten-year period, or at the end of three years after it has ceased to be regarded as a developing country, whichever period expires later.

4. Any copies of a work already made under the exceptions provided for in Articles Vter and Vquater may continue to be distributed after the expiration of the period for which notifications under this Article were effective until their stock is exhausted.

5. Any Contracting State that has deposited a notification in accordance with Article XIII with respect to the application of this Convention to a particular country or territory, the situation of which can be regarded as analogous to that of the States referred to in paragraph 1 of this Article, may also deposit notifications and renew them in accordance with the provisions of this Article with respect to any such country or territory. During the effective period of such notifications, the provisions of Articles Vter and Vquater may be applied with respect to such country or territory. The sending of copies from the country or territory to the Contracting State shall be considered as export within the meaning of Articles Vter and Vquater.

Article Vter

1. (a) Any Contracting State to which Article Vbis (1) applies may substitute for the period of seven years provided for in Article V (2) a period of three years or any longer period prescribed by its legislation. However, in the case of a translation into a language not in general use in one or more developed countries that are party to this Convention or only the 1952 Convention, the period shall be one year instead of three.

(b) A Contracting State to which Article Vbis (1) applies may, with the unanimous agreement of the developed countries party to this

Convention or only the 1952 Convention and in which the same language is in general use, substitute, in the case of translation into that language, for the period of three years provided for in sub-paragraph (a) another period as determined by such agreement but not shorter than one year. However, this sub-paragraph shall not apply where the language in question is English, French or Spanish. Notification of any such agreement shall be made to the Director-General.

(c) The licence may only be granted if the applicant, in accordance with the procedure of the State concerned, establishes either that he has requested, and been denied, authorization by the owner of the right of translation, or that, after due diligence on his part, he was unable to find the owner of the right. At the same time as he makes his request he shall inform either the International Copyright Information Center established by the United Nations Educational, Scientific and Cultural Organization or any national or regional information centre which may have been designated in a notification to that effect deposited with the Director-General by the government of the State in which the publisher is believed to have his principal place of business.

(d) If the owner of the right of translation cannot be found, the applicant for a licence shall send, by registered airmail, copies of this application to the publisher whose name appears on the work and to any national or regional information center as mentioned in sub-paragraph (c). If no such center is notified he shall also send a copy to the international copyright information center established by the United Nations Educational, Scientific and Cultural Organization.

2. (a) Licences obtainable after three years shall not be granted under this Article until a further period of six months has elapsed and licences obtainable after one year until a further period of nine months has elapsed. The further period shall begin either from the date of the request for permission to translate mentioned in paragraph 1 (c) or, if the identity or address of the owner of the right of translation is not known, from the date of dispatch of the copies of the application for a licence mentioned in paragraph 1 (d).

(b) Licences shall not be granted if a translation has been published by the owner of the right of translation or with his authorization during the said period of six or nine months.

3. Any licence under this Article shall be granted only for the purpose of teaching, scholarship or research.

4. (a) Any licence granted under this Article shall not extend to the export of copies and shall be valid only for publication in the territory of the Contracting State where it has been applied for.

(b) Any copy published in accordance with a licence granted under this Article shall bear a notice in the appropriate language stating that the copy is available for distribution only in the Contracting State granting the licence. If the writing bears the notice specified in Article III (1) the copies shall bear the same notice.

(c) The prohibition of export provided for in sub-paragraph (a) shall not apply where a governmental or other public entity of a State which has granted a licence under this Article to translate a work into a language other than English, French or Spanish sends copies of a translation prepared under such licence to another country if:

- (i) the recipients are individuals who are nationals of the Contracting State granting the licence, or organizations grouping such individuals;
- (ii) the copies are to be used only for the purpose of teaching, scholarship or research;
- (iii) the sending of the copies and their subsequent distribution to recipients is without the object of commercial purpose; and
- (iv) the country to which the copies have been sent has agreed with the Contracting State to allow the receipt, distribution or both and the Director-General has been notified of such agreement by any one of the governments which have concluded it.

5. Due provision shall be made at the national level to ensure:

(a) that the licence provides for just compensation that is consistent with standards of royalties normally operating in the case of licences freely negotiated between persons in the two countries concerned; and

(b) payment and transmittal of the compensation; however, should national currency regulations intervene, the competent authority shall make all efforts, by the use of international machinery, to ensure transmittal in internationally convertible currency or its equivalent.

6. Any licence granted by a Contracting State under this Article shall terminate if a translation of the work in the same language with substantially the same content as the edition in respect of which the licence was granted is published in the said State by the owner of the right of translation or with his authorization, at a price reasonably related to that normally charged in the same State for comparable works. Any copies already made before the licence is terminated may continue to be distributed until their stock is exhausted.

7. For works which are composed mainly of illustrations a licence to translate the text and to reproduce the illustrations may be granted only if the conditions of Article Vquater are also fulfilled.

8. (a) A licence to translate a work protected under this Convention, published in printed or analogous forms of reproduction, may also be granted to a broadcasting organization having its headquarters in a Contracting State to which Article Vbis (1) applies, upon an application made in that State by the said organization under the following conditions:

(i) the translation is made from a copy made and acquired in accordance with the laws of the Contracting State;

(ii) the translation is for use only in broadcasts intended exclusively for teaching or for the dissemination of the results of specialized technical or scientific research to experts in a particular profession;

(iii) the translation is used exclusively for the purposes set out in condition (ii), through broadcasts lawfully made which are intended for recipients on the territory of the Contracting State, including broadcasts made through the medium of sound or visual recordings lawfully and exclusively made for the purpose of such broadcasts;

(iv) sound or visual recordings of the translation may be exchanged only between broadcasting organizations having their headquarters in the Contracting State granting the licence; and

(v) all uses made of the translation are without any commercial purpose.

(b) Provided all of the criteria and conditions set out in sub-paragraph (a) are met, a licence may also be granted to a broadcasting organization to translate any text incorporated in an audio-visual fixation which was itself prepared and published for the sole purpose of being used in connexion with systematic instructional activities.

(c) Subject to sub-paragraphs (a) and (b), the other provisions of this Article shall apply to the grant and exercise of the licence.

9. Subject to the provisions of this Article, any licence granted under this Article shall be governed by the provisions of Article V, and shall continue to be governed by the provisions of Article V and of this Article, even after the seven-year period provided for in Article V (2) has expired. However, after the said period has expired, the licensee shall be free to request that the said licence be replaced by a new licence governed exclusively by the provisions of Article V.

Article Vquater

1. Any Contracting State to which Article Vbis (1) applies may adopt the following provisions:

(a) If, after the expiration of (i) the relevant period specified in sub-paragraph (c) commencing from the date of first publication of a particular edition of a literary, scientific or artistic work referred to in paragraph 3, or (ii) any longer period determined by national legislation of the State; copies of such edition have not been distributed in that State to the general public or in connexion with systematic instructional activities at a price reasonably related to that normally charged in the State for comparable works, by the owner of the right of reproduction or with his authorization, any national of such State may obtain a non-exclusive licence from the competent authority to publish such edition at that or a lower price for use in connexion with systematic instructional activities. The licence may only be granted if such national, in accordance with the procedure of the State concerned, establishes either that he has requested, and been denied, authorization by the proprietor of the right to publish such work, or that, after due diligence on his part, he was unable to find the owner of the right. At the same time as he makes his request he shall inform either the international copyright information center established by the United Nations Educational, Scientific and Cultural Organization or any national or regional information center referred to in sub-paragraph (d).

(b) A licence may also be granted on the same conditions if, for a period of six months, no authorized copies of the edition in question have been on sale in the State concerned to the general public or in connexion with systematic instructional activities at a price reasonably related to that normally charged in the State for comparable works.

(c) The period referred to in sub-paragraph (a) shall be five years except that:

(i) for works of the natural and physical sciences, including mathematics, and of technology, the period shall be three years;
(ii) for works of fiction, poetry, drama and music, and for art books, the period shall be seven years.

(d) If the owner of the right of reproduction cannot be found, the applicant for a licence shall send, by registered air mail, copies of his application to the publisher whose name appears on the work and to any national or regional information centre identified as such in a notification deposited with the Director-General by the State in which the publisher is believed to have his principal place of business. In the absence of any such notification, he shall also send a copy to the international copyright information center established by the United Nations Educational, Scientific and Cultural Organization. The licence shall not be granted before the expiration of a period of three months from the date of dispatch of the copies of the application.

(e) Licences obtainable after three years shall not be granted under this Article:

(i) until a period of six months has elapsed from the date of the request for permission referred to in sub-paragraph (a) or, if the identity or address of the owner of the right of reproduction is unknown, from the date of the dispatch of the copies of the application for a licence referred to in sub-paragraph (d);
(ii) if any such distribution of copies of the edition as is mentioned in sub-paragraph (a) has taken place during that period.

(f) The name of the author and the title of the particular edition of the work shall be printed on all copies of the published reproduction. The licence shall not extend to the export of copies and shall be valid only for publication in the territory of the Contracting State where it has been applied for. The licence shall not be transferable by the licensee.

(g) Due provision shall be made by domestic legislation to ensure an accurate reproduction of the particular edition in question.

(h) A licence to reproduce and publish a translation of a work shall not be granted under this Article in the following cases:

(i) where the translation was not published by the owner of the right of translation or with his authorization;
(ii) where the translation is not in a language in general use in the State with power to grant the licence.

2. The exceptions provided for in paragraph 1 are subject to the following additional provisions:

(a) Any copy published in accordance with a licence granted under this Article shall bear a notice in the appropriate language stating that the copy is available for distribution only in the Contracting State to which the said licence applies. If the edition bears the notice specified in Article III (1), the copies shall bear the same notice.

(b) Due provision shall be made at the national level to ensure:

(i) that the licence provides for just compensation that is consistent with standards of royalties normally operating in the case of licences freely negotiated between persons in the two countries concerned; and

(ii) payment and transmittal of the compensation; however, should national currency regulations intervene, the competent authority shall make all efforts, by the use of international machinery, to ensure transmittal in internationally convertible currency or its equivalent.

(c) Whenever copies of an edition of a work are distributed in the Contracting State to the general public or in connexion with systematic instructional activities, by the owner of the right of reproduction or with his authorization, at a price reasonably related to that normally charged in the, State for comparable works, any licence granted under this Article shall terminate if such edition is in the same language and is substantially the same in content as the edition published under the licence. Any copies already made before the licence is terminated may continue to be distributed until their stock is exhausted.

(d) No licence shall be granted when the author has withdrawn from circulation all copies of the edition in question.

3. (a) Subject to sub-paragraph (b), the literary, scientific or artistic works to which this Article applies shall be limited to works published in printed or analogous forms of reproduction.

(b) The provisions of this Article shall also apply to reproduction in audio-visual form of lawfully made audio-visual fixations including any protected works incorporated therein and to the translation of any incorporated text into a language in general use in the State with power to grant the licence; always provided that the audio-visual fixations in question were prepared and published for the sole purpose of being used in connexion with systematic instructional activities.

Article VI

'Publication', as used in this Convention, means the reproduction in tangible form and the general distribution to the public of copies of a work from which it can be read or otherwise visually perceived.

Article VII

This Convention shall not apply to works or rights in works which, at the effective date of this Convention in a Contracting State where protection is claimed, are permanently in the public domain in the said Contracting State.

Article VIII

1. This Convention, which shall bear the date of 24 July 1971, shall be deposited with the Director-General and shall remain open for signature by all States party to the 1952 Convention for a period of 120 days after the date of this Convention. It shall be subject to ratification or acceptance by the signatory States.

2. Any State which has not signed this Convention may accede thereto.

3. Ratification, acceptance or accession shall be effected by the deposit of an instrument to that effect with the Director-General.

Article IX

1. This Convention shall come into force three months after the deposit of twelve instruments of ratification, acceptance or accession.

2. Subsequently, this Convention shall come into force in respect of each State three months after that State has deposited its instrument of ratification, acceptance or accession.

3. Accession to this Convention by a State not party to the 1952 Convention shall also constitute accession to that Convention; however, if its instrument of accession is deposited before this Convention comes into force, such State may make its accession to the 1952 Convention conditional upon the coming into force of this Convention. After the coming into force of this Convention, no State may accede solely to the 1952 Convention.

4. Relations between States party to this Convention and States that are party only to the 1952 Convention, shall be governed by the 1952 Convention. However, any State party only to the 1952 Convention may, by a notification deposited with the Director-General, declare that it will admit the application of the 1971 Convention to works of its nationals or works first published in its territory by all States party to this Convention.

Article X

1. Each Contracting State undertakes to adopt, in accordance with its Constitution, such measures as are necessary to ensure the application of this Convention.

2. It is understood that at the date this Convention comes into force in respect of any State, that State must be in a position under its domestic law to give effect to the terms of this Convention.

Article XI

1. An Intergovernmental Committee is hereby established with the following duties:

(a) to study the problems concerning the application and operation of the Universal Copyright Convention;

(b) to make preparation for periodic revisions of this Convention;

(c) to study any other problems concerning the international protection of copyright, in co-operation with the various interested international organizations, such as the United Nations Educational, Scientific and Cultural Organization, the International Union for the Protection of Literary and Artistic Works and the Organization of American States;

(d) to inform States party to the Universal Copyright Convention as to its activities.

2. The Committee shall consist of the representatives of eighteen States party to this Convention or only to the 1952 Convention.

3. The Committee shall be selected with due consideration to a fair balance of national interests on the basis of geographical location, population, languages and stage of development.

4. The Director-General of the United Nations Educational, Scientific and Cultural Organization, the Director-General of the World Intellectual Property Organization and the Secretary-General of the Organization of American States, or their representatives, may attend meetings of the Committee in an advisory capacity.

Article XII

The Intergovernmental Committee shall convene a conference for revision whenever it deems necessary, or at the request of at least ten States party to this Convention.

Article XIII

1. Any Contracting State may, at the time of deposit of its instrument of ratification, acceptance or accession, or at any time thereafter, declare by notification addressed to the Director-General that this Convention shall apply to all or any of the countries or territories for the international relations of which it is responsible and this Convention shall thereupon apply to the countries or territories named in such notification after the expiration of the term of three months provided for in Article IX. In the absence of such notification, this Convention shall not apply to any such country or territory.

2. However, nothing in this Article shall be understood as implying the recognition or tacit acceptance by a Contracting State of the factual situation concerning a country or territory to which this Convention is made applicable by another Contracting State in accordance with the provisions of this Article.

Article XIV

1. Any Contracting State may denounce this Convention in its own name or on behalf of all or any of the countries or territories with respect to which a notification has been given under Article XIII. The denunciation shall be made by notification addressed to the Director-General. Such denunciation shall also

constitute denunciation of the 1952 Convention.

2. Such denunciation shall operate only in respect of the State or of the country or territory on whose behalf it was made and shall not take effect until twelve months after the date of receipt of the notification.

Article XV

A dispute between two or more Contracting States concerning the interpretation or application of this Convention, not settled by negotiation, shall, unless the States concerned agree on some other method of settlement, be brought before the International Court of Justice for determination by it.

Article XVI

1. This Convention shall be established in English, French and Spanish. The three texts shall be signed and shall be equally authoritative.

2. Official texts of this Convention shall be established by the Director-General, after consultation with the governments concerned, in Arabic, German, Italian and Portuguese.

3. Any Contracting State or group of Contracting States shall be entitled to have established by the Director-General other texts in the language of its choice by arrangement with the Director-General.

4. All such texts shall be annexed to the signed texts of this Convention.

Article XVII

1. This Convention shall not in any way affect the provisions of the Berne Convention for the Protection of Literary and Artistic Works or membership in the Union created by that Convention.

2. In application of the foregoing paragraph, a declaration has been annexed to the present Article. This declaration is an integral part of this Convention for the States bound. by the Berne Convention on 1 January 1951, or which have or may become bound to it at a later date. The signature of this Convention by such States shall also constitute signature of the said declaration, and ratification, acceptance or accession by such States shall include the declaration, as well as this Convention.

Article XVIII

This Convention shall not abrogate multilateral or bilateral copyright conventions or arrangements that are or may be in effect exclusively between two or more American Republics. In the event of any difference either between the provisions of such existing conventions or arrangements and the provisions of this Convention, or between the provisions of this Convention and those of any new convention or arrangement which may be formulated between two or more American Republics after this Convention comes into force, the convention or arrangement most recently formulated shall prevail between the parties thereto. Rights in works acquired in any Contracting State under existing conventions or arrangements before the date this Convention comes into force in such ' State shall not be affected.

Article XIX

This Convention shall not abrogate multilateral or bilateral conventions or arrangements in effect between two or more Contracting States. In the event of any difference between the provisions of such existing conventions or arrangements and the provisions of this Convention, the provisions of this Convention shall prevail. Rights in works acquired in any Contracting State under existing conventions or arrangements before the date on which this Convention comes into force in such State shall not be affected. Nothing in this Article shall affect the provisions of Articles XVII and XVIII.

Article XX

Reservations to this Convention shall not be permitted.

Article XXI

1. The Director-General shall send duly certified copies of this Convention to the States

interested and to the Secretary-General of the United Nations for registration by him.

2. He shall also inform all interested States of the ratifications, acceptances and accessions which have been deposited, the date on which this Convention comes into force, the notifications under this Convention and denunciations under Article XIV.

Appendix declaration relating to Article XVII.

The States which are members of the International Union for the Protection of Literary and Artistic Works (hereinafter called 'the Berne Union') and which are signatories to this Convention,

Desiring to reinforce their mutual relations on the basis of the said Union and to avoid any conflict which might result from the co-existence of the Berne Convention and the Universal Copyright Convention,

Recognizing the temporary need of some States to adjust their level of copyright protection in accordance with their stage of cultural, social and economic development,

Have, by common agreement, accepted the terms of the following declaration:

(a) Except as provided by paragraph (b), works which, according to the Berne Convention, have as their country of origin a country which has withdrawn from the Berne Union after 1 January 1951, shall not be protected by the Universal Copyright Convention in the countries of the Berne Union;

(b) Where a Contracting State is regarded as a developing country in conformity with the established practice of the General Assembly of the United Nations, and has deposited with the Director-General of the United Nations Educational, Scientific and Cultural Organization, at the time of its withdrawal from the Berne Union, a notification to the effect that it regards itself as a developing country, the provisions of paragraph (a) shall not be applicable as long as such State may avail itself of the exceptions provided for by this Convention in accordance with Article Vbis;

(c) The Universal Copyright Convention shall not be applicable to the relationships among countries of the Berne Union in so far as it relates to the protection of works having as their country of origin, within the meaning of the Berne Convention, a country of the Berne Union.

Resolution concerning Article XI

The Conference for Revision of the Universal Copyright Convention,

Having considered the problems relating to the Intergovernmental Committee provided for in Article XI of this Convention, to which this resolution is annexed,

Resolves that:

1. At its inception, the Committee shall include representatives of the twelve States members of the Intergovernmental Committee established under Article XI of the 1952 Convention and the resolution annexed to it, and, in addition, representatives of the following States: Algeria, Australia, Japan, Mexico, Senegal and Yugoslavia.

2. Any States that are not party to the 1952 Convention and have not acceded to this Convention before the first ordinary session of the Committee following the entry into force of this Convention shall be replaced by other States to be selected by the Committee at its first ordinary session in conformity with the provisions of Article XI (2) and (3).

3. As soon as this Convention comes into force the Committee as provided for in paragraph 1 shall be deemed to be constituted in accordance with Article XI of this Convention.

4. A session of the Committee shall take place within one year after the coming into force of this Convention; thereafter the Committee shall meet in ordinary session at intervals of not more than two years.

5. The Committee shall elect its Chairman and two Vice-Chairmen. It shall establish its Rules of Procedure having regard to the following principles:

(a) The normal duration of the term of office of the members represented on the Committee shall be six years with one-third retiring every two years, it being however understood that, of the original terms of office, one-third shall expire at the end of the Committee's second ordinary session which will follow the entry into force of this Convention, a further third at the end of its third ordinary session, and the remaining third at the end of its fourth ordinary session.

(b) The rules governing the procedure whereby the Committee shall fill vacancies, the order in which terms of membership expire, eligibility for re-election, and election procedures, shall be based upon a balancing of the needs for continuity of membership and rotation of representation, as well as the considerations set out in Article XI (3).

Expresses the wish that the United Nations Educational, Scientific and Cultural Organization provide its Secretariat.

IN FAITH WHEREOF the undersigned, having deposited their respective full powers, have signed this Convention.

Done at Paris, this twenty-fourth day of July 1971, in a single copy.

APPENDIX 4

Rome Convention for the Protection of Performers, Producers of Phonograms and Broadcasting Organizations 1961

Done at Rome on October 26, 1961

The Contracting States, moved by the desire to protect the rights of performers, producers of phonograms, and broadcasting organizations,

Have agreed as follows:

Article 1

[Safeguard of Copyright Proper]

Protection granted under this Convention shall leave intact and shall in no way affect the protection of copyright in literary and artistic works. Consequently, no provision of this Convention may be interpreted as prejudicing such protection.

Article 2

[Protection given by the Convention. Definition of National Treatment]

1. For the purposes of this Convention, national treatment shall mean the treatment accorded by the domestic law of the Contracting State in which protection is claimed:

(a) to performers who are its nationals, as regards performances taking place, broadcast, or first fixed, on its territory;

(b) to producers of phonograms who are its nationals, as regards phonograms first fixed or first published on its territory;

(c) to broadcasting organizations which have their headquarters on its territory, as regards broadcasts transmitted from transmitters situated on its territory.

2. National treatment shall be subject to the protection specifically guaranteed, and the limitations specifically provided for, in this Convention.

Article 3

[Definitions: (a) Performers; (b) Phonogram; (c) Producers of Phonograms; (d) Publication; (e) Reproduction; (f) Broadcasting; (g) Rebroadcasting]

For the purposes of this Convention:

(a) 'performers' means actors, singers, musicians, dancers, and other persons who act, sing, deliver, declaim, play in, or otherwise perform literary or artistic works;

(b) 'phonogram' means any exclusively aural fixation of sounds of a performance or of other sounds;

(c) 'producer of phonograms' means the person who, or the legal entity which, first fixes the sounds of a performance or other sounds;

(d) 'publication' means the offering of copies of a phonogram to the public in reasonable quantity;

(e) 'reproduction' means the making of a copy or copies of a fixation;

(f) 'broadcasting' means the transmission by wireless means for public reception of sounds or of images and sounds;

(g) 'rebroadcasting' means the simultaneous broadcasting by one broadcasting organization of the broadcast of another broadcasting organization.

Article 4
[Performances Protected. Points of Attachment for Performers]

Each Contracting State shall grant national treatment to performers if any of the following conditions is met:

(a) the performance takes place in another Contracting State;

(b) the performance is incorporated in a phonogram which is protected under *Article 5* of this Convention;

(c) the performance, not being fixed on a phonogram, is carried by a broadcast which is protected by *Article 6* of this Convention.

Article 5
[Protected Phonograms: 1. Points of Attachment for Producers of Phonograms; 2. Simultaneous Publication; 3. Power to exclude certain Criteria]

1. Each Contracting State shall grant national treatment to producers of phonograms if any of the following conditions is met:

(a) the producer of the phonogram is a national of another Contracting State (criterion of nationality);

(b) the first fixation of the sound was made in another Contracting State (criterion of fixation);

(c) the phonogram was first published in another Contracting State (criterion of publication).

2. If a phonogram was first published in a non-contracting State but if it was also published, within thirty days of its first publication, in a Contracting State (simultaneous publication), it shall be considered as first published in the Contracting State.

3. By means of a notification deposited with the Secretary-General of the United Nations, any Contracting State may declare that it will not apply the criterion of publication or, alternatively, the criterion of fixation. Such notification may be deposited at the time of ratification, acceptance or accession, or at any time thereafter; in the last case, it shall become effective six months after it has been deposited.

Article 6
[Protected Broadcasts: 1. Points of Attachment for Broadcasting Organizations; 2. Power to Reserve]

1. Each Contracting State shall grant national treatment to broadcasting organizations if either of the following conditions is met:

(a) the headquarters of the broadcasting organization is situated in another Contracting State;

(b) the broadcast was transmitted from a transmitter situated in another Contracting State.

2. By means of a notification deposited with the Secretary-General of the United Nations, any Contracting State may declare that it will protect broadcasts only if the headquarters of the broadcasting organization is situated in another Contracting State and the broadcast was transmitted from a transmitter situated in the same Contracting State. Such notification may be deposited at the time of ratification, acceptance or accession, or at any time thereafter; in the last case, it shall become effective six months after it has been deposited.

Article 7
[Minimum Protection for Performers: 1. Particular Rights; 2. Relations between Performers and Broadcasting Organizations]

1. The protection provided for performers by this Convention shall include the possibility of preventing:

(a) the broadcasting and the communication to the public, without their consent, of their performance, except where the performance used in the broadcasting or the public communication is itself already a broadcast performance or is made from a fixation;

(b) the fixation, without their consent, of their unfixed performance;

(c) the reproduction, without their consent, of a fixation of their performance:

(i) if the original fixation itself was made without their consent;
(ii) if the reproduction is made for purposes different from those for which the performers gave their consent;
(iii) if the original fixation was made in accordance with the provisions of *Article 15*, and the reproduction is made for purposes different from those referred to in those provisions.

2. (1) If broadcasting was consented to by the performers, it shall be a matter for the domestic law of the Contracting State where protection is claimed to regulate the protection against rebroadcasting, fixation for broadcasting purposes and the reproduction of such fixation for broadcasting purposes.

(2) The terms and conditions governing the use by broadcasting organizations of fixations made for broadcasting purposes shall be determined in accordance with the domestic law of the Contracting State where protection is claimed.

(3) However, the domestic law referred to in *sub-paragraphs (1)* and *(2)* of this paragraph shall not operate to deprive performers of the ability to control, by contract, their relations with broadcasting organisations.

Article 8
[Performers acting jointly]

Any Contracting State may, by its domestic laws and regulations, specify the manner in which performers will be represented in connection with the exercise of their rights if several of them participate in the same performance.

Article 9
[Variety and Circus Artists]

Any Contracting State may, by its domestic laws and regulations, extend the protection provided for in this Convention to artists who do not perform literary or artistic works.

Article 10
[Right of Reproduction for Phonogram Producers]

Producers of phonograms shall enjoy the right to authorize or prohibit the direct or indirect reproduction of their phonograms.

Article 11
[Formalities for Phonograms]

If, as a condition of protecting the rights of producers of phonograms, or of performers, or both, in relation to phonograms, a Contracting State, under its domestic law, requires compliance with formalities, these shall be considered as fulfilled if all the copies in commerce of the published phonogram or their containers bear a notice consisting of the symbol (P), accompanied by the year date of the first publication, placed in such a manner as to give reasonable notice of claim of protection; and if the copies or their containers do not identify the producer or the licensee of the producer (by carrying his name, trade mark or other appropriate designation), the notice shall also include the name of the owner of the rights of the producer; and, furthermore, if the copies or their containers do not identify the principal performers, the notice shall also include the name of the person who, in the country in which the fixation was effected, owns the rights of such performers.

Article 12
[Secondary Uses of Phonograms]

If a phonogram published for commercial purposes, or a reproduction of such phonogram, is used directly for broadcasting or for any communication to the public, a single equitable remuneration shall be paid by the user to the performers, or to the producers of the phonograms, or to both. Domestic law may, in the absence of agreement between these parties, lay down the conditions as to the sharing of this remuneration.

Article 13
[Minimum Rights for Broadcasting Organizations]

Broadcasting organizations shall enjoy the right to authorize or prohibit:

(a) the rebroadcasting of their broadcasts;

(b) the fixation of their broadcasts;

(c) the reproduction:

(i) of fixations, made without their consent, of their broadcasts;
(ii) of fixations, made in accordance with the provisions of *Article 15*, of their broadcasts, if the reproduction is made for purposes different from those referred to in those provisions;

(d) the communication to the public of their television broadcasts if such communication is made in places accessible to the public against payment of an entrance fee; it shall be a matter for the domestic law of the State where protection of this right is claimed to determine the conditions under which it may be exercised.

Article 14
[Minimum Duration of Protection]

The term of protection to be granted under this Convention shall last at least until the end of a period of twenty years computed from the end of the year in which:

(a) the fixation was made—for phonograms and for performances incorporated therein;

(b) the performance took place—for performances not incorporated in phonograms;

(c) the broadcast took place—for broadcasts.

Article 15
[Permitted Exceptions: 1. Specific Limitations; 2. Equivalents with copyright]

1. Any Contracting State may, in its domestic laws and regulations, provide for exceptions to the protection guaranteed by this Convention as regards:

(a) private use;

(b) use of short excerpts in connection with the reporting of current events;

(c) ephemeral fixation by a broadcasting organisation by means of its own facilities and for its own broadcasts;

(d) use solely for the purposes of teaching or scientific research.

2. Irrespective of *paragraph 1* of this Article, any Contracting State may, in its domestic laws and regulations, provide for the same kinds of limitations with regard to the protection of performers, producers of phonograms and broadcasting organizations, as it provides for, in its domestic laws and regulations, in connection with the protection of copyright in literary and artistic works. However, compulsory licences may be provided for only to the extent to which they are compatible with this Convention.

Article 16
[Reservations]

1. Any State, upon becoming party to this Convention, shall be bound by all the obligations and shall enjoy all the benefits thereof. However, a State may at any time, in a notification deposited with the Secretary-General of the United Nations, declare that:

(a) as regards *Article 12*:

(i) it will not apply the provisions of that Article;
(ii) it will not apply the provisions of that Article in respect of certain uses;
(iii) as regards phonograms the producer of which is not a national of another Contracting State, it will not apply that Article;
(iv) as regards phonograms the producer of which is a national of another Contracting State, it will limit the protection provided for by that Article to the extent to which, and to the term for which, the latter State grants protection to phonograms first fixed by a national of the State making the declaration; however, the fact that the Contracting State of which the producer is a national does not grant the protection to the same beneficiary or beneficiaries as the State making the declaration shall not be considered as a difference in the extent of the protection;

(b) as regards *Article 13*, it will not apply *item (d) of that Article*; if a Contracting State makes such a declaration, the other Contracting States shall not be obliged to grant the right referred to in *Article 13, item (d)*, to broadcasting organizations whose headquarters are in that State.

2. If the notification referred to in *paragraph 1* of this Article is made after the date of the deposit of the instrument of ratification, acceptance or accession, the declaration will become effective six months after it has been deposited.

Article 17
[Certain countries applying only the 'fixation' criterion]

Any State which, on October 26, 1961, grants protection to producers of phonograms solely on the basis of the criterion of fixation may, by a notification deposited with the Secretary-General of the United Nations at the time of ratification, acceptance or accession, declare that it will apply, for the purposes of *Article 5*, the criterion of fixation alone and, for the purposes of *paragraph 1(a)(iii)* and *(iv) of Article 16*, the criterion of fixation instead of the criterion of nationality.

Article 18
[Withdrawal of reservations]

Any State which has deposited a notification under *paragraph 3 of Article 5, paragraph 2 of Article 6, paragraph 1 of Article 16* or *Article 17*, may, by a further notification deposited with the Secretary-General of the United Nations, reduce its scope or withdraw it.

Article 19
[Performers' Rights in Films]

Notwithstanding anything in this Convention, once a performer has consented to the incorporation of his performance in a visual or audio-visual fixation, *Article 7* shall have no further application.

Article 20
[Non-retroactivity]

1. This Convention shall not prejudice rights acquired in any Contracting State before the date of coming into force of this Convention for that State.

2. No Contracting State shall be bound to apply the provisions of this Convention to performances or broadcasts which took place, or to phonograms which were fixed, before the date of coming into force of this Convention for that State.

Article 21
[Protection by other means]

The protection provided for in this Convention shall not prejudice any protection otherwise secured to performers, producers of phonograms and broadcasting organizations.

Article 22
[Special agreements]

Contracting States reserve the right to enter into special agreements among themselves in so far as such agreements grant to performers, producers of phonograms or broadcasting organizations more extensive rights than those granted by this Convention or contain other provisions not contrary to this Convention.

Article 23
[Signature and deposit]

This Convention shall be deposited with the Secretary-General of the United Nations. It shall be open until June 30, 1962, for signature by any State invited to the Diplomatic Conference on the International Protection of Performers, Producers of Phonograms and Broadcasting Organizations which is a party to the Universal Copyright Convention or a member of the International Union for the Protection of Literary and Artistic Works.

Article 24
[Becoming Party to the Convention]

1. This Convention shall be subject to ratification or acceptance by the signatory States.

2. This Convention shall be open for accession by any State invited to the Conference referred to in *Article 23*, and by any State Member of the United Nations, provided that in either case such State is a party to the Universal Copyright Convention or a member of the International Union for the Protection of Literary and Artistic Works.

3. Ratification, acceptance or accession shall be effected by the deposit of an instrument to that effect with the Secretary-General of the United Nations.

Article 25
[Entry into force]

1. This Convention shall come into force three months after the date of deposit of the sixth instrument of ratification, acceptance or accession.

2. Subsequently, this Convention shall come into force in respect of each State three months after the date of deposit of its instrument of ratification, acceptance or accession.

Article 26
[Implementation of the Convention by the Provision of Domestic Law]

1. Each Contracting State undertakes to adopt, in accordance with its Constitution, the measures necessary to ensure the application of this Convention.

2. At the time of deposit of its instrument of ratification, acceptance or accession, each State must be in a position under its domestic law to give effect to the terms of this Convention.

Article 27
[Applicability of the Convention to Certain Territories]

1. Any State may, at the time of ratification, acceptance or accession, or at any time thereafter, declare by notification addressed to the Secretary-General of the United Nations that this Convention shall extend to all or any of the territories for whose international relations it is responsible, provided that the Universal Copyright Convention or the International Convention for the Protection of Literary and Artistic Works applies to the territory or territories concerned. This notification shall take effect three months after the date of its receipt.

2. The notifications referred to in *paragraph 3 of Article 5, paragraph 2 of Article 6, paragraph 1 of Article 16* and *Articles 17* and *18*, may be extended to cover all or any of the territories referred to in *paragraph 1* of this Article.

Article 28
[Denunciation of the Convention]

1. Any Contracting State may denounce this Convention, on its own behalf or on behalf of all or any of the territories referred to in *Article 27*.

2. The denunciation shall be effected by a notification addressed to the Secretary-General of the United Nations and shall take effect twelve months after the date of receipt of the notification.

3. The right of denunciation shall not be exercised by a Contracting State before the expiry of a period of five years from the date on which the Convention came into force with respect to that State.

4. A Contracting State shall cease to be a party to this Convention from that time when it is neither a party to the Universal Copyright Convention nor a member of the International Union for the Protection of Literary and Artistic Works.

5. This Convention shall cease to apply to any territory referred to in *Article 27* from that time when neither the Universal Copyright Convention nor the International Convention for the Protection of Literary and Artistic Works applies to that territory.

Article 29
[Revision of the Convention]

1. After this Convention has been in force for five years, any Contracting State may, by notification addressed to the Secretary-General of the United Nations, request that a conference be convened for the purpose of revising the Convention. The Secretary-General shall notify all Contracting States of this request. If, within a period of six months following the date of notification by the Secretary-General of the United Nations, not less than one half of the Contracting States notify him of their concurrence with the request, the Secretary-General shall inform the Director-General of the International Labor Office, the Director-

General of the United Nations Educational, Scientific and Cultural Organization and the Director of the Bureau of the International Union for the Protection of Literary and Artistic Works, who shall convene a revision conference in co-operation with the Intergovernmental Committee provided for in *Article 32*.

2. The adoption of any revision of this Convention shall require an affirmative vote by two-thirds of the States attending the revision conference, provided that this majority includes two-thirds of the States which, at the time of the revision conference, are parties to the Convention.

3. In the event of adoption of a Convention revising this Convention in whole or in part, and unless the revising Convention provides otherwise:

(a) this Convention shall cease to be open to ratification, acceptance or accession as from the date of entry into force of the revising Convention;

(b) this Convention shall remain in force as regards relations between or with Contracting States which have not become parties to the revising Convention.

Article 30
[Settlement of disputes]

Any dispute which may arise between two or more Contracting States concerning the interpretation or application of this Convention and which is not settled by negotiation shall, at the request of any one of the parties to the dispute, be referred to the International Court of Justice for decision, unless they agree to another mode of settlement.

Article 31
[Limits on Reservations]

Without prejudice to the provisions of *paragraph 3 of Article 5, paragraph 2 of Article 6, paragraph 1 of Article 16* and *Article 17*, no reservation may be made to this Convention.

Article 32
[Intergovernmental Committee]

1. An Intergovernmental Committee is hereby established with the following duties:

(a) to study questions concerning the application and operation of this Convention; and

(b) to collect proposals and to prepare documentation for possible revision of this Convention.

2. The Committee shall consist of representatives of the Contracting States, chosen with due regard to equitable geographical distribution. The number of members shall be six if there are twelve Contracting States or less, nine if there are thirteen to eighteen Contracting States and twelve if there are more than eighteen Contracting States.

3. The Committee shall be constituted twelve months after the Convention comes into force by an election organized among the Contracting States, each of which shall have one vote, by the Director-General of the International Labor Office, the Director-General of the United Nations Educational, Scientific and Cultural Organization and the Director of the Bureau of the International Union for the Protection of Literary and Artistic Works, in accordance with rules previously approved by a majority of all Contracting States.

4. The Committee shall elect its Chairman and officers. It shall establish its own rules of procedure. These rules shall in particular provide for the future operation of the Committee and for a method of selecting its members for the future in such a way as to ensure rotation among the various Contracting States.

5. Officials of the International Labor Office, the United Nations Educational, Scientific and Cultural Organization and the Bureau of the International Union for the Protection of Literary and Artistic Works, designated by the Directors-General and the Director thereof, shall constitute the Secretariat of the Committee.

6. Meetings of the Committee, which shall be convened whenever a majority of its members deems it necessary, shall be held successively

at the headquarters of the International Labor Office, the United Nations Educational, Scientific and Cultural Organization and the Bureau of the International Union for the Protection of Literary and Artistic Works.

7. Expenses of members of the Committee shall be borne by their respective Governments.

Article 33
[Languages]

1. The present Convention is drawn up in English, French and Spanish, the three texts being equally authentic.

2. In addition, official texts of the present Convention shall be drawn up in German, Italian and Portuguese.

Article 34
[Notifications]

1. The Secretary-General of the United Nations shall notify the States invited to the Conference referred to in *Article 23* and every State Member of the United Nations, as well as the Director-General of the International Labor Office, the Director-General of the United Nations Educational, Scientific and Cultural Organization and the Director of the Bureau of the International Union for the Protection of Literary and Artistic Works:

(a) of the deposit of each instrument of ratification, acceptance or accession;

(b) of the date of entry into force of the Convention;

(c) of all notifications, declarations or communications provided for in this Convention;

(d) if any of the situations referred to in *paragraphs 4* and *5 of Article 28* arise.

2. The Secretary-General of the United Nations shall also notify the Director-General of the International Labor Office, the Director-General of the United Nations Educational, Scientific and Cultural Organization and the Director of the Bureau of the International Union for the Protection of Literary and Artistic Works of the requests communicated to him in accordance with *Article 29*, as well as of any communication received from the Contracting States concerning the revision of the Convention.

IN FAITH WHEREOF, the undersigned, being duly authorised thereto, have signed this Convention.

DONE at Rome, this twenty-sixth day of October 1961, in a single copy in the English, French and Spanish languages. Certified true copies shall be delivered by the Secretary-General of the United Nations to all the States invited to the Conference referred to in *Article 23* and to every State Member of the United Nations, as well as to the Director-General of the International Labor Office, the Director-General of the United Nations Educational, Scientific and Cultural Organization and the Director of the Bureau of the International Union for the Protection of Literary and Artistic Works.

APPENDIX 5

Convention for the Protection of Producers of Phonograms Against Unauthorized Duplication of their Phonograms

of October 29, 1971

The Contracting States,

concerned at the widespread and increasing unauthorized duplication of phonograms and the damage this is occasioning to the interests of authors, performers and producers of phonograms;

convinced that the protection of producers of phonograms against such acts will also benefit the performers whose performances, and the authors whose works, are recorded on the said phonograms;

recognizing the value of the work undertaken in this field by the United Nations Educational, Scientific and Cultural Organization and the World Intellectual Property Organization;

anxious not to impair in any way international agreements already in force and in particular in no way to prejudice wider acceptance of the Rome Convention of October 26, 1961, which affords protection to performers and to broadcasting organizations as well as to producers of phonograms;

have agreed as follows:

Article 1
[Definitions]

For the purposes of this Convention:

(a) 'phonogram' means any exclusively aural fixation of sounds of a performance or of other sounds;

(b) 'producer of phonograms' means the person who, or the legal entity which, first fixes the sounds of a performance or other sounds;

(c) 'duplicate' means an article which contains sounds taken directly or indirectly from a phonogram and which embodies all or a substantial part of the sounds fixed in that phonogram;

(d) 'distribution to the public' means any act by which duplicates of a phonogram are offered, directly or indirectly, to the general public or any section thereof.

Article 2
[Obligations of Contracting States; Whom they must protect and against what]

Each Contracting State shall protect producers of phonograms who are nationals of other Contracting States against the making of duplicates without the consent of the producer and against the importation of such duplicates, provided that any such making or importation is for the purpose of distribution to the public, and against the distribution of such duplicates to the public.

Article 3
[Means of Implementation by Contracting States]

The means by which this Convention is implemented shall be a matter for the domestic law of each Contracting State and shall include one or more of the following: protection by means of the grant of a copyright or other specific right; protection by means of the law relating to unfair competition; protection by means of penal sanctions.

Article 4
[Term of Protection]

The duration of the protection given shall be a matter for the domestic law of each Contracting State. However, if the domestic law prescribes a specific duration for the protection, that duration shall not be less than twenty years from the end either of the year in which the sounds embodied in the phonogram were first fixed or of the year in which the phonogram was first published.

Article 5
[Formalities]

If, as a condition of protecting the producers of phonograms, a Contracting State, under its domestic law, requires compliance with formalities, these shall be considered as fulfilled if all the authorized duplicates of the phonogram distributed to the public or their containers bear a notice consisting of the symbol (P), accompanied by the year date of the first publication, placed in such manner as to give reasonable notice of claim of protection; and, if the duplicates or their containers do not identify the producer, his successor in title or the exclusive licensee (by carrying his name, trademark or other appropriate designation), the notice shall also include the name of the producer, his successor in title or the exclusive licensee.

Article 6
[Limitations on Protection]

Any Contracting State which affords protection by means of copyright or other specific right, or protection by means of penal sanctions, may in its domestic law provide, with regard to the protection of producers of phonograms, the same kinds of limitations as are permitted with respect to the protection of authors of literary and artistic works. However, no compulsory licenses may be permitted unless all of the following conditions are met:

(a) the duplication is for use solely for the purpose of teaching or scientific research;
(b) the license shall be valid for duplication only within the territory of the Contracting State whose competent authority has granted the license and shall not extend to the export of duplicates;
(c) the duplication made under the license gives rise to an equitable remuneration fixed by the said authority taking into account, inter alia, the number of duplicates which will be made.

Article 7
[*Savings*: 1. Safeguard of Copyright and Neighboring Rights; 2. Protection for Performers; 3. Non-Retroactivity; 4. Substitution of the Criterion of Fixation]

(1) This Convention shall in no way be interpreted to limit or prejudice the protection otherwise secured to authors, to performers, to producers of phonograms or to broadcasting organizations under any domestic law or international agreement.

(2) It shall be a matter for the domestic law of each Contracting State to determine the extent, if any, to which performers whose performances are fixed in a phonogram are entitled to enjoy protection and the conditions for enjoying any such protection.

(3) No Contracting State shall be required to apply the provisions of this Convention to any phonogram fixed before this Convention entered into force with respect to that State.

(4) Any Contracting State which, on October 29, 1971, affords protection to producers of phonograms solely on the basis of the place of first fixation may, by a notification deposited with the Director General of the World Intellectual Property Organization, declare that it will apply this criterion instead of the criterion of the nationality of the producer.

Article 8
[Secretariat]

(1) The International Bureau of the World Intellectual Property Organization shall assemble and publish information concerning the protection of phonograms. Each Contracting State shall promptly communicate to the International Bureau all new laws and official texts on this subject.

(2) The International Bureau shall, on request, furnish information to any Contracting State on matters concerning this Convention, and shall conduct studies and provide services designed to facilitate the protection provided for therein.

(3) The International Bureau shall exercise the functions enumerated in *paragraph (1)* and *paragraph (2)* above in cooperation, for matters within their respective competence, with the United Nations Educational, Scientific and Cultural Organization and the International Labour Office.

Article 9

[*Joining the Convention*: 1. Signature and Deposit; 2 and 3. Ratification and Accession; 4. States' Obligations as to their Domestic Law]

(1) This Convention shall be deposited with the Secretary–General of the United Nations. It shall be open until April 30, 1972, for signature by any State that is a member of the United Nations, any of the Specialized Agencies brought into relationship with the United Nations, or the International Atomic Energy Agency, or is a party to the Statute of the International Court of Justice.

(2) This Convention shall be subject to ratification or acceptance by the signatory States. It shall be open for accession by any State referred to in *paragraph (1)* of this Article.

(3) Instruments of ratification, acceptance or accession shall be deposited with the Secretary–General of the United Nations.

(4) It is understood that, at the time a State becomes bound by this Convention, it will be in a position in accordance with its domestic law to give effect to the provisions of the Convention.

Article 10

[Reservations]

No reservations to this Convention are permitted.

Article 11

[*Entry into Force and Applicability*: 1 and 2. Entry into Force of the Convention; 3 and 4. Applicability of the Convention to Certain Territories]

(1) This Convention shall enter into force three months after deposit of the fifth instrument of ratification, acceptance or accession.

(2) For each State ratifying, accepting or acceding to this Convention after the deposit of the fifth instrument of ratification, acceptance or accession, the Convention shall enter into force three months after the date on which the Director General of the World Intellectual Property Organization informs the States, in accordance with *Article 13, paragraph (4)*, of the deposit of its instrument.

(3) Any State may, at the time of ratification, acceptance or accession or at any later date, declare by notification addressed to the Secretary–General of the United Nations that this Convention shall apply to all or any one of the territories for whose international affairs it is responsible. This notification will take effect three months after the date on which it is received.

(4) However, the preceding paragraph may in no way be understood as implying the recognition or tacit acceptance by a Contracting State of the factual situation concerning a territory to which this Convention is made applicable by another Contracting State by virtue of the said paragraph.

Article 12

[Denunciation of the Convention]

(1) Any Contracting State may denounce this Convention, on its own behalf or on behalf of any of the territories referred to in *Article 11, paragraph (3)*, by written notification addressed to the Secretary–General of the United Nations.

(2) Denunciation shall take effect twelve months after the date on which the Secretary–General of the United Nations has received the notification.

Article 13
[Languages and Notifications]

(1) This Convention shall be signed in a single copy in English, French, Russian and Spanish, the four texts being equally authentic.

(2) Official texts shall be established by the Director General of the World Intellectual Property Organization, after consultation with the interested Governments, in the Arabic, Dutch, German, Italian and Portuguese languages.

(3) The Secretary–General of the United Nations shall notify the Director General of the World Intellectual Property Organization, the Director–General of the United Nations Educational, Scientific and Cultural Organization and the Director–General of the International Labour Office of:

(a) signatures to this Convention;
(b) the deposit of instruments of ratification, acceptance or accession;
(c) the date of entry into force of this Convention;
(d) any declaration notified pursuant to *Article 11, paragraph (3)*;
(e) the receipt of notifications of denunciation.

(4) The Director General of the World Intellectual Property Organization shall inform the States referred to in *Article 9, paragraph (1)*, of the notifications received pursuant to the preceding paragraph and of any declarations made under *Article 7, paragraph (4)*. He shall also notify the Director–General of the United Nations Educational, Scientific and Cultural Organization and the Director–General of the International Labour Office of such declarations.

(5) The Secretary–General of the United Nations shall transmit two certified copies of this Convention to the States referred to in *Article 9, paragraph (1)*.

APPENDIX 6

Convention Relating to the Distribution of Programme-Carrying Signals Transmitted by Satellite (Brussels Satellites Convention 1974)

(Done at Brussels on May 21, 1974)

The Contracting States,

Aware that the use of satellites for the distribution of programme-carrying signals is rapidly growing both in volume and geographical coverage;

Concerned that there is no world-wide system to prevent distributors from distributing programme-carrying signals transmitted by satellite which were not intended for those distributors, and that this lack is likely to hamper the use of satellite communications;

Recognizing, in this respect, the importance of the interests of authors, performers, producers of phonograms and broadcasting organizations;

Convinced that an international system should be established under which measures would be provided to prevent distributors from distributing programme-carrying signals transmitted by satellite which were not intended for those distributors;

Conscious of the need not to impair in any way international agreements already in force, including the International Telecommunication Convention and the Radio Regulations annexed to that Convention, and in particular in no way to prejudice wider acceptance of the Rome Convention of October 26, 1961, which affords protection to performers, producers of phonograms and broadcasting organizations,

Have agreed as follows:

Article 1

For the purposes of this Convention:

(i) 'signal' is an electronically-generated carrier capable of transmitting programmes;

(ii) 'programme' is a body of live or recorded material consisting of images, sounds or both, embodied in signals emitted for the purpose of ultimate distribution;

(iii) 'satellite' is any device in extraterrestrial space capable of transmitting signals;

(iv) 'emitted signal' or 'signal emitted' is any programme-carrying signal that goes to or passes through a satellite;

(v) 'derived signal' is a signal obtained by modifying the technical characteristics of the emitted signal, whether or not there have been one or more intervening fixations;

(vi) 'originating organization' is the person or legal entity that decides what programme the emitted signals will carry;

(vii) 'distributor' is the person or legal entity that decides that the transmission of the derived signals to the general public or any section thereof should take place;

(viii) 'distribution' is the operation by which a distributor transmits derived signals to the general public or any section thereof.

Article 2

(1) Each Contracting State undertakes to take adequate measures to prevent the distribution on or from its territory of any programme-carrying signal by any distributor for whom the signal emitted to or passing through the satellite is not intended. This obligation shall apply where the originating organization is a national of another Contracting State

and where the signal distributed is a derived signal.

(2) In any Contracting State in which the application of the measures referred to in *paragraph (1)* is limited in time, the duration thereof shall be fixed by its domestic law. The Secretary-General of the United Nations shall be notified in writing of such duration at the time of ratification, acceptance or accession, or if the domestic law comes into force or is changed thereafter, within six months of the coming into force of that law or of its modification.

(3) The obligation provided for in *paragraph (1)* shall not apply to the distribution of derived signals taken from signals which have already been distributed by a distributor for whom the emitted signals were intended.

Article 3

This Convention shall not apply where the signals emitted by or on behalf of the originating organization are intended for direct reception from the satellite by the general public.

Article 4

No Contracting State shall be required to apply the measures referred to in *Article 2(1)* where the signal distributed on its territory by a distributor for whom the emitted signal is not intended

(i) carries short excerpts of the programme carried by the emitted signal, consisting of reports of current events, but only to the extent justified by the informatory purpose of such excerpts, or
(ii) carries, as quotations, short excerpts of the programme carried by the emitted signal, provided that such quotations are compatible with fair practice and are justified by the informatory purpose of such quotations, or
(iii) carries, where the said territory is that of a Contracting State regarded as a developing country in conformity with the established practice of the General Assembly of the United Nations, a programme carried by the emitted signal, provided that the distribution is solely for the purpose of teaching, including teaching in the framework of adult education, or scientific research.

Article 5

No Contracting State shall be required to apply this Convention with respect to any signal emitted before this Convention entered into force for that State.

Article 6

This Convention shall in no way be interpreted to limit or prejudice the protection secured to authors, performers, producers of phonograms, or broadcasting organizations, under any domestic law or international agreement.

Article 7

This Convention shall in no way be interpreted as limiting the right of any Contracting State to apply its domestic law in order to prevent abuses of monopoly.

Article 8

(1) Subject to *paragraphs (2)* and *(3)*, no reservation to this Convention shall be permitted.

(2) Any Contracting State whose domestic law, on May 21, 1974, so provides may, by a written notification deposited with the Secretary-General of the United Nations, declare that, for its purposes, the words 'where the originating organization is a national of another Contracting State' appearing in *Article 2(1)* shall be considered as if they were replaced by the words 'where the signal is emitted from the territory of another Contracting State.'

(3) (a) Any Contracting State which, on May 21, 1974, limits or denies protection with respect to the distribution of programme-carrying signals by means of wires, cable or other similar communications channels to subscribing members of the public may, by a written notification deposited with the Secretary–General of the United Nations, declare that, to the extent that and as long as its domestic law limits or denies protection, it will

not apply this Convention to such distributions.

(b) Any State that has deposited a notification in accordance with *subparagraph (a)* shall notify the Secretary-General of the United Nations in writing, within six months of their coming into force, of any changes in its domestic law whereby the reservation under that subparagraph becomes inapplicable or more limited in scope.

Article 9

(1) This Convention shall be deposited with the Secretary-General of the United Nations. It shall be open until March 31, 1975, for signature by any State that is a member of the United Nations, any of the Specialized Agencies brought into relationship with the United Nations, or the International Atomic Energy Agency, or is a party to the Statute of the International Court of Justice.

(2) This Convention shall be subject to ratification or acceptance by the signatory States. It shall be open for accession by any State referred to in *paragraph (1)*.

(3) Instruments of ratification, acceptance or accession shall be deposited with the Secretary-General of the United Nations.

(4) It is understood that, at the time a State becomes bound by this Convention, it will be in a position in accordance with its domestic law to give effect to the provisions of the Convention.

Article 10

(1) This Convention shall enter into force three months after the deposit of the fifth instrument of ratification, acceptance or accession.

(2) For each State ratifying, accepting or acceding to this Convention after the deposit of the fifth instrument of ratification, acceptance or accession, this Convention shall enter into force three months after the deposit of its instrument.

Article 11

(1) Any Contracting State may denounce this Convention by written notification deposited with the Secretary-General of the United Nations.

(2) Denunciation shall take effect twelve months after the date on which the notification referred to in *paragraph (1)* is received.

Article 12

(1) This Convention shall be signed in a single copy in English, French, Russian and Spanish, the four texts being equally authentic.

(2) Official texts shall be established by the Director-General of the United Nations Educational, Scientific and Cultural Organization and the Director General of the World Intellectual Property Organization, after consultation with the interested Governments, in the Arabic, Dutch, German, Italian and Portuguese languages.

(3) The Secretary-General of the United Nations shall notify the States referred to in *Article 9(1)*, as well as the Director-General of the United Nations Educational, Scientific and Cultural Organization, the Director General of the World Intellectual Property Organization, the Director-General of the International Labour Office and the Secretary-General of the International Telecommunication Union, of

- (i) signatures to this Convention;
- (ii) the deposit of instruments of ratification, acceptance or accession;
- (ii) the date of entry into force of this Convention under *Article 10(1)*;
- (iv) the deposit of any notification relating to *Article 2(2)* or *Article 8(2)* or *(3)*, together with its text;
- (v) the receipt of notifications of denunciation.

(4) The Secretary-General of the United Nations shall transmit two certified copies of this Convention to all States referred to in *Article 9(1)*.

APPENDIX 7

WIPO Copyright Treaty 1996

(adopted in Geneva on December 20, 1996)[1]

Preamble

The Contracting Parties,

Desiring to develop and maintain the protection of the rights of authors in their literary and artistic works in a manner as effective and uniform as possible,

Recognizing the need to introduce new international rules and clarify the interpretation of certain existing rules in order to provide adequate solutions to the questions raised by new economic, social, cultural and technological developments,

Recognizing the profound impact of the development and convergence of information and communication technologies on the creation and use of literary and artistic works,

Emphasizing the outstanding significance of copyright protection as an incentive for literary and artistic creation,

Recognizing the need to maintain a balance between the rights of authors and the larger public interest, particularly education, research and access to information, as reflected in the Berne Convention,

Have agreed as follows:

[1] *Entry into force:* 6 March 2002.
Source: International Bureau of WIPO.
Note: The agreed statements of the Diplomatic Conference that adopted the Treaty (WIPO Diplomatic Conference on Certain Copyright and Neighbouring Rights Questions) concerning certain provisions of the WCT are reproduced in the notes below.

Article 1

[Relation to the Berne Convention]

(1) This Treaty is a special agreement within the meaning of *Article 20 of the Berne Convention* for the Protection of Literary and Artistic Works, as regards Contracting Parties that are countries of the Union established by that Convention. This Treaty shall not have any connection with treaties other than the Berne Convention, nor shall it prejudice any rights and obligations under any other treaties.

(2) Nothing in this Treaty shall derogate from existing obligations that Contracting Parties have to each other under the Berne Convention for the Protection of Literary and Artistic Works.

(3) Hereinafter, 'Berne Convention' shall refer to the Paris Act of July 24, 1971 of the Berne Convention for the Protection of Literary and Artistic Works.

(4) Contracting Parties shall comply with *Articles 1* to *21* and the *Appendix of the Berne Convention.*[2]

[2] Agreed statements concerning Article 1(4): The reproduction right, as set out in Article 9 of the Berne Convention, and the exceptions permitted thereunder, fully apply in the digital environment, in particular to the use of works in digital form. It is understood that the storage of a protected work in digital form in an electronic medium constitutes a reproduction within the meaning of Article 9 of the Berne Convention.

Article 2
[Scope of Copyright Protection]

Copyright protection extends to expressions and not to ideas, procedures, methods of operation or mathematical concepts as such.

Article 3
[Application of *Articles 2* to *6 of the Berne Convention*]

Contracting Parties shall apply *mutatis mutandis* the provisions of *Articles 2* to *6 of the Berne Convention* in respect of the protection provided for in this Treaty.[3]

Article 4
[Computer Programs]

Computer programs are protected as literary works within the meaning of *Article 2 of the Berne Convention.* Such protection applies to computer programs, whatever may be the mode or form of their expression.[4]

Article 5
[Compilations of Data (Databases)]

Compilations of data or other material, in any form, which by reason of the selection or arrangement of their contents constitute intellectual creations, are protected as such. This protection does not extend to the data or the material itself and is without prejudice to any copyright subsisting in the data or material contained in the compilation.[5]

Article 6
[Right of Distribution]

(1) Authors of literary and artistic works shall enjoy the exclusive right of authorizing the making available to the public of the original and copies of their works through sale or other transfer of ownership.

(2) Nothing in this Treaty shall affect the freedom of Contracting Parties to determine the conditions, if any, under which the exhaustion of the right in *paragraph (1)* applies after the first sale or other transfer of ownership of the original or a copy of the work with the authorization of the author.[6]

Article 7
[Right of Rental]

(1) Authors of

(i) computer programs;
(ii) cinematographic works; and
(iii) works embodied in phonograms, as determined in the national law of Contracting Parties,

---

[3] Agreed statements concerning Article 3: It is understood that in applying Article 3 of this Treaty, the expression 'country of the Union' in Articles 2 to 6 of the Berne Convention will be read as if it were a reference to a Contracting Party to this Treaty, in the application of those Berne Articles in respect of protection provided for in this Treaty. It is also understood that the expression 'country outside the Union' in those Articles in the Berne Convention will, in the same circumstances, be read as if it were a reference to a country that is not a Contracting Party to this Treaty, and that this Convention in Articles 2(8), 2*bis*(2), 3, 4 and 5 of the Berne Convention will be read as if it were a reference to the Berne Convention and this Treaty. Finally, it is understood that a reference in Articles 3 to 6 of the Berne Convention to a 'national of one of the countries of the Union' will, when these Articles are applied to this Treaty, mean, in regard to an intergovernmental organization that is a Contracting Party to this Treaty, a national of one of the countries that is member of that organization.

[4] Agreed statements concerning Article 4: The scope of protection for computer programs under Article 4 of this Treaty, read with Article 2, is consistent with Article 2 of the Berne Convention and on a par with the relevant provisions of the TRIPS Agreement.

[5] Agreed statements concerning Article 5: The scope of protection for compilations of data (databases) under Article 5 of this Treaty, read with Article 2, is consistent with Article 2 of the Berne Convention and on a par with the relevant provisions of the TRIPS Agreement.

[6] Agreed statements concerning Articles 6 and 7: As used in these Articles, the expressions 'copies' and 'original and copies', being subject to the right of distribution and the right of rental under the said Articles, refer exclusively to fixed copies that can be put into circulation as tangible objects.

shall enjoy the exclusive right of authorizing commercial rental to the public of the originals or copies of their works.

(2) *Paragraph (1)* shall not apply

(i) in the case of computer programs, where the program itself is not the essential object of the rental; and

(ii) in the case of cinematographic works, unless such commercial rental has led to widespread copying of such works materially impairing the exclusive right of reproduction.

(3) Notwithstanding the provisions of *paragraph (1)*, a Contracting Party that, on April 15, 1994, had and continues to have in force a system of equitable remuneration of authors for the rental of copies of their works embodied in phonograms may maintain that system provided that the commercial rental of works embodied in phonograms is not giving rise to the material impairment of the exclusive right of reproduction of authors.[7, 8]

Article 8

[Right of Communication to the Public]

Without prejudice to the provisions of *Articles 11(1)(ii), 11bis(1)(i)* and *(ii), 11ter(1)(ii), 14(1)(ii)* and *14bis(1) of the Berne Convention*, authors of literary and artistic works shall enjoy the exclusive right of authorizing any communication to the public of their works, by wire or wireless means, including the making available to the public of their works in such a way that members of the public may access these works from a place and at a time individually chosen by them.[9]

Article 9

[Duration of the Protection of Photographic Works]

In respect of photographic works, the Contracting Parties shall not apply the provisions of *Article 7(4) of the Berne Convention.*

Article 10

[Limitations and Exceptions]

(1) Contracting Parties may, in their national legislation, provide for limitations of or exceptions to the rights granted to authors of literary and artistic works under this Treaty in certain special cases that do not conflict with a normal exploitation of the work and do not unreasonably prejudice the legitimate interests of the author.

(2) Contracting Parties shall, when applying the Berne Convention, confine any limitations of or exceptions to rights provided for therein to certain special cases that do not conflict with a normal exploitation of the work and do not unreasonably prejudice the legitimate interests of the author.[10]

---

[7] Agreed statements concerning Articles 6 and 7: As used in these Articles, the expressions 'copies' and 'original and copies', being subject to the right of distribution and the right of rental under the said Articles, refer exclusively to fixed copies that can be put into circulation as tangible objects.

[8] Agreed statements concerning Article 7: It is understood that the obligation under Article 7(1) does not require a Contracting Party to provide an exclusive right of commercial rental to authors who, under that Contracting Party's law, are not granted rights in respect of phonograms. It is understood that this obligation is consistent with Article 14(4) of the TRIPS Agreement.

[9] Agreed statements concerning Article 8: It is understood that the mere provision of physical facilities for enabling or making a communication does not in itself amount to communication within the meaning of this Treaty or the Berne Convention. It is further understood that nothing in Article 8 precludes a Contracting Party from applying Article 11*bis*(2).

[10] Agreed statement concerning Article 10: It is understood that the provisions of Article 10 permit Contracting Parties to carry forward and appropriately extend into the digital environment limitations and exceptions in their national laws which have been considered acceptable under the Berne Convention. Similarly, these provisions should be understood to permit Contracting Parties to devise new exceptions and limitations that are appropriate in the digital network environment.

It is also understood that Article 10(2) neither reduces nor extends the scope of applicability of the limitations and exceptions permitted by the Berne Convention.

Article 11
[Obligations concerning Technological Measures]

Contracting Parties shall provide adequate legal protection and effective legal remedies against the circumvention of effective technological measures that are used by authors in connection with the exercise of their rights under this Treaty or the Berne Convention and that restrict acts, in respect of their works, which are not authorized by the authors concerned or permitted by law.

Article 12
[Obligations concerning Rights Management Information]

(1) Contracting Parties shall provide adequate and effective legal remedies against any person knowingly performing any of the following acts knowing, or with respect to civil remedies having reasonable grounds to know, that it will induce, enable, facilitate or conceal an infringement of any right covered by this Treaty or the Berne Convention:

(i) to remove or alter any electronic rights management information without authority;

(ii) to distribute, import for distribution, broadcast or communicate to the public, without authority, works or copies of works knowing that electronic rights management information has been removed or altered without authority.

(2) As used in this Article, 'rights management information' means information which identifies the work, the author of the work, the owner of any right in the work, or information about the terms and conditions of use of the work, and any numbers or codes that represent such information, when any of these items of information is attached to a copy of a work or appears in connection with the communication of a work to the public.[11]

[11] Agreed statements concerning Article 12: It is understood that the reference to 'infringement of any right covered by this Treaty or the Berne Convention' includes both exclusive rights and rights of remuneration.

It is further understood that Contracting Parties will not rely on this Article to devise or implement rights management systems that would have the effect of imposing formalities which are not permitted under the Berne Convention or this Treaty, prohibiting the free movement of goods or impeding the enjoyment of rights under this Treaty.

Article 13
[Application in Time]

Contracting Parties shall apply the provisions of *Article 18 of the Berne Convention* to all protection provided for in this Treaty.

Article 14
[Provisions on Enforcement of Rights]

(1) Contracting Parties undertake to adopt, in accordance with their legal systems, the measures necessary to ensure the application of this Treaty.

(2) Contracting Parties shall ensure that enforcement procedures are available under their law so as to permit effective action against any act of infringement of rights covered by this Treaty, including expeditious remedies to prevent infringements and remedies which constitute a deterrent to further infringements.

Article 15
[Assembly]

(1) (a) The Contracting Parties shall have an Assembly.

(b) Each Contracting Party shall be represented by one delegate who may be assisted by alternate delegates, advisors and experts.

(c) The expenses of each delegation shall be borne by the Contracting Party that has appointed the delegation. The Assembly may ask the World Intellectual Property Organization (hereinafter referred to as 'WIPO') to grant financial assistance to facilitate the participation of delegations of Contracting Parties that are regarded as developing countries in conformity with the established practice of the General Assembly of the United Nations or that are countries in transition to a market economy.

(2) (a) The Assembly shall deal with matters concerning the maintenance and development of this Treaty and the application and operation of this Treaty.

(b) The Assembly shall perform the function allocated to it under *Article 17(2)* in respect of the admission of certain intergovernmental organizations to become party to this Treaty.

(c) The Assembly shall decide the convocation of any diplomatic conference for the revision of this Treaty and give the necessary instructions to the Director General of WIPO for the preparation of such diplomatic conference.

(3) (a) Each Contracting Party that is a State shall have one vote and shall vote only in its own name.

(b) Any Contracting Party that is an intergovernmental organization may participate in the vote, in place of its Member States, with a number of votes equal to the number of its Member States which are party to this Treaty. No such intergovernmental organization shall participate in the vote if any one of its Member States exercises its right to vote and *vice versa.*

(4) The Assembly shall meet in ordinary session once every two years upon convocation by the Director General of WIPO.

(5) The Assembly shall establish its own rules of procedure, including the convocation of extraordinary sessions, the requirements of a quorum and, subject to the provisions of this Treaty, the required majority for various kinds of decisions.

Article 16
[International Bureau]

The International Bureau of WIPO shall perform the administrative tasks concerning the Treaty.

Article 17
[Eligibility for Becoming Party to the Treaty]

(1) Any Member State of WIPO may become party to this Treaty.

(2) The Assembly may decide to admit any intergovernmental organization to become party to this Treaty which declares that it is competent in respect of, and has its own legislation binding on all its Member States on, matters covered by this Treaty and that it has been duly authorized, in accordance with its internal procedures, to become party to this Treaty.

(3) The European Community, having made the declaration referred to in the preceding paragraph in the Diplomatic Conference that has adopted this Treaty, may become party to this Treaty.

Article 18
[Rights and Obligations under the Treaty]

Subject to any specific provisions to the contrary in this Treaty, each Contracting Party shall enjoy all of the rights and assume all of the obligations under this Treaty.

Article 19
[Signature of the Treaty]

This Treaty shall be open for signature until December 31, 1997, by any Member State of WIPO and by the European Community.

Article 20
[Entry into Force of the Treaty]

This Treaty shall enter into force three months after 30 instruments of ratification or accession by States have been deposited with the Director General of WIPO.

Article 21
[Effective Date of Becoming Party to the Treaty]

This Treaty shall bind:

(i) the 30 States referred to in *Article 20*, from the date on which this Treaty has entered into force;

(ii) each other State from the expiration of three months from the date on which the State has deposited its instrument with the Director General of WIPO;

(iii) the European Community, from the expiration of three months after the deposit of its instrument of ratification or accession if such instrument has been deposited after the entry into force of this Treaty according to *Article 20*, or, three months after the entry into force of this Treaty if such instrument has been deposited before the entry into force of this Treaty;

(iv) any other intergovernmental organization that is admitted to become party to this Treaty, from the expiration of three months after the deposit of its instrument of accession.

Article 22
[No Reservations to the Treaty]

No reservation to this Treaty shall be admitted.

Article 23
[Denunciation of the Treaty]

This Treaty may be denounced by any Contracting Party by notification addressed to the Director General of WIPO. Any denunciation shall take effect one year from the date on which the Director General of WIPO received the notification.

Article 24
[Languages of the Treaty]

(1) This Treaty is signed in a single original in English, Arabic, Chinese, French, Russian and Spanish languages, the versions in all these languages being equally authentic.

(2) An official text in any language other than those referred to in *paragraph (1)* shall be established by the Director General of WIPO on the request of an interested party, after consultation with all the interested parties. For the purposes of this paragraph, 'interested party' means any Member State of WIPO whose official language, or one of whose official languages, is involved and the European Community, and any other intergovernmental organization that may become party to this Treaty, if one of its official languages is involved.

Article 25
[Depositary]

The Director General of WIPO is the depositary of this Treaty.

APPENDIX 8

WIPO Performances and Phonograms Treaty 1996

(adopted in Geneva on December 20, 1996)*

Preamble

The Contracting Parties,

Desiring to develop and maintain the protection of the rights of performers and producers of phonograms in a manner as effective and uniform as possible,

Recognizing the need to introduce new international rules in order to provide adequate solutions to the questions raised by economic, social, cultural and technological developments,

Recognizing the profound impact of the development and convergence of information and communication technologies on the production and use of performances and phonograms,

Recognizing the need to maintain a balance between the rights of performers and producers of phonograms and the larger public interest, particularly education, research and access to information,

Have agreed as follows:

Chapter I—General Provisions

Article 1

[Relation to Other Conventions]

(1) Nothing in this Treaty shall derogate from existing obligations that Contracting Parties have to each other under the International Convention for the Protection of Performers, Producers of Phonograms and Broadcasting Organizations done in Rome, October 26, 1961 (hereinafter the 'Rome Convention').

(2) Protection granted under this Treaty shall leave intact and shall in no way affect the protection of copyright in literary and artistic works. Consequently, no provision of this Treaty may be interpreted as prejudicing such protection.[1]

(3) This Treaty shall not have any connection with, nor shall it prejudice any rights and obligations under, any other treaties.

Article 2

[Definitions]

For the purposes of this Treaty:

(a) 'performers' are actors, singers, musicians, dancers, and other persons who act, sing,

---

* *Entry into force:* 20 May 2002.

Source: International Bureau of WIPO.

Note: The agreed statements of the Diplomatic Conference that adopted the Treaty (WIPO Diplomatic Conference on Certain Copyright and Neighboring Rights Questions) concerning certain provisions of the WPPT, are reproduced in the notes below.

[1] *Agreed statement concerning Article 1(2):* It is understood that Article 1(2) clarifies the relationship between rights in phonograms under this Treaty and copyright in works embodied in the phonograms. In cases where authorization is needed from both the author of a work embodied in the phonogram and a performer or producer owning rights in the phonogram, the need for the authorization of the author does not cease to exist because the authorization of the performer or producer is also required, and vice versa.

It is further understood that nothing in Article 1(2) precludes a Contracting Party from providing exclusive rights to a performer or producer of phonograms beyond those required to be provided under this Treaty.

deliver, declaim, play in, interpret, or otherwise perform literary or artistic works or expressions of folklore;

(b) 'phonogram' means the fixation of the sounds of a performance or of other sounds, or of a representation of sounds, other than in the form of a fixation incorporated in a cinematographic or other audiovisual work;[2]

(c) 'fixation' means the embodiment of sounds, or of the representations thereof, from which they can be perceived, reproduced or communicated through a device;

(d) 'producer of a phonogram' means the person, or the legal entity, who or which takes the initiative and has the responsibility for the first fixation of the sounds of a performance or other sounds, or the representations of sounds;

(e) 'publication' of a fixed performance or a phonogram means the offering of copies of the fixed performance or the phonogram to the public, with the consent of the rightholder, and provided that copies are offered to the public in reasonable quantity;[3]

(f) 'broadcasting' means the transmission by wireless means for public reception of sounds or of images and sounds or of the representations thereof; such transmission by satellite is also 'broadcasting'; transmission of encrypted signals is 'broadcasting' where the means for decrypting are provided to the public by the broadcasting organization or with its consent;

(g) 'communication to the public' of a performance or a phonogram means the transmission to the public by any medium, otherwise than by broadcasting, of sounds of a performance or the sounds or the representations of sounds fixed in a phonogram. For the purposes of *Article 15*, 'communication to the public' includes making the sounds or representations of sounds fixed in a phonogram audible to the public.

Article 3

[Beneficiaries of Protection under this Treaty]

(1) Contracting Parties shall accord the protection provided under this Treaty to the performers and producers of phonograms who are nationals of other Contracting Parties.

(2) The nationals of other Contracting Parties shall be understood to be those performers or producers of phonograms who would meet the criteria for eligibility for protection provided under the Rome Convention, were all the Contracting Parties to this Treaty Contracting States of that Convention. In respect of these criteria of eligibility, Contracting Parties shall apply the relevant definitions in *Article 2* of this Treaty.[4]

(3) Any Contracting Party availing itself of the possibilities provided in *Article 5(3)* of the Rome Convention or, for the purposes of *Article 5* of the same Convention, *Article 17* thereof shall make a notification as foreseen in those provisions to the Director General of the World Intellectual Property Organization (WIPO).[5]

[2] *Agreed statement concerning Article 2(b):* It is understood that the definition of phonogram provided in Article 2(b) does not suggest that rights in the phonogram are in any way affected through their incorporation into a cinematographic or other audiovisual work.

[3] *Agreed statement concerning Articles 2(e), 8, 9, 12, and 13:* As used in these Articles, the expressions 'copies' and 'original and copies,' being subject to the right of distribution and the right of rental under the said Articles, refer exclusively to fixed copies that can be put into circulation as tangible objects.

[4] *Agreed statement concerning Article 3(2):* For the application of Article 3(2), it is understood that fixation means the finalization of the master tape ('bande-mère').

[5] *Agreed statement concerning Article 3:* It is understood that the reference in Articles 5(a) and 16(a)(iv) of the Rome Convention to 'national of another Contracting State' will, when applied to this Treaty, mean, in regard to an intergovernmental organization that is a Contracting Party to this Treaty, a national of one of the countries that is a member of that organization.

Article 4
[National Treatment]

(1) Each Contracting Party shall accord to nationals of other Contracting Parties, as defined in *Article 3(2)*, the treatment it accords to its own nationals with regard to the exclusive rights specifically granted in this Treaty, and to the right to equitable remuneration provided for in *Article 15* of this Treaty.

(2) The obligation provided for in *paragraph (1)* does not apply to the extent that another Contracting Party makes use of the reservations permitted by *Article 15(3)* of this Treaty.

Chapter II—Rights of Performers

Article 5
[Moral Rights of Performers]

(1) Independently of a performer's economic rights, and even after the transfer of those rights, the performer shall, as regards his live aural performances or performances fixed in phonograms, have the right to claim to be identified as the performer of his performances, except where omission is dictated by the manner of the use of the performance, and to object to any distortion, mutilation or other modification of his performances that would be prejudicial to his reputation.

(2) The rights granted to a performer in accordance with *paragraph (1)* shall, after his death, be maintained, at least until the expiry of the economic rights, and shall be exercisable by the persons or institutions authorized by the legislation of the Contracting Party where protection is claimed. However, those Contracting Parties whose legislation, at the moment of their ratification of or accession to this Treaty, does not provide for protection after the death of the performer of all rights set out in the preceding paragraph may provide that some of these rights will, after his death, cease to be maintained.

(3) The means of redress for safeguarding the rights granted under this Article shall be governed by the legislation of the Contracting Party where protection is claimed.

Article 6
[Economic Rights of Performers in their Unfixed Performances]

Performers shall enjoy the exclusive right of authorizing, as regards their performances:

(i) the broadcasting and communication to the public of their unfixed performances except where the performance is already a broadcast performance; and

(ii) the fixation of their unfixed performances.

Article 7
[Right of Reproduction]

Performers shall enjoy the exclusive right of authorizing the direct or indirect reproduction of their performances fixed in phonograms, in any manner or form.[6]

Article 8
[Right of Distribution]

(1) Performers shall enjoy the exclusive right of authorizing the making available to the public of the original and copies of their performances fixed in phonograms through sale or other transfer of ownership.

(2) Nothing in this Treaty shall affect the freedom of Contracting Parties to determine the conditions, if any, under which the exhaustion of the right in *paragraph (1)* applies after the first sale or other transfer of ownership of the original or a copy of the fixed performance with the authorization of the performer.[7]

---

[6] *Agreed statement concerning Articles 7, 11 and 16:* The reproduction right, as set out in Articles 7 and 11, and the exceptions permitted thereunder through Article 16, fully apply in the digital environment, in particular to the use of performances and phonograms in digital form. It is understood that the storage of a protected performance or phonogram in digital form in an electronic medium constitutes a reproduction within the meaning of these Articles.

[7] *Agreed statement concerning Articles 2(e), 8, 9, 12, and 13:* As used in these Articles, the expressions 'copies' and 'original and copies,' being subject to the right of distribution and the right of rental under the said Articles, refer exclusively to fixed copies that can be put into circulation as tangible objects.

Article 9
[Right of Rental]

(1) Performers shall enjoy the exclusive right of authorizing the commercial rental to the public of the original and copies of their performances fixed in phonograms as determined in the national law of Contracting Parties, even after distribution of them by, or pursuant to, authorization by the performer.

(2) Notwithstanding the provisions of *paragraph (1)*, a Contracting Party that, on April 15, 1994, had and continues to have in force a system of equitable remuneration of performers for the rental of copies of their performances fixed in phonograms, may maintain that system provided that the commercial rental of phonograms is not giving rise to the material impairment of the exclusive right of reproduction of performers.[8]

Article 10
[Right of Making Available of Fixed Performances

Performers shall enjoy the exclusive right of authorizing the making available to the public of their performances fixed in phonograms, by wire or wireless means, in such a way that members of the public may access them from a place and at a time individually chosen by them.

Chapter III—Rights of Producers of Phonograms

Article 11
[Right of Reproduction]

Producers of phonograms shall enjoy the exclusive right of authorizing the direct or indirect reproduction of their phonograms, in any manner or form.[9]

Article 12
[Right of Distribution]

(1) Producers of phonograms shall enjoy the exclusive right of authorizing the making available to the public of the original and copies of their phonograms through sale or other transfer of ownership.

(2) Nothing in this Treaty shall affect the freedom of Contracting Parties to determine the conditions, if any, under which the exhaustion of the right in *paragraph (1)* applies after the first sale or other transfer of ownership of the original or a copy of the phonogram with the authorization of the producer of the phonogram.[10]

Article 13
[Right of Rental]

(1) Producers of phonograms shall enjoy the exclusive right of authorizing the commercial rental to the public of the original and copies of their phonograms, even after distribution of them, by or pursuant to, authorization by the producer.

(2) Notwithstanding the provisions of *paragraph (1)*, a Contracting Party that, on April 15, 1994, had and continues to have in force a system of equitable remuneration of producers of phonograms for the rental of copies of their phonograms, may maintain that system provided that the commercial rental

---

[8] *Agreed statement concerning Articles 2(e), 8, 9, 12, and 13:* As used in these Articles, the expressions 'copies' and 'original and copies,' being subject to the right of distribution and the right of rental under the said Articles, refer exclusively to fixed copies that can be put into circulation as tangible objects.

[9] *Agreed statement concerning Articles 7, 11 and 16:* The reproduction right, as set out in Articles 7 and 11, and the exceptions permitted thereunder through Article 16, fully apply in the digital environment, in particular to the use of performances and phonograms in digital form. It is understood that the storage of a protected performance or phonogram in digital form in an electronic medium constitutes a reproduction within the meaning of these Articles.

[10] *Agreed statement concerning Articles 2(e), 8, 9, 12, and 13:* As used in these Articles, the expressions 'copies' and 'original and copies,' being subject to the right of distribution and the right of rental under the said Articles, refer exclusively to fixed copies that can be put into circulation as tangible objects.

of phonograms is not giving rise to the material impairment of the exclusive rights of reproduction of producers of phonograms.[11]

Article 14
[Right of Making Available of Phonograms]

Producers of phonograms shall enjoy the exclusive right of authorizing the making available to the public of their phonograms, by wire or wireless means, in such a way that members of the public may access them from a place and at a time individually chosen by them.

Chapter IV—Common Provisions

Article 15
[Right to Remuneration for Broadcasting and Communication to the Public]

(1) Performers and producers of phonograms shall enjoy the right to a single equitable remuneration for the direct or indirect use of phonograms published for commercial purposes for broadcasting or for any communication to the public.

(2) Contracting Parties may establish in their national legislation that the single equitable remuneration shall be claimed from the user by the performer or by the producer of a phonogram or by both. Contracting Parties may enact national legislation that, in the absence of an agreement between the performer and the producer of a phonogram, sets the terms according to which performers and producers of phonograms shall share the single equitable remuneration.

(3) Any Contracting Party may, in a notification deposited with the Director General of WIPO, declare that it will apply the provisions of *paragraph (1)* only in respect of certain uses, or that it will limit their application in some other way, or that it will not apply these provisions at all.

(4) For the purposes of this Article, phonograms made available to the public by wire or wireless means in such a way that members of the public may access them from a place and at a time individually chosen by them shall be considered as if they had been published for commercial purposes.[12,13]

Article 16
[Limitations and Exceptions]

(1) Contracting Parties may, in their national legislation, provide for the same kinds of limitations or exceptions with regard to the protection of performers and producers of phonograms as they provide for, in their national legislation, in connection with the protection of copyright in literary and artistic works.

(2) Contracting Parties shall confine any limitations of or exceptions to rights provided for in this Treaty to certain special cases which do not conflict with a normal exploitation of the performance or phonogram and do not unreasonably prejudice the legitimate interests

[11] *Agreed statement concerning Articles 2(e), 8, 9, 12, and 13:* As used in these Articles, the expressions 'copies' and 'original and copies,' being subject to the right of distribution and the right of rental under the said Articles, refer exclusively to fixed copies that can be put into circulation as tangible objects.

[12] *Agreed statement concerning Article 15:* It is understood that Article 15 does not represent a complete resolution of the level of rights of broadcasting and communication to the public that should be enjoyed by performers and phonogram producers in the digital age. Delegations were unable to achieve consensus on differing proposals for aspects of exclusivity to be provided in certain circumstances or for rights to be provided without the possibility of reservations, and have therefore left the issue to future resolution.

[13] *Agreed statement concerning Article 15:* It is understood that Article 15 does not prevent the granting of the right conferred by this Article to performers of folklore and producers of phonograms recording folklore where such phonograms have not been published for commercial gain.

of the performer or of the producer of the phonogram.[14,15]

Article 17
[Term of Protection]

(1) The term of protection to be granted to performers under this Treaty shall last, at least, until the end of a period of 50 years computed from the end of the year in which the performance was fixed in a phonogram.

(2) The term of protection to be granted to producers of phonograms under this Treaty shall last, at least, until the end of a period of 50 years computed from the end of the year in which the phonogram was published, or failing such publication within 50 years from fixation of the phonogram, 50 years from the end of the year in which the fixation was made.

Article 18
[Obligations concerning Technological Measures]

Contracting Parties shall provide adequate legal protection and effective legal remedies against the circumvention of effective technological measures that are used by performers or producers of phonograms in connection with the exercise of their rights under this Treaty and that restrict acts, in respect of their performances or phonograms, which are not authorized by the performers or the producers of phonograms concerned or permitted by law.

Article 19
[Obligations concerning Rights Management Information]

(1) Contracting Parties shall provide adequate and effective legal remedies against any person knowingly performing any of the following acts knowing, or with respect to civil remedies having reasonable grounds to know, that it will induce, enable, facilitate or conceal an infringement of any right covered by this Treaty:

(i) to remove or alter any electronic rights management information without authority;

(ii) to distribute, import for distribution, broadcast, communicate or make available to the public, without authority, performances, copies of fixed performances or phonograms knowing that electronic rights management information has been removed or altered without authority.

(2) As used in this Article, 'rights management information' means information which identifies the performer, the performance of the performer, the producer of the phonogram, the phonogram, the owner of any right in the performance or phonogram, or information about the terms and conditions of use of the performance or phonogram, and any numbers or codes that represent such information, when any of these items of information is attached to a copy of a fixed performance or a phonogram or appears in connection with the

---

[14] *Agreed statement concerning Articles 7, 11 and 16:* The reproduction right, as set out in Articles 7 and 11, and the exceptions permitted thereunder through Article 16, fully apply in the digital environment, in particular to the use of performances and phonograms in digital form. It is understood that the storage of a protected performance or phonogram in digital form in an electronic medium constitutes a reproduction within the meaning of these Articles.

[15] *Agreed statement concerning Article 16:* The agreed statement concerning Article 10 (on Limitations and Exceptions) of the WIPO Copyright Treaty is applicable *mutatis mutandis* also to Article 16 (on Limitations and Exceptions) of the WIPO Performances and Phonograms Treaty. [The text of the agreed statement concerning Article 10 of the WCT reads as follows: 'It is understood that the provisions of Article 10 permit Contracting Parties to carry forward and appropriately extend into the digital environment limitations and exceptions in their national laws which have been considered acceptable under the Berne Convention. Similarly, these provisions should be understood to permit Contracting Parties to devise new exceptions and limitations that are appropriate in the digital network environment.

'It is also understood that Article 10(2) neither reduces nor extends the scope of applicability of the limitations and exceptions permitted by the Berne Convention.']

communication or making available of a fixed performance or a phonogram to the public.[16]

Article 20
[Formalities]

The enjoyment and exercise of the rights provided for in this Treaty shall not be subject to any formality.

Article 21
[Reservations]

Subject to the provisions of *Article 15(3)*, no reservations to this Treaty shall be permitted.

Article 22
[Application in Time]

(1) Contracting Parties shall apply the provisions of *Article 18 of the Berne Convention, mutatis mutandis*, to the rights of performers and producers of phonograms provided for in this Treaty.

(2) Notwithstanding *paragraph (1)*, a Contracting Party may limit the application of *Article 5* of this Treaty to performances which occurred after the entry into force of this Treaty for that Party.

[16] *Agreed statement concerning Article 19:* The agreed statement concerning Article 12 (on Obligations concerning Rights Management Information) of the WIPO Copyright Treaty is applicable *mutatis mutandis* also to Article 19 (on Obligations concerning Rights Management Information) of the WIPO Performances and Phonograms Treaty. [The text of the agreed statement concerning Article 12 of the WCT reads as follows: 'It is understood that the reference to "infringement of any right covered by this Treaty or the Berne Convention" includes both exclusive rights and rights of remuneration.

'It is further understood that Contracting Parties will not rely on this Article to devise or implement rights management systems that would have the effect of imposing formalities which are not permitted under the Berne Convention or this Treaty, prohibiting the free movement of goods or impeding the enjoyment of rights under this Treaty.']

Article 23
[Provisions on Enforcement of Rights]

(1) Contracting Parties undertake to adopt, in accordance with their legal systems, the measures necessary to ensure the application of this Treaty.

(2) Contracting Parties shall ensure that enforcement procedures are available under their law so as to permit effective action against any act of infringement of rights covered by this Treaty, including expeditious remedies to prevent infringements and remedies which constitute a deterrent to further infringements.

Chapter V—Administrative and Final Clauses

Article 24
[Assembly]

(1) (a) The Contracting Parties shall have an Assembly.

(b) Each Contracting Party shall be represented by one delegate who may be assisted by alternate delegates, advisors and experts.

(c) The expenses of each delegation shall be borne by the Contracting Party that has appointed the delegation. The Assembly may ask WIPO to grant financial assistance to facilitate the participation of delegations of Contracting Parties that are regarded as developing countries in conformity with the established practice of the General Assembly of the United Nations or that are countries in transition to a market economy.

(2) (a) The Assembly shall deal with matters concerning the maintenance and development of this Treaty and the application and operation of this Treaty.

(b) The Assembly shall perform the function allocated to it under *Article 26(2)* in respect of the admission of certain intergovernmental organizations to become party to this Treaty.

(c) The Assembly shall decide the convocation of any diplomatic conference for the revision of this Treaty and give the necessary instructions to the Director General of WIPO for the preparation of such diplomatic conference.

(3) (a) Each Contracting Party that is a State shall have one vote and shall vote only in its own name.

(b) Any Contracting Party that is an intergovernmental organization may participate in the vote, in place of its Member States, with a number of votes equal to the number of its Member States which are party to this Treaty. No such intergovernmental organization shall participate in the vote if any one of its Member States exercises its right to vote and vice versa.

(4) The Assembly shall meet in ordinary session once every two years upon convocation by the Director General of WIPO.

(5) The Assembly shall establish its own rules of procedure, including the convocation of extraordinary sessions, the requirements of a quorum and, subject to the provisions of this Treaty, the required majority for various kinds of decisions.

Article 25
[International Bureau]

The International Bureau of WIPO shall perform the administrative tasks concerning the Treaty.

Article 26
[Eligibility for Becoming Party to the Treaty]

(1) Any Member State of WIPO may become party to this Treaty.

(2) The Assembly may decide to admit any intergovernmental organization to become party to this Treaty which declares that it is competent in respect of, and has its own legislation binding on all its Member States on, matters covered by this Treaty and that it has been duly authorized, in accordance with its internal procedures, to become party to this Treaty.

(3) The European Community, having made the declaration referred to in the preceding paragraph in the Diplomatic Conference that has adopted this Treaty, may become party to this Treaty.

Article 27
[Rights and Obligations under the Treaty]

Subject to any specific provisions to the contrary in this Treaty, each Contracting Party shall enjoy all of the rights and assume all of the obligations under this Treaty.

Article 28
[Signature of the Treaty]

This Treaty shall be open for signature until December 31, 1997, by any Member State of WIPO and by the European Community.

Article 29
[Entry into Force of the Treaty]

This Treaty shall enter into force three months after 30 instruments of ratification or accession by States have been deposited with the Director General of WIPO.

Article 30
[Effective Date of Becoming Party to the Treaty]

This Treaty shall bind:

(i) the 30 States referred to in *Article 29*, from the date on which this Treaty has entered into force;

(ii) each other State from the expiration of three months from the date on which the State has deposited its instrument with the Director General of WIPO;

(iii) the European Community, from the expiration of three months after the deposit of its instrument of ratification or accession if such instrument has been deposited after the entry into force of this Treaty according to *Article 29*, or, three months after the entry into force of this Treaty if such instrument has been deposited before the entry into force of this Treaty;

(iv) any other intergovernmental organization that is admitted to become party to this Treaty, from the expiration of three months after the deposit of its instrument of accession.

Article 31
[Denunciation of the Treaty]

This Treaty may be denounced by any Contracting Party by notification addressed to the Director General of WIPO. Any denunciation shall take effect one year from the date on which the Director General of WIPO received the notification.

Article 32
[Languages of the Treaty]

(1) This Treaty is signed in a single original in English, Arabic, Chinese, French, Russian and Spanish languages, the versions in all these languages being equally authentic.

(2) An official text in any language other than those referred to in *paragraph (1)* shall be established by the Director General of WIPO on the request of an interested party, after consultation with all the interested parties. For the purposes of this paragraph, 'interested party' means any Member State of WIPO whose official language, or one of whose official languages, is involved and the European Community, and any other intergovernmental organization that may become party to this Treaty, if one of its official languages is involved.

Article 33
[Depositary]

The Director General of WIPO is the depositary of this Treaty.

APPENDIX 9

Agreement on Trade-Related Aspects of Intellectual Property Rights ('TRIPs') 1994 (relevant extracts)

Agreement on Trade-Related Aspects of Intellectual Property Rights

Members,

Desiring to reduce distortions and impediments to international trade, and taking into account the need to promote effective and adequate protection of intellectual property rights, and to ensure that measures and procedures to enforce intellectual property rights do not themselves become barriers to legitimate trade;

Recognizing, to this end, the need for new rules and disciplines concerning:

(a) the applicability of the basic principles of GATT 1994 and of relevant international intellectual property agreements or conventions;

(b) the provision of adequate standards and principles concerning the availability, scope and use of trade-related intellectual property rights;

(c) the provision of effective and appropriate means for the enforcement of trade-related intellectual property rights, taking into account differences in national legal systems;

(d) the provision of effective and expeditious

procedures for the multilateral prevention and settlement of disputes between governments; and

(e) transitional arrangements aiming at the fullest participation in the results of the negotiations;

Recognizing the need for a multilateral framework of principles, rules and disciplines dealing with international trade in counterfeit goods;

Recognizing that intellectual property rights are private rights;

Recognizing the underlying public policy objectives of national systems for the protection of intellectual property, including developmental and technological objectives;

Recognizing also the special needs of the least-developed country Members in respect of maximum flexibility in the domestic implementation of laws and regulations in order to enable them to create a sound and viable technological base;

Emphasizing the importance of reducing tensions by reaching strengthened commitments to resolve disputes on trade-related intellectual property issues through multilateral procedures;

Desiring to establish a mutually supportive relationship between the WTO and the World Intellectual Property Organization (referred to in this Agreement as 'WIPO') as well as other relevant international organizations;

Hereby agree as follows:

Part I General Provisions and Basic Principles

Article 1

[Nature and Scope of Obligations]

1. Members shall give effect to the provisions of this Agreement. Members may, but shall not be obliged to, implement in their law more extensive protection than is required by this Agreement, provided that such protection does not contravene the provisions of this Agreement. Members shall be free to determine the appropriate method of implementing the provisions of this Agreement within their own legal system and practice.

2. For the purposes of this Agreement, the term 'intellectual property' refers to all categories of intellectual property that are the subject of Sections 1 through 7 of Part II.

3. Members shall accord the treatment provided for in this Agreement to the nationals of other Members.[1] In respect of the relevant intellectual property right, the nationals of other Members shall be understood as those natural or legal persons that would meet the criteria for eligibility for protection provided for in the Paris Convention (1967), the Berne Convention (1971), the Rome Convention and the Treaty on Intellectual Property in Respect of Integrated Circuits, were all Members of the WTO members of those conventions.[2] Any Member availing itself of the possibilities provided in paragraph 3 of Article 5 or paragraph 2 of Article 6 of the Rome Convention shall make a notification as foreseen in those provisions to the Council for Trade-Related Aspects of Intellectual Property Rights (the 'Council for TRIPS').

---

[1] When 'nationals' are referred to in this Agreement, they shall be deemed, in the case of a separate customs territory Member of the WTO, to mean persons, natural or legal, who are domiciled or who have a real and effective industrial or commercial establishment in that customs territory.

[2] In this Agreement, 'Paris Convention' refers to the Paris Convention for the Protection of Industrial Property; 'Paris Convention (1967)' refers to the Stockholm Act of this Convention of 14 July 1967. 'Berne Convention' refers to the Berne Convention for the Protection of Literary and Artistic Works; 'Berne Convention (1971)' refers to the Paris Act of this Convention of 24 July 1971. 'Rome Convention' refers to the International Convention for the Protection of Performers, Producers of Phonograms and Broadcasting Organizations, adopted at Rome on 26 October 1961. 'Treaty on Intellectual Property in Respect of Integrated Circuits' (IPIC Treaty) refers to the Treaty on Intellectual Property in Respect of Integrated Circuits, adopted at Washington on 26 May 1989. 'WTO Agreement' refers to the Agreement Establishing the WTO.

Article 2
[Intellectual Property Conventions]

1. In respect of Parts II, III and IV of this Agreement, Members shall comply with Articles 1 through 12, and Article 19, of the Paris Convention (1967).

2. Nothing in Parts I to IV of this Agreement shall derogate from existing obligations that Members may have to each other under the Paris Convention, the Berne Convention, the Rome Convention and the Treaty on Intellectual Property in Respect of Integrated Circuits.

Article 3
[National Treatment]

1. Each Member shall accord to the nationals of other Members treatment no less favourable than that it accords to its own nationals with regard to the protection[3] of intellectual property, subject to the exceptions already provided in, respectively, the Paris Convention (1967), the Berne Convention (1971), the Rome Convention or the Treaty on Intellectual Property in Respect of Integrated Circuits. In respect of performers, producers of phonograms and broadcasting organizations, this obligation only applies in respect of the rights provided under this Agreement. Any Member availing itself of the possibilities provided in Article 6 of the Berne Convention (1971) or paragraph 1(b) of Article 16 of the Rome Convention shall make a notification as foreseen in those provisions to the Council for TRIPS.

2. Members may avail themselves of the exceptions permitted under paragraph 1 in relation to judicial and administrative procedures, including the designation of an address for service or the appointment of an agent within the jurisdiction of a Member, only where such exceptions are necessary to secure compliance with laws and regulations which are not inconsistent with the provisions of this Agreement and where such practices are not applied in a manner which would constitute a disguised restriction on trade.

Article 4
[Most-Favoured-Nation Treatment]

With regard to the protection of intellectual property, any advantage, favour, privilege or immunity granted by a Member to the nationals of any other country shall be accorded immediately and unconditionally to the nationals of all other Members. Exempted from this obligation are any advantage, favour, privilege or immunity accorded by a Member:

(a) deriving from international agreements on judicial assistance or law enforcement of a general nature and not particularly confined to the protection of intellectual property;
(b) granted in accordance with the provisions of the Berne Convention (1971) or the Rome Convention authorizing that the treatment accorded be a function not of national treatment but of the treatment accorded in another country;
(c) in respect of the rights of performers, producers of phonograms and broadcasting organizations not provided under this Agreement;
(d) deriving from international agreements related to the protection of intellectual property which entered into force prior to the entry into force of the WTO Agreement, provided that such agreements are notified to the Council for TRIPS and do not constitute an arbitrary or unjustifiable discrimination against nationals of other Members.

Article 5
[Multilateral Agreements on Acquisition or Maintenance of Protection]

The obligations under Articles 3 and 4 do not apply to procedures provided in multilateral agreements concluded under the auspices of WIPO relating to the acquisition or maintenance of intellectual property rights.

[3] For the purposes of Articles 3 and 4, 'protection' shall include matters affecting the availability, acquisition, scope, maintenance and enforcement of intellectual property rights as well as those matters affecting the use of intellectual property rights specifically addressed in this Agreement.

Article 6
[Exhaustion]

For the purposes of dispute settlement under this Agreement, subject to the provisions of Articles 3 and 4 nothing in this Agreement shall be used to address the issue of the exhaustion of intellectual property rights.

Article 7
[Objectives]

The protection and enforcement of intellectual property rights should contribute to the promotion of technological innovation and to the transfer and dissemination of technology, to the mutual advantage of producers and users of technological knowledge and in a manner conducive to social and economic welfare, and to a balance of rights and obligations.

Article 8
[Principles]

1. Members may, in formulating or amending their laws and regulations, adopt measures necessary to protect public health and nutrition, and to promote the public interest in sectors of vital importance to their socio-economic and technological development, provided that such measures are consistent with the provisions of this Agreement.

2. Appropriate measures, provided that they are consistent with the provisions of this Agreement, may be needed to prevent the abuse of intellectual property rights by right holders or the resort to practices which unreasonably restrain trade or adversely affect the international transfer of technology.

Part II Standards concerning the Availability, Scope and Use of Intellectual Property Rights

Section 1: Copyright and related rights

Article 9
[Relation to the Berne Convention]

1. Members shall comply with Articles 1 through 21 of the Berne Convention (1971) and the Appendix thereto. However, Members shall not have rights or obligations under this Agreement in respect of the rights conferred under Article 6*bis* of that Convention or of the rights derived therefrom.

2. Copyright protection shall extend to expressions and not to ideas, procedures, methods of operation or mathematical concepts as such.

Article 10
[Computer Programs and Compilations of Data]

1. Computer programs, whether in source or object code, shall be protected as literary works under the Berne Convention (1971).

2. Compilations of data or other material, whether in machine readable or other form, which by reason of the selection or arrangement of their contents constitute intellectual creations shall be protected as such. Such protection, which shall not extend to the data or material itself, shall be without prejudice to any copyright subsisting in the data or material itself.

Article 11
[Rental Rights]

In respect of at least computer programs and cinematographic works, a Member shall provide authors and their successors in title the right to authorize or to prohibit the commercial rental to the public of originals or copies of their copyright works. A Member shall be excepted from this obligation in respect of cinematographic works unless such rental has led to widespread copying of such works which is materially impairing the exclusive right of reproduction conferred in that Member on authors and their successors in title. In respect of computer programs, this obligation does not apply to rentals where the program itself is not the essential object of the rental.

Article 12
[Term of Protection]

Whenever the term of protection of a work, other than a photographic work or a work of applied art, is calculated on a basis other than the life of a natural person, such term shall be no less than 50 years from the end of the calendar year of authorized publication, or, failing such authorized publication within 50 years from the making of the work, 50 years from the end of the calendar year of making.

Article 13

[Limitations and Exceptions]

Members shall confine limitations or exceptions to exclusive rights to certain special cases which do not conflict with a normal exploitation of the work and do not unreasonably prejudice the legitimate interests of the right holder.

Article 14

[Protection of Performers, Producers of Phonograms (Sound Recordings) and Broadcasting Organizations]

1. In respect of a fixation of their performance on a phonogram, performers shall have the possibility of preventing the following acts when undertaken without their authorization: the fixation of their unfixed performance and the reproduction of such fixation. Performers shall also have the possibility of preventing the following acts when undertaken without their authorization: the broadcasting by wireless means and the communication to the public of their live performance.

2. Producers of phonograms shall enjoy the right to authorize or prohibit the direct or indirect reproduction of their phonograms.

3. Broadcasting organizations shall have the right to prohibit the following acts when undertaken without their authorization: the fixation, the reproduction of fixations, and the rebroadcasting by wireless means of broadcasts, as well as the communication to the public of television broadcasts of the same. Where Members do not grant such rights to broadcasting organizations, they shall provide owners of copyright in the subject matter of broadcasts with the possibility of preventing the above acts, subject to the provisions of the Berne Convention (1971).

4. The provisions of Article 11 in respect of computer programs shall apply *mutatis mutandis* to producers of phonograms and any other right holders in phonograms as determined in a Member's law. If on 15 April 1994 a Member has in force a system of equitable remuneration of right holders in respect of the rental of phonograms, it may maintain such system provided that the commercial rental of phonograms is not giving rise to the material impairment of the exclusive rights of reproduction of right holders.

5. The term of the protection available under this Agreement to performers and producers of phonograms shall last at least until the end of a period of 50 years computed from the end of the calendar year in which the fixation was made or the performance took place. The term of protection granted pursuant to paragraph 3 shall last for at least 20 years from the end of the calendar year in which the broadcast took place.

6. Any Member may, in relation to the rights conferred under paragraphs 1, 2 and 3, provide for conditions, limitations, exceptions and reservations to the extent permitted by the Rome Convention. However, the provisions of Article 18 of the Berne Convention (1971) shall also apply, *mutatis mutandis*, to the rights of performers and producers of phonograms in phonograms.

. . . .

Part III Enforcement of Intellectual Property Rights

Section 1: General obligations

Article 41

1. Members shall ensure that enforcement procedures as specified in this Part are available under their law so as to permit effective action against any act of infringement of intellectual property rights covered by this Agreement, including expeditious remedies to prevent infringements and remedies which constitute a deterrent to further infringements. These procedures shall be applied in such a manner as to

avoid the creation of barriers to legitimate trade and to provide for safeguards against their abuse.

2. Procedures concerning the enforcement of intellectual property rights shall be fair and equitable. They shall not be unnecessarily complicated or costly, or entail unreasonable time-limits or unwarranted delays.

3. Decisions on the merits of a case shall preferably be in writing and reasoned. They shall be made available at least to the parties to the proceeding without undue delay. Decisions on the merits of a case shall be based only on evidence in respect of which parties were offered the opportunity to be heard.

4. Parties to a proceeding shall have an opportunity for review by a judicial authority of final administrative decisions and, subject to jurisdictional provisions in a Member's law concerning the importance of a case, of at least the legal aspects of initial judicial decisions on the merits of a case. However, there shall be no obligation to provide an opportunity for review of acquittals in criminal cases.

5. It is understood that this Part does not create any obligation to put in place a judicial system for the enforcement of intellectual property rights distinct from that for the enforcement of law in general, nor does it affect the capacity of Members to enforce their law in general. Nothing in this Part creates any obligation with respect to the distribution of resources as between enforcement of intellectual property rights and the enforcement of law in general.

Section 2: Civil and administrative procedures and remedies

Article 42
[Fair and Equitable Procedures]

Members shall make available to right holders[4] civil judicial procedures concerning the enforcement of any intellectual property right covered by this Agreement. Defendants shall have the right to written notice which is timely and contains sufficient detail, including the basis of the claims. Parties shall be allowed to be represented by independent legal counsel, and procedures shall not impose overly burdensome requirements concerning mandatory personal appearances. All parties to such procedures shall be duly entitled to substantiate their claims and to present all relevant evidence. The procedure shall provide a means to identify and protect confidential information, unless this would be contrary to existing constitutional requirements.

Article 43
[Evidence]

1. The judicial authorities shall have the authority, where a party has presented reasonably available evidence sufficient to support its claims and has specified evidence relevant to substantiation of its claims which lies in the control of the opposing party, to order that this evidence be produced by the opposing party, subject in appropriate cases to conditions which ensure the protection of confidential information.

2. In cases in which a party to a proceeding voluntarily and without good reason refuses access to, or otherwise does not provide necessary information within a reasonable period, or significantly impedes a procedure relating to an enforcement action, a Member may accord judicial authorities the authority to make preliminary and final determinations, affirmative or negative, on the basis of the information presented to them, including the complaint or the allegation presented by the party adversely affected by the denial of access to information, subject to providing the parties an opportunity to be heard on the allegations or evidence.

Article 44
[Injunctions]

1. The judicial authorities shall have the authority to order a party to desist from an infringement, *inter alia* to prevent the entry

[4] For the purpose of this Part, the term 'right holder' includes federations and associations having legal standing to assert such rights.

into the channels of commerce in their jurisdiction of imported goods that involve the infringement of an intellectual property right, immediately after customs clearance of such goods. Members are not obliged to accord such authority in respect of protected subject matter acquired or ordered by a person prior to knowing or having reasonable grounds to know that dealing in such subject matter would entail the infringement of an intellectual property right.

2. Notwithstanding the other provisions of this Part and provided that the provisions of Part II specifically addressing use by governments, or by third parties authorized by a government, without the authorization of the right holder are complied with, Members may limit the remedies available against such use to payment of remuneration in accordance with subparagraph (h) of Article 31. In other cases, the remedies under this Part shall apply or, where these remedies are inconsistent with a Member's law, declaratory judgments and adequate compensation shall be available.

Article 45
[Damages]

1. The judicial authorities shall have the authority to order the infringer to pay the right holder damages adequate to compensate for the injury the right holder has suffered because of an infringement of that person's intellectual property right by an infringer who knowingly, or with reasonable grounds to know, engaged in infringing activity.

2. The judicial authorities shall also have the authority to order the infringer to pay the right holder expenses, which may include appropriate attorney's fees. In appropriate cases, Members may authorize the judicial authorities to order recovery of profits and/or payment of pre-established damages even where the infringer did not knowingly, or with reasonable grounds to know, engage in infringing activity.

Article 46
[Other Remedies]

In order to create an effective deterrent to infringement, the judicial authorities shall have the authority to order that goods that they have found to be infringing be, without compensation of any sort, disposed of outside the channels of commerce in such a manner as to avoid any harm caused to the right holder, or, unless this would be contrary to existing constitutional requirements, destroyed. The judicial authorities shall also have the authority to order that materials and implements the predominant use of which has been in the creation of the infringing goods be, without compensation of any sort, disposed of outside the channels of commerce in such a manner as to minimize the risks of further infringements. In considering such requests, the need for proportionality between the seriousness of the infringement and the remedies ordered as well as the interests of third parties shall be taken into account. In regard to counterfeit trademark goods, the simple removal of the trademark unlawfully affixed shall not be sufficient, other than in exceptional cases, to permit release of the goods into the channels of commerce.

Article 47
[Right of Information]

Members may provide that the judicial authorities shall have the authority, unless this would be out of proportion to the seriousness of the infringement, to order the infringer to inform the right holder of the identity of third persons involved in the production and distribution of the infringing goods or services and of their channels of distribution.

Article 48
[Indemnification of the Defendant]

1. The judicial authorities shall have the authority to order a party at whose request measures were taken and who has abused enforcement procedures to provide to a party wrongfully enjoined or restrained adequate compensation for the injury suffered because of such abuse. The judicial authorities shall

also have the authority to order the applicant to pay the defendant expenses, which may include appropriate attorney's fees.

2. In respect of the administration of any law pertaining to the protection or enforcement of intellectual property rights, Members shall only exempt both public authorities and officials from liability to appropriate remedial measures where actions are taken or intended in good faith in the course of the administration of that law.

Article 49

[Administrative Procedures]

To the extent that any civil remedy can be ordered as a result of administrative procedures on the merits of a case, such procedures shall conform to principles equivalent in substance to those set forth in this Section.

Section 3: Provisional measures

Article 50

1. The judicial authorities shall have the authority to order prompt and effective provisional measures:

(a) to prevent an infringement of any intellectual property right from occurring, and in particular to prevent the entry into the channels of commerce in their jurisdiction of goods, including imported goods immediately after customs clearance;

(b) to preserve relevant evidence in regard to the alleged infringement.

2. The judicial authorities shall have the authority to adopt provisional measures *inaudita altera parte* where appropriate, in particular where any delay is likely to cause irreparable harm to the right holder, or where there is a demonstrable risk of evidence being destroyed.

3. The judicial authorities shall have the authority to require the applicant to provide any reasonably available evidence in order to satisfy themselves with a sufficient degree of certainty that the applicant is the right holder and that the applicant's right is being infringed or that such infringement is imminent, and to order the applicant to provide a security or equivalent assurance sufficient to protect the defendant and to prevent abuse.

4. Where provisional measures have been adopted *inaudita altera parte*, the parties affected shall be given notice, without delay after the execution of the measures at the latest. A review, including a right to be heard, shall take place upon request of the defendant with a view to deciding, within a reasonable period after the notification of the measures, whether these measures shall be modified, revoked or confirmed.

5. The applicant may be required to supply other information necessary for the identification of the goods concerned by the authority that will execute the provisional measures.

6. Without prejudice to paragraph 4, provisional measures taken on the basis of paragraphs 1 and 2 shall, upon request by the defendant, be revoked or otherwise cease to have effect, if proceedings leading to a decision on the merits of the case are not initiated within a reasonable period, to be determined by the judicial authority ordering the measures where a Member's law so permits or, in the absence of such a determination, not to exceed 20 working days or 31 calendar days, whichever is the longer.

7. Where the provisional measures are revoked or where they lapse due to any act or omission by the applicant, or where it is subsequently found that there has been no infringement or threat of infringement of an intellectual property right, the judicial authorities shall have the authority to order the applicant, upon request of the defendant, to provide the defendant appropriate compensation for any injury caused by these measures.

8. To the extent that any provisional measure can be ordered as a result of administrative procedures, such procedures shall conform to principles equivalent in substance to those set forth in this Section.

Section 4: Special requirements related to border measures[5]

Article 51
[Suspension of Release by Customs Authorities]

Members shall, in conformity with the provisions set out below, adopt procedures[6] to enable a right holder, who has valid grounds for suspecting that the importation of counterfeit trademark or pirated copyright goods[7] may take place, to lodge an application in writing with competent authorities, administrative or judicial, for the suspension by the customs authorities of the release into free circulation of such goods. Members may enable such an application to be made in respect of goods which involve other infringements of intellectual property rights, provided that the requirements of this Section are met. Members may also provide for corresponding procedures concerning the suspension by the customs authorities of the release of infringing goods destined for exportation from their territories.

Article 52
[Application]

Any right holder initiating the procedures under Article 51 shall be required to provide adequate evidence to satisfy the competent authorities that, under the laws of the country of importation, there is *prima facie* an infringement of the right holder's intellectual property right and to supply a sufficiently detailed description of the goods to make them readily recognizable by the customs authorities. The competent authorities shall inform the applicant within a reasonable period whether they have accepted the application and, where determined by the competent authorities, the period for which the customs authorities will take action.

Article 53
[Security or Equivalent Assurance]

1. The competent authorities shall have the authority to require an applicant to provide a security or equivalent assurance sufficient to protect the defendant and the competent authorities and to prevent abuse. Such security or equivalent assurance shall not unreasonably deter recourse to these procedures.

2. Where pursuant to an application under this Section the release of goods involving industrial designs, patents, layout-designs or undisclosed information into free circulation has been suspended by customs authorities on the basis of a decision other than by a judicial or other independent authority, and the period provided for in Article 55 has expired without the granting of provisional relief by the duly empowered authority, and provided that all other conditions for importation have been complied with, the owner, importer, or consignee of such goods shall be entitled to their release on the posting of a security in an amount sufficient to protect the right holder for any infringement. Payment of such security shall not prejudice any other remedy available to the right holder, it being understood that

[5] Where a Member has dismantled substantially all controls over movement of goods across its border with another Member with which it forms part of a customs union, it shall not be required to apply the provisions of this Section at that border.

[6] It is understood that there shall be no obligation to apply such procedures to imports of goods put on the market in another country by or with the consent of the right holder, or to goods in transit.

[7] For the purposes of this Agreement: (a) 'counterfeit trademark goods' shall mean any goods, including packaging, bearing without authorization a trademark which is identical to the trademark validly registered in respect of such goods, or which cannot be distinguished in its essential aspects from such a trademark, and which thereby infringes the rights of the owner of the trademark in question under the law of the country of importation; (b) 'pirated copyright goods' shall mean any goods which are copies made without the consent of the right holder or person duly authorized by the right holder in the country of production and which are made directly or indirectly from an article where the making of that copy would have constituted an infringement of a copyright or a related right under the law of the country of importation.

the security shall be released if the right holder fails to pursue the right of action within a reasonable period of time.

Article 54
[Notice of Suspension]

The importer and the applicant shall be promptly notified of the suspension of the release of goods according to Article 51.

Article 55
[Duration of Suspension

If, within a period not exceeding 10 working days after the applicant has been served notice of the suspension, the customs authorities have not been informed that proceedings leading to a decision on the merits of the case have been initiated by a party other than the defendant, or that the duly empowered authority has taken provisional measures prolonging the suspension of the release of the goods, the goods shall be released, provided that all other conditions for importation or exportation have been complied with; in appropriate cases, this time-limit may be extended by another 10 working days. If proceedings leading to a decision on the merits of the case have been initiated, a review, including a right to be heard, shall take place upon request of the defendant with a view to deciding, within a reasonable period, whether these measures shall be modified, revoked or confirmed. Notwithstanding the above, where the suspension of the release of goods is carried out or continued in accordance with a provisional judicial measure, the provisions of paragraph 6 of Article 50 shall apply.

Article 56
[Indemnification of the Importer and of the Owner of the Goods]

Relevant authorities shall have the authority to order the applicant to pay the importer, the consignee and the owner of the goods appropriate compensation for any injury caused to them through the wrongful detention of goods or through the detention of goods released pursuant to Article 55.

Article 57
[Right of Inspection and Information]

Without prejudice to the protection of confidential information, Members shall provide the competent authorities the authority to give the right holder sufficient opportunity to have any goods detained by the customs authorities inspected in order to substantiate the right holder's claims. The competent authorities shall also have authority to give the importer an equivalent opportunity to have any such goods inspected. Where a positive determination has been made on the merits of a case, Members may provide the competent authorities the authority to inform the right holder of the names and addresses of the consignor, the importer and the consignee and of the quantity of the goods in question.

Article 58
[Ex Officio Action]

Where Members require competent authorities to act upon their own initiative and to suspend the release of goods in respect of which they have acquired *prima facie* evidence that an intellectual property right is being infringed:

(a) the competent authorities may at any time seek from the right holder any information that may assist them to exercise these powers;
(b) the importer and the right holder shall be promptly notified of the suspension. Where the importer has lodged an appeal against the suspension with the competent authorities, the suspension shall be subject to the conditions, *mutatis mutandis*, set out at Article 55;
(c) Members shall only exempt both public authorities and officials from liability to appropriate remedial measures where actions are taken or intended in good faith.

Article 59
[Remedies]

Without prejudice to other rights of action open to the right holder and subject to the right of the defendant to seek review by a judicial authority, competent authorities shall have the authority to order the destruction or disposal of infringing goods in accordance with the principles set out in Article 46. In regard to counterfeit trademark goods, the authorities shall not allow the re-exportation of the infringing goods in an unaltered state or subject them to a different customs procedure, other than in exceptional circumstances.

Article 60

[De Minimis Imports]

Members may exclude from the application of the above provisions small quantities of goods of a non-commercial nature contained in travellers' personal luggage or sent in small consignments.

Section 5: Criminal procedures

Article 61

Members shall provide for criminal procedures and penalties to be applied at least in cases of wilful trademark counterfeiting or copyright piracy on a commercial scale. Remedies available shall include imprisonment and/or monetary fines sufficient to provide a deterrent, consistently with the level of penalties applied for crimes of a corresponding gravity. In appropriate cases, remedies available shall also include the seizure, forfeiture and destruction of the infringing goods and of any materials and implements the predominant use of which has been in the commission of the offence. Members may provide for criminal procedures and penalties to be applied in other cases of infringement of intellectual property rights, in particular where they are committed wilfully and on a commercial scale.

. . . .

Part V Dispute Prevention and Settlement

Article 63

[Transparency]

1. Laws and regulations, and final judicial decisions and administrative rulings of general application, made effective by a Member pertaining to the subject matter of this Agreement (the availability, scope, acquisition, enforcement and prevention of the abuse of intellectual property rights) shall be published, or where such publication is not practicable made publicly available, in a national language, in such a manner as to enable governments and right holders to become acquainted with them. Agreements concerning the subject matter of this Agreement which are in force between the government or a governmental agency of a Member and the government or a governmental agency of another Member shall also be published.

2. Members shall notify the laws and regulations referred to in paragraph 1 to the Council for TRIPS in order to assist that Council in its review of the operation of this Agreement. The Council shall attempt to minimize the burden on Members in carrying out this obligation and may decide to waive the obligation to notify such laws and regulations directly to the Council if consultations with WIPO on the establishment of a common register containing these laws and regulations are successful. The Council shall also consider in this connection any action required regarding notifications pursuant to the obligations under this Agreement stemming from the provisions of Article 6*ter* of the Paris Convention (1967).

3. Each Member shall be prepared to supply, in response to a written request from another Member, information of the sort referred to in paragraph 1. A Member, having reason to believe that a specific judicial decision or administrative ruling or bilateral agreement in the area of intellectual property rights affects its rights under this Agreement, may also request in writing to be given access to or be informed in sufficient detail of such specific judicial decisions or administrative rulings or bilateral agreements.

4. Nothing in paragraphs 1, 2 and 3 shall require Members to disclose confidential information which would impede law enforcement or otherwise be contrary to the public interest or would prejudice the legitimate commercial interests of particular enterprises, public or private.

Article 64
[Dispute Settlement]

1. The provisions of Articles XXII and XXIII of GATT 1994 as elaborated and applied by the Dispute Settlement Understanding shall apply to consultations and the settlement of disputes under this Agreement except as otherwise specifically provided herein.

2. Subparagraphs 1(b) and 1(c) of Article XXIII of GATT 1994 shall not apply to the settlement of disputes under this Agreement for a period of five years from the date of entry into force of the WTO Agreement.

3. During the time period referred to in paragraph 2, the Council for TRIPS shall examine the scope and modalities for complaints of the type provided for under subparagraphs 1(b) and 1(c) of Article XXIII of GATT 1994 made pursuant to this Agreement, and submit its recommendations to the Ministerial Conference for approval. Any decision of the Ministerial Conference to approve such recommendations or to extend the period in paragraph 2 shall be made only by consensus, and approved recommendations shall be effective for all Members without further formal acceptance process.

Part VI Transitional Arrangements

Article 65
[Transitional Arrangements]

1. Subject to the provisions of paragraphs 2, 3 and 4, no Member shall be obliged to apply the provisions of this Agreement before the expiry of a general period of one year following the date of entry into force of the WTO Agreement.

2. A developing country Member is entitled to delay for a further period of four years the date of application, as defined in paragraph 1, of the provisions of this Agreement other than Articles 3, 4 and 5.

3. Any other Member which is in the process of transformation from a centrally-planned into a market, free-enterprise economy and which is undertaking structural reform of its intellectual property system and facing special problems in the preparation and implementation of intellectual property laws and regulations, may also benefit from a period of delay as foreseen in paragraph 2.

4. To the extent that a developing country Member is obliged by this Agreement to extend product patent protection to areas of technology not so protectable in its territory on the general date of application of this Agreement for that Member, as defined in paragraph 2, it may delay the application of the provisions on product patents of Section 5 of Part II to such areas of technology for an additional period of five years.

5. A Member availing itself of a transitional period under paragraphs 1, 2, 3 or 4 shall ensure that any changes in its laws, regulations and practice made during that period do not result in a lesser degree of consistency with the provisions of this Agreement.

Article 66
[Least-Developed Country Members]

1. In view of the special needs and requirements of least-developed country Members, their economic, financial and administrative constraints, and their need for flexibility to create a viable technological base, such Members shall not be required to apply the provisions of this Agreement, other than Articles 3, 4 and 5, for a period of 10 years from the date of application as defined under paragraph 1 of Article 65. The Council for TRIPS shall, upon duly motivated request by a least-developed country Member, accord extensions of this period.

2. Developed country Members shall provide incentives to enterprises and institutions in their territories for the purpose of promoting and encouraging technology transfer to least-developed country Members in order to enable them to create a sound and viable technological base.

Article 67
[Technical Cooperation]

In order to facilitate the implementation of this Agreement, developed country Members shall provide, on request and on mutually agreed terms and conditions, technical and financial cooperation in favour of developing and least-developed country Members. Such cooperation shall include assistance in the preparation of laws and regulations on the protection and enforcement of intellectual property rights as well as on the prevention of their abuse, and shall include support regarding the establishment or reinforcement of domestic offices and agencies relevant to these matters, including the training of personnel.

Part VII Institutional Arrangements; Final Provisions

Article 68

[Council for Trade-Related Aspects of Intellectual Property Rights]

The Council for TRIPS shall monitor the operation of this Agreement and, in particular, Members' compliance with their obligations hereunder, and shall afford Members the opportunity of consulting on matters relating to the trade-related aspects of intellectual property rights. It shall carry out such other responsibilities as assigned to it by the Members, and it shall, in particular, provide any assistance requested by them in the context of dispute settlement procedures. In carrying out its functions, the Council for TRIPS may consult with and seek information from any source it deems appropriate. In consultation with WIPO, the Council shall seek to establish, within one year of its first meeting, appropriate arrangements for cooperation with bodies of that Organization.

Article 69

[International Cooperation]

Members agree to cooperate with each other with a view to eliminating international trade in goods infringing intellectual property rights. For this purpose, they shall establish and notify contact points in their administrations and be ready to exchange information on trade in infringing goods. They shall, in particular, promote the exchange of information and cooperation between customs authorities with regard to trade in counterfeit trademark goods and pirated copyright goods.

Article 70

[Protection of Existing Subject Matter]

1. This Agreement does not give rise to obligations in respect of acts which occurred before the date of application of the Agreement for the Member in question.

2. Except as otherwise provided for in this Agreement, this Agreement gives rise to obligations in respect of all subject matter existing at the date of application of this Agreement for the Member in question, and which is protected in that Member on the said date, or which meets or comes subsequently to meet the criteria for protection under the terms of this Agreement. In respect of this paragraph and paragraphs 3 and 4, copyright obligations with respect to existing works shall be solely determined under Article 18 of the Berne Convention (1971), and obligations with respect to the rights of producers of phonograms and performers in existing phonograms shall be determined solely under Article 18 of the Berne Convention (1971) as made applicable under paragraph 6 of Article 14 of this Agreement.

3. There shall be no obligation to restore protection to subject matter which on the date of application of this Agreement for the Member in question has fallen into the public domain.

4. In respect of any acts in respect of specific objects embodying protected subject matter which become infringing under the terms of legislation in conformity with this Agreement, and which were commenced, or in respect of which a significant investment was made, before the date of acceptance of the WTO Agreement by that Member, any Member may provide for a limitation of the remedies available to the right holder as to the continued performance of such acts after the date of application of this Agreement for that Member. In such cases the Member shall, however, at least provide for the payment of equitable remuneration.

5. A Member is not obliged to apply the provisions of Article 11 and of paragraph 4 of Article 14 with respect to originals or copies purchased prior to the date of application of this Agreement for that Member.

6. . . .

. . . .

Article 71
[Review and Amendment]

1. The Council for TRIPS shall review the implementation of this Agreement after the expiration of the transitional period referred to in paragraph 2 of Article 65. The Council shall, having regard to the experience gained in its implementation, review it two years after that date, and at identical intervals thereafter. The Council may also undertake reviews in the light of any relevant new developments which might warrant modification or amendment of this Agreement.

2. Amendments merely serving the purpose of adjusting to higher levels of protection of intellectual property rights achieved, and in force, in other multilateral agreements and accepted under those agreements by all Members of the WTO may be referred to the Ministerial Conference for action in accordance with paragraph 6 of Article X of the WTO Agreement on the basis of a consensus proposal from the Council for TRIPS.

Article 72
[Reservations]

Reservations may not be entered in respect of any of the provisions of this Agreement without the consent of the other Members.

Article 73
[Security Exceptions]

Nothing in this Agreement shall be construed:

(a) to require a Member to furnish any information the disclosure of which it considers contrary to its essential security interests; or

(b) to prevent a Member from taking any action which it considers necessary for the protection of its essential security interests;

   (i) relating to fissionable materials or the materials from which they are derived;

   (ii) relating to the traffic in arms, ammunition and implements of war and to such traffic in other goods and materials as is carried on directly or indirectly for the purpose of supplying a military establishment;

   (iii) taken in time of war or other emergency in international relations; or

(c) to prevent a Member from taking any action in pursuance of its obligations under the United Nations Charter for the maintenance of international peace and security.

APPENDIX 10

Understanding on Rules and Procedures Governing the Settlement of Disputes (Annexe 2 to the WTO Agreement)

Members hereby *agree* as follows:

Article 1
[Coverage and Application]

1. The rules and procedures of this Understanding shall apply to disputes brought pursuant to the consultation and dispute settlement provisions of the agreements listed in Appendix 1 to this Understanding (referred to in this Understanding as the 'covered agreements'). The rules and procedures of this Understanding shall also apply to consultations and the settlement of disputes between Members concerning their rights and obligations under the provisions of the Agreement Establishing the World Trade Organization (referred to in this Understanding as the 'WTO Agreement') and of this Understanding taken in isolation or in combination with any other covered agreement.

2. The rules and procedures of this Understanding shall apply subject to such special or additional rules and procedures on dispute settlement contained in the covered agreements as are identified in Appendix 2 to this Understanding. To the extent that there is a difference between the rules and procedures of this Understanding and the special or additional rules and procedures set forth in Appendix 2, the special or additional rules and procedures in Appendix 2 shall prevail. In disputes involving rules and procedures under more than one covered agreement, if there is a conflict between special or additional rules and procedures of such agreements under review, and where the parties to the dispute cannot agree on rules and procedures within 20 days of the establishment of the panel, the Chairman of the Dispute Settlement Body provided for in paragraph 1 of Article 2 (referred to in this Understanding as the 'DSB'), in consultation with the parties to the dispute, shall determine the rules and procedures to be followed within 10 days after a request by either Member. The Chairman shall be guided by the principle that special or additional rules and procedures should be used where possible, and the rules and procedures set out in this Understanding should be used to the extent necessary to avoid conflict.

Article 2
[Administration]

1. The Dispute Settlement Body is hereby established to administer these rules and procedures and, except as otherwise provided in a covered agreement, the consultation and dispute settlement provisions of the covered agreements. Accordingly, the DSB shall have the authority to establish panels, adopt panel and Appellate Body reports, maintain surveillance of implementation of rulings and recommendations, and authorize suspension of concessions and other obligations under the covered agreements. With respect to disputes arising under a covered agreement which is a Plurilateral Trade Agreement, the term 'Member' as used herein shall refer only to those Members that are parties to the relevant Plurilateral Trade Agreement. Where the DSB administers the dispute settlement provisions of a Plurilateral Trade Agreement, only those Members that are parties to that Agreement may participate in decisions or actions taken by the DSB with respect to that dispute.

2. The DSB shall inform the relevant WTO Councils and Committees of any developments in disputes related to provisions of the respective covered agreements.

3. The DSB shall meet as often as necessary to carry out its functions within the time-frames provided in this Understanding.

4. Where the rules and procedures of this Understanding provide for the DSB to take a decision, it shall do so by consensus.[1]

Article 3
[General Provisions]

1. Members affirm their adherence to the principles for the management of disputes heretofore applied under Articles XXII and XXIII of GATT 1947, and the rules and procedures as further elaborated and modified herein.

2. The dispute settlement system of the WTO is a central element in providing security and predictability to the multilateral trading system. The Members recognize that it serves to preserve the rights and obligations of Members under the covered agreements, and to clarify the existing provisions of those agreements in accordance with customary rules of interpretation of public international law. Recommendations and rulings of the DSB cannot add to or diminish the rights and obligations provided in the covered agreements.

3. The prompt settlement of situations in which a Member considers that any benefits accruing to it directly or indirectly under the covered agreements are being impaired by measures taken by another Member is essential to the effective functioning of the WTO and the maintenance of a proper balance between the rights and obligations of Members.

4. Recommendations or rulings made by the DSB shall be aimed at achieving a satisfactory settlement of the matter in accordance with the rights and obligations under this Understanding and under the covered agreements.

5. All solutions to matters formally raised under the consultation and dispute settlement provisions of the covered agreements, including arbitration awards, shall be consistent with those agreements and shall not nullify or impair benefits accruing to any Member under those agreements, nor impede the attainment of any objective of those agreements.

6. Mutually agreed solutions to matters formally raised under the consultation and dispute settlement provisions of the covered agreements shall be notified to the DSB and the relevant Councils and Committees, where any Member may raise any point relating thereto.

7. Before bringing a case, a Member shall exercise its judgement as to whether action under these procedures would be fruitful. The aim of the dispute settlement mechanism is to secure a positive solution to a dispute. A solution mutually acceptable to the parties to a dispute and consistent with the covered agreements is clearly to be preferred. In the absence of a mutually agreed solution, the first objective of the dispute settlement mechanism is usually to secure the withdrawal of the measures concerned if these are found to be inconsistent with the provisions of any of the covered agreements. The provision of compensation should be resorted to only if the immediate withdrawal of the measure is impracticable and as a temporary measure pending the withdrawal of the measure which is inconsistent with a covered agreement. The last resort which this Understanding provides to the Member invoking the dispute settlement procedures is the possibility of suspending the application of concessions or other obligations under the covered agreements on a discriminatory basis vis-à-vis the other Member, subject to authorization by the DSB of such measures.

8. In cases where there is an infringement of the obligations assumed under a covered agreement, the action is considered *prima facie* to constitute a case of nullification or impairment. This means that there is normally a presumption that a breach of the rules has an adverse impact on other Members parties to

[1] The DSB shall be deemed to have decided by consensus on a matter submitted for its consideration, if no Member, present at the meeting of the DSB when the decision is taken, formally objects to the proposed decision.

that covered agreement, and in such cases, it shall be up to the Member against whom the complaint has been brought to rebut the charge.

9. The provisions of this Understanding are without prejudice to the rights of Members to seek authoritative interpretation of provisions of a covered agreement through decision-making under the WTO Agreement or a covered agreement which is a Plurilateral Trade Agreement.

10. It is understood that requests for conciliation and the use of the dispute settlement procedures should not be intended or considered as contentious acts and that, if a dispute arises, all Members will engage in these procedures in good faith in an effort to resolve the dispute. It is also understood that complaints and counter-complaints in regard to distinct matters should not be linked.

11. This Understanding shall be applied only with respect to new requests for consultations under the consultation provisions of the covered agreements made on or after the date of entry into force of the WTO Agreement. With respect to disputes for which the request for consultations was made under GATT 1947 or under any other predecessor agreement to the covered agreements before the date of entry into force of the WTO Agreement, the relevant dispute settlement rules and procedures in effect immediately prior to the date of entry into force of the WTO Agreement shall continue to apply.[2]

12. Notwithstanding paragraph 11, if a complaint based on any of the covered agreements is brought by a developing country Member against a developed country Member, the complaining party shall have the right to invoke, as an alternative to the provisions contained in Articles 4, 5, 6 and 12 of this Understanding, the corresponding provisions of the Decision of 5 April 1966 (BISD 14S/18), except that where the Panel considers that the time-frame provided for in paragraph 7 of that Decision is insufficient to provide its report and with the agreement of the complaining party, that time-frame may be extended. To the extent that there is a difference between the rules and procedures of Articles 4, 5, 6 and 12 and the corresponding rules and procedures of the Decision, the latter shall prevail.

Article 4
[Consultations]

1. Members affirm their resolve to strengthen and improve the effectiveness of the consultation procedures employed by Members.

2. Each Member undertakes to accord sympathetic consideration to and afford adequate opportunity for consultation regarding any representations made by another Member concerning measures affecting the operation of any covered agreement taken within the territory of the former.[3]

3. If a request for consultations is made pursuant to a covered agreement, the Member to which the request is made shall, unless otherwise mutually agreed, reply to the request within 10 days after the date of its receipt and shall enter into consultations in good faith within a period of no more than 30 days after the date of receipt of the request, with a view to reaching a mutually satisfactory solution. If the Member does not respond within 10 days after the date of receipt of the request, or does not enter into consultations within a period of no more than 30 days, or a period otherwise mutually agreed, after the date of receipt of the request, then the Member that requested the holding of consultations may proceed directly to request the establishment of a panel.

4. All such requests for consultations shall be notified to the DSB and the relevant Councils

[2] This paragraph shall also be applied to disputes on which panel reports have not been adopted or fully implemented.

[3] Where the provisions of any other covered agreement concerning measures taken by regional or local governments or authorities within the territory of a Member contain provisions different from the provisions of this paragraph, the provisions of such other covered agreement shall prevail.

and Committees by the Member which requests consultations. Any request for consultations shall be submitted in writing and shall give the reasons for the request, including identification of the measures at issue and an indication of the legal basis for the complaint.

5. In the course of consultations in accordance with the provisions of a covered agreement, before resorting to further action under this Understanding, Members should attempt to obtain satisfactory adjustment of the matter.

6. Consultations shall be confidential, and without prejudice to the rights of any Member in any further proceedings.

7. If the consultations fail to settle a dispute within 60 days after the date of receipt of the request for consultations, the complaining party may request the establishment of a panel. The complaining party may request a panel during the 60-day period if the consulting parties jointly consider that consultations have failed to settle the dispute.

8. In cases of urgency, including those which concern perishable goods, Members shall enter into consultations within a period of no more than 10 days after the date of receipt of the request. If the consultations have failed to settle the dispute within a period of 20 days after the date of receipt of the request, the complaining party may request the establishment of a panel.

9. In cases of urgency, including those which concern perishable goods, the parties to the dispute, panels and the Appellate Body shall make every effort to accelerate the proceedings to the greatest extent possible.

10. During consultations Members should give special attention to the particular problems and interests of developing country Members.

11. Whenever a Member other than the consulting Members considers that it has a substantial trade interest in consultations being held pursuant to paragraph 1 of Article XXII of GATT 1994, paragraph 1 of Article XXII of GATS, or the corresponding provisions in other covered agreements[4], such Member may notify the consulting Members and the DSB, within 10 days after the date of the circulation of the request for consultations under said Article, of its desire to be joined in the consultations. Such Member shall be joined in the consultations, provided that the Member to which the request for consultations was addressed agrees that the claim of substantial interest is well-founded. In that event they shall so inform the DSB. If the request to be joined in the consultations is not accepted, the applicant Member shall be free to request consultations under paragraph 1 of Article XXII or paragraph 1 of Article XXIII of GATT 1994, paragraph 1 of Article XXII or paragraph 1 of Article XXIII of GATS, or the corresponding provisions in other covered agreements.

Article 5

[Good Offices, Conciliation and Mediation]

1. Good offices, conciliation and mediation are procedures that are undertaken voluntarily if the parties to the dispute so agree.

2. Proceedings involving good offices, conciliation and mediation, and in particular posi-

[4] The corresponding consultation provisions in the covered agreements are listed hereunder: Agreement on Agriculture, Article 19; Agreement on the Application of Sanitary and Phytosanitary Measures, paragraph 1 of Article 11; Agreement on Textiles and Clothing, paragraph 4 of Article 8; Agreement on Technical Barriers to Trade, paragraph 1 of Article 14; Agreement on Trade-Related Investment Measures, Article 8; Agreement on Implementation of Article VI of GATT 1994, paragraph 2 of Article 17; Agreement on Implementation of Article VII of GATT 1994, paragraph 2 of Article 19; Agreement on Preshipment Inspection, Article 7; Agreement on Rules of Origin, Article 7; Agreement on Import Licensing Procedures, Article 6; Agreement on Subsidies and Countervailing Measures, Article 30; Agreement on Safeguards, Article 14; Agreement on Trade-Related Aspects of Intellectual Property Rights, Article 64.1; and any corresponding consultation provisions in Plurilateral Trade Agreements as determined by the competent bodies of each Agreement and as notified to the DSB.

tions taken by the parties to the dispute during these proceedings, shall be confidential, and without prejudice to the rights of either party in any further proceedings under these procedures.

3. Good offices, conciliation or mediation may be requested at any time by any party to a dispute. They may begin at any time and be terminated at any time. Once procedures for good offices, conciliation or mediation are terminated, a complaining party may then proceed with a request for the establishment of a panel.

4. When good offices, conciliation or mediation are entered into within 60 days after the date of receipt of a request for consultations, the complaining party must allow a period of 60 days after the date of receipt of the request for consultations before requesting the establishment of a panel. The complaining party may request the establishment of a panel during the 60-day period if the parties to the dispute jointly consider that the good offices, conciliation or mediation process has failed to settle the dispute.

5. If the parties to a dispute agree, procedures for good offices, conciliation or mediation may continue while the panel process proceeds.

6. The Director-General may, acting in an *ex officio* capacity, offer good offices, conciliation or mediation with the view to assisting Members to settle a dispute.

Article 6
[Establishment of Panels]

1. If the complaining party so requests, a panel shall be established at the latest at the DSB meeting following that at which the request first appears as an item on the DSB's agenda, unless at that meeting the DSB decides by consensus not to establish a panel.[5]

2. The request for the establishment of a panel shall be made in writing. It shall indicate whether consultations were held, identify the specific measures at issue and provide a brief summary of the legal basis of the complaint sufficient to present the problem clearly. In case the applicant requests the establishment of a panel with other than standard terms of reference, the written request shall include the proposed text of special terms of reference.

Article 7
[Terms of Reference of Panels]

1. Panels shall have the following terms of reference unless the parties to the dispute agree otherwise within 20 days from the establishment of the panel:

> 'To examine, in the light of the relevant provisions in (name of the covered agreement(s) cited by the parties to the dispute), the matter referred to the DSB by (name of party) in document . . . and to make such findings as will assist the DSB in making the recommendations or in giving the rulings provided for in that/those agreement(s).'

2. Panels shall address the relevant provisions in any covered agreement or agreements cited by the parties to the dispute.

3. In establishing a panel, the DSB may authorize its Chairman to draw up the terms of reference of the panel in consultation with the parties to the dispute, subject to the provisions of paragraph 1. The terms of reference thus drawn up shall be circulated to all Members. If other than standard terms of reference are agreed upon, any Member may raise any point relating thereto in the DSB.

Article 8
[Composition of Panels]

1. Panels shall be composed of well-qualified governmental and/or non-governmental individuals, including persons who have served on or presented a case to a panel, served as a representative of a Member or of a contracting party to GATT 1947 or as a representative to the Council or Committee of any covered agreement or its predecessor agreement, or in the

[5] If the complaining party so requests, a meeting of the DSB shall be convened for this purpose within 15 days of the request, provided that at least 10 days' advance notice of the meeting is given.

Secretariat, taught or published on international trade law or policy, or served as a senior trade policy official of a Member.

2. Panel members should be selected with a view to ensuring the independence of the members, a sufficiently diverse background and a wide spectrum of experience.

3. Citizens of Members whose governments[6] are parties to the dispute or third parties as defined in paragraph 2 of Article 10 shall not serve on a panel concerned with that dispute, unless the parties to the dispute agree otherwise.

4. To assist in the selection of panelists, the Secretariat shall maintain an indicative list of governmental and non-governmental individuals possessing the qualifications outlined in paragraph 1, from which panelists may be drawn as appropriate. That list shall include the roster of non-governmental panelists established on 30 November 1984 (BISD 31S/9), and other rosters and indicative lists established under any of the covered agreements, and shall retain the names of persons on those rosters and indicative lists at the time of entry into force of the WTO Agreement. Members may periodically suggest names of governmental and non-governmental individuals for inclusion on the indicative list, providing relevant information on their knowledge of international trade and of the sectors or subject matter of the covered agreements, and those names shall be added to the list upon approval by the DSB. For each of the individuals on the list, the list shall indicate specific areas of experience or expertise of the individuals in the sectors or subject matter of the covered agreements.

5. Panels shall be composed of three panelists unless the parties to the dispute agree, within 10 days from the establishment of the panel, to a panel composed of five panelists. Members shall be informed promptly of the composition of the panel.

6. The Secretariat shall propose nominations for the panel to the parties to the dispute. The parties to the dispute shall not oppose nominations except for compelling reasons.

7. If there is no agreement on the panelists within 20 days after the date of the establishment of a panel, at the request of either party, the Director-General, in consultation with the Chairman of the DSB and the Chairman of the relevant Council or Committee, shall determine the composition of the panel by appointing the panelists whom the Director-General considers most appropriate in accordance with any relevant special or additional rules or procedures of the covered agreement or covered agreements which are at issue in the dispute, after consulting with the parties to the dispute. The Chairman of the DSB shall inform the Members of the composition of the panel thus formed no later than 10 days after the date the Chairman receives such a request.

8. Members shall undertake, as a general rule, to permit their officials to serve as panelists.

9. Panelists shall serve in their individual capacities and not as government representatives, nor as representatives of any organization. Members shall therefore not give them instructions nor seek to influence them as individuals with regard to matters before a panel.

10. When a dispute is between a developing country Member and a developed country Member the panel shall, if the developing country Member so requests, include at least one panelist from a developing country Member.

11. Panelists' expenses, including travel and subsistence allowance, shall be met from the WTO budget in accordance with criteria to be adopted by the General Council, based on recommendations of the Committee on Budget, Finance and Administration.

Article 9

[Procedures for Multiple Complainants]

1. Where more than one Member requests the establishment of a panel related to the same matter, a single panel may be established to

[6] In the case where customs unions or common markets are parties to a dispute, this provision applies to citizens of all member countries of the customs unions or common markets.

examine these complaints taking into account the rights of all Members concerned. A single panel should be established to examine such complaints whenever feasible.

2. The single panel shall organize its examination and present its findings to the DSB in such a manner that the rights which the parties to the dispute would have enjoyed had separate panels examined the complaints are in no way impaired. If one of the parties to the dispute so requests, the panel shall submit separate reports on the dispute concerned. The written submissions by each of the complainants shall be made available to the other complainants, and each complainant shall have the right to be present when any one of the other complainants presents its views to the panel.

3. If more than one panel is established to examine the complaints related to the same matter, to the greatest extent possible the same persons shall serve as panelists on each of the separate panels and the timetable for the panel process in such disputes shall be harmonized.

Article 10
[Third Parties]

1. The interests of the parties to a dispute and those of other Members under a covered agreement at issue in the dispute shall be fully taken into account during the panel process.

2. Any Member having a substantial interest in a matter before a panel and having notified its interest to the DSB (referred to in this Understanding as a 'third party') shall have an opportunity to be heard by the panel and to make written submissions to the panel. These submissions shall also be given to the parties to the dispute and shall be reflected in the panel report.

3. Third parties shall receive the submissions of the parties to the dispute to the first meeting of the panel.

4. If a third party considers that a measure already the subject of a panel proceeding nullifies or impairs benefits accruing to it under any covered agreement, that Member may have recourse to normal dispute settlement procedures under this Understanding. Such a dispute shall be referred to the original panel wherever possible.

Article 11
[Function of Panels]

The function of panels is to assist the DSB in discharging its responsibilities under this Understanding and the covered agreements. Accordingly, a panel should make an objective assessment of the matter before it, including an objective assessment of the facts of the case and the applicability of and conformity with the relevant covered agreements, and make such other findings as will assist the DSB in making the recommendations or in giving the rulings provided for in the covered agreements. Panels should consult regularly with the parties to the dispute and give them adequate opportunity to develop a mutually satisfactory solution.

Article 12
[Panel Procedures]

1. Panels shall follow the Working Procedures in Appendix 3 unless the panel decides otherwise after consulting the parties to the dispute.

2. Panel procedures should provide sufficient flexibility so as to ensure high-quality panel reports, while not unduly delaying the panel process.

3. After consulting the parties to the dispute, the panelists shall, as soon as practicable and whenever possible within one week after the composition and terms of reference of the panel have been agreed upon, fix the timetable for the panel process, taking into account the provisions of paragraph 9 of Article 4, if relevant.

4. In determining the timetable for the panel process, the panel shall provide sufficient time for the parties to the dispute to prepare their submissions.

5. Panels should set precise deadlines for written submissions by the parties and the parties should respect those deadlines.

6. Each party to the dispute shall deposit its written submissions with the Secretariat for immediate transmission to the panel and to the

other party or parties to the dispute. The complaining party shall submit its first submission in advance of the responding party's first submission unless the panel decides, in fixing the timetable referred to in paragraph 3 and after consultations with the parties to the dispute, that the parties should submit their first submissions simultaneously. When there are sequential arrangements for the deposit of first submissions, the panel shall establish a firm time-period for receipt of the responding party's submission. Any subsequent written submissions shall be submitted simultaneously.

7. Where the parties to the dispute have failed to develop a mutually satisfactory solution, the panel shall submit its findings in the form of a written report to the DSB. In such cases, the report of a panel shall set out the findings of fact, the applicability of relevant provisions and the basic rationale behind any findings and recommendations that it makes. Where a settlement of the matter among the parties to the dispute has been found, the report of the panel shall be confined to a brief description of the case and to reporting that a solution has been reached.

8. In order to make the procedures more efficient, the period in which the panel shall conduct its examination, from the date that the composition and terms of reference of the panel have been agreed upon until the date the final report is issued to the parties to the dispute, shall, as a general rule, not exceed six months. In cases of urgency, including those relating to perishable goods, the panel shall aim to issue its report to the parties to the dispute within three months.

9. When the panel considers that it cannot issue its report within six months, or within three months in cases of urgency, it shall inform the DSB in writing of the reasons for the delay together with an estimate of the period within which it will issue its report. In no case should the period from the establishment of the panel to the circulation of the report to the Members exceed nine months.

10. In the context of consultations involving a measure taken by a developing country Member, the parties may agree to extend the periods established in paragraphs 7 and 8 of Article 4. If, after the relevant period has elapsed, the consulting parties cannot agree that the consultations have concluded, the Chairman of the DSB shall decide, after consultation with the parties, whether to extend the relevant period and, if so, for how long. In addition, in examining a complaint against a developing country Member, the panel shall accord sufficient time for the developing country Member to prepare and present its argumentation. The provisions of paragraph 1 of Article 20 and paragraph 4 of Article 21 are not affected by any action pursuant to this paragraph.

11. Where one or more of the parties is a developing country Member, the panel's report shall explicitly indicate the form in which account has been taken of relevant provisions on differential and more-favourable treatment for developing country Members that form part of the covered agreements which have been raised by the developing country Member in the course of the dispute settlement procedures.

12. The panel may suspend its work at any time at the request of the complaining party for a period not to exceed 12 months. In the event of such a suspension, the time-frames set out in paragraphs 8 and 9 of this Article, paragraph 1 of Article 20, and paragraph 4 of Article 21 shall be extended by the amount of time that the work was suspended. If the work of the panel has been suspended for more than 12 months, the authority for establishment of the panel shall lapse.

Article 13
[Right to Seek Information]

1. Each panel shall have the right to seek information and technical advice from any individual or body which it deems appropriate. However, before a panel seeks such information or advice from any individual or body within the jurisdiction of a Member it shall inform the authorities of that Member. A Member should respond promptly and fully to any request by a panel for such information as the panel considers necessary and appropriate. Confidential information which is provided

shall not be revealed without formal authorization from the individual, body, or authorities of the Member providing the information.

2. Panels may seek information from any relevant source and may consult experts to obtain their opinion on certain aspects of the matter. With respect to a factual issue concerning a scientific or other technical matter raised by a party to a dispute, a panel may request an advisory report in writing from an expert review group. Rules for the establishment of such a group and its procedures are set forth in Appendix 4.

Article 14
[Confidentiality]

1. Panel deliberations shall be confidential.

2. The reports of panels shall be drafted without the presence of the parties to the dispute in the light of the information provided and the statements made.

3. Opinions expressed in the panel report by individual panelists shall be anonymous.

Article 15
[Interim Review Stage]

1. Following the consideration of rebuttal submissions and oral arguments, the panel shall issue the descriptive (factual and argument) sections of its draft report to the parties to the dispute. Within a period of time set by the panel, the parties shall submit their comments in writing.

2. Following the expiration of the set period of time for receipt of comments from the parties to the dispute, the panel shall issue an interim report to the parties, including both the descriptive sections and the panel's findings and conclusions. Within a period of time set by the panel, a party may submit a written request for the panel to review precise aspects of the interim report prior to circulation of the final report to the Members. At the request of a party, the panel shall hold a further meeting with the parties on the issues identified in the written comments. If no comments are received from any party within the comment period, the interim report shall be considered the final panel report and circulated promptly to the Members.

3. The findings of the final panel report shall include a discussion of the arguments made at the interim review stage. The interim review stage shall be conducted within the time-period set out in paragraph 8 of Article 12.

Article 16
[Adoption of Panel Reports]

1. In order to provide sufficient time for the Members to consider panel reports, the reports shall not be considered for adoption by the DSB until 20 days after the date they have been circulated to the Members.

2. Members having objections to a panel report shall give written reasons to explain their objections for circulation at least 10 days prior to the DSB meeting at which the panel report will be considered.

3. The parties to a dispute shall have the right to participate fully in the consideration of the panel report by the DSB, and their views shall be fully recorded.

4. Within 60 days after the date of circulation of a panel report to the Members, the report shall be adopted at a DSB meeting[7] unless a party to the dispute formally notifies the DSB of its decision to appeal or the DSB decides by consensus not to adopt the report. If a party has notified its decision to appeal, the report by the panel shall not be considered for adoption by the DSB until after completion of the appeal. This adoption procedure is without prejudice to the right of Members to express their views on a panel report.

Article 17
[Appellate Review]

Standing Appellate Body

1. A standing Appellate Body shall be established by the DSB. The Appellate Body shall

[7] If a meeting of the DSB is not scheduled within this period at a time that enables the requirements of paragraphs 1 and 4 of Article 16 to be met, a meeting of the DSB shall be held for this purpose.

hear appeals from panel cases. It shall be composed of seven persons, three of whom shall serve on any one case. Persons serving on the Appellate Body shall serve in rotation. Such rotation shall be determined in the working procedures of the Appellate Body.

2. The DSB shall appoint persons to serve on the Appellate Body for a four-year term, and each person may be reappointed once. However, the terms of three of the seven persons appointed immediately after the entry into force of the WTO Agreement shall expire at the end of two years, to be determined by lot. Vacancies shall be filled as they arise. A person appointed to replace a person whose term of office has not expired shall hold office for the remainder of the predecessor's term.

3. The Appellate Body shall comprise persons of recognized authority, with demonstrated expertise in law, international trade and the subject matter of the covered agreements generally. They shall be unaffiliated with any government. The Appellate Body membership shall be broadly representative of membership in the WTO. All persons serving on the Appellate Body shall be available at all times and on short notice, and shall stay abreast of dispute settlement activities and other relevant activities of the WTO. They shall not participate in the consideration of any disputes that would create a direct or indirect conflict of interest.

4. Only parties to the dispute, not third parties, may appeal a panel report. Third parties which have notified the DSB of a substantial interest in the matter pursuant to paragraph 2 of Article 10 may make written submissions to, and be given an opportunity to be heard by, the Appellate Body.

5. As a general rule, the proceedings shall not exceed 60 days from the date a party to the dispute formally notifies its decision to appeal to the date the Appellate Body circulates its report. In fixing its timetable the Appellate Body shall take into account the provisions of paragraph 9 of Article 4, if relevant. When the Appellate Body considers that it cannot provide its report within 60 days, it shall inform the DSB in writing of the reasons for the delay together with an estimate of the period within which it will submit its report. In no case shall the proceedings exceed 90 days.

6. An appeal shall be limited to issues of law covered in the panel report and legal interpretations developed by the panel.

7. The Appellate Body shall be provided with appropriate administrative and legal support as it requires.

8. The expenses of persons serving on the Appellate Body, including travel and subsistence allowance, shall be met from the WTO budget in accordance with criteria to be adopted by the General Council, based on recommendations of the Committee on Budget, Finance and Administration.

Procedures for Appellate Review

9. Working procedures shall be drawn up by the Appellate Body in consultation with the Chairman of the DSB and the Director-General, and communicated to the Members for their information.

10. The proceedings of the Appellate Body shall be confidential. The reports of the Appellate Body shall be drafted without the presence of the parties to the dispute and in the light of the information provided and the statements made.

11. Opinions expressed in the Appellate Body report by individuals serving on the Appellate Body shall be anonymous.

12. The Appellate Body shall address each of the issues raised in accordance with paragraph 6 during the appellate proceeding.

13. The Appellate Body may uphold, modify or reverse the legal findings and conclusions of the panel.

Adoption of Appellate Body Reports

14. An Appellate Body report shall be adopted by the DSB and unconditionally accepted by the parties to the dispute unless the DSB decides by consensus not to adopt the Appellate Body report within 30 days following its

circulation to the Members.[8] This adoption procedure is without prejudice to the right of Members to express their views on an Appellate Body report.

Article 18
[Communications with the Panel or Appellate Body]

1. There shall be no *ex parte* communications with the panel or Appellate Body concerning matters under consideration by the panel or Appellate Body.

2. Written submissions to the panel or the Appellate Body shall be treated as confidential, but shall be made available to the parties to the dispute. Nothing in this Understanding shall preclude a party to a dispute from disclosing statements of its own positions to the public. Members shall treat as confidential information submitted by another Member to the panel or the Appellate Body which that Member has designated as confidential. A party to a dispute shall also, upon request of a Member, provide a non-confidential summary of the information contained in its written submissions that could be disclosed to the public.

Article 19
[Panel and Appellate Body Recommendations]

1. Where a panel or the Appellate Body concludes that a measure is inconsistent with a covered agreement, it shall recommend that the Member concerned[9] bring the measure into conformity with that agreement.[10] In addition to its recommendations, the panel or Appellate Body may suggest ways in which the Member concerned could implement the recommendations.

2. In accordance with paragraph 2 of Article 3, in their findings and recommendations, the panel and Appellate Body cannot add to or diminish the rights and obligations provided in the covered agreements.

Article 20
[Time-frame for DSB Decisions]

Unless otherwise agreed to by the parties to the dispute, the period from the date of establishment of the panel by the DSB until the date the DSB considers the panel or appellate report for adoption shall as a general rule not exceed nine months where the panel report is not appealed or 12 months where the report is appealed. Where either the panel or the Appellate Body has acted, pursuant to paragraph 9 of Article 12 or paragraph 5 of Article 17, to extend the time for providing its report, the additional time taken shall be added to the above periods.

Article 21
[Surveillance of Implementation of Recommendations and Rulings]

1. Prompt compliance with recommendations or rulings of the DSB is essential in order to ensure effective resolution of disputes to the benefit of all Members.

2. Particular attention should be paid to matters affecting the interests of developing country Members with respect to measures which have been subject to dispute settlement.

3. At a DSB meeting held within 30 days[11] after the date of adoption of the panel or Appellate Body report, the Member concerned shall inform the DSB of its intentions in respect of implementation of the recommendations and rulings of the DSB. If it is impracticable to comply immediately with the recommendations and rulings, the Member concerned shall have a reasonable period of time in which to do so. The reasonable period of time shall be:

---

[8] If a meeting of the DSB is not scheduled during this period, such a meeting of the DSB shall be held for this purpose.

[9] The 'Member concerned' is the party to the dispute to which the panel or Appellate Body recommendations are directed.

[10] With respect to recommendations in cases not involving a violation of GATT 1994 or any other covered agreement, see Article 26.

[11] If a meeting of the DSB is not scheduled during this period, such a meeting of the DSB shall be held for this purpose.

(a) the period of time proposed by the Member concerned, provided that such period is approved by the DSB; or, in the absence of such approval,
(b) a period of time mutually agreed by the parties to the dispute within 45 days after the date of adoption of the recommendations and rulings; or, in the absence of such agreement,
(c) a period of time determined through binding arbitration within 90 days after the date of adoption of the recommendations and rulings.[12] In such arbitration, a guideline for the arbitrator[13] should be that the reasonable period of time to implement panel or Appellate Body recommendations should not exceed 15 months from the date of adoption of a panel or Appellate Body report. However, that time may be shorter or longer, depending upon the particular circumstances.

4. Except where the panel or the Appellate Body has extended, pursuant to paragraph 9 of Article 12 or paragraph 5 of Article 17, the time of providing its report, the period from the date of establishment of the panel by the DSB until the date of determination of the reasonable period of time shall not exceed 15 months unless the parties to the dispute agree otherwise. Where either the panel or the Appellate Body has acted to extend the time of providing its report, the additional time taken shall be added to the 15-month period; provided that unless the parties to the dispute agree that there are exceptional circumstances, the total time shall not exceed 18 months.

5. Where there is disagreement as to the existence or consistency with a covered agreement of measures taken to comply with the recommendations and rulings such dispute shall be decided through recourse to these dispute settlement procedures, including wherever possible resort to the original panel. The panel shall circulate its report within 90 days after the date of referral of the matter to it. When the panel considers that it cannot provide its report within this time frame, it shall inform the DSB in writing of the reasons for the delay together with an estimate of the period within which it will submit its report.

6. The DSB shall keep under surveillance the implementation of adopted recommendations or rulings. The issue of implementation of the recommendations or rulings may be raised at the DSB by any Member at any time following their adoption. Unless the DSB decides otherwise, the issue of implementation of the recommendations or rulings shall be placed on the agenda of the DSB meeting after six months following the date of establishment of the reasonable period of time pursuant to paragraph 3 and shall remain on the DSB's agenda until the issue is resolved. At least 10 days prior to each such DSB meeting, the Member concerned shall provide the DSB with a status report in writing of its progress in the implementation of the recommendations or rulings.

7. If the matter is one which has been raised by a developing country Member, the DSB shall consider what further action it might take which would be appropriate to the circumstances.

8. If the case is one brought by a developing country Member, in considering what appropriate action might be taken, the DSB shall take into account not only the trade coverage of measures complained of, but also their impact on the economy of developing country Members concerned.

Article 22

[Compensation and the Suspension of Concessions]

1. Compensation and the suspension of concessions or other obligations are temporary measures available in the event that the recommendations and rulings are not implemented within a reasonable period of time. However, neither compensation nor the suspension of

---

[12] If the parties cannot agree on an arbitrator within ten days after referring the matter to arbitration, the arbitrator shall be appointed by the Director-General within ten days, after consulting the parties.

[13] The expression 'arbitrator' shall be interpreted as referring either to an individual or a group.

concessions or other obligations is preferred to full implementation of a recommendation to bring a measure into conformity with the covered agreements. Compensation is voluntary and, if granted, shall be consistent with the covered agreements.

2. If the Member concerned fails to bring the measure found to be inconsistent with a covered agreement into compliance therewith or otherwise comply with the recommendations and rulings within the reasonable period of time determined pursuant to paragraph 3 of Article 21, such Member shall, if so requested, and no later than the expiry of the reasonable period of time, enter into negotiations with any party having invoked the dispute settlement procedures, with a view to developing mutually acceptable compensation. If no satisfactory compensation has been agreed within 20 days after the date of expiry of the reasonable period of time, any party having invoked the dispute settlement procedures may request authorization from the DSB to suspend the application to the Member concerned of concessions or other obligations under the covered agreements.

3. In considering what concessions or other obligations to suspend, the complaining party shall apply the following principles and procedures:

(a) the general principle is that the complaining party should first seek to suspend concessions or other obligations with respect to the same sector(s) as that in which the panel or Appellate Body has found a violation or other nullification or impairment;

(b) if that party considers that it is not practicable or effective to suspend concessions or other obligations with respect to the same sector(s), it may seek to suspend concessions or other obligations in other sectors under the same agreement;

(c) if that party considers that it is not practicable or effective to suspend concessions or other obligations with respect to other sectors under the same agreement, and that the circumstances are serious enough, it may seek to suspend concessions or other obligations under another covered agreement;

(d) in applying the above principles, that party shall take into account:
   (i) the trade in the sector or under the agreement under which the panel or Appellate Body has found a violation or other nullification or impairment, and the importance of such trade to that party;
   (ii) the broader economic elements related to the nullification or impairment and the broader economic consequences of the suspension of concessions or other obligations;

(e) if that party decides to request authorization to suspend concessions or other obligations pursuant to subparagraphs (b) or (c), it shall state the reasons therefor in its request. At the same time as the request is forwarded to the DSB, it also shall be forwarded to the relevant Councils and also, in the case of a request pursuant to subparagraph (b), the relevant sectoral bodies;

(f) for purposes of this paragraph, 'sector' means:
   (i) with respect to goods, all goods;
   (ii) with respect to services, a principal sector as identified in the current 'Services Sectoral Classification List' which identifies such sectors;[14]
   (iii) with respect to trade-related intellectual property rights, each of the categories of intellectual property rights covered in Section 1, or Section 2, or Section 3, or Section 4, or Section 5, or Section 6, or Section 7 of Part II, or the obligations under Part III, or Part IV of the Agreement on TRIPS;

(g) for purposes of this paragraph, 'agreement' means:
   (i) with respect to goods, the agreements listed in Annex 1A of the WTO Agreement, taken as a whole as well as the Plurilateral Trade Agreements in

---

[14] The list in document MTN.GNS/W/120 identifies eleven sectors.

so far as the relevant parties to the dispute are parties to these agreements;

(ii) with respect to services, the GATS;

(iii) with respect to intellectual property rights, the Agreement on TRIPS.

4. The level of the suspension of concessions or other obligations authorized by the DSB shall be equivalent to the level of the nullification or impairment.

5. The DSB shall not authorize suspension of concessions or other obligations if a covered agreement prohibits such suspension.

6. When the situation described in paragraph 2 occurs, the DSB, upon request, shall grant authorization to suspend concessions or other obligations within 30 days of the expiry of the reasonable period of time unless the DSB decides by consensus to reject the request. However, if the Member concerned objects to the level of suspension proposed, or claims that the principles and procedures set forth in paragraph 3 have not been followed where a complaining party has requested authorization to suspend concessions or other obligations pursuant to paragraph 3(b) or (c), the matter shall be referred to arbitration. Such arbitration shall be carried out by the original panel, if members are available, or by an arbitrator[15] appointed by the Director-General and shall be completed within 60 days after the date of expiry of the reasonable period of time. Concessions or other obligations shall not be suspended during the course of the arbitration.

7. The arbitrator[16] acting pursuant to paragraph 6 shall not examine the nature of the concessions or other obligations to be suspended but shall determine whether the level of such suspension is equivalent to the level of nullification or impairment. The arbitrator may also determine if the proposed suspension of concessions or other obligations is allowed under the covered agreement. However, if the matter referred to arbitration includes a claim that the principles and procedures set forth in paragraph 3 have not been followed, the arbitrator shall examine that claim. In the event the arbitrator determines that those principles and procedures have not been followed, the complaining party shall apply them consistent with paragraph 3. The parties shall accept the arbitrator's decision as final and the parties concerned shall not seek a second arbitration. The DSB shall be informed promptly of the decision of the arbitrator and shall upon request, grant authorization to suspend concessions or other obligations where the request is consistent with the decision of the arbitrator, unless the DSB decides by consensus to reject the request.

8. The suspension of concessions or other obligations shall be temporary and shall only be applied until such time as the measure found to be inconsistent with a covered agreement has been removed, or the Member that must implement recommendations or rulings provides a solution to the nullification or impairment of benefits, or a mutually satisfactory solution is reached. In accordance with paragraph 6 of Article 21, the DSB shall continue to keep under surveillance the implementation of adopted recommendations or rulings, including those cases where compensation has been provided or concessions or other obligations have been suspended but the recommendations to bring a measure into conformity with the covered agreements have not been implemented.

9. The dispute settlement provisions of the covered agreements may be invoked in respect of measures affecting their observance taken by regional or local governments or authorities within the territory of a Member. When the DSB has ruled that a provision of a covered agreement has not been observed, the responsible Member shall take such reasonable measures as may be available to it to ensure its observance. The provisions of the covered agreements and this Understanding relating to compensation and suspension of concessions or other obligations apply in cases where

[15] The expression 'arbitrator' shall be interpreted as referring either to an individual or a group.

[16] The expression 'arbitrator' shall be interpreted as referring either to an individual or a group or to the members of the original panel when serving in the capacity of arbitrator.

it has not been possible to secure such observance.[17]

Article 23

[Strengthening of the Multilateral System]

1. When Members seek the redress of a violation of obligations or other nullification or impairment of benefits under the covered agreements or an impediment to the attainment of any objective of the covered agreements, they shall have recourse to, and abide by, the rules and procedures of this Understanding.

2. In such cases, Members shall:

(a) not make a determination to the effect that a violation has occurred, that benefits have been nullified or impaired or that the attainment of any objective of the covered agreements has been impeded, except through recourse to dispute settlement in accordance with the rules and procedures of this Understanding, and shall make any such determination consistent with the findings contained in the panel or Appellate Body report adopted by the DSB or an arbitration award rendered under this Understanding;

(b) follow the procedures set forth in Article 21 to determine the reasonable period of time for the Member concerned to implement the recommendations and rulings; and

(c) follow the procedures set forth in Article 22 to determine the level of suspension of concessions or other obligations and obtain DSB authorization in accordance with those procedures before suspending concessions or other obligations under the covered agreements in response to the failure of the Member concerned to implement the recommendations and rulings within that reasonable period of time.

[17] Where the provisions of any covered agreement concerning measures taken by regional or local governments or authorities within the territory of a Member contain provisions different from the provisions of this paragraph, the provisions of such covered agreement shall prevail.

Article 24

[Special Procedures Involving Least-Developed Country Members]

1. At all stages of the determination of the causes of a dispute and of dispute settlement procedures involving a least-developed country Member, particular consideration shall be given to the special situation of least-developed country Members. In this regard, Members shall exercise due restraint in raising matters under these procedures involving a least-developed country Member. If nullification or impairment is found to result from a measure taken by a least-developed country Member, complaining parties shall exercise due restraint in asking for compensation or seeking authorization to suspend the application of concessions or other obligations pursuant to these procedures.

2. In dispute settlement cases involving a least-developed country Member, where a satisfactory solution has not been found in the course of consultations the Director-General or the Chairman of the DSB shall, upon request by a least-developed country Member offer their good offices, conciliation and mediation with a view to assisting the parties to settle the dispute, before a request for a panel is made. The Director-General or the Chairman of the DSB, in providing the above assistance, may consult any source which either deems appropriate.

Article 25

[Arbitration]

1. Expeditious arbitration within the WTO as an alternative means of dispute settlement can facilitate the solution of certain disputes that concern issues that are clearly defined by both parties.

2. Except as otherwise provided in this Understanding, resort to arbitration shall be subject to mutual agreement of the parties which shall agree on the procedures to be followed. Agreements to resort to arbitration shall be notified to all Members sufficiently in advance of the actual commencement of the arbitration process.

3. Other Members may become party to an arbitration proceeding only upon the agreement of the parties which have agreed to have recourse to arbitration. The parties to the proceeding shall agree to abide by the arbitration award. Arbitration awards shall be notified to the DSB and the Council or Committee of any relevant agreement where any Member may raise any point relating thereto.

4. Articles 21 and 22 of this Understanding shall apply *mutatis mutandis* to arbitration awards.

Article 26

[1. *Non-Violation Complaints of the Type Described in Paragraph 1(b) of Article XXIII of GATT 1994*]

Where the provisions of paragraph 1(b) of Article XXIII of GATT 1994 are applicable to a covered agreement, a panel or the Appellate Body may only make rulings and recommendations where a party to the dispute considers that any benefit accruing to it directly or indirectly under the relevant covered agreement is being nullified or impaired or the attainment of any objective of that Agreement is being impeded as a result of the application by a Member of any measure, whether or not it conflicts with the provisions of that Agreement. Where and to the extent that such party considers and a panel or the Appellate Body determines that a case concerns a measure that does not conflict with the provisions of a covered agreement to which the provisions of paragraph 1(b) of Article XXIII of GATT 1994 are applicable, the procedures in this Understanding shall apply, subject to the following:

(a) the complaining party shall present a detailed justification in support of any complaint relating to a measure which does not conflict with the relevant covered agreement;
(b) where a measure has been found to nullify or impair benefits under, or impede the attainment of objectives, of the relevant covered agreement without violation thereof, there is no obligation to withdraw the measure. However, in such cases, the panel or the Appellate Body shall recommend that the Member concerned make a mutually satisfactory adjustment;
(c) notwithstanding the provisions of Article 21, the arbitration provided for in paragraph 3 of Article 21, upon request of either party, may include a determination of the level of benefits which have been nullified or impaired, and may also suggest ways and means of reaching a mutually satisfactory adjustment; such suggestions shall not be binding upon the parties to the dispute;
(d) notwithstanding the provisions of paragraph 1 of Article 22, compensation may be part of a mutually satisfactory adjustment as final settlement of the dispute.

[2. *Complaints of the Type Described in Paragraph 1(c) of Article XXIII of GATT 1994*]

Where the provisions of paragraph 1(c) of Article XXIII of GATT 1994 are applicable to a covered agreement, a panel may only make rulings and recommendations where a party considers that any benefit accruing to it directly or indirectly under the relevant covered agreement is being nullified or impaired or the attainment of any objective of that Agreement is being impeded as a result of the existence of any situation other than those to which the provisions of paragraphs 1(a) and 1(b) of Article XXIII of GATT 1994 are applicable. Where and to the extent that such party considers and a panel determines that the matter is covered by this paragraph, the procedures of this Understanding shall apply only up to and including the point in the proceedings where the panel report has been circulated to the Members. The dispute settlement rules and procedures contained in the Decision of 12 April 1989 (BISD 36S/61–67) shall apply to consideration for adoption, and surveillance and implementation of recommendations and rulings. The following shall also apply:

(a) the complaining party shall present a detailed justification in support of any argument made with respect to issues covered under this paragraph;

(b) in cases involving matters covered by this paragraph, if a panel finds that cases also involve dispute settlement matters other than those covered by this paragraph, the panel shall circulate a report to the DSB addressing any such matters and a separate report on matters falling under this paragraph.

Article 27

[Responsibilities of the Secretariat]

1. The Secretariat shall have the responsibility of assisting panels, especially on the legal, historical and procedural aspects of the matters dealt with, and of providing secretarial and technical support.

2. While the Secretariat assists Members in respect of dispute settlement at their request, there may also be a need to provide additional legal advice and assistance in respect of dispute settlement to developing country Members. To this end, the Secretariat shall make available a qualified legal expert from the WTO technical cooperation services to any developing country Member which so requests. This expert shall assist the developing country Member in a manner ensuring the continued impartiality of the Secretariat.

3. The Secretariat shall conduct special training courses for interested Members concerning these dispute settlement procedures and practices so as to enable Members' experts to be better informed in this regard.

APPENDIX 1—Agreements covered by the understanding

(A) Agreement Establishing the World Trade Organization

(B) Multilateral Trade Agreements

Annex 1A: Multilateral Agreements on Trade in Goods

Annex 1B: General Agreement on Trade in Services

Annex 1C: Agreement on Trade-Related Aspects of Intellectual Property Rights

Annex 2: Understanding on Rules and Procedures Governing the Settlement of Disputes

(C) Plurilateral Trade Agreements

Annex 4: Agreement on Trade in Civil Aircraft
Agreement on Government Procurement
International Dairy Agreement
International Bovine Meat Agreement

The applicability of this Understanding to the Plurilateral Trade Agreements shall be subject to the adoption of a decision by the parties to each agreement setting out the terms for the application of the Understanding to the individual agreement, including any special or additional rules or procedures for inclusion in Appendix 2, as notified to the DSB.

. . . .

APPENDIX 3—Working procedures

1. In its proceedings the panel shall follow the relevant provisions of this Understanding. In addition, the following working procedures shall apply.

2. The panel shall meet in closed session. The parties to the dispute, and interested parties, shall be present at the meetings only when invited by the panel to appear before it.

3. The deliberations of the panel and the documents submitted to it shall be kept confidential. Nothing in this Understanding shall preclude a party to a dispute from disclosing statements of its own positions to the public. Members shall treat as confidential information submitted by another Member to the panel which that Member has designated as confidential. Where a party to a dispute submits a confidential version of its written submissions to the panel, it shall also, upon request of a Member, provide a non-confidential summary of the information contained in its submissions that could be disclosed to the public.

4. Before the first substantive meeting of the panel with the parties, the parties to the dispute shall transmit to the panel written submissions in which they present the facts of the case and their arguments.

5. At its first substantive meeting with the parties, the panel shall ask the party which has brought the complaint to present its case. Subsequently, and still at the same meeting, the party against which the complaint has been brought shall be asked to present its point of view.

6. All third parties which have notified their interest in the dispute to the DSB shall be invited in writing to present their views during a session of the first substantive meeting of the panel set aside for that purpose. All such third parties may be present during the entirety of this session.

7. Formal rebuttals shall be made at a second substantive meeting of the panel. The party complained against shall have the right to take the floor first to be followed by the complaining party. The parties shall submit, prior to that meeting, written rebuttals to the panel.

8. The panel may at any time put questions to the parties and ask them for explanations either in the course of a meeting with the parties or in writing.

9. The parties to the dispute and any third party invited to present its views in accordance with Article 10 shall make available to the panel a written version of their oral statements.

10. In the interest of full transparency, the presentations, rebuttals and statements referred to in paragraphs 5 to 9 shall be made in the presence of the parties. Moreover, each party's written submissions, including any comments on the descriptive part of the report and responses to questions put by the panel, shall be made available to the other party or parties.

11. Any additional procedures specific to the panel.

12. Proposed timetable for panel work:

(a) Receipt of first written submissions of the parties:
  (1) complaining Party: ____ 3–6 weeks
  (2) Party complained against: ____ 2–3 weeks

(b) Date, time and place of first substantive meeting with the parties; third party session: ____ 1–2 weeks

(c) Receipt of written rebuttals of the parties: ____ 2–3 weeks

(d) Date, time and place of second substantive meeting with the parties: ____ 1–2 weeks

(e) Issuance of descriptive part of the report to the parties: ____ 2–4 weeks

(f) Receipt of comments by the parties on the descriptive part of the report: ____ 2 weeks

(g) Issuance of the interim report, including the findings and conclusions, to the parties: ____ 2–4 weeks

(h) Deadline for party to request review of part(s) of report: ____ 1 week

(i) Period of review by panel, including possible additional meeting with parties: ____ 2 weeks

(j) Issuance of final report to parties to dispute: ____ 2 weeks

(k) Circulation of the final report to the Members: ____ 3 weeks

The above calendar may be changed in the light of unforeseen developments. Additional meetings with the parties shall be scheduled if required.

APPENDIX 4—Expert review groups

The following rules and procedures shall apply to expert review groups established in accordance with the provisions of paragraph 2 of Article 13.

1. Expert review groups are under the panel's authority. Their terms of reference and detailed working procedures shall be decided by the panel, and they shall report to the panel.

2. Participation in expert review groups shall be restricted to persons of professional standing and experience in the field in question.

3. Citizens of parties to the dispute shall not serve on an expert review group without the joint agreement of the parties to the dispute, except in exceptional circumstances when the panel considers that the need for specialized scientific expertise cannot be fulfilled otherwise. Government officials of parties to the dispute shall not serve on an expert review group. Members of expert review groups shall serve in their individual capacities and not as government representatives, nor as representatives of any organization. Governments or organizations shall therefore not give them instructions with regard to matters before an expert review group.

4. Expert review groups may consult and seek information and technical advice from any source they deem appropriate. Before an expert review group seeks such information or advice from a source within the jurisdiction of a Member, it shall inform the government of that Member. Any Member shall respond promptly and fully to any request by an expert review group for such information as the expert review group considers necessary and appropriate.

5. The parties to a dispute shall have access to all relevant information provided to an expert review group, unless it is of a confidential nature. Confidential information provided to the expert review group shall not be released without formal authorization from the government, organization or person providing the information. Where such information is requested from the expert review group but release of such information by the expert review group is not authorized, a non-confidential summary of the information will be provided by the government, organization or person supplying the information.

6. The expert review group shall submit a draft report to the parties to the dispute with a view to obtaining their comments, and taking them into account, as appropriate, in the final report, which shall also be issued to the parties to the dispute when it is submitted to the panel. The final report of the expert review group shall be advisory only.

APPENDIX 11

Agreement between WIPO and WTO 1994

(of December 22, 1995)

Preamble

The World Intellectual Property Organization (WIPO) and the World Trade Organization (WTO),

Desiring to establish a mutually supportive relationship between them, and with a view to establishing appropriate arrangements for cooperation between them,

Agree as follows:

Article 1
[Abbreviated Expressions]

For the purposes of this Agreement:

(i) 'WIPO' means the World Intellectual Property Organization;
(ii) 'WTO' means the World Trade Organization;
(iii) 'International Bureau' means the International Bureau of WIPO;
(iv) 'WTO Member' means a party to the Agreement Establishing the World Trade Organization;
(v) 'the TRIPS Agreement' means the Agreement on Trade-Related Aspects of Intellectual Property Rights, *Annex 1C to the Agreement Establishing the World Trade Organization*
(vi) 'Paris Convention' means the Paris Convention for the Protection of Industrial Property of March 20, 1883, as revised;
(vii) 'Paris Convention (1967)' means the Paris Convention for the Protection of Industrial Property of March 20, 1883, as revised at Stockholm on July 14, 1967;
(viii) 'emblem' means, in the case of a WTO Member, any armorial bearing, flag and other State emblem of that WTO Member, or any official sign or hallmark indicating control and warranty adopted by it, and, in the case of an international intergovernmental organization, any armorial bearing, flag, other emblem, abbreviation or name of that organization.

Article 2
[Laws and Regulations]

(1) [*Accessibility of Laws and Regulations in the WIPO Collection by WTO Members and Their Nationals*] The International Bureau shall, on request, furnish to WTO Members and to nationals of WTO Members copies of laws and regulations, and copies of translations thereof, that exist in its collection, on the same terms as apply to the Member States of WIPO and to nationals of the Member States of WIPO, respectively.

(2) [*Accessibility of the Computerized Database*] WTO Members and nationals of WTO Members shall have access, on the same terms as apply to the Member States of WIPO and to nationals of the Member States of WIPO, respectively, to any computerized database of the International Bureau containing laws and regulations. The WTO Secretariat shall have access, free of any charge by WIPO, to any such database.

(3) [*Accessibility of Laws and Regulations in the WIPO Collection by the WTO Secretariat and the Council for TRIPS*]

(a) Where, on the date of its initial notification of a law or regulation under *Article 63.2 of the TRIPS Agreement*, a WTO Member has already communicated that law or regulation, or a translation thereof, to the International Bureau and that WTO Member has sent to the WTO Secretariat a statement to that effect, and that law, regulation or translation actually exists in the collection of the International Bureau, the International Bureau shall, on request of the WTO Secretariat, give, free of charge, a copy of the said law, regulation or translation to the WTO Secretariat.

(b) Furthermore, if, for the purposes of carrying out its obligations under *Article 68 of the TRIPS Agreement*, such as monitoring the operation of the TRIPS Agreement or providing assistance in the context of dispute settlement procedures, the Council for TRIPS of the WTO requires a copy of a law or regulation, or a copy of a translation thereof, which had not previously been given to the WTO Secretariat under *subparagraph (a)*, and which exists in the collection of the International Bureau, the International Bureau shall, upon request of either the Council for TRIPS or the WTO Secretariat, give to the WTO Secretariat, free of charge, the requested copy.

(c) The International Bureau shall, on request, furnish to the WTO Secretariat on the same terms as apply to Member States of WIPO any additional copies of the laws, regulations and translations given under *subparagraph (a)* or *(b)*, as well as copies of any other laws and regulations, and copies of translations thereof, which exist in the collection of the International Bureau.

(d) The International Bureau shall not put any restriction on the use that the WTO Secretariat may make of the copies of laws, regulations and translations transmitted under *subparagraph (a)*, *(b)* or *(c)*.

(4) [*Laws and Regulations Received by the WTO Secretariat from WTO Members*]

(a) The WTO Secretariat shall transmit to the International Bureau, free of charge, a copy of the laws and regulations received by the WTO Secretariat from WTO Members under *Article 63.2 of the TRIPS Agreement* in the language or languages and in the form or forms in which they were received, and the International Bureau shall place such copies in its collection.

(b) The WTO Secretariat shall not put any restriction on the further use that the International Bureau may make of the copies of the laws and regulations transmitted under *subparagraph (a)*.

(5) [*Translation of Laws and Regulations*] The International Bureau shall make available to developing country WTO Members which are not Member States of WIPO the same assistance for translation of laws and regulations for the purposes of *Article 63.2 of the TRIPS Agreement* as it makes available to Members of WIPO which are developing countries.

Article 3

[Implementation of *Article 6ter of the Paris Convention* for the Purposes of the TRIPS Agreement]

(1) [*General*]

(a) The procedures relating to communication of emblems and transmittal of objections under the TRIPS Agreement shall be administered by the International Bureau in accordance with the procedures applicable under *Article 6ter of the Paris Convention* (1967).

(b) The International Bureau shall not recommunicate to a State party to the Paris Convention which is a WTO Member an emblem which had already been communicated to it by the International Bureau under *Article 6ter of the Paris Convention* prior to January 1, 1996, or, where that State became a WTO Member after January 1, 1996, prior to the date on which it became a WTO Member, and the International Bureau shall not transmit any objection received from the said WTO Member concerning the said emblem if the objection is received by the International Bureau more than 12 months after receipt of the communication of the said emblem under *Article 6ter of the Paris Convention* by the said State.

(2) [*Objections*] Notwithstanding *paragraph (1)(a)*, any objection received by the International Bureau from a WTO Member which concerns an emblem that had been communicated to the International Bureau by another WTO Member where at least one of the said WTO Members is not party to the Paris Convention, and any objection which concerns an emblem of an international intergovernmental organization and which is received by the International Bureau from a WTO Member not party to the Paris Convention or not bound under the Paris Convention to protect emblems of international intergovernmental organizations, shall be transmitted by the International Bureau to the WTO Member or international intergovernmental organization concerned regardless of the date on which the objection had been received by the International Bureau. The provisions of the preceding sentence shall not affect the time limit of 12 months for the lodging of an objection.

(3) [*Information to Be Provided to the WTO Secretariat*] The International Bureau shall provide to the WTO Secretariat information relating to any emblem communicated by a WTO Member to the International Bureau or communicated by the International Bureau to a WTO Member.

Article 4
[Legal-Technical Assistance and Technical Cooperation]

(1) [*Availability of Legal-Technical Assistance and Technical Cooperation*] The International Bureau shall make available to developing country WTO Members which are not Member States of WIPO the same legal-technical assistance relating to the TRIPS Agreement as it makes available to Member States of WIPO which are developing countries. The WTO Secretariat shall make available to Member States of WIPO which are developing countries and are not WTO Members the same technical cooperation relating to the TRIPS Agreement as it makes available to developing country WTO Members.

(2) [*Cooperation Between the International Bureau and the WTO Secretariat*] The International Bureau and the WTO Secretariat shall enhance cooperation in their legal-technical assistance and technical cooperation activities relating to the TRIPS Agreement for developing countries, so as to maximize the usefulness of those activities and ensure their mutually supportive nature.

(3) [*Exchange of Information*] For the purposes of *paragraphs (1)* and *(2)*, the International Bureau and the WTO Secretariat shall keep in regular contact and exchange non-confidential information.

Article 5
[Final Clauses]

(1) [*Entry into Force of this Agreement*] This Agreement shall enter into force on January 1, 1996.

(2) [*Amendment of this Agreement*] This Agreement may be amended by common agreement of the parties to this Agreement.

(3) [*Termination of this Agreement*] If one of the parties to this Agreement gives the other party written notice to terminate this Agreement, this Agreement shall terminate one year after receipt of the notice by the other party, unless a longer period is specified in the notice or unless both parties agree on a longer or a shorter period.

[Entry into force: 1 January 1996. Source: Communication from the International Bureau of WIPO and the WTO Secretariat.]

APPENDIX 12

Vienna Convention on the Law of Treaties

(Vienna, 23 May 1969)

THE STATES PARTIES TO THE PRESENT CONVENTION,

CONSIDERING the fundamental role of treaties in the history of international relations,

RECOGNIZING the ever-increasing importance of treaties as a source of international law and as a means of developing peaceful co-operation among nations, whatever their constitutional and social systems,

NOTING that the principles of free consent and of good faith and the *pacta sunt servanda* rule are universally recognized,

AFFIRMING that disputes concerning treaties, like other international disputes, should be settled by peaceful means and in conformity with the principles of justice and international law,

RECALLING the determination of the peoples of the United Nations to establish conditions under which justice and respect for the obligations arising from treaties can be maintained,

HAVING IN MIND the principles of international law embodied in the Charter of the United Nations, such as the principles of the equal rights and self-determination of peoples, of the sovereign equality and independence of all States, of non-interference in the domestic affairs of States, of the prohibition of the threat or use of force and of universal respect for, and observance of, human rights and fundamental freedoms for all,

BELIEVING that the codification and progressive development of the law of treaties achieved in the present Convention will promote the purposes of the United Nations set forth in the Charter, namely, the maintenance of international peace and security, the development of friendly relations and the achievement of co-operation among nations,

AFFIRMING that the rules of customary international law will continue to govern questions not regulated by the provisions of the present Convention,

HAVE AGREED as follows:

Part I Introduction

Article 1
[Scope of the present Convention]

The present Convention applies to treaties between States.

Article 2
[Use of terms]

1. For the purposes of the present Convention:

(a) 'treaty' means an international agreement concluded between States in written form and governed by international law, whether embodied in a single instrument or in two or more related instruments and whatever its particular designation;
(b) 'ratification', 'acceptance', 'approval' and 'accession' mean in each case the international act so named whereby a State establishes on the international plane its consent to be bound by a treaty;
(c) 'full powers' means a document emanating from the competent authority of a State designating a person or persons to represent the State for negotiating, adopting or authenticating the text of a treaty, for expressing the consent of the State to be bound by a treaty, or for accomplishing any other act with respect to a treaty;

(d) 'reservation' means a unilateral statement, however phrased or named, made by a State, when signing, ratifying, accepting, approving or acceding to a treaty, whereby it purports to exclude or to modify the legal effect of certain provisions of the treaty in their application to that State;
(e) 'negotiating State' means a State which took part in the drawing up and adoption of the text of the treaty;
(f) 'contracting State' means a State which has consented to be bound by the treaty, whether or not the treaty has entered into force;
(g) 'party' means a State which has consented to be bound by the treaty and for which the treaty is in force;
(h) 'third State' means a State not a party to the treaty;
(i) 'international organization' means an intergovernmental organization.

2. The provisions of paragraph 1 regarding the use of terms in the present Convention are without prejudice to the use of those terms or to the meanings which may be given to them in the internal law of any State.

Article 3
[International agreements not within the scope of the present Convention]

The fact that the present Convention does not apply to international agreements concluded between the States and other subjects of international law or between such other subjects of international law, or to international agreements not in written form, shall not affect:

(a) the legal force of such agreements;
(b) the application to them of any of the rules set forth in the present Convention to which they would be subject under international law independently of the Convention;
(c) the application of the Convention to the relations of States as between themselves under international agreements to which other subjects of international law are also parties.

Article 4
[Non-retroactivity of the present Convention]

Without prejudice to the application of any rules set forth in the present Convention to which treaties would be subject under international law independently of the Convention, the Convention applies only to treaties which are concluded by States after the entry into force of the present Convention with regard to such States.

Article 5
[Treaties constituting international organizations and treaties adopted within an international organization]

The present Convention applies to any treaty which is the constituent instrument of an international organization and to any treaty adopted within an international organization without prejudice to any relevant rules of the organization.

Part II Conclusion and Entry into Force of Treaties

Section 1: Conclusion of treaties

Article 6
[Capacity of States to conclude treaties]

Every State possesses capacity to conclude treaties.

Article 7
[Full powers]

1. A person is considered as representing a State for the purpose of adopting or authenticating the text of a treaty or for the purpose of expressing the consent of the State to be bound by a treaty if:

(a) he produces appropriate full powers; or
(b) it appears from the practice of the States concerned or from other circumstances that their intention was to consider that person as representing the State for such purposes and to dispense with full powers.

2. In virtue of their functions and without having to produce full powers, the following are considered as representing their State:

(a) Heads of State, Heads of Government and Ministers for Foreign Affairs, for the purpose of performing all acts relating to the conclusion of a treaty;
(b) heads of diplomatic missions, for the purpose of adopting the text of a treaty between the accrediting State and the State to which they are accredited;
(c) representatives accredited by States to an international conference or to an international organization or one of its organs, for the purpose of adopting the text of a treaty in that conference, organization or organ.

Article 8
[Subsequent confirmation of an act performed without authorization]

An act relating to the conclusion of a treaty performed by a person who cannot be considered under article 7 as authorized to represent a State for that purpose is without legal effect unless afterwards confirmed by that State.

Article 9
[Adoption of the text]

1. The adoption of the text of a treaty takes place by the consent of all the States participating in its drawing up except as provided in paragraph 2.

2. The adoption of the text of a treaty at an international conference takes place by the vote of two thirds of the States present and voting, unless by the same majority they shall decide to apply a different rule.

Article 10
[Authentication of the text]

The text of a treaty is established as authentic and definitive:

(a) by such procedures as may be provided for in the text or agreed upon by the States participating in its drawing up; or
(b) failing such procedure, by the signature, signature *ad referendum* or initialling by the representatives of those States of the text of the treaty or of the Final Act of a conference incorporating the text.

Article 11
[Means of expressing consent to be bound by a treaty]

The consent of a State to be bound by a treaty may be expressed by signature, exchange of instruments constituting a treaty, ratification, acceptance, approval or accession, or by any other means if so agreed.

Article 12
[Consent to be bound by a treaty expressed by signature]

1. The consent of a State to be bound by a treaty is expressed by the signature of its representative when:

(a) the treaty provides that signature shall have that effect;
(b) it is otherwise established that the negotiating States were agreed that signature should have that effect; or
(c) the intention of the State to give that effect to the signature appears from the full powers of its representative or was expressed during the negotiation.

2. For the purposes of paragraph 1:

(a) the initialling of a text constitutes a signature of the treaty when it is established that the negotiating States so agreed;
(b) the signature *ad referendum* of a treaty by a representative, if confirmed by his State, constitutes a full signature of the treaty.

Article 13
[Consent to be bound by a treaty expressed by an exchange of instruments constituting a treaty]

The consent of States to be bound by a treaty constituted by instruments exchanged between them is expressed by that exchange when;

(a) the instruments provide that their exchange shall have that effect; or
(b) it is otherwise established that those States were agreed that the exchange of instruments should have that effect.

Article 14

[Consent to be bound by a treaty expressed by ratification, acceptance or approval]

1. The consent of a State to be bound by a treaty is expressed by ratification when:

(a) the treaty provides for such consent to be expressed by means of ratification;
(b) it is otherwise established that the negotiating States were agreed that ratification should be required;
(c) the representative of the State has signed the treaty subject to ratification; or
(d) the intention of the State to sign the treaty subject to ratification appears from the full powers of its representative or was expressed during the negotiation.

2. The consent of a State to be bound by a treaty is expressed by acceptance or approval under conditions similar to those which apply to ratification.

Article 15

[Consent to be bound by a treaty expressed by accession]

The consent of a State to be bound by a treaty is expressed by accession when:

(a) the treaty provides that such consent may be expressed by that State by means of accession;
(b) it is otherwise established that the negotiating States were agreed that such consent may be expressed by that State by means of accession; or
(c) all the parties have subsequently agreed that such consent may be expressed by that State by means of accession.

Article 16

[Exchange or deposit of instruments of ratification, acceptance, approval or accession]

Unless the treaty otherwise provides, instruments of ratification, acceptance, approval or accession establish the consent of a State to be bound by a treaty upon:

(a) their exchange between the contracting States;
(b) their deposit with the depositary; or
(c) their notification to the contracting States or to the depositary, if so agreed.

Article 17

[Consent to be bound by part of a treaty and choice of differing provisions]

1. Without prejudice to articles 19 to 23, the consent of a State to be bound by part of a treaty is effective only if the treaty so permits or the other contracting States so agree.

2. The consent of a State to be bound by a treaty which permits a choice between differing provisions is effective only if it is made clear to which of the provisions the consent relates.

Article 18

[Obligation not to defeat the object and purpose of a treaty prior to its entry into force]

A State is obliged to refrain from acts which would defeat the object and purpose of a treaty when:

(a) it has signed the treaty or has exchanged instruments constituting the treaty subject to ratification, acceptance or approval, until it shall have made its intention clear not to become a party to the treaty; or
(b) it has expressed its consent to be bound by the treaty, pending the entry into force of the treaty and provided that such entry into force is not unduly delayed.

Section 2: Reservations

Article 19

[Formulation of reservations]

A State may, when signing, ratifying, accepting, approving or acceding to a treaty, formulate a reservation unless:

(a) the reservation is prohibited by the treaty;
(b) the treaty provides that only specified reservations, which do not include the reservation in question, may be made; or
(c) in cases not falling under sub-paragraphs (a) and (b), the reservation is incompatible with the object and purpose of the treaty.

Article 20
[Acceptance of and objection to reservations]

1. A reservation expressly authorized by a treaty does not require any subsequent acceptance by the other contracting States unless the treaty so provides.

2. When it appears from the limited number of the negotiating States and the object and purpose of a treaty that the application of the treaty in its entirety between all the parties is an essential condition of the consent of each one to be bound by the treaty, a reservation requires acceptance by all the parties.

3. When a treaty is a constituent instrument of an international organization and unless it otherwise provides, a reservation requires the acceptance of the competent organ of that organization.

4. In cases not falling under the preceding paragraphs and unless the treaty otherwise provides:

(a) acceptance by another contracting State of a reservation constitutes the reserving State a party to the treaty in relation to that other State if or when the treaty is in force for those States;

(b) an objection by another contracting State to a reservation does not preclude the entry into force of the treaty as between the objecting and reserving States unless a contrary intention is definitely expressed by the objecting State;

(c) an act expressing a State's consent to be bound by the treaty and containing a reservation is effective as soon as at least one other contracting State has accepted the reservation.

5. For the purposes of paragraphs 2 and 4 and unless the treaty otherwise provides, a reservation is considered to have been accepted by a State if it shall have raised no objection to the reservation by the end of a period of twelve months after it was notified of the reservation or by the date on which it expressed its consent to be bound by the treaty, whichever is later.

Article 21
[Legal effects of reservations and of objections to reservations]

1. A reservation established with regard to another party in accordance with articles 19, 20 and 23:

(a) modifies for the reserving State in its relations with that other party the provisions of the treaty to which the reservation relates to the extent of the reservation; and

(b) modifies those provisions to the same extent for that other party in its relations with the reserving State.

2. The reservation does not modify the provisions of the treaty for the other parties to the treaty *inter se*.

3. When a State objecting to a reservation has not opposed the entry into force of the treaty between itself and the reserving State, the provisions to which the reservation relates do not apply as between the two States to the extent of the reservation.

Article 22
[Withdrawal of reservations and of objections to reservations]

1. Unless the treaty otherwise provides, a reservation may be withdrawn at any time and the consent of a State which has accepted the reservation is not required for its withdrawal.

2. Unless the treaty otherwise provides, an objection to a reservation may be withdrawn at any time.

3. Unless the treaty otherwise provides, or it is otherwise agreed:

(a) the withdrawal of a reservation becomes operative in relation to another contracting State only when notice of it has been received by that State;

(b) the withdrawal of an objection to a reservation becomes operative only when notice of it has been received by the State which formulated the reservation.

Article 23
[Procedure regarding reservations]

1. A reservation, an express acceptance of a reservation and an objection to a reservation must be formulated in writing and communicated to the contracting States and other States entitled to become parties to the treaty.

2. If formulated when signing the treaty subject to ratification, acceptance or approval, a reservation must be formally confirmed by the reserving State when expressing its consent to be bound by the treaty. In such a case the reservation shall be considered as having been made on the date of its confirmation.

3. An express acceptance of, or an objection to, a reservation made previously to confirmation of the reservation does not itself require confirmation.

4. The withdrawal of a reservation or of an objection to a reservation must be formulated in writing.

Section 3: Entry into force and provisional application of treaties

Article 24
[Entry into force]

1. A treaty enters into force in such manner and upon such date as it may provide or as the negotiating States may agree.

2. Failing any such provision or agreement, a treaty enters into force as soon as consent to be bound by the treaty has been established for all the negotiating States.

3. When the consent of a State to be bound by a treaty is established on a date after the treaty has come into force, the treaty enters into force for that State on that date, unless the treaty otherwise provides.

4. The provisions of a treaty regulating the authentication of its text, the establishment of the consent of States to be bound by the treaty, the manner or date of its entry into force, reservations, the functions of the depositary and other matters arising necessarily before the entry into force of the treaty apply from the time of the adoption of its text.

Article 25
[Provisional application]

1. A treaty or a part of a treaty is applied provisionally pending its entry into force if:

(a) the treaty itself so provides; or
(b) the negotiating States have in some other manner so agreed.

2. Unless the treaty otherwise provides or the negotiating States have otherwise agreed, the provisional application of a treaty or a part of a treaty with respect to a State shall be terminated if that State notifies the other States between which the treaty is being applied provisionally of its intention not to become a party to the treaty.

Part III Observance, Application and Interpretation of Treaties

Section 1: Observance of treaties

Article 26
[*Pacta sunt servanda*]

Every treaty in force is binding upon the parties to it and must be performed by them in good faith.

Article 27
[Internal law and observance of treaties]

A party may not invoke the provisions of its internal law as justification for its failure to perform a treaty. This rule is without prejudice to article 46.

Section 2: Application of treaties

Article 28
[Non-retroactivity of treaties]

Unless a different intention appears from the treaty or is otherwise established, its provisions do not bind a party in relation to any act or fact which took place or any situation which ceased to exist before the date of the entry into force of the treaty with respect to that party.

Article 29
[Territorial scope of treaties]

Unless a different intention appears from the treaty or is otherwise established, a treaty is binding upon each party in respect of its entire territory.

Article 30

[Application of successive treaties relating to the same subject-matter]

1. Subject to article 103 of the Charter of the United Nations, the rights and obligations of States parties to successive treaties relating to the same subject-matter shall be determined in accordance with the following paragraphs.

2. When a treaty specifies that it is subject to, or that it is not to be considered as incompatible with, an earlier or later treaty, the provisions of that other treaty prevail.

3. When all the parties to the earlier treaty are parties also to the later treaty but the earlier treaty is not terminated or suspended in operation under article 59, the earlier treaty applies only to the extent that its provisions are compatible with those of the later treaty.

4. When the parties to the later treaty do not include all the parties to the earlier one:

(a) as between States parties to both treaties the same rule applies as in paragraph 3;

(b) as between a State party to both treaties and a State party to only one of the treaties, the treaty to which both States are parties governs their mutual rights and obligations.

5. Paragraph 4 is without prejudice to article 41, or to any question of the termination or suspension of the operation of a treaty under article 60 or to any question of responsibility which may arise for a State from the conclusion or application of a treaty the provisions of which are incompatible with its obligations towards another State under another treaty.

Section 3: Interpretation of treaties

Article 31

[General rule of interpretation]

1. A treaty shall be interpreted in good faith in accordance with the ordinary meaning to be given to the terms of the treaty in their context and in the light of its object and purpose.

2. The context for the purpose of the interpretation of a treaty shall comprise, in addition to the text, including its preamble and annexes:

(a) any agreement relating to the treaty which was made between all the parties in connexion with the conclusion of the treaty;

(b) any instrument which was made by one or more parties in connexion with the conclusion of the treaty and accepted by the other parties as an instrument related to the treaty.

3. There shall be taken into account, together with the context:

(a) any subsequent agreement between the parties regarding the interpretation of the treaty or the application of its provisions;

(b) any subsequent practice in the application of the treaty which establishes the agreement of the parties regarding its interpretation;

(c) any relevant rules of international law applicable in the relations between the parties.

4. A special meaning shall be given to a term if it is established that the parties so intended.

Article 32

[Supplementary means of interpretation]

Recourse may be had to supplementary means of interpretation, including the preparatory work of the treaty and the circumstances of its conclusion, in order to confirm the meaning resulting from the application of article 31, or to determine the meaning when the interpretation according to article 31:

(a) leaves the meaning ambiguous or obscure; or

(b) leads to a result which is manifestly absurd or unreasonable.

Article 33

[Interpretation of treaties authenticated in two or more languages]

1. When a treaty has been authenticated in two or more languages, the text is equally authoritative in each language, unless the treaty provides or the parties agree that, in case of divergence, a particular text shall prevail.

2. A version of the treaty in a language other than one of those in which the text was authenticated shall be considered an authentic text only if the treaty so provides or the parties so agree.

3. The terms of the treaty are presumed to have the same meaning in each authentic text.

4. Except where a particular text prevails in accordance with paragraph 1, when a comparison of the authentic texts discloses a difference of meaning which the application of articles 31 and 32 does not remove, the meaning which best reconciles the texts, having regard to the object and purpose of the treaty, shall be adopted.

Section 4: Treaties and third states

Article 34
[General rule regarding third States]

A treaty does not create either obligations or rights for a third State without its consent.

Article 35
[Treaties providing for obligations for third States]

An obligation arises for a third State from a provision of a treaty if the parties to the treaty intend the provision to be the means of establishing the obligation and the third State expressly accepts that obligation in writing.

Article 36
[Treaties providing for rights for third States]

1. A right arises for a third State from a provision of a treaty if the parties to the treaty intend the provision to accord that right either to the third State, or to a group of States to which it belongs, or to all States, and the third State assents thereto. Its assent shall be presumed so long as the contrary is not indicated, unless the treaty otherwise provides.

2. A State exercising a right in accordance with paragraph 1 shall comply with the conditions for its exercise provided for in the treaty or established in conformity with the treaty.

Article 37
[Revocation or modification of obligations or rights of third States]

1. When an obligation has arisen for a third State in conformity with article 35, the obligation may be revoked or modified only with the consent of the parties to the treaty and of the third State, unless it is established that they had otherwise agreed.

2. When a right has arisen for a third State in conformity with article 36, the right may not be revoked or modified by the parties if it is established that the right was intended not to be revocable or subject to modification without the consent of the third State.

Article 38
[Rules in a treaty becoming binding on third States through international custom]

Nothing in articles 34 to 37 precludes a rule set forth in a treaty from becoming binding upon a third State as a customary rule of international law, recognized as such.

Part IV Amendment and Modification of Treaties

Article 39
[General rule regarding the amendment of treaties]

A treaty may be amended by agreement between the parties. The rules laid down in Part II apply to such an agreement except in so far as the treaty may otherwise provide.

Article 40
[Amendment of multilateral treaties]

1. Unless the treaty otherwise provides, the amendment of multilateral treaties shall be governed by the following paragraphs.

2. Any proposal to amend a multilateral treaty as between all the parties must be notified to all the contracting States, each one of which shall have the right to take part in:

(a) the decision as to the action to be taken in regard to such proposal;

(b) the negotiation and conclusion of any agreement for the amendment of the treaty.

3. Every State entitled to become a party to the treaty shall also be entitled to become a party to the treaty as amended.

4. The amending agreement does not bind any State already a party to the treaty which does not become a party to the amending agreement; article 30, paragraph 4(b), applies in relation to such State.

5. Any State which becomes a party to the treaty after the entry into force of the amending agreement shall, failing an expression of a different intention by that State:

(a) be considered as a party to the treaty as amended; and
(b) be considered as a party to the unamended treaty in relation to any party to the treaty not bound by the amending agreement.

Article 41
[Agreements to modify multilateral treaties between certain of the parties only]

1. Two or more of the parties to a multilateral treaty may conclude an agreement to modify the treaty as between themselves alone if:

(a) the possibility of such a modification is provided for by the treaty; or
(b) the modification in question is not prohibited by the treaty and:
    (i) does not affect the enjoyment by the other parties of their rights under the treaty or the performance of their obligations;
    (ii) does not relate to a provision, derogation from which is incompatible with the effective execution of the object and purpose of the treaty as a whole.

2. Unless in a case falling under paragraph 1(a) the treaty otherwise provides, the parties in question shall notify the other parties of their intention to conclude the agreement and of the modification to the treaty for which it provides.

Part V Invalidity, Termination and Suspension of the Operation of Treaties

Section 1: General provisions

Article 42
[Validity and continuance in force of treaties]

1. The validity of a treaty or of the consent of a State to be bound by a treaty may be impeached only through the application of the present Convention.

2. The termination of a treaty, its denunciation or the withdrawal of a party, may take place only as a result of the application of the provisions of the treaty or of the present Convention. The same rule applies to suspension of the operation of a treaty.

Article 43
[Obligations imposed by international law independently of a treaty]

The invalidity, termination or denunciation of a treaty, the withdrawal of a party from it, or the suspension of its operation, as a result of the application of the present Convention or of the provisions of the treaty, shall not in any way impair the duty of any State to fulfil any obligation embodied in the treaty to which it would be subject under international law independently of the treaty.

Article 44
[Separability of treaty provisions]

1. A right of a party, provided for in a treaty or arising under article 56, to denounce, withdraw from or suspend the operation of the treaty may be exercised only with respect to the whole treaty unless the treaty otherwise provides or the parties otherwise agree.

2. A ground for invalidating, terminating, withdrawing from or suspending the operation of a treaty recognized in the present Convention may be invoked only with respect to the whole treaty except as provided in the following paragraphs or in article 60.

3. If the ground relates solely to particular clauses, it may be invoked only with respect to those clauses where:

(a) the said clauses are separable from the remainder of the treaty with regard to their application;
(b) it appears from the treaty or is otherwise established that acceptance of those clauses was not an essential basis of the consent of the other party or parties to be bound by the treaty as a whole; and
(c) continued performance of the remainder of the treaty would not be unjust.

4. In cases falling under articles 49 and 50 the State entitled to invoke the fraud or corruption may do so with respect either to the whole treaty or, subject to paragraph 3, to the particular clauses alone.

5. In cases falling under articles 51, 52 and 53, no separation of the provisions of the treaty is permitted.

Article 45

[Loss of a right to invoke a ground for invalidating, terminating, withdrawing from or suspending the operation of a treaty]

A State may no longer invoke a ground for invalidating, terminating, withdrawing from or suspending the operation of a treaty under articles 46 to 50 or articles 60 and 62 if, after becoming aware of the facts:

(a) it shall have expressly agreed that the treaty is valid or remains in force or continues in operation, as the case may be; or
(b) it must by reason of its conduct be considered as having acquiesced in the validity of the treaty or in its maintenance in force or in operation, as the case may be.

Section 2: Invalidity of treaties

Article 46

[Provisions of internal law regarding competence to conclude treaties]

1. A State may not invoke the fact that its consent to be bound by a treaty has been expressed in violation of a provision of its internal law regarding competence to conclude treaties as invalidating its consent unless that violation was manifest and concerned a rule of its internal law of fundamental importance.

2. A violation is manifest if it would be objectively evident to any State conducting itself in the matter in accordance with normal practice and in good faith.

Article 47

[Specific restrictions on authority to express the consent of a State]

If the authority of a representative to express the consent of a State to be bound by a particular treaty has been made subject to a specific restriction, his omission to observe that restriction may not be invoked as invalidating the consent expressed by him unless the restriction was notified to the other negotiating States prior to his expressing such consent.

Article 48

[Error]

1. A State may invoke an error in a treaty as invalidating its consent to be bound by the treaty if the error relates to a fact or situation which was assumed by that State to exist at the time when the treaty was concluded and formed an essential basis of its consent to be bound by the treaty.

2. Paragraph 1 shall not apply if the State in question contributed by its own conduct to the error or if the circumstances were such as to put that State on notice of a possible error.

3. An error relating only to the wording of the text of a treaty does not affect its validity; article 79 then applies.

Article 49

[Fraud]

If a State has been induced to conclude a treaty by the fraudulent conduct of another negotiating State, the State may invoke the fraud as invalidating its consent to be bound by the treaty.

Article 50
[Corruption of a representative of a State]

If the expression of a State's consent to be bound by a treaty has been procured through the corruption of its representative directly or indirectly by another negotiating State, the State may invoke such corruption as invalidating its consent to be bound by the treaty.

Article 51
[Coercion of a representative of a State]

The expression of a State's consent to be bound by a treaty which has been procured by the coercion of its representative through acts or threats directed against him shall be without any legal effect.

Article 52
[Coercion of a State by the threat or use of force]

A treaty is void if its conclusion has been procured by the threat or use of force in violation of the principles of international law embodied in the Charter of the United Nations

Article 53
[Treaties conflicting with a peremptory norm of general international law (*jus cogens*)]

A treaty is void if, at the time of its conclusion, it conflicts with a peremptory norm of general international law. For the purposes of the present Convention, a peremptory norm of general international law is a norm accepted and recognized by the international community of States as a whole as a norm from which no derogation is permitted and which can be modified only by a subsequent norm of general international law having the same character.

Section 3: Termination and suspension of the operation of treaties

Article 54
[Termination of or withdrawal from a treaty under its provisions or by consent of the parties]

The termination of a treaty or the withdrawal of a party may take place:

(a) in conformity with the provisions of the treaty; or
(b) at any time by consent of all the parties after consultation with the other contracting States.

Article 55
[Reduction of the parties to a multilateral treaty below the number necessary for its entry into force]

Unless the treaty otherwise provides, a multilateral treaty does not terminate by reason only of the fact that the number of the parties falls below the number necessary for its entry into force.

Article 56
[Denunciation of or withdrawal from a treaty containing no provision regarding termination, denunciation or withdrawal]

1. A treaty which contains no provision regarding its termination and which does not provide for denunciation or withdrawal is not subject to denunciation or withdrawal unless:

(a) it is established that the parties intended to admit the possibility of denunciation or withdrawal; or
(b) a right of denunciation or withdrawal may be implied by the nature of the treaty.

2. A party shall give not less than twelve months' notice of its intention to denounce or withdraw from a treaty under paragraph 1.

Article 57
[Suspension of the operation of a treaty under its provisions or by consent of the parties]

The operation of a treaty in regard to all the parties or to a particular party may be suspended:

(a) in conformity with the provisions of the treaty; or
(b) at any time by consent of all the parties after consultation with the other contracting States.

Article 58

[Suspension of the operation of a multilateral treaty by agreement between certain of the parties only]

1. Two or more parties to a multilateral treaty may conclude an agreement to suspend the operation of provisions of the treaty, temporarily and as between themselves alone, if:

(a) the possibility of such a suspension is provided for by the treaty; or
(b) the suspension in question is not prohibited by the treaty and:
 (i) does not affect the enjoyment by the other parties of their rights under the treaty or the performance of their obligations;
 (ii) is not incompatible with the object and purpose of the treaty.

2. Unless in a case falling under paragraph 1(a) the treaty otherwise provides, the parties in question shall notify the other parties of their intention to conclude the agreement and of those provisions of the treaty the operation of which they intend to suspend.

Article 59

[Termination or suspension of the operation of a treaty implied by conclusion of a later treaty]

1. A treaty shall be considered as terminated if all the parties to it conclude a later treaty relating to the same subject-matter and:

(a) it appears from the later treaty or is otherwise established that the parties intended that the matter should be governed by that treaty; or
(b) the provisions of the later treaty are so far incompatible with those of the earlier one that the two treaties are not capable of being applied at the same time.

2. The earlier treaty shall be considered as only suspended in operation if it appears from the later treaty or is otherwise established that such was the intention of the parties.

Article 60

[Termination or suspension of the operation of a treaty as a consequence of its breach]

1. A material breach of bilateral treaty by one of the parties entitles the other to invoke the breach as a ground for terminating the treaty or suspending its operation in whole or in part.

2. A material breach of a multilateral treaty by one of the parties entitles:

(a) the other parties by unanimous agreement to suspend the operation of the treaty in whole or in part or to terminate it either:
 (i) in the relations between themselves and the defaulting State, or
 (ii) as between all the parties;
(b) a party specially affected by the breach to invoke it as a ground for suspending the operation of the treaty in whole or in part in the relations between itself and the defaulting State;
(c) any party other than the defaulting State to invoke the breach as a ground for suspending the operation of the treaty in whole or in part with respect to itself if the treaty is of such a character that a material breach of its provisions by one party radically changes the position of every party with respect to the further performance of its obligations under the treaty.

3. A material breach of a treaty, for the purposes of this article, consists in:

(a) a repudiation of the treaty not sanctioned by the present Convention; or
(b) the violation of a provision essential to the accomplishment of the object or purpose of the treaty.

4. The foregoing paragraphs are without prejudice to any provision in the treaty applicable in the event of a breach.

5. Paragraphs 1 to 3 do not apply to provisions relating to the protection of the human person contained in treaties of a humanitarian character, in particular to provisions prohibiting any form of reprisals against persons protected by such treaties.

Article 61

[Supervening impossibility of performance]

1. A party may invoke the impossibility of performing a treaty as a ground for terminating

or withdrawing from it if the impossibility results from the permanent disappearance or destruction of an object indispensable for the execution of the treaty. If the impossibility is temporary, it may be invoked only as a ground for suspending the operation of the treaty.

2. Impossibility of performance may not be invoked by a party as a ground for terminating, withdrawing from or suspending the operation of a treaty if the impossibility is the result of a breach by that party either of an obligation under the treaty or of any other international obligation owed to any other party to the treaty.

Article 62

[Fundamental change of circumstances]

1. A fundamental change of circumstances which has occurred with regard to those existing at the time of the conclusion of a treaty, and which was not foreseen by the parties, may not be invoked as a ground for terminating or withdrawing from the treaty unless:

(a) the existence of those circumstances constituted an essential basis of the consent of the parties to be bound by the treaty; and

(b) the effect of the change is radically to transform the extent of obligations still to be performed under the treaty.

2. A fundamental change of circumstances may not be invoked as a ground for terminating or withdrawing from a treaty:

(a) if the treaty establishes a boundary; or

(b) if the fundamental change is the result of a breach by the party invoking it either of an obligation under the treaty or of any other international obligation owed to any other party to the treaty.

3. If, under the foregoing paragraphs, a party may invoke a fundamental change of circumstances as a ground for terminating or withdrawing from a treaty it may also invoke the change as a ground for suspending the operation of the treaty.

Article 63

[Severance of diplomatic or consular relations]

The severance of diplomatic or consular relations between parties to a treaty does not affect the legal relations established between them by the treaty except in so far as the existence of diplomatic or consular relations is indispensable for the application of the treaty

Article 64

[Emergence of a new peremptory norm of general international law (*jus cogens*)]

If a new peremptory norm of general international law emerges, any existing treaty which is in conflict with that norm becomes void and terminates.

Section 4: Procedure

Article 65

[Procedure to be followed with respect to invalidity, termination, withdrawal from or suspension of the operation of a treaty]

1. A party which, under the provisions of the present Convention, invokes either a defect in its consent to be bound by a treaty or a ground for impeaching the validity of a treaty, terminating it, withdrawing from it or suspending its operation, must notify the other parties of its claim. The notification shall indicate the measure proposed to be taken with respect to the treaty and the reasons therefor.

2. If, after the expiry of a period which, except in cases of special urgency, shall not be less than three months after the receipt of the notification, no party has raised any objection, the party making the notification may carry out in the manner provided in article 67 the measure which it has proposed.

3. If, however, objection has been raised by any other party, the parties shall seek a solution through the means indicated in Article 33 of the Charter of the United Nations.

4. Nothing in the foregoing paragraphs shall affect the rights or obligations of the parties under any provisions in force binding the parties with regard to the settlement of disputes.

5. Without prejudice to article 45, the fact that a State has not previously made the notification prescribed in paragraph 1 shall not prevent it from making such notification in answer to another party claiming performance of the treaty or alleging its violation.

Article 66

[Procedures for judicial settlement, arbitration and conciliation]

If, under paragraph 3 of article 65, no solution has been reached within a period of twelve months following the date on which the objection was raised, the following procedures shall be followed:

(a) any one of the parties to a dispute concerning the application or the interpretation of article 53 or 64 may, by a written application, submit it to the International Court of Justice for a decision unless the parties by common consent agree to submit the dispute to arbitration;
(b) any one of the parties to a dispute concerning the application or the interpretation of any of the other articles in Part V of the present Convention may set in motion the procedure specified in the Annex to the Convention by submitting a request to that effect to the Secretary-General of the United Nations.

Article 67

[Instruments for declaring invalid, terminating, withdrawing from or suspending the operation of a treaty]

1. The notification provided for under article 65, paragraph 1 must be made in writing.

2. Any act declaring invalid, terminating, withdrawing from or suspending the operation of a treaty pursuant to the provisions of the treaty or of paragraphs 2 or 3 of article 65 shall be carried out through an instrument communicated to the other parties. If the instrument is not signed by the Head of State, Head of Government or Minister for Foreign Affairs, the representative of the State communicating it may be called upon to produce full powers.

Article 68

[Revocation of notifications and instruments provided for in articles 65 and 67]

A notification or instrument provided for in article 65 or 67 may be revoked at any time before it takes effect.

Section 5: Consequences of the invalidity, termination or suspension of the operation of a treaty

Article 69

[Consequences of the invalidity of a treaty]

1. A treaty the invalidity of which is established under the present Convention is void. The provisions of a void treaty have no legal force.

2. If acts have nevertheless been performed in reliance on such a treaty:

(a) each party may require any other party to establish as far as possible in their mutual relations the position that would have existed if the acts had not been performed;
(b) acts performed in good faith before the invalidity was invoked are not rendered unlawful by reason only of the invalidity of the treaty.

3. In cases falling under articles 49, 50, 51 or 52, paragraph 2 does not apply with respect to the party to which the fraud, the act of corruption or the coercion is imputable.

4. In the case of the invalidity of a particular State's consent to be bound by a multilateral treaty, the foregoing rules apply in the relations between that State and the parties to the treaty.

Article 70

[Consequences of the termination of a treaty]

1. Unless the treaty otherwise provides or the parties otherwise agree, the termination of a treaty under its provisions or in accordance with the present Convention:

(a) releases the parties from any obligation further to perform the treaty;
(b) does not affect any right, obligation or legal situation of the parties created

through the execution of the treaty prior to its termination.

2. If a State denounces or withdraws from a multilateral treaty, paragraph 1 applies in the relations between that State and each of the other parties to the treaty from the date when such denunciation or withdrawal takes effect.

Article 71

[Consequences of the invalidity of a treaty which conflicts with a peremptory norm of general international law]

1. In the case of a treaty which is void under article 53 the parties shall:

(a) eliminate as far as possible the consequences of any act performed in reliance on any provision which conflicts with the peremptory norm of general international law; and
(b) bring their mutual relations into conformity with the peremptory norm of general international law.

2. In the case of a treaty which becomes void and terminates under article 64, the termination of the treaty:

(a) releases the parties from any obligation further to perform the treaty;
(b) does not affect any right, obligation or legal situation of the parties created through the execution of the treaty prior to its termination; provided that those rights, obligations or situations may thereafter be maintained only to the extent that their maintenance is not in itself in conflict with the new peremptory norm of general international law.

Article 72

[Consequences of the suspension of the operation of a treaty]

1. Unless the treaty otherwise provides or the parties otherwise agree, the suspension of the operation of a treaty under its provisions or in accordance with the present Convention:

(a) releases the parties between which the operation of the treaty is suspended from the obligation to perform the treaty in their mutual relations during the period of the suspension;
(b) does not otherwise affect the legal relations between the parties established by the treaty.

2. During the period of the suspension the parties shall refrain from acts tending to obstruct the resumption of the operation of the treaty.

Part VI Miscellaneous Provisions

Article 73

[Cases of State succession, State responsibility and outbreak of hostilities]

The provisions of the present Convention shall not prejudge any question that may arise in regard to a treaty from a succession of States or from the international responsibility of a State or from the outbreak of hostilities between States.

Article 74

[Diplomatic and consular relations and the conclusion of treaties]

The severance or absence of diplomatic or consular relations between two or more States does not prevent the conclusion of treaties between those States. The conclusion of a treaty does not in itself affect the situation in regard to diplomatic or consular relations.

Article 75

[Case of an aggressor State]

The provisions of the present Convention are without prejudice to any obligation in relation to a treaty which may arise for an aggressor State in consequence of measures taken in conformity with the Charter of the United Nations with reference to that State's aggression.

Part VII Depositaries, Notifications, Corrections and Registration

Article 76

[Depositaries of treaties]

1. The designation of the depositary of a treaty may be made by the negotiating States, either in the treaty itself or in some other

manner. The depositary may be one or more States, an international organization or the chief administrative officer of the organization.

2. The functions of the depositary of a treaty are international in character and the depositary is under an obligation to act impartially in their performance. In particular, the fact that a treaty has not entered into force between certain of the parties or that a difference has appeared between a State and a depositary with regard to the performance of the latter's functions shall not affect that obligation.

Article 77

[Functions of depositaries]

1. The functions of a depositary, unless otherwise provided in the treaty or agreed by the contracting States, comprise in particular:

(a) keeping custody of the original text of the treaty and of any full powers delivered to the depositary;
(b) preparing certified copies of the original text and preparing any further text of the treaty in such additional languages as may be required by the treaty and transmitting them to the parties and to the States entitled to become parties to the treaty;
(c) receiving any signatures to the treaty and receiving and keeping custody of any instruments, notifications and communications relating to it;
(d) examining whether the signature or any instrument, notification or communication relating to the treaty is in due and proper form and, if need be, bringing the matter to the attention of the State in question;
(e) informing the parties and the States entitled to become parties to the treaty of acts, notifications and communications relating to the treaty;
(f) informing the States entitled to become parties to the treaty when the number of signatures or of instruments of ratification, acceptance, approval or accession required for the entry into force of the treaty has been received or deposited;
(g) registering the treaty with the Secretariat of the United Nations;
(h) performing the functions specified in other provisions of the present Convention.

2. In the event of any difference appearing between a State and the depositary as to the performance of the latter's functions, the depositary shall bring the question to the attention of the signatory States and the contracting States or, where appropriate, of the competent organ of the international organization concerned.

Article 78

[Notifications and communications]

Except as the treaty or the present Convention otherwise provide, any notification or communication to be made by any State under the present Convention shall:

(a) if there is no depositary, be transmitted direct to the States for which it is intended, or if there is a depositary, to the latter;
(b) be considered as having been made by the State in question only upon its receipt by the State to which it was transmitted or, as the case may be, upon its receipt by the depositary;
(c) if transmitted to a depositary, be considered as received by the State for which it was intended only when the latter State has been informed by the depositary in accordance with article 77, paragraph 1(e).

Article 79

[Correction of errors in texts or in certified copies of treaties]

1. Where, after the authentication of the text of a treaty, the signatory States and the contracting States are agreed that it contains an error, the error shall, unless they decide upon some other means of correction, be corrected:

(a) by having the appropriate correction made in the text and causing the correction to be initialled by duly authorized representatives;
(b) by executing or exchanging an instrument or instruments setting out the correction which it has been agreed to make; or
(c) by executing a corrected text of the whole

treaty by the same procedure as in the case of the original text.

2. Where the treaty is one for which there is a depositary, the latter shall notify the signatory States and the contracting States of the error and of the proposal to correct it and shall specify an appropriate time-limit within which objection to the proposed correction may be raised. If, on the expiry of the time-limit:

(a) no objection has been raised, the depositary shall make and initial the correction in the text and shall execute a *procès-verbal* of the rectification of the text and communicate a copy of it to the parties and to the States entitled to become parties to the treaty;
(b) an objection has been raised, the depositary shall communicate the objection to the signatory States and to the contracting States.

3. The rules in paragraphs 1 and 2 apply also where the text has been authenticated in two or more languages and it appears that there is a lack of concordance which the signatory States and the contracting States agree should be corrected.

4. The corrected text replaces the defective text *ab initio*, unless the signatory States and the contracting States otherwise decide.

5. The correction of the text of a treaty that has been registered shall be notified to the Secretariat of the United Nations.

6. Where an error is discovered in a certified copy of a treaty, the depositary shall execute a *procès-verbal* specifying the rectification and communicate a copy of it to the signatory States and to the contracting States.

Article 80
[Registration and publication of treaties]

1. Treaties shall, after their entry into force, be transmitted to the Secretariat of the United Nations for registration or filing and recording, as the case may be, and for publication.

2. The designation of a depositary shall constitute authorization for it to perform the acts specified in the preceding paragraph.

Part VIII Final Provisions

Article 81
[Signature]

The present Convention shall be open for signature by all States Members of the United Nations or of any of the specialized agencies or of the International Atomic Energy Agency or parties to the Statute of the International Court of Justice, and by any other State invited by the General Assembly of the United Nations to become a party to the Convention, as follows: until 30 November 1969, at the Federal Ministry for Foreign Affairs of the Republic of Austria, and subsequently, until 30 April 1970, at United Nations Headquarters New York

Article 82
[Ratification]

The present Convention is subject to ratification. The instruments of ratification shall be deposited with the Secretary-General of the United Nations.

Article 83
[Accession]

The present Convention shall remain open for accession by any State belonging to any of the categories mentioned in article 81. The instruments of accession shall be deposited with the Secretary-General of the United Nations.[1]

Article 84
[Entry into force]

1. The present Convention shall enter into force on the thirtieth day following the date

[1] Instrument of accession deposited for Australia 13 June 1974, with the following declaration:

> 'In acceding to the Vienna Convention on the Law of Treaties the Government of Australia declares its understanding that nothing in Article 66 of the Convention is intended to exclude the jurisdiction of the International Court of Justice where such jurisdiction exists under any provisions in force binding the parties with regard to the settlement of disputes.'

of deposit of the thirty-fifth instrument of ratification or accession.[2]

2. For each State ratifying or acceding to the Convention after the deposit of the thirty-fifth instrument of ratification or accession, the Convention shall enter into force on the thirtieth day after deposit by such State of its instrument of ratification or accession.

Article 85
[Authentic texts]

The original of the present Convention, of which the Chinese, English, French Russian and Spanish texts are equally authentic, shall be deposited with the Secretary-General of the United Nations.

IN WITNESS WHEREOF the undersigned Plenipotentiaries, being duly authorized thereto by their respective Governments, have signed the present Convention.

DONE AT VIENNA, this twenty-third day of May, one thousand nine hundred and sixty-nine.

[Signatures not reproduced here.]

ANNEX

1. A list of conciliators consisting of qualified jurists shall be drawn up and maintained by the Secretary-General of the United Nations. To this end, every State which is a Member of the United Nations or a party to the present Convention shall be invited to nominate two conciliators, and the names of the persons so nominated shall constitute the list. The term of a conciliator, including that of any conciliator nominated to fill a casual vacancy, shall be five years and may be renewed. A conciliator whose term expires shall continue to fulfil any function for which he shall have been chosen under the following paragraph.

2. When a request has been made to the Secretary-General under article 66, the Secretary-General shall bring the dispute before a conciliation commission constituted as follows:

The State or States constituting one of the parties to the dispute shall appoint:

(a) one conciliator of the nationality of that State or of one of those States, who may or may not be chosen from the list referred to in paragraph 1; and
(b) one conciliator not of the nationality of that State or of any of those States, who shall be chosen from the list.

The State or States constituting the other party to the dispute shall appoint two conciliators in the same way. The four conciliators chosen by the parties shall be appointed within sixty days following the date on which the Secretary-General receives the request.

The four conciliators shall, within sixty days following the date of the last of their own appointments, appoint a fifth conciliator chosen from the list, who shall be chairman.

If the appointment of the chairman or of any of the other conciliators has not been made within the period prescribed above for such appointment, it shall be made by the Secretary-General within sixty days following the expiry of that period. The appointment of the chairman may be made by the Secretary-General either from the list or from the membership of the International Law Commission. Any of the periods within which appointments must be made may be extended by agreement between the parties to the dispute.

Any vacancy shall be filled in the manner prescribed for the initial appointment.

3. The Conciliation Commission shall decide its own procedure. The Commission, with the consent of the parties to the dispute, may invite any party to the treaty to submit to it its views orally or in writing. Decisions and recommendations of the Commission shall be made by a majority vote of the five members.

4. The Commission may draw the attention of the parties to the dispute to any measures which might facilitate an amicable settlement.

5. The Commission shall hear the parties, examine the claims and objections, and make proposals to the parties with a view to reaching an amicable settlement of the dispute.

[2] The Convention entered into force for Australia and generally 27 January 1980.

6. The Commission shall report within twelve months of its constitution. Its report shall be deposited with the Secretary-General and transmitted to the parties to the dispute. The report of the Commission, including any conclusions stated therein regarding the facts or questions of law, shall not be binding upon the parties and it shall have no other character than that of recommendations submitted for the consideration of the parties in order to facilitate an amicable settlement of the dispute.

7. The Secretary-General shall provide the Commission with such assistance and facilities as it may require. The expenses of the Commission shall be borne by the United Nations.

APPENDIX 13

Draft Treaty on Databases (Geneva Conference, 1996) Document CRNR/DC/6 (30 August 1996)

Basic Proposal for the Substantive Provisions of the Treaty on Intellectual Property in Respect of Databases to be Considered by the Diplomatic Conference

prepared by the Chairman of the Committees of Experts on a Possible Protocol to the Berne Convention and on a Possible Instrument for the Protection of the Rights of Performers and Producers of Phonograms

Note: The text of the draft treaty follows, but the accompanying commentary has been omitted.

Preamble

The Contracting Parties,

Desiring to enhance and stimulate the production, distribution and international trade in databases,

Recognizing that databases are a vital element in the development of a global information infrastructure and an essential tool for promoting economic, cultural and technological advancement,

Recognizing that the making of databases requires the investment of considerable human, technical and financial resources but that such databases can be copied or accessed at a fraction of the cost needed to design them independently,

Desiring to establish a new form of protection for databases by granting rights adequate to enable the makers of databases to recover the investment they have made in their databases and by providing international protection in a manner as effective and uniform as possible,

Emphasizing that nothing in this Treaty shall derogate from existing obligations that Contracting Parties may have to each other under treaties in the field of intellectual property, and in particular, that nothing in this Treaty shall in any way prejudice the rights granted to authors in the Berne Convention for the Protection of Literary and Artistic Works,

Have agreed as follows:

Article 1
[Scope]

(1) Contracting Parties shall protect any database that represents a substantial investment in the collection, assembly, verification, organization or presentation of the contents of the database.

(2) The legal protection set forth in this Treaty extends to a database regardless of the form or medium in which the database is embodied, and regardless of whether or not the database is made available to the public.

(3) The protection granted under this Treaty shall be provided irrespective of any protection provided for a database or its contents by copyright or by other rights granted by Contracting Parties in their national legislation.

(4) The protection under this Treaty shall not extend to any computer program as such, including without limitation any computer program used in the manufacture, operation or maintenance of a database.

Article 2
[Definitions]

For the purposes of this Treaty:

(i) 'database' means a collection of independent works, data or other materials arranged in a systematic or methodical way and capable of being individually accessed by electronic or other means;
(ii) 'extraction' means the permanent or temporary transfer of all or a substantial part of the contents of a database to another medium by any means or in any form;
(iii) 'maker of the database' means the natural or legal person or persons with control and responsibility for the undertaking of a substantial investment in making a database;
(iv) 'substantial investment' means any qualitatively or quantitatively significant investment of human, financial, technical or other resources in the collection, assembly, verification, organization or presentation of the contents of the database;
(v) 'substantial part', in reference to the contents of a database, means any portion of the database, including an accumulation of small portions, that is of qualitative or quantitative significance to the value of the database;
(vi) 'utilization' means the making available to the public of all or a substantial part of the contents of a database by any means, including by the distribution of copies, by renting, or by on-line or other forms of transmission, including making the same available to the public at a place and at a time individually chosen by each member of the public.

Article 3
[Rights]

(1) The maker of a database eligible for protection under this Treaty shall have the right to authorize or prohibit the extraction or utilization of its contents.

(2) Contracting Parties may, in their national legislation, provide that the right of utilization provided for in paragraph (1) does not apply to distribution of the original or any copy of any database that has been sold or the ownership of which has been otherwise transferred in that Contracting Party's territory by or pursuant to authorization.

Article 4
[Rightholders]

(1) The rights provided under this Treaty shall be owned by the maker of the database.

(2) The rights provided under this Treaty shall be freely transferable.

Article 5
[Exceptions]

(1) Contracting Parties may, in their national legislation, provide exceptions to or limitations of the rights provided in this Treaty in certain special cases that do not conflict with the normal exploitation of the database and do not unreasonably prejudice the legitimate interests of the rightholder.

(2) It shall be a matter for the national legislation of Contracting Parties to determine the protection that shall be granted to databases made by governmental entities or their agents or employees.

Article 6
[Beneficiaries of Protection]

(1) Each Contracting Party shall protect according to the terms of this Treaty makers of databases who are nationals of a Contracting Party.

(2) The provisions of paragraph (1) shall also apply to companies, firms and other legal entities formed in accordance with the laws of a Contracting Party or having their registered office, central administration or principal place of business within a Contracting Party; however, where such a company, firm or other legal entity has only its registered office in the territory of a Contracting Party, its operations must be genuinely linked on an on-going basis with the economy of a Contracting Party.

Article 7
[National Treatment and Independence of Protection]

(1) The maker of a database shall enjoy in respect of the protection provided for in this Treaty, in Contracting Parties other than the Contracting Party of which he is a national, the rights which their respective laws do now or may hereafter grant to their nationals as well as the rights specially granted by this Treaty.

(2) Protection of a database in the Contracting Party of which the maker of the database is a national shall be governed by national legislation.

(3) The enjoyment and the exercise of rights under this Treaty shall be independent of the existence of protection in the Contracting Party of which the maker of a database is a national. Apart from the provisions of this Treaty, the extent of protection, as well as the means and extent of redress, shall be governed exclusively by the laws of the Contracting Party where protection is claimed.

(4) Makers of databases who are not nationals of a Contracting Party but who have their habitual residence in a Contracting Party shall, for the purposes of this Treaty, be assimilated to nationals of that Contracting Party.

Article 8
[Term of Protection]

(1) The rights provided for in this Treaty shall attach when a database meets the requirements of Article 1(1) and shall endure for at least

Alternative A: 25
Alternative B: 15

years from the first day of January in the year following the date when the database first met the requirements of Article 1(1).

(2) In the case of a database that is made available to the public, in whatever manner, before the expiry of the period provided for in paragraph (1), the term of protection shall endure for at least

Alternative A: 25
Alternative B: 15

years from the first day of January in the year following the date when the database was first made available to the public.

(3) Any substantial change to the database, evaluated qualitatively or quantitatively, including any substantial change resulting from the accumulation of successive additions, deletions, verifications, modifications in organization or presentation, or other alterations, which constitute a new substantial investment, shall qualify the database resulting from such investment for its own term of protection.

Article 9
[Formalities]

The enjoyment and exercise of the rights provided for in this Treaty shall not be subject to any formality.

Article 10
[Obligations concerning Technological Measures]

(1) Contracting Parties shall make unlawful the importation, manufacture or distribution of protection-defeating devices, or the offer or performance of any service having the same effect, by any person knowing or having reasonable grounds to know that the device or service will be used for, or in the course of, the exercise of rights provided under this Treaty that is not authorized by the rightholder or the law.

(2) Contracting Parties shall provide for appropriate and effective remedies against the unlawful acts referred to in paragraph (1).

(3) As used in this Article, 'protection-defeating device' means any device, product or

component incorporated into a device or product, the primary purpose or primary effect of which is to circumvent any process, treatment, mechanism or system that prevents or inhibits any of the acts covered by the rights under this Treaty.

Article 11
[Application in Time]

(1) Contracting Parties shall also grant protection pursuant to this Treaty in respect of databases that met the requirements of Article 1(1) at the date of the entry into force of this Treaty for each Contracting Party. The duration of such protection shall be determined by the provisions of Article 8.

(2) The protection provided for in paragraph (1) shall be without prejudice to any acts concluded or rights acquired before the entry into force of this Treaty in each Contracting Party.

(3) A Contracting Party may provide for conditions under which copies of databases which were lawfully made before the date of the entry into force of this Treaty for that Contracting Party may be distributed to the public, provided that such provisions do not allow distribution for a period longer than two years from that date.

Article 12
[Relation to Other Legal Provisions]

The protection accorded under this Treaty shall be without prejudice to any other rights in, or obligations with respect to, a database or its contents, including laws in respect of copyright, rights related to copyright, patent, trademark, design rights, antitrust or competition, trade secrets, data protection and privacy, access to public documents and the law of contract.

Article 13
[Special Provisions on Enforcement of Rights]

(1) Special provisions regarding the enforcement of rights are included in the Annex to the Treaty.

(2) The Annex forms an integral part of this Treaty.

Alternative B

Contracting Parties shall ensure that the enforcement procedures specified in Part III, Articles 41 to 61, of the Agreement on Trade-Related Aspects of Intellectual Property Rights, Including Trade in Counterfeit Goods, Annex 1C, of the Marrakesh Agreement Establishing the World Trade Organization, concluded on April 15, 1994 (the 'TRIPS Agreement'), are available under their national laws so as to permit effective action against any act of infringement of the rights provided under this Treaty, including expeditious remedies to prevent infringements, and remedies that constitute a deterrent to further infringements. To this end, Contracting Parties shall apply *mutatis mutandis* the provisions of Articles 41 to 61 of the TRIPS Agreement.

ANNEX

. . .

Note: The draft provisions on enforcement contained here are not set out as they were modelled largely upon those in articles 41–61 of the TRIPs Agreement.

APPENDIX 14

Proposal for Instrument on the Protection of Audiovisual Performances (WIPO Document IAVP/DC/3, 1 August 2000)

Basic Proposal for the Substantive Provisions of an Instrument on the Protection of Audiovisual Performances to be Considered by the Diplomatic Conference

prepared by the Chairman of the Standing Committee on Copyright and Related Rights

Note: the draft text of the proposed treaty only is set out below, with various proposed alternatives.

Alternative A

Draft Protocol to the WIPO Performances and Phonograms Treaty concerning Audiovisual Performances

Alternative B

Draft WIPO Audiovisual Performances Treaty

Preamble

The Contracting Parties,

Desiring to develop and maintain the protection of rights of performers in their audiovisual performances in a manner as effective and uniform as possible,

Recognizing the need to introduce new international rules in order to provide adequate solutions to the questions raised by economic, cultural and technological developments,

Recognizing the profound impact of the development and convergence of information and communication technologies on the production and use of audiovisual performances,

Recognizing the need to maintain a balance between the rights of performers in their audiovisual performances and the larger public interest, particularly education, research and access to information,

Recognizing that the WIPO Performances and Phonograms Treaty done in Geneva, December 20, 1996, does not extend protection to performers in respect of their audiovisual performances,

Referring to the Resolution concerning Audiovisual Performances adopted by the Diplomatic Conference on Certain Copyright and Neighboring Rights Questions on December 20, 1996,

Have agreed as follows:

Article 1
[Relation to Other Conventions and Treaties]

Alternative A

(1) This Treaty constitutes a Protocol to the WIPO Performances and Phonograms Treaty done in Geneva, December 20, 1996.

[Paragraphs (2) and (3) follow below]
(4) This Treaty shall not have any connection with treaties other than the WIPO Performances and Phonograms Treaty, nor shall it prejudice any rights and obligations under any other treaties.

Alternative B

(1) [No such provision]

[Paragraphs (2) and (3) follow below]

(4) This Treaty shall not have any connection with, nor shall it prejudice any rights and obligations under, any other treaties.

(2) Nothing in this Treaty shall derogate from existing obligations that Contracting Parties have to each other under the WIPO Performances and Phonograms Treaty or the International Convention for the Protection of Performers, Producers of Phonograms and Broadcasting Organizations done in Rome, October 26, 1961.

(3) Protection granted under this Treaty shall leave intact and shall in no way affect the protection of copyright in literary and artistic works. Consequently, no provision of this Treaty may be interpreted as prejudicing such protection.

Article 2
[Definitions]

For the purposes of this Treaty:

(a) 'performers' are actors, singers, musicians, dancers, and other persons who act, sing, deliver, declaim, play in, interpret, or otherwise perform literary or artistic works or expressions of folklore;
(b) 'audiovisual performances' (hereinafter 'performances') mean performances that can be embodied in audiovisual fixations;
(c) 'audiovisual fixation' means the embodiment of moving images, whether or not accompanied by sound or by the representations thereof, from which they can be perceived, reproduced or communicated through a device;
(d) 'broadcasting' means the transmission by wireless means for public reception of sounds or images or images and sounds or the representations of sounds; such transmission by satellite is also 'broadcasting'; transmission of encrypted signals is 'broadcasting' where the means for decrypting are provided to the public by the broadcasting organization or with its consent;

(e) 'communication to the public' of a performance means the transmission to the public by any medium, otherwise than by broadcasting, of an unfixed performance, or of a performance fixed in an audiovisual fixation. For the purposes of Article 11, 'communication to the public' includes making a performance fixed in an audiovisual fixation audible or visible or audible and visible to the public.

Article 3
[Beneficiaries of Protection]

(1) Contracting Parties shall accord the protection granted under this Treaty to performers who are nationals of other Contracting Parties.

(2) Performers who are not nationals of one of the Contracting Parties but who have their habitual residence in one of them shall, for the purposes of this Treaty, be assimilated to nationals of that Contracting Party.

Article 4
[National Treatment]

Alternative C

(1) Each Contracting Party shall accord to nationals of other Contracting Parties, in respect of the subject matter protected under this Treaty, the treatment it accords to its own nationals with regard to:

(i) the rights specifically granted in this Treaty; and
(ii) such additional rights as it accords to its own nationals.

(2) A Contracting Party shall be entitled, in respect of nationals of any other Contracting Party, to limit the protection provided for in subparagraph (ii) of paragraph (1) to the extent to which, and to the term for which, the latter Contracting Party grants such rights to the nationals of the former Contracting Party.

Alternative D

(1) Each Contracting Party shall accord to nationals of other Contracting Parties the treatment it accords to its own nationals with regard to the exclusive rights specifically granted in this Treaty and the right to equitable remuneration provided for in Article 11 of this Treaty.

(2) The obligation provided for in paragraph (1) does not apply to the extent that another Contracting Party makes use of the reservations permitted by Article 11(3) of this Treaty.

Article 5
[Moral Rights]

(1) Independently of a performer's economic rights, and even after the transfer of those rights, the performer shall have the right

(i) to claim to be identified as the performer of his performances, except where omission is dictated by the manner of the use of the performance; and
(ii) to object to any distortion, mutilation or other modification of his performances that would be prejudicial to his reputation. Modifications consistent with the normal exploitation of a performance in the course of a use authorized by the performer shall not be considered prejudicial to the performer's reputation.

(2) The rights granted to a performer in accordance with paragraph (1) shall, after his death, be maintained, at least until the expiry of the economic rights, and shall be exercisable by the persons or institutions authorized by the legislation of the Contracting Party where protection is claimed. However, those Contracting Parties whose legislation, at the moment of their ratification of or accession to this Treaty, does not provide for protection after the death of the performer of all rights set out in the preceding paragraph may provide that some of these rights will, after his death, cease to be maintained.

(3) The means of redress for safeguarding the rights granted under this Article shall be governed by the legislation of the Contracting Party where protection is claimed.

Article 6
[Economic Rights of Performers in their Unfixed Performances]

Performers shall enjoy the exclusive right of authorizing, as regards their performances:

(i) the broadcasting and communication to the public of their unfixed performances except where the performance is already a broadcast performance; and
(ii) the audiovisual fixation of their unfixed performances.

Article 7
[Right of Reproduction]

Performers shall enjoy the exclusive right of authorizing the direct or indirect reproduction of their performances fixed in audiovisual fixations, in any manner or form.

Article 8
[Right of Distribution]

(1) Performers shall enjoy the exclusive right of authorizing the making available to the public of the original and copies of their performances fixed in audiovisual fixations through sale or other transfer of ownership.

(2) Nothing in this Treaty shall affect the freedom of Contracting Parties to determine the conditions, if any, under which the exhaustion of the right in paragraph (1) applies after the first sale or other transfer of ownership of the original or a copy of the fixed performance with the authorization of the performer.

Article 9
[Right of Rental]

(1) Performers shall enjoy the exclusive right of authorizing the commercial rental to the public of the original and copies of their performances fixed in audiovisual fixations even after distribution of them by, or pursuant to, authorization by the performer.

(2) Contracting Parties are exempt from the obligation of paragraph (1) unless the commercial rental has led to widespread copying of such fixations materially impairing the exclusive right of reproduction of performers.

Article 10
[Right of Making Available of Fixed Performances]

Performers shall enjoy the exclusive right of authorizing the making available to the public of their performances fixed in audiovisual fixations, by wire or wireless means, in such a way that the members of the public may access them from a place and at a time individually chosen by them.

Article 11
[Right of Broadcasting and Communication to the Public]

(1) Performers shall enjoy the exclusive right of authorizing the broadcasting and communication to the public of their performances fixed in audiovisual fixations.

(2) Contracting Parties may establish, instead of the right of authorization provided for in paragraph (1), a right to equitable remuneration for the direct or indirect use of performances fixed in audiovisual fixations for broadcasting or for communication to the public. Contracting Parties may in their legislation set conditions for the exercise of the right to equitable remuneration.

(3) Any Contracting Party may in a notification deposited with the Director General of WIPO, declare that it will apply the provisions of paragraph (2) only in respect of certain uses, or that it will limit their application in some other way, or that it will not apply the provisions of paragraphs (1) and (2) at all.

Article 12

Alternative E

[Transfer]

Once a performer has consented to the incorporation of his performance in an audiovisual fixation, he shall be deemed to have transferred all exclusive rights of authorization provided for in this Treaty with respect to that particular fixation to its producer, subject to written contractual clauses to the contrary.

Alternative F

[Entitlement to Exercise Rights]

In the absence of written contractual clauses to the contrary, once the performer has consented to the audiovisual fixation of his performance, the producer shall be deemed to be entitled to exercise the exclusive rights of authorization provided for in this Treaty with respect to that particular fixation.

Alternative G

[Law Applicable to Transfers]

(1) In the absence of any contractual clauses to the contrary, a transfer to the producer of an audiovisual fixation of a performance, by agreement or operation of law, of any of the exclusive rights of authorization granted under this Treaty, shall be governed by the law of the country most closely connected with the particular audiovisual fixation.

(2) The country most closely connected with a particular audiovisual fixation shall be

(i) the Contracting Party in which the producer of the fixation has his headquarters or habitual residence; or

(ii) where the producer does not have his headquarters or habitual residence in a Contracting Party, or where there is more than one producer, the Contracting Party of which the majority of performers are nationals; or

(iii) where the producer does not have his headquarters or habitual residence in a Contracting Party, or where there is more than one producer, and where there is no single Contracting Party of which a majority of the performers are nationals, the principal Contracting Party in which the photography takes place.

Alternative H

[No such provision]

Article 13
[Limitations and Exceptions]

(1) Contracting Parties may, in their national legislation, provide for the same kinds of limitations and exceptions with regard to the protection of performers as they provide for, in their national legislation, in connection with the protection of copyright in literary and artistic works.

(2) Contracting Parties shall confine any limitations of or exceptions to rights provided for in this Treaty to certain special cases which do not conflict with a normal exploitation of the performance and do not unreasonably prejudice the legitimate interests of the performer.

Article 14
[Term of Protection]

The term of protection to be granted to performers under this Treaty shall last, at least, until the end of a period of 50 years computed from the end of the year in which the performance was fixed in an audiovisual fixation.

Article 15
[Obligations concerning Technological Measures]

Contracting Parties shall provide adequate legal protection and effective legal remedies against the circumvention of effective technological measures that are used by performers in connection with the exercise of their rights under this Treaty and that restrict acts, in respect of their performances, which are not authorized by the performers concerned or permitted by law.

Article 16
[Obligations concerning Rights Management Information]

(1) Contracting Parties shall provide adequate and effective legal remedies against any person knowingly performing any of the following acts knowing, or with respect to civil remedies having reasonable grounds to know, that it will induce, enable, facilitate, or conceal an infringement of any right covered by this Treaty:

(i) to remove or alter any electronic rights management information without authority;

(ii) to distribute, import for distribution, broadcast, communicate or make available to the public, without authority, unfixed performances or performances fixed in audiovisual fixations knowing that electronic rights management information has been removed or altered without authority.

(2) As used in this Article, 'rights management information' means information which identifies the performer, the performance of the performer, or the owner of any right in the performance, or information about the terms and conditions of use of the performance, and any numbers or codes that represent such information, when any of these items of information is attached to a performance fixed in an audiovisual fixation.

Article 17
[Formalities]

The enjoyment and exercise of the rights provided for in this Treaty shall not be subject to any formality.

Article 18
[Reservations]

Subject to the provisions of Article 11(3), no reservations to this Treaty shall be permitted.

Article 19
[Application in Time]

(1) Contracting Parties shall accord the protection granted under this Treaty to fixed performances that exist at the moment of the entry into force of this Treaty and to all performances that occur after the entry into force of this Treaty for each Contracting Party.

(2) Notwithstanding the provisions of paragraph (1), a Contracting Party may choose not to apply the provisions of Articles 6 to 11 of this Treaty to fixed performances that existed at the moment of the entry into force of this Treaty for each Contracting Party. In respect of such Contracting Party, other Contracting Parties may limit the application of Articles 4 and 6 to 11 of this Treaty to performances that occurred after the entry into force of this Treaty.

(3) The protection provided for in this Treaty shall be without prejudice to any acts committed, agreements concluded or rights acquired before the entry into force of this Treaty for each Contracting Party.

(4) Contracting Parties may in their legislation establish transitional provisions under which any person who, prior to the entry into force of this Treaty, engaged in lawful acts with respect to a performance, may undertake with respect to the same performance acts within the scope of the rights provided for in Articles 6 to 11 after the entry into force of this Treaty for the respective Contracting Parties.

Article 20
[Provisions on Enforcement of Rights]

(1) Contracting Parties undertake to adopt, in accordance with their legal systems, the measures necessary to ensure the application of this Treaty.

(2) Contracting Parties shall ensure that enforcement procedures are available under their law so as to permit effective action against any act of infringement of rights covered by this Treaty, including expeditious remedies to prevent infringements and remedies which constitute a deterrent to further infringements.

SELECT BIBLIOGRAPHY

Authors' note

As the adjective in the title indicates, this is only a selection of the sources that have been consulted and relied upon during the preparation of this edition. Many more, in particular electronic versions, are referred to in the footnotes at the relevant parts of the principal text and have not been enumerated here for reasons of space and also because these addresses are often changed as they are updated. However, as noted in the preface to this edition, commentators on matters relating to 'Berne and Beyond' are exceptionally fortunate now in relation to the ready availability of online versions of important primary documents, through the WIPO, WTO, and other international organization websites.

Documents

Records of the various revision conferences

Actes de la Conférence internationale pour la protection des Droits d'auteur réunie à Berne du 8 au 19 septembre 1884, International Office, Berne (1884)

Actes de la 2me Conférence internationale pour la protection des oeuvres littéraires et artistiques réunie à Berne du 7 au 18 septembre 1885, International Office, Berne (1885)

Actes de la 3me Conférence internationale pour la protection des oeuvres littéraires et artistiques réunie à Berne du 6 au 9 septembre 1886, International Office, Berne (1886)

Actes de la Conférence de Paris de 1896, International Office, Berne (1897)

Actes de la Conférence de Berlin 1908, International Office, Berne (1909)

Actes de la Conférence réunie à Rome du 7 mai au 2 juin 1928, International Office, Berne (1929)

Documents de la Conférence réunie à Bruxelles du 5 au 26 juin 1948, International Office, Berne (1951)

Records of the Intellectual Property Conference of Stockholm, June 11 to July 14, 1967 (2 vols), WIPO, Geneva (1971)

Records of the Paris Conference 1971 (Paris, July 5 to 24, 1971), WIPO, Geneva (1974)

The Berne Convention for the Protection of Literary and Artistic Works from 1886 to 1986, WIPO, Geneva (1986) (the 'Berne Centenary Volume', which contains all the reports of the various revision conferences together with other selected documents)

Preparatory documents for conferences

Romberg, E, *Compte-rendu des travaux du congrès de la propriété littéraire et artistique*, Flateau, Brussels (1859)

Union internationale pour la protection des oeuvres littéraires et artistiques, *Études sur diverses questions relative à la revision de Convention de Berne (Droit de traduction. Instruments de musique mécaniques. Oeuvres d'architecture. Oeuvres photographiques. Principe fondamental de la Convention. Reproduction des articles de journaux. Protection des auteurs non-unionistes)*, Gollin, Berne (1896)

International Bureau of the Union for the Protection of Literary and Artistic Works, *Conférence de Berlin—Documents préliminaires*, Berne (1907) (English translation made also by E Cutler KC and printed for private circulation by the UK Copyright Association)

'Les travaux préparatoires de la conférence de Bruxelles' [1933] *DA* 73, 90, 97, 112, 121

Report of the Authors' Consultative Commission (1963), Document DA 20/4 (Authors' Consultative Commission)

Report of the Sub-Committee charged with the study of sanctions and reciprocity in the Convention of Berne, submitted to the fifth meeting of the Authors' Consultative Committee, 28 February and 1 March 1963

BIRPI, *General Report of the Swedish/BIRPI Study Group established at 1st June 1963*, Document DA/20/2 (1963 Study Group)

Stockholm Conference Committee of Experts (November 1963), Report of the Debates, Document DA/20/29rev (1963 Committee of Experts)

BIRPI, *General Report of the Swedish/BIRPI Study Group established at 1st July 1964*, Document DA/22/2 (1964 Study Group)

Diplomatic Conference of Stockholm 1967, Committee of Governmental Experts (1965) Report of the Debates, Document DA/22/33 (1965 Committee of Governmental Experts)

Collections of treaties and conventions

Delalain, J, *Recueil des Conventions conclues par la France pour la Reconnaissance de la Properiété Littéraire et Artistique*, Université, Paris (1866)

Lyon-Caen, C and Delalain, P, *Lois françaises et étrangères sur la propriété littéraire et artistique suivie des conventions internationales conclues par la France pour la protection des oeuvres de littérature et d'art* (2 vols), Pichon, Paris (1889)

International Copyright Office, *Recueil des conventions et traités concernant la propriété littéraire et artistique, publiés en français et dans les langues des pays contractants avec une introduction et des notices*, Berne (1904)

WIPO/UNESCO, *Copyright Laws and Treaties of the World* (3 vols), UNESCO, Paris, Bureau of National Affairs, Washington (from 1956 onwards)

BIRPI, *Recueil des accords de travail entre les BIRPI et les autres organisations internationales*, WIPO Library (1967)

WIPO, *Copyright Law Survey* (1979, 1981, 1982, 1983)

Other reports and documents

Copyright Commission, *The Royal Commissions and the Report of the Commissioners*, presented to both Houses of Parliament by command of Her Majesty, C-2036, HMSO, London (1878)

Switzerland No 1 (1886), Correspondence respecting the Formation of an International Copyright Union, presented to both Houses of Parliament by command of Her Majesty, January 1886, C-4606, London (1886)

Switzerland No 2 (1886), Further Correspondence respecting the Formation of an International Copyright Union, presented to both Houses of Parliament by command of Her Majesty, August 1886, C-4856, London (1886)

Switzerland No 3 (1886), Further Correspondence respecting the Formation of an International Copyright Union, presented to both Houses of Parliament by command of Her Majesty, September 1886, C-4910, London (1886)

Commercial No 6 (1897), Correspondence respecting the Copyright Conference at Paris, presented to both Houses of Parliament by command of Her Majesty, August 1897, C-8441, HMSO, London (1897)

Annexe au journal de la conférence spéciale convoquée sur l'ordre de sa majesté l'empereur pour étudier la question des conventions littéraires (1907) (Russia)

Miscellaneous No 2 (1909), Correspondence respecting the Revised Convention of Berne for the Protection of Literary and Artistic Works, signed at Berlin, November 13, 1908, presented to both Houses of Parliament by command of His Majesty, February 1909, C-4467, HMSO, London (1909)

Dominions No 3, Imperial Copyright Conference, 1910: Memorandum of Proceedings, presented to both Houses of Parliament by command of His Majesty, July 1910, Cd 5272, HMSO, London, (1910)

Report of the Australian Delegate (Sir W Harrison Moore), presented to the Parliament of the Commonwealth of Australia and printed by command 31 August 1928, No 255

Board of Trade, *Report of the Departmental Committee on International Copyright*, unpublished, London (1935)

Compte-rendu du Congrès International de Droit Photographique organisé a l'exposition universelle de Bruxelles du 12 au 16 juin 1935, Syndicat de la propriété artistique, Paris (1936)

Report of the Committee appointed by the Attorney-General of the Commonwealth to Consider what Alterations are Desirable to the Copyright Law of the Commonwealth (1965), Canberra (1965) (Australia)

US Copyright Office, *Report for the Subcommittee on Patents, Copyright and Trademarks, Committee of the Judiciary, US Senate* (Dec 1984)

Intellectual Property and Innovation, Cmnd 9712, HMSO, London (1986)

Final Report of the Ad Hoc Working Group on US Adherence to the Berne Convention (1986) 10 *Columbia-VLA Journal of Law & the Arts* 513

US Government, *Green Paper—Intellectual Property and the National Information Infrastructure: A Preliminary Draft of the Report of the Working Group on Intellectual Property Rights*, July 1994

Agency of Cultural Affairs, Japan, *A Report on Discussions by the Working Group of the Subcommittee on Multimedia Copyright, Copyright Council: Study of Institutional Issues regarding Multimedia*, February 1995

Commission of the European Community, *Green Paper—Copyright and Related Rights in the Information Society*, Document COM(95) 385, 19 July 1995

US Government, *White Paper—Intellectual Property and the National Information Infrastructure: The Report of the Working Group on Intellectual Property Rights*, September 1995

Commission of the European Community, *Communication from the Commission: Follow-up to the Green Paper—Copyright and Related Rights in the Information Society*, Document COM(96) 568, 20 November 1996

Documents relating to other conventions on copyright and neighbouring rights

Documents for the Use of Delegations to the Seventh International Conference of American States (Montevideo, Uruguay, 3 December 1933), No 5, Pan-American Union, Washington (1934)

Documents préliminaires publiés par l'Administration belge et l'Institut international de Cooperation intellectuelle, Fascicule I, Brussels (1938)

Records of the Intergovernmental Conference, Geneva 1952, UNESCO, Paris (1954)

Records of the Diplomatic Conference on the International Protection of Performers, Producers of Phonograms and Broadcasting Organizations, Rome, 10–26 October 1961 (Geneva), UNESCO, Paris and BIRPI, Geneva) (1968)

Records of the Conference for Revision of the Universal Copyright Convention, Unesco House, Paris, 5 to 24 July 1971, UNESCO, Paris (1973)

Records of the International Conference of States on the Protection of Phonograms, Geneva 18 to 29 October 1971, WIPO, Geneva (1972)

Records of the International Conference of States on the Distribution of Programme-Carrying Signals Transmitted by Satellite, Brussels, 6–21 May 1974, UNESCO, Paris and WIPO, Geneva (1977)

Records of the Diplomatic Conference on Certain Copyright and Neighboring Rights Questions, Geneva 1996, WIPO, Geneva (1999) (2 vols)

Reports and Documents of BIRPI and WIPO

Summary of replies to Professor Lyon-Caen's Report [1959] *DA* 225 [1960] *DA* 6, 28, 58

Rapport, Groupe d'étude pour la protection internationale des oeuvres cinématographiques (Geneva, 20–3 June and Madrid 26–9 September 1961) [1962] *DA* 38

Committee of African Experts to Study a Draft Model Copyright Law (Geneva, 10 November–4 December 1964), General Report—Draft Provisions and Resolutions [1965] *Copyright* 31–39

Hispano-American Legal Seminar (Copyright) (UNESCO/BIRPI) (Madrid, 30 May–5 June 1966) [1966] *Copyright* 179–81

East Asian Seminar on Copyright (New Delhi, 23–30 January 1967), Reports of Debates [1967] *Copyright* 42–53

Working Group on Copyright Problems of Satellite Communications (Geneva, 14–16 October 1968) [1968] *Copyright* 230–3

Committee of Experts on the Photographic Reproduction of Protected Works (Paris, 1–5 July 1968), Report [1968] *Copyright* 195–201

African Committee of Experts to Draft a Model Statute of Authors' Societies (Abidjan, 9–12 June 1969), Report and Draft Statute [1969] *Copyright* 167–73

Symposium on Practical Aspects of Copyright (Geneva, 25–9 November 1968) [1969] *Copyright* 11–13

Final Report, Ad Hoc Committee for the Revision of the Berne Convention (Geneva, 19–21 May 1970) [1970] *Copyright* 145

Information Meeting of International Non-Governmental Organisations (Paris, 16 March 1970) [1971] *Copyright* 66–67

Committee of Government Experts on Problems in the Field of Copyright Protection of Performers, Productions of Phonograms and Broadcasting carried by Transmission via Space Satellites (Lausanne, 21–30 April 1971), Report and Draft Convention [1971] *Copyright* 102–15

Committee of Experts for the Protection of Type Faces, fifth meeting (Geneva, 22–6 February 1971), Note [1971] *Copyright* 100–102

Advisory Group of Government Experts on the Protection of Computer Programs (Geneva, 8–12 March 1971), Report [1971] *Copyright* 35–40

African Seminar on Intellectual Property (Navisti, 16–20 October 1972) [1972] *Copyright* 239–240

Second Committee of Government Experts on Problems in the Field of Copyright Protection of Performers, Producers of Phonograms and Broadcasting raised by Transmission via Space Satellites (Paris, 9–17 May 1972), Report and Draft Convention [1972] *Copyright* 142–54

Committee of Experts for the Protection of Type Faces, sixth meeting (Geneva, 13–16 March 1972), Note [1972] *Copyright* 87–8

Working Group on Reprographic Reproduction of Works Protected by Copyright (Paris, 2–4 May 1973), Report of Recommendations [1973] *Copyright* 172–180

Committees of Government Experts on Problems in the Field of Copyright and of the Protection of Performers, Producers of Phonograms and Broadcasting raised by Transmission via Satellite, Commentary on Draft Convention (adapted by Second Committee of Experts, Paris, 9–17 May 1972); Third Committee of Experts (Nairobi, 2–11 July 1973) [1973] *Copyright* 9

Advisory Group of Non-Governmental Experts on the Protection of Computer Programs (Geneva, 17–20 June 1974), Report of Recommendations [1974] *Copyright* 226–32

Sub-committee of the Executive Committee of the International Union for the Protection of Literary and Artistic Works on Reprographic Reproduction sitting together with the sub-committee of the Intergovernmental Committee on Reprographic Reproduction (Washington, 16–21 June 1975), Statements and Report [1975] *Copyright* 159–76

Advisory Group of Non-Governmental Experts on the Protection of Computer Programs, second session (Geneva, 23–7 June 1975), Note [1975] *Copyright* 183–5

Committee of Governmental Experts to Prepare a Model Law on Copyright for Developing Countries (Tunis, 23 February–2 March 1976), Report and Model Law with Commentary [1976] *Copyright* 139–52, 165–86

Advisory Group of Non-Governmental Experts on the Protection of Computer Programs, third session (Geneva, 17–20 May 1976), Note [1976] *Copyright* 163–4

Advisory Group of Non-Governmental Experts on the Protection of Computer Programs, fourth session (Geneva, 1–3 June 1977) [1977] *Copyright* 271

Working Group on the Problems in the Field of Copyright and Neighbouring Rights raised by the Distribution of Television Programmes by Cable (Paris, 13–17 June 1977), Report [1977] *Copyright* 246–51

Working Group on the Legal Problems arising from the Use of Videocassettes and Audiovisual Discs (Geneva, 21–5 February 1977), Report [1977] *Copyright* 87–92

Committees of Governmental Experts (Paris, 3 November 1975 and 8–16 December 1976) [1977] *Copyright* 42

Seminar on Copyright for Arab Countries (Rabbat, Morocco, 23–6 May 1977) [1977] *Copyright* 147

Group of Non-Governmental Experts, Model Provisions on the Protection of Computer Software [1978] *Copyright* 6–19

Subcommittee of the Executive Committee of the Berne Union and of the Intergovernmental Committee of the Universal Copyright Convention on Legal Problems arising from the Use of Videocassettes and Audiovisual Discs (Paris, 13, 14, and 19 September 1978), Report and Inventory of Problems [1978] *Copyright* 406–12

Third Committee of Governmental Experts on Double Taxation of Copyright Royalties Remitted from one Country to Another (Paris, 19–30 June 1978), Report, Draft Convention, and Resolutions [1978] *Copyright* 270–6

Sub-committee of the Executive Committee of the Berne Union and of the Intergovernmental Committee of the UCC on Television by Cable (Geneva, 3, 4, and 7 July 1978), Report [1978] *Copyright* 203–12

Regional Seminar on Copyright and Neighbouring Rights for Asian and Pacific States and Territories (New Delhi, 18–22 December 1978), Note of Recommendations of Participants [1979] *Copyright* 22–5

UNESCO Meeting of Governmental Experts on International Arrangements in the Space Communications Field [1979] *Copyright* 57

Working Group on Copyright Problems Arising from the Use of Computers (Geneva, 28–31 May 1979), Report [1979] *Copyright* 186–90

Working Group on the Overall Problems Posed for Developing Countries by Access to Works Protected under the Copyright Conventions (Paris, 2–6 July 1979), Report and Recommendations [1979] *Copyright* 247–50

Working Group on the Support of National Authors and Performers (Geneva, 17–20 September 1979), Report and Recommendations [1979] *Copyright* 267–70

Regional Copyright Seminar for Latin American and Caribbean Countries (Buenos Aires, 5–9 November 1979), Report and Recommendations [1979] *Copyright* 291–3

Expert Group on the Legal Protection of Computer Software, first session (Geneva, 27–30 November 1979), Note and List of Participants [1980] *Copyright* 36–7

Working Group on the Intellectual Property Aspects of Folklore Protection (Geneva, 7–9 January 1980), Note [1980] *Copyright* 110–12

Group of Independent Experts on the Impact of Cable Television in the Sphere of Copyright (Geneva, 10–13 March 1980), Report and Statement of Experts [1980] *Copyright* 154–7

Seminar on Intellectual Property for Newly Independent African Countries (Bissau, 19–22 May 1980) [1980] *Copyright* 280–1

Committee of Experts to Draft Model Statutes for Institutions Administering Authors' Rights in Developing Countries (Paris, 9–13 June 1980), Report and Model Statutes [1980] *Copyright* 271–80

Working Group on the Formulation of Guiding Principles Governing the Problems Posed by the Practical Implementation of the Licensing Procedure for Translations and Reproductions under the Copyright Conventions (Geneva, 17–21 November 1980) [1981] *Copyright* 9

Committee of Governmental Experts on Copyrights Problems Arising from the Use of Computers for Access to, or the Creation of Works (Paris, 15–19 December 1980), Report [1981] *Copyright* 73–9

Group of Independent Experts on the Impact of Cable Television in the Sphere of Copyright and Neighbouring Rights, second session (Geneva, 25–7 May 1981), Note [1981] *Copyright* 218–19

Committee of Experts on Means of Implementation of Model Provisions for National Laws, Intellectual Property Aspects of the Protection of Expressions of Folklore and

Traditional Folk Culture in the Latin American and Caribbean Countries (Bogotá, 14–16 October 1981), Report [1981] *Copyright* 308–10

Joint UNESCO/WIPO Consultative Committee on the Access by Developing Countries to Works Protected by Copyright, first ordinary session (Paris, 2–4 September 1981), Report [1981] *Copyright* 281–5

WIPO Worldwide Forum on the Piracy of Sound and Audiovisual Recordings (Geneva, 25–7 March 1981), Note and List of Participants [1981] *Copyright* 191–7

Regional Seminar of WIPO and Economic Community of the Great Lakes Countries (Gisenyi, 2–4 March 1981) (Rwanda), Report and Recommendations [1981] *Copyright* 173–5

Working Group on Intellectual Property Aspects of Folklore Protection, second meeting (Paris, 9–13 February 1981), Report and Model Provisions [1981] *Copyright* 111–17

African Regional Seminars on Copyright and Neighbouring Rights (Lomé, 1–5 December 1980) (Togo), Report and 'Wishes' [1981] *Copyright* 53–6

Views of International Non-Governmental Organizations—On Private Copying—On Private Reproduction of Printed Matter [1982] *Copyright* 211, 332

Working Group on Access by the Visually and Auditory Handicapped to Material Reproducing Works, Protected by Copyright (Paris, 25–7 October 1982), Report and Model Provisions [1982] *Copyright* 354–6

Consultative Committee on the Question of Copyright Ownership and its Consequences for the Relation Between Employed or Salaried Authors (Geneva, 1–3 September 1982), Report [1982] *Copyright* 322–3

Second Committee of Government Experts on Copyright Problems Arising from the Use of Computers for Access to or the Creation of Works (Paris, 7–11 June 1982), Report and Recommendations [1982] *Copyright* 239–47

Committee of Non-Governmental Experts on the 'Domanie Public Payant' (Geneva, 26–9 April 1982), Report [1982] *Copyright* 179–84

Committee of Government Experts on the Intellectual Property Aspects of the Protection of Folklore (Geneva, 28 June–2 July 1982), Report and Model Provisions [1982] *Copyright* 278

Regional Seminar on Copyright for English-Speaking Caribbean States (Kingston, 19–23 October 1981), Report and Recommendations [1982] *Copyright* 5–8

Sub-committees of the Executive Committee of the Berne Union, Intergovernmental Committee of the Rome Convention on Television by Cable (Paris, 13–17 December 1982) [1983] *Copyright* 80–1

Working Group on Formulation of Guidelines on the System of Translation and Reproduction Licences for Developing Countries under the Copyright Conventions (Paris, 6–10 December 1982), Report and Advisory Notes on Implementation [1983] *Copyright* 123–35

Committee of Governmental Experts on the Drafting of Model Statutes for Institutions Administering Authors' Rights in Developing Countries (Geneva, 17–21 October 1983), Report and Model Statutes for Public Institutions and Private Societies [1983] *Copyright* 345–58

Joint UNESCO-WIPO Consultative Committee on the Access by Developing Countries to Works Protected by Copyright, second ordinary session (Geneva, 4–7 July 1983), Report [1983] *Copyright* 280–6

Committee of Experts on the Legal Protection of Computer Software, second session (Geneva, 13–17 June 1983), Report [1983] *Copyright* 271–9

Seminar on Intellectual Property Rights of Performers—WIPO/FLAIE (Buenos Aires, 25–8 May 1983), Report and Recommendations [1983] *Copyright* 239–40

WIPO Worldwide Forum on the Piracy of Broadcasts and the Printed Word (Geneva, 16–18 March 1983), Note [1983] *Copyright* 159–64

Regional Committee of Experts on Means of Implementation in Africa of Model Provisions of Intellectual Property Aspects of Protection of Expressions of Folklore (Dakar, 23–5 February 1983) [1983] *Copyright* 235–8

Regional Committee of Experts on Means of Implementation in Asia of Model Provisions on Intellectual Property Aspects of Protection of Expressions of Folklore (31 January–2 February 1983), Report [1983] *Copyright* 195–200

Working Group on Model Contracts concerning Co-Publishing of Commissioned Works (Geneva, 8–12 November 1982), Note [1983] *Copyright* 6

Sub-committee of the Executive Committee of the Berne Union, of the Intergovernmental Committee of the UCC and of the Intergovernmental Committee of the Rome Convention on Television by Cable (Geneva, 5–7 December 1983): Annotated Principles of Protection of Authors, Performers, Producers of Phonograms and of Broadcasting Organizations in Connection with Distribution of Programs by Cable [1984] *Copyright* 131

Regional Committee of Experts on Means of Implementation in the Arab States of Model Provisions on Intellectual Property Aspects of Protection of Expressions of Folklore (Doha, 8–10 October 1984), Note [1984] *Copyright* 452

Group of Experts on Unauthorized Private Copying of Recordings, Broadcasts and Printed Matter (Geneva, 4–8 June 1984), Report [1984] *Copyright* 280

WIPO/Arab States Broadcasting Union (ASBU) Workshop on Copyright and Neighbouring Rights (Geneva, 8–10 May 1984) [1984] *Copyright* 252

Second Working Group on Model Contracts Concerning Co-Publishing and Commissioned Works (Paris, 2–6 April 1984) [1984] *Copyright* 250–1

Working Group on Model Provisions for National Laws on Publishing Contracts for Literary Works (Geneva, 18–22 June 1984), Report and Draft Provisions and Excerpts from Preparatory Document [1984] *Copyright* 307–20

Group of Experts on the Copyright Aspects of Direct Broadcasting by Satellite (Paris, 18–22 March 1985), Report [1985] *Copyright* 180–9

Group of Experts on the Copyright Aspects of the Protection of Computer Software (Geneva, 25 February–1 March 1985), Report and Annexes (Legal Protection of Computer Programs, Survey and Analysis of National Legislation and Case Law) [1985] *Copyright* 146–57

Group of Experts on the Rental of Phonograms and Videograms (Paris, 26–30 November 1984) Report, Annexe A (Conclusion) [1985] *Copyright* 16–21

Seminar on Copyright and Neighbouring Rights for Central American and Caribbean States (Masui City, 19–22 February 1985) [1985] *Copyright* 142

Group of Experts on the International Protection of Expressions of Folklore by Intellectual Property (Paris, 10–14 December 1984), Report and Draft Treaty [1985] *Copyright* 40

Committee of Governmental Experts on Model Provisions for National Laws on Employed Authors (Geneva, 27–31 January 1986), Report [1986] *Copyright* 72–7

Committee of Governmental Experts on Model Provisions for National Laws on Publishing Contracts for Literary Works (Paris, 2–6 December 1985), Note [1986] *Copyright* 40–1

WIPO/UNESCO Committee of Experts on Audiovisual Works and Phonograms (Paris, 2–6 June 1986) [1986] *Copyright* 218

WIPO Worldwide Symposium on the Impact of Digital Technology on Copyright and Neighbouring Rights, Harvard University, March–April 1993, WIPO publication no 723(E), 1993.

WIPO Worldwide Symposium on the Future of Copyright and Neighbouring Rights, Louvre, Paris, June 1994, WIPO publication no 731(E), 1994.

WIPO Worldwide Symposium on Copyright in the Global Information Infrastructure, Mexico City, May 1995, WIPO publication no 746(E/S), 1995.

WIPO World Forum on the Protection of Intellectual Creations in the Information Society, Naples, October 1995, WIPO publication no 751(E), 1996

Books and Monographs

American Law Institute Restatement of the Law, 3d, Foreign Relations Law of the United States, Philadelphia (1987)

Association littéraire et artistique internationale, *Avant-projet de révision de la Convention d'Union de Berne*, Paris (1907)

Association littéraire et artistique internationale: Son histoire, Ses travaux (1878–1889), Bibliothèque Chaconac, Paris (1889)

Azzi, Tristan, *Recherche sur la loi applicable aux droits voisins du droit d'auteur en droit international privé*, LGDJ, Paris (2005)

Baetzmann, F, *Union internationale pour la protection des oeuvres littéraires et artistiques. Convention de Berne: Concordance des textes de 1883, 1884 et 1885*, Kugelmann, Paris (1889)

Bappert, W, and Wager, E, *Internationales Urheberrecht: Kommentar*, Beck, Munich and Berlin (1956)

Bappert, W, Maunz, T, Schricker, G, *Verlagsrecht, Kommentar zum Gesetz über das Verlagsrecht vom 19.6.1901*, 2nd edn, Beck, Munich (1984)

Barker, R E, *Copyright: The New International Conventions*, Publisher's Association, London (1971)

Barnes, J J, *Authors, Publishers and Politicians: The Quest for an Anglo-American Copyright Agreement 1815–1854*, Routledge and Kegan Paul, London (1974)

Bastide, L, *L'Union de Berne de 1886 et la protection internationale des droits des auteurs et des artistes suivie du texte de l'avant-projet de la Conférence de Berne de 1883, de la Convention définitive du 9 septembre 1886, de la loi espagnole du 9 jan 1879 sur la propriété intellectuelle et la loi belge du 22 mars 1886 sur le droit d'auteur*, Giard, Paris (1890)

Baum, A, *The Brussels Conference for the Revision of the Berne Convention*, Library of Congress, Washington, DC (1949) (trans by W Strauss from [1949] *GRUR* 1)

Beguin, G, *La Clause juridictionnelle du nouvel art 27bis de la Convention de Berne pour la protection des oeuvres littéraires et artistiques*, extract from (1949) 6 *Annuaire suisse du droit international* 282, Ed polygraphiques, Zurich (1950)

Beier, F, and Schricker, G (eds), *GATT or WIPO? New Ways in the International Protection of Intellectual Property*, IIC Studies, Munich, VCH (1989)

Beier, F-K, and Schricker, G (eds), *From GATT to TRIPS, The Agreement on Trade Related Aspects of Intellectual Property*, 18 IIC Studies, Munich, VCH (1996)

Bently, L, and Sherman, B, *Intellectual Property Law*, 2nd edn, Oxford University Press (2004)

Bergé, Jean-Sylvestre, *La protection internationale et communautaire du droit d'auteur: Essai d'une analyse conflictuelle*, LGDJ-Monchrestien, Paris (1998)

BIRPI, *Le cinéma dans la Convention de Berne: The cinema in the Berne Convention*, BIRPI, Geneva (1960)

Blaisdale, W M, 'Size of Copyright Industries', in *Studies in Copyright*, vol I, Rothman and Bobbs-Merrill, New Jersey and New York (1963)

Blakeney, M, *Trade Related Aspects of Intellectual Property Rights*, Sweet & Maxwell, London, (1996)

Bodenhausen, G H C, *Guide to the Application of the Paris Convention for the Protection of Industrial Property*, BIRPI, Geneva (1968)

Bodenhausen, G H C, *Developing Countries and International Copyright* (Address at New Delhi, 23 October 1973), WIPO, Geneva (1973)

Boele-Woelki, K, and Kessedjian, C (eds), *Internet, Which Court Decides, Which Law Applies?* Molengraaf Institut voor Privaatrecht, Utrecht (1998)

Bogsch, A, *The Law of Copyright under the Universal Copyright Convention*, 3rd rev edn, Sijthoff, Leyden, and Bowker, New York (1968)

Boguslavsky, M, *The USSR and International Copyright Protection* (trans from Russian), Progress Publishers, Moscow (1979)

Bolla, P, *The Berne Convention for the Protection of Literary and Artistic Works in the Text Revised at Brussels*, US Copyright Office (trans from *DA*), Library of Congress, Washington, DC (1949)

Borchgrave, J, *Les Résultats de la Convention de Berlin et le Rapport de M Taillefer au Syndicat pour la Protection de la Properiété intellectuelle*, Bruylants, Brussels (1909)

Börsenverein des Deutschen Buchhandels and International Publishers Association, *International Copyright Symposium, Heidelberg, 24–25 April 1986*, Schweitzer, Munich (1986)

Boutet, M, and Plaisant, R, *Régime International du droit d'auteur: La Convention de Berne, révisée à Bruxelles*, Juris-Classeurs, Libraire de la Cour de cassation, Paris (1950)

Bowett, D W, *The Law of International Institutions*, 4th edn, Stevens, London (1982)

Boytha, G, *Reciprocity in International Copyright Law*, Hungarian Branch of the International Law Association, Budapest (1968)

Boytha, G, *Interrelationship of Conventions on Copyright and Neighbouring Rights*, Hungarian Academy of Sciences, Budapest (1983)

Braderman, E, *International Copyright: A World View*, extract from (1970) 62 *Department of State Bulletin*, No 1607, 486

Brennan, D J, *Retransmission and US Compliance with TRIPS*, Kluwer Law International, The Hague, London, and New York (2003)

Bricon, E, *Des droits d'auteur dans les rapports internationaux*, Rousseau, Paris (1888)

Briggs, A, *The BBC: The First Fifty Years*, Oxford University Press, Oxford and New York (1985)

Briggs, W, *The Law of International Copyright*, Stevens and Haynes, London (1906)

Brownlie, I, *Principles of Public International Law*, 5th edn, Oxford University Press, Oxford (1998), and 6th edn (2003)

Burke, P, *The Law of International Copyright between England and France in Literature, the Drama, Music and the Fine Arts . . .*, Sampson Low, London (1852)

Carmichael, V C H, *The Paris International Literary Congress*, London (1878)

Carotti, F, *Le Projet de Convention pour l'Union Générale Littéraire et Artistique: Considérations dediées à Mm les Délégues des Gouvernements Adhérents à la Conférence de Berne (8 septembre 1884)*, Civelli, Florence (1884)

Carreau, C, *Mérite et droit d'auteur*, LGDJ Paris (1981)

Cavali, J, *La Genèse de la Convention de Berne pour la protection des oeuvres littéraires et artistiques du 9 septembre 1886*, Imprimeries Réunies, Lausanne (1986)

Ciampi, A, *La durée du droit d'auteur dans le cadre de l'intégration européenne: La durata del diritto d'autore nel quadro dell'integrazione europea*, 2nd edn, Casa Editrice Dr Francesco Vallardi, Società Editrice Libraria, Milan (1974)

Claude, I L, *Swords into Ploughshares: The Problems and Progress of International Organisation*, 4th edn, Random House, New York (1982)

Clunet, E, *Étude sur la Convention d'Union internationale pour la protection des oeuvres littéraires et artistiques . . .*, Marchal and Billard, Paris (1887)

Codding, G A, *The International Telecommunications Unions: An Experiment in International Co-operation*, Leyden (1952)

Codding, G A, *The Universal Postal Union: Co-ordination of the International Mails*, New York University Press, New York (1964)

Cohen, B A, *The Law of Copyright*, Jordan, London (1896)

Columbet, C, *Propriété littéraire et artistique*, 2nd edn, Dalloz, Paris (1980)

Constant, C, *Union internationale pour la protection des oeuvres littéraires et artistiques. Convention de Berne du 9 septembre 1886 et Acte Additionnel de Paris du 4 mai 1896: Textes et documents, publiés avec quelques observations*, Agence générale, Paris (1897)

Constant, C, *Protection internationale des oeuvres artistiques*, Société des artistes françaises, Paris (1914)

Copinger, W A, *The Law of Copyright in Works of Literature and Arts*, 2nd edn, Stevens and Haynes, London (1881)

Coppetiers de Gibson, D, *La Conférence diplomatique du droit d'auteur (Bruxelles 5–26 juin 1948)*, Goemaere, Brussels (1948)

Copyright Association (UK), *The Articles of the International Copyright Union*, Longmans, Green and Co, London (1887)

Correa, C M, and Ysef, A A (eds), *Intellectual Property and Trade: The TRIPS Agreement*, Kluwer Law International, London (1998)

Crawford, J, *The Creation of States in International Law*, Clarendon Press, Oxford (1979)

Darras, A, *Du droit des auteurs et des artistes dans les rapports internationaux*, Rousseau, Paris (1887)

Darras, A, *Rapport sur la deuxième conférence réunie à Berne par l'Association littéraire et artistique internationale*, Pichon, Paris (1890)

Davies, G, *Private Copying of Sound and Audio-Visual Recordings*, ESC, Oxford (1984)

Davies, G, *Piracy of Phonograms*, 2nd edn, ESC, Oxford (1986)

Davies, G, and Hung, M E, *Music and Video Private Copying: An International Survey of the Problem and the Law*, Sweet & Maxwell, London (1993)

Davison, M, *The Legal Protection of Databases*, Cambridge Studies in Intellectual Property Rights, Cambridge University Press, Cambridge (2003)

Deàk, F, *Report on the Status of International Copyright Protection and on the Brussels Meeting of the Committee of Experts*, Committee for the Study of Copyright, Sub-committee of the American National Committee of International Intellectual Co-operation, Columbia University Press, New York (1938)

Deliyanni, Elsa, *Le droit de représentation des auteurs face à la télévision transfrontalière par satellite et par cable*, LGDJ-Montcrestien, Paris (1998)

Desbois, H, *Le droit d'auteur*, 1st edn, Dalloz, Paris (1950)
Desbois, H, *Le droit d'auteur en France*, 3rd edn, Dalloz, Paris (1978)
Desbois, H, Françon, A, and Kéréver, A, *Les Conventions internationales du droit d'auteur et des droits voisins*, Dalloz, Paris (1976)
Desjeux, X, *La Convention de Rome (10–26 octobre 1961): Etude de la protection des artistes, interprètes ou exécutants, des producteurs de phonogrammes et des organisms de radiodiffusion*, Pichon and Durand-Auzias, Paris (1966)
Dicey and Morris, *The Conflict of Laws*, 13th edn, by Trevor C Hartley et al, Sweet & Maxwell, London (2000)
Dietz, A, *Copyright Law in the European Community*, Sijthoff and Noordhoff, Alphen aan den Rijn, Netherlands (1978)
Dietz, A, *Urheberrecht und Entwicklungsländer*, Beck, Munich (1981)
Dinwoodie, G, Hennessey, W, and Perlmutter, S, *International Intellectual Property Law and Policy*, Lexis Nexis, Newark (2001)
Dittrich, R, *Die Stockholmer Fassung der Berner Übereinkunft*, Internationale Gesellschaft für Urheberrecht, Schriftenreihe, Band 40 Berlin-Frankfurt/Maín (1968)
Dock, M C, *Etude sur le droit d'auteur*, Pichon and Durand-Auzias, Paris (1963)
Duchemin, J-L, *Le droit de suite des artistes*, Recueil Sirey, Thuilles, Belgium (1948)
Durrande, S, *La détermination du pays d'origine de l'oeuvre en droit international privé*, Doctoral thesis presented to the University of Paris, 1980 (copy held in WIPO Library, Geneva)
Dusollier, S, *Droit d'auteur et protection des oeuvres dans l'univers numérique: Droits et exceptions à la lumière des dispositifs de verrouillage des oeuvres*, Larcier, Brussels (2005)
Ekedi-Samnik, J, *L'Organisation mondiale de la propriété intellectuelle (OMPI)*, Bruylant, Brussels (1975)
Elias, T O, *The International Court of Justice and Some Contemporary Problems*, Nijhoff, The Hague, Boston and London (1983)
Emiowe Esezobar, J, *The Implications of International Copyright for Developing Countries in Africa*, doctoral thesis for University of Ibadan, 1975 (copy held in WIPO Library, Geneva)
Fabiani, M, 'Conflicts of Law in International Copyright Assignments' [1998] *Ent L Rev* 157
Fawcett, J J, and Torremans, P, *Intellectual Property and Private International Law*, Oxford Monographs in Private International Law, Oxford University Press, Oxford (1998)
Ficsor, M, *The Law of Copyright and the Internet: The 1996 WIPO Treaties, Their Interpretation and Implementation*, Oxford University Press, Oxford (2002)
Fisher, W, *Promises to Keep: Technology, Law, and the Future of Entertainment*, Stanford University Press (2004)
Fleischmann, A, *Die Berner Übereinkunft zum Schutze des Urheberrechts*, extract from (1888) *Unsere Zeit-Deutsche Revue der Gegenwart* 314, Brockhaus, Leipzig (1888)
Fliniaux, C, *Essai sur les droits des auteurs étrangers en France et des auteurs françaises en pays étrangers*, Thorin, Paris (1879)
de Freitas, D, *The Copyright System: Practice and Problems in Developing Countries*, Commonwealth Secretariat, London (1983)
Gervais, D, *La notion d'oeuvre dans la Convention de Berne et en droit comparé*, Librarie Droz, Geneva (1998)
Gervais, D, *The TRIPS Agreement: Drafting History and Analysis*, 2nd edn, Sweet & Maxwell, London (2003)

Gilbert, M, *Recent Historical Atlas 1860 to 1960*, revd edn (1977)

Ginsburg, J C, and Lucas, A, *Study on Transfer of Rights of Performers to Producers of Audiovisual Fixations*, General Appreciation, AVP/IM/03/4Add (WIPO, 2004), http://www.wipo.int/documents/en/meetings/2003/avp_im/doc/avp_im_03_4add.doc

Goldbaum, W, *Berner Übereinkunft zum Schutze von Werken der Literatur und Kunst, vom 2 juni 1928*, Stilke, Berlin (1928)

Goldbaum, W, *Verfall und Auflösung der sogenannten Berner Union und Uebereinkunft zum Schutz von Werken der Literatur und Kunst*, Vahlen, Berlin and Frankfurt (1959)

Goldstein, P, *International Copyright: Principles, Law, and Practice*, Oxford University Press, New York (2001)

Grassin, F, *Compte rendu des travaux du Congrès artistique d'Anvers* (1862)

Grunebaum-Ballin, P, *Le droit moral des auteurs et des artistes. Commentaire d'un projet des textes sur le droit moral à inserter dans la Convention de Berne revisée, suivi des textes proposés*, Imprimerie du Palais, Paris (1928)

Guibault, L, *Copyright Limitations and Contracts: An Analysis of the Contractual Overridability of Limitations on Copyright*, Information Law Series, vol 9 (2002)

Hachette, L, *Modifications apportées à la Convention de Berne de 1913 à 1931: Rapport présenté à la IXme Session du Congrès des éditeurs à Paris*, Cercle de la librairie, Paris (1931)

Harper, J H, *The House of Harper: A Century of Publishing*, Harper, New York (1912)

Helberger, N, *Neighbouring Rights Protection of Broadcasting Organisations: Current Problems and Possible Lines of Action* (report prepared for the Council of Europe) (1999), http://www.ivir.nl/publications/helberger/coe.doc

Hoffman, W, *Die Berner Uebereinkunft zum Schutze von Werken der Literatur und Kunst vom 9.September 1886 revidiert in Berlin am 13 November 1908 und in rom am 2 June 1928*, Springer, Berlin (1935)

Holdsworth, W, *A History of English Law*, 2nd edn, Sweet and Maxwell, London (1939, reprinted 1966)

Hommage à Henri Desbois, études de propriété intellectuelle, Dalloz, Paris (1974)

Huard, G, *Etude sur les modifications apportées à la Convention de Berne par la Conférence réunie à Paris, du 15 avril au 1er mai 1896*, extract from *Bulletin de la Société de législation comparée*, Pichon, Paris (1897)

Hubman, H, *Urheber- und Verlagsrecht*, 5th edn, Beck, Munich (1984)

Imbert, P-H, *Les Réserves aux Traités Multilatéraux*, Publications de la Revue générale de droit international public, Nouvelle série no 31, Pedone, Paris (1978)

Institut de Droit International, *Révision de la Convention de Berne du 9 septembre 1886 créant une Union internationale pour la protection des oeuvres littéraires et artistiques: Conclusions présentées au nom de la commission par Mm Roguin rapporteur et Renault co-rapporteur*

International Institute of Intellectual Co-operation, *La Protection internationale du droit d'auteur*, Fontenay, Paris (1928)

Janlet, V, *De la Protection des oeuvres de la pensée: Créations littéraires*, Moens, Brussels (1888)

Jarrold, S, *A Handbook of English and Foreign Copyright in Literary and Dramatic Works*, Chatto and Windus, London (1881)

Jehoram, H C (ed), *Design Protection*, Monographs on Industrial Property and Copyright, Sijhoff, Leyden (1976)

Jehoram, H C, Keuchenius, P, and Brownlee, L M (eds), *Trade Related Aspects of Copyright*, Kluwer, Deventer (1996)

Jenks, C W, *The Proper Law of International Organisations*, Stevens, London and Oceana, Dobbs Ferry, New York (1962)

Josselin-Gall, M, *Les Contrats d'Exploitation de Droit de Propriété Littéraire et Artistique* (1995)

Junker, C, *Die Berner Konvention zum Schutze der Werken der Literatur und Kunst und Österreich-Ungarn*, Hölder, Vienna (1900)

Kamina, P, *Film Copyright in the European Union*, Cambridge University Press, Cambridge (2002)

Kase, J R, *Copyright Thought in Continental Europe: Its Development, Legal Theories and Philosophy; a Selected and Annotated Bibliography*, Rothman, South Hackensack, New York (1967)

Katzenberger, P, *Das Folgerecht im deutschen und ausländischen Urheberrecht*, Beck, Munich (1970)

Kerr, S P, *The Copyright 1911*, Jordan, London (1912)

Kinder, H, and Hilgemann, W, (trans by Menze, E A), *The Penguin Atlas of World History, Volume Two (French Revolution to the Present)*, Penguin, Harmondsworth (1978)

Kohler, J, *Die Immaterialgüter im internationalen Recht*, Duncker and Humblot, Leipzig (1896)

Kohler, J, *Urheberrecht an Schriftwerken und Verlagsrecht*, Enke, Stuttgart (1906–7)

Kupferman, T R, and Foner, M, *Universal Copyright Convention Analyzed*, Federal Legal Publications, New York (1955)

Ladas, S P, *The International Protection of Literary and Artistic Property* (2 vols), Harvard Studies in International Law, Macmillan, New York (1938)

Ladas, S P, *Patents, Trademarks, and Related Rights: National and International Protection*, Harvard University Press, Cambridge, Mass (1975)

Laddie, H, Prescott, P, and Vitoria, M, *The Modern Law of Copyright and Designs*, 3rd edn, Butterworths, London (2000)

Lahore, J C, *Intellectual Property in Australia: Copyright*, Butterworths, Sydney (1977) (now Lahore, J C, and Rothnie, W A, *Copyright and Designs*, looseleaf service, Butterworths, Sydney (2003–)

Lavollée, R, *Propriété littéraire et la Convention de Berne*, extract from *Journal des économistes*, 15 mars 1887, Guillaumin, Paris (1887)

Lermina, J, *Convention de Berne: Unification des Législations—Historique de l'Association littéraire et artistique internationale*, Baer, Bucarest (1906)

Lucas, A, and Lucas, H-J, *Traité de la Propriété Littéraire et Artistique*, 2nd edn, Litec, Paris (2001)

Macaulay, T, *Speeches on Copyright*, ed C Gaston, London (1914)

McFarlane, G, *Copyright: The Development and Exercise of the Performing Right*, Oxford, London (1980)

McNair, Lord, *The Law of Treaties*, Clarendon Press, Oxford (1961)

Majoros, F, *Les arrangements bilatéraux en matière de droit d'auteur*, Pedone, Paris (1971)

Makeen, M K, *Copyright in a Global Information Society: The Scope of Copyright Protection Under International, US, UK and French Law*, Kluwer Law International (2001)

Malaplate, L, *Le Droit d'auteur, sa protection dans les rapports franco-étrangers*, Sirey, Paris (1931)

Marks, D, and Bruce Turnbull, B, *Technical Protection Measures: The Intersection of*

Technology, Law and Commercial Licenses, WIPO Workshop on Implementation Issues of the WIPO Copyright Treaty (WCT) and the WIPO Performances and Phonograms Treaty (WPPT), Geneva 6–7 December, 1999, WIPO Document WCT-WPPT/IMP/3

Marwitz, B, *Die Berner Uebereinkunft und die Römische Konferenz*, Vahlen, Berlin (1928)

Marzano, P, *Diritto d'Autore e Digital Technologies*, Giuffrè, Milan (2005)

Masouyé, C, *Guide to the Berne Convention for the Protection of Literary and Artistic Works*, trans W Wallace, WIPO, Geneva (1978)

Masouyé, C, *Guide to the Rome Convention and to the Phonograms Convention*, trans W Wallace, WIPO, Geneva (1981)

Moynier, G, *Les bureaux internationaux des unions universelles*, Cherbuliez, Geneva and Fischbacher, Geneva (1892)

Nimmer, M, *The United States Copyright Law and the Berne Convention: The Implications of the Prospective Revision of Each*, BIRPI, Geneva (1966)

Nimmer, M B and Geller, P E, *International Copyright Law and Practice*, LexisNexis, Newark and San Francisco (2003)

Nimmer, D and Nimmer, M B, *Nimmer on Copyright*, Mathew Bender, New York (1995–)

Nordemann, W, Vinck, K, and Hertin, P W, *Internationales Urheberrecht und Leistungsschutzrecht der deutschaprachigen Länder unter Berücksichtigung auch der Staaten der Europäischen Gemeinschaft, Kommentar*, Werner, Düsseldorf (1977). Also published in French under the title of *Droit d'auteur international et droits voisins: Commentaire* (trans by J Tournier), Bruylant, Brussels (1983) and in an English version with Dr G Meyer (trans by R Livingston), with extensive revisions and updates, as *International Copyright and Neighbouring Rights Law*, VCH, Weinheim (1990)

O'Connell, D P, *State Succession in Municipal and International Law* (2 vols), Cambridge University Press, Cambridge (1967)

Ohanian, T A, and Phillips, M E, *Digital Filmmaking: The Changing Art and Craft of Making Motion Pictures*, 2nd edn, Focal Press (2000)

Orelli, A D, *La Conférence internationale pour la protection des droits d'auteur réunie à Berne du 8 au 19 septembre 1884*, Murquardt, Brussels and Leipzig (1884)

Orelli, A D, *La deuxième Conférence internationale pour la protection des oeuvres littéraires et artistiques réunie à Berne du 7 au 18 septembre 1885*, no publisher given (1885), also published in [1886] *Revue de droit international* 37

Pataille and Huget *Code international*, 1st edn, Maresque and Dujardin, Paris (1885)

Perot-Morel, M A, *Les Principes de Protection des Dessins et Modèles dans les pays du Marché Commun* (1968)

Peter, F-W, *Das Stockholmer Protokoll für die Entwicklungsländer: Gefahr für das internationale Urheberrecht*, Börsenverein des Deutschen Buchhandels, Frankfurt am Main (1970)

Petit, A, *Étude sur la Convention de Berlin de 1908 pour la protection des oeuvres littéraires et artistiques. Le point de vue littéraire*, Jardin, Paris (1911)

Phillips, J, *The Economic Importance of Copyright*, Common Law Institute of Intellectual Property, London (1985)

Plaisant, M, and Pichot, O, *La Conférence de Rome: Commentaire pratique de la nouvelle Convention pour la protection internationale de la propriété littéraire et artistique*, Recueil Sirey, Paris (1934)

Plaisant, R, *Propriété littéraire et artistique*, Delmas, Paris (1985)
Poinsard, L, *Études de droit international conventionnel*, Première série, Transports, Transmissions, Relations Economiques Internationales, Propriété Intellectuelle, Pichon, Paris (1894)
Poinsard, L, *Les Unions et ententes internationales*, 2nd edn, Baumgart, Berne (1901)
Poinsard, L, *La propriété artistique et littéraire et la Conférence de Berlin (1910)*, extract from *Annales des Sciences Politiques, Revue bimestrielle*, January 1910, Alcan, Paris (1910)
Pollaud-Dulian, F, *Le droit de destination: le sort des exemplaires en droit d'auteur*, LGDJ-Montchrestien, Paris (1989)
Potu, E, *La Convention de Berne pour la protection des oeuvres littéraires et artistiques: Revisée à Berlin le 13 novembre 1908, et la Protocol additionnel de Berne du 20 mars 1914*, Rousseau, Paris (1914)
Pouillet, E, *Traité théorique et pratique de la propriété littéraire et artistique et du droit de représentation*, 2nd edn, Marchal and Billard, Paris (1894)
Pouillet, E, *Traité théorique et pratique des dessins et modèles*, 5th edn, by A Taillifer and C Claro, Marchal and Godde, Paris (1911)
'Publisher, A', *Copyright, National and International, with some remarks on the Position of Authors and Publishers*, Sampson Low, Marston, Searle and Rivington, London (1887)
Putnam, G H, *International Copyright: Considered in Some of its Relations to Ethics and Political Economy*, Putnams, New York (1879)
Putnam, G H, *The Question of Copyright*, 2nd edn, Putnams, New York (1896)
Putnam, G H, *Memories of a Publisher 1865–1915*, Putnams, New York (1915)
Raestad, A, *La Convention de Berne révisée à Rome 1928 pour la protection de la littérature, de la musique, des arts figuratifs, de l'architecture, de l'art appliqué à l'industrie et des oeuvres de photographie et de cinématographie, contenant des dispositions relatives à la reproduction mécanique des sons, à la radiodiffusion et au droit de réimpression de la presse*, Editions internationales, Paris (1931)
Recht, P, *Le Droit d'Auteur, une nouvelle forme de propriété. Histoire et théorie*, Libraire générale de droit et de jurisprudence Paris and Duclot, Gembloux (1969)
Regensteiner, L, *Schutz des Urhebers eines literarischen Werkes gegen Bearbeitung seines Werkes nach deutschem Recht und nach der revidierten Berner Konvention*, Himmer, Augsburg (1913)
Rehbinder, M, and Larese, W (eds), *Die Berner Übereinkunft und die Schweitz*, Stampfli, Berne (1986)
Reimann, M, *Conflict of Laws in Western Europe: A Guide Through the Jungle*, Transnational Publishers, Ardsley, New York, (1995)
Reinbothe, J, and von Lewinski, S, *The WIPO Treaties 1996*, Butterworths/Lexis Nexis, London (2002)
Renault, L, *De la propriété littéraire et artistique au point de vue international*, Paris (1879)
Report of the United States Observer Delegation to the International Conference for the Revision of the Berne Convention . . . Held in Brussels, Washington (1949)
Richardson, J B, *The Law of Copyright*, Jordan, London (1913)
Ricketson, S, *The Law of Intellectual Property*, Law Book Co, Sydney (1984)
Ricketson, S, and Creswell, C, *The Law of Intellectual Property: Copyright, Designs and Confidential Information*, 2nd edn, Law Book Co, Sydney (1999)
Ricketson, S, *The Three-step Test, Deemed Quantities, Libraries and Closed Exceptions*,

advice prepared for the Centre of Copyright Studies Ltd, Centre for Copyright Studies, Sydney (2003)

Ricketson, S, *WIPO Study on Exceptions and Limitations of Copyright and Related Rights in the Digital Environment* SCCR/97 (5 April 2003)

Rivière, L, *La Protection internationale des oeuvres littéraires et artistiques: Etude de législation comparée*, Fonteming, Paris (1897)

Robertson, G S, *The Law of Copyright*, Clarendon Press, Oxford (1912)

Roeber, G (ed), *Die Pariser Revisionen der Übereinkünfte zum internationalen Urheberrecht*, Schweitzer, Berlin (1975)

Rose, M, *Authors and Owners: The Invention of Copyright*, Harvard University Press, Cambridge, Mass (1995)

Rosenne, S, *The Law and Practice of the International Court*, Sijthoff, Leyden (1965)

Röthlisberger, E, *Schriftstellerische Postulate zur Revision der Berner Konvention vom 9 September 1886*, Heymanns, Berlin (1893)

Röthlisberger, E, *Préparation de la seconde Conférence diplomatique de révision de la Convention de Berne: Le Colloque de Berlin (novembre 1905)*, Berne (1905)

Röthlisberger, E, *Die Berner Übereinkunft zum Schutze von Werken der Literatur und Kunst und die Zusatzabkommen. Geschichtlich und rechtlich beleuchtet und kommentiert*, Francke, Berne (1906)

Röthlisberger, E, *Der interne und internationale Schutz des Urheberrechts in den Ländern des Erdballs*, 4th edn, by C Hillig and G Greuner, Leipzig (1931)

Rubin, M R, *The Copyright Industries in the United States*, an economic report prepared for the American Copyright Council (1985)

Ruffini, F, *De la protection internationale des droits sur les oeuvres littéraires et artistiques*, Extrait du Recueil des Cours, Hachette, Paris (1927)

Saenger, A, *Verhältnis der Berner Konvention zum innerstaatlichen Urheberrecht*, Vlg für Recht und Gesellschaft, Bale (1940)

SBS World Guide: The Complete Fact File on Every Country, 12th edn, Hardie Grant Book, South Yarra, Victoria, Australia (2004)

Schermers, H C, *International Institutional Law*, Alphen aan den Rijn, Netherlands (1980)

Schulze, E, *The Forthcoming Stockholm Revision Conference 1967* (also in German and French), Internationale Gesellschaft für Urheberrecht, Schriftenreihe, Band 36, Vahlen, Berlin and Frankfurt (1964)

Schulze, E, *Intellectual Property Conference of Stockholm 1967* (also in German and French), Internationale Gesellschaft für Urheberrecht, Schriftenreihe, Band 39, Vahlen, Berlin and Frankfurt (1967)

Schulze, E, *Advancement of World Copyright through Aid to Developing Countries*, also in German and French, Internationale Gesellschaft für Urheberrecht, Schriftenreihe, Band 44, Vahlen, Berlin and Frankfurt (1970)

Schulze, E, *Revision of the International Copyright* (also in French and German), Internationale Gesellschaft für Urheberrecht, Schriftenreihe, Band 46, Vahlen, Munich (1971)

Scrutton, T E, *The Laws of Copyright: An Examination of the Principles which Regulate Literary and Artistic Property in England and Other Countries*, John Murray, London (1883)

Seignette, J, *Challenges to the Creator Doctrine: Authorship, Copyright Ownership and the Exploitation of Creative Works in The Netherlands, Germany, and the United States*, Information Law Series, Kluwer Law International, The Hague (1994)

Senftleben, M, *Copyright, Limitations and the Three-Step Test: An Analysis of the Three-Step Test in International and EC Copyright Law*, Kluwer Law International, The Hague, London, New York (2004)

Sherman, B, and Bently, L, *The Making of Modern Intellectual Property Law: The British Experience, 1760–1911*, Cambridge University Press, Cambridge (1999)

Sherman, B, and Strowel, A (eds), *Of Authors and Origins: Essays on Copyright*, Oxford University Press, Oxford (1994)

Sidjanski, D, and Castanos, S, *Droit d'auteur ou copyright: Les rapports entre les différents systèmes en vigueur*, Rouge, Lausanne (1954)

Sinclair, I, *The Vienna Convention on the Law of Treaties*, 2nd edn, Melland Schill Monographs in International Law, Manchester University Press, Manchester (1984)

Sirinelli, P, *Exceptions and Limitations to Copyright and Neighboring Rights*, report presented to the Workshop on Implementation Issues of the WIPO Copyright Treaty (WCT) and the WIPO Performers and Phonograms (WPPT), Geneva, 6–7 December 1999, WIPO Doc WCT-WPPT/IMP/1 p 28 (3 Dec 1999)

Skone, E P, Mummery, J F, and Rayner James, J, *Copinger and Skone James on Copyright*, 12th edn, Sweet & Maxwell, London (1980)

Solberg, T, *Report on the Berlin Conference of 1908*, US Copyright Office, Washington, DC (1908)

Solberg, T, *The Development of International Copyright Relations between the United States and Foreign Countries*, Berlin (1933)

Soldan, C, *L'Union internationale pour la protection des oeuvres littéraires et artistiques: Commentaire de la Convention de Berne du 9 Septembre, 1886*, Thorin, Paris (1888), also in (1887) *Revue générale du droit, de la legislation et de la jurisprudence en France et à l'étrangère*, 392–424, 493–520

Spoor, J H, Cornish, W R, and Nolan, P F, *Copies in Copyright*, Monographs on Industrial Property and Copyright, Sijhoff and Noordhoff, Netherlands and Germantown, Maryland, USA (1980)

Sterling, J A L, *World Copyright Law*, Sweet & Maxwell, London (2003)

Sterling, J A L, and Carpenter, M C L, *Copyright Law in the United Kingdom and the Rights of Performers, Authors and Composers in Europe*, Legal Books, Sydney and London (1986)

Stewart, S M, *International Copyright and Neighbouring Rights*, 2nd edn, Butterworths, London (1989)

Stewart, T R (ed), *The GATT Uruguay Round: A Negotiating History (1986–1992)*, Kluwer, Deventer (1993)

Straschnov, G, *Le droit d'auteur et les droits connexes en radiodiffusion*, Bruylant, Brussels (1948)

Strömholm, S, *Le droit moral de l'auteur en droit allemand, français et scandinave avec un aperçu de l'évolution internationale* (published in three parts), Norstedt and Söners, Stockholm (1966, 1967, and 1973)

Talfourde, T N, *Three Speeches Delivered in The House of Commons in Favour of a Measure for an Extension of Copyright*, Moxon, London (1840)

Thompson, D, *Europe since Napoleon*, revd edn, Penguin, London (1966)

Tomlinson, J D, *The International Control of Radiocommunications*, Imprimerie du Journal de Genève (1938), Kraus Reprint Co, New York (1972)

Ulmer, E, *Intellectual Property Rights and the Conflict of Laws*, Kluwer/Commission of the European Communities, Netherlands and Luxembourg (1978) (original in German)

Ulmer, E, *Urheber- und Verlagsrecht*, 3rd edn, Springer, Berlin, Heidelberg, and New York (1980)

L'Union internationale pour la protection des oeuvres littéraires et artistiques: Sa fondation et son développement, 1886–1936, Mémoire, Bureau de l'Union, Berne (1936)

Vaunois, A, *Note sur la Convention de Berne de 1886 relative aux oeuvres littéraires et artistiques (Texte révisée à Berlin en 1908)*, Association des inventeurs et artistes industriels, Paris (1908)

Vaunois, A, *Protection internationale des oeuvres littéraires et artistiques d'après la Convention d'Union de Berne révisée signée à Berlin le 13 novembre 1908*, 2e ed, Guyonnard, Paris (1910)

van Eechoud, M, *Choice of Law in Copyright and Related Rights: Alternatives to the Lex Protectionis*, Information Law Series, Kluwer Law International, The Hague (2003)

Wauwermans, P, *Le droit des auteurs en Belgique*, Brussels (1894)

Wauwermans, P, *La Convention de Berne (révisée à Berlin) pour la protection des oeuvres littéraires et artistiques*, Rivière, Paris, and Misch and Thron, Brussels (1910)

Whale, R F, *The Stockholm Act of the Berne Copyright Union: Protocol Regarding the Developing Countries*, British Copyright Council, London (1968)

Wildhaber, L, *Treaty-Making Power and Constitutions: An International and Comparative Study*, Juristische Fakultät der Universität Basel, Schriftenreihe Recht und Internationale Beziehungen, Heft 16, Helling and Lichtenhain, Basel and Stuttgart (1971)

Wood, G S, *Preliminary Observations upon, and Arguments against, the Amendments to the Berne Convention of 1886 . . . proposed by the Italian Government in conjunction with the Office of the International Union for the Protection of Literary and Artistic Works, with General Suggestions for Revision of that Convention along Different Lines*, Mechanical Music Industry of Great Britain, London (1927)

Journal Articles and Chapters in Books

Adeney, E, 'Moral Rights and Substantiality: Some Questions of Integration' (2002) 13 *Australian Intellectual Property Journal* 5

'A propos des droits musico-mécaniques' [1926] *DA* 87

'Les arrangements particuliers entre pays de l'Union (Des effets des articles 15 et 17 de la Convention de Berne)' [1892] *DA* 105

'L'article 7 de la conférence de Berne révisée et la future conférence de Rome' [1928] *DA* 49

Article 18 of the Berne Convention: Correspondence Between WIPO Director General Arpad Bogsch and Assistant Secretary of Commerce and Commissioner of Patents & Trademarks Bruce Lehman (1995) 43 *J Copyr Soc USA* 181

Australian Copyright Council, 'The Protection of Aboriginal Folklore: Report of the Working Party' (31 May 1983) *Bulletin No* 44

Austin, G W, 'The Infringement of Foreign Intellectual Property Rights' (1997) 113 *Law Quarterly Review* 321

Austin, G W, 'Domestic Laws and Foreign Rights: Choice of Law in Transnational Copyright Infringement Litigation' (1999) 23 *Colum-VLA J L & Arts* 1.

Austin, G W, 'The Berne Convention as a Model of Construction: Moral Rights after *Datstar*' [2005] *Annual Survey of American Law* 101

Bappert, W, and Wagner, E, 'Le droit de traduction dans la Convention de Berne et dans la Convention universelle sur le droit d'auteur' [1958] *DA* 27, 41

Bariatti, S, 'Internet e il diritto internazionale privato: aspetti relativi all a disciplina del diritto d'autore' (1996) *AIDA* 59

Barker, R, 'The Stockholm Conference', *The Bookseller*, 8 July 1967

Baum, A, 'Berner Konvention und Landesgesetze' [1928] *GRUR* 648

Baum, A, 'Droit international public, Convention de Berne et lois nationales' [1946] *DA* 85, 101, 114

Baum, A, 'Völkerrecht, Berner Konvention und Landesgesetze' [1950] *GRUR* 437, 451

Baumgarten, J, 'Primer on the Principles of International Copyright' in *Fourth Annual U.S. Copyright Office Speaks: Contemporary Copyright and Intellectual Property Issues* (1992) 470

Beguin, G, 'L'organisation des Bureaux internationaux réunis pour la protection de la propriété industrielle, littéraire et artistique' [1962] *DA* 9

Bella, C, 'Oeuvres des arts appliqués et dessins ou modèles industriels: vers une solution internationale nouvelle' (1959) 24 *RIDA* 55

Bercovitz, A, 'The Relationship between the Berne Convention and Intellectual Property Law in Spain' [1986] *Copyright* 345

Bergne, H G, 'The International Copyright Union' (1887) 3 *LQR* 14

Bergström, S, 'A propos de l'interprétation de l'article 9, alinéa (3), de la Convention de Berne' [1964] *DA* 93

Bergström, S, 'Schutzprinzipien der Berner Übereinkunft nach der Stockhom-Pariser Fassung' [1973] *GRUR Int* 238

Bernard, A, and Boytha, G, 'Socialist Copyright Law: A Theoretical Approach' (1976) *RIDA* 45

'The Berne Union and International Copyright and Neighbouring Rights in 1975' [1976] *Copyright* 14

Besek, J, 'Anti-Circumvention Laws and Copyright: A Report From the Kernochan Center for Law, Media and the Arts' (2004) 27 *Colum J L & the Arts* 389

'La bilan de la guerre mondiale en matière de propriété intellectuelle' [1920] *DA* 37, 50, and 66

BIRPI Study, 'The Protection of Cinematographic Works' [1961] *DA* 19, 62, 86

Bodenhausen, G H C, 'Evolution of the United International Bureaux' [1963] *DA*, General Studies 91 (in French in [1963] *DA* 105)

Bogsch, A, 'L'article XIX de la Convention universelle' [1953] *DA* 144 (Part I), [1954] *DA* 9 (Part II), [1954] *DA* 48 (Part III), [1954] *DA* 67 (Part IV)

Bogsch, A, 'Study Group on so-called "Neighbouring Rights" '[1956] *DA* May Supplement 49

Bogsch, A, 'The First Hundred Years of the Berne Convention for the Protection of Literary and Artistic Works' [1986] *Copyright* 291

Boytha, G, 'The Draft Convention Adopted at Nairobi Relating to the Distribution of Programme-Carrying Signals Transmitted by Satellite Seen from the Angle of the Protection of Authors' Rights' [1974] *Copyright* 70

Boytha, G, 'The Berne Convention and the Socialist Countries with Particular Reference to Hungary' [1986] 11 *Colum-VLA JL & Arts* 57

Braderman, E M, 'International Copyright: A World View' (1970) 17 *Bull Cop Soc USA* 147

Bradley, C, 'Territorial Intellectual Property Rights in an Age of Globalism' (1997) 37 *Va J Int'l L* 505

Breyer, S, 'The Uneasy Case for Copyright: A Study of Copyright in Books, Photocopies and Computer Programs' (1970) 84 *Harv L Rev* 281

Burchfiel, K J, 'The Effect of United States Trade Legislation on Intellectual Property Rights' (1988) 19 *IIC* 295
Burger, P F, 'The New Photocopy Remuneration Provisions in the Federal Republic of Germany and their Application to Foreign Authors under International Copyright Law' (1988) 19 *IIC* 488
Casellati, A M, 'The Evolution of Article 6.4 of the European Information Society Copyright Directive' (2001) 24 *Colum J Law & the Arts* 369
Castelain, R, 'Cinéma et révision de la Convention de Berne' (1962) 36 *RIDA* 53
Chafee, Z, 'Reflections on the Law of Copyright' (1945) 45 *Columbia Law Rev* 503
Chalton, S, 'The Copyright and Rights in Databases Regulations 1997: Some Outstanding Issues on Implementation of the Database Directive' (1998) 20 *EIPR* 178
Chua, A T, 'Precedent and Principles of WTO Panel Jurisprudence' (1998) 2 *Berkeley Journal of International Law* 171
'CISAC's Comments on the Draft Text for the Revision of the Berne Convention' [1972] *Interauteurs* 23
Cohen, J E, 'Copyright and The Jurisprudence of Self-Help' (1998) 13 *Berkeley Tech LJ* 1089
Cohen, J E, 'WIPO Copyright Treaty Implementation in the United States: Will Fair Use Survive' (1999) *EIPR* 236
Cohen Jehoram, H, 'Designs Laws in Continental Europe and their Relation to Copyright' [1981] *EPIR* 235, 237
Collovà, T and Tournier, J-L, 'Des sanctions et la notion de réciprocité dans la Convention de Berne' [1964] *DA* 11
'La Convention de Berne et le droit de reproduction en matière de journaux et de publications périodiques' [1926] *DA* 73
'La Convention de Berne révisée, du 13 novembre 1908' [1909] *DA* 34, 45; [1910] *DA* 2, 18, 29, 59, 76, 93 (commentaries on the Berlin Revision)
'La Convention de Berne révisée et les lois nationales plus favorables' [1929] *DA* 50, 62
'La Conférence de Berlin, ses travaux et ses résultats' [1909] *DA* 1, 19
'La Conference de Rome: Etudes' [1928] *DA* 80, 90
'Copyright and Folk Music: A Perplexing Problem' (1962) 12 *Bull Cop Soc USA* 277
Corbet, J, 'The Berne Convention and the Belgian Copyright Law' [1986] *Copyright* 260
Cornish, W R, 'Intellectual Property Infringement and Private International Law: Changing the Common Law Approach' (1996) *GRUR Int* 285
Cornish, W R, 'The Author as Risk-Sharer' (2002) 26 *Colum J L & the Arts* 1
Crewe, G B, 'National Treatment as the Basis for a Universal Copyright Convention' *UNESCO Copyright Bulletin*, vol III, no 1, 6
Cunard, J, 'Technological Protection of Copyrighted Works and Copyright Management Systems: A Brief Survey of the Landscape', in Ginsburg, J, and Besek, J (eds), *Adjuncts and Alternatives to Copyright: Proceedings of the 2001 ALAI Congress*, Kernochan Center for Law, Media and the Arts, New York (2002)
Da Costa, J F, 'Some Reflections on the Rome Convention' [1976] *Copyright* 80
Da Silva, R J, 'Droit Moral and the Amoral Copyright' (1981) 28 *Bull Cop Soc USA* 1
Davies, G, 'The Rome Convention 1961: A Brief Summary of its Development and Prospect' [1979] *EIPR* 154
Davies, G, 'Technical Devices as a Solution to Private Copying', in Stamatudi, I and Torremans, P (eds), *Copyright in the New Digital Environment*, Sweet & Maxwell, London (2000)

Davis, I, 'A Century of Copyright: The United Kingdom and the Berne Convention' (1986) 11 *Colum-VLA JL & Arts* 33
Davis-Ferid, H, 'Copyright in Technical Drawings under German Law' [1980] *EIPR* 26
'Les délais de protection dans les diverses législations' [1925] *DA* 98, 113, 122, [1926] *DA* 15, 26, 37, 49
Desbois, H, 'Les oeuvres cinématographiques dans le cadre de la Convention de Berne révisée à Stockholm en 1967' (1968) 95 *Journal du droit international* 646
Desbois, H, 'L'organisation mondiale de la propriété intellectuelle' (1967–8) 54–5 *RIDA* 573 (F, E, & S)
Desjeux, X, ' "The Narrow Gate": Commentary on Article 16(1)(a)(i) Rome Convention' [1965] *Copyright* 151
Dessemontet, F, 'Internet, la propriété intellectuelle et le droit international privé', in Boele-Woelki, K, and Kessedjian, C (eds), *Internet, Which Court Decides, Which Law Applies?* (1998)
Dietz, A, 'The Social Endeavours of Writers and Artists and the Copyright Law' (1972) 3 *IIC* 451
Dietz, A, 'Letter from the Federal Republic of Germany' [1974] *Copyright* 87
Dietz, A, 'The Public Lending Right in the Federal Republic of Germany: Education and Regulation' (1976) 7 *ICC* 220
Dietz, A, 'Letter from the Federal Republic of Germany: Report on the Development of Copyright Between 1972 and 1979' [1980] *Copyright* 85, 129
Dietz, A, 'A propos de l'harmonisation des législation nationales dans les pays de la CEA' (1983) 117 *RIDA* 48 (F, E, & S)
Dietz, A, 'The Shortcomings and Positive Evolution of National Copyright Legislation in View of International Satellite Transmission' (1985) XXIV *Estratto de Diritto Communitario e Degli Scambi Internazionale* 365
Dietz, A, 'The United States and Moral Rights: Idiosyncrasy or Approximation? Observations on a Problematical Relationship Underlying United States Adherence to the Berne Convention' (1989) 142 *RIDA* 222
Dietz, A, 'The Concept of Author Under the Berne Convention' (1993) 155 *RIDA* 2
Dittrich, R, 'The Brussels Satellite Convention' [1974] *EBU Legal Rev* 60
Dittrich, R, 'On the Interpretation of Article 11bis(1) and (2) of the Berne Convention' [1982] *Copyright* 294
Dock, M-C, 'Genèse et évolution de la notion de propriété littéraire' (1974) *RIDA* 127 (F, E, & S)
'Le droit d'auteur en Russie' [1899] *DA* 40
'Droit d'auteur et droit voisins' [1952] *DA* 133
'Droit d'auteur et radiophonie' [1925] *DA* 14
'Le droit moral dans les pays de l'Union' [1929] *DA* 110, 123, [1931] *DA* 98, and [1932] *DA* 112, 122
'Les droits des auteurs étrangers en Russie' [1894] *DA* 21
Droz, N, 'Conférence diplomatique de Berne dans le but de constituer une Union pour la protection des droits d'auteur' (1884) 11 *JDIPJC (Clunet)* 441
Droz, N, 'Deuxième conférence diplomatique de Berne dans le but de constituer une Union pour la protection des oeuvres littéraires et artistiques' (1885) 12 *JDIPJC (Clunet)* 481
Droz, N, 'Reponse aux observations du syndicat des sociétés littéraires et artistiques sur le projet de convention international relatif à la constitution d'une Union pour la protection des droits d'auteur' (1885) *JDIPJC (Clunet)* 163

'Du droit à la plus-value des oeuvres artistiques' [1914] *DA* 34, 57
Duchemin, J-L, 'La protection internationale des oeuvres des arts appliqués' (1956) 12 *RIDA* 85
Duchemin, J-L, 'Droit de suite' (1967–8) 54–5 *RIDA* 369 (F, E, & S)
Duchemin, J-L, 'Le droit de suite aux artists' (1969) 62 *RIDA* 78
Duchemin, W, 'Le droit de suite' (1974) 80 *RIDA* 4 (F, E, & S)
Durrande, S, 'The Concept of Publication in the International Conventions' (1982) 111 *RIDA* 72
Dworkin, G, 'The Moral Right and English Copyright Law' (1981) 12 *IIC* 476
Dworkin, G, 'Moral Rights in English Law: The Shape of Rights to Come' [1986] *EIPR* 329
Dworkin, G 'Moral Rights and the Common Law Tradition' (1994) 5 *Australian Intellectual Property Journal* 5
Elkin-Koren, N, 'Copyrights in Cyberspace: Rights Without Laws?' (1998) 73 *Chi-Kent L Rev* 1155
'Les emprunts licites, étude générale du régime de l'Union et des législations intérieures' [1924] *DA* 37, 52, 67, 77, 87
Englert, B, 'The Law of Industrial Designs in Germany: Actual State and Reform Proposals' (1981) *IIC* 773
'Les enregistrements éphémères selon l'article 11*bis* de la Convention de Berne révisée à Bruxelles' [1951] *DA* 37
'Essai de Classification des conventions et arrangements conclues entre les divers pays pour la protection de la protection de la propriété intellectuelle' [1907] *DA* 57
'Etat actuel de la question des instruments de musique mécaniques' [1908] *DA* 107
'Etude des dispositions de l'article 14 de la convention du 9 september 1986 du chiffre 4 du protocole de clôture qui s'y rattache (Rétroactivité)' [1888] *DA* 61, 73, 88, 105, 117
Evans, A E, 'Self-executing Treaties in the United States of America' (1954) 31 *BYIL* 179
Fabiani, M, 'Le droit de reproduction et la révision de la Convention de Berne' [1964] *DA* 286
Fernay, R, 'Oeuvres cinématographiques et télévisuelles' (1967–8) 54–5 *RIDA* 319
Fernay, R, 'La recommendation de Washington' (1970) 63 *RIDA* 87
Fernay, R, 'Paris 1971, ou les aventures d'un "package deal" ' (1971) 70 *RIDA* 3 (F, E, & S)
Fernay, R, 'Grandeur, misère et contradictions du droit d'auteur' (1980) *RIDA* 138 (F, E, & S)
Ferrara-Santamaria, M, 'Régime juridique des oeuvres cinématographiques après le révision de Stockholm' (1968) 56 *RIDA* 83
Ficsor, M, 'Disquieting Report from the Maginot Line of Authors' Copyright' [1982] *Copyright* 104
Ficsor, M, 'Technological Progress and Crisis Tendencies in Copyright' [1982] *Copyright* 104
Ficsor, M, 'Development and Objectives of Collective Administration of Authors' Rights' [1985] *Copyright* 341
Ficsor, M, 'Copyright for the Digital Era: The WIPO "Internet Treaties" ' (Manges Lecture) (1997) 21 *Colum-VLA JL & Arts* 197, 204
Finniss, C, 'The Theory of "Unity of Art" and the Protection of Designs and Models in French Law' (1964) 46 *JPOS* 615
Foged, T, 'U.S. v E.U. Anti-Circumvention Legislation: Preserving the Public's Privileges in the Digital Age?' [2003] *European Intellectual Property Review* 525

Françon, A, 'A propos d'une éventuelle modification de l'article 4 alineá (3) de la Convention de Berne sur le pays d'origine de l'oeuvre publiée' [1963] *DA* 32
Françon, A, 'Le droit d'auteur et les pays en voie de développement' (1968) 95 *Journal du droit international* 889
Françon, A, 'Actes de Paris portant révision des Conventions internationales sur la propriété littéraire et artistique' (1976) 103 *Journal du droit international* 29
Françon, A, 'The Legal Situation Concerning Reprography Internationally and in France' (1984) 15 *IIC* 679
Françon, A, 'Letter from France' [1986] *Copyright* 359
Frowein, J A, 'Legal Problems of the German Ostpolitik' (1974) 23 *ICLQ* 105
Furler, H, 'Sur l'interprétation de l'article 2, alinéa 5, la Convention de Berne revisée à Bruxelles' [1951] *DA* 111
Gamble, J K, 'Reservations to Multilateral Treaties: A Macroscopic View of State Practice' [1980] *AJIL* 372
Gansser, G R, 'Violations of the Paris Convention for the Protection of Industrial Property' (1980) 11 *IIC* 1
Garilov, E P, 'The Legal Protection of Works of Folklore' [1984] *Copyright* 76
Gaubiac, Y, 'La théorie de l'unité de l'art' (1982) 11 *RIDA* 2 (F, E, & S)
Gaudel-Gruyer, D, 'The Assimilation of Televisual Works to Cinematographic Works and the Régime of Cinematographic Works in the Stockholm Act of the Berne Convention' [1968] *Copyright* 205
Gaudrat, P, 'Protection de l'auteur lors d'une retransmission spatiale de son oeuvre' (1980) 104 *RIDA* 3 (F, E, & S)
Gautier, P-Y, 'Du droit applicable dans le "village planétaire", au titre de l'usage immatériel des oeuvres' D.1996.131
Gautier, P-Y, 'Private International Law Aspects: France', in Baulch, L et al (eds), *ALAI Study Days: Copyright in Cyberspace* 298–9, Amsterdam (1996)
Geller, P E, 'Conflict of Laws in Cyberspace: Rethinking International Copyright in a Digitally Networked World' (1996) 20 *Colum-VLA JL & Arts* 571
Ginsburg, J C, 'Les conflits de lois relatifs au titulaire initial du droit d'auteur' (1986) 5 *Revue du droit de la propriété industrielle* 26
Ginsburg, J C, 'Copyright in the 101st Congress: Commentary on the Visual Artists Rights Act and the Architectural Works Copyright Protection Act of 1990' (1990) 14 *Colum-VLA J L & the Arts* 477
Ginsburg, J C, 'Moral Rights in a Common Law System' (1990) 4 *Entertainment Law Review* 121
Ginsburg, J C, 'Four Reasons and a Paradox: The Manifest Superiority of Copyright over Sui Generis Protection of Computer Software' (1994) 94 *Colum L Rev* 2559
Ginsburg, J C, 'A Tale of Two Copyrights: Literary Property in Revolutionary France and America', in Sherman, B and Strowel, A (eds), *Of Authors and Origins: Essays on Copyright*, Oxford University Press, Oxford (1994)
Ginsburg, J C, 'Global Use/Territorial Rights: Private International Law Questions of the Global Information Infrastructure' (1995) 42 *J Copyr Soc* 318
Ginsburg, J C, 'The Private International Law of Copyright in an Era of Technological Change' (1999) *Recueil des Cours* 273
Ginsburg, J C, 'International Copyright: From a "Bundle" of National Copyright Laws to a Supranational Code?' (2000) 47 *J Copyr Soc* 265
Ginsburg, J C, 'Copyright and Control over New Technologies of Dissemination' (2001) 101 *Colum L Rev* 1613

Ginsburg, J C, 'Have Moral Rights Come of (Digital) Age in the U.S.?', in 'Symposium: The Art and Cultural Property Wars' (2001) 19 *Cardozo Arts & Ent L J* 9
Ginsburg, J C 'Towards Supranational Copyright Law? The WTO Panel: Decision and the "Three-Step Test" for Copyright Exceptions' (2001) 187 *RIDA* 3
Ginsburg, J C, 'The Concept of Authorship in Comparative Copyright Law' (2003) 52 *de Paul L Rev* 1063.
Ginsburg, J C, 'The (New?) Right of Making Available to the Public', in Vaver, D, and Bently, L (eds), *Intellectual Property in the New Millennium: Essays in Honour of William R Cornish*, Cambridge University Press, Cambridge (2004)
Ginsburg, J C, 'The Right to Claim Authorship in US Copyright and Trademarks Law' (2004) 41 *U Houston L Rev* 263
Ginsburg, J C and Kernochan, J M, '102 Years Later: The US Joins the Berne Convention' (1988) 13 *Columbia-VLA Journal of Law & the Arts* 1
Gorman, R A, 'Copyright Courts and Merit Judgments: Abuse or Necessity' (2002) 25 *Colum J L & the Arts* 1
Gotzen, F, 'Cable Television and Copyright in Belgium: A Study of the Belgian Law in Relation to the Berne Convention and the Treaty of Rome' [1982] *Copyright* 307
Gou Shoukang, 'China and the Berne Convention' (1986) 11 *Colum-VLA JL & Arts* 121
Greuze, M, 'The TRIPS Council and Implementation of the TRIPS Agreement', in Jehoram, H C, Keuchenius, P, and Brownlee, L M (eds), *Trade Related Aspects of Copyright*, Kluwer, Deventer (1996)
Grosheide, F W, 'Copyright Law from a User's Perspective: Access Rights for Users' [2001] *European Intellectual Property Review* 321
'Grundfragen der künftigen Medienordnung: Urheberrechtlichte Aspekte' [1984] *Film und Recht* 63
Guibault, L M C R, 'Contract and Copyright Exemptions', in Hugenholtz and Koelman (eds), *Copyright and Electronic Commerce*, Information Law Series, Kluwer Law International, The Hague (2000)
Hadl, R, 'Toward International Copyright Revision: Report on the Meetings in Paris and Geneva, September 1970' (1970) 18 *Bull Cop Soc USA* 183
Hansmann, H, and Marina Santilli, M, 'Authors' and Artists' Moral Rights: A Comparative Legal and Economic Analysis' (1997) 26 *J Legal Stud* 95
Hardy, J, 'The Interpretation of Plurilingual Treaties by International Courts and Tribunals' (1961) XXXVII *BYIL* 73
Hauser, R E, 'French *droit de suite*: The Problem of Protection for the Underprivileged Artist under the Copyright Law' (1959) 6 *Bull Cop Soc USA* 94
Hazan, V, ' "The Body Other than the Original Broadcaster" in Cable Transmission: Article 11*bis*(1)(ii) of the Berne Convention' [1984] *Copyright* 228
Heide, T, 'Copyright in the E.U. and United States: What "Access Right?" '[2001] *European Intellectual Property Review* 469
Henn, H G, 'The Quest for International Copyright Protection' (1953) 39 *Cornell Law Quarterly* 43
Henneburg, I, 'Scope of Protection according to the Stockholm Act of the Berne Convention' [1968] *Copyright* 167
Hepp, F, 'La protection internationale des arts appliqués' (1957) 14 *RIDA* 115
Hepp, F, 'Royalties from Works of the Fine Arts: Origin of the Concept of *droit de suite* in Copyright Law' (1959) 6 *Bull Cop Soc USA* 94
Herman, G, 'Grenzüberschreitende Fernseh- und Hörfunksendungen im Gemeinsamen Markt' [1984] *GRUR Int* 578

Hesser, T, 'Quelques questions concernant la future révision de la Convention de Berne' [1961] *DA* 238

'Historical Outline of the Preparations of the Revision of the UCC and the Berne Convention' [1971] *Copyright* 19

Hoffmann, W, 'Berner Übereinkunft und Landesgesetze' [1928] *GRUR* 897

Howell, H A, 'International Copyright Relations of the United States' (1917) 27 *Yale L J* 348

Huard, A, 'La prochaine Conférence de Paris' [1893] *DA* 81

Hugenholtz, P B, 'Comment: Electronic Rights and Wrongs in Germany and the Netherlands' (1998) 22 *Colum-VLA JL & Arts* 151

Hugenholtz, P B, 'Why the Copyright Directive is Unimportant, and Possibly Invalid' [2000] *EIPR* 501

'The Implications of the TRIPS Agreement on Treaties administered by WIPO', published in [1996] *Industrial Property and Copyright* 164

Ionasco, O, 'Protection du droit d'auteur dans les pays socialistes' (1973) 75 *RIDA* 84 (F, E, & S)

Isacker, van, F, 'Letter from Belgium' [1967] *Copyright* 135

Jenks, C W, 'The Legal Personality of International Organizations' (1945) 22 *BYIL* 267

Jenks, C W, 'State Succession in Respect of Law Making Treaties' (1952) 29 *BYIL* 105

Jennings, A, 'Cables and Satellites' (1986) 11 *Colum-VLA JL & Arts* 129

Johnson, C F, 'The Origins of the Stockholm Protocol' (1970) 18 *Bull Cop Soc USA* 91

Joubert, C, 'Applicabilité des actes successifs de la Convention d'Union de Berne' (1968) 58 *RIDA* 4 (F, E, & S)

Joubert, C, 'Les clauses administratives et les clauses finales' (1967–8) 54–5 *RIDA* 427 (F, E, & S)

Kaminstein, A, 'The Phonogram Convention' (1972) 19 *Bull Cop Soc USA* 175

Kampelman, M, 'The United States and International Copyright' (1947) 41 *Am Jo Int Law* 406

Karnell, G, 'The Relations between Authors and Organizations Administering their Rights' [1986] *Copyright* 45

Katzenberger, P, 'The Droit de Suite in Copyright Law' (1973) 4 *IIC* 361

Katzenberger, P, 'Urheberrechtsfragen der elektronischen Textkommunikation' [1983] 85 *GRUR Int* 895

Katzenberger, P, 'Copyright Problems of Reprographic Reproduction: Access to Scientific Literature for Research Purposes' (1984) 15 *IIC* 693

Kaufmann-Kohler, G, 'Internet: Mondialisation de la communication: mondialisation de la résolution des litiges?', in Kessedjian, C, and Boele-Woelki, K (eds), *Internet, Which Court Decides, Which Law Applies?*, Molengraaf Institut voor Privaatrecht, Utrecht (1998)

Kéréver, A, 'The International Copyright Conventions and Reprography' [1976] *DA* 188

Kéréver, A, 'Is Copyright an Anachronism?' [1983] *Copyright* 368

Kéréver, A, 'Droit d'auteur et satellites spatiaux' (1984) 121 *RIDA* 26

Keziak, D P, 'Copyright Registration for Aleatory and Indeterminate Musical Compositions' (1971) 18 *Bull Cop Soc of the USA* 311

Klaver, F, 'Current Developments in Wire Television: Copyright and Neighbouring Rights Problems' [1969] *Copyright* 56

Koelman, K, 'A Hard Nut to Crack: The Protection of Technological Measures' (2000) 22 *EIPR* 272

Kolle, G, 'Reprography and Copyright Law: A Comparative Law Study Concerning the Role of Copyright Law in the Age of Information' (1975) 6 *IIC* 382

Koumantos, G A, 'The Notion of Publication in the Berne Convention' (1964) 40 *RIDA* 4

Koumantos, G A, 'Remarques sur l'application de l'article 14*bis* de la Convention de Berne (Stockholm)' (1969) 60 *RIDA* 27 (F, E, & S)

Koumantos, G, 'Challenges and Promises of the Mass Media for Copyright' [1981] *Copyright* 16

Koumantos, G A, 'Le droit d'auteur et la rémunération équitable' [1983] 85 *GRUR Int* 424

Koumantos, G, 'The Future of the Berne Convention' [1986] 11 *Colum-VLA JL & Arts* 225

Koumantos, G, 'Private International Law and the Berne Convention' (1988) 24 *Copyright* 415

Koumantos, G, 'Copyright and Private International Law in the Face of the International Diffusion of Works', in *WIPO Worldwide Symposium on the Future of Copyright and the Neighboring Rights*, 233 (1994) (WIPO publication no 731(E))

Kreile, R, 'Collection and Distribution of the Statutory Remuneration of Private Copying . . . in Germany' (1992) 23 *IIC* 449

Kumar, N M, 'Cultural Imperialism and Third World Publishing' [1983] *Copyright* 17

Kunz-Hallstein, H P, 'Recent Trends in Copyright Legislation of Developing Countries' (1982) 13 *IIC* 689

Ladd, D, 'To Cope with the World Upheaval in Copyright' [1983] *Copyright* 289

Lee, Tae-Hee, 'Intellectual Property Laws in Korea', Korean-American Business Institute, Annual Seminar on Doing Business in Korea (Seoul, Korea, 6–7 November, 1986)

'La législation et les traités en matière de protection littéraire et artistique' [1896] *DA* 51

Lemley, M A, 'Dealing with Overlapping Copyrights On the Internet' (1997) 22 *U Dayton L Rev* 547

'Lettre de Belgique' [1898] *DA* 103

'Lettre de France' [1934] *DA* 105

von Lewinski, S, 'WIPO Diplomatic Conference on Audiovisual Performances: A First Resume' [2001] *European Intellectual Property Review* 333

Limpberg, T, 'Les problèmes de la reprographie des oeuvres imprimées protegées par le droit d'auteur' (1973) 120 *RIDA* 120

Litman, J, 'The Exclusive Right to Read' (1994) 13 *Cardozo Arts & Ent LJ* 29

Litman, J, 'Sharing and Stealing' (2004) 27 *Hastings Comm & Ent LJ* 1

Llewellyn, D, 'Computers, Software and International Protection' (1986) 11 *Columbia-VLA Journal of Law and the Arts* 183

Lokrantz-Bernitz, A, 'Les télésatellites et le droit d'auteur' (1970) 68 *RIDA* 68 (F, E, & S)

Loughlan, P, 'The Right of Integrity: What is in that Word Honour? What is in that Word Reputation?' (2001) 12 *Australian Intellectual Property Journal* 189

Lucas, A, 'Private International Law Aspects of the Protection of Works and Objects of Related Rights Transmitted Through Digital Networks' (1998), available at http://www.wipo.int/documents/en/meetings/1998/gcpic/pdf/gcpic_1.pdf

Lucas, A, 'La loi applicable aux contrats d'exploitation des droits d'auteur et des droits voisins', in *Mélanges Victor Nabhan*, Editions Yvon Blais, Montreal (2004)

Lucas-Schloetter, A, 'Folklore', in von Lewinski, S (ed), *Indigenous Heritage and Intellectual Property: Genetic Resources, Traditional Knowledge and Folklore* (2003); WIPO,

Consolidated Analysis of the Legal Protection of Traditional Cultural Expressions/Folklore, Background Paper No 1 (2003), available at http://www.wipo.int/tk/en/publications/785e_tce_background.pdf
Lund, T, 'Photocopie, droit d'auteur et usage privé' (1957) 14 *RIDA* 137
Luzzati, M G E, 'Réforme des clauses administratives des unions et l'institution de l'organisation mondiale de la propriété intellectuelle' (1967) 101 *Annales de la propriété industrielle, artistique et littéraire* 338
Lyon-Caen, C, 'Le cinéma dans la Convention de Berne' [1959] *DA* 217
Lyon-Caen, C, 'Nouvelles observations au sujet de la protection internationale des oeuvres cinématographiques' [1962] *DA* 153
McCrae, D M, 'The Legal Effect of Interpretative Declarations' (1978) XLIV *BYIL* 154
McFarlane, G, 'The Public Lending Right Act 1979 in the United Kingdom' [1979] *Copyright* 313
McFarlane, G, 'The Public Lending Right: A Comparison of National Approaches' [1980] *Copyright* 335
Maggs, P B, 'New Directions in US–USSR Copyright Relations' (1974) 68 *Am Jo Int Law* 391
Maillard, G, 'Conférence de Rome' *ALAI Bulletin*, October 1928
Majoros, F, 'Some Considerations on the Future of International Copyright Arising upon the Paris Acts of 1971' (1978) 49 *Diritto di Autore* 291
Malaplate, L, and Vilbois, J, 'Réforme de la structure administrative des Unions de Berne et de Paris et des Bureaux réunis' (1965) 46 *RIDA* 5
Mann, F A, 'Germany's Present Legal Status Revisited' (1967) 16 *ICLQ* 761
Masouyé, C, 'Les prolongations de guerre' (1953) 3 *RIDA* 49 (Part I), (1954) 4 *RIDA* 80 (Part II), (1955) 9 *RIDA* 82 (Part III), (1957) 14 *RIDA* 109 (Part IV), (1958) 20 *RIDA* 59 (Part V) (F, E, & S)
Masouyé, C, 'Décolonisation, indépendence et droit d'auteur' (1962) 36 *RIDA* 85 (F, E, & S)
Masouyé, C, 'La prochaine conférence de Stockholm' (1962) 31 *RIDA* 3
Masouyé, C, 'Perspectives de révision de la Convention' de Berne (1964) 43 *RIDA* 5 (F, E, & S)
Masouyé, C, 'Les droits des artistes interprétes ou exécutants dans la Convention de Rome' (1965) *RIDA* 161 (F, E, & S)
Masouyé, C, 'Nouveau régime international des oeuvres cinématographiques et télévisuelles dans la Convention de Berne (Paris, du 5 au 24 juillet 1971)' (1972) 65 *AUFT* 11
Masouyé, C, 'A New International Convention on the Protection of Phonograms' [1972] *EBU Legal Rev* 59
Masouyé, C, 'Quid du droit d'auteur dans l'utilisation des satellites spateaux?' [1972] 72 *RIDA* 10 (F, E, & S)
Masouyé, C, 'The Role of *ALAI* in the Development of International Copyright Law' [1978] *Copyright* 120
Masouyé, C, 'Droit d'auteur: Horizon 2000' (1979) *Diritto di autore* 163
Masouyé, C, 'Protection des expressions du folklore' (1983) 115 *RIDA* 2 (F, E, & S)
Massa, C-H and Strowel, A, 'Community Design: Cinderella Revamped [2003] *EIPR* 68
Mendelsohn, M H, 'Diminutive States in the United Nations' (1972) 21 *ICLQ* 609
Mentha, B, 'A Glance at the Principal Substantive Clauses of the Berne Convention Adopted at Stockholm on July 14, 1967' [1967] *Copyright* 321
'Model Law Concerning the Protection of Performers, Producers or Phonograms and Broadcasting Organizations' [1974] *Copyright* 163

Mott, K M, 'Analysis of the "Unity of Art" Concept in European Legal Systems' (1964) 11 *Bull Cop Soc USA* 242
Nabhan, V, 'Reprography and Education' [1983] *Copyright* 207
Nabhan, V, 'Satellites and Copyright in Canada' (1984) 120 *RIDA* 2
Ndiaye, N, 'Influence du droit d'auteur sur le développement de la culture dans les pays en voie de développement' (1975) 86 *RIDA* 59
Ndiaye, N, 'The Berne Convention and the Developing Countries' (1986) 11 *Colum-VLA JL and Arts* 47
Netanel, N, 'Impose a Noncommercial Use Levy to Allow Free Peer-to-Peer File Sharing' (2003) 17 *Harv JL & Tech* 1
Netterville, V S, 'Copyright and Tort Aspects of Parody, Mimicry and Humorous Commentary' [1962] 35 *So Cal LR* 25
'New International Organization for Intellectual Property? Efforts to Modify the Structure of the Paris and Berne Unions' [1966] *Industrial Property* 37
Niedzielska, M, 'Intellectual Property Aspects of Folklore Protection' [1980] *Copyright* 339
Nimmer, M B, 'Who is the Copyright Owner When the Laws Conflict?' (1974) 5 *IIC* 62
Nimmer, M B, 'Simultaneous Publication as a Route to Berne Protection for non-Berne Nationals' [1979] *Diritto di Autore* 704
Nordemann, W, 'The 1972 Amendment of the German Copyright Law' (1973) 4 *IIC* 179
Nordemann, W, 'Public Lending Right in Federal Germany' (1976) 90 *RIDA* 61
Nordemann, W, The "Droit de Suite" in Art 14*ter* of the Berne Convention and in the Copyright Law of the Federal Republic of Germany' [1977] *Copyright* 342
Nordemann, W, 'Right to Control or Merely to Payment? Towards a Logical Copyright System' [1980] 11 *IIC* 49
Nordemann, W, 'Determining the Country of Origin According to the Berne Convention' (1984) 121 *RIDA* 2 (F, E, & S)
Nordemann, W, 'New Imperative Contract Rules Implemented Into the German Copyright Law', in *Mélanges Victor Nabhan*, Editions Yvon Blais, Montreal 309 (2004)
'Le nouveau décret-loi italien sur le droit d'auteur du 7 november 1925' [1926] *DA* 91, 99, 109
'Le nouveau Protocole additionnel, à la Convention de Berne révisée de 1908' [1914] *DA* 79, 93
O'Connell, D P, 'Independence and Succession to Treaties' (1962) 38 *BYIL* 84
O'Connell, D P, 'State Succession and the Effect upon Treaties of Entry into a Composite Relationship' (1963) 39 *BYIL* 54
O'Hara, S D, ' "Developing Countries": A Definitional Exercise' (1967) 15 *Bull Cop Soc USA* 83
Olian, I A, 'International Copyright and the Needs of Developing Countries: The Awakening at Stockholm and Paris' (1974) 7 *Cornell Int LJ* 81
Olssen, A H, 'Copyright in the National Economy' [1982] *Copyright* 130
Ong, B, 'Why Moral Rights Matter: Recognizing the Intrinsic Value of Integrity Rights' (2003) 26 *Colum JL & Arts* 297
D'Orelli, A, 'Les dispositions impératives et normatives de la Convention internationale du 9 september 1886 et leur influence sur la législation intérieure des pays de l'Union' [1889] *DA* 1

D'Orelli, A, 'Le vingt-cinquième anniversaire de la Convention de Berne du 9 September 1886' [1911] *DA* 116, 129
Ostertag, F, 'Nouvelles Propositions pour la Conférence de Bruxelles' [1939] *DA* 62
Ostertag, F, 'La Convention de Berne et le droit national' [1941] *DA* 29, 37
Otten, A, 'Implementation of the TRIPS Agreement and Prospects for its Further Development' (1998) 1 *Journal of International Economic Law* 523
Palmeter, D, 'National Sovereignty and the World Trade Organization' (1999) 2 *Journal of World Intellectual Property* 77
'The Performing Artist, The Recording Manufacturer, The Broadcaster' [1956] *DA* April supplement
Perkins, A, 'United States Still No Closer to Database Legislation' [2000] *EIPR* 366
Perlmutter, S, 'Resale Royalties for Artists: An Analysis of the Register of Copyrights' Report' (1992) 16 *Colum-VLA JL & Arts* 157
Phillips, J, 'Copyright: Towards a Positive Approach?' (1974) 82 *RIDA* 34
Phillips, J, 'The Concept of "Author" in Copyright Law: Some Reflections on the Basis of Copyright in the UK' [1990] *Copyright* 26
Plaisant, R, 'Les droits sur les phonogrammes' [1956] *DA* August and September Supplements 61 and 69
Plaisant, R, 'La protection des arts appliqués: Besoins nouveaux, idées nouvelles' [1957] *DA* 160, 192
Plaisant, R, 'Protection des oeuvres d'art appliquée à l'industrie' [1964] *DA* 96
Plaisant, R, 'Droit de suite' [1969] *Copyright* 157
Plaisant, R, 'Propriété intellectuelle et communications par satellite' (1971) 70 *RIDA* 79
Plaisant, R, 'Loi n 85–660 du 3 juillet 1985 relative aux droits d'auteur . . .' [1986] *Propriété Littéraire et Artistique* Fasc 80
Plant, Sir Arnold, 'The Economic Aspects of Copyright in Books', *Economica*, May 1934
Plenter, S, 'Choice of Law Rules for Copyright Infringements in the Global Information Infrastructure: A Never-Ending Story' [2003] 23 *EIPR* 313
Price, M E, 'Government Policy and Economic Security for Artists: The Case of the droit de suite' (1968) 77 *Yale LJ* 1333
'Les propositions arrêtés en vue de la Conférence de Rome pour les Gouvernements allemand, autrichien, brittanique, français et suisse' [1927] *DA* 116, 126, 137
'La propriété intellectuelle en Russie' [1897] *DA* 99, 112
'La protection internationale des droits voisins du droit d'auteur (Etat actuel de la question)' [1940] *DA* 109, 121, 133
Püschel, H, 'The International Law of the Berne Convention and the National Copyright Law of Member States with Particular Reference to the Legislation of the German Democratic Republic' [1986] *Copyright* 144
'Quelques conditions prélables pour que soit viables un accord international sur les droits voisins' [1957] *DA* 22
'La question des instruments de musique mécaniques' [1895] *DA* 54
Radojokovic, Z, 'Legal Character of "Moral Right" ' [1965] *Copyright* 203
Radojokovic, Z, 'The Historical Development of "Moral Right" ' [1966] *Copyright* 168
Radojokovic, Z, 'Legal Character of "Moral Right" ' [1966] *Copyright* 168
'La ratification, par les Etats-unis d'Amérique de la Convention universelle sur le droit d'auteur' [1955] *DA* 63
Rauscher auf Weeg, H von, 'The Rome Convention Rights: A Comparative Review of Legislation and International Legal Developments over 12 Years' (1974) 21 *Bull Cop Soc US* 237

Recht, P, 'Le droit de suite est-il un droit d'auteur?' (1950) 3 *UNESCO Copyright Bulletin* 61, 70
Recht, P, 'Should the Berne Convention Include a Definition of the Right of Reproduction?' [1965] *Copyright* 82
Recht, P, 'Article 6*bis* of the Berne Convention (Moral Rights)' [1968] *Copyright* 15
Recht, P, 'Copyright: A New Form of Property' [1969] *Copyright* 94
Reichman, J H, 'Design Protection in Domestic and Foreign Copyright Law; From the Berne Revision of 1948 to the Copyright Act of 1976' [1983] *Duke Law Journal* 1143
Reichman, J H, 'Designs Protection after the Copyright Act 1976: A Comparative View of the Emerging Interim Models' (1984) 31 *Jo Cop Soc USA* 267
Reichman, J H, 'Intellectual Property in International Trade: Opportunities and Risks of a GATT Connection' (1989) 22 *Vanderbilt Journal of Transnational Law* 747
Reichman, J H, 'The TRIPS Component of the GATT's Uruguay Round: Competitive Prospects for Intellectual Property Owners in an Integrated World Market' (1993) IV *Fordham Intellectual Property, Media & Entertainment Law Journal* 171
Reimer, D, 'Filmrechtliche Fragen in Rahmen des Berner Union' [1959] *GRUR* 639
Reimer, D, 'The Right of Distribution with Special Reference to the Hiring and Lending of Books and Records' [1973] *Copyright* 56
Reindl, A, 'Choosing Law in Cyberspace: Copyright Conflicts on Global Networks' (1998) 19 *Mich J Int'l L* 799
'Request for Views on a Universal Copyright Convention' (1950) *UNESCO Copyright Bulletin*, vol III, no 2, 47
'Retransmission des émissions' (1963) 41 *RIDA* 101
'De la rétroactivité prévue par l'article 18 de la Convention d'Union' [1926] *DA* 114
Ricketson, S, 'The Birth of the Berne Union' (1986) 11 *Colum-VLA JL & Arts* 9
Ricketson, S, 'People or Machines: The Berne Convention and the Changing Concept of Authorship' (1991) 16 *Colum-VLA JL & the Arts* 1
Ricketson, S, 'The Boundaries of Copyright: Its Proper Limitations and Exceptions—International Conventions and Treaties' (1999) *Intellectual Property Quarterly* 56
Ricketson, S, 'The Berne Convention: The Continued Relevance of an Ancient Text', in Vaver, D, and Bently, L (eds), *Intellectual Property in the New Millennium: Essays in Honour of William R Cornish*, Cambridge University Press, Cambridge (2004)
Ringer, B, 'Recent Developments in International Copyright: The Paris Meetings of February 1969' (1968–9) 16 *Bull Cop Soc USA* 223
Ringer, B, 'The Role of the United States in International Copyright' [1968] *Copyright* 215
Ringer, B, 'Report of the General Rapporteur, Satellites Convention' [1974] *Copyright* 267
Ringer, B, 'Copyright and the Future of Authorship' [1976] *Copyright* 155
Ringer, B, 'Copyright in the 1980s' (1976) *Bull Cop Soc USA* 299
Ringer, B 'The Role of the United States in International Copyright: Past, Present and Future' (1986) 56 *Georgetown Law Journal* 1050
Roeder, M A, 'The Doctrine of Moral Right: A Study in the Law of Artists, Authors and Creators' (1940) 53 *Harv L Rev* 554
Rollin, H, and Troller, A, 'Consultation sur l'adhésion de la République Démocratique Allemande aux Conventions Internationales pour la protection de la propriété intellectuelle' (1967) 16 *Staat und Recht* 1293
Ronga, G, 'Les colonies et l'Union de Berne' [1956] *DA* 21

Ronga, G, 'The Position in the Berne Union of Countries which have Recently Become Independent' [1960] *DA* 320 (E & F)
Ronga, G, 'Règle de l'unanimité pour la révision des Conventions de Paris et de Berne' (1961) 33 *RIDA* 13
Rothnie, W A, 'Moral Rights: Consents and Waivers' (2002) 20 *Copyright Reporter* 145
Roussel, G, 'The Copyright of Salaried and Employed Authors: A Comparative Study of National Laws' [1990] *Copyright* 221
Rousselet, M, 'Droit moral de l'auteur' (1962) 35 *RIDA* 3 (F, E, & S)
Rumphorst, W, 'Cable Distribution of Broadcasts' [1983] *Copyright* 301
'Russie: Etat de la réforme législative en matière de droit d'auteur; la Russie et la Convention de Berne' [1907] *DA* 94
'La Russie et la Convention de Berne' [1888] *DA* 122
'La Russie et la protection internationale des auteurs; opinions et ideés récentes' [1904] *DA* 46
Sacks, H D, 'Crisis in International Copyright: The Protocol Regarding Developing Countries' [1969] *JBL* 26
Samuelson, P, 'The U.S. Digital Agenda at WIPO' (1997) 37 *University of Virginia Law Journal of International Law* 369
Samuelson, P et al, 'A Manifesto Concerning the Legal Protection of Computer Programs' (1994) 94 *Colum L Rev* 2308
Sanctis, de, V, 'Lettre d'Italie' [1956] *DA* 127
Sanctis, de, V, 'L'avenir du droit d'auteur international à la lumière des conférences de révision de juillet 1971' [1972] *Interauteurs* 39
Sanctis, de, V, 'Paris Revisions (July 1971) of the UCC and the Berne Convention' [1972] *Copyright* 241
Sanctis, de, V, 'Some General Considerations on the Recent Geneva Convention for the Protection of Phonograms' [1972] *Copyright* 111
Sandison, H, 'The Berne Union and the Universal Copyright Convention: The American Experience' (1986) 11 *Colum-VLA JL & Arts* 89
Sarraute, R, 'Current Theory on the Moral Right of Authors and Artists under French Law' (1968) 16 *Am Jo of Comp Law* 487
Sawer, G, 'Australia: Embarrassing Interlude' (1964) 11 *Bull Cop Soc USA* 313
Schlotelburg, M, 'The Community Design: First Experience with Registrations' [2003] *EIPR* 383
Schönherr, F, 'On the Interpretation of Article 5(2) of the Berne Convention: Taking as an Example the Greek Antipiracy Law of July 15, 1980' [1981] *Copyright* 294
Schønning, P, 'Applicable Law in Transfrontier On-Line Transmissions' (1996) 170 *RIDA* 21
Schrader, D M, 'Analysis of the Protocol Regarding Developing Countries' (1970) 17 *Bull Cop Soc USA* 166
Schricker, G, 'Grenzüberschreitende Fernseh- und Hörfunksendungen im Gemeinsamen Markt' [1984] *GRUR Int* 592
Secretan, J, 'L'évolution structurelle des Unions internationales pour la protection de la propriété intellectuelle' [1962] *DA* 131
Seltzer, E M, 'The Future of Section 337 of the Tariff Act of 1930: The Response of the United States Trade Representative to the GATT Panel Report' (1992) *IIC* 352
Sher, Z, 'Reflections on Copyright in Developing Countries' (1968–9) 16 *Bull Cop Soc USA* 201

Sherman, B, and Bently, L, 'Great Britain and the Signing of the Berne Convention in 1886' (2000) *Journal of the Copyright Society of the USA* 311
'De la situation des droits d'auteur et d'édition durant et après la guerre' [1917] *DA* 15, 29, 60
'La situation des pays sous mandat dans les Unions pour la protection de la propriété industrielle et des droits des auteurs' [1926] *DA* 62
Solberg, T, 'The International Copyright Union' (1926) 36 *Yale Law Journal* 68
Spoor, J H, 'The Copyright Approach to Copying on the Internet: (Over)stretching the Reproduction Right', in Hungenhotz, P B (ed), *The Future of Copyright in a Digital Environment*, Information Law Series, Kluwer Law International, The Hague (1996)
Spoor, J H, 'General Aspects of Exceptions and Limitations to Copyright: General Report', in Baulch, L et al (eds), *ALAI Study Days: The Boundaries of Copyright: Its Proper Limitations and Exceptions* (1998)
Stewart, S, 'The Geneva Convention for the Protection of Phonograms' [1973] *Copyright* 100
Stewart, S, 'International Copyright in the 1980s' (1981) 28 *Bull Cop Soc USA* 351
Straschnov, G, 'L'article 11ter de la Convention de Berne révisée à Bruxelles' [1951] *DA* 73
Straschnov, G, 'Rapports entre la Convention de Berne et la Convention universelle' [1953] *DA* 37
Straschnov, G, 'La loi ghanéenne sur le droit d'auteur' [1962] *DA* 156
Straschnov, G, 'The Broadcast-Satellite Service in Private Law' [1977] *EBU Legal Rev* 97
Strauss, W, 'The Moral Right of the Author' (1955) 4 *Am Jo of Comp Law* 506
Strauss, W, 'Le droit moral et la protection des droits personnels de l'auteur' [1955] *DA* 173, 185, [1956] *DA* 6
Strömholm, S, 'The "Right of Putting into Circulation" in Relation to Copyright: A Study of Comparative Law' [1967] *Copyright* 266
Strömholm, S, 'Droit Moral: The International and Comparative Scene from a Scandinavian Viewpoint' (1983) 14 *IIC* 1
Strowel, A, 'La protection des mesures techniques: une couche en trop?' (2001) *Auteurs & Médias* 90
Szilagyi, I, 'Questions of Broadcasting by Satellite with Special Reference to Authors' Rights' [1981] *Copyright* 222
'Tableau de la législation et des traités concernant la protection des oeuvres littéraires et artistiques' [1900] *DA* 58
Tan, D, 'Seeing Red over Stravinsky's Firebird' (1996) 7 *Australian Property Journal* 63
Teran, J M, 'International Copyright Developments: A Third World Perspective' (1982) 30 *J Cop Soc USA* 129
Thompson, E, 'Twenty Years of the Rome Convention' [1981] *Copyright* 270
Tocups, N M, 'The Development of Special Provisions in International Copyright Law for the Benefit of Developing Countries' (1982) 29 *J Cop Soc USA* 402
Tournier, A, 'The Out-of-Date Notion of Publication in the Berne Convention' (1963) 39 *RIDA* 3 (F, E, & S)
Tournier, A, 'La Conférence de révision de Stockholm: Cinéma et télévision' (1965) 45 *RIDA* 5 (F, E, & S)
Tournier, J-L, 'Ryksdag 67, or the End of a Myth' (1968) 54–5 *RIDA* 663 (F, E, & S)
Tournier, J-L, and Joubert, C, 'Collective Administration and Competition Law' [1986] *Copyright* 96

'Les traités et arrangements bilatéraux en matière de propriété littéraire et artistique' [1919] *DA* 92

'Les traités particuliers entre pays unionistes et la révision future de la Convention d'Union' [1906] *DA* 113

Troller, A, 'Aufgabe und Organisation des Berner Verbandes zum Schutze der Rechte der Urheber an ihren Werken der Literatur und Kunst' (1950) 39 *UFITA* 173

Troller, A, 'The Hundredth Anniversary of the Berne Convention: The Development of Law in the Copyright Field through the Interaction of the Convention and Swiss Legislation' [1986] *Copyright* 208

Trotter Hardy, I, 'Property (and Copyright) in Cyberspace' (1996) *U Chi Legal F* 217

Tyerman, B, 'The Economic Rationale for Copyright Protection for Published Books: A Reply to Professor Breyer' (1971) 18 *UCLA Law Review* 1100

Uchtenhagen, U, 'The GATT Negotiations Concerning Copyright and Intellectual Property Protection' (1990) 21 IIC 765

Ulmer, E, 'Consultation sur le cinématographie et le droit d'auteur' [1953] *DA* 97

Ulmer, E, 'Letter from Germany' [1965] *Copyright* 275

Ulmer, E, 'The Revision of the Copyright Conventions in the light of the Washington Recommendation' (1970) 1 *IIC* 235

Ulmer, E, 'The Revisions of the Copyright Conventions' (1971) 2 *IIC* 345

Ulmer, E, 'The Convention for the Protection of Producers of Phonograms' (1972) 3 *IIC* 317

Ulmer, E, 'International Copyright after the Paris Revisions' (1972) 19 *Bull Cop Soc USA* 263

Ulmer, E, 'The "Droit de Suite" in International Copyright Law' (1975) 6 *IIC* 12

Ulmer, E, 'Protection des auteurs lors de la transmission par satellite des programmes de radiodiffusion' (1977) 93 *RIDA* 4 (F, E, & S)

Ungern-Sternberg, von, J, 'Transmission d'émissions de radiodiffusion par satellites et le droit d'auteur' (1973) 75 *RIDA* 2 (F, E, & S)

'L'Union internationale après la guerre' [1918] *DA* 15

'Union internationale: les rapports unionistes pendant la guerre' [1915] *DA* 5, 116

US Copyright Office, *Droit de Suite: The Artist's Resale Royalty* (1992 report), summarized at (1992) 16 *Colum-VLA JL & Arts* 318

Vaver, D, 'Authors' Moral Rights in Canada' (1983) 14 *IIC* 329

Vaver, D, 'The National Treatment Requirements of the Berne and Universal Copyright Conventions: Part One' (1986) 17 *IIC* 577; 'Part Two' (1986) 17 *IIC* 715

Vermulst, E, and Drierssen, B, 'An Overview of the WTO Dispute Settlement System and its Relationship with the Uruguay Round Agreement: Nice on Paper but Too Much Stress for the System?' (1995) 29 *Journal of World Trade* 131

Views of the International Non-Governmental Organisations on Private Copying [1982] *Copyright* 211

Vijne, T C, 'Copyright Imperilled?' (1999) 21 *EIPR* 192

Vilbois, J, 'La procédure de révision de la Convention de Berne' (1962) 36 *RIDA* 33 (F, E, & S)

Vivant, V, 'Cybermonde: Droit et droits des reseaux', JCP 1996.I.3969

Walter, M W, 'Telediffusion and Wire-Distribution Systems: Berne Convention and Copyright Legislation in Europe' [1974] *Copyright* 302

Walter, M W, 'Contractual Freedom in the Field of Copyright and Conflicts of Laws' (1976) 44 *RIDA* 87 (F, E, & S)

Walter, M W, 'Cable Television in the Austrian Copyright Amendment Law 1980' [1982] *Copyright* 254
de Werra, J, 'The Legal System of Technological Protection Measures under the WIPO Treaties, the Digital Millennium Copyright Act, the European Union Directives, and other National Laws, (Japan, Australia)', in *Adjuncts and Alternatives to Copyright: Proceedings of the 2001 ALAI Congress*, Kernochan Center for Law Media and the Arts, New York (2002)
Yankwich, L R, 'Parody and Burlesque in the Law of Copyright' (1955) 33 *CBR* 1130
Yasseen, M K, 'La Convention de Vienne sur la Succession d'États en Matière de Traités' [1978] 24 *Annuaire français de droit international* 59, 108

INDEX